Mediation Theory and Practice

By

James J. Alfini
Professor of Law
Northern Illinois University College of Law

Sharon B. Press
Director, Florida Dispute Resolution Center
Tallahassee, Florida

Jean R. Sternlight
Professor of Law
University of Missouri-Columbia School of Law

Joseph B. Stulberg
Professor of Law
Ohio State University College of Law

CASEBOOK SERIES

LEXIS Publishing™

LEXIS®·NEXIS®· MARTINDALE-HUBBELL®
MATTHEW BENDER®· MICHIE™· SHEPARD'S®

Library of Congress Cataloging-in-Publication Data

Mediation theory and practice\James J. Alfini . . [et al.].
        p. m.—(Legal text series)
    Includes bibliographical references and index.
    ISBN 0-8205-4264-4 (hardbound)
    1. Mediation--United States. 2. Dispute and resolution (Law)--United States.
3. Compromise (Law)—United States. I.Alfini, James J. II. Series.

KF9084 .M444 2001
347.73'9—dc21   2001029196

This publication is designed to provide accurate and authoritative information in regard to the subject matter covered. It is sold with the understanding that the publisher is not engaged in rendering legal, accounting, or other professional services. If legal advice or other expert assistance is required, the services of a competent professional should be sought.

LEXIS, NEXIS, *Shepard's* and Martindale-Hubbell are registered trademarks, LEXIS Publishing and MICHIE are trademarks, and *lexis.com* is a service mark of Reed Elsevier Properties Inc., used under license. Matthew Bender is a registered trademark of Matthew Bender Properties Inc.

Editorial Offices
744 Broad Street, Newark, NJ 07102 (973) 820-2000
201 Mission St., San Francisco, CA 94105-1831 (415) 908-3200
701 East Water Street, Charlottesville, VA 22902-7587 (804) 972-7600
www.lexis.com

.

(Pub.1179)

To
Barry, Carol, Midge, and Sylvia

PREFACE

Mediation, as a distinct course of study, is a newcomer to the law school curriculum. Over the past decade, the number of law school courses in mediation has increased exponentially. Ten years ago, those law students who were introduced to mediation generally learned about it in a one hour discussion of alternative dispute resolution in their Civil Procedure course. Today, law faculty have recognized that the richness of its subject matter and the widespread use of this dispute resolution alternative in many legal practice settings warrants giving mediation its own place in the law school curriculum.

Our objective in preparing this book has been to capture the richness of mediation as a field of study and to present this subject matter in a manner suitable for examination as a full semester law school course. We shared a belief that mediation theory, policy concerns, and practice skills are complementary and should be presented as such in a law school text. If we have been successful in this endeavor, it is because we sought to include materials that encompass our varying theoretical, policy and practice perspectives. Thus, working on this book has truly been a "transformative" experience. We "recognized" each other's distinctive contributions to this joint enterprise and were "empowered" by the process of reviewing and commenting on each other's work. (Apologies to Bush and Folger.)

We were also helped by the camaraderie and collegiality of our fellow academics and practitioners in the mediation field. Although those with whom we consulted while working on various chapters are too numerous to mention here, we thank them for their input and hope that they see their imprint on this final product.

Our home institutions also provided needed encouragement and support. We thank our colleagues at the Florida Dispute Resolution Center, the University of Missouri-Columbia, Northern Illinois University, and Ohio State University for accommodating our research, resource, and emotional needs. We are also grateful to our students for providing important feedback on ideas and drafts. A special expression of gratitude is due our research assistants: Kate McCabe at Northern Illinois University College of Law; and Brian Beatte at the University of Missouri-Columbia School of Law. For their excellent word-processing assistance, we thank Jean Myers, Becky LeNeau, and Lisa Hoebing at Northern Illinois.

We are indebted to Lexis Publishing for agreeing that there is a need for a book on this "new" subject matter and for providing important editorial support. In particular, we thank Leslie Levin for her excellent editorial judgment and patience.

Finally, we thank our partners in life. They not only provided advice and encouragement, but endured weekend absences and other annoyances. This book is dedicated to them.

v

TABLE OF CONTENTS

Chapter 1
HISTORICAL CONTEXT AND CONCEPTUAL FRAMEWORK

Chapter 2
NEGOTIATION

Chapter 3
MEDIATION PROCESS AND SKILLS

Chapter 4
MEDIATOR ROLES, ORIENTATIONS, AND STYLES

Chapter 5
LEGAL ISSUES IN MEDIATION

Chapter 6
DIVERSITY, POWER, AND FAIRNESS

Chapter 7
MEDIATOR CERTIFICATION AND ETHICS

Chapter 8
MEDIATION AND THE LAWYER

Chapter 9
THE INSTITUTIONALIZATION OF MEDIATION

Chapter 11
MEDIATION'S PROMISE

Chapter 1
HISTORICAL CONTEXT AND CONCEPTUAL FRAMEWORK

Mantei BP Facilitate of discussion /Negotiation

§ A INTRODUCTION

[1] DEFINITION

Mediation is a procedure for resolving controversies. It is a process in which an impartial intervener assists two or more negotiating parties identify matters of concern and then develop mutually acceptable proposals to deal with the concerns. Mediation is a process that takes seriously the philosophy of democratic decision-making. Three of mediation's essential features must be underscored in order to understand its history: first, a mediator has no preference for what the parties' settlement terms shall be; second, a mediator has no authority to impose a binding decision on the parties; and third, parties do not reach complete agreement in mediation unless each party accepts every settlement term.

[2] HISTORICAL PERSPECTIVE

Mediation has a distinguished history of use, both internationally and in the United States. International diplomacy features political leaders and institutions that assume a mediating role to facilitate negotiations aimed at stopping hostilities among warring parties or creating economic development packages among national partners. Indigenous tribal groups in Central America and Africa call upon family elders to assume a mediating role to promote problem solving among disputing community members. And contemporary China employs mediation as its primary process for resolving a range of interpersonal controversies.

In the United States, religious, immigrant and trade groups in colonial New England sustained their ethical and religious traditions in part by using mediation to resolve conflicts among group members. More formal use of mediation took hold in the early twentieth century with the emergence of formal union-management relations in the railroad industry. Following World War II, the United States Congress, with the goal of sustaining industrial stability, created the Federal Mediation and Conciliation Service (FMCS). FMCS' continuing mandate is to provide mediation services to private sector union and management personnel engaged in collective bargaining.

But mediation's prominence and expanded use emerged in the United States in the late 1960's as part of the "movement" known as "Alternative Dispute Resolution." (ADR). ADR proponents endorsed using dispute resolution processes that were "alternatives" to traditional trials and their accompanying litigation processes. They encouraged parties, courts, government agencies, and private sector businesses to use negotiation, mediation, arbitration, elections, summary jury trials, and early neutral evaluation processes to address controversies for which the traditional trial process appeared ill-suited. Mediation became the "darling child" of this movement in large measure because it reserves to the parties the ultimate authority to "settle" the matter. People concluded that since disputing parties can always refuse to accept settlement terms proposed in mediation, no one could be hurt by using it. We will examine that conclusion in more detail in subsequent chapters, but certainly that belief encouraged policy makers to support using mediation, either in the form of an experimental program or through statutory or court rule mandate, to address disputes ranging from interpersonal, commercial, and family matters to public policy controversies involving complex environmental claims or the political budgeting process.

This explosion of mediation's use in the United States has served as the basis for recent analysis and adaptation by persons in Western Europe, Central and Eastern Europe, Latin America, selected African nations, and the Far East who are interested in studying and implementing democratically-based dispute resolution processes in their countries. Many U.S. scholars, mediation trainers, and court administrative experts have served as consultants to court-reform and democracy-building groups in these nations, and throughout the 1990's, the presence of United States mediation practitioners and scholars dominated presentations at national and international professional meetings. Although it is culturally myopic to believe that only the United States' experience is relevant to the study of mediation, there is legitimate support, given its influence, for studying its experience in detail. Two other reasons support this perspective: first, practicing lawyers must know the dynamics and strategies relevant to the mediation process as it operates in the United States in order to capably serve their clients; second, the United States' experience itself has been infused and shaped by its own rich diversity of participants and perspectives that other countries find relevant to their own adaptation.

What follows, then, is the United States' story.

§ B   MEDIATION: THE FOUNDATIONAL YEARS OF THE 1960s AND 1970s.

[1]   THE CHALLENGES

Beginning in the late 1960s, people used mediation to resolve many different types of controversies. Consider the challenges described in the following sections.

[a]   A Hot City Night

Police officers are conducting a routine patrol of a city street that teems with people in bars and entertainment centers. Young car owners cruise the streets strutting their wheels. Crowds mingle. It is a typical, hot Saturday evening in August in one of the nation's medium-sized urban areas.

Suddenly, two Caucasian police officers are involved in a scuffle with three female African American teenagers. Amid screaming and shouting of "pigs" and "honkeys go home," police try to wrestle the three to the ground to handcuff and arrest them on charges of drug dealing. They fiercely resist. Police aggressively use billy clubs to subdue them. By the time police officers shove the three girls into the car, the girls' faces are notably bruised and one is spitting up blood. Thirty onlookers, all shouting hate slogans at the police, begin to "rock" the police car before it can pull away. The police officers fire warning shots into the air, then accelerate the car; regrettably, one protester did not jump back in time and is fatally injured.

Pictures of the three arrested women appear in the next day's newspaper. Two have swollen jaws, later determined to be broken. The third has a swollen eye; it is reported that this third individual, a fifteen-year-old, was six months pregnant but suffered a spontaneous abortion during the prior night's activity.

On Sunday morning, through church sermons and local news programming, the leadership of the African American community action agency calls upon all "decent members of the community" to participate in a mass demonstration in front of police headquarters on the following day, Monday, at 12:00 noon. The goal is to "protest acts of police brutality" and demand that "the Police Commissioner create an independent citizen review board to investigate both the Saturday night incident as well as any future citizen complaint of police misconduct." The Police Commissioner, in a television interview that night, states that "all citizens have a right to engage in free speech and assembly, but if they are disruptive, they will be arrested." He further noted that the internal affairs division of the police department was already investigating the situation and that an independent citizen board was both unnecessary and contrary to guidelines established in the collective bargaining agreement with the police union. The family of the fatally injured individual announces it will sue the city and the individual police officers.

You are a lawyer and concerned citizen of the community. You receive a telephone call from the Mayor on Sunday evening. She describes the above scenario and then asks: Can you help us solve these matters? How would you respond?

[b] Not in My Backyard

Seventy-five families live in single–family houses in a quiet, residential neighborhood of tree-lined streets. Many moved to that area so that their children could attend the highly-acclaimed elementary and middle schools. Yesterday, residents awoke to read a surprising and startling story in their newspaper: the home in their neighborhood that had been sold last week by their friends had been purchased at a very substantial price by a non-profit organization which will operate a "half-way" house for twenty-five mentally-challenged adults. These persons, previously committed to large institutional settings to receive therapeutic treatment for psychological and developmental disorders, would become neighborhood residents; they would live in a super-vised living setting, engage in routine daily activities, and assume, to the degree possible, a "normal," conventional lifestyle.

Many residents are upset and concerned. Some are afraid that the presence of such neighbors will deflate their property values. Some fear that their school-age children will not be able to play with one another in a carefree, unsupervised setting on the neighborhood street and sidewalks. And still others, particularly senior citizens, fear for their physical safety.

These neighborhood residents contact you, a lawyer, to obtain guidance. There are no apparent zoning ordinances that prohibit a home in that area from being used in this way. How might you proceed?

[c] Neighborhood Citizenship

As the new academic year begins, four seniors, living in an off-campus apartment for the first time in their college career, hosted a "welcome-back-to-campus" party. The party began on Friday evening and concluded Sunday afternoon! As the hosts described it: "lots of fun—football in the backyard, and food, television, dancing, music, booze, and sex throughout the house."

The party did not endear the students to the Smiths, their neighbors and thirty-three-year residents of the neighborhood. Several times during the weekend, the Smiths visited the house and requested that the noise abate; that seemed only to enhance the volume. Complaints to the police, as far as the Smiths were concerned, were ineffective. Officers stopped by to talk with the students, but no arrests were made and the noise seemed to increase as soon as the police left.

Similar incidents continued throughout the fall. Tensions were exacerbated by the fact that the Smiths and their college neighbors shared a common driveway. The Smiths often left their car in the middle of the driveway close to their side-entrance door; only when students complained to them that they could not get their cars out of the driveway would the Smiths move their car to their garage in the back.

One morning in mid-October, a student resident bolted from the house to his car, needing to get to the university to take a mid-term exam. The Smith's car was blocking the driveway. The student frantically rang the doorbell. Mr. Smith answered, but took five minutes "to find his car keys" before moving his car. The delay made it difficult for the student to find an available parking spot at the university. As a result, he arrived at the mid-term exam fifteen minutes after the test had started, and he felt rushed and upset when completing the exam. The following week, he learned that he had failed the exam. Since he was certain that Smith had been slow to find his keys just to harass him, the student hosted "a very loud party for Mr. and Mrs. Smith's benefit" on the following Saturday evening. That night was an uncomfortable, aggravating one for the Smiths.

The next day, three of the student residents were playing catch with a football on their front lawn. An errant pass landed on Mr. Smith's front lawn. As a student went to retrieve the football, Mr. Smith, standing by his porch with his metal-prong rake, threw the rake at the student, yelling: "get off our lawn." By all accounts, the rake's prongs narrowly missed hitting the student's face.

The next day, Mr. and Mrs. Smith filed a criminal complaint for harassment against their college-student neighbors. The Smiths must prove beyond a reasonable doubt that the defendants, with the requisite mental culpability, committed the acts of which they are accused.

The trial court administrator contacts you, describes the situation, and asks for your advice on "how to handle this—and lots of cases like it that don't seem to belong in court." What is your response?

[d] Working for Local Government

A group of 275 persons work for the sanitation department of a large city in the northern U.S. Their working conditions are multifaceted. In brutally cold weather, workers find it difficult to keep their truck operating and their hands warm; heavy snowfall complicates picking up the bags as well as making each bag heavier to lift. During the summer months, their challenge is to beat the heat: hot, humid weather makes sustained physical activity difficult; garbage left on hot sidewalks becomes infested with rodents; and, at a day's end, employees reek of garbage aroma and their clothes are frequently not salvageable.

Workplace operations also involve personal dynamics. Tempers routinely flare among co-workers who approach their tasks with varying degrees of persistence. Supervisors generate animosity and low morale by assigning overtime work to their friends or by rewarding favored employees with desirable vacation schedules. Some employees complain that their health insurance coverage is inadequate, while others assert that intemperate supervisor treatment of employees is grounded in racial bias.

A group of these employees decide that they could improve their working conditions if they addressed their employer with a unified voice, so they seek recognition as a union. The city leaders balk, claiming that such recognition would undercut their sovereign prerogative. The employees respond by engaging in a work stoppage. For one week, employees refuse to collect garbage; it piles up on the streets and avenues of the city and its neighborhoods, generating a concern about citizens' health. News media reports are split: some editorialize that the employees are greedy and should be terminated while others accuse the city administration of promoting sub-optimal workforce productivity by ignoring legitimate concerns regarding supervisor mistreatment of subordinates.

The Mayor contacts you, a local leader of the Bar Association, and asks for your thoughts about the most constructive way to proceed. How would you respond?

[2] THE EXISTING REPERTOIRE OF RESPONSES

[a] Overview

How did our legal and political systems handle such matters? As would be expected, they responded within the strengths and constraints of their institutional values and competence. For such matters as "Hot City Night" and "Not In My Backyard," the physically injured parties or their estates sued one another; to address the policy matters, community action agencies or neighborhoods would engage in coalition-building political strategies to develop local government responses to answer their concerns. The disputing neighbors in "Neighborhood Citizenship" situations would file criminal misdemeanor charges against one another. And for situations recounted in "Working for Local Government," public employees would work in partnership with supervisors to secure incremental change on a unit-by-unit basis within individual governmental jurisdictions or seek, through their state legislatures, new statutory authority authorizing public employees to join unions.

The fundamental flaw in each approach was identical: the parties at interest were not able to trigger discussion on the very matters that meant the most to them with those persons who were in a position to effectively address their concerns. Why does this occur and what are the consequences?

[b] Hot City Night/Not in My Backyard

For incidents such as "Hot City Night," only the injured parties can initiate litigation, so the leaders of the community activist organizations have no voice in that discussion. But the "problem" they want to have addressed—thoughtful, effective, non-discriminatory law enforcement practices—would not be fully addressed in that forum. If, heeding the call of community organization activists, dozens of protestors appeared at the Monday rally and were arrested for disorderly conduct, they, too, in their criminal court hearing, would be limited to discussing, the particular criminal charges, not their broader concerns surrounding the Saturday night events. The primary mechanism—indeed, the only one—by which the community activists can express their concerns about community policing practices and advance their proposal to create a citizen review board is through the local political process. Similar dynamics operate in the "Not in My Backyard" situations.

On one version of political theory, of course, such situations as "Hot City Night," and "Not in My Backyard" are precisely those which democracy and representative government are designed to address. The courts are not the right forum for handling all disputes. Neither do we necessarily want those citizens with the loudest voices to command public attention and resources; let them, we say, work through accepted processes with elected or appointed officials to have their matters addressed. But there is a fundamental weakness to this response: it assumes that all participants have comparable access to, and influence on, political leadership. Yet when access and voice are not comparable, persons sometimes resort to physical action, such as protests, boycotts, and harassment, to communicate their message. There is a strong history of such responses in the United States, with the Boston Tea Party being one shining example. Persons with strong beliefs and passionately-felt convictions who feel "voiceless" will express their concerns by engaging in conduct that garners attention. And when that happens, the response is comparably distorted, for it addresses the responsive actions, not the primary message. That, regrettably, was the routine paradigm for responding to the extraordinary challenges triggered by the various protest "movements" of the 1960s and 1970s: efforts to achieve civil rights for various racial and ethnic groups and for women, student demands for educational reform, and anti-Vietnam war efforts. While each of these movements achieved some consider-able success, they also resulted in a dangerous alienation of citizens both from one another and from their fundamental institutions.

[c]   Neighborhood Citizenship

The "neighborhood citizenship" situation is typically addressed by one neighbor filing a criminal complaint for harassment against her neighbors. Many such complaints are not prosecuted for lack of corroborating witnesses. When the complaint is not even processed, the complaining neighbors lose faith that their justice system can help them. If the complaint is processed and proceeds to a preliminary hearing at which a trial date is to be set, a judge might sustain a request to adjourn the case in contemplation of dismissal. Under that arrangement, if the defendants agree not to commit acts similar to those of which they have been accused for a six-month period, then the original complaint will be dismissed. Of course, when such an adjournment is granted, the defendants, incensed by having to hire attorneys and wanting to humiliate their neighbors, will inaccurately report to anyone they meet that their case was "thrown out of court"; the complaining parties, quite justifiably, believe that no official in the system took their case seriously.

Finally, if the prosecuting attorney does take the case to trial, there are two possible outcomes. First, if the prosecutor prevails, the question turns to identifying an effective remedy. Since such charges are normally classified as misdemeanors, the offender faces a possible fine, probation order, or a maximum one-year jail sentence. Empirically, for almost all of the "neighbor-hood citizenship" cases, the likely penalty the court would impose is probation. To the victim of the criminal conduct, that result is viewed as ineffective and a flagrant example of the justice system's failure to effectively punish or correct an undesirable situation. The other possible trial outcome, of course, is that the defendant prevails. If that happens, the defendants celebrate and often engage in conduct designed to humiliate the complaining parties among friends and neighbors. Both trial results generate undesirable outcomes, for the neighbors return to their prior living arrangements with their relationship now intensely fueled by the "losing party's" anger and hostility for having lost.

Again, what is most notable about these developments is that the parties to the controversy—and the persons most able to concretely and creatively address their concerns—have never discussed with one another how their behavior could be adjusted to meet one another's interests.

[d]   Working for Local Government

Public sector employment in the United States has historically been viewed as a privilege, not a right. The government as employer establishes conditions governing wages, work hours, insurance, vacations, promotional opportuni-ties, and workplace safety; if an employee is not satisfied with the arrange-ment, she is free to look for work elsewhere. In 1935, Congress established the right of private sector employees to join or form a union in order to engage in collective bargaining with their employer over wages, hours, and other terms and conditions of employment. If efforts to reach acceptable collective decisions about these matters reached an impasse, employees had the legal right to strike and employers had the option of locking out employees to encourage the union to accept their bargaining proposals. But workers in the public sector, be they school teachers, police officers, firefighters, or recreation workers, had never been extended such rights.

Once more, persons who had concerns about the fairness or adequacy of particular employment practices confronted a Hobson's choice: either "suffer the perceived injustice" or look elsewhere for employment. There was no sustained forum in which persons with differing viewpoints on how to most effectively and fairly develop policies to govern these employment conditions could meet to hammer out their differences. So employees engaged in "illegal" work stoppages or slowdowns to garner attention to their concerns.

[3] THE GRAND EXPERIMENT: USING MEDIATION AS AN "ALTERNATIVE DISPUTE RESOLUTION" FORUM

[a] Introduction

The fundamental drawback to using our traditional legal and political processes to meet each of these challenges was identical: the parties most affected by the matters in question were not able to discuss the concerns that mattered most to them with the persons or institutional representatives who were in a position to effectively address the matter. In short, parties living with the problems were effectively shut off from participating in their resolution. Their concerns were redefined as legal or political issues in ways that left those living with the fundamental controversies alienated from being able to address them directly and resolve them constructively. The era of mediation's use in the 1970s is best viewed, then, as an experimental, then structured, response to meet this fundamental "participation" challenge.

[b] Community Conflicts

To respond to the "hot disputes," religious, civic, and governmental organizations seized the initiative to become neutral interveners—"peacemakers"—motivated by a passion to secure civil stability and promote social welfare. Congress created the Community Relations Service (CRS) of the U.S. Department of Justice under the 1964 Civil Rights Act, a unit whose purpose was to recruit, train and deploy persons skilled at developing and advancing the use of conciliation and mediation to resolve controversies in which racial and ethnic tensions pierced the environment. Its mandate, then and now, is to foster dialogue and bargaining among parties in interest to work out mutually acceptable settlement terms. CRS's history includes intervening in such matters as the citizen disruptions and chaos surrounding the implementation of the Boston School desegregation orders, the march of the Ku Klux Klan in the predominantly Jewish Chicago suburb of Skokie, Native American land claim negotiations, and the civic and neighborhood tensions arising from the negotiations among Federal governmental agencies, lawyers, families, and concerned citizens focusing on the custody and immigration status of Elian Gonzalez.

In the private sector, the Ford Foundation and the William and Flora Hewlett Foundation assumed the leadership role in providing substantial financial support to non-profit organizations dedicated to experimenting with the use of mediation to resolve these social conflicts. Working with established organizations, such as the American Arbitration Association (AAA), persons experimented with using mediation to resolve the "hot disputes" and urban disruptions that dotted city and state agendas.

The persons who assumed leadership or visible mediation roles in these early efforts came from strikingly different backgrounds: James Laue, an eminent theologian and activist academician; Theodore Kheel and Ronald Haughton, each nationally prominent labor mediators and arbitrators; Sam Jackson and Willoughby Abner, two African American community and political activists who became the first and second directors of the National Center for Dispute Settlement of the American Arbitration Association; Linda Singer and Michael Lewis, attorneys with a commitment to experimenting with mediation's use in prison settings; Raymond Shonholtz, a former public defender who became founder and first director of the nationally-acclaimed, albeit controversial, Community Boards Program in San Francisco with its distinctive commitment to citizen participation in the identification and mediation of disputes; and George Nicolau and Joseph B. Stulberg, each of whom directed regional, then national, comprehensive mediation centers and became widely known as pre-eminent mediation trainers.

These persons, and others like them, intervened in disputes involving controversies between police departments and citizen groups, environmentalists and builders, school districts and parents, universities and protesting students, and Native Americans and United States citizens. Their involvement was fluid; defining and measuring what constituted "success" was part of the experiment. Results were uneven, though everyone appreciated how significant a resource investment was required to sustain such efforts. But what energized such experiments was a common vision that structured participation by disputing parties enhanced the dignity of citizens' lives and cemented their perspectives as democratic partners, that dialogue engendered accountability, and that accountability was the foundation for unleashing citizen imagination to design and implement effective relationships, programs, and institutions.

[c] "Minor Disputes"

To respond to interpersonal disputes among neighbors, many court systems created and experimented with using volunteer citizens to mediate such cases. Beginning with the experimental Night Prosecutor's Program in Columbus, Ohio, the Arbitration as an Alternative ("4-A") program of the American Arbitration Association (AAA), and the Citizen Dispute Settlement (CDS) programs in selected Florida counties, mediation proponents and sympathetic judicial personnel offered a new approach and philosophy for servicing the "Neighborhood Citizenship" cases that were crowding court calendars. The approach can be simply described: Bring all the neighbors into a room. Have them meet with one another in the presence of a community resident trained in conducting problem-solving dialogues. Try, through that discussion, to have the parties discuss their concerns, communicate their aspirations to one another, and work out arrangements acceptable to each. If the matter can be resolved in this manner, the case is removed from the court docket. Such programs quickly established dramatic results: settlement rates often exceeded 75 % of the cases, and numerous studies confirmed striking evidence of party satisfaction with both the process and the results.

The "simple description" of using mediation to resolve these disputes masks the fundamental reorientation required in our thinking about how to resolve them. The process—mediation—requires people to listen to one another, accord respect to and concern for each other's viewpoint, place fault-finding in perspective, and engage in problem solving discussions that enable participants to resolve their immediate concerns and stabilize future interactions. Doing all those things is neither easy nor straightforward; it takes time, commitment, and skill from the parties, their representatives, and the mediator. The benefits, though, are obvious and tangible: it empowers persons and families to interact constructively as neighbors; it enables persons to regain command of discussing the things that matter most to them; and it requires each individual to be accountable for her conduct.

These court-related mediation experimental programs received critical impetus from Harvard Law Professor Frank Sander's presentation entitled "Varieties of Dispute Processing" at the 1976 Pound Conference, amplified by the comments of then U.S. Supreme Court Chief Justice Warren Burger who encouraged all lawyers and judicial administrators to utilize multiple processes for resolving disputes. In 1977, the U.S. Department of Justice gave prominence to the early local initiatives by launching three experimental Neighborhood Justice Centers (NJC) in Kansas City, Missouri, Atlanta, Georgia, and Los Angeles, California. While each of these programs adopted a differing design model, their common feature was a commitment to use mediation to resolve the "Neighborhood Problem" noted above and to use citizens from a broad range of backgrounds and training as volunteer mediators. NJCs, variously referred to as Citizen Dispute Centers or Community Dispute Resolution Centers, now number more than four hundred and are permanently incorporated by state statute into a number of jurisdictions. All retain the features of using mediation with volunteer citizens to service the disputes.

[d] Public Employment: State and Local Government

The most explosive growth in the use of mediation during the late 1960s and 1970s occurred in public sector labor relations. Historically, laws in the United States have separated the treatment of private enterprise employment practices from those operative when the government is employer. Social attitudes changed notably, though, during the 1960s, as leading voices articulated workplace concerns that seemed common to all working women and men: safety; wages, benefits and opportunities for workplace training; equitable policies governing job promotions or layoffs; and the use of prompt, informal dispute resolution systems (notably, arbitration) for efficiently and fairly addressing employer or employee concerns.

While still recognizing important differences between public and private sector workplace operations, various state legislatures passed laws authorizing public sector employees to join unions and engage in collective bargaining over wages, hours, and other terms and conditions of employment. The statutes created administrative agencies, variously referred to as Public Employment Relations Boards (PERB) or Public Employment Relations Commissions (PERC), to oversee the implementation of collective negotiations among state and local government personnel. To address predictable disagreements between employers and employee representatives, statutes provided for "impasse procedures," including mediation, that parties could use to resolve their disputes. Administrative agencies quickly recruited and trained staff employees to serve as mediators and also developed "panels" of individuals whom administrative agency personnel would appoint to serve as mediators on a per case basis.

[4]   LESSONS AND LEGACIES OF THE FOUNDATIONAL YEARS

The heritage of mediation's use during this time of significant social and political change falls into three categories: practice; policy; and professional development.

[a]   Practice

Using mediation to address this broad range of disputes seemed ideal for multiple reasons: (1) it permitted stakeholders to the controversy to establish the discussion agenda—that is, they could "put on the table for discussion" whatever concerns mattered the most to them, whether or not they fit within existing "legal," "political," or "administrative" categories; (2) it was an inclusive process, permitting participation not only by trained advocates but also those persons or organizations which had to abide by the resolution; (3) it required persons to be accountable for designing solutions to problems, not just complaining about them; (4) it supported the belief, later to be substantiated empirically, that meaningful, direct participation enhances participant respect for the fairness of the process and strengthens participant compliance with negotiated outcomes; and (5) it appeared to be both a harmless ("no harm in talking since the mediator can't make us do anything") and minimally costly process.

One striking feature regarding mediation's use during this period was that, to a substantial degree, non-lawyers, more than lawyers, advocated its use and implementation. This was due, in part, to the nature of the controversies in which mediators became involved: "hot disputes" were viewed as social, not legal, conflicts, and collective bargaining impasses were contractual, not legal. While there were many individual lawyers and judges who supported mediation's use in these early years, the legal profession did not signal its sustained support until the mid-1970s when the U.S. Attorney General initiated the Neighborhood Justice Center experiment and the American Bar Association created its Special Committee on the Resolution of Minor Disputes. Although the attitude and role of the legal profession has changed dramatically during the past twenty-five years, its early support focused almost exclusively on endorsing mediation to handle "minor" disputes—the "neighborhood case" described above. The difficult, complex cases in which lawyers' expertise and acumen were vital were not touched. All that would change in less than a decade.

[b] Policy

Three important themes emerged from these early developments. First, the central emphasis was on the negotiation process (cited in some statutes as collective bargaining) rather than a trial. In "unassisted" negotiations, stakeholders to the controversy, either directly or through their spokespersons, participate actively in discussing issues and shaping the resolutions that govern their lives; mediation efforts were designed to "assist" negotiators reach a successful outcome.

Second, persons recognized that the "value-added" of the mediation process resided in the mediator's neutrality. Many persons were skeptical that controversies could be resolved without there being someone "with authority" to decide the matter. But mediation's expanded use confirmed the contribution that an intervener without decision-making authority makes to sustaining constructive dialogue, clarifying misunderstandings, and developing imaginative, yet practical, solutions to significant problems. Mediator neutrality, later incorporated in all mediator ethical codes, anchored its success and confirmed the dominant conception of mediation as a process designed to facilitate dialogue among negotiating parties.

Third, mediators were individuals drawn broadly from the community who reflected a diverse range of professional training and life experiences. Persons with extensive labor relations or human resource management experience were sought by parties who were embroiled in workplace controversies. Multi-dimensional mediation teams consisting of clergy, lawyers, and media personnel served effectively as the intermediaries for such explosive disputes as prison inmate riots; and school teachers, business persons, community activists, and lawyers, among others, were trained to mediate "Neighborhood Citizenship" cases.

As mediation has expanded to different contexts in the following decades, these three themes have been challenged or altered.

[c]   Professional Development

During this formative period, there were no commanding "mediation paradigms" to which mediation trainers turned for guidance. Mediator trainers developed their training programs by drawing on materials used to train private sector labor-management mediators, marriage counselors, and international peace-keepers. The theoretical literature was even more sparse. Mediator training and insights proceeded from experimenting and sharing "war stories" with one another. As activities coalesced during the 1970s, several important efforts to improve practice and theory emerged.

[i] The Society of Professionals in Dispute Resolution (SPIDR)

In 1972, mediator practitioners in these emerging practice areas felt the need to establish an organization that would promote dialogue, study and education among practitioners. The National Academy of Arbitrators had been established as a professional organization for private sector labor arbitrators, but there was no comparable professional organization for mediators. SPIDR was created to meet that need. Its early membership consisted heavily of mediators serving in the rapidly expanding environment of public sector labor relations; Robert Helsby, SPIDR's first president, was the Chair of New York State's Public Employment Relations Board. But persons serving as mediators in social policy and court-annexed programs were eligible for membership as well.

[ii] The Special Committee on the Resolution of Minor Disputes of the American Bar Association

In 1977, the American Bar Association created a Special Committee to study the growth of court-annexed citizen dispute settlement programs. Its first chair, Talbot D'Alemberte, later to be President of the ABA, helped shape the Committee and its staff as a comprehensive, national resource for providing materials or technical assistance to lawyers, judges, and court personnel interested in developing program initiatives in this area.

[iii] Scholarship

Dispute resolution scholarship, from World War II through the 1970s, focused on analyzing dispute resolution processes operative in private sector labor-management relations. It was conducted largely by economists, political scientists, psychologists, and industrial relations scholars and concentrated on studying the dynamics of collective bargaining, not mediation. Legal scholarship examined the interplay between the courts and the arbitration process, and law school courses focused almost exclusively on the theory and practice of grievance arbitration in the private sector union-management arena. As mediation's use in multiple contexts grew in the 1970s and accelerated in the 1980s, there was no traditional intellectual discipline in which dispute resolution research was based. The setting, therefore, was ripe for the rise of multi-disciplinary and inter-disciplinary scholarship.

§ C   THE 1980s: A DECADE OF PROGRAM STABILIZATION AND EXPANSION

[1]   INTRODUCTION

During the 1980s, mediation's use would accelerate onto a flight path that would make its presence and use pervasive. By the decade's end and thereafter, no lawyer would be able to conduct a traditional law practice without being able to counsel clients about mediation or represent them in a mediation conference. For some individuals, the prospect of developing a career as a mediator became viable. But that panorama was not clear as the decade began.

Mediation's use during this decade spread in several ways. Successful experiments were transformed into permanent components of the social justice system, and mediation's use extended to new arenas. With each of these developments, new questions about process use and service delivery arose.

[2] PROGRAM STABILIZATION

Social experiments, including dispute resolution projects, are designed, implemented, and then evaluated. For initiatives deemed successful and valuable, program planners pursue efforts to stabilize ("institutionalize") their presence. For initiatives that fail, program planners try to learn from program weaknesses so that subsequent efforts, if any, avoid those pitfalls.

Program evaluation of dispute resolution projects generated several consequences. First, for a successful experiment, program advocates focused on developing strategies to stabilize the program's status and, in appropriate ways, to incorporate it into the justice system. Second, program advocates encouraged the replication of successful projects in other jurisdictions. And third, for experiments that failed, practitioners tried to distill the lessons so that mediation's use in new substantive arenas would be informed by those lessons. Mediation's use was deemed successful and valuable in almost every area of use. The degree to which it was institutionalized, though, varied.

For *Public Sector Labor Relations,* many legislatures passed statutes granting various public employees the right to form and join unions and engage in collective bargaining. The statutory framework created administrative agencies to administer activities and provide, among other things, mediation services. Such agencies at the state and local government level are now conventional elements of government service.

Similarly, efforts to stabilize mediation's use for handling *Neighborhood Citizenship* cases received strong judicial endorsement during the 1980s; several state legislatures promulgated statutes providing for mediation's use and allocated funding to judicial budgets to sustain these programs; Colorado and New York were among the jurisdictions to lead this movement. In other jurisdictions, such as Florida, judges promulgated court rules to support local efforts to sustain these programs.

It was only in the area of *Community Disputes* that financial support for mediation withered. Although the Community Relations Service of the U.S. Department of Justice remained intact and expanded its service, those mediation experiments funded through private foundation support began to recede. The reasons were multiple: it was costly; the controversies, by their very nature, involved at least some parties who would not be capable of paying for such services; the results of the intervention were difficult to quantify; and the need for such services was unpredictable. New efforts in the 1980s tried to address these shortcomings.

[3] EXPANDED AREAS OF PRACTICE

The practice of mediation expanded in two different directions during this decade: one direction embraced controversies involving groups and public agencies; the other was focused on individuals.

[a] Public Disputes

The social conflicts of the 1960s and 1970s had their counterparts during the 1980s, with one significant difference: for these "newer" conflicts, a public agency often was a party to the controversy or had responsibility for governing its resolution. Disputes arose both among governmental agencies at various levels and between governmental agencies and private parties.

Disputes among governmental agencies arise in multiple ways. Federal monies become available to state and local governments for various community development projects, but conflicts arise among the federal monitors and local recipients regarding which projects should take priority, be they highway construction, infrastructure development, or other economic development training and development projects. Historically, governmental representatives spoke in terms of trying to coordinate service delivery, but that language masked the fact that governmental representatives had specific, and often conflicting interests and goals; rather than coordinating efforts, the more accurate portrayal of their interaction was that they often had to negotiate the resolution of their conflicting obligations.

The Kettering Foundation built on that recognition by funding an experiment in which negotiations between Federal, State, and Local officials were mediated by selected individuals. The first experiment took place in St. Paul, Minnesota; William Usery, former Director of the Federal Mediation and Conciliation Service, was selected to mediate negotiations among governmental representatives focusing on establishing community development project priorities and funding formula. Similar initiatives occurred in Columbus, Ohio, Gary, Indiana, and, in a modified form, the State of Connecticut, with Lawrence Susskind, James Laue, and Joseph Stulberg serving, respectively, as the mediators. The projects were widely cited as successful models for predicating inter-governmental interaction on the basis of negotiated discussions. During the 1990s, these projects, with appropriate adaptation, served as important examples of democratic institution-building initiatives in Central and Eastern Europe.

Disputes in which a governmental unit is a party to a controversy with private parties also abound. For example, conflicts erupt over the manner in which administrative agencies, such as the U.S. Environmental Protection Agency or the Occupational Safety and Health Administration, develop rules to regulate fossil fuel emissions or workplace safety matters. State and federal offices responsible for regulating environmental laws routinely become embroiled in controversies between environmentalists and developers.

With financial support from the National Institute of Dispute Resolution (itself a program originally funded by the William and Flora Hewlett Foundation and the Ford Foundation), a small number of "State Offices of Dispute Resolution" were created as part of state government bureaucracies to test whether the development and delivery of mediation services for these and other types of public policy matters would be helpful. These offices operate in a manner similar to public sector labor relations agencies and, more appropriately, the Community Relations Service of the U.S. Department of Justice, though the scope of their service is broader,

The impact of these experimental projects and state-office initiatives was important in several ways: their use solidified public awareness that mediation could be used regularly to resolve complex matters; and they introduced the mediation process to a segment of the practicing Bar whose clients were involved in these controversies. They served to legitimize mediation's routine use to resolve important matters.

[b]   Disputes Among Individuals

[i]   Overview/Children and the Family

In the private sector, the faltering economic climate of the 1980s triggered the movement of corporate downsizing and a rush to privatization of services. For businesses attempting to compete effectively in a rapidly developing global economy, any effort to improve total quality management was examined. If disputes could be handled more efficiently by a process such as mediation, it would be viewed favorably. If mediation's use could result in less destructive business relationships following the resolution of particular controversies (thereby not losing dissatisfied customers in the process), that was also welcomed.

The result, then, was not surprising. Large organizations, such as insurance companies, developed and implemented mediation programs to handle a variety of customer complaints. They developed comparable programs to address internal workplace controversies. General counsel of large corporations publicly subscribed to the Center for Public Resource's call for a "Pledge" to explore using alternative dispute resolution procedures, including mediation, to resolve business and legal controversies in which they were involved. Trade and professional organizations within the construction industry, a prominent user of arbitration processes, developed and encouraged the use of mediation as a "pre-arbitration" step to resolve disputes arising from the construction of residential and commercial projects.

These initiatives, albeit cautious, were becoming abundant and widespread. But, perhaps not surprisingly in retrospect, the trigger area that would catapult mediation's use comprehensively into the court system, was, broadly speaking, children and the family. It surfaced in three distinct ways.

[ii]   Children and the Schools: Special Education

In 1973, Congress passed the Rehabilitation Act. The statute, among its provisions, required school districts to develop individualized educational plans for each student certified to be in need of special services, with the overall goal being to integrate that student into the normal tempo of school life to the maximum feasible extent. Typical issues arising included: If a student were hearing impaired, could she best learn by having the school district provide her with a sign language interpreter for each class, by grouping her in a special classroom with students from all grade levels who had the same disability, or by sending her to a private school, at the public school district's expense, that could provide her with the necessary services? The key element of the statutory framework was that the district's plan had to be acceptable to the student's parents. What would happen if the district and parents could not agree on the elements of a plan: could the district impose its plan unilaterally? Must the parents file a lawsuit to contest the proposed plan and have a judge decide the matter? The statute took a different route; it encouraged the use of mediation to resolve such matters. Why? The idea was that persons "closest" to the dispute should be involved in discussing and resolving it; a mediator could help to pierce disagreements among the district personnel and parents without removing the decision-making authority from them. To implement the statutory mandate, some school districts hired lawyers to serve as mediators while other districts trained school-based staff to mediate these situations. Taking a different tack, states such as Massachusetts hired full-time staff mediators into their department of education to handle these controversies.

Importantly, now, a significant federal statute supported the systematic use of mediation. While this was occurring, mediation proponents also entered the school system using a different route.

[iii]   Children and the Schools: Peer Mediation

Our schools are an important social institution in large measure because they are a primary place in which young persons grow into adults. All the physical, emotional, and intellectual challenges of becoming a person are experienced inside the school environment: students mature biologically; they experience the joys and sorrows of falling in and out of love with a peer; they deal with disappointment or resentment when they are ignored or closed out by peers or when they fail to earn a spot on the varsity athletic team or a role in the school play; they learn citizenship skills for interacting effectively with diverse classmates. As if these challenges were not sufficient, they must also develop the skills and discipline necessary to do the intellectual work demanded of them. But, of course, there is much more.

Many commentators have observed that the social challenges of the larger society are imported into our school systems. Acts of violence, drug use, health diseases, and other challenges do not respect school walls. Whatever the sources of the challenge—poverty, racism, class, ethnicity, or illiteracy—the social problems they spawn appear routinely in our school environments.

So, a typical day in a high school could easily include the following incidents:

— two students get into a hallway fight because one allegedly "dissed" the other's friend;

— two boys get into a fight because the first accuses the second of not having returned a SONY Walkman that he had borrowed 3 weeks ago;

— a teacher, frustrated by three students who are talkative, loud and otherwise disruptive in a classroom, sends all of them to the counselor's office for discipline.

— A 'bully' mercilessly teases a new student about her physical appearance; the next day, the new student's sister confronts the "bully" on the playground and attempts to gain revenge by physically attacking him.

— Two groups of students quarrel with one another over which one gets to use the school playground's basketball court during recess; the "bigger kids" always seem to win.

— A youth who is not a student waits on the school playground, with a knife concealed in his backpack, to take revenge against a student who had 'stolen his girlfriend' at a weekend party.

— Drug runners wait outside a school building at the beginning of a school day to peddle their products.

What can school administrators, teachers and students do to respond to such situations? There is the normal set of responses: the classroom teacher tries to gain a student's cooperation for the 40-minute period by ignoring her interruptions, playfully cajoling or asking the student to stop the offending behavior, standing by the student's desk, sending her to the back of the room, or threatening to impose a punishment on her, such as additional homework. But for some situations, the teacher, at her wit's end, deploys a different response: she suspends the student from school, hoping to "teach her a lesson" as well as enable her to teach the other students without interruption. For many school districts, the minimum suspension is five school days. From the parent's perspective or that of the larger community, the question immediately surfaces: what will that student do for five days?

Such an environment led mediation advocates to believe that using mediation in innovative ways might be helpful to address such situations. Specifically, Community Boards (San Francisco) and Safe Horizons (New York City) developed programs in which they trained high school students to become mediators; these student mediators, under supervised conditions, then mediated cases involving students—the "peers"—who had been involved in disruptive behavior. The mediation process became a "safety valve" for the school; it was an affirmative response for dealing with conflicts that was both an alternative to suspension and a learning process in which student participants had to take responsibility for dealing with their situation. These Peer Mediation programs incorporated the lessons of the 1970s experiments: create a meeting space in which the persons involved in the problem talk with one another; have a neutral third party whom the parties view as trustworthy, helpful, and understanding, conduct those discussions; and structure the conversation so that those involved with the problem become accountable for developing its solution.

Many questions and challenges have surfaced in the ensuing years regarding the precise focus and effectiveness of such programs, but one thing is certain: peer mediation programs have become ubiquitous in middle schools and high schools in the United States. Indeed, many students entering law schools today became familiar with mediation through their service as peer mediators.

But it was mediation's use in an important area of family relations—matrimonial dissolutions—that paved the way for expanding the legal system's connection with the process.

[iv] Mediation of Matrimonial Dissolutions

(a) Context

Divorce is an extraordinary human experience. Even when desired by one or both partners, it often triggers a profound range of turbulence that persists into the indefinite future.

To obtain a civil divorce in the United States requires one to fulfill the statutory requirements of a particular state's jurisdiction. Even with the widespread presence of "no-fault" divorce that eliminates the need for one party to predicate the divorce on such grounds as adultery or abandonment, parties still need to resolve matters relating to real and personal property, debts and other financial matters, spousal and child financial support, and, where appropriate, parenting arrangements. As the divorce rate in the United States increased during the 1980s, the experience of obtaining a legal divorce became more visibly excruciating. Stereotypically, clients would report that after they had retained a lawyer, all further discussions between spouses occurred only through their lawyers. As offers and counteroffers regarding financing and parenting arrangements were exchanged among the lawyers, the parties developed increasingly bitter pictures of how their spouse was being selfish, manipulative, or mean. If the parties contested the proposed arrangements and submitted their controversy to a judge, parties frequently perceived the decision to be neither fair nor congruent with their own values. Hence, the legal divorce process became costly financially and psychologically. The post-divorce period was frequently checkered with one party petitioning the court either to secure or contest compliance with various provisions of the divorce decree, and the cost of how parental conduct during the divorce process and beyond affected their children's psychological health remained unknown.

This adversarial climate paralleled that of the social controversies from the earlier period: participants felt that their legal arguments prevented them from discussing their central concerns; resolutions were not sensitively crafted to meet the parties' particular circumstances; and those who had to live with the outcome were removed from important aspects of the negotiating and decision-making process. Mediation proponents cautiously urged its experimental use in this setting. O.J. Coogler, based in Atlanta, Georgia, was the first person to design and use a "structured mediation process" for handling divorces. Leaders of the AAA soon developed its Family Mediation programs. Dr. John Haynes, a psychologist, encouraged its development and use by practicing mental health professionals. All persons aligned with this initiative believed that using mediation to assist parties seeking a divorce would be a more attractive option than the default forum.

The era of "divorce mediation" had arrived. And with it, significant challenges to the "lessons" of mediation practice from the prior decade; we note these challenges here but address them in depth in subsequent chapters.

(b) New Challenges

(1) Mediator Qualifications

What type of person is best able to mediate a divorce? Prior mediation initiatives had not imposed any formal requirements on persons serving as mediators. But mental health professionals poignantly argued that a divorce mediator, to be effective, needed training and expertise regarding the manner in which emotional turbulence and family dynamics reinforce power inequities among divorcing spouses. Just as persuasively, lawyers asserted that divorcing spouses had to resolve complex matters involving property transfers, pensions, and taxes, all of which bear significant legal consequences. So who is qualified to mediate such matters? Both groups shared the presumption that only members of their respective professions were qualified to provide this service; they effectively convinced policy makers that most of those individuals who had mediated the social disputes of the prior decade—be they clergy, educators, or citizens with unusually rich life experiences—were too uneven in qualifications to be used regularly in this area.

(2) Professional Dilemmas

If mental health professionals practiced divorce mediation, would they be properly accused of practicing law without a license? If lawyers assumed the mediator's role for a divorcing couple, would they be violating the Code of Professional Responsibility by representing conflicting interests simultaneously? These were new questions for mediators.

(3) Fees and Fee Structure

Therapists and attorneys in private practice are remunerated for their traditional professional services. Who would pay for divorce mediation services? The experimental use of mediation in the 1970s was funded either through taxpayer dollars (CRS or FMCS) or by private grants; the mediators either were paid from these sources or served *gratis*. Parties did not pay. Divorce mediation changed that practice.

Further, the traditional fee structure in these professions is to charge a client at an hourly rate. Since time frames carry economic consequences, divorce mediators scheduled conferences in defined time-blocks: two hours, six hours, or whatever seemed appropriate. This practice sharply introduced the possibility that a mediator might terminate the process before the parties had reached either agreement or impasse because they had exhausted their financial capacity to pay for the service.

(4) Payment and Neutrality

The historical practice in labor arbitration was that each party, management and labor, pay fifty percent (50%) of the arbitrator's fee. That practice was designed to minimize the possible perception that an arbitrator would skew her decision to favor the paying party. That principle governed the design and implementation of mediation initiatives in the 1970s, as program personnel or interveners would make certain that independent funding sources financed the mediation effort if not all parties had capacity to pay. But private divorce mediators embraced the fee structure of their traditional service, and that raised two immediate challenges: first, is it fair to require persons with unequal resources to share the expense of mediation, and second, if parties did not share equally in financing mediation, would that fact jeopardize the mediator's neutrality, either in fact or in party perception?

(5) Servicing a Case

When mediating a social policy dispute or a neighborhood citizenship case, what constituted a "case" was ambiguous and fluid. Defining the relevant issues, deciding the appropriate timing for entry, and identifying appropriate "parties" to the dispute were often themselves important topics of negotiation; their combination made each situation significantly different for the intervener. Further, as the earlier account indicates, parties to these controversies did not know what might happen if they did not reach a resolution. By contrast, the "case" in divorce mediation was definite and circumscribed: resolve those matters that are required to obtain a legal divorce. While divorce mediation advocates used the rhetoric of party participation and empowerment to promote mediation's use, that masked a fundamental shift, for if parties in a divorce mediation were not able to resolve all the legal issues, they could proceed to court to litigate their claims. Parties to a divorce mediation were negotiating in the shadow of a trial.

———

Divorce mediation practice took hold and expanded. Organizations such as the Academy of Family Mediators (AFM) were created to promote professional standards of excellence in the practice. Private practices developed, and court planners supported efforts to make mediation mandatory for all matrimonial cases, particularly those involving minor children. It was only a matter of time until parties involved in virtually any civil action filed in court would be encouraged or required to use mediation. And that dam broke in Florida in 1988.

[v] Disputes among Individuals/Entities: A Comprehensive Court System of Mediation

(a) Questions Raised

By 1988, a variety of mediation initiatives dotted the Florida landscape: citizen dispute settlement programs; family and divorce mediation; peer mediation; consumer mediation; and public policy mediation. The legislature assumed a leadership role in promulgating legislation which authorized civil trial court judges to promote pre-trial settlement by referring almost any civil court filing to mediation. The message was clarion: any case, large or small, "simple" or "complex," "important" or "unimportant," might be resolved through mediated negotiations. The Florida Supreme Court was responsible for implementing the statute. It created a committee comprised of practicing lawyers, judges, mediators, and court administrators and charged it with creating rules and standards for realizing the statute's promise. Professor James Alfini, then of Florida State University School of Law, together with Michael Bridenback and Sharon Press, then Director and Associate Director of the Dispute Resolution Center of the Florida Supreme Court, served as the technical faculty and staff resources to the court for implementing this unprecedented initiative. The committee worked rapidly, and, in consultation with a broad range of professionals from across the nation, developed a governing framework for implementing this comprehensive initiative. Its central features, several of which remain controversial, included the following:

1. *Eligible Cases.* With very limited exceptions, a court can refer any civil case to mediation. Mandating party participation in mediation does not constitute a denial of a party's state constitutional right to a jury trial. If a judge orders a case to mediation, the burden is on the party seeking an exemption to file a motion setting forth the grounds as to why mediation for that particular case is ill-suited or unwarranted.

2. *Mediator Qualifications.* Parties and their counsel are allowed to select whomever they wish to serve as their mediator. However, if an individual wants to be a court-certified mediator, he or she must satisfactorily complete a court-approved mediator performance skill-training program. Persons serving as mediators for neighborhood citizenship cases must complete a twenty-hour training program; those persons mediating family matters or civil cases involving claims of more than five thousand dollars must complete forty hours of training. In addition, persons who are court-certified to mediate the neighborhood citizenship cases reflect a broad range of vocational backgrounds and training; those who are court-certified to mediate civil circuit or matrimonial cases must be either a lawyer licensed to practice law in Florida or a mental health professional, and he or she must also satisfy a minimum length of years in practice requirement.

3. *Fees.* For cases involving claims below a prescribed dollar amount, mediators provide their service on a volunteer basis. For family cases and larger civil cases, mediators can establish whatever fee schedule they desire, subject to court approval of those fees as "reasonable fees." The standard practice is to charge an hourly rate.

4. *Program Administration.* State and local offices supervise, coordinate and monitor the delivery of mediation services. For a substantial number of cases, particularly in the family area involving parties with low to modest incomes, court personnel conduct the mediation hearings. For cases handled by private mediators, no public reporting requirements exist.

Within ten years of operation, Florida reported that more than three thousand persons had been certified as mediators and that mediations had been conducted in more than one hundred twenty thousand cases per year. The legal culture in Florida has embraced its use, deploying mediation to resolve cases ranging from typical personal injury and breach of contract cases to medical malpractice claims and multi-party construction project disputes.

Florida's approach serves as an important benchmark against which other state initiatives during the 1990s were measured. Its approach also raised challenges not encountered in prior decades; some were referenced above, but a range of matters dealing with ensuring quality performance surfaced with particular urgency. These matters include such questions as the following:

1. If all mediation sessions are conducted in a confidential setting, how is the public to learn about, and gain confidence in, this segment of the justice system?

2. If a court system effectively mandates parties to use mediation before they can go to trial, what does the court do to insure that parties have qualified mediators to serve them?

3. While lawyers represent parties in many cases going to mediation, what special rules or protections are required in mediation to protect the *pro se* (unrepresented) party?

[4]   LESSONS AND LEGACIES OF THE 1980s

Spiraling practice and policy questions emerged as mediation's expansion accelerated. The more significant concerns are highlighted below.

[a]   Practice Challenges

Urgent questions regarding mediator practice surfaced during this decade. Some presented the challenge of trying to reconcile new practice twists with earlier approaches and values; others presented new, unforeseen challenges:

[i]   Reconciling New Practices with Existing Patterns

(a)   Mediator Qualifications

As the use of mediation expanded to address public disputes and court-annexed questions, the question of who was qualified to mediate these cases arose. The debate was frequently framed as whether a mediator needed "substantive expertise" as well as "process expertise." For public disputes, parties asked who could effectively assist them to resolve controversies involving technical issues relating to water pollution or the delivery of public utilities; comparable questions arose for servicing individual disputes that ranged from matrimonial dissolutions to contract disputes involving complex construction issues. A related question was whether or not a mediator could be a generalist or needed to specialize in a particular area of work.

(b)   Defining and Servicing a "Case"

With the substantial shift to servicing individual disputants, mediators and parties defined a "case" as matters consisting of legal claims; this quickly led to a mediator requiring all parties to "focus" on and resolve the "same" matters in each case. The capacity to develop innovative, creative resolutions for individual cases was curtailed by the weight of repetitive practice.

(c)   Maintaining Process Flexibility

One of mediation's strengths lies in the freedom of the mediators and parties to create or adapt rules and procedures to meet the particular dynamics of an individual dispute. Efficiency, though, is also an important value. As the types of mediation cases in a mediator's practice became repetitive (all "divorces," for example), the practitioner adopted forms and rules to address them. Process flexibility was subdued by the need for efficient business practices.

[ii] Challenges of New Domains

The practice issues that arose as mediation's use moved to service different constituents included the following:

(a) Financing Mediator Services

Before the onset of divorce mediation and comprehensive statewide mediation programs, parties did not underwrite a mediator's compensation; rather, proponents sought financial support from government or private foundation sources. That principle was incorporated into the development of state offices of mediation which addressed public disputes, but the operative mechanism for dealing with mediation's use for individual controversies was the private market place. And that generated traditional questions of distributive justice: If parties had to pay their share of the mediator's fee in addition to paying their lawyer fees, could the financial burden be justified? Would some people choose, or be compelled, to use their dispute resolution financial budget to pay for mediators rather than their lawyer, thereby being effectively deprived of their right to counsel? Are persons without capacity to pay denied access to mediation? Policy makers had to make hard choices when confronting these dilemmas.

(b) Insuring Quality Performance by Mediators

As the state courts' role expanded in encouraging or mandating parties to use mediation, their responsibility for ensuring quality services increased. Court officials became responsible for educating the parties about the mediation process and for supervising its efficient, fair implementation. Discharging these responsibilities raised new questions. For instance, if mediation conferences are confidential, is it appropriate for a judge to ask the parties about what occurred during the mediation in order to supervise that mediator's performance? Conversely, if the parties fail to reach resolution in mediation and proceed to trial, is it appropriate for the judge to ask the mediator for his or her insights about the case? Additionally, in systems where courts assign a mediator to a case, would the mediator deliberately or inadvertently exert extra pressure on the parties to settle their case in mediation in order to impress the judge with his or her mediator skills? These and other challenges raised important questions about program design and service delivery.

(c) Integrating Competing Professional Values into the Mediation Process

Mediation's expansion into a state-wide comprehensive system forced a re-examination of the conception of the mediator's role. Mediator neutrality had been the signal value of the early mediation experiments. Now, though, parties began to look to the mediator as someone who was an expert in the matter under discussion; parties involved in a personal injury accident would select as their mediator a lawyer experienced in that area of the law. How was the mediator to remain neutral while simultaneously drawing upon her professional expertise and experience to assist the parties?

In conjunction with these developing practice and policy issues, a more fundamental shift was occurring. The early proponents of mediation were individuals and social institutions committed to using mediation as a participatory process to address prominent social conflicts within a community; it is fair to characterize them as social activists. But the persons behind mediation's expanded use during the 1980s were institutional players: legislators, business leaders, mental health professionals, educational leaders, and governmental agency and court administrators. Each had their reasons for using mediation to meet identifiable needs. As noted above, while there was important overlap and consistency in mediator values, practices, and policies among the early innovators and their institutional successors, there was not a perfect congruence. This led some commentators to bemoan the "co-optation" of mediation by the "system" while others embraced mediation's growing presence as a recognition of its success.

[b] Policy

With mediation practice penetrating multiple contexts, new policy questions emerged. Some of the more significant of these policy questions are discussed in the following sections.

[i] Mediator Qualifications

While this matter affected one's practice, in that persons deemed not qualified to help would not be hired or selected by the parties as a mediator, the topic also generate a significant policy question: must one possess certain qualifications in order to mediate certain types of disputes? During the "Foundational" period of the 1960s and 1970s, a person's qualifications related to life experiences and communication skills, not professional training and academic degrees. As mediation came to be used in such defined contexts as matrimonial dissolution or court-filed cases, the relevance of professional training gained salience because the courts properly perceived themselves to be the guarantor of providing qualified individuals as mediators. One significant policy ramification of the movement to use educational credentials to establish mediator qualifications is that policy's impact on the diversity of the mediator pool. That concern for ensuring broad-based access to the mediation profession fuels the debate about mediator certification that appears in Chapter 7, *infra*.

[ii] Ethical Standards

With persons beginning to establish private mediation practices came the need to articulate ethical standards of conduct. Mediator advertising and fee structures had to be addressed, as did the more urgent matter of clarifying how the practice of mediation differed from rendering legal, psychological, or other professional services.

[c] Professional Development

Mediation's expanded use was triggered, shaped, and evaluated by persons committed to ensuring informed policy and practice.

[i] Professional Organizations and Activities

(a) The Society of Professionals in Dispute Resolution (SPIDR)

The growth in SPIDR's membership and activities reflected mediation's expanding range of activity. By the end of the 1980s, attendance at SPIDR's annual conference grew from several hundred to almost a thousand partici-pants; its membership roster was growing to what would ultimately exceed three thousand persons in the following decade; and it developed specialty areas so that mediators active in labor relations, court programs, schools, family, or the environment would all have a place within the organization. Program activities were also conducted through its local chapters.

(b) Other Professional Organizations

Other professional organizations were also formed during this period. The Academy of Family Mediators was created to monitor and establish perfor-mance standards for mediating family disputes. It developed a journal, the *Mediation Quarterly*, for contributors to share research and practice insights. Program directors of Community Dispute Resolution Centers formed state-wide organizations and coalitions to share information and adopt strategies to ensure program growth. And Bar Associations at the national, state and local levels established committees to explore and monitor mediation's growth in their respective jurisdictions. The ABA solidified its growing recognition and support for these developments by converting its Special Committee into an on-going Standing Committee and staffed it accordingly; by the 1990s, this Committee would become a new Section of the ABA.

[ii] Scholarship

Scholarship on mediation was transformed during the 1980s; perhaps more remarkably, scholarship transformed practice. This development occurred in three distinct ways.

(a) Theory Centers

The William and Flora Hewlett Foundation provided leadership and finan-cial support to create Theory Centers in Dispute Resolution; it wanted to help move the dispute resolution field beyond "sharing experiences" to understand-ing its basic structures and values. The Foundation's commitment was to provide financial support to a limited number of universities at which there were groups of scholars interested in analyzing conceptual and theoretical aspects of dispute resolution processes from multiple perspectives; its hope was that such institutions would sustain these activities through other financial resources once the Foundation's grant expired.

The Program on Negotiation (PON), a consortium of faculty from Harvard University, Massachusetts Institute of Technology, and Tufts University, was created with this Hewlett Foundation support and remains, perhaps, its best known center. PON was located administratively at Harvard Law School, where prominent professors Roger Fisher and Frank E.A. Sander were engaged in pathbreaking work in the area; a faculty member from each of the participating institutions served on a rotating basis as Executive Director. Other universities who were among the initial Theory Center recipients were Northwestern, Stanford, the University of Michigan, and George Mason. Scholars at these centers focused their work on examining negotiation, mediation and other forms of third-party intervention in a variety of contexts: business settings; social conflict; and international affairs; courts.

Among the work products of PON was a book on negotiation authored by Roger Fisher and William Ury entitled, *Getting to Yes*. Published in 1981, its impact on the dispute resolution field in general, and mediation in particular, was electrifying, immediate, and pervasive. The book introduced the concept of "principled" or "interest-based" bargaining. By the end of the decade, the Federal Mediation and Conciliation Service (FMCS) had introduced "interest-based" negotiation training for its staff mediators and encouraged parties to collective bargaining sessions to engage in "interest-based bargaining." Mediator trainers in other sectors quickly incorporated the Fisher/Ury thesis into their programs. Several other books written by PON participating scholars soon appeared, including *The Art and Science of Negotiation*, by Howard Raiffa, and *The Manager as Negotiator* by David Lax and James Sebenius, and there was renewed interest in and discussion of the classic, *A Behavioral Theory of Labor Negotiations*, by Richard Walton and Robert McKersie. Mediator practitioners could no longer complain that there were no "standard" materials in the field that they should read.

The Hewlett Foundation has sustained and expanded this program to support comparable scholarly and policy work through eighteen university-based theory centers. While the Theory Centers provided important impetus for scholarship, they were not its only source. Before the 1980s concluded, there were new books on the mediation process that focused on its general use in social policy or court programs as well as its deployment in such specific settings as divorce.

(b) Legal Scholarship

During this decade, legal scholars and law schools became active, significant contributors to the emerging dispute resolution field. In 1984, The Ohio State University College of Law and the Benjamin Cardozo School of Law implemented the nation's first clinical mediation programs using law students as mediators to resolve neighborhood citizenship disputes and small claims court cases. The first law school courses in dispute resolution, and their accompanying casebooks, emerged in the middle 1980s. And in the late 1980s, the faculty at the University of Missouri-Columbia School of Law led by Professor

Leonard Riskin, developed a broad-based curriculum in which materials for studying ADR processes were introduced into each course of the traditional first–year curriculum.

Two law reviews devoted exclusively to dispute resolution scholarship were launched during the decade: *The Journal of Dispute Resolution* was started at the University of Missouri-Columbia School of Law, and *The Ohio State Journal on Dispute Resolution* was published at the College of Law at The Ohio State University. Together with PON's *Negotiation Journal* and AFM's *Mediation Quarterly*, these journals became the focused, dedicated resources for scholarship and practice commentary.

(c) Degree Programs

The emergence in the 1980s of University advanced degree programs in conflict resolution was important. It represented a signal shift away from the traditional academic home for dispute resolution scholarship, Industrial Relations, to a multi-disciplinary or eclectic approach. George Mason University established the first Master of Arts and Doctor of Philosophy degree programs in Conflict Resolution. Offered through its newly-established Institute of Conflict Analysis and Resolution (ICAR), the curriculum reflected a broad-based offering of courses dealing with theoretical and practical issues arising in such diverse disputing contexts as international affairs and community-based interpersonal problems. Among its initial faculty members were the late James Laue, a trained theologian and sociologist who was a pioneer in mediation's use in its Foundational years. The ICAR program is committed to an inter-disciplinary study of conflict and conflict resolution processes, with persons trained in political science, law, sociology and psychology serving as its faculty; the practitioner experience of the Foundational years in public sector labor relations remains notably absent from this, and subsequent, degree programs. That curricular shape has been repeated in the design of most conflict resolution degree and certificate programs established thereafter.

§ D 1990s: MEDIATION AND DEMOCRATIC GOVERNANCE

[1] OVERVIEW

Mediation's systemic growth during the 1980s targeted activities primarily at the state and local level. This was particularly true for court initiatives involving mediation. Following Florida's lead, states such as Texas, Indiana, North Carolina and others embraced a commitment to the comprehensive use of mediation to resolve a broad range of cases on their court docket. Some states passed legislation that required mediation's use in particular areas, such as disputes between mobile-home owners and their park landlords; more comprehensively, other states required the litigating parties to affirmatively indicate that they had examined using some form of ADR (including mediation) but for compelling reasons related to their specific case believed such a route inappropriate or ill-timed to be of assistance.

Mediation programs connected to court services were developed to address a dizzying array of cases: "Victim Offender Reconciliation Programs" brought together the crime victim with its perpetrator to discuss ways of engaging in reconciliation initiatives. Complex Child Dependency and Neglect matters involving social workers, guardians ad litem, and parents and their lawyers were sent to mediation to explore designing acceptable plans that could lead to the child being safely reassigned to live with the responsible parent.

With expanding mandates to mediate, the range of controversies being resolved through mediation duplicated the world of litigation. Intellectual property disputes, international business transactions, and class-action law suits were resolved in the privacy of mediated discussions. And the numbers of professionals, particularly lawyers, who developed full-time private mediation practices notably expanded.

As mentioned earlier, with the demise of the Soviet Union at the decade's dawn, leaders of democracy-building efforts in South Africa, Central and Eastern Europe, and the Far East surveyed effective processes and perspectives for strengthening democratic values into their governance structures. As a part of this effort, they solicited training, technical, and scholarly assistance from the leading mediation practitioners, trainers, scholars, and professional organizations within the United States. These collaborations generated new legislation incorporating mediation into governmental decision-making processes, created court-annexed mediation programs, developed new university curricular offerings in conflict resolution, and produced multiple training programs in negotiation, mediation, and collaborative problem-solving skills for leaders of both non-governmental organizations (NGOs) who led the reform efforts as well as for newly elected public officials. The extensive U.S. experience of using mediation in multiple settings for more than two decades constituted a significant base for analyzing and meeting these multiple needs.

As the century concluded, two additional arenas for mediation's use in the United States emerged: the last major governmental player—the Federal Government—weighed in, and parties began to glimpse the future of mediation's use in cyberspace.

[2] THE ROLE OF THE FEDERAL GOVERNMENT

[a] Overview

In a significant way, the U.S. federal government legitimized and endorsed the use of mediation when, in 1947, it created the Federal Mediation and Conciliation Service to provide impasse services to private sector companies and unions engaged in collective bargaining. Comparable services afforded under the Railway Labor Act to resolve workplace disputes in the railroad and airline industries stand as a continuous reminder of mediation's role in resolving vital controversies that affect the nation's well-being. Finally, through sustained funding of the Community Relations Service of the U.S. Department of Justice, the federal government cemented its support for using mediation to resolve social policy issues. But the commitment of the federal government to use mediation either within the federal court system or more expansively throughout the executive agencies was, until the 1990s, subdued. That has now changed.

[b] Federal Agencies

In 1990, Congress passed two laws affecting the use of alternative dispute resolution processes in federal agencies. The Negotiated Rulemaking Act established a framework whereby a federal government agency responsible for issuing various rules (e.g. the Environmental Protection Agency or the Federal Communications Commission) could engage a neutral third-party intervener (mediator) to facilitate rule-development. Within this framework (referred to as "Reg-Neg") the selected mediator meets with those parties who will be affected or regulated by the rule. The intervener's role is to manage the negotiations between those interested parties and the federal agency decision-makers so that all the stakeholders collectively identify regulatory needs, the strengths and weaknesses of various approaches for addressing those needs, and, to the extent possible, mutually develop and agree upon regulatory guidelines. In short, the statutory purpose is to facilitate the development of governmental regulations through assisted negotiations as an alternative to the traditional, and adversarial, "notice and comment" procedure. Though the use of the "reg-neg" process has been uneven, it continues.

Congress also passed the Administrative Dispute Resolution Act in 1990. The Act authorizes and encourages each federal agency to consider using various dispute resolution processes, including mediation, to resolve any of the multiple issues that constitute their work, from intra-agency controversies to agency/public interactions. This initiative has received additional support from Executive Orders from Presidents George P. Bush (1991) and Bill Clinton (1998), directing or encouraging agencies and their litigation counsel to explore various resolution procedures in addition to traditional litigation.

[c] Federal Courts

With the passage of the Civil Justice Reform Act of 1990 and the Alternative Dispute Resolution Act in 1998, Congress aligned the federal district courts with the ADR movement. However, unlike the state court initiatives which encouraged or mandated mediation's use, the federal approach required federal district courts to establish a more general ADR program; mediation, advisory arbitration, mini-trials, or summary jury trials were among the processes that district courts could make available. The 1998 Act also mandated that litigants consider the use of ADR at an appropriate time. Several district courts quickly adopted advisory arbitration programs; soon thereafter, selected district courts adopted experimental mediation programs using volunteer attorneys as mediators. One important, unusual twist that has developed in the federal sector is the use of mediation within the federal circuit courts of appeal; a designated court employee serves full-time as a mediator of cases that are on appeal, conducting some mediation conferences in person and others by telephone.

[3] TECHNOLOGY AND MEDIATION

Technology permeates the practice of dispute resolution in two ways. While digital telephones, fax machines, and cable television bands permit rapid communication or dialogue among multiple parties, the Internet revolution increases that capacity in ways not yet fully explored. Electronic mail, chat rooms, and mobile communication apparatus permit people to communicate with one another from virtually anywhere in the world. These tools reduce the need to find mutually acceptable meeting dates or wait for documents to be transmitted through normal postal services, and thereby diminishes the delays that might otherwise occur in conducting conversations between disputing parties and among the mediator and the parties. Cable television access allows for all members of a community to watch public discussion of important, public policy issues. The Internet, via list-serves, offers the possibility of facilitating broad-based participation and discussion of policy matters by any interested person throughout the world; indeed, the world is a community. These are important efficiency contributions for expediting the transmission of information and ideas.

But the Internet technology also promises to take the need for dispute resolution—and possibly mediation—into uncharted waters, and there was a glimpse of that environment as the new millennium started. Experiments using the Internet to mediate disputes began in the late 1990s. For example, parties to a consumer-merchant dispute could submit their controversy to mediation conducted entirely via the computer. Parties identified their concerns, advanced proposed solutions, and then, through guided questioning and discussion by a mediator, considered possible outcomes. All these conversations were conducted electronically. This approach did not fundamentally change the structure of mediation's use: identifiable parties who had personally engaged in an unsuccessful transaction submitted their controversy through the Internet to a mediator. What was unusual, though, was that the parties were not personally acquainted with the selected mediator, nor were they restricted to resolving their controversy in a particular jurisdiction; disputes among parties in the state of Oregon could be resolved via the Internet with a mediator from Massachusetts. The development of E-commerce, though, promises to change the structure of disputes and the format of the mediation process that is shaped to resolve such disputes.

E-commerce occurs entirely via technology. A typical example is the following: a consumer in the United States orders a product from a French vendor who uses a Brazilian supplier to fill the order. If the customer is dissatisfied with the product (or, worse yet, never receives it but has already paid for it on her credit card), how is he or she to gain satisfaction? These are uncharted territories. The consumer does not know the vendor; the vendor can refuse to acknowledge the consumer's e-mail complaints; and the consumer is unlikely to travel personally to France or Brazil to locate his or her contractual counterpart and contest the matter. What happens? No one has yet developed appropriate, effective dispute resolution protocols for such situations. In some ways, these transactions mirror a routine international business transaction for which parties frequently stipulate to use arbitration to resolve controversies arising from such transactions. But in those business to business situations, the parties have usually retained lawyers to negotiate contracts that include these arbitral provisions, and those lawyers attend to these details with traditional professional care. In contrast, E-commerce is routinely conducted directly between businesses and consumers; most consumers cannot be expected to pay attention to designing dispute settlement mechanisms to resolve their controversies, and, even if they did, it is not clear how they would enforce such contractual provisions. Whether and how mediation can be useful in this domain will be answered only through the experience of the early years of the twenty-first century.

§ E THE CHALLENGES OF GROWTH: LESSONS AND LEGACIES AT THE MILLENNIUM

The enthusiasm which has accompanied the meteoric rise of mediation must be tempered by an appropriate demand for accountability. Important studies raise questions regarding the degree to which mediation meets some or all of its goals, beginning fundamentally with concerns regarding whether parties are treated fairly in mediation. These questions warrant careful analysis. What is exciting to realize, though, is that the study of the design and implementation of these dispute resolution processes in the new millennium commands the interest and skill of the practicing lawyer to a substantially larger degree than has historically been the case.

Another consequence of these multiple mediation initiatives is that more than 2200 statutes and court rules now reference "mediation." This situation poses important challenges. Lawyers practicing across state jurisdictions must know which law governs their mediation process and whether different states approach mediation with a consistent vision. In an attempt to provide clarity and consistency to these matters, the National Conference of Commissioners on Uniform State Laws and the American Bar Association's Section on Dispute Resolution initiated in 1997 an unprecedented partnership geared to develop a Uniform Mediation Statute. The draft statute is currently scheduled for discussion and possible adoption by NCCUSL in July, 2001. The proposed statute, whether or not adopted by the various states, constitutes an important benchmark in the development of law, policy and practice in mediation.

A final dimension of mediation's growth and stability lies in professional development. Law student training in mediation is now standard at most U.S. law schools, and similar courses are offered in graduate school training in disciplines ranging from environmental science and city planning to health care. Professional associations have expanded their membership and activity. In the early 1990s, representatives of the ABA's Section on Dispute Resolution, AAA, and SPIDR developed a model code of ethical conduct for mediators; the multi-faceted goal was to articulate standards of conduct for mediators and sustain public confidence in the integrity of the mediation. *See* Chapter 7 *infra*. And as the new century begins, representatives from SPIDR, AFM, and CREnet (mediators for school-based programs) voted to merge their organizations in order to create one comprehensive professional association that would meet the professional needs of persons who mediate all types of cases. The new organization is to be called the Association for Conflict Resolution ("ACR").

All practicing lawyers in the United States in the twenty-first century must know about mediation, for they will be involved in counseling their clients about its dynamics, representing clients in such conferences, or serving as mediators themselves. Lawyers have much to contribute to sustaining the quality of mediation's use, for they are trained to analyze and shape human interactions in a manner congruent with principles of fair treatment, resourceful problem-solving, and fidelity to community ideals. Lawyers have contributed significantly to mediation's recent development, and they must continue their responsible stewardship of its use.

Chapter 2
NEGOTIATION

§ A OVERVIEW

It is essential that the student of the mediation process have some familiarity with negotiation theory and practice strategies. Mediation is generally defined by relating it to negotiation. Some commentators, for example, have defined mediation as negotiation in the presence of a third-party neutral (the mediator). Moreover, the parties to a mediation will often have attempted to negotiate a settlement prior to the mediation and may therefore arrive at the mediation with firmly entrenched negotiation postures and positions.

This chapter introduces some of the thinking about the negotiation process, particularly those commentaries that would be helpful to the lawyer mediator or the lawyer representing a party in mediation. During the past few decades, an extensive literature on the subject of negotiation has evolved. A rich scholarly literature explores such topics as psychological barriers to settlement and negotiator styles. As well, neighborhood bookstores carry popular treatments of negotiation that offer tips on how to negotiate on a wide range of subjects and from a number of different perspectives.

As you read through the materials on negotiation theory, pay particular attention to the vocabulary that emerges. Phrases such as "win-win solutions," "integrative versus distributive bargaining," "cooperative versus competitive negotiations," "positional bargaining," and "collaborative problem-solving" are used extensively throughout the mediation literature.

This chapter is arranged into three sections that offer a sampling from the literature on negotiation intended for lawyers. Section B focuses on negotiation strategies and behavior. Section C addresses the ethics of negotiation, particularly the issue of lying in negotiations. Section D explores psychological and economic analyses of negotiation.

NOTE ON NEGOTIATION TERMINOLOGY

As noted above, negotiation theorists have developed a distinctive vocabulary. Although this terminology may initially seem somewhat confusing, each of the authors whose writings are excerpted in this chapter views the negotiation process somewhat differently and is seeking to develop a conceptual framework for understanding how people *negotiate*, or *bargain*. Indeed, commentators generally use the terms *negotiation* and *bargaining* as if they are interchangeable. We mention some of these terms at the outset to emphasize that these words and phrases are not necessarily interdependent but merely represent varying perspectives on how to describe or analyze the negotiation process.

In Section B of this chapter, we will encounter the notion of *principled negotiation*. As espoused by Fisher and Ury, particularly in their landmark book, *Getting to YES, principled negotiation* is an approach to bargaining that permits "the pie" that is the subject of the negotiation to be expanded, resulting in so-called *win-win solutions*. This approach is often also referred to as *integrative bargaining*.

Fisher and Ury also introduced the concept of *BATNA* (Best Alternative to a Negotiated Agreement). The term *BATNA*, when encountered in the literature, should not be confused with one's *bottom line*. *Bottom line* generally refers to the very minimum for which you will settle. *Bottom line* is also sometimes referred to as your *reservation price*. *BATNA*, on the other hand, is not the minimum that you think you should get but what you will do if you don't get that minimum. What will you do if you are unable to negotiate an agreement? For attorneys attempting to negotiate a settlement in a court case, their clients' *BATNA* is often that of trying the case in court.

Those who ascribe to *principled negotiation*, or *integrative bargaining*, generally distinguish it from other forms of negotiation that are focused on dividing a limited resource. Specifically, *integrative bargaining* can be contrasted to *distributive bargaining*, *positional negotiations* or *hard bargaining*, where parties are more rigidly locked into positions as they attempt to split up a fixed pie.

Thus, James White criticizes *principled negotiation* because it fails to consider the *distributional* aspects of negotiation. Rather than assuming that the pie is expandable, *distributive bargaining* assumes *zero-sum negotiations*, where plus one for me equals minus one for you.

The *integrative-distributive* dichotomy may be juxtaposed with the *cooperative-competitive* dichotomy discussed by Gerald Williams and Gary Goodpaster. Do the *cooperative* negotiators fit neatly into the *integrative bargaining* package and the *competitive* negotiators into the *distributive bargaining* package? Not necessarily. Each of these commentators on the negotiation process is using a different framework for discussing negotiation behavior. What is important is that you understand the author's use of each term and phrase well enough to be able to consider how they overlap and how they can be distinguished from one another.

Some theorists distinguish negotiation behaviors from negotiation processes. For example, in explaining *problem-solving negotiation*, Carrie Menkel-Meadow states that *cooperative* or *collaborative negotiation* are terms that refer to behaviors that people exhibit while negotiating. The *problem-solving* approach to negotiation, on the other hand, refers to a more comprehensive process. She suggests that "[t]he conceptualization used in planning problem-solving negotiation is useful in all negotiation, regardless of the particular behaviors chosen in the executory stages."

Having a clear understanding of these terms and phrases is crucial to an attorney's being able to adopt a comprehensive, flexible approach to representing a client's interests in a negotiation or mediation. Indeed, some lawyers may use multiple, seemingly inconsistent, approaches in a single negotiation. For example, a lawyer may decide that her client's interests can best be served by taking an *integrative* approach at the outset of a negotiation and then switching to *distributive bargaining*. Or, a lawyer might commence a negotiation using an *adversarial competitive approach* and then become more *problem solving* when it appears that no deal is forthcoming. As you read through the materials in this chapter, consider whether and how such combination of approaches might be sensible.

§ B NEGOTIATION STRATEGIES AND BEHAVIOR

The materials below introduce some of the more prominent prescriptions and descriptions of negotiation strategy and behavior. Readings discussing and critiquing "principled negotiation" are excerpted in Section [1]. Section [2] presents materials on cooperative vs. competitive negotiation, and Section [3] outlines the "problem solving" approach to negotiation, which calls upon lawyers to rethink certain basic assumptions about lawyering.

[1] PRINCIPLED NEGOTIATION

Getting to YES: Negotiating Agreement Without Giving In by Roger Fisher and William Ury is perhaps the most well-known work in the extensive negotiation literature. While it can usually be found in the neighborhood bookstore, *Getting to YES* has also been the focus of considerable commentary by legal scholars. It argues for a "principled" approach to negotiation. The essential method presented by Fisher and Ury calls upon the negotiator to *"separate the people from the problem," "focus on interests rather than positions," "invent options for mutual gain,"* and *"insist on using objective criteria."* *Getting to Yes* also introduced the acronym *BATNA*—Best Alternative to a Negotiated Agreement—into the ADR vocabulary.

In the first excerpt, Robert Condlin reviews these precepts from the standpoint of the lawyer's role. James White then critiques *Getting to YES* from a distributive bargaining perspective, Roger Fisher comments on White's analysis, and Condlin offers additional critical commentary.

Proponents of principled negotiation discredit the "positional" approach to bargaining that is perhaps most consistent with a lawyer's training. In our adversarial system, lawyers are trained to develop and advance "positions" on behalf of their clients with adversarial zeal. Principled bargainers urge lawyers to abandon negotiation strategies and behaviors that require rigid adherence to their positions and argue that they adopt the precepts of the "principled" approach to negotiation.

BARGAINING IN THE DARK: THE NORMATIVE INCOHERENCE OF LAWYER DISPUTE BARGAINING ROLE

51 Md. L. Rev. 1, 23-26 (1992) ·

By Robert J. Condlin

. . . [P]rincipled bargaining theory asserts that successful bargainers are those who "separate the people from the problem," "focus on interests, not positions," "invent options for mutual gain," and "insist on objective criteria."

Separating the people from the problem involves preventing perceptual and psychological errors in communication and interpretation from skewing analysis of the substantive issues presented by the bargaining problem. Principled bargainers recognize that "[n]egotiators are people first," who get angry, depressed, fearful, hostile, frustrated, and offended. They have egos that are easily threatened. They see the world from their own personal vantage point, and they frequently confuse perceptions with reality. Routinely, they fail to interpret what you say in the way you intend and do not mean what you understand them to say.

To protect against such potential disasters, principled bargainers are encouraged to "see the situation as the other side sees it," with the aid of a set of interactive rules of thumb (e.g., do not deduce their intentions from your fears; recognize, identify, and discuss emotion explicitly; confirm interpretations before acting on them; and the like), which make overinterpretation difficult and projection less likely. When bargainers identify communicative incompetence and isolate its effects, proponents of principled bargaining claim, the bargaining conversation will deal naturally and successfully with satisfying the parties' respective interests.

The directive to focus on interests rather than positions is a more elusive notion. Interests are "the silent movers behind the hubbub of positions," what causes one to decide on a position, and the "needs, desires, concerns, and fears" that underlie expressed statements of what one wants. In the principled view, reconciling interests, not positions, is the basic problem of bargaining, but it is a more manageable problem because for every interest several positions usually exist that would satisfy it, and behind opposed positions lie more shared interests than conflicting ones. While principled bargainers are soft on people, they are hard on interests. They commit to interests, and make them come alive with all of their "aggressive energies." This is because "two negotiators, each pushing hard for their interests, will often stimulate each other's creativity in thinking up mutually advantageous solutions."

Inventing options for mutual gain consists of identifying and mulling over multiple solutions to the bargaining problem, and comparing, contrasting, and refining such solutions until a mutually satisfactory outcome is found. It includes "brainstorming," in which bargainers hypothesize outcomes but do not evaluate them until all imaginable possibilities are on the table, and perspective shifts, where bargainers consider the bargaining problem from the differing vantage points of description, analysis, diagnosis, and prescription, and through the intellectual frameworks of different disciplines and professions. Principled bargainers alter and re-alter the scope and strength of potential agreements, expand bargaining stakes until there is something for everyone, identify and match shared and dovetailing interests, and treat agreements as tentative and subject to improvement. . . . The object of this process is to discover a configuration of the (continuingly redefined) bargaining pot that leaves all parties with those items or parts of items they value most, and each party with a payoff that is roughly equivalent (or at least perceived to be) to the other's.

Principled bargaining's distinctive characteristic, however, is its insistence on the use of objective criteria (the "principle" from which the theory takes its name), as the basis for settlement. To proponents of principled bargaining, objective criteria are important because they allow parties to arrive at lasting agreements amicably and efficiently. . . . Objective criteria consist of "fair standards and fair procedures." Standards and procedures are fair when they are "independent of" each side's will, are "legitimate and practical," and pass the test of "reciprocal application"—that is, each side would use the same standards and procedures if bargaining positions were reversed. Examples of fair standards include market value, replacement cost, depreciated book value, competitive prices, scientific judgment, precedent, community practice, what a court would decide, tradition, moral norms, and other consensus standards accepted by the bargaining parties and the community in which they bargain. Examples of fair procedures include "taking turns, drawing lots, letting someone else decide, and so on."

When more than one objective criterion is available as the basis for settlement, or when parties advance different criteria, as will usually be the case, bargainers should "look for an objective basis for deciding between them, such as which standard has been used by the parties in the past or which standard is more widely applied." If there are two (or more) standards that produce different results, but which seem equally legitimate, the parties should "split the difference or otherwise compromise between the results" suggested by the standards. Throughout the bargaining process, bargainers should "be open to reason" and yield "only to principle." Such a stance has the "power of legitimacy" and allows bargainers to prevail on the all-important issue of negotiation style. It allows them to shift discussion from positional bargaining to a search for a solution based on merit, and as such, is a dominant strategy over positional bargaining, giving principled bargainers an edge. "It is a form of 'right makes might.' "

The concept of principled bargaining has great analytical power and appeal. It builds on the idea of "legal astuteness," identified, but not elaborated upon, in the theory of cordial bargaining, and in the process adds an important normative dimension to the idea of cooperation. Being cooperative now means adhering to authoritative substantive norms—legal, moral and political— which form the backdrop of dispute settlement and make its outcomes legitimate and fair. It is no longer enough that bargainers be cordial, predictable, and nice; they must do justice as well. This normative addition transforms bargaining theory from a theory of strategy and manners to one also of morality and politics, and in so doing, helps justify bargaining's place in the system of adjudicatory justice.

THE PROS AND CONS OF "GETTING TO YES"

34 J. Legal Educ. 115, 115–120 (1984)[*]

By James J. White

Getting to YES is a puzzling book. On the one hand it offers a forceful and persuasive criticism of much traditional negotiating behavior. It suggests a variety of negotiating techniques that are both clever and likely to facilitate effective negotiation. On the other hand, the authors seem to deny the existence of a significant part of the negotiation process, and to oversimplify or explain away many of the most troublesome problems inherent in the art and practice of negotiation. The book is frequently naive, occasionally self-righteous, but often helpful.

. . . Unfortunately the book's emphasis upon mutually profitable adjustment, on the "problem solving" aspect of bargaining, is also the book's weakness. It is a weakness because emphasis of this aspect of bargaining is done to almost total exclusion of the other aspect of bargaining, "distributional bargaining," where one for me is minus one for you. Schelling, Karrass and other students of negotiation have long distinguished between that aspect of bargaining in which modification of the parties' positions can produce benefits for one without significant cost to the other, and on the other hand, cases where benefits to one come only at significant cost to the other. They have variously described the former as "exploring for mutual profitable adjustments," "the efficiency aspect of bargaining," or "problem solving." The other has been characterized as "distributional bargaining" or "share bargaining." Thus some would describe a typical negotiation as one in which the parties initially begin by cooperative or efficiency bargaining, in which each gains something with each new adjustment without the other losing any significant benefit. Eventually, however, one comes to bargaining in which added benefits to one impose corresponding significant costs on the other. For example, in a labor contract one might engage in cooperative bargaining by the modification of a medical plan so that the employer could engage a less expensive medical insurance provider, yet one that offered improved services. Each side gains by that change from the old contract. Ultimately parties in a labor negotiation will come to a raw economic exchange in which additional wage dollars for the employees will be dollars subtracted from the corporate profits, dollars that cannot be paid in dividends to the shareholders.

One can concede the authors' thesis (that too many negotiators are incapable of engaging in problem solving or in finding adequate options for mutual gain), yet still maintain that the most demanding aspect of nearly every negotiation is the distributional one in which one seeks more at the expense of the other. My principal criticism of the book is that it seems to overlook the ultimate hard bargaining. Had the authors stated that they were dividing the negotiation process in two and were dealing with only part of it, that omission would be excusable. That is not what they have done. Rather they seem to assume that a clever negotiator can make any negotiation into problem solving and thus completely avoid the difficult distribution. . . . To my mind this is naive. By so distorting reality, they detract from their powerful and central thesis.

Chapter 5, entitled "Insist on Objective Criteria," is a particularly naive misperception or rejection of the guts of distributive negotiation. Here, as elsewhere, the authors draw a stark distinction between a negotiator who simply takes a position without explanation and sticks to it as a matter of "will," and the negotiator who is reasonable and insists upon "objective criteria." Of course the world is hardly as simple as the authors suggest. Every party who takes a position will have some rationale for that position; every able negotiator rationalizes every position that he takes. Rarely will an effective negotiator simply assert "X" as his price and insist that the other party meet it.

The suggestion that one can find objective criteria (as opposed to persuasive rationalizations) seems quite inaccurate. . . . [T]he distributive aspect of the negotiation often turns on the relative power of the parties. One who could sell his automobile to a particular person for $6,000 could not necessarily sell it for more than $5,000 to another person, not because of principle, but because of the need of the seller to sell and the differential need of the two buyers to buy. To say that there are objective criteria that call for a $5,000 or $6,000 price, or in the case of a personal injury suit for a million dollars or an $800,000 judgment, is to ignore the true dynamics of the situation and to exaggerate the power of objective criteria. Any lawyer who has been involved in a personal injury suit will marvel at the capacity of an effective plaintiff's lawyer to appear to do what the authors seem to think possible, namely to give the superficial appearance of certainty and objectivity to questions that are inherently imponderable. For example, an effective plaintiff's lawyer will sometimes fix a certain dollar amount per week for the pain and suffering which one might suffer. He will then multiply that amount by the number of weeks per year and the number of years in the party's life expectancy. Thus he produces a series of tables and columns full of "hard" numbers. These have the appearance of objectivity, but in fact they are subjective, based (if on anything) on a judgment about how a jury would react to the case. Every lawyer who has ever been involved in a lawsuit in which experts have been hired by each side will have a deep skepticism about the authors' appeal to scientific merit as a guide in determining a fair outcome in the negotiation of any hotly disputed problem.

In short, the authors' suggestion in Chapter 5 that one can avoid "contests of will" and thereby eliminate the exercise of raw power is at best naive and at worst misleading. Their suggestion that the parties look to objective criteria to strengthen their cases is a useful technique used by every able negotiator. Occasionally it may do what they suggest: give an obvious answer on which all can agree. Most of the time it will do no more than give the superficial appearance of reasonableness and honesty to one party's position.

. . . [B]ecause the book almost totally disregards distributive bargaining, it necessarily ignores a large number of factors that probably have a significant impact on the outcome of negotiations.

. . . On the one hand the book promises an entirely new technique of negotiation, but it delivers only interesting techniques and insights. On the other hand the book delivers more than it promises in that its argument rests on a series of unarticulated moral premises. In sum, the book is useful; it contains interesting techniques and valid criticism of much negotiator behavior. However, its overstatement and its facile denial of some of the serious difficulties involved in negotiation detract from its quality.

COMMENT

34 J. Legal Educ. 120, 120–124 (1984) *

By Roger Fisher

. . . To some extent, I believe, White is more concerned with the way the world is, and I am more concerned with what intelligent people ought to do. One task is to teach the truth—to tell students the unpleasant facts of life, including how people typically negotiate. But I want a student to negotiate better than his or her father. I see my task as to give the best possible prescriptive advice, taking into account the way other human beings are likely to behave as well as one's own emotions and psychological state.

Suppose a husband and wife come to an expert in negotiation asking advice on how best to negotiate the terms of a separation agreement that will involve children and jointly-held property. What is the best advice that such an expert could give to both about the process—about the manner of negotiating that would be most likely to produce a wise and fair outcome while maximizing their ability to deal with future problems, and minimizing their costs in terms of time, resources, and emotional stress? If one of them alone asked for such advice, in what ways would wise recommendations differ? These are the questions I am interested in.

The world is a rough place. It is also a place where, taken collectively, we are incompetent at resolving our differences in ways that efficiently and amicably serve our mutual interests. It is important that students learn about bluffing and hard bargaining, because they will certainly encounter it. It is also important that our students become more skillful and wise than most people in dealing with differences. Thus, to some extent, White and I are emphasizing different aspects of what needs to be taught.

Are distributional issues amenable to joint problem solving? The most fundamental difference between White's way of thinking and mine seems to concern the negotiation of distributional issues "where one for me is minus one for you." We agree on the importance of cooperation, imagination, and the search for creative options where the task is to reconcile substantive interests that are compatible. White, however, sees the joint problem-solving approach as limited to that area. In his view, the most demanding aspect of nearly every negotiation is the distributional one in which one seeks more at the expense of the other. Distributional matters, in his view, must be settled by the ultimate hard bargaining. He regards it as a distortion of reality to suggest that problem solving is relevant to distributional negotiation.

Here we differ. By focusing on the substantive issues (where the parties' interests may be directly opposed), White overlooks the shared interest that the parties continue to have in the process for resolving that substantive difference. How to resolve the substantive difference is a shared problem. Both parties have an interest in identifying quickly and amicably a result acceptable to each, if one is possible. How to do so is a problem. A good solution to that process-problem requires joint action.

The guts of the negotiation problem, in my view, is not who gets the last dollar, but what is the best process for resolving that issue. It is certainly a mistake to assume that the only process available for resolving distributional questions is hard bargaining over positions. In my judgment it is also a mistake to assume that such hard bargaining is the best process for resolving differences efficiently and in the long-term interest of either side.

Two men in a lifeboat quarreling over limited rations have a distributional problem. One approach to resolving that problem is to engage in hard bargaining. A can insist that he will sink the boat unless he gets 60 percent of the rations. B can insist that he will sink the boat unless he gets 80 percent of the rations. But A's and B's shared problem is not just how to divide the rations; rather it is how to divide the rations without tipping over the boat and while getting the boat to safer waters. In my view, to treat the distributional issue as a shared problem is a better approach than to treat it as a contest of will in which a more deceptive, more stubborn, and less rational negotiator will tend to fare better. Treating the distributional issue as a problem to be solved ("How about dividing the rations in proportion to our respective weights?" or "How about a fixed portion of the rations for each hour that one of us rows?") is likely to be better for both than a contest over who is more willing to sink the boat.

Objective criteria. It is precisely in deciding such distributional issues that objective criteria can play their most useful role. Here is a second area of significant disagreement. White finds it useful to deny the existence of objective standards: "The suggestion that one can find objective criteria (as opposed to persuasive rationalizations) seems quite inaccurate." To his way of thinking the only approach is for a negotiator first to adopt a position and later to develop rationalizations for it: ". . . every able negotiator rationalizes every position that he takes."

No one has suggested that in most negotiations there is a single objective criterion that both parties will quickly accept as determinative. The question is rather what should be treated as the essence of the negotiation, and what attitude should be taken toward arguments advanced in the discussion. White thinks it better to treat positions of the parties as the essence of the negotiation, and objective standards advanced by either party as mere rationalizations. That is one approach. A different approach is possible and, I believe, preferable.

Two judges, in trying to reach agreement, will be looking for standards that should decide the case. They may have their predispositions and even strongly-held views, but they will jointly look for an agreed basis for decision. Each will typically advance law, precedent, and evidence not simply as rationalizations for positions adopted for other reasons, but honestly, as providing a fair basis for decision. White's example of litigation is the very one I would advance to demonstrate that however great the disagreement, the wise approach is to insist upon using objective criteria as the basis for decision. It is better for the parties in court to be advancing objective standards which they suggest ought to be determinative than to be telling the court that they won't take less (or pay more) than so many dollars. The same, I believe, is true for negotiators.

Two negotiators can be compared with two judges, trying to decide a case. There won't be a decision unless they agree. It is perfectly possible for fellow negotiators, despite their self-interest, to behave like fellow judges, in that they advance reasoned arguments seriously, and are open to persuasion by better arguments. They need not advance standards simply as rationalizations for positions, but as providing a genuine basis for joint decision.

What we are suggesting is that in general a negotiator should seek to persuade by coming up with better arguments on the merits rather than by simply trying to convince the other side that he is the more stubborn. A good guideline is for a negotiator to advance arguments as though presenting them to an impartial arbitrator, to press favorable bases for decision, but none so extreme as to damage credibility. (On the receiving side, a good guideline is for a negotiator to listen to arguments as though he were an impartial arbitrator, remaining open to persuasion despite self-interest and preconceptions.) My experience suggests that this method is often more efficient and amicable than hard positional bargaining and more often leads to satisfactory results for both parties.

. . . *Changed thinking. Getting to YES* says "Don't Bargain Over Positions." Students have now taught me that there are categories of negotiations where positional bargaining is the best way to proceed. On single-issue negotiations among strangers where the transaction costs of exploring interest would be high and where each side is protected by competitive opportunities, haggling over positions may work better than joint problem solving. A typical case would be negotiating a sale on the New York Stock Exchange.

Another chapter heading, "Separate the People from the Problem," also puts the matter too broadly. In some cases the people *are* the problem; negotiating a good relationship with them may be more important than the substantive outcome of any one negotiation. And good relations can ease future substantive negotiations. I still think that relationship issues and substantive issues should be separated to the following extent: One should not threaten a relationship as a means of trying to coerce a substantive concession; nor should one make an otherwise unjustified concession in hopes of buying a good relationship.

Getting to YES as a whole, I believe, blurs a desirable distinction between descriptive analysis and prescriptive advice. Descriptively, it sorts facts into useful categories: positions vs. interests; people issues vs. substantive ones; inventing vs. deciding; discussing what negotiators will or won't do vs. discussing what they ought to do. Those distinctions, like distinctions between reptiles and mammals, or between short snakes and long snakes, are objectively true and, despite possible difficulties in drawing lines, exist as facts in the real world. Whether or not they are useful is another question.

We go beyond suggesting these descriptive categories by advancing some prescriptive rules of thumb, indicated by the chapter headings in the book. These are not advanced as guidelines that will in every case produce the desired result. No such guidelines can exist, since negotiators who deal with each other often desire different results. The rules of thumb we advanced are the best we could come up with. Without knowing the particular subject matter of a negotiation or the identity of the people on the other side, what is the best advice one can give to a negotiator? People may prefer to ask different questions, but I have not yet heard better answers to the question on which we were and are working.

I am confident, however, that with the continued stimulating participation of people such as Jim White, we jointly will be able to produce both better questions and better answers.

BARGAINING IN THE DARK: THE NORMATIVE INCOHERENCE OF LAWYER DISPUTE BARGAINING ROLE

51 Md. L. Rev. 1, 26–34 (1992)[*]

By Robert J. Condlin

While a major advance . . . principled bargaining also has weaknesses in each of its core principles. For example, in discussing the importance of separating the people from the problem, the leading proponents of principled bargaining recommend both that bargainers identify with the other side ("see the situation as the other side sees it"),[84] and that they manipulate the other side when it is possible to do so. "Manipulate" is my characterization but it seems fair. For example, a principled bargainer is encouraged to "devote substantial time to working out the practical arrangements" of concessions so as to provide the other bargainer "with an impressive achievement and a real incentive to reach agreement on other issues.[85] Drag out concession-making, in other words, even when one is ready to concede, so that the other side will think it has accomplished more than it has and be correspondingly grateful. This may be instrumentally useful advice, but it encourages bargainers to be strategically inauthentic, and it seems slightly out of place in a bargaining method based on mutual cooperation and empathic identification with the other side. Following the dictates of principled bargaining is not always easy, in part, because the theory is not always clear about whether it is a genuine alternative to discredited positional bargaining, or a set of more sophisticated techniques for operating successfully within the positional mode.

Similarly, the advice to focus on interests rather than positions is based on an unargued premise, that the two are different in some significant sense, which is convincing to proponents of principled bargaining for reasons that ordinary language seems not to explain. In bargaining, all statements of interest are not very thinly disguised statements of position (i.e., that the interest must be provided for by some explicit term in the agreement), and statements of position are inarticulate but usually discernible statements of interest (i.e., that the money or whatever else is being discussed is desired for some particular reason or reasons—to feel vindicated, be made whole, take revenge, or the like). It simply is not possible for conversation of any sophistication to be about just one or the other. Principled bargaining implicitly admits this impossibility when it acknowledges that bargaining ultimately must

---

[84] *See* FISHER & URY, at 23. [ROGER FISHER & WILLIAM URY, GETTING TO YES, (1981)]
[85] *Id.* at 27.

involve the discussion of and agreement on settlement terms (positions), and describes a range of rhetorical and psychological techniques designed to help in this process. Given this acknowledgment, it is perhaps a bit disingenuous to suggest that "focusing on interests not positions" will make bargaining more productive.

Presumably, proponents of principled bargaining make the distinction between interest and position to emphasize the need for flexibility in defining bargaining objectives, and thus to encourage bargainers to take different approaches to solving the bargaining problem when necessary in order to avoid unproductive conflict, polarization, or deadlock. If flexibility is the goal, however, it is promoted by bargainer offer-and concession-making that is imaginative, contingent, and respectful. It is skill in formulating, discussing, refining, and discarding settlement terms (whether thought of or expressed as interests or positions), not skill in labeling them, that is critical. When the end is avoiding polarization, the means must be more than terminological.

There is an understanding of the interest-position distinction that proponents of principled bargaining may recognize, but do not discuss. In this view, interests are the ultimate ends of bargaining, the objectives one would pursue if perfectly and finally aware of what is to one's greatest advantage, judged from the vantage point of perfect information and the perspective of all of time. Positions are intermediate or provisional expressions of those ends, based on imperfect information and incomplete perspective. Ultimate ends are often different from intermediate ones, in the same manner that destinations are often different from way stations, because knowing perfectly what will be in one's ultimate interest is frequently not possible in any real or trustworthy sense within the time frame of bargaining.

For example, the lawyer bargainer must determine which of the client's many selves to consult in determining what to seek from a bargaining transaction. The pleasure-seeking self will want something different than the citizen self, the short term self something different than the long term self, and the public self something different than the private one. The client may want most not to have to decide at all, and wish only that the problem had never arisen. Asked today, she may want one thing, but tomorrow (or yesterday) another. Even when expressed, the description of interests is often likely to be a function of how, by whom, and under what circumstances the questions were asked. Moreover, statements of interests even when made are inevitably at the mercy of new information not taken into account in formulating the statements, and can be shaken to the core, even to the point of being repudiated, by such information. This is a particular concern in dispute negotiation where bargaining interests are partly a function of what outcomes are available, and where the information and understanding necessary to make that determination change constantly as bargaining proceeds. Only after a negotiation has concluded will a client know better what she wanted during it, and she may not know best for months or years to come. The problem with bargaining is that it forces one to articulate objectives that are mixed, contingent, tentative, fuzzy, and incomplete, as if they were discrete, fixed, tangible, and exhaustive. But this is true whether one thinks of objectives as interests or positions, and it is the real problem in understanding and articulating bargaining goals.

Principled bargaining's third foundational rule, the directive to invent options for mutual gain by expanding the bargaining pie and looking for shared and dovetailing interests, is often a helpful guide in resolving particular disputes, but of more limited use in constructing a general theory of bargaining. Bargainers sometimes get locked into unnecessarily zero-sum conceptions of their situations, and see conflicts where none exist, and when this happens, it can help to redefine issues, clarify goals, and expand the pie. Conceptually, however, this is not bargaining. Bargaining begins at the point where differences must be reconciled, accomodated, or compromised. It is not the same as individual bargainer interest clarification (i.e., learning), and is not needed when interest clarification will suffice. Inventing options for mutual gain is about avoiding the need to bargain, an important practical topic, but of limited significance in the theoretical task of explaining bargaining.

Finally, and most interestingly, there are weaknesses in the most controversial part of principled bargaining theory: its insistence on the use of "objective criteria" for determining outcome. "Objective" is an emotionally evocative term, with positive associations for most, but it is ambiguous in an important sense, which the theory of principled bargaining trades on, but does not discuss. Objective can mean neutral or nonpartisan, in the sense of treating each side's interests equally. Flipping a coin or splitting the difference is objective in this sense. Or it can mean fair and legitimate, in the sense of respecting recognized entitlements of the parties, and reconciling conflicts between them through the use of principles, procedures, and substantive norms that are accepted as authoritative. Neutrality and fairness are not always the same, however, as it is possible to be both neutral and unfair, and fair but biased. The theory of principled bargaining does not say so directly, and there may be some waffling, but its suggested examples of objective criteria, such as splitting techniques that divide pots into rough equivalents, consensus community practices, or the parties' past behavior, seem based on an understanding of objectivity as neutrality. Like "neutral" mechanisms generally, however, such criteria have a strong bias in favor of status quo distributions, and the status quo is not always fair, particularly to those who reasonably reject existing definitions of worth, received distributions of resources and power, consensus procedures, or the wisdom of past behavior, their own included. Principled bargaining cannot simply assume that neutral principles will be fair, and if it intends to stand on this proposition, then it must argue for it, directly and at length.

A second problem with objective criteria, as principled bargaining acknowledges, is that often there will be more than one objective criterion (by whatever definition) available to settle a dispute. In choosing among them, principled bargainers are told to look for second level criteria, or meta-criteria, that will tell one which is the appropriate first level norm. But principled bargaining does not explain why it is reasonable to expect the problem of more than one criterion to go away at the appellate level, or in other words, why it is reasonable to expect to find only one meta-criterion. . . .

In principled bargaining, objective criteria are important because they enable bargainers to avoid contests of will, those wasteful and degrading ego spats that cause unnecessary conflict and delay, and leave parties with the sense that their claims have not been understood or respected. Like many things in bargaining, however, avoiding contests of will is good advice to a point, and in principled bargaining, the point is sometimes missed. Objective criteria, like any criteria, are open-ended and indeterminate, and parties must deduce and debate their relevance and meaning on a case-by-case basis. Even noncontroversial points that eventually are accepted may take time to be understood, and a bargainer's resolve in discussing or debating the points is frequently decisive in influencing the extent to which the points are recognized and accepted. In a significant sense then, objective criteria do not exist independently of will, and it is a mistake to think that bargainer resolve plays no role in principled (or any other kind of) bargaining. Some contest of will must always be fought, not for their own sake, but because some points are true and yet some bargainers will be slow or reluctant to accept them.

By proposing a kind of bilateral, private adjudication as the proper understanding of cooperative bargaining, the theory of principled bargaining advances the idea of cooperation beyond the overly simple level of social style and explains the central role of authoritative substantive norms in determining the outcome of bargaining interactions. But for many who think that the resolution of differences from the perspective of individual, self-interested points of view (whether expressed as interests or positions) is destined to fail, principled bargaining's reluctance to jettison the adjudicatory model completely, and its incorporation of some features of adversary advocacy, prevent it from being the final word. This view requires a new orientation to bargaining, one that defines the bargaining task in terms of a mutual effort toward a common goal, and one that does not get sidetracked, however well-intended, into a destructive quest for correct answers to the question of whose substantive views are right and whose wrong. That is where the theory of problem-solving bargaining comes in.

NOTES AND QUESTIONS

(1) White's general criticism of Fisher and Ury's "principled," or "integrative," approach to negotiation is that it fails to account for the "distributional" aspects of a negotiation. The integrative approach is oriented toward achieving a win-win solution, while distributive bargaining assumes a zero-sum game where plus one for me means minus one for you. Is White correct when he argues that although one may wish to begin a negotiation with an integrative approach, ultimately you need to reckon with the distributive aspects of the negotiation? Even in those negotiations where the distributive aspects are clear, is it possible to take an integrative approach? That is, although integrative and distributive approaches to bargaining provide distinct communication frameworks, are they reconcilable? How? Which of these communication frameworks do you think would be most suitable for a mediation? Why?

(2) Both Condlin and White criticize Fisher and Ury's insistence on the use of "objective criteria." Why? Why does White argue in favor of "persuasive rationalizations"? Is this more in line with what a lawyer is trained to do?

(3) Condlin also criticizes Fisher and Ury for insisting on "separating the people from the problem," particularly through the use of "manipulative" techniques such as dragging out concession-making. However, there is no doubt that people problems, such as a growing dislike for the personality or attitude of the lawyer for the other side, may get in the way of one's ability to stay focused on one's client's interests. One of the more difficult people problems to deal with during a negotiation may arise when the lawyer for the other side makes offensive or demeaning comments. For a helpful analytical framework for dealing with such comments, see Andrea Kupfer Schneider, *Effective Responses to Offensive Comments*, 1994 Negotiation J. 107.

(4) As you read the material in the next section, consider how the integrative/distributive dichotomy meshes with the cooperative/competitive dichotomy.

[2] COOPERATIVE VERSUS COMPETITIVE NEGOTIATION

The behaviors that people exhibit when they negotiate or bargain have been the subject of considerable interest to social scientists. One set of research has sought to identify styles or patterns of negotiating behavior that might be deemed most "effective." Although there has never been a clear consensus over what is meant by negotiation effectiveness, these earlier studies have been very helpful in identifying varying negotiation styles or types. In particular, the identification of cooperative versus competitive negotiating styles emerged from this research. In the selections that follow, Professor Gerald Williams discusses the distinguishing characteristics of competitive and cooperative negotiators; Professor Gary Goodpaster argues for a clearer understanding of competitive behavior in negotiation; and Professor Williams reports on the similarities between effective, cooperative negotiators and effective, competitive negotiators.

Gerald R. Williams, LEGAL NEGOTIATION AND SETTLEMENT (1983), pp. 48–54 *

The experimental literature on negotiation contains a running debate between two opposing schools of thought: one arguing generally for a "cooperative" approach to negotiation and the other for a "tough" or "competitive" approach. . . .

What are the ingredients of a "tough" approach? As defined in social psychological literature, they include:[16]

1. making high initial demands;

2. maintaining a high level of demands in the course of the negotiation;

3. making few concessions;

---

* Copyright © 1983 by West Publishing. Reprinted from *Legal Negotiations and Settlement*, Gerald R. Williams, 1983, with permission of the West Group.

[16] I. Morley and G. Stephenson, *The Social Psychology of Bargaining* (1977).

4. making small concessions (when concessions are made); and

5. having a generally high level of aspiration.

*   *   *   *   *   *

What we have learned so far about competitive negotiators is brought to life by the insights of Herbert W. Simons. In *Persuasion: Understanding, Practice and Analysis*, pp. 133–134 (1976), he observes that the underlying dynamic of combative strategies is to move psychologically against the other person by word or action. Videotapes of competitive lawyers engaged in negotiating do show a definite pattern of behavior of moving psychologically against the other (non-competitive) attorney. They make very high demands and few (if any) concessions. They use exaggeration, ridicule, threat, bluff, and accusation to create high levels of tension and pressure on the opponent.

What are the effects of these tactics? If used effectively, the tactics cause the opposing attorney to lose confidence in himself and his case, to reduce his expectations of what he will be able to obtain in the case, and to accept less than he otherwise would as a settlement outcome. As Simons observed, the combative approach is a manipulative approach, designed to intimidate the opponent into accepting the combative's demands. . . .

The elements of the cooperative approach also come from insights of Simons. The basic dynamic of the cooperative negotiator is to move psychologically *toward* the opposing attorney. Cooperative negotiators seek common ground. They communicate a sense of shared interests, values, and attitudes using rational, logical persuasion as a means of seeking cooperation. They promote a trusting atmosphere appearing to seek no special advantage for self or client. The explicit goal is to reach a fair resolution of the conflict based on an objective analysis of the facts and law.

Osgood observed a crucial dynamic here: the cooperative negotiator shows his own trust and good faith by making unilateral concessions. Making unilateral concessions is risky, but cooperative negotiators believe it creates a moral obligation in the other to reciprocate. The cooperative strategy is calculated (subconsciously) to induce the other party to reciprocate: to co-operate in openly and objectively resolving the problem; to forego aggression, and to make reciprocal concessions until a solution is reached.

Cooperative negotiators feel a high commitment to fairness, objecting to the competitive view of negotiation as a game. To a cooperative, the gamesmanship view is ethically suspect. They fell that to move psychologically *against* another person to promote one's own interest is manipulative and an affront to human dignity. On the other hand, cooperatives move psychologically *toward* other people to achieve their preferred outcome. Competitive negotiators have reason to ask whether this is any less manipulative. Their manipulation is designed to induce or permit the opponent to trust, cooperate with, and make concessions to the manipulator.

The strengths of the cooperative approach as identified in the literature are that cooperative strategies are often more effective than tough strategies for two primary reasons: they produce more favorable outcomes, and they result in fewer ultimate breakdowns in bargaining (in the legal context, resort to trial). . . .

The cooperative strategy, like the competitive, has limitations. Its major disadvantage is its vulnerability to exploitation, a problem compounded by the apparent inability of some cooperative types to recognize it when it happens. When a cooperative negotiator attempts to establish a cooperative, trusting atmosphere, in a negotiation with a tough, non-cooperative opponent, the cooperative attorney has an alarming tendency to ignore the lack of cooperation and to pursue his cooperative strategy unilaterally. The strategy requires him to continue discussing the case fairly and objectively, to make concessions about the weaknesses of his case, and refrain from self-serving behavior. In this situation, the tough negotiator is free to accept all of the fairness and cooperation without giving anything in return. In fact, it would be irrational to do anything else. On these facts, the cooperative has placed himself at a serious disadvantage. He has forgone attacking the other's position, he has conceded the weaknesses of his own position, and he has received no reciprocal value in return.

A PRIMER ON COMPETITIVE BARGAINING

1996 J. Disp. Resol. 325, 325–326, 341–343, 370–377 *

By Gary Goodpaster

One cannot understand negotiation without understanding competitive behavior in negotiation. It is not that competing is a good way to negotiate; it may or may not be, depending on the circumstances. Understanding competition in negotiation is important simply because many people do compete when they negotiate, either by choice or happenstance.

. . . Competitive bargaining, sometimes called hard, distributive, positional, zero-sum or win-lose bargaining, has the purpose of maximizing the competitive bargainer's gain over the gain of those with whom he negotiates. He is, in effect, trying to "come out ahead of," or "do better than," all other parties in the negotiation. For this reason, we sometimes refer to this competitive bargaining strategy as a *domination* strategy, meaning that the competitive bargainer tends to treat negotiations as a kind of contest to win.

The competitive negotiator tends to define success in negotiation rather narrowly. It is simply getting as much as possible for himself: the cheapest price, the most profit, the least cost, the best terms and so on. In its simplest form, this strategy focuses on immediate gain and is not much concerned with the relationship between the negotiating parties. A more complex version of this strategy focuses on long-term gain. This focus usually requires some effort to maintain or further a relationship and usually moderates the competitive, often aggressive, behavior that jeopardizes relationships and possibilities of long-term gain. . . .

People bargain competitively essentially for three reasons, which often overlap. First, by inclination or calculation, they view the negotiation as a kind of competition, in which they wish to win or gain as much as possible. Secondly, they do not trust the other party. Where parties are non-trusting, they are non-disclosing and withhold information, which leads to further distrust and defensive or self-protective moves. Parties may be non-trusting because they are unfamiliar with the other party or because they are generally or situationally non-trusting. Finally, a party may bargain competitively as a defense to, or retaliation for, competitive moves directed at it.

. . . The competitive negotiator adopts a risky strategy which involves the taking of firm, almost extreme positions, making few and small concessions, and withholding information that may be useful to the other party. The intention, and hoped-for effect, behind this basic strategy is to persuade the other party that it must make concessions if it is to get an agreement. In addition to this basic strategy, competitive negotiators may also use various ploys or tactics aimed at pressuring, unsettling, unbalancing or even misleading the other party to secure an agreement with its demands.

In an important sense, the competitive negotiator plays negotiation as an information game. In this game, the object is to get as much information from the other party as possible while disclosing as little information as possible. Alternatively, a competitive negotiator sometimes provides the other party with misleading clues, bluffs, and ambiguous assertions with multiple meanings, which are not actually false, but nevertheless mislead the other party into drawing incorrect conclusions that are beneficial to the competitor.

The information the competitive negotiator seeks is the other party's bottom line. How much he will maximally give or minimally accept to make a deal. On the other hand, the competitive negotiator wants to persuade the other side about the firmness of the negotiator's own *asserted* bottom line. The competitive negotiator works to convince the other party that it will settle only at some point that is higher (or lower, as the case may be) than its *actual* and unrevealed bottom line. . . . Taking a firm position and conceding little will incline the other party to think the competitor has little to give. Thus, if there is to be a deal, then the other party must give or concede more.

. . . Competitive and cooperative bargaining strategies conflict. A simple cooperative strategy leaves the cooperator vulnerable to exploitation by a competitor. There is also good evidence that competitive negotiators who use the high demand, firmness, small concession strategy get better negotiation results than cooperators, at least where "better" means getting the most immediate gain.

Cooperative bargainers vary greatly in their sophistication. Innocent cooperators who, consciously or unconsciously, uncritically adopt the premise that cooperation begets cooperation may unwittingly engage in behavior that exposes them to possible exploitation. Potentially detrimental information disclosures, unilateral concessions, or excessive concession making are all examples of this kind of behavior. Some cooperators may even exhibit invariant, non-adaptive or "pathological" cooperation. That is, they either consistently and detrimentally misinterpret the other party's exploitive moves, or otherwise always respond to persistent hard bargaining with increasing defer-ence or reasonableness and with more, or greater, concessions.

If the hard bargainer overreaches too much, the cooperator may feel pushed beyond his own boundaries of reasonableness and cooperation and break off the negotiations out of frustration and anger at the other party's unreason-ableness. A canny, hard bargainer, however, who is skilled in reading the other party and sensitive to the possibility of pushing too far, can always take advantage of a naive and inexperienced cooperative negotiator. Innocent or naive cooperators tend to assume that the other party is bargaining non-exploitively. They want to be trusted and tend to trust others. In their desire to be reasonable and friendly, they assume that the other party will act the same way, even in the face of contrary evidence.

Cooperators may worry more about having a good relationship and keeping things calm, reasonable, and agreeable than they do about getting exactly what they want. Indeed, going into the negotiation, they may not specifically know what they would deem a good disposition. Instead, rather than enter the negotiation with certain figures or positions in mind as desirable results, they may enter with vaguer, more malleable and manipulable notions that they only want "what's fair" or "what's reasonable" under the circumstances. The lack of a clear reference point makes them less able to discern their own interest and, therefore, more vulnerable to competitive claiming.

The cooperator's desire to be a certain kind of person—noncompetitive, non-aggressive, fair, decent, honorable—may also result in turning the other cheek to the other party's hard-bargaining tactics. In fact, naive cooperators may undercut getting what they want by assuming that they must make unilateral concessions or compromises without a return just to get an agreement. They sometimes fail to distinguish between their behavior toward others and their behavior toward the problem they are trying to resolve. In other words, they are "soft on the people" and "soft on the problem."

The cooperator faces a dilemma: the reasonable, compromising conduct in which he wishes to engage in order to obtain a fair and just agreement also puts him at risk. If the other party is also cooperative, all is well and good. The other party, however, may not be cooperative. Instead, the other party may either be overtly competitive or cooperative in demeanor and competitive in substance. If, for example, to be reasonable and attempt to have the union understand its point of view, management volunteers important information, such as planning a plant expansion, the union may simply take the informa-tion and use it to its advantage without volunteering information in return or reciprocating in any other way. Similarly, if Susan, being cooperative, makes a concession hoping to trigger a concession from Jerry, Jerry may simply take the concession and either give nothing in return or give a non-commensurate concession. Indeed, the cooperator's concession may encourage the other side to seek more or greater concessions. In this situation, the truly naive coopera-tor may respond by conceding more in the hope of inducing a concession and movement toward an agreeable settlement rather than by noting the lack of reciprocity and adjusting his own behavior to protect himself.

The cooperator faces the dilemma that the way he wants to negotiate may put him at risk of being taken or exploited. Obviously, cooperative negotiators should not naively *assume* that the other party will also act cooperatively. Indeed, they must recognize that they cannot successfully bargain cooperatively unless the other party cooperates. They also need to devise ways to protect themselves from the other party's possible competitive moves that are often masked or hidden by a genial, reasonable, or cooperative demeanor.

Aware of the potential risks involved in their cooperative behavior, a negotiator could adopt a hard bargaining strategy. This strategy would certainly not be necessary in all cases. In fact, many negotiators might object to hard bargaining in principle. How does a wise and careful cooperative negotiator protect herself from competitive bargainers?

Defensive cooperativeness. During the initial stages of a negotiation the parties feel each other out, not only to gain information respecting positions, wants, and desires, but also to get a sense of whether, and how far, they can trust one another. Since trust, or providing security that one can trust, is a key issue, cooperators should try to anticipate negotiations, develop information about the other party, and build a relationship with the other party prior to negotiation.

Because cooperative behavior promotes trust, it tends to induce reciprocal cooperative behavior. Once in a negotiation, the careful cooperator adopts a cooperative, yet wary, demeanor and indicates a general posture of flexibility on issues. This may signal or hint at a willingness to make concessions on certain issues. Nevertheless, the defensive or cautious cooperator does not make significant concessions before determining whether the other party is trustworthy.

Fractionating concessions. A careful negotiator can, in part, fashion a self-protective concession strategy by fractionating concessions. One fractionates concessions by dividing an issue into smaller issues and, therefore, into smaller concessions where one gives on an issue. Using this method, the negotiator can make a small concession and wait to see how the other party responds. If the other party makes an equivalent concession, the negotiator can proceed.

Ambiguous or disownable signals. A negotiator makes a "disownable" concession move by making an ambiguous statement that suggests a willingness to make a concession but which can also be plausibly interpreted as not expressing such willingness. If the other party interprets the statement as offering a concession and reciprocates, then the negotiator confirms the other side's interpretation in some way. If the other party seeks to grab the assumed concession without offering a return, the negotiator denies making it. Suppose, for example, that one party has repeatedly argued that two conditions had to be met before he would consider changing his position. After a time, however, he begins to mention only one condition, thereby, signaling a willingness to drop the unmentioned condition.

This sort of signaling is, in effect, a testing of the other party. This test, however, does not run the actual risk of making a concession or exposing weakness. At most, it is an unclear expression of a contingent willingness to concede. As another example, consider two parties negotiating over contract terms. The buyer wants the seller to give her the same discount on equipment that the seller gives some of its other, much larger customers. The seller says, "We can write something like a 'favored nations' clause into the contract." The buyer responds, "I'll take that, and I appreciate getting the same discount as your larger customers," but he makes no concession in return. The seller then responds, "Well, you can have the clause, but it doesn't apply to discounts." Alternatively, had the buyer shown a willingness to concede, the seller could let the buyer's first interpretation of the statement stand.

If there is little trust, this process of signaling can be quite subtle because the target of the signal may be uncertain whether to interpret a statement as expressing a willingness to concede. If the target is uncertain, he may fear responding in a way which clearly shows his willingness to reciprocate because that may put him at risk. Consequently, the parties sometimes engage in trading ambiguous statements until one party feels secure enough to make a clear proposal or until both parties simultaneously make a clear move.

"Directional" information. Sometimes a negotiator may encourage cooperative bargaining simply by indicating on which issues the other party should improve its proposals. This tactic provides the other party with some information about the negotiator's priorities but without clearly committing to anything.

Demanding reasoned justifications. A negotiator should make a practice of asking the other party to justify its positions in terms of some objective criteria. If the other party simply behaves competitively and attempts to extract whatever gains it can, it may have difficulty in stating satisfactory justifications for its positions.

Contingent cooperativeness and the reformed sinner strategy. There is good evidence that even those who wish to bargain cooperatively can succeed with competitive negotiators by adopting a shifting "competitive to cooperative" or "reformed sinner" strategy. This strategy involves making a high, initial demand, remaining firm initially, and then moving to a "contingently cooperative" strategy. Contingent cooperativeness involves behaving cooperatively if the other party reciprocates cooperative behavior and increasing cooperative behavior as the other party does so. Interestingly, the cooperator's initial firmness may signal to the other party that competitive behavior will not work. . . .

The contingently competitive strategy appears to work by giving the other party evidence that its own cooperative behavior, but not its competitive behavior, has a desirable effect. In carrying out this general strategy, the cooperator may expressly negotiate over the negotiation ground rules and seek the other party's commitment to negotiate cooperatively as well, but, in any case, asserting a norm and expectation of cooperative behavior. The cooperator may then attempt to structure the negotiation to handle small issues first, where the risk of loss is not great. When ready to take some risks, the cooperator makes contingent proposals. The proposal expressly offers a concession or adopts a position closer to the other party's demands yet contingent on some specific concession or change of position from the other party.

Strategy imitation or tit-for-tat. Response—in-kind or tit-for-tat is a form of contingent cooperation a negotiator can use to handle a competitor. If the cooperator observes competitive tactics, she can call attention to them and state that she knows how to bargain that way too and will respond in kind unless the other party bargains cooperatively. Alternatively, the cooperator can just respond in kind by using tit-for-tat to discipline the other party.

Tit-for-tat is a negotiation strategy designed to shape the other party's bargaining behavior. One dilemma negotiators face is figuring out whether to bargain cooperatively or competitively. If one wishes to be reasonable and bargain cooperatively, there is a risk that the other party will bargain competitively and gain an advantage. Using tit-for-tat, a negotiator solves that problem by competing just as the other party does and, in effect, sends the message that "I will bargain the way you bargain and will use the same tactics you use." This teaches the other party that it cannot get away with anything, and may lead to cooperative behavior.

In general, using a tit-for-tat or matching strategy appears to be an effective way to induce cooperation. The strategy makes it clear to the other party that it risks retaliation and increasing conflict if it continues to bargain competitively.

Time-outs. Negotiating parties deadlock when no party is willing to make a further concession to bring the parties closer together. When the parties are nearing a deadline and are deadlocked, they may realize that the negotiation will fail completely unless they cooperate. Declaring a time-out when a deadlock is apparent gives the parties time to assess the situation without continued conflict, reconsider their reading of the negotiation thus far, and determine more rationally whether to risk trusting the other party. Often enough, when the parties return to formal negotiation, each side signals a willingness to move towards an agreement or make concessions leading to an agreement.

Because people bargain competitively for various reasons, negotiators and mediators need to understand competition in negotiation in order to respond appropriately. Some people bargain competitively without giving much conscious attention to the matter. Others compete in response to the other party's competitive behavior. In this response, they follow the common pattern that a particular kind of behavior elicits a similar behavior in response. In other words, one party frames the negotiation as a contest, and the other party picks up the competitive cues and behaves accordingly. Further, people naturally incline to competitive bargaining when they are non-trusting. In such situations, in order to avoid putting themselves at risk, non-trusting people act guardedly and adopt elements of the competitive strategy, for example, withholding information or misrepresenting a position. Finally, one can readily imagine ambiguous bargaining situations, in which at least one party is non-trusting, quickly devolving into a competitive negotiation between both parties. The non-trusting party acts defensively, and the other party senses this as competitive behavior and, therefore, acts in a similar fashion.

Negotiators, however, can also consciously adopt a competitive strategy. Negotiators are most likely to compete purposefully when

- the parties have an adversarial relationship;
- a negotiator has a bargaining power advantage and can dominate the situation;

- a negotiator perceives an opportunity for gain at the expense of the other party;
- the other party appears susceptible to competitive tactics;
- the negotiator is defending against competitive moves; or
- there is no concern for the future relationship between the parties.

This list suggests that competitive bargaining most likely occurs in situations such as labor and lawsuit negotiations, insurance and similar claims type settlements, and in one-time transactions between a relatively experienced party and a relatively inexperienced party. One would, for example, expect to see it in sales transactions where the parties will probably not see each other again.

Representative bargaining or bargaining for a constituency may also prompt competitive bargaining even when there will be future negotiations between equally sophisticated parties. The negotiator's accountability may override relationship concerns and reasons for cooperation. The concerned audience, consisting of a client, constituency, coalition partner, or other phantom party at the table, is, in effect, looking over the negotiator's shoulder. The negotiator, therefore, takes positions and makes moves she believes her client either expects or would approve. International negotiations between countries, union-management, lawsuit negotiations, and negotiations between different parties in interest-group coalition negotiations sometimes evidence this pattern.

Aside from circumstantial or situational pressures, there are some parties who bargain competitively because they believe that is the way to conduct business. There are also parties who are simply predisposed to bargain competitively and will incline to do so opportunistically in any bargaining situation if possible.

Finally, it is important to note that one can bargain competitively in a negotiation on some issues and cooperatively on others. In other words, a negotiator can selectively use competitive strategy or tactics on particular issues, while using a cooperative or problem-solving strategy on other issues. In such a case, extracting gain competitively may not greatly endanger future relationships. At least, there is a judgment call concerning this. The negotiator attempts to calculate the net effect of the overall results and skews the benefits, insofar as possible, to his side. In this kind of calculation, it is clear that there is some kind of assessment or balancing of short-term versus long-term gain. Again, there is no formula to calculate these gains, and the parties probably follow rules of thumb prevalent in the industry and developed from prior experience, or they calculate these gains based on hopes or individualized assessments.

Similarly, it is possible for negotiators to use an integrative or problem-solving bargaining strategy in order to increase the amount of gain possible to the parties. At some point, however, notwithstanding cooperation to produce greater gain, the parties will have to distribute or divide the gain. Therefore, they may also engage in competitive bargaining.

Obviously, competitive bargaining covers a continuum of behaviors from the simplest, unreflective adversarial actions to highly conscious and virtually scripted contests. As such, competitive bargaining moves are natural responses in some negotiation situations and advantageous or profitable actions in others. This being so, what are the downsides to competitive negotiation?

At least in its full-blown form, competitive negotiation is risky bargaining. The competitor takes risks in order to secure gains. Among these is the risk that there will be no gains at all. The competitive strategy of staking out a position and holding firm, particularly when joined with various devious tactics, runs the risk of alienating, frustrating, or angering the other party and, thus, precluding a possible agreement.

Even if there is an agreement, it may not be a sustainable one. On reflection, the other party may conclude that it does not really like the deal or feels that it was "taken" in some way. Furthermore, even if there is a deal and it survives, the bargaining that occurred may adversely affect future relations between the parties. This is certain to happen if one party discovers that the other party actively misled or manipulated it. It may also happen just because of residual hard feelings or mistrust arising from the tactics used.

Beyond these concerns, competitive bargaining is neither efficient nor productive bargaining. It is inefficient and nonproductive because parties who withhold and manipulate information miss possibilities of cooperating to find or create additional value to divide between them. As a result, they can be said "to leave gains on the table."

Along this line, genuine cooperation and positive relationships are two real gains that competitive negotiators are unlikely to ever realize and bring to bear in immediate or prospective negotiations between themselves and others. Put another way, although a competitive negotiator may realize a gain in a particular negotiation, he may forgo far greater possible gains in doing so.

Gerald R. Williams, LEGAL NEGOTIATION AND SETTLEMENT (1983), pp. 25–30 *

[Ed. Note: Gerald Williams' research studied the negotiating behaviors of practicing attorneys in Denver, Colorado and Phoenix, Arizona. While Williams found that these lawyers could generally be placed in either the cooperative or the competitive category in terms of their negotiating behaviors, he concluded that there were effective and ineffective negotiators in both categories. That is, use of a cooperative style could, in and of itself, no more guarantee negotiating effectiveness than the use of a competitive style.]

In contrast to the friendly, trustworthy approach of cooperative effectives, effective/competitives are seen as dominating, competitive, forceful, tough, arrogant, and uncooperative. They make high opening demands, they use threats, they are willing to stretch the facts in favor of their clients' positions, they stick to their positions, and they are parsimonious with information about the case. They are concerned not only with maximizing the outcome for their client but they appear to take a gamesmanship approach to negotiation, having a principle objective of outdoing or outmaneuvering their opponent.

Thus, rather than seeking an outcome that is "fair" to both sides, they want to outdo the other side; to score a clear victory. . . .

While there are differences in approach between the two types of effective negotiators, both types are, in fact, rated as highly effective. Our interest is in what makes them effective, i.e., what traits they have in common. Common traits have particular importance, since law students and attorneys can seek to understand and emulate them irrespective of which pattern they prefer to follow. . . .

Both types of effective negotiators are ranked as highly experienced. This comes as no surprise, since we normally assume that negotiating effectiveness improves with experience. Its meaning here is illuminated by the comment of a responding attorney, who wrote: "it is important to have enough experience in order that you have confidence in yourself and be able to convey that confidence."

More importantly, both types are seen as ethical, trustworthy and honest, thus dispelling any doubt about the ethical commitments of effective/competitives. However, the priority of these traits is ranked much higher for cooperatives (3rd, 6th and 1st in priority) than for competitives (15th, 20th and 11th in priority). Given the current interest and concern about professional responsibility in the Bar, the high ratings on ethical and trustworthy for both effective groups are worthy of notice. Although literature on professional responsibility generally argues that high ethical standards are a precondition to success in practice, many law students and some practicing attorneys continue to believe or suspect that they must compromise their ethical standards in order to effectively represent their clients and attain success in practice. The findings of this survey suggest such compromises may be not only unnecessary, but actually counterproductive to one's effectiveness in negotiation situations.

In the same vein, we see that both types are careful to observe the customs and courtesies of the bar. While some attorneys have argued that there are tactical advantages in deliberately departing from the etiquette of the profession, as a general rule effective negotiators observe it. . . .

Although effective/competitives were seen as taking unrealistic opening positions, in general they share with cooperatives the traits of being realistic, rational, and analytical. These three attributes become very important in interpreting negotiator behavior. They mean more than the idea of "thinking like a lawyer"; they impose limits on how far a negotiator may credibly go in such things as interpretation of facts, claims about damages and other economic demands, and levels of emotional involvement in the case.

Both effective types are seen as thoroughly prepared on the facts and the law of the case. They are also described as legally astute. This, again, is something to be expected. But it bears emphasis because, as we shall see, ineffective negotiators lack these qualities. One attorney had these traits in mind when he wrote, "In my experience, the most important part of negotiation is thorough preparation and a complete knowledge of the strengths and weaknesses of your position. . . . I feel individual personality traits (e.g. loud, forceful, quiet, reserved) are unimportant."

Legal astuteness means they have not only done their homework by informing themselves about the legal and procedural ramifications of the case, but they also have acquired good judgment about how and when to act with respect to this information.

Both types of effective attorneys are rated as creative, versatile, and adaptable. This is true even though competitive effectives are also labeled rigid. Apparently there is a distinction between being tough (which competitive attorneys are) and being obstinate. An attorney should not be so rigid that he is unable to seek creative solutions to problems. The flavor of the terms is suggested in a comment by an attorney representing a party who was involved in a very acrimonious dispute with a neighbor over an irrigation ditch. He wrote, "Our problem was solved by a simple relocation agreement executed by the parties and recorded. The opposition attorney and myself, after great study and much effort, came up with the simple solution of simply relocating the ditch."

Both types are self-controlled. . . .

One of the more important marks of effective negotiators is skill in reading their opponent's cues. This refers not only to the ability to judge an opponent's reactions in negotiating situations, but to affirmatively learn from the opponent. The old saying is that experience is the best teacher. Experience is only a good teacher for those who are skillful at learning from it. In the course of interviews connected with Denver attorneys, they were routinely asked what they did when they were faced with an inexperienced opponent—an opponent fresh out of law school. Their responses were very informative. One group of attorneys would get a sly grin on their face, their eyes would light up, and they would say "I hammer them into the ground". By far the larger number of attorneys responded quite differently, however. They said that when they had a "green" opponent, they slowed the case way down, tried to spell everything out as they went, and tried generally to show the younger attorney the right way to go about handling a case.

Consider this problem from the perspective of law graduates recently admitted to the bar. During the first few months of practice, they encounter some attorneys who hammer them into the ground, exploiting and taking advantage of them at every turn, and others who are trying to teach them how to be good lawyers. The experience is not calculated to engender trust in fellow officers of the court. Rather, the tendency in young lawyers is to develop a mild paranoia and to distrust everyone. This is unfortunate, because *some* opponents are providing valuable information, albeit in subtle ways. The key, then, is to learn to observe and "read" the opposing attorney and know who can be trusted and who cannot and then learn from both types without being misled by either.

Competitive and cooperative effectives are rated as perceptive, a term that goes hand in hand with skill in reading cues. It relates in part to the ability to perceive an opponent's strategy and his subjective reaction to your strategy. It also has a larger connotation, referring to the accuracy of one's perception of the whole case. One attorney in our study gave a telling description of his perception of a recently completed case: "I lost the case. Though my opponent was ineffective in preparation and presentation— and was a drunk—the judge *disbelieved* my key witness, a fundamentalist Minister, and the plaintiff got every cent he had wrongly demanded from my client."

Finally, it must be stressed that both types of effective negotiators are also rated as effective trial attorneys. As mentioned earlier, the alternative to settlement is trial. If an attorney is known as a weak trial attorney, it will often be more profitable for his opponent to take him to trial than agree to a reasonable settlement. This creates an awkward and troublesome dynamic, because the weak trial attorney knows that his client would be poorly served by an inept trial of the case. The weak attorney discounts the case as an inducement to the other side to settle and avoid the costs (and benefits) of trial. The interplay between fear of trial and discounting of the case is not healthy. There appears to be only one solution: to be taken seriously, lawyers who negotiate legal disputes (as opposed to non-actionable matters) must either develop substantial expertise as trial attorneys, or must openly associate themselves (whether by partnership, a referral system, or some other way) with very effective trial counsel.

NOTES AND QUESTIONS

(1) Would you characterize your negotiation style as cooperative or competitive? Why?

(2) Do Professor Goodpaster's suggestions for dealing with a competitive negotiator ("defensive cooperativeness," etc.) make you feel more comfortable about adopting a cooperative bargaining posture? Why or why not?

[3] PROBLEM-SOLVING NEGOTIATION

TOWARD ANOTHER VIEW OF LEGAL NEGOTIATION: THE STRUCTURE OF PROBLEM-SOLVING

31 UCLA L. Rev. 754, 817–829 (1984) [*]

By Carrie Menkel-Meadow

C. The Process of Problem-Solving Negotiation

The process of problem-solving negotiation is likely to be very different from the linear, reciprocal concession patterns leading to compromise in adversarial negotiation. This section reviews how problem-solving negotiation processes are likely to differ from adversarial negotiation.

---

1. Planning

As the discussion thus far should indicate, the crux of the problem-solving approach is the conceptualization and planning which precede any execution of the negotiation. A problem-solving conception of negotiation should be distinguished from cooperative or collaborative negotiation. The latter refers to particular behaviors engaged in during the negotiation, such as "being flexible, disclosing information and establishing good relationships with the other negotiator." These behaviors may be useful in problem-solving negotiations, but they can also be used as tactics in adversarial negotiations where their purpose is to achieve greater individual gain. The conceptualization used in planning problem-solving negotiation is useful in all negotiation, regardless of the particular behaviors chosen in the executory stages. Planning may indicate that needs are truly incompatible and call for the use of adversarial strategies to maximize individual gain, or that resort to adjudication is necessary.

Although economic evaluation of the case and some prediction of how a court would rule in a dispute resolution will still be appropriate, potential solutions need not be limited to some prediction of the mid-point compromise between estimated first offers. Instead, the planning stages of a problem-solving negotiation resemble the brainstorming process described by Fisher & Ury in *Getting To YES*. The process emphasizes exploring and considering both parties' underlying needs and objectives and the devices suggested earlier in this Article for expanding resources. The problem solver who has engaged in a brainstorming planning session is likely to approach a negotiation with a number of possible proposals which can be offered for two-sided brainstorming with the other party. While the planning stages of an adversarial negotiation may narrow and make the offers more precise, the problem solving planning stages are more likely to result in a broadening of solutions. As Fisher & Ury point out, the key to creative problem solving is to separate the creative stages of planning from the necessarily more rigid judgment stages.[257] The more potential solutions a negotiator is able to bring to the bargaining table, the more probable it is that agreement will be reached; stalemate and rejection are less likely to occur. In the legal context these brainstorming sessions should include the client, as she may have some solutions of her own, as well as important insights into what the other party desires.

The planning discussed above is primarily substantive planning focused on potential solutions rather than strategic planning focused on what positions to take in the negotiation. Strategic planning may depend on how willing the other party is to depart from the more familiar adversarial negotiation process. At the intersection of substantive and strategic planning are considerations of what information about the other party's needs is necessary to plan for solutions acceptable to the other party. An example best illustrates this point.

Suppose that in a lawsuit based on concealment of a leaky roof in the sale of a residence, the plaintiff has sued for $10,000, the cost of repairing the roof. However, a more extensive portion of the roof was repaired than that which

---

[257] R. Fisher & W. Ury at 62–66. [R. Fisher & W. Ury, Getting to YES (1981)]

seemed necessary to prevent leaks. The plaintiff has been forced to take out a bank loan in order to repair the roof. This is a further encumbrance on the property, and the plaintiff is having a great deal of difficulty making all of the payments on the house. In addition, the plaintiff is concerned that her parents will learn she bought the house without following their advice to have an inspection made. The defendant seller of the house needs to make payments on her own house and is worried about the possibility of rescission. A bona fide dispute about the facts is whether the defendant misrepresented the facts, and if so, whether he did so negligently or intentionally. The seller holds a second mortgage on the house and the plaintiff now threatens to withhold payment. The plaintiff has taken the deposition of the defendant's former housekeeper who does remember a leaky roof when the defendant was in possession.

Assuming that we represent the plaintiff in this case, there are a number of needs that can be identified. Economically, the plaintiff would like to recover the cost of the roof repair, probably with a minimum of transaction costs. Depending on her dealings and relationship with the defendant, the plaintiff might wish to have the defendant's actions declared legally fraudulent. Recall, however, that in this example the defendant holds a second mortgage on the house so that the plaintiff and the defendant will have a continuing relationship if the plaintiff remains in the house. The plaintiff's social needs may include preventing her parents from discovering that she bought the house without an inspection. Psychologically, it is possible that the plaintiff feels both foolish for not discovering the leak and angry because it was hidden. Furthermore, the plaintiff may feel that the defendant's deception was morally wrong and she may want an apology, payment as punishment, and/or an assurance that this is the only undisclosed defect.

At this point all we know of the defendant's needs may be what we learned from our client, the plaintiff. We know, for example, that the defendant needs the money from the second mortgage to pay the mortgage on her own new home. We may know that the defendant would prefer not to have a legal judgment of fraud entered against her because it will damage her credit rating. Similarly, the defendant may not want a lawsuit for fraud to become public because it could damage her relationship with business associates or her reputation in the community. Finally, it is possible that because the housekeeper has already given testimony against her, the defendant fears losing a lawsuit and may feel regretful or guilty about what she has done. Note that many of the assumptions or speculations about the defendant's needs have to be more fully discovered, either in pretrial discovery or in informal investigation, or tested in the negotiation.

Having identified the parties' needs, we can now begin to consider a number of general solutions. These may include such things as settling the case privately because both parties fear publicity, an apology and new promise that nothing else is defective, and perhaps a delayed or installment payment from defendant to plaintiff, or a reduction on the plaintiff's obligation on the second mortgage. The one remaining issue which is likely to result in conflicting views, the amount of the settlement, can be made less difficult either by having an independent determination of the proper amount to repair the original damage or by expanding the resources through time payments and tax structures that may permit the plaintiff to realize more dollars than the defendant actually pays out.

The structure of this example may not work in all cases, but it illustrates how the analysis of both parties' needs may lead to a number of possible solutions.

2. Execution

To the extent that both parties engage in a problem-solving negotiation structure, the negotiation is likely to resemble a fluid brainstorming session. Even if only one party has engaged in a problem-solving planning process, the negotiation need not be reduced to an adversarial exercise. First, the parties may begin with a greater number of possible solutions simply because two heads are better than one. In addition, as empirical research has demonstrated, when both parties approach negotiation with the objective of working collaboratively, more of the information reflecting the parties' needs may be revealed, facilitating the search for solutions. Thus, in the case of the leaky roof, the amount of damages might be easier to determine if both parties approached the problem by looking for ways to reach agreement than if one approached the problem as simply maximizing or minimizing payment, using litigation as a threat. On the other hand, even a single problem solver can propose alternative ways of measuring liability that may eventually be successful, if she has accurately determined the other party's needs.

When the problem solver is able to present a number of different solutions which potentially satisfy at least some of the other party's needs, it is more likely that the adversarial concession and argumentation pattern can be avoided than if she presents a single demand. The parties can consider variations of each of the proposals using the techniques of game theorists who simply alter the coordinates slightly at each play to see if a more efficient solution can be achieved. Thus, the negotiation game may be played on a multi-dimensional field rather than on one that is linear, or two dimensional. In the leaky roof case one party may suggest a number of different methods of payment, such as reduction of the second mortgage, lump-sum, or installment payments at different discount factors, rather than simply demanding $10,000.

In addition to the different offer structure, problem-solving negotiations are likely to have different information sharing processes. As discussed above, many conventional works on negotiation urge the negotiator not to reveal information. The problem solver recognizes that he is more likely to develop solutions which meet the parties' needs by revealing his own needs or objectives, while at the same time trying to learn about the other party's. In short, there is no incentive to dissemble. When this is the goal, the process consists of asking questions in search of clarification and information, rather than making statements or arguments designed to persuade the other party to accept one's own world view.

On the other hand, totally uninhibited information sharing may be as dysfunctional as withholding information. In experimental simulations Pruitt

& Lewis found that there was not necessarily a correlation between free information exchange and joint profit.[268] Instead, joint profit was associated with information processing—that is, the ability to listen to, receive, and understand the information and how it related concretely to the problem. Furthermore, information sharing in a thoughtless and unrestricted fashion may lead to the sharpening of conflict as value differences are revealed in competing goals and needs. In problem-solving negotiation it is crucial to understand the usefulness and function of particular pieces of information—such as exploring how strongly one party desires something—because each piece is related to possible solutions. Problem solvers must determine what information is needed and why, and must be able to absorb information from the other side to test assumptions about needs, goals or objectives.

An example taken from my negotiation course can illustrate. In negotiating a partnership agreement, students are given information about each of the prospective partners. One partner has an immediate need for a relatively high salary because he must provide for a disabled child. The other partner would also like a high salary, but is more concerned about creating the partnership because he is excited about entering a new business. Students, who in my experience are more likely to be adversarial negotiators, have tended to approach the salary negotiation as a conventional zero-sum negotiation. When, as happens occasionally, one side reveals why the salary is needed, a greater variety of solutions seem to come unlocked, such as sliding scales, deferred versus immediate compensation, special provisions for the child, and salary trade-offs for other items. In this situation the party who learns of the disabled child either may be moved by sympathy or by the more instrumental realization that if this is of concern to his future partner it should be dealt with now so it is not a future drain on the partnership. Whatever the motivation, the new information can serve as a source of new solutions ending an otherwise stalemated salary negotiation. Obviously, not all negotiation problems will contain such useful information, but the problem solver is willing to share information about needs that may facilitate such solutions. Thus, problem solving produces a more sophisticated calculus concerning what information should be revealed.

Related to the information flow is the process by which the proposals are evaluated during the negotiation. Fisher & Ury describe this process in a problem-solving environment as principled movements which are reasoned, justified statements about why a particular proposal is important. Fisher & Ury distinguish such movements from the arguments over position which occur in conventional adversarial negotiation. In conventional negotiation, each party takes a position such as the first offer or target position, argues for it, and then makes unprincipled concessions to reach a compromise.

Even conventional adversarial negotiation, however, may be justified by principled movements. One of the most valuable contributions of the growing clinical literature on legal negotiation has been the analysis of using reasons for concessions. Thus, in order to avoid the pitfalls of totally unjustified concessions, negotiators are told that "it is important that the pattern and

---

[268] PRUITT & LEWIS at 170-72. [PRUITT & LEWIS, *The Psychology of Integrative Bargaining*, in NEGOTIATIONS: SOCIAL-PSYCHOLOGICAL PERSPECTIVES (D. Druckman ed. 1977)]

content of . . . justifications [for concessions] will be well thought out in advance" as "the justification offered for a particular concession invariably will be assessed by one's opponent. . . ."[276] These suggestions about principled movement in the adversarial context, however, have been used largely to justify movements up and down the limited linear plane. Thus, although useful even in adversarial negotiation, principled movements are of a different sort and used for different purposes in a problem-solving negotiation.

According to Fisher & Ury, in the problem-solving context the negotiator will use principled movements to justify proposals and suggestions in terms of their relationship to the parties' underlying interests or objectives. Reconciling interests will be more effective than arguing over positions, they say, because "for every interest there usually exist several possible positions that could satisfy it. . . . Reconciling interests rather than compromising between positions also works because behind opposed positions lie many more shared interests than conflicting ones."[278]

In the process of considering possibilities, the problem solver articulates reasons why a particular solution is acceptable or unacceptable, rather than simply rejecting an offer or making a concession. Articulating reasons during the negotiation facilitates agreement in a number of ways. First, it establishes standards for judging whether a particular solution is sensible and should be accepted. If the reason is focused on the parties' underlying needs, the negotiator can consider whether the proposal is satisfactory to the parties. She need not be concerned with such conventional evaluation as "Is this the most I can get?" or its counterpart, "Is this the least I can get away with?" Second, principled proposals focus attention on solving the problem by meeting the parties' needs, rather than winning an argument. Furthermore, continuously focusing justification on the parties' needs may cause negotiators to see still other solutions, rather than simply to respond with arguments about particular offers. The use of principled proposals can decrease the likelihood that unjustified and unnecessary concessions will be made simply to move toward agreement. Finally, the use of principled proposals causes the parties to share information about their preferences that they might otherwise be reluctant to reveal.

Principled negotiations in the legal context may be more complex, however. In addition to proposals based on the parties' underlying needs, negotiators can focus on the legal merits as a justification for a particular proposal. Indeed, negotiators are told to use "the law" or "the facts" to make arguments or justify positions in analyzing how concessions can be justified in adversarial negotiations. For example, in deciding whether to accept a particular settlement offer a negotiator might say: "We might not agree on the percentage of responsibility, but in this jurisdiction there is comparative negligence so it is unlikely that our contributory negligence will bar recovery. My client is entitled to something." In some sense, all legal negotiations are measured against the legal merits because, in deciding whether to accept a particular proposal, the negotiator must also decide whether the negotiated agreement

---

276 G. BELLOW & B. MOULTON. [G. BELLOW & B. MOULTON, THE LAWYERING PROCESS: NEGOTIATION (1981)]

278 R. FISHER & W. URY at 11, 41–57. [R. FISHER & W. URY, GETTING TO YES (1981)]

is better than the one which would be achieved at trial or in a form contract. In Fisher & Ury's parlance this is termed one of the BATNAs (Best Alternative to a Negotiated Agreement). All proposals in litigation negotiations will be measured against predictions about what the court might order.

Proposals justified by the legal merits can be problematic. Given a dispute where the parties have widely divergent views of the merits and how they will be determined by a factfinder, negotiators may find themselves involved in precisely the sort of unproductive argumentation inherent in adversarial negotiation. Indeed, as some have argued, one of the primary advantages of negotiation over adjudication is that no judgment need be made about whose argument is right or wrong. Parties can agree to settle on principles such as community norms or values that are broader than those the court can consider. On the other hand, focusing on the merits as a justification still may be more productive than adhering to arbitrary positions simply out of competitive stubbornness.

Ideally, of course, proposals should be justifiable on a basis which integrates the parties' needs and the legal merits. Returning to the leaky roof example, consider how a demand by the plaintiff for $10,000 "because your client defrauded mine" contrasts with the following proposal to the defendant:

> "One solution here might be for your client to pay my client $7,000 by reducing the monthly payment on the second mortgage over the term of the five year mortgage. It seems to me that this is fair because if we go to trial I think the court will find the defendant liable for at least $7,000 of the damages to the roof. The housekeeper's testimony will make it clear the defendant knew of the leak and the court will believe the housekeeper because she has no reason to lie. A payment of $7,000 is fair because it cost $3,000 to repair the roof, $3,000 to replaster the room and $1,000 to replace the ruined rugs. The proposal seems fair because it fits the needs of both of the parties. My client needs a reduction in her total monthly payments to meet all of her obligations, including the second mortgage payment to your client, and your client won't be out of any immediate cash to settle this case. If you prefer some other method of payment or other formulation, I'd be happy to discuss it with you."

The defendant's lawyer is now able to respond to the assessment of the legal merits and his client's needs and may modify this proposal, perhaps by offering a small cash payment with less of a reduction on the second mortgage to insure some future income. In addition, by presenting proposals with such justifications, each party reveals its assumptions about the other party's needs and legal positions, and can be corrected where wrong. When proposals are not justified in this way, the problem-solving negotiator should ask on what basis the proposal is made to be sure the principles are articulated and not assumed. Notice that the proposal is sufficiently flexible and indeterminate in terms of how the $7,000 second mortgage reduction will be structured. Both parties, therefore, can modify the proposal and contribute to the final solution without having to accept or reject the general principle of the solution.

Thus, although the relationship of the legal merits to the parties' underlying needs may be more problematic and complex than a simpler justification on the basis of the parties' underlying interests, these articulated rationales for negotiation proposals may be more likely to produce acceptable solutions.

Finally, a word should be said about the process of problem-solving negotiation from the perspective of the behavior of the parties. Problem-solving conceptions of negotiation do not necessarily result in weak or conciliatory strategies or tactics. As Fisher & Ury have stated, "being nice'" is not the answer to unproductive adversarial negotiations. Negotiating styles and behaviors are the means or procedures by which negotiation results and solutions are achieved, but they are not synonymous concepts. An overly cooperative negotiator may be just as likely to produce an ineffective compromise by giving in without basis as would a competitive negotiator who stubbornly holds to an unreasonable position. Some game theory suggests that cooperative strategies positively affect joint outcomes. Empirical studies of the effectiveness of cooperative versus competitive behaviors, however, are more complex and as yet inconclusive, both in legal negotiation and in more general negotiations studied by social psychologists. It is beyond the scope of this Article to discuss particular behaviors, other than in the context of negotiation structure. Furthermore, the state of negotiation art and science is not sufficiently advanced to permit accurate generalizations about specific behavioral choices.

Because problem-solving negotiations are likely to result in a greater number of potential solutions not contemplated in advance, the client in such negotiations is more likely to become involved in evaluating proposals. This will be particularly true where a client's objectives or needs may change over time, or need to be reevaluated as new proposals are forthcoming. Thus, the increased fluidity and emphasis on the parties' underlying interests may result in greater client involvement in the legal negotiation process. One of the key differences between the conventional adversarial model and the problem-solving model is the extent to which the parties and their lawyers engage in a continually interactive negotiation process, using the opportunity to seek new solutions rather than simply moving along a predetermined linear scale of compromise.

NOTES AND QUESTIONS

(1) Professor Menkel-Meadow states that the planning stage of problem-solving negotiation resembles a "fluid brainstorming session" and that in the execution stage the problem-solving negotiator should offer reasons why a solution may be acceptable or unacceptable. How are these aspects of the two stages related?

(2) May a problem solving approach be used in connection with both integrative and distributive bargaining? By both cooperative and competitive negotiators?

§ C   NEGOTIATION ETHICS

Although a number of ethical issues may confront a lawyer who is negotiating on behalf of a client, the most troubling is the extent to which a lawyer may engage in deception. A number of commentators have argued that the ABA Model Rules of Professional Conduct do not offer adequate guidance to the practicing lawyer. The materials in this section wrestle with this notion. Ruth Fleet Thurman argues that Model Rule 4.1 does not present a clear standard as to what is acceptable in negotiations. She suggests that lawyers should generally adhere to a higher standard of truth-telling. Charles Craver is more accepting of Rule 4.1 and draws a line between deception and dishonesty. While he also believes that lawyers should avoid deception and adhere to high standards, he would apparently leave it up to lawyers to police themselves.

CHIPPING AWAY AT LAWYER VERACITY: THE ABA'S TURN TOWARD SITUATION ETHICS IN NEGOTIATIONS

1990 J. Disp. Resol. 103, 103–115 [*]

By Ruth Fleet Thurman

Should the legal profession permit lawyers to lie when negotiating on behalf of clients? The virtually unequivocal position of the profession and commentators is "no," and such a position is generally followed by the American Bar Association Model Rules of Professional Conduct (Model Rules). [*] The Preamble to the Model Rules states, "[a]s a negotiator a lawyer seeks a result advantageous to the client but consistent with the requirements of *honest dealings with others.*" Model Rule 8.4(c) declares that dishonesty, fraud, deceit and misrepresentation constitute professional misconduct, and is based on a similar rule in the earlier American Bar Association Code of Professional Responsibility (Model Code). The Model Code also mandates that a lawyer shall not knowingly make a false statement of law or fact.

When the American Bar Association (ABA) adopted the Model Rules in 1983, the Model Code provision was included. However, the Model Rules language reads, "false statement of *material* law or fact" in Model Rule 3.3, Candor Toward the Tribunal, and in Model Rule 4.1, Truthfulness in Statements to Others. The narrowing of the veracity requirement in negotiations is clearly set forth in the official Comment to Model Rule 4.1. (Comments are intended as 'guides to interpretation.") The Comment declares, A "lawyer is required to be truthful when dealing with others on a client's behalf, but generally has no affirmative duty to inform an opposing party of relevant facts." The Comment continues, "[w]hether a particular statement should be regarded as one of fact can depend on the circumstance. *Under generally accepted conventions in negotiations* certain types of statements ordinarily are not taken as statements of material fact." The Comment then singles out three

---

[*] MODEL RULES OF PROFESSIONAL CONDUCT (1983, revised 1989). [hereinafter MODEL RULES].

exceptions to the veracity requirement for negotiators: (1) Estimates of price or value placed on the subject of a transaction; (2) a party's intentions as to an acceptable settlement of a claim; and (3) the existence of an undisclosed principal except where nondisclosure of the principal would constitute fraud. The reason for developing these three particular items as exceptions is unclear and is certainly inconsistent with the Preamble's *honest dealings with others* precept, and Model Rule 8.4's proscription against dishonesty, deceit and misrepresentation. . . .

. . .

A fundamental precept of effective lawyering is assisting clients in realistically appraising their situation and evaluating the probability of achieving a desired result. The lawyer's experience, objective viewpoint, and ability to weigh competing alternatives assist clients in making decisions. Although clients make the ultimate decisions regarding the objectives of representation, clients are entitled to the lawyer's honest assessments and straightforward advice. In negotiating, lawyers serve as "go-betweens" for the client in dealing with other parties. By conducting themselves in a conscientious and forthright manner, lawyers elevate the negotiation process to a higher plane. Likewise, if lawyers apply a lower standard of conduct during negotiations, the process is demeaned.

Devising enforceable standards of ethical behavior for the legal profession is not an easy task. As commentators point out, if ethical norms are routinely violated, this will weaken the force of the norms, thus making it more difficult for the bar to follow, let alone enforce, its ethical rules. This difficulty, however, should not dictate the rejection of "better and more desirable rules for poorer ones." Arguably, it would be preferable to have no rules, rather than poor rules. Since rules of ethics are normative and thereby shape expectations and behavior, great care should be taken to ensure that the rules adopted are consonant with the high level of trust and confidence that the public reposes in the practicing bar. Consequently, rules allowing lawyers to engage in puffery, deception, and lying are inappropriate and unacceptable because the public's trust and confidence in lawyers will diminish. In addition, allowing such conduct is inconsistent with a lawyer's obligation of integrity as an "officer of the legal system.". . .

Ethics is more than a matter of external compulsion. "Ethics is a form of critical reasoning, not a matter of indoctrination or blind obedience to external authority, but an internal development of natural cognitive and emotional capacities which express our moral nature in the form of principles that we accept for ourselves and universalize for others."[34]

When lawyers devise ethical standards that affect others as well as themselves, they must step back and examine the relevant issues and options from an objective viewpoint. What is sought to be accomplished by a standard? What are lawyers' aspirations and highest concerns in serving the public? The

---

[34] Richards, *Moral Theory, the Developmental Psychology of Ethical Autonomy and Professionalism*, 31 J. LEGAL EDUC. 359, 373 (1981). *See also, e.g.,* Lowenthal at 413. [Lowenthal, *The Bar's Failure to Require Truthful Bargaining by Lawyers*, 2 GEO. J. LEGAL ETHICS 411, 425-26 (1988)] "The concept of an ethic, a principal of desirable conduct that is morally binding on the conscience of the professional, is not limited to legal duties." *Id.*

nature of the lawyer's varied roles in society raises important issues of moral responsibility. Professor Charles Fried and others ask the question, "Can a lawyer be a good person?"[36] In other words, can the lawyer conform to the traditional concept of a professional—one devoted to his client's interests and authorized, if not required, to do some things for the client that the lawyer would not do for himself—and at the same time live up to "the ideal that one's life should be lived in fulfillment of the most demanding moral principles, and not just barely within the law."[37] Fried answers the question affirmatively, reasoning that, by preserving clients' autonomy and legal rights, the lawyer acts morally. The lawyer may not, however, *lie* or cheat for a client. Fried describes lying in negotiations as an offense to both the integrity of the victim as a rational and moral being, and to the lawyer's own moral status.

Despite strong moral arguments such as Fried's and traditional prohibitions against lawyers' engaging in deceit or misrepresentation, the ABA House of Delegates sanctioned this behavior in negotiations by adopting Model Rule 4.1 and its accompanying Comment. Model Rule 4.1, as previously mentioned, forbids lawyers while representing clients from knowingly making a false statement of *material* fact to a third person and from failing "to disclose a *material* fact to a third person when disclosure is necessary to avoid assisting a criminal or fraudulent act by a client," unless disclosure is prohibited by the ABA's rule on confidentiality. The Comment to Rule 4.1 states in part that during negotiations, some statements are not to be considered statements of "material fact," thus logically (under the rule) exempting them from the requirement of truthfulness and disclosure . . .

In a thoughtful commentary, Judge Alvin B. Rubin questions the wisdom of allowing "rules of the game" to govern law practice.[55] He deplores equating negotiation to a game and insists that lawyers act honestly and in good faith, so that persons dealing with them need not be as cautious as if trading in a bazaar. An ethic, he notes, is morally binding and not just a rule of the game.

A less stringent view is espoused by Professor James White. According to White, successful negotiators must be able to mislead like poker players, and even the most honest and trustworthy do so. White discusses five cases showing the difficulty of formulating a rule that will cover all types of lying during negotiations.[59] In the first example, the lawyer misrepresents his true opinion about the meaning of a case or a statute. The second case involves distortion of the value of a case or the subject matter involved. In the third case, a negotiator includes a series of false demands to trade for concessions from the other side. In the fourth case, the plaintiff's lawyer says, "I think

---

[36] Fried, *The Lawyer as Friend: The Moral Foundations of the Lawyer-Client Relation*, 85 YALE L.J. 1060 (1976).

[37] *Id.* at 1060-61.

[55] Rubin, *A Causerie on Lawyers' Ethics in Negotiation*, 35 LA. LAW REV. 577, 586 (1975).

To most practitioners it appears that anything sanctioned by the rules of the game is appropriate. From this point of view, negotiations are merely, as the social scientists have viewed it, a form of game; observance of the expected rules, not professional ethics, is the guiding precept. But gamesmanship is not ethics.

Id.

[59] White at 927. [White, *Machiavelli and the Bar: Ethical Limitations on Lying in Negotiation*, AM. B. FOUND. RES. J. 926 (1980)].

$90,000 will settle this case. Will your client give $90,000?" The defense lawyer has authority to settle for that amount, but wants to settle for less. In the fifth case, the lawyer represents three persons charged with shoplifting. Two have told him they will plead guilty and one says that he will not. The lawyer informs the prosecutor that the two will plead guilty *only if* the third is allowed to go free.

White found the first three cases easy. In the first case, he said it is all right in or out of court to argue an interpretation of a case or statute favorable to a client's position even if the lawyer does not personally agree with that interpretation. White is correct as long as the law is not being falsely represented. The Model Code and Model Rules permit good faith argument for extension, modification or reversal of existing law. Such argument is not "frivolous" even though the lawyer personally does not believe the argument will ultimately prevail.

In the second case, White thinks that distortion of the value of a case or other subject matter by the lawyer is permissible even though it conflicts with his "dispassionate analysis of the value of his case."[70] He cited section 2-313 of the Uniform Commercial Code as permitting *general* statements concerning value to be made without the law treating them as warranties. Exception must be taken to White's conclusion, because distortion of value of the subject of the negotiation need not rise to the level of warranty before it is improper. It is wrong for a lawyer to lie for a client.

The third case involves what White considers a "false demand;" a technique in multiple-issue bargaining in which one side includes a series of demands about which "it cares little or not at all. The purpose of including these demands is to increase one's supply of negotiating currency. One hopes to convince the other party that one or more of these false demands is important and thus successfully to trade it for some significant concession."[73]

White believes false demands are an acceptable negotiating technique. He states, "Such behavior is untruthful in the broadest sense; yet at least in collective bargaining negotiation its use is a standard part of the process and is not thought to be inappropriate by any experienced bargainer."[75] White further states, "[a] layman might say that this behavior falls within the ambit of 'exaggeration,' a form of behavior that while not necessarily respected is not regarded as morally reprehensible in our society."[76]

Again, exception must be taken to White's conclusion because this negotiating technique can become morally reprehensible and can cause great harm. In working out a divorce or separation settlement, for example, one may legitimately include in a list of demands those items the client would really like to have. One should, however, draw the line at encouraging a client to demand custody of children purely for purposes of gaining bargaining leverage. Demand for custody by a parent who does not, in fact, want custody (usually because he or she realizes that the children are better off with the

---

[70] White at 932.

[73] *Id.*

[75] *Id.* at 932.

[76] *Id.* at 934.

other parent), is likely to create hostility and cause the divorce proceedings to escalate into hotly contested, expensive, and emotionally charged litigation. All this is done in an effort to gain concessions from the other side. The considerable harm done to the parties by this maneuver is nothing compared to the harm done to the children.

The last two cases White finds troubling. In response to the question, "Will your client give $90,000?" White reports that many, and perhaps most, lawyers will be forced to lie or to reveal that they have been given such authority. He adds, "Some might say that the rules of the game provide for such distortion, but I suspect that many lawyers would say that such lies are out of bounds and are not part of the rules of the game."[78] White correctly concludes that a lawyer should not lie, but turn aside such questions and avoid any inference from his silence.

As to the plea bargaining in the fifth case, White asks, "Is it conceivable that the act can be justified on the ground that it is part of the game in this context in that prosecutors as well as defense lawyers routinely misstate what they, their witnesses, and clients can or will do? None of these answers seems persuasive."[79] White is correct that it is not permissible to lie to the prosecutor in negotiating the plea bargain.

White appears to countenance lying by negotiators in some of these cases because of what he sees as limits on what the law can do. He states, "[i]n a sense rules governing these cases may simply arise from a recognition by the law of its limited power to shape human behavior."[80] He figuratively throws in the towel when he concedes, "[b]y tolerating exaggeration and puffing in the sales transaction, by refusing to make misstatements of one's intentions actionable, the law may simply have recognized the bounds of its control over human behavior."[81]

The error in both this suggestion, and the exception for lying in negotiations provided in Rule 4.1, is in the notion that rules of ethics must be set so that they accommodate the lowest possible threshold of professional behavior. Lawyers should abide by high and aspirational standards of conduct. Lawyers' influential position in society, together with their fiduciary responsibilities, demand uncompromising levels of trust, integrity, and veracity. Countenancing puffery, exaggeration, distortion and outright lying in negotiations is inconsistent with this high standard, especially in light of the indispensable role of lawyers in our legal system. Lawyers ought not be compelled to lie for clients or to compensate for the lies of opposing counsel who comfortably exploit the exception to veracity as set out in the Comment to Model Rule 4.1.

White suggests that truthfulness ought to be determined contextually by the subject matter of the negotiation, and the region and background of the negotiators, and type of law practice. This thinking represents another outgrowth of a *situational ethics* framework of analysis. The difficulty of devising standards applicable to the wide range of activities embraced by

---

[78] *Id.* at 934.

[79] *Id.*

[80] *Id.*

[81] *Id.*

negotiation and the wide range of proficiency, skill, and sophistication among lawyers from divergent backgrounds, contrary to White's suggestion, does not justify relaxing requirements of integrity and veracity in negotiations.

Is White correct in his assertion that successful negotiators must be able to mislead like poker players and that even the most honest and trustworthy do so? Is misleading the same as lying? What is a lie? What is the harm in a little lying? Webster defines a "lie" as "an assertion of something known or believed by the speaker to be untrue with intent to deceive . . . an untrue or inaccurate statement that may or may not be believed true by the speaker . . . something that misleads or deceives."

 Philosopher Sissela Bok defines a "lie" as "an intentionally deceptive message in the form of a *statement*."[89] When she began her study of lying, Bok wrote that she looked to moral philosophers for guidance and concluded that in addition to hurting the liar and the victim, lies harm society by lowering the level of trust and social cooperation. Relations among human beings are founded on some degree of veracity, without which institutions collapse.

Bok recommends a "test of publicity"[92] which asks which lies, if any, would reasonable persons justify. The test requires reasonable persons to look for non-deceptive alternatives and moral reasons for and against the lie from the perspective of those potentially deceived or affected by the lie. The test also considers the value to society of veracity and accountability, and whether informed consent to be deceived has been freely given (as in playing poker or bargaining in a bazaar where each tries to outwit the other). The reasonable persons would consider the harm to persons outside the deceptive situations, such as distrust, loss of personal standards, and spreading of deception by others in retaliation or limitation.

Consent, Bok observes, must be based on adequate information, ability to make a choice, and freedom to opt out. Informed consent eliminates the discrepancy between liar and dupe. Thus, reasonable persons would probably have no objection to buyer and seller trying to outwit each other by bargaining deceptively in a bazaar.

Even if Bok's test of publicity countenanced lying in a bazaar or a poker game, the question remains whether negotiations by lawyers should be placed on a par with bargaining in a bazaar or playing poker. Looking beyond the liars and dupes to the harm to persons outside the situation, one can see that lying spreads and multiplies the harm and abuse, thereby increasing the damage. Moreover, the absence of clear-cut standards as to what is acceptable increases the likelihood of abuse.

It is easy to see that blatant deception in negotiations can produce these harmful results. Even trivial puffery, if told with the objective of shading the truth or in an effort to distort or mislead, undermines the integrity of the liar, who will then find it easier to slide into a more serious level of lying and distortion. Like pedestrians crossing the street against red lights or automobile drivers exceeding the speed limit, law abiding citizens find themselves

---

[89] S. Bok, Lying: Moral Choice in Public and Private Life 15 (1978) (emphasis in original).
[92] *Id.* at 100.

falling into the same practices when they observe large numbers of persons violating the law. If many lawyers shade the truth when they negotiate in behalf of clients, the practice will spread by imitation or retaliation and will spill over into more serious distortions. The ultimate outcome is loss of trust and goodwill toward lawyers and the law. Bar association public relations campaigns may be able to dispel *myths* about lawyers, but not matters for which there is a *factual* basis.

To avoid this insidious cycle, lawyers engaged in negotiations should make it a practice to weigh their statements before speaking and ask themselves: Is this statement true? Is it necessary? Do I have an alternative? May I say nothing or tell the truth? Like the social white lie, told usually out of good intentions to be polite or save someone's feelings, puffery, exaggeration, or simple misstatements in negotiations can become ingrained and habitual. At that point, duplicity becomes a way of life. These types of deception can be reduced by consciously looking for alternatives, even without clear-cut standards as to what is acceptable.

NEGOTIATION ETHICS: HOW TO BE DECEPTIVE WITHOUT BEING DISHONEST/HOW TO BE ASSERTIVE WITHOUT BEING OFFENSIVE

38 S. Tex. L. Rev. 713, 714–715, 718–720, 724–731, 733–734 (1997) [*]

By Charles Craver

Most attorneys feel some degree of professional discomfort when they negotiate with other lawyers. If they hope to achieve beneficial results for their clients, they must convince their opponents that those parties must offer more generous terms than they must actually offer if agreements are to be generated. To accomplish this objective, lawyers usually employ some deceptive tactics. Take for example two parties bargaining over the purchase/sale of a small business. The Seller is willing to accept $500,000, while the Buyer is willing to pay $575,000. The Seller's attorney initially indicates that the Seller must obtain $600,000, with the Buyer's lawyer suggesting that the Buyer cannot go above $450,000. Once these preliminary offers have been exchanged, the parties are pleased with the successful way in which they have begun their discussions. Yet both have begun with position statements designed to mislead the other side. Have they behaved unethically? Are they obliged to disclose their true bargaining needs and intentions to preserve their professional reputations? May they never reject offers they know their clients will accept?

During their subsequent discussions, the Seller's representative is likely to embellish the value of the business being sold, while the Buyer's advocate undervalues that firm. Must the Seller's attorney admit that the Seller believes that future competition from foreign firms is likely to diminish the economic value of his company? Must the Buyer's lawyer disclose the Buyer's innovative plan to enhance the competitive position and future value of this particular firm? When does the Seller-advocate's embellishment exceed the bounds of bargaining propriety? To what extent may the Buyer's representative disingenuously undervalue the company being discussed? Are the Buyer and Seller representatives ethically obliged to ensure a "fair" price for the business? If the Seller is willing to accept less than the Buyer anticipated or the Buyer is willing to pay more than the Seller imagined, would the lawyer representing the other side be duty bound to disclose this fact and attempt to moderate the other side's "unrealistic" beliefs?

Some advocates may try to advance client interests through tactics that are designed to make their opponents feel uncomfortable. They may be rude or inconsiderate, or may employ overly aggressive bargaining tactics. A few may resort to abrasive or even hostile behavior they hope will disconcert unsuspecting adversaries. To what extent may Buyer or Seller representatives employ highly competitive or adversarial negotiating techniques in an effort to obtain beneficial client results? At what point would such conduct transcend the bounds of appropriate behavior?

. . . Although the ABA Model Rules unambiguously proscribe all lawyer prevarication, they reasonably, but confusingly, exclude mere "puffing" and dissembling regarding one's true minimum objectives. These important exceptions appropriately recognize that disingenuous behavior is indigenous to most legal negotiations and could not realistically be prevented due to the nonpublic nature of bargaining interactions.

If one negotiator lies to another, only by happenstance will the other discover the lie. If the settlement is concluded by negotiation, there will be no trial, no public testimony by conflicting witnesses, and thus no opportunity to examine the truthfulness of assertions made during the negotiation. Consequently, in negotiation, more than in other contexts, ethical norms can probably be violated with greater confidence that there will be no discovery and punishment.   *   *   *   *

One of the inherent conflicts with regard to this area concerns the fact that what people label acceptable "puffing" when they make value-based representations during legal negotiations may be considered improper mendacity when uttered by opposing counsel.

Even though advocate prevarication during legal negotiations rarely results in bar disciplinary action, practitioners must recognize that other risks are created by truly dishonest bargaining behavior. Attorneys who deliberately deceive opponents regarding material matters or who withhold information they are legally obliged to disclose may be guilty of fraud. Contracts procured through fraudulent acts of commission or omission are voidable, and the responsible advocates and their clients may be held liable for monetary damages. It would be particularly embarrassing for lawyers to make misrepresentations that could cause their clients additional legal problems transcending those the attorneys were endeavoring to resolve. Since the adversely affected clients might thereafter sue their culpable former counsel for legal malpractice, the ultimate injury to the reputations and practices of the deceptive attorneys could be momentous. Legal representatives who employ clearly improper bargaining tactics may even subject themselves to judicial sanctions.

Most legal representatives always conduct their negotiations with appropriate candor, because they are moral individuals and/or believe that such professional behavior is mandated by the applicable ethical standards. A few others, however, do not feel so constrained. These persons should consider the practical risks associated with disreputable bargaining conduct. Even if their deceitful action is not reported to the state bar and never results in personal liability for fraud or legal malpractice, their aberrational behavior is likely to be eventually discovered by their fellow practitioners. As other attorneys learn that particular lawyers are not minimally trustworthy, future interactions become more difficult for those persons. Factual and legal representations are no longer accepted without time-consuming and expensive verification. Oral agreements on the telephone and handshake arrangements are no longer acceptable. Executed written documents are required for even rudimentary transactions. Attorneys who contemplate the employment of unacceptable deception to further present client interests should always be cognizant of the fact that their myopic conduct may seriously jeopardize their future effectiveness. No short-term gain achieved through deviant behavior should ever be permitted to outweigh the likely long-term consequences of those improper actions.

When lawyers negotiate, they must constantly decide whether they are going to divulge relevant legal and/or factual information to opposing counsel. If they decide to disclose some pertinent information, may they do so partially or is complete disclosure required? They must also determine the areas they may permissibly misrepresent and the areas they may not distort.

. . . .

Negotiators regularly use selective disclosures to enhance their positions. They divulge the legal doctrines and factual information beneficial to their claims, while withholding circumstances that are not helpful. In most instances, these selective disclosures are expected by opponents and are considered an inherent aspect of bargaining interactions. When attorneys emphasize their strengths, opposing counsel must attempt to ascertain their undisclosed weaknesses. They should carefully listen for verbal leaks and look for nonverbal signals that may indicate the existence of possible opponent problems. Probing questions may be used to elicit some negative information, and external research may be employed to gather other relevant data. These efforts are particularly important when opponents carefully limit their disclosures to favorable circumstances, since their partial disclosures may cause listeners to make erroneous assumptions.

When I discuss negotiating ethics with legal practitioners, I often ask if lawyers are obliged to disclose information to correct erroneous factual or legal assumptions made by opposing counsel. Most respondents perceive no duty to correct legal or factual misunderstandings generated solely by the carelessness of opposing attorneys. Respondents only hesitate when opponent misperceptions may have resulted from misinterpretations of seemingly honest statements made by them. For example, when a plaintiff attorney embellishes the pain being experienced by a client with a severely sprained ankle, the defense lawyer may indicate how painful broken ankles can be. If the plaintiff representative has said nothing to create this false impression, should he or she be obliged to correct the obvious defense counsel error? Although a respectable minority of respondents believe that an affirmative duty to correct the misperception may exist here—due to the fact plaintiff embellishments may have inadvertently contributed to the misunderstanding—most respondents feel no such obligation. So long as they have not directly generated the erroneous belief, it is not their duty to correct it. They could not, however, include their opponent's misunderstanding in their own statements, since this would cause them to improperly articulate knowing misrepresentations of material fact.

When opponent misperceptions concern legal doctrines, almost no respondents perceive a duty to correct those misconceptions. They indicate that each side is obliged to conduct its own legal research. If opposing counsel make incorrect assumptions or carelessly fail to locate applicable statutes or cases, those advocates do not have the right to expect their adversaries to provide them with legal assistance. The more knowledgeable advocates may even continue to rely on precedents supporting their own claims, so long as they do not distort those decisions or the opinions supporting the other side's positions.

Under some circumstances, partial answers may mislead opposing counsel as effectively as direct misrepresentations. For example, the plaintiff in Spaulding, discussed in Section A [omitted], sustained cracked ribs and fractured clavicles in an automobile accident. After the ribs and clavicles had healed, the defense lawyers had the plaintiff examined by their own medical expert who detected an aorta aneurysm that plaintiff attorneys did not know about. While defense counsel were probably under no ethical obligation to voluntarily disclose existence of the aneurysm and they could use evasive responses to avoid answering opponent inquiries regarding the plaintiff's condition, they could not overtly misrepresent their physician's findings by stating that the plaintiff was in perfect health. Could defendant attorneys respond to plaintiff counsel questions by indicating that "the ribs and the clavicles have healed nicely?" Would this partial disclosure constitute a deliberate misrepresentation of material fact, because the defendant lawyers realize that plaintiff counsel are interpreting this statement in a more expansive manner? Most practitioners have indicated that they would refuse to provide partial responses that would mislead plaintiff counsel into believing the plaintiff had completely recovered. While they could decline to answer questions regarding the plaintiff's health, they should not be permitted to provide partial responses they know will deceive plaintiff counsel. Nonetheless, recipients of answers limited to such specific conditions should become suspicious and ask follow-up inquiries about other problems that may have been discovered.

. . . .

When lawyers are asked if negotiators may overtly misrepresent legal or factual matters, most immediately reply in the negative. Many lawyers cite Model Rule 4.1 and suggest that this prohibition covers all intentional misrepresentations. While attorneys are correct with respect to deliberate misstatements by negotiators concerning material legal doctrines, they are not entirely correct with respect to factual issues. Almost all negotiators expect opponents to engage in "puffing" and "embellishment." Advocates who hope to obtain $50,000 settlements may initially insist upon $150,000 or even

$200,000. They may also embellish the pain experienced by their client, so long as their exaggerations do not transcend the bounds of expected propriety. Individuals involved in a corporate buy out may initially over-or under-value the real property, the building and equipment, the inventory, the accounts receivable, the patent rights and trademarks, and the goodwill of the pertinent firm.

It is clear that lawyers may not intentionally misrepresent material facts, but it is not always apparent what facts are "material." The previously noted Comment to Rule 4.1 explicitly acknowledges that "estimates of price or value placed on the subject of a transaction and a party's intentions as to an acceptable settlement of a claim" do not constitute material facts under that provision. It is thus ethical for legal negotiators to misrepresent the value their client places on particular items. For example, attorneys representing one spouse involved in a marital dissolution may indicate that their client wants joint custody of the children, when in reality he or she does not. Lawyers representing a party attempting to purchase a particular company may understate their client's belief regarding the value of the goodwill associated with the target firm. So long as the statement conveys their side's belief—and does not falsely indicate the view of an outside expert, such as an accountant—no Rule 4.1 violation would occur.

Legal negotiators may also misrepresent client settlement intentions. They may ethically suggest to opposing counsel that an outstanding offer is unacceptable, even though they know the proposed terms would be accepted if no additional concessions could be generated. Nonetheless, it is important to emphasize that this Rule 4.1 exception does not wholly excuse all misstatements regarding client settlement intentions. During the early stages of bargaining interactions, most practitioners do not expect opponents to disclose exact client desires. As negotiators approach final agreements, however, they anticipate a greater degree of candor. If negotiators were to deliberately deceive adversaries about this issue during the closing stage of their interaction, most attorneys would consider them dishonest, even though the Rule 4.1 proscription would remain inapplicable.

The relevant Comments to Rule 4.1 are explicitly restricted to negotiations with opposing counsel. Outside that narrow setting, statements pertaining to client settlement objectives may constitute "material" fact. ABA Commission on Ethics and Professional Responsibility, Formal Opinion 370 indicated that knowing misrepresentations regarding client settlement intentions to judges during pretrial settlement discussions would be impermissible because the misstatements would not be confined to adversarial bargaining interactions.

When material facts are involved, attorneys may not deliberately misrepresent the actual circumstances. They may employ evasive techniques to avoid answering opponent questions, but they may not provide false or misleading answers. If they decide to respond to inquiries pertaining to material facts, they must do so honestly. They must also be careful not to issue partially correct statements they know will be misinterpreted by their opponents, since such deliberate deception would be likely to contravene Rule 4.1.

A crucial distinction is drawn between statements of lawyer opinion and statements of material fact. When attorneys merely express their opinions—for example, "I think the defendant had consumed too much alcohol" and "I believe the plaintiff will encounter future medical difficulties"—they are not constrained by Rule 4.1. Opposing counsel know that these recitations only concern the personal views of the speakers. Thus, personal view statements are critically different from lawyer statements indicating that they have witnesses who can testify to these matters. If representations regarding witness information is knowingly false, the misstatements would clearly violate Rule 4.1.

A frequently debated area concerns representations about one's authorized limits. Many attorneys refuse to answer "unfair" questions concerning their authorized limits because these inquiries pertain to confidential attorney-client communications. If negotiators decide to respond to these queries, must they do so honestly? Some lawyers believe that truthful responses are required, since they concern material facts. Other practitioners assert that responses about client authorizations merely reflect client valuations and settlement intentions and are thus excluded from the scope of Rule 4.1 by the drafter's Comment. For this reason, these practitioners think that attorneys may distort these matters.

Negotiators who know they cannot avoid the impact of questions concerning their authorized limits by labeling them "unfair" and who find it difficult to provide knowingly false responses can employ an alternative approach. If the plaintiff lawyer who is demanding $120,000 asks the defendant attorney who is presently offering $85,000 whether he or she is authorized to provide $100,000, the recipient may treat the $100,000 figure as a new plaintiff proposal. That individual can reply that the $100,000 sum suggested by plaintiff counsel is more realistic but still exorbitant. The plaintiff attorney may become preoccupied with the need to clarify the fact that he or she did not intend to suggest any reduction in his or her outstanding $120,000 demand. That person would probably forego further attempts to ascertain the authorized limits possessed by the defendant attorney!

. . . .

In recent years, a number of legal representatives—especially in large urban areas— have decided to employ highly offensive tactics to advance client interests. They may be rude, sarcastic, or nasty. These individuals erroneously equate discourteous actions with effective advocacy. They use these techniques as a substitute for lawyering skill. Proficient practitioners recognize that impolite behavior is the antithesis of competent representation.

Legal representatives should eschew tactics that are merely designed to humiliate or harass opponents. ABA Model Rule 4.4 expressly states that "[A] lawyer shall not use means that have no substantial purpose other than to embarrass, delay, or burden a third person. . . ." Demented win-lose negotiators occasionally endeavor to achieve total annihilation of adversaries through the cruel and unnecessary degradation of opposing counsel. When advocates obtain munificent settlement terms for their client, there is no reason for them to employ tactics intended to discomfort their adversaries. Not only is such behavior morally reprehensible, but it needlessly exposes the offensive perpetrators to future recriminations that could easily be avoided through common courtesy. This approach also guarantees the offensive actors far more nonsettlements than are experienced by their more cooperative cohorts, and it tends to generate less efficient bargaining distributions.

Many practicing attorneys seem to think that competitive/adversarial negotiators—who use highly competitive tactics to maximize their own client returns—achieve more beneficial results for their clients than their cooperative/problem-solving colleagues—who employ more cooperative techniques designed to maximize the joint return to the parties involved. An empirical study, conducted by Professor Gerald Williams, of legal practitioners in Denver and Phoenix contradicts this notion. Professor Williams found that sixty-five percent of negotiators are considered cooperative/problem-solvers by their peers, twenty-four percent are viewed as competitive/adversarial, and eleven percent did not fit in either category. [43] When the respondents were asked to indicate which attorneys were "effective," "average," and "ineffective" negotiators, the results were striking. While fifty-nine percent of the cooperative/problem-solving lawyers were rated "effective," only twenty-five percent of competitive/adversarial attorneys were rated effective. On the other hand, while a mere three percent of cooperative/problem-solvers were considered "ineffective," thirty-three percent of competitive/adversarial bargainers were rated "ineffective."

In his study, Professor Williams found that certain traits were shared by both effective cooperative/problem-solving negotiators and effective competitive/adversarial bargainers. Successful negotiators from both groups are thoroughly prepared, behave in an honest and ethical manner, are perceptive readers of opponent cues, are analytical, realistic, and convincing, and observe the courtesies of the bar. The proficient negotiators from both groups also sought to maximize their own client's return. Since this is the quintessential characteristic of competitive/adversarial bargainers, it would suggest that a number of successful negotiators may be adroitly masquerading as sheep in wolves' clothing. They exude a cooperative style, but seek competitive objectives.

Most successful negotiators are able to combine the most salient traits associated with the cooperative/problem-solving and the competitive/adversarial styles. They endeavor to maximize client returns, but attempt to accomplish this objective in a congenial and seemingly ingenuous manner. They look for shared values in recognition of the fact that by maximizing joint returns, they are more likely to obtain the best settlements for their own clients. Although successful negotiators try to manipulate opponent perceptions, they rarely resort to truly deceitful tactics. They know that a loss of credibility will undermine their ability to achieve beneficial results. Despite the fact successful negotiators want as much as possible for their own clients, they are not "win-lose" negotiators who judge their results, not by how well they have done, but by how poorly they think their opponents have done. They realize that the imposition of poor terms on opponents does not necessarily benefit their own clients. All factors being equal, they want to maximize opponent satisfaction. So long as it does not require significant concessions on their part, they acknowledge the benefits to be derived from this approach.

---

[43] Gerald R. Williams, Legal Negotiation and Settlement 19 (1983).

The more satisfied opponents are, the more likely those parties will accept proposed terms and honor the resulting agreements.

These eclectic negotiators employ a composite style. They may be characterized as competitive/problem-solvers. They seek competitive goals (maximum client returns), but endeavor to accomplish these objectives through problem-solving strategies. They exude a cooperative approach and follow the courtesies of the legal profession. They avoid rude or inconsiderate behavior, recognizing that such openly adversarial conduct is likely to generate competitive/adversarial responses from their opponents. They appreciate the fact that individuals who employ wholly inappropriate tactics almost always induce opposing counsel to work harder to avoid exploitation by these openly opportunistic bargainers. Legal negotiators who are contemplating the use of offensive techniques should simply ask themselves how they would react if similar tactics were employed against them.

. . . .

Despite the contrary impression of some members of the general public, I have generally found attorneys to be conscientious and honorable people. I have encountered few instances of questionable behavior. I would thus like to conclude with the admonitions I impart to my Legal Negotiating students as they prepare to enter the legal profession. Lawyers must remember that they have to live with their own consciences, and not those of their clients or their partners. They must employ tactics they are comfortable using, even in those situations in which other people encourage them to employ less reputable behavior. If they adopt techniques they do not consider appropriate, not only will they experience personal discomfort, but they will also fail to achieve their intended objective due to the fact they will not appear credible when using those tactics. Attorneys must also acknowledge that they are members of a special profession and owe certain duties to the public that transcend those that may be owed by people engaged in other businesses. Even though ABA Model Rule 1.3 states that "[a] lawyer shall act with reasonable diligence," Comment One expressly recognizes that "a lawyer is not bound to press for every advantage that might be realized for a client. A lawyer has professional discretion in determining the means by which a matter [shall] be pursued."

Popular negotiation books occasionally recount the successful use of questionable techniques to obtain short-term benefits. The authors glibly describe the way they have employed highly aggressive, deliberately deceptive, or equally opprobrious bargaining tactics to achieve their objectives. They usually conclude these stories with parenthetical admissions that their bilked adversaries would probably be reluctant to interact with them in the future. When negotiators engage in such questionable behavior such that they would find it difficult, if not impossible, to transact future business with their adversaries, they have usually transcended the bounds of propriety. No legal representatives should be willing to jeopardize long-term professional relationships for the narrow interests of particular clients. Zealous representation should never be thought to require the employment of personally compromising techniques.

Lawyers must acknowledge that they are not guarantors—they are only legal advocates. They are not supposed to guarantee client victory no matter how disreputably they must act to do so. They should never countenance witness perjury or the withholding of subpoenaed documents. While they should zealously endeavor to advance client interests, they should recognize their moral obligation to follow the ethical rules applicable to all attorneys.

Untrustworthy advocates encounter substantial difficulty when they negotiate with others. Their oral representations must be verified and reduced to writing, and many opponents distrust their written documents. Their negotiations become especially problematic and cumbersome. If nothing else moves practitioners to behave in an ethical and dignified manner, their hope for long and successful legal careers should induce them to avoid conduct that may undermine their future effectiveness.

Attorneys should diligently strive to advance client objectives while simultaneously maintaining their personal integrity. This philosophy will enable them to optimally serve the interests of both their clients and society. Legal practitioners who are asked about their insistence on ethical behavior may take refuge in an aphorism of Mark Twain: "Always do right. This will gratify some people, and astonish the rest[!]"

NOTES AND QUESTIONS

(1) In the excerpt from her article, Professor Thurman states: "If many lawyers shade the truth when they negotiate in behalf of clients, the practice will spread by imitation or retaliation and will spill over into more serious distortions. The ultimate outcome is loss of trust and goodwill toward lawyers and the law." Is this concern heightened with the increased use of mediation by lawyers? In his thoughtful article, *Telling the Truth in Mediation: Mediator Owed Duty of Candor*, Disp. Resol. Mag., Winter, 1997, Bruce E. Meyerson quotes a prominent mediator: "Don't believe anything a lawyer will tell you during a mediation!" Meyerson goes on to argue for a higher standard of truth-telling in the mediation setting. Do you think it is feasible to have one standard of truth-telling in mediation, another in negotiation, and still another in court?

(2) The increasingly widespread use of mediation by lawyers also makes the lack of clarity in Model Rule 4.1 more problematic. In a recent article, James Alfini argues that there is a need to revise Rule 4.1 to create a more suitable ethics infrastructure to support mediation and other ADR proceedings. His suggested revision is reprinted below. Do you think the practicing bar would find this revision acceptable? Why or why not?

SETTLEMENT ETHICS AND LAWYERING IN ADR PROCEEDINGS: A PROPOSAL TO REVISE RULE 4.1

19 N. Ill. U. L. Rev. 255, 270-271 (1999) *

By James Alfini

RULE 4.1 TRUTHFULNESS IN STATEMENTS TO OTHERS

[Alfini Proposal]

In the course of representing a client a lawyer shall not knowingly:

(a) make a false statement of ~~material~~ fact or law to a third person; or

(b) assist the client in reaching a settlement agreement that is based on reliance upon a false statement of fact made by the lawyer's client; or

~~(b)~~ (c) fail to disclose a material fact to a third person when disclosure is necessary to avoid assisting a criminal or fraudulent act by a client, unless disclosure is prohibited by Rule 1.6.

Comment

Misrepresentation

[1] A lawyer is required to be truthful when dealing with others on a client's behalf, but generally has no affirmative duty to inform an opposing party of relevant facts. A misrepresentation can occur if the lawyer incorporates or affirms a statement of another person that the lawyer knows is false. Misrepresentations can also occur by failure to act.

~~Statements of Fact~~

[2] ~~This Rule refers to statements of fact. Whether a particular statement should be regarded as one of fact can depend on the circumstances. Under generally accepted conventions in negotiation, certain types of statements ordinarily are not taken as statements of material fact. Estimates of price or value placed on the subject of a transaction and a party's intentions as to an acceptable settlement of a claim are in this category, and so is the existence of an undisclosed principal except where nondisclosure of the principal would constitute fraud.~~

Alternative Dispute Resolution

[2] A lawyer's duty of truthfulness applies beyond formal tribunals (see Rule 3.3) to less formal settings. The obligation to be truthful is particularly

essential with the increased use by courts of dispute resolution alternatives such as mediation, arbitration, mini-trial, and summary jury trial to effect settlement. When representing a client in these less formal settings, the lawyer may often encounter situations where both the lawyer and his or her client participate freely in open and frank discussions unconstrained by rules of evidence or procedure. The lawyer should therefore inform the client of the lawyer's duty to be truthful and the lawyer's inability to assist the client in reaching a settlement agreement that is procured in whole or in part as a result of a false statement of material fact or law made by the client.

Fraud by Client

[3] Paragraph (b) recognizes that substantive law may require a lawyer to disclose certain information to avoid being deemed to have assisted the client's crime or fraud. The requirement of disclosure created by this paragraph is, however, subject to the obligations created by Rule 1.6.

§ D   PSYCHOLOGICAL AND ECONOMIC ANALYSES

In recent years, social science researchers, particularly from psychology and economics, have offered new insights into negotiation behavior. Much of this research is referred to as "barriers" research, because it seeks to identify and analyze various barriers or obstacles to the settlement of cases. The authors of the materials in this section apply these research findings to the negotiation practice setting.

PSYCHOLOGICAL PRINCIPLES IN NEGOTIATING CIVIL SETTLEMENTS

4 Harv. Negot. L. Rev., 1, 2-4, 39–56 (1999) *

By Richard Birke & Craig R. Fox

This article focuses on psychological obstacles to the rational resolution of legal disputes. Our purpose is to alert legal scholars and practitioners to the psychological principles most relevant to legal negotiation, particularly those that apply to civil litigation. In so doing, we adapt a well-established body of psychological literature to legal negotiations. Because there have been few attempts to date to adapt these principles specifically to the realm of legal decisionmaking, our applications of some of these principles to legal negotiations are necessarily speculative. Nonetheless, we believe that awareness of these principles will help practitioners achieve more efficient and desirable settlements. The psychological principles that we present in this article operate in a similar manner to optical illusions in that they typically involve automatic, subconscious processes that are difficult to subvert. However, we think that increased awareness of psychological principles will make any lawyer a better negotiator, as awareness can help lawyers identify situations in which they might consciously choose to override or attempt to compensate for their instinctive reactions. Moreover, understanding of these tendencies can help lawyers anticipate bias in the behavior of others.

. . . .

This article is organized around a series of questions that lawyers are likely to ask themselves as they guide cases from intake through to settlement.

. . . .

Question 7: Should I make the first offer, and if so, what should it be?

Your wrongful death case is proceeding. A pre-trial ruling has made the possibility of punitive damages near zero, and given that the heirs are distant relatives, the likelihood of any "loss of consortium" damages is slight. The death came relatively quickly, so you estimate that "pain and suffering" will not yield vast amounts of money from a jury.

Nonetheless, because your case on liability is strong, the other side has offered to settle, upon conditions. They will admit to liability if you can agree to actuarial damages (the amount she would have earned over the rest of her life) plus some token amounts for the other aspects of the case. In preparation for negotiation over the amount of actuarial damages, you have discovered some interesting facts. The deceased had worked as a waitress, earning approximately $20,000 per year, but she had finished two years of law school at a reasonably prestigious school, and was on the "Dean's list" every term. She was enrolled and ready to start her final year of school at the time of her death.

Attorneys in the case have a meeting with you later this week to discuss possible settlement. Will you make the first offer? Will you invite them to make it? If you do, what will it be?

When considering the question of whether to make the first offer or wait for an opponent to make the first offer, the traditional practice has been for the moving party (the plaintiff or the prosecution) to make a proposal that is rejected by the defendant, and the rejection is followed by a counter. Positional bargaining may cause an iterated chain of steps toward a mid-point, and if the mid-point is agreed upon, a settlement occurs. Otherwise, a trial is likely.

The first "offer" is generally the demand stated in the complaint as the request for damages. However, this amount is often an over stated figure that is included to prevent a jurisdictional challenge and to get the attention of the defendant. It is rarely seen by defendants as a credible settlement offer. Similarly, some defendants respond to the complaint with an offer to settle the case for its nuisance value. Again, this figure is so starkly low relative to the ultimate settlement value of most cases that it is not a perceived as an offer to settle. It is an announcement of aspiration, not valuation.

When the time comes to make sincere offers, someone has to go first, but most attorneys prefer to hold their cards close to their vests. The question looms—how to start?

1. Psychological Considerations

There is little empirical research on the question of whether it is best to make the first offer. Two psychological phenomena may be relevant. In situations where one's counterpart has only a vague sense of what is reasonable (e.g., because there is little or no judicial precedent), making the first offer may afford an opportunity to exploit . . . anchoring bias, and draw the counterpart into an order of magnitude that is more favorable to the offeror before the counterpart makes an offer that anchors both parties in a range that favors him. On the other hand, a pervasive norm that governs negotiation behavior is that of reciprocity, according to which one should reciprocate concessions made by others. In fact, distributive negotiations typically settle roughly midway between the opening offers to the extent that this midpoint is feasible for both sides. Hence, making the second offer can afford the negotiator an opportunity to define where that midpoint lies. In general, whether one makes the first offer in order to exploit anchoring, or makes the second offer in order to leave room for concessions and exploit reciprocity, it is good strategy to make as extreme an opening offer as can be gotten away with, but not so extreme that the offeror appears to be negotiating in bad faith.

In cases where opposing counsel has no clear notion of the value of the claim, she will be more susceptible to anchoring bias. The case of the "waitress/lawyer," for example, might provide an opportunity to anchor opposing counsel to a higher number than she might otherwise have considered. Valuing the career worth of a law student is a highly speculative enterprise, as her chosen career path may have been a lucrative corporate career or a lower-salaried career in public interest law. Furthermore, long-term success in her chosen path is largely a matter of guesswork. Hence, a high first offer might draw opposing counsel into a debate about how successful a law career the deceased would have had, rather than a discussion on whether she would have finished law school at all.

In cases where opposing counsel has a reasonable idea concerning the value of the claim, it may behoove the lawyer to wait for the other side to make the first offer so that the lawyer can respond with a counter-offer that defines a midpoint favorable to him. Had the deceased been an established attorney with a stable income, it might make sense to let opposing counsel make the first offer. In such an instance, if opposing counsel offered four million dollars as a settlement, and the lawyer aspired to settle at eight million, she should counter at twelve.

2. Remediation

To protect against being exploited by one's counterpart, we suggest that attorneys gather as much information as possible that might help them assess the value of the claim in question. The more information one has at his fingertips, the less likely he is to be drawn into accepting an inequitable offer due to an anchoring bias. Furthermore, we suggest that attorneys decide in advance on their reservation price (in consultation with the client, of course), and that they base this price on a carefully researched estimate of what is likely to happen if the case goes to court. Adjustments are appropriate only as relevant new information comes to light. Finally, we suggest that attorneys can use the norm of reciprocity to their advantage by insisting that their own concessions be followed by concessions from their counterpart. In our experience, people tend to be more sensitive to the rate of concessions than they are to the magnitude of those concessions.

Question 8: How should I frame the offer?

The wrongful death case is close to settlement. They've agreed that if you will compromise on the expected wages then they will compensate you for other aspects of the claim—provided that they "feel okay with the offer." The other attorney wants to see your offer in writing.

There are a number of aspects of your demand—loss of consortium, expected wages, medical bills, funeral costs, attorneys fees, etc. Some of the bills are in—e.g., funeral costs—and you are waiting for others—e.g. medical bills. Furthermore, although you can compile some of your attorney's fees, you haven't gotten all the hourly work bills from your associates, and you still have bills coming in from expert consultants and investigators. Do you send the information piecemeal, or wait to collect all the information and send one bill?

Traditional economic analysis suggests that people should be sensitive to the impact of offers on final states of wealth, and that the particulars of how those offers are communicated should not matter. Empirical studies of attorneys suggest that describing an offer in terms of gains versus losses can affect a lawyer's willingness to accept the offer. Certainly, lawyers choose words carefully, and this tendency extends to the crafting and communication of offers. However, for the most part, attorneys use this skill to avoid admitting or denying liability, or to avoid the accidental creation of exploitable weaknesses in their cases. Less thought goes into the question of how to frame an offer so that it is most likely to be accepted.

1. The Psychology of Value and Framing

Behavioral decision theorists have documented systematic violations of the standard economic assumption that people evaluate options in terms of their impact on one's final state of wealth. In particular, prospect theory assumes that people adapt to their present state of wealth and are sensitive to changes with respect to that endowment.

Second, people exhibit diminishing sensitivity to increasing gains and losses. For example, increasing an award from zero to $1000 is more pleasurable than increasing an award from $1000 to $2000; increasing an award from $2000 to $3000 is even less pleasurable, and so forth. Similarly, increasing a payment from zero to $1000 is more painful than increasing a payment from $1000 to $2000, and so on. One key implication of this pattern is that people's willingness to take risks differs for losses versus gains. For example, because $1000 is more than half as attractive as $2000, people typically prefer to receive $1,000 for sure than face a fifty-fifty chance of receiving $2,000 or nothing (i.e., they are "risk-averse" for medium probability gains). In contrast, because losing $1000 is more than half as painful as losing $2000, people typically prefer to risk a 50-50 chance of losing $2,000 or losing nothing to losing $1,000 for sure (i.e., they are "risk-seeking" for medium probability losses).

Third, prospect theory asserts that losses have more impact on choices than do equivalent gains. For example, most people do not think that a fifty percent chance of gaining $100 is sufficient to compensate a fifty percent chance of losing $100. In fact, people typically require a 50% chance of gaining as much as $200 or $300 to offset a 50% chance of losing $100.

. . . .

Taken together, the way in which a problem is framed in terms of losses or gains can have a substantial impact on behavior in negotiations. First, loss aversion contributes to a bias in favor of the status quo because relative disadvantages of alternative outcomes loom larger than relative advantages. Hence, negotiators are often reluctant to make the tradeoffs necessary for them to achieve joint gains. To illustrate, consider the case of two partners in a failing consulting firm. The joint office space and secretarial support costs are unduly burdensome, and each could operate productively out of their homes with minimal overhead costs. If they could divide their territory and agree not to compete, each could have a profitable career—but each would have to agree to give up half the firm's client base. Each partner may view the territory they retain as a gain that doesn't compensate adequately for the territory they must relinquish. Yet failure to make such a split consigns them to continuation in a losing venture.

Second, both loss aversion and the pattern of risk seeking for losses may lead to more aggressive bargaining when the task is viewed as minimizing losses rather than maximizing gains. Indeed, in laboratory studies, negotiators whose payoffs are framed in terms of gains (e.g., they were instructed to maximize revenues) tended to be more risk-averse than those whose payoffs are framed in terms of losses (e.g., they were instructed to minimize costs): the first group tended to be more concessionary but completed more transactions. Recently, Professor Rachlinski documented greater willingness to accept settlement offers in legal contexts when the offer is perceived as a gain compared to when it is perceived as a loss.[182]

Third, the attractiveness of potential agreements may be influenced by the way in which gains and losses are packaged and described. In particular, if a negotiator wants to present a proposal in its best possible light to a counterpart, he or she should attempt to integrate each aspect of the agreement on which the counterpart stands to lose (in order to exploit the fact that people experience diminishing sensitivity to each additional loss) and segregate each aspect of the agreement on which the counterpart stands to gain (in order to avoid the tendency of people to experience diminishing sensitivity to each additional gain). For instance, in the partnership dissolution example, it would be most effective to describe the territory forgone as a single unit (e.g., "everything west of highway 6 is mine") and the territory obtained in component parts (e.g., "and you will have the Heights neighborhood, the eastern section of downtown, everything north of there to the river, South

---

182 *See* Rachlinski at 128. [Jeffrey J. Rachlinski, *Gains, Losses, and the Psychology of Litigation*, 70 S. Cal. L. Rev. 113, 13–58 (1996).]

Village, etc."), and least effective to describe the territory foregone in component parts (e.g. "I keep the west side of downtown, the riverfront, North village, and everything between downtown and Ballard Square . . .") and the territory obtained as a single unit (e.g., "everything east of highway 6 is yours").

2. Remediation: Protecting Against Framing Effects

Knowledge of the psychology of value can help a negotiator make offers appear more desirable to her counterpart, as described above. As for defending against inconsistency or manipulations by others, a negotiator should be aware that aspirations, past history, or previous offers may influence the frame of reference against which a negotiator perceives losses and gains; as a result, risk attitudes may be influenced by these transitory perceptions, which in turn influence how aggressively a negotiator bargains. Furthermore, negotiators must consciously overcome their natural reluctance to make concessions in order to exploit opportunities for trades that make both sides better off. Finally, in order to protect against mental accounting manipulations by others, a negotiator might develop a scoring system for each of the issues under consideration or translate everything into a unified dollar metric. By adding up points or dollars across all issues, the negotiator can focus on the value of the aggregate outcome to her client, rather than a piecemeal melange of incremental gains and losses that may have been creatively framed by her counterpart.

Returning to our hypothetical question of whether to wait and send one bill or to send the bills as they come in, our advice is to wait and send one bill. If one bill came in for expenses to date and then a second bill came in for medical expenses and so forth, the recipient of the bills would have to endure a series of segregated losses rather than a single, integrated loss.

Question 9: How should I evaluate their offers?

You have been discussing with your client two possible settlement packages in your "hot pie" case. Package A would require the company to pay a cash amount of $100,000, and Package B would require an agreement by the company to pay all of your client's current and future medical bills, change the temperature at which they serve their pies, and give her a cash payment of $50,000. Your client has expressed, in confidence, a mild preference for the $100,000 cash.

While you are out of town on other business and before you could communicate these offers to your counterpart, the opposing counsel leaves you a message offering $100,000 to settle the case. When you call your client to communicate this news, rather than show elation, she expresses concern and suggests that the other deal now seems more appealing. How do you counsel your client?

When an attorney receives an offer from the other side, he is ethically obligated to transmit that offer to his client.[185] He is not obligated to show

---

[185] MODEL RULES OF PROFESSIONAL CONDUCT Rule 1.2(a), 1.4 (1995).

the client a letter or play a voice-mail message or recite verbatim the offer with appropriate inflections. As the lawyer communicates the offer, the lawyer inevitably, if unwittingly, introduces a spin on the offer that may influence the client to consider it favorably or unfavorably. Usually the attorney's impression (and indeed, the client's) of the offer will be influenced to some degree by the identity of the offeror. In particular, if the attorney's dealings with the other side have been rancorous, the attorney may view any offer with a great deal of suspicion. Sometimes the relationship impedes impartial evaluation of an offer, causing a negotiator to reject an offer from an adversary that he should have accepted.

1. Psychology of Reactive Devaluation

Fixed-pie bias (i.e., the assumption that what is good for my counterpart must be bad for me) may contribute to reactive devaluation, which is a tendency to evaluate proposals less favorably after they have been offered by one's adversary. In one classic study conducted during the days of Apartheid, researchers solicited students' evaluations of two university plans for divestment from South Africa.[187] The first plan called for partial divestment, and the second increased investments in companies that had left South Africa. Both plans, which fell short of the students' demand for full divestment, were rated before and after the university announced that it would adopt the partial divestment plan. The results were dramatic: students rated the university plan less positively after it was announced by the university and the alternative plan more positively.

We hasten to note that the source of an offer may be diagnostic of its quality. It may be reasonable to view an offer more critically when the source is one's opponent, particularly if there is an unpleasant history between the parties. However, evidence from the aforementioned studies suggests that people tend to experience a knee-jerk overreaction to the source of the offer. If negotiators routinely under value concessions made their counterparts, it will inhibit their ability to exploit tradeoffs that might result in more valuable agreements.

Consider an example of how reactive devaluation might manifest itself in a negotiation between lawyers. Imagine a simplified environmental cleanup action in which the parties are a governmental enforcement agency (represented by a single person) and a single responsible polluter. There may be two solutions to their problem. In one, the government effectuates the cleanup and sends a bill to the polluter. In the second, the polluter does the cleanup and the government inspects. Perhaps solution one meets more of the polluters' interests than solution two. One might suppose that the polluter would prefer this solution regardless of how it emerges as the agreed method. However, studies of reactive devaluation suggest that once the government tentatively agrees to that particular solution, the polluter may view the alternative solution more favorably. The apparent thought process is "if they held it back, it must be worse for them and therefore better for me than the

---

187 See Stillinger et al. [Constance Stillinger et al., The Reactive Devaluation Barrier to Conflict Resolution, unpublished manuscript, Stanford University (1990) (on file with authors).] For a description of the study, see Mnookin & Ross [Robert H. Mnookin & Lee Ross, *Introduction* to BARRIERS TO CONFLICT RESOLUTION 3 (Kenneth J. Arrow et al. eds, 1995).]

one offered." The polluter may irrationally reorder her priorities and reject a deal simply be cause it was offered freely by an opponent.

2. *Remediation*

Resisting the destructive effects of reactive devaluation will require negotiators to unlearn a pervasive assumption that most people carry with them. Negotiations are rarely fixed-sum and it is simply not true that what is good for one side is necessarily bad for the other. As mentioned above, both parties often have congruent interests or a mutual interest in exploiting tradeoffs on issues that they prioritize differently. To resist reactive devaluation, one must short-circuit a deeply ingrained habit. It is natural to react against freedom to choose, and when an opponent holds back one offer in favor of another, it's natural to yearn for the alternative option. However, it would be wise to critically examine this natural impulse and ask if this impulse is a rational response to a truly inferior offer or an emotional reaction against the other side's initiative.

Even if a lawyer can restrain herself from reactive devaluation, it may be very difficult to buffer this response in his counterpart. Certainly, it first may help to cultivate a cordial relationship with one's counterpart to the extent that this is possible, so that offers are regarded with less suspicion. Second, it may be helpful to ask a mutually trusted intermediary to convey a proposal. Some commentators have suggested that reactive devaluation can be overcome with the help of a mediator. Finally, if a party crafts a settlement package that would be mutually beneficial, it may be helpful to work with opposing counsel to make them feel as if the solution was jointly initiated or even that it was the opposing counsel's idea.

Returning to the hypothetical, the client may be experiencing reactive devaluation. It may behoove the attorney to counsel her client to consider whether her change of heart was a result of the fact that her original package was offered by her opponent in the litigation or is a result of other factors. If her reaction was driven by its source, the attorney should make sure she understands that she is rejecting her formerly-preferred deal solely because it was offered by an adversary, and not necessarily because it fails to meet her interests.

Question 10: How can I get people to accept my offers?

You are submitting your offer on the harassment case. To what extent do you think that each of the following might help get your offer accepted by opposing counsel? Why?

1) "Of course, we put a lot of time and energy into crafting this offer, and we've conceded at least five different times on the amount that we are willing to take. We're asking you to concede just once from your initial offer."

2) "You once told me that money was a secondary issue, that it was confidentiality that mattered most to your client. We've agreed to give you that. Isn't your statement still true?"

3) "I've run this offer by six other people in this firm, all of whom used to work with you before you took your present job. They all thought that the offer was one that your client should accept."

4) "We've been friends for a long time, so how about helping me make this one go away? Once we get it done, I'll take you out for a beer."

5) "And while I don't want to put any pressure on you, you probably know that we hired Justice Brown from the local court where our case is filed. I showed him our offer just to get his feedback, and he thought your client would be foolish not to accept."

6) "This offer is open for forty-eight hours. After that, all bets are off."

Negotiation is, in part, a game of mutual influence. Many attorneys are naturally gifted in the art of social influence while others are less comfortable with this dimension of lawyering. We believe that the study of social influence tactics can help attorneys protect them selves against exploitation.

1. Psychology of Social Influence

A vast literature in social psychology examines how individuals persuade others to accede to their requests. Psychologist Robert Cialdini[191] organizes the literature into six pervasive principles of social influence that we describe below. Cialdini observed these tactics in his study of salespeople, fund-raisers, advertisers, and other professionals.[192] We believe that these principles apply with equal force to negotiations of civil settlements by attorneys.

a. Reciprocation

One should repay, in kind, what another person has provided. Even uninvited favors and gifts leave people with a sense of indebtedness that they feel they must reciprocate. In negotiation, there is a strong norm that a party should respond to each concession that his or her counterpart makes with a concession of his or her own, even if the initial offer was rather extreme.

The tendency to reciprocate is not in itself problematic, but when one side reciprocates relatively trivial concessions with meaningful concessions, such as a significant reduction in what was already a reasonable request, she may be committing a negotiation error. A skillful negotiator knows that people tend to reciprocate acts of kindness, even when the original kindness is uninvited and of no value to the recipient. Lawyers bargain over both substantive and logistical matters, such as discovery schedules, stipulations, deposition schedules, compliance with orders, and the possible settlement of the action. They rarely get everything they want, and the result of these interactions generally involves some degree of compromise from both sides. Occasionally, a logistical concession from one attorney may elicit a substantive concession from opposing counsel.

Two suggestions are in order. First, as noted in Question 7, the lawyer should make an optimistic first offer in order to leave room for concessions

---

[191] *See* Cialdini. [ROBERT B. CIALDINI, INFLUENCE: THE PSYCHOLOGY OF PERSUASION (1993)]
[192] *See id.*

that will be expected by the other side (in response to concessions that they will make). Second, it is important to resist the temptation to reciprocate meaningless or negligible concessions.

Returning to our hypothetical, it is easy to see that the first phrase employed by the attorney is an attempt to exploit the reciprocation norm. The speaker draws attention to previous concessions, thereby putting pressure on the respondent to reciprocate.

b. Commitment and Consistency

Once a person makes a choice or takes a stand, she encounters personal and interpersonal pressure to behave consistently with that commitment. There are at least three manifestations of this principle in negotiation. First, a public commitment to a statement of principles, an aspiration, or a criterion of fairness is difficult to abnegate at a later time. Second, after a negotiator gets her "foot in the door" by having her counterpart accede to a small initial request, later cooperation becomes more likely. Third, after investing significant time and energy into crafting a tentative agreement, negotiators are more likely to give in to last-minute requests by their counterparts.

Sometimes lawyers decrease the possibility of negotiated settlement by publicly committing to an unrealistic aspiration. They often promise an optimistic result before they have all of the relevant facts, typically in an effort to get retain a potential client. For example, a plaintiff's attorney might tell his client that the case should not settle for less than $100,000. The client and attorney may then become wedded to this aspiration level. Suppose the lawyer later discovers that the objective value of the case is $50,000. It may be an embarrassment at this point for the attorney to recommend accepting an offer that is even as high as $80,000.

In addition to commitments made in valuation, commitments made in reaction to offers can be detrimental to the negotiating process. A lawyer often rejects offers made by the other side, or prematurely commits to an unrealistic "walk-away" price. If she later wishes to accept the offer or relax her reservation price, she must either admit that she was wrong or come up with a reason why circumstances have changed. We recommend that lawyers be circumspect in making public commitments, and that they help provide opponents with face-saving reasons to back down from commitments opponents may have made (e.g., provide reasons why circumstances have changed).

It is quite common for negotiators to force endgame concessions. For instance, when a real estate deal is near consummation, it is common for sellers and mortgage companies to reveal myriad small costs that were not discussed earlier. Lawyers may try at the last moment to tack on attorney's fees and court costs to a settlement. Provided that these costs are small relative to settlement amounts, the recipient of such a request may feel that it is better to concede rather than to scuttle the whole deal and "go back to square one." Again, one useful means to defend against such exploitation is to decide in advance on a reservation price and to resist temptations to back off of this value unless additional information justifies doing so.

Returning to the hypothetical, it is easy to see that the use of the phrases "You once told me that . . ." and "Isn't your statement still true?" are attempts to pressure the recipient to remain consistent with prior statements and offers.

c. Social Proof

People view a behavior as correct in a given situation to the degree that they see others performing it. The reactions of others thus serves as "proof" that the behavior is appropriate. For example, canned laughter has been shown to elicit more laughter in audiences and cause them to rate material as funnier than they do in its absence. In general, people are more likely to follow the behavior of others when the situation is unclear or ambiguous or when people are unsure of themselves. Moreover, people are more likely to follow the example of others whom they perceive to be similar to themselves. Senior lawyers in large firms inculcate junior associates into practice, in part, by modeling a great many behavioral characteristics that are not necessarily effective, but which are nonetheless deeply ingrained. When and where to meet for negotiations, how to dress for work, and how to interview clients are all matters that are typically transmitted uncritically from one generation of firm lawyers to the next.

In settlement negotiations, lawyers can exploit past precedents and examples of other litigants who have accepted similar terms in attempts to gain compliance. In order to defend against such tactics, we encourage lawyers to seek out for themselves information concerning comparable cases and values in order to effectively evaluate the case at bar.

Returning to our hypothetical, the reference to the "other six people" who approved the offer is an attempt to influence the recipient to conform to social proof. These former colleagues provide cues for appropriate behavior in a circumstance in which the proper response is unclear.

d. Liking

People prefer to say yes to others they know and like. Several factors promote liking: physical attractiveness, similarity, compliments, cooperation, and familiarity. Contrary to the popular belief that a successful negotiator ruthlessly intimidates and exploits her counterparts, a positive relationship can be more effective for achieving mutually beneficial and equitable outcomes. Moreover, leading economists have argued that cooperation and honesty tend to promote long-term success in bargaining. And studies of lawyers negotiating prove that those who are cooperative (a trait that engenders liking) are rated as more effective, on average, than lawyers who are not.

The fourth statement in our hypothetical is a transparent attempt to leverage "liking" in order to influence the recipient to accept the settlement offer. The more the recipient likes the offeror, the more likely she will be to accept.

e. Authority

People are more likely to accede to the request of a perceived authority figure. The best known illustration of this principle is Milgram's work, which demonstrated the willingness of ordinary people to administer what they thought were dangerous levels of electrical shocks to a person with an alleged heart condition merely because an "experimenter" in a white laboratory coat insisted that "the experiment requires that [they] continue."[206] Equally sobering is the demonstration by Hofling and his colleagues in which a researcher identified himself over the phone as a hospital physician and asked hospital nurses to administer a dangerous dose of an unauthorized drug to a specific patient; in this case 95 percent of the nurses attempted to comply.[207] Not only do titles tend to promote compliance and deference, but so do uniforms and other trappings, such as fancy automobiles. Certainly, most trial attorneys will agree that the judge's physically elevated status and somber, traditional robe reinforce a courtroom hierarchy in which the judge enjoys the greatest status. Even a retired judge or a sufficiently senior partner may lend an air of authority to a position or an offer, as might a "home turf" advantage.

In our hypothetical, the reference to Justice Brown is meant to lend an air of authority to the offer. To the extent that the recipient regards the Justice in esteem or believes him to be a figure of authority in the community, the offer may be more readily accepted.

f. Scarcity

Opportunities often seem more valuable when they are less available. According to psychological reactance theory, when people are proscribed from making a certain choice, they desire that choice more and work harder to obtain it. This is the principle underlying the success of the ubiquitous "limited time offer" in consumer advertising. Threats to freedom can take the form of time limits, supply limits, and competition. In negotiation, these tactics can be a particularly effective means of gaining compliance. Savvy negotiators can dramatize their alternatives by entertaining competing bids, or they can strategically impose artificial time limits for negotiation.

In our hypothetical, the time limit attached to the offer may trigger a response by the other side. They may be more willing to accept the offer in reaction to the threat of its imminent disappearance.

---

[206] *See* STANLEY MILGRAM, OBEDIENCE TO AUTHORITY (1974).

[207] *See* Charles K. Hofling et al., *An Experimental Study of Nurse Physician Relationships*, 143 J. NERVOUS & MENTAL DISEASE 171 (1966).

WHY NEGOTIATIONS FAIL: AN EXPLORATION OF BARRIERS TO THE RESOLUTION OF CONFLICT

8 Ohio St. J. on Disp. Resol. 235, 238–249 (1993) [*]

By Robert H. Mnookin

Why is it that under circumstances where there are resolutions that better serve disputants, negotiations often fail to achieve efficient resolutions? In other words, what are the barriers to the negotiated resolution of conflict?

. . . I will explore four such barriers. Each of these barriers reflect somewhat different theoretical perspectives on negotiation and dispute resolution. The first barrier is a *strategic barrier*, which is suggested by game theory and the economic analysis of bargaining. The barrier relates to an underlying dilemma inherent in the negotiation process. Every negotiation characteristically involves a tension between: (a) discovering shared interests and maximizing joint gains, and (b) maximizing one's own gains where more for one side will necessarily mean less for the other. The second barrier arises as a result of the *principal/agent* problem. In many disputes, principals do not negotiate on their own behalf but instead act through agents who may have somewhat different incentives than their principals. This work draws on research concerning the "principal/agent" problem in law and economics and transaction cost economics. The third barrier is *cognitive*, and relates to how the human mind processes information, especially in evaluating risks and uncertainty. My discussion here draws on recent work in cognitive psychology, especially the pathbreaking research of my colleague, Amos Tversky and his collaborator, Daniel Kahneman.[14] The fourth and final barrier, "*reactive devaluation*," draws on the social psychological research of my colleague Lee Ross, and relates to the fact that bargaining is an interactive social process in which each party is constantly drawing inferences about the intentions, motives, and good faith of the other.[15]

As should be obvious, I am not attempting to provide a comprehensive list of barriers or an all-encompassing classification scheme. Instead, my purpose is to show that the concept of barriers provides a useful and necessarily interdisciplinary vantage point for exploring why negotiations sometimes fail. After describing these four barriers and their relevance to the study of negotiation, I will briefly suggest a variety of ways that neutral third parties might help overcome each of these barriers.

A. Strategic Barriers

The first barrier to the negotiated resolution of conflict is inherent in a central characteristic of negotiation. Negotiation can be metaphorically

---

[14] *See* JUDGMENT UNDER UNCERTAINTY: HEURISTICS AND BIASES, (Daniel Kahneman et al. eds., 1982).

[15] Constance A. Stillinger et al., *The Reactive Devaluation Barrier to Conflict Resolution*, J. OF PERSONALITY AND SOC. PSYCHOL. (under review).

compared to making a pie and then dividing it up. The process of conflict resolution affects both the size of the pie, and who gets what size slice.

The disputants' behavior may affect the size of the pie in a variety of ways. On the one hand, spending on avoidable legal fees and other process costs shrinks the pie. On the other hand, negotiators can together "create value" and make the pie bigger by discovering resolutions in which each party contributes special complementary skills that can be combined in a synergistic way, or by exploiting differences in relative preferences that permit trades that make both parties better off. Books like "Getting to Yes" and proponents of "win-win negotiation" emphasize the potential benefits of collaborative problem-solving approaches to negotiation which allow parties to maximize the size of the pie. [17]

Negotiation also involves issues concerning the distribution of benefits, and, with respect to pure distribution, both parties cannot be made better off at the same time. Given a pie of fixed size, a larger slice for you means a smaller one for me.

Because bargaining typically entails both efficiency issues (that is, how big the pie can be made) and distributive issues (that is, who gets what size slice), negotiation involves an inherent tension—one that David Lax and James Sebenius have dubbed the "negotiator's dilemma." [18] In order to create value, it is critically important that options be created in light of both parties' underlying interests and preferences. This suggests the importance of openness and disclosure, so that a variety of options can be analyzed and compared from the perspectives of all concerned. However, when it comes to the distributive aspects of bargaining, full disclosure—particularly if unreciprocated by the other side—can often lead to outcomes in which the more open party receives a comparatively smaller slice. To put it another way, unreciprocated approaches to creating value leave their maker vulnerable to claiming tactics. On the other hand, focusing on the distributive aspects of bargaining can often lead to unnecessary deadlocks and, more fundamentally, a failure to discover options or alternatives that make both sides better off. A simple example can expose the dilemma. The first involves what game theorists call "information asymmetry." This simply means each side to a negotiation characteristically knows some relevant facts that the other side does not know.

Suppose I have ten apples and no oranges, and Nancy Rogers has ten oranges and no apples. (Assume apples and oranges are otherwise unavailable to either of us.) I love oranges and hate apples. Nancy likes them both equally well. I suggest to Nancy that we might both be made better off through a trade. If I disclose to Nancy that I love oranges and don't eat apples, and Nancy wishes to engage in strategic bargaining, she might simply suggest that her preferences are the same as mine, although, in truth, she likes both. She might propose that I give her nine apples (which she says have little value to her) in exchange for one of her very valuable oranges. Because it is often very difficult for one party to know the underlying preferences of the other party, parties in a negotiation may puff, bluff, or lie about their underlying interests

---

[17] ROGER FISHER, WILLIAM URY, & BRUCE PATTON, GETTING TO YES (2nd ed. 1991).

[18] DAVID A. LAX & JAMES K. SEBENIUS, THE MANAGER AS NEGOTIATOR (1986).

and preferences. Indeed, in many negotiations, it may never be possible to know whether the other side has honestly disclosed its interests and preferences. I have to be open to create value, but my openness may work to my disadvantage with respect to the distributive aspect of the negotiation.

Even when both parties know all the relevant information, and that potential gains may result from a negotiated deal, strategic bargaining over how to divide the pie can still lead to deadlock (with no deal at all) or protracted and expensive bargaining, thus shrinking the pie. For example, suppose Nancy has a house for sale for which she has a reservation price of $245,000. I am willing to pay up to $295,000 for the house. Any deal within a bargaining range from $245,000 to $295,000 would make both of us better off than no sale at all. Suppose we each know the other's reservation price. Will there be a deal? Not necessarily. If we disagree about how the $50,000 "surplus" should be divided (each wanting all or most of it), our negotiation may end in a deadlock. We might engage in hardball negotiation tactics in which each tried to persuade the other that he or she was committed to walking away from a beneficial deal, rather than accept less than $40,000 of the surplus. Nancy might claim that she won't take a nickel less than $285,000, or even $294,999 for that matter. Indeed, she might go so far as to give a power of attorney to an agent to sell only at that price, and then leave town in order to make her commitment credible. Of course, I could play the same type of game and the result would then be that no deal is made and that we are both worse off. In this case, the obvious tension between the distribution of the $50,000 and the value creating possibilities inherent in any sale within the bargaining range may result in no deal.

Strategic behavior—which may be rational for a self-interested party concerned with maximizing the size of his or her own slice—can often lead to inefficient outcomes. Those subjected to claiming tactics often respond in kind, and the net result typically is to push up the cost of the dispute resolution process. (Buchwald v. Paramount Pictures Corp.,[21] is a good example of a case in which the economic costs of hardball litigation obviously and substantially shrunk the pie.) Parties may be tempted to engage in strategic behavior, hoping to get more. Often all they do is shrink the size of the pie. Those experienced in the civil litigation process see this all the time. One or both sides often attempt to use pre-trial discovery as leverage to force the other side into agreeing to a more favorable settlement. Often the net result, however, is simply that both sides spend unnecessary money on the dispute resolution process.

B. The Principal/Agent Problem

The second barrier is suggested by the recent work relating to transaction cost economics, and is sometimes called the "principal/agent" problem. Notwithstanding the jargon, the basic idea is familiar to everyone in this room. The basic problem is that the incentives for an agent (whether it be a lawyer, employee, or officer) negotiating on behalf of a party to a dispute may induce behavior that fails to serve the interests of the principal itself. The relevant

---

[21] No. C 706083, 1990 WL 357611 (Cal. Superior Jan. 8, 1990).

research suggests that it is no simple matter—whether by contract or custom—to align perfectly the incentives for an agent with the interests of the principal. This divergence may act as a barrier to efficient resolution of conflict.

Litigation is fraught with principal/agent problems. In civil litigation, for example— particularly where the lawyers on both sides are being paid by the hour—there is very little incentive for the opposing lawyers to cooperate, particularly if the clients have the capacity to pay for trench warfare and are angry to boot. Commentators have suggested that this is one reason many cases settle on the courthouse steps, and not before: for the lawyers, a late settlement may avoid the possible embarrassment of an extreme outcome, while at the same time providing substantial fees.

The Texaco/Pennzoil dispute may have involved a principal/agent problem of a different sort. My colleague Bob Wilson and I have argued that the interests of Texaco officers and directors diverged from those of the Texaco shareholders in ways that may well have affected the conduct of that litigation.[25] Although the shareholders would have benefitted from an earlier settlement, the litigation was controlled by the directors, officers, and lawyers whose interests differed in important respects. A close examination of the incentives for the management of Texaco in particular suggests an explanation for the delay in settlement.

The directors and officers of Texaco were themselves defendants in fourteen lawsuits, eleven of them derivative shareholder actions, brought after the original multi-billion Pennzoil verdict in the Texas trial court. These lawsuits essentially claimed that Texaco's directors and officers had violated their duty of care to the corporation by causing Texaco to acquire Getty Oil in a manner that led to the multi-billion dollar Texas judgment. After this verdict, and for the next several years, the Texaco management rationally might have preferred to appeal the Pennzoil judgment and seek complete vindication, even though a speedy settlement for the expected value of the litigation might have better served their shareholders. Because they faced the risk of personal liability, the directors and officers of Texaco acted in such a way as to suggest they would prefer to risk pursuing the case to the bitter end (with some slight chance of complete exoneration) rather than accept a negotiated resolution, even though in so doing they risked subjecting the corporation to a ten billion dollar judgment. The case ultimately did settle, but only through a bankruptcy proceeding in which the bankruptcy court eliminated the risk of personal liability for Texaco's officers and directors.

C. Cognitive Barriers.

The third barrier is a by-product of the way the human mind processes information, deals with risks and uncertainties, and makes inferences and judgments. Research by cognitive psychologists during the last fifteen years suggests several ways in which human reasoning often departs from that suggested by theories of rational judgment and decision making. Daniel

---

[25] MNOOKIN & WILSON at 295, 315–323. [Robert H. Mnookin & Robert R. Wilson, *Rational Bargaining and Market Efficiency: Understanding* Pennzoil v. Texaco, 75 VA. L. REV. 295 (1989)]

Kahneman and Amos Tversky had done research on a number of cognitive biases that are relevant to negotiation.[29] This evening, I would like to focus on two aspects of their work: those relating to loss aversion and framing effects.

Suppose everyone attending this evening's lecture is offered the following happy choice: At the end of my lecture you can exit at the north end of the hall or the south end. If you choose the north exit, you will be handed an envelope in which there will be a crisp new twenty dollar bill. Instead, if you choose the south exit, you will be given a sealed envelope randomly pulled from a bin. One quarter of these envelopes contain a $100 bill, but three quarters are empty. In other words, you can have a sure gain of $20 if you go out the north door, or you can instead gamble by choosing the south door where you will have a 25% chance of winning $100 and a 75% chance of winning nothing. Which would you choose? A great deal of experimental work suggests that the overwhelming majority of you would choose the sure gain of $20, even though the "expected value" of the second alternative, $25, is slightly more. This is a well known phenomenon called "risk aversion." The principle is that most people will take a sure thing over a gamble, even where the gamble may have a somewhat higher "expected" payoff.

Daniel Kahneman and Amos Tversky have advanced our understanding of behavior under uncertainty with a remarkable discovery. They suggest that, in order to avoid what would otherwise be a sure loss, many people will gamble, even if the expected loss from the gamble is larger. Their basic idea can be illustrated by changing my hypothetical. Although you didn't know this when you were invited to this lecture, it is not free. At the end of the lecture, the doors are going to be locked. If you go out the north door, you'll be required to *pay* $20 as an exit fee. If you go out the south door, you'll participate in a lottery by drawing an envelope. Three quarters of the time you're going to be let out for free, but one quarter of the time you're going to be required to pay $100. Rest assured all the money is going to the Dean's fund—a very good cause. What do you choose? There's a great deal of empirical research, based on the initial work of Kahneman and Tversky, suggesting that the majority of this audience would choose the south exit—i.e., most of you would gamble to avoid having to lose $20 for sure.[30] Kahneman and Tversky call this "loss aversion."

Now think of these two examples together. Risk aversion suggests that most of you would not gamble for a gain, even though the expected value of $25 exceeds the sure thing of $20. On the other hand, most of you would gamble to avoid a sure loss, even though, on the average, the loss of going out the south door is higher. Experimental evidence suggests that the proportion of people who will gamble to avoid a loss is much greater than those who would gamble to realize a gain.

---

[29] For a discussion of various cognitive barriers, see Daniel Kahneman and Amos Tversky, *Conflict Resolution: A Cognitive Perspective*, in BARRIERS TO CONFLICT RESOLUTION (K. Arrow et al. eds.).

[30] Amos Tversky & Richard Thaler, *Anomalies: Preference Reversals*, 4 J. ECON. PERSPECTIVES 201 (Spring 1990); Amos Tversky et al., *The Causes of Preference Reversals*, 80 AM. ECON. REV. 204 (March 1990).

Loss aversion can act as a cognitive barrier to the negotiated resolution of conflict for a variety of reasons. For example, both sides may fight on in a dispute in the hope that they may avoid any losses, even though the continuation of the dispute involves a gamble in which the loss may end up being far greater. Loss aversion may explain Lyndon Johnson's decision, in 1965, to commit additional troops to Vietnam as an attempt to avoid the sure loss attendant to withdrawal, and as a gamble that there might be some way in the future to avoid any loss at all. Similarly, negotiators may, in some circumstances, be adverse to offering a concession in circumstances where they view the concession as a sure loss. Indeed, the notion of rights or entitlements may be associated with a more extreme form of loss aversion that Kahneman and Tversky call "enhanced loss aversion," because losses "compounded by outrage are much less acceptable than losses that are by misfortune or by legitimate actions of others."[31]

One of the most striking features of loss aversion is that whether something is viewed as a gain or loss—and what kind of gain or loss it is considered—depends upon a reference point, and the choice of a reference point is sometimes manipulable. Once again, a simple example suggested by Kahneman and Tversky, can illustrate.

Suppose you and a friend decide to go to Cleveland for a big night out on the town. You've made reservations at an elegant restaurant that will cost $100 a couple. In addition, you've bought two superb seats—at $50 each—to hear the Cleveland orchestra. You set off for Cleveland, thinking you have your symphony tickets and $100, but no credit cards.

Imagine that you park your car in Cleveland and make a horrifying discovery—you've lost the tickets. Assume that you cannot be admitted to the symphony without tickets. Also imagine that someone is standing in front of the Symphony Hall offering to sell two tickets for $100. You have a choice. You can use the $100 you intended for the fancy dinner to buy the tickets to hear the concert, or you can skip the concert and simply go to dinner. What would you do?

Consider a second hypothetical. After you park the car, you look in your wallet and you realize to your horror that the $100 is gone, but the tickets are there. In front of the Symphony Hall is a person holding a small sign indicating she would like to buy two tickets for $100. What do you do? Do you sell the tickets and go to dinner? Or do you instead skip dinner and simply go to the concert?

Experimental research suggests that in the first example many more people would skip the symphony and simply go out to dinner, while in the second example, the proportions are nearly reversed; most people would skip dinner and go to the concert. The way we keep our mental accounts is such that, in the first instance, to buy the tickets a second time would somehow be to overspend our ticket budget. "and, yet, an economist would point out that the two situations are essentially identical because there is a ready and efficient market in which you can convert tickets to money or money to tickets.

---

[31] Kahneman et al.

The purpose of the hypotheticals is to suggest that whether or not an event is framed as a loss can often affect behavior. This powerful idea concerning "framing" has important implications for the resolution of disputes to which I will return later.

D. "Reactive Devaluation" of Compromises and Concessions.

The final barrier I wish to discuss is "reactive devaluation," and is an example of a social/psychological barrier that arises from the dynamics of the negotiation process and the inferences that negotiators draw from their interactions. My Stanford colleague, psychology Professor Lee Ross, and his students have done experimental work to suggest that, especially between adversaries, when one side offers a particular concession or proposes a particular exchange of compromises, the other side may diminish the attractiveness of that offer or proposed exchange simply because it originated with a perceived opponent. The basic notion is a familiar one, especially for lawyers. How often have you had a client indicate to you in the midst of litigation, "If only we could settle this case for $7,000. I'd love to put this whole matter behind me." Lo and behold, the next day, the other side's attorney calls and offers to settle for $7,000. You excitedly call your client and say, "Guess what—the other side has just offered to settle this case for $7,000." You expect to hear jubilation on the other end of the phone, but instead there is silence. Finally, your client says, "Obviously they must know something we don't know. If $7,000 is a good settlement for them, it can't be a good settlement for us."

Both in laboratory and field settings, Ross and his colleagues have marshalled interesting evidence for "reactive devaluation." They have demonstrated both that a given compromise proposal is rated less positively when proposed by someone on the other side than when proposed by a neutral or an ally. They also demonstrated that a concession that is actually offered is rated lower than a concession that is withheld, and that a compromise is rated less highly after it has been put on the table by the other side than it was beforehand.[33]

. . . Ross has described a range of cognitive and motivational processes that may account for the reactive devaluation phenomenon.[35] Whatever its roots, reactive devaluation certainly can act as a barrier to the efficient resolution of conflict. It suggests that the exchange of proposed concessions and compromises between adversaries can be very problematic. When one side unilaterally offers a concession that it believes the other side should value and the other side reacts by devaluing the offer, this can obviously make resolution difficult. The recipient of a unilateral concession is apt to believe that her adversary has given up nothing of real value and may therefore resist any notion she should offer something of real value in exchange. On the other hand, the failure to respond may simply confirm the suspicions of the original

---

[33] *See* Stillinger et al. *See also*, Lee Ross & Constance Stillinger, *Barriers to Conflict Resolution*, 7 NEGOTIATION J. 389 (Oct. 1991).

[35] *Id.* [Rob J. Robinson et al., *Misconstruing the Views of the "Other Side": Real and Perceived Differences in Three Ideological Conflicts*, Stanford Center on Conflict and Negotiation Working Paper No. 18 (June 1990).

offeror, who will believe that her adversary is proceeding in bad faith and is
being strategic.

III OVERCOMING STRATEGIC BARRIERS: THE ROLES OF NEGOTIA-TORS AND MEDIATORS

The study of barriers can do more than simply help us understand why
negotiations sometimes fail when they should not. It can also contribute to
our understanding of how to overcome these barriers. Let me illustrate this
by using the preceding analysis of four barriers briefly to explore the role of
mediators, and to suggest why neutrals can often facilitate the efficient
resolution of disputes by overcoming these specific barriers.

First, let us consider the strategic barrier. To the extent that a neutral third
party is trusted by both sides, the neutral may be able to induce the parties
to reveal information about their underlying interests, needs, priorities, and
aspirations that they would not disclose to their adversary. This information
may permit a trusted mediator to help the parties enlarge the pie in circumstances where the parties acting alone could not. Moreover, a mediator can
foster a problem-solving atmosphere and lessen the temptation on the part
of each side to engage in strategic behavior. A skilled mediator can often get
parties to move beyond political posturing and recriminations about past
wrongs and to instead consider possible gains from a fair resolution of the
dispute.

A mediator also can help overcome barriers posed by principal/agent
problems. A mediator may bring clients themselves to the table, and help them
understand their shared interest in minimizing legal fees and costs in
circumstances where the lawyers themselves might not be doing so. In
circumstances where a middle manager is acting to prevent a settlement that
might benefit the company, but might be harmful to the manager's own career,
an astute mediator can sometimes bring another company representative to
the table who does not have a personal stake in the outcome.

A mediator can also promote dispute resolution by helping overcome
cognitive barriers. Through a variety of processes, a mediator can often help
each side understand the power of the case from the other side's perspective.
Moreover, by reframing the dispute and suggesting a resolution that avoids
blame and stresses the positive aspects of a resolution, a mediator may be
able to lessen the effects of loss aversion. My colleague Tversky thinks that
cognitive barriers are like optical illusions—knowing that an illusion exists
does not necessarily enable us to see things differently.[36] Nevertheless, I
believe that astute mediators can dampen loss aversion through reframing,
by helping a disputant reconceptualize the resolution. By emphasizing the
potential gains to both sides of the resolution and de-emphasizing the losses
that the resolution is going to entail, mediators (and lawyers) often facilitate
resolution.

With respect to the fourth barrier, reactive devaluation, mediators can plan
an important and quite obvious role. Reactive devaluation can often be
sidestepped if the source of a proposal is a neutral—not one of the parties.
Indeed, one of the trade secrets of mediators is that after talking separately

---

[36] Tversky & Thaler, *supra* note 30.

to each side about what might or might not be acceptable, the mediator takes responsibility for making a proposal. This helps both parties avoid reactive devaluation by allowing them to accept as sensible a proposal that they might have rejected if it had come directly from their adversary.

NOTES AND QUESTIONS

(1) Although the usefulness of interdisciplinary research to negotiation practice is well demonstrated in the foregoing articles, certain limitations have also been noted. Some commentators have pointed to less tangible factors that may influence negotiation behavior but have not been considered by social science researchers. In *The Role of Hope in Negotiation*, 44 UCLA L. Rev. 1661, 1684–1685 (1997)[*], Jennifer Gerarda Brown criticizes economic theories of negotiation for failing to recognize a role for hope:

Hope is part emotion, part preference structure, part cognitive process. Hope affects people's behavior, as much in negotiation as in any other context. . . .

Hope may not be easily subject to manipulation. Even if hope is not fixed, we may be unable to find and operate the mechanism that moves hope up or down. So if hope is not malleable—or if we are unable to change malleable hopes—why focus on it? Why not just take hope as a psychological wild-card—like pride, anger, or love—that may affect the negotiation, but not in a manner that economists would study or care about?

Even if we cannot manipulate hope, we might want to include it in models of negotiation because more inclusive models will be better predictors of negotiation processes and outcomes. . . .

Similarly, hopeless models that fail to incorporate optimism will overestimate the probability of settlement, because they will wrongly assume that negotiators accurately calculate the probable distribution of the other side's reservation price. Realizing that an optimistic seller might inflate the range of the buyer's possible reservation prices will show that such parties are less likely to come to terms than we might at first predict.

Measuring hope—even if we cannot manipulate it—might also be useful. Negotiators should try to assess the other side's optimism or satiation point if these variables might affect behavior in negotiation. For example, if a buyer was able to discover that a seller might be sated easily, this could affect the buyer's first and subsequent offers. Or if the buyer knew that the seller had an unrealistically optimistic view of the buyer's reservation price, the buyer might plan to bring to the negotiation some "proof" that would educate the seller away from her optimism. In either case, measuring hope prior to a negotiation might help a negotiator prepare more thoroughly. . . .

For an argument that economists should move away from the standard neoclassical assumptions by recognizing that people exhibit bounded

---

rationality, bounded self-interest, and bounded willpower, see Christine Jolls et al., *A Behavioral Approach to Law Economics*, 50 Stan. L. Rev. 1471 (1998).

(2) Professor Mnookin explores different ways in which the addition of a third-party neutral (a mediator) to the negotiation setting may overcome barriers to settlement. For other discussions of the value of adding a mediator, see Robert A. Baruch Bush, *"What Do We Need a Mediator For?": Mediation's "Value-Added" for Negotiators,* 12 Ohio St. J. on Disp. Resol. 1 (1997), and Jean R. Sternlight, *Lawyers' Representation of Clients in Mediation: Using Economics and Psychology to Structure Advocacy in a Nonadversarial Setting,* 14 Ohio St. J. on Disp. Resol. 269 (1999).

(3) As you read, analyze and discuss the materials in the following chapters, consider how mediation may "add value" to negotiations.

Chapter 3

MEDIATION PROCESS AND SKILLS

§ A INTRODUCTION

This chapter will highlight the substantive skills and strategies which shape the distinctive role of the mediator. It identifies possible contributions and constraints of taking an impartial role in dispute resolution, points out deliberate strategies which the mediator may adopt in attempting to build a settlement and indicates the activities which the mediator must avoid. Beyond the skills required for effective mediation, additional characteristics are important, because mediation is mostly an art, not a science. Each mediator has a distinctive mediation style, which will be defined by the mediator's individual personality traits. A wide range of styles enriches the mediation process and constitutes one of its compelling strengths as a dispute resolution mechanism.

As you will read in Chapter 4, *infra*, there are many different styles and orientations to which mediators subscribe. The most widely used approaches are facilitative, evaluative, and transformative. For purposes of understanding the skills of the mediator, this chapter will focus primarily on the facilitative style of mediation for several reasons. First, the facilitative style of mediation most underscores the differences between the role a mediator plays and that of an attorney or judge. The facilitative style emphasizes skills that generally are not learned in law school. Second, it is the style used in all mediation settings outside the conventional lawsuit. Third, even the most evaluative mediators acknowledge that their first efforts in a mediation are usually facilitative. They would move into an "evaluative" framework if the parties desire that type of intervention. The final section of this chapter will briefly highlight the tansformative and evaluative approaches for comparison purposes.

§ B INITIAL CONSIDERATIONS

[1] MEDIATION PROCESS

There are many different theories concerning the number of steps within the mediation process. Some scholars identify three or four stages, and others assert twelve or more. At a minimum, it is helpful to consider certain discrete stages of a mediation, as set out below.

[a] The Beginning

This includes the pre-mediation set-up, any review the mediator makes of the preliminary information about the facts and circumstances of the mediation, and the mediator's opening statement. If the mediation is scheduled after the parties have filed a lawsuit, some mediators will review the court file. If the mediation is conducted either "pre-suit" or under the auspices of a mediation program, an in-take person or the mediator may have had some preliminary conversations with the parties, and possibly their attorneys, if the parties are represented.

[b] Accumulating Information

This includes the parties, and possibly their attorneys (if represented), recounting what happened to bring them to mediation. This part of the mediation may continue throughout the process.

[c] Developing an Initial Agenda

Based on the initial identification by the parties of their needs, interests and concerns, the mediator will assist the parties in organizing their conversation. Providing structure will often assist the parties to keep focused. The agenda is always subject to revision as the mediation proceeds.

[d] Generating Movement

Often parties in dispute are trapped in the way they are thinking about their dispute. One of the benefits a mediator brings to the process is the ability to help the parties understand their situation in a new way and consider creative alternatives for addressing their issues. In addition, the parties may find it useful during the mediation to meet with the mediator individually in a separate session (caucus). This too can happen at varying times during the mediation and may occur more than once.

[e] Ending the Mediation

This includes any of the following possible endings (or some combination): a full resolution with a written agreement signed by all of the parties; a full resolution of the dispute with no written agreement (may include a dismissal of the underlying case if one had already been filed in court); a partial resolution which is written and signed by the parties; a cessation of the mediation session with an agreement to return to mediation and continue the discussion at a scheduled future date; or no agreement with no future plans to mediate further.

In learning the skills of the mediator, it is easier to understand the process in a linear format, i.e. you start at the beginning, gather information, develop the agenda, generate movement and finally reach a conclusion. In actuality, the middle stages of mediation are often cyclical rather than linear. The mediation will always have a beginning and an ending, but in the middle it may loop back and forth between these artificial stages. For purposes of learning the process, we will discuss each phase as a separate and distinct part of the mediation. Keep in mind, however, that when mediating a "real" case, the phases will often meld together. Although this segmented approach to understanding and learning mediation is widely held, it has not been universally adopted. For example, mediators who subscribe to the transformative school of mediation, reject this stage model as a means of understanding the process since a mediation will follow the needs of the individual parties rather than some pre-determined model.

[2] THE MEDIATOR

Before returning to the mediation process to study it in greater depth, we will focus on the mediator—both the role and qualities or characteristics of the individual which contribute to his/her effectiveness. The role of the mediator and the definition of the term can vary depending on the type of mediation, program goals, and local practice. According to one state statue, "the role of the mediator includes, but is not limited to, assisting the parties in identifying issues, fostering joint problem solving, and exploring settlement alternatives." Section 44.1011(2), Florida Statutes. The draft Uniform Mediation Act defines a "mediator" as "an individual, of any profession or background, who conducts a mediation." February 2001 Draft.

A definition, however, cannot capture the wide range of dynamics, strategies and techniques a mediator employs when attempting to assist parties in negotiating their dispute. In discussing the role of a mediator, it is fitting to examine the skills, abilities and other attributes that are required to perform the role effectively. While the following is not an exhaustive list, it represents the thinking of a diverse group of mediators who worked for five years in a consensus-based effort as part of the Test Design Project to provide mediation programs, courts and other interested parties with improved tools for selecting, training, and evaluating mediators. While the desired traits were normally referred to as KSAOs or Knowledge, Skills, Abilities and Other Attributes, the Test Design Project chose not to identify particular types of required legal or procedural subject matter knowledge because "they are specific to the situation (e.g. type of mediation program, state law), and because for some types of program little or no substantive knowledge is required prior to selection."

PERFORMANCE-BASED ASSESSMENT: A METHODOLOGY, FOR USE IN SELECTING, TRAINING AND EVALUATING MEDIATORS

The Test Design Project, 19 (1995) [*]

Skills, Abilities, and Other Attributes

1. Reasoning: To reason logically and analytically, effectively distinguishing issues and questioning assumptions.

2. Analyzing: To assimilate large quantities of varied information into logical ideas or concepts.

[*] Copyright © 1995 by the National Institute of Dispute Resolution. Reprinted with permission.

most critical

3. Problem Solving: To generate, assess and prioritize alternative solutions to a problem, or help the parties to do so.

4. Reading Comprehension: To read and comprehend written materials.

5. Writing: To write clearly and concisely, using neutral language.

6. Oral Communication: To speak with clarity, and to listen carefully and empathetically.

7. Non-verbal Communication: To use voice inflection, gestures, and eye contact appropriately.

8. Interviewing: To obtain and process information from others, eliciting information, listening actively, and facilitating an exchange of information.

9. Emotional stability/maturity: To remain calm and level-headed in stressful and emotional situations.

10. Sensitivity: To recognize a variety of emotions and respond appropriately.

11. Integrity: To be responsible, ethical and honest.

12. Recognizing Values: To discern own and others' strongly held values.

13. Impartiality: To maintain an open mind about different points of view.

14. Organizing: To manage effectively activities, records and other materials.

15. Following procedure: To follow agreed-upon procedures.

16. Commitment: Interest in helping others to resolve conflict.

[3] MEDIATOR FUNCTIONS

The functions of a mediator are very much tied to the goals and expectations of the parties or mediation program, the context in which the mediation takes place, and the style of the mediator. In underscoring this point, the Test Design's Report stated in bold print "The resulting lists [of mediator tasks and KSAOs] are not exhaustive, and they do not reflect reality for every program. They are intended merely as a starting point to encourage any given program to prepare a modified list that reflects its actual practices." The Report identified seven major tasks, which each involved several sub-tasks:

Gathering Background Information

Facilitating Communication

Communicating Information to Others

Analyzing Information

Facilitating Agreement

Managing Cases

Documenting Information

NOTES AND QUESTIONS

(1) What other characteristics do you think would be important for a mediator to possess? Of those that are listed, which are the most important to the mediation process? How do these correspond to ethical duties of a mediator?

(2) Some claim that anyone can be a good mediator, if suitably trained. Do you agree?

(3) It was noted in the Test Design's publication that the terms used "arise out of the predominant North American culture, and may not apply to another society or even to indigenous or minority cultures within North America." What are the cultural assumptions made in identifying the list of attributes and the tasks? Are there other attributes which may be important in other cultural contexts?

[4]   BEGINNING THE MEDIATION PROCESS

There are no restrictions on where a mediation can be held. Usually, though, a mediation takes place in a conference room—either the mediator's or one of the attorney's. If the mediation is court-ordered, it may take place in a courthouse. As with traditional negotiation practices, a mediator should give some thought to the location (neutrality of the setting, accessibility, comfort, etc.) and room set up.

Normally, when the mediator invites the parties into the room, the mediator will tell them where to sit (either verbally or by motioning to a particular grouping of chairs on one side of the table). The seating should reflect a structure conducive to the process of communication which the mediator is trying to create; if one party sits at the table but the other sits in the corner, the process is skewed. A mediator will often sit so that, from the parties' perspective, the mediator is "in the middle." Sometimes, parties bring other people with them to mediation, such as an attorney. If other people are in the mediation room, they should sit with the persons whom they are accompanying. Here are some options:

Possible Seating Arrangements (mediator and 2 disputants)

D = Disputant; M = Mediator

Possible Seating Arrangements (mediator, two parties and an attorney)

P = Party, M = Mediator, A = Attorney

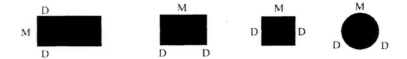

Possible Seating Arrangements (mediator, two parties and an attorney)
P = Party, M = Mediator, A = Attorney

Note that there are many different possibilities; to some extent the decision will depend on the mediator's own personal style and preference, as well as what shape table is available. Some mediators prefer not to use any table at all or a only a low coffee table in a "living room" type setting. This is most commonly seen in divorce or other family–issue type mediations. It is important to keep in mind the following general principles when determining seating:

- the mediator should be equidistant between the disputants (and everyone should be seated on similar chairs)
- the parties should be able to look at each other and the mediator comfortably
- the parties should be far enough apart that they are not bumping into each other nor able to read each other's notes.

But how does the mediator decide whether someone should be in the mediation room or not?

Typically, in most mediations, the following persons are entitled to be in the mediation:

- the mediator
- the people in dispute (if there is a court case, this will usually be defined as the "named parties")
- attorneys for the disputants (if applicable)

- a sign language interpreter or other Americans with Disabilities Act representative (if necessary)

- foreign language interpreter (if necessary).

Other individuals often appear at mediation; these include family members, bailiffs, members of the media, friends, moral supporters, observers, and witnesses. Whether these individuals are admitted into the mediation usually is dependent upon agreement of the disputants. Any of the disputants has a right to object to the inclusion of someone else at the mediation. The mediator may wish to discuss with the disputants the ramifications of such a disagreement by noting that mediation requires active participation by the disputants, that participation in mediation is voluntary, and that if one or more of the disputants are unwilling to proceed because of the presence or absence of non-entitlement members, the mediation might be immediately concluded.

Whether to permit such persons into the mediation session is a decision for the parties to make. However, the extent of their participation, once admitted, is strongly influenced by the mediator's responsibility for conducting a constructive dialogue.

The use of a witness is of primary importance at trial because the parties need to present evidence to convince the fact finder, whether judge or jury, of the correctness of their positions. In mediation, the only person a disputant needs to convince is the other person. As a result, witnesses tend to be useful only if both disputants want to hear from them.

NOTES AND QUESTIONS

(1) The illustrated seating arrangements when an attorney is representing one of the parties suggests that the attorney sit next to his or her client and that the parties (or disputants) sit between the attorney and the mediator. What are the pros and cons of such an arrangement?

(2) Identify additional people who may participate in the mediation and how you would set up the room to accommodate their participation. (e.g. interpreters, co-mediators, moral supporters, etc.)

(3) Note that in some cultures it is expected that members of the extended family or community will attend the mediation. See, e.g. James Wall, Ho'oponopono: Some Lessons From Hawaiian Mediation. *infra* Chapter 10.

§ C MEDIATION PROCESS

[1] MEDIATOR'S OPENING STATEMENT

A mediation will typically begin with the mediator providing an "opening statement." Even if the parties have participated in mediations before, it is not advisable to skip the opening statement. There are several reasons for beginning the mediation in this fashion:

- to establish the ground rules and the mediator's role
- to put people at ease
- to convey a sense of mediator competence and skill, thereby inviting trust and comfort with the process and the mediator
- to reconcile any conflicting expectations regarding what will happen in mediation
- to satisfy ethical requirements (if applicable)

Typically, there are six basic components to an opening statement:

- Introductions of the mediator, disputants and others present
- Establishing credibility and impartiality
- Explaining the process of mediation and the role of the mediator
- Explaining the procedures which will govern the process (including, if applicable the possibility of meeting separately with the parties)
- Explaining the extent to which the process is confidential or inviting parties to set terms of confidentiality
- Asking the parties if they have any questions

The mediator's opening statement should be clear and concise. A mediator should try to avoid using "jargon" or technical words that the disputants are unlikely to understand (e.g., plaintiff, defendant, claimant, respondent, pro se). Even if the parties are represented by attorneys and the attorneys are present, it is a good idea for the mediator to focus the opening statement on the parties and to ensure their understanding of the process. Although delivering an opening statement should not consume a lot of time, a mediator should not rush through it. The mediator's opening statement is important—it must be long enough to cover all of the elements clearly and completely, and short enough not to lose the interest of the parties.

Delivering the mediator's opening statement is deceptively difficult. One cannot underestimate the importance of starting the mediation in an articulate, informative and calming manner. This is the one part of the mediation which can be practiced in advance.

In developing an opening statement, a mediator should recognize that an opening statement need not be structured in any particular order, but it should flow and sound like the individual mediator. It also may vary depending on the type of mediation and the context of the mediation. With these caveats in mind, a mediator should consider the following suggestions.

[a] Introductions

Before the mediation begins, the mediator should decide how he or she wants to be addressed. For example, are first names appropriate? What about titles or degrees (e.g., Dr., Colonel, attorney . . .)? As a general rule, the mediator should only tell the parties the information they need to know. Generally, parties do not need to know the titles or degrees a mediator holds. In fact, sometimes this information can be harmful to the mediation process as the disputants may look to the mediator for legal or technical advice rather than just facilitation. On the other hand, if the parties are represented by attorneys who are present, it might make everyone more comfortable to know the legal qualifications of the mediator. Also, mediators who practice in a more evaluative or directive style may have been chosen for their subject matter expertise, and therefore should disclose this information. In addressing the disputants, generally the mediator will use last names; however, this is not a firm rule. For example, if the disputants are on a first name basis and request that the mediator use first names, it would be appropriate to do so.

[b] Establishing Credibility and Impartiality

It is important for the mediator to establish credibility in order to give the disputants confidence that the mediator and the process of mediation may be of assistance to them. The focus should be on the mediator's mediation experience—not the mediator's unrelated experience or expertise. As noted above, depending on the circumstances, lawyers and law students might want to refrain from revealing their expertise. The easiest (and safest) way for the mediator to establish credibility is to provide the disputants with information about the mediator's experience as a mediator. For example, if the mediator is "certified" as a mediator, stating that fact would be a quick and easy way to establish credibility. Mediators should not be falsely modest about their experience, but they must not forget that the disputants are there to resolve their disputes and not listen to a long dissertation about the mediator's experience, no matter how impressive it may be.

In order to gain the disputants' trust and confidence, a mediator should assure the disputants of the mediator's impartiality about the dispute and the individuals involved. The most concise, credible way to do this is to provide the participants with information regarding the mediator's previous experience and knowledge about the dispute and then let the parties draw their own conclusion. This can be accomplished with this simple sentence: "I have not met either of you before and have no previous knowledge of the events which brought you to mediation today." Most people will conclude that the mediator is impartial if the mediator does not know either of them and has no preconceived notion about the dispute. This approach works best when mediating community or small claims disputes. For more complex disputes, the mediator may have received information in advance from the parties to review and may have been chosen by the parties and/or their attorneys based on their previous experience with the mediator; this requires a modified approach.

In situations in which the mediator knows one or more of the parties or attorneys, the mediator should conduct a two-part analysis. First, the mediator should assess how well he/she knows the individual and if this relationship raises any concerns for the mediator regarding his/her ability to remain impartial. If the mediator believes that his or her impartiality might be compromised, or perceived to be so, then the mediator should not conduct the mediation. A mediator should attempt to make this assessment as soon as possible in order to create the least disturbance for the disputants. When in doubt, it is better to err on the side of caution and decline the mediation.

If the mediator analyzes the prior relationship and concludes that it does not jeopardize the integrity of the process, then the mediator moves to the second part of the test, namely disclosing the contact to the parties. While the exact requirements of ethical rules vary, a mediator is often prohibited from mediating any case in which the parties express concern regarding previous contact or in some cases if the relationship is "too close." The ethical constraints placed on the mediator will be discussed in greater detail in Chapter 7, *infra*.

[c] Explaining Mediation and the Role of the Mediator

Next the mediator will explain what mediation is and what the disputants can expect in this process. In defining mediation, and depending on the circumstances, the mediator should typically strive to use the simplest terms possible. Often it is helpful to highlight the difference between mediation and the traditional court process since most people are more familiar with litigation as a form of dispute resolution. It might also be helpful to discuss the mediator's and the parties' roles in the process.

For example:

Mediation provides you with an opportunity to talk with one another with the help of another person, a mediator, who is not involved in the dispute. As mediator, my job is to assist you in talking to each other so that you can gain a better understanding of what happened. It is not my job, nor am I permitted, to decide who is right or wrong or to tell you how to resolve your conflict. Rather, in mediation you have the ability to develop a resolution that makes sense to each of you. If you develop options that each of you find acceptable, we will write them into an agreement that each of you can sign and the matter will then be closed. If you are unable to resolve it here, you will [return to the judge who will make a decision for you—if court-ordered] or [need to choose another means of handling your dispute—if private].

[d] Explaining the Procedures That Will Govern the Process

The mediator should discuss the following procedural guidelines:

- *Speaking Order*: If the mediation is of a case already filed in court, generally, the plaintiff will be asked to speak first. Typically, the person who filed the claim has the obligation to let the other person know why he/she filed the case. If the mediation is not taking place under the shadow of the courts, the mediator may ask the person who requested mediation to begin or alternatively, ask the disputants who would like to begin. The person who begins does have an advantage in framing the dispute; therefore, whoever speaks second should be given latitude to share not only a response, but also to describe any other concerns which the disputant has. *See* Chapter 8, *infra*, for a further discussion of how an attorney might divide these responsibilities with a client.

- *Separate Sessions (Caucus)*: Sometimes it will be useful for the mediator to meet with the disputants (and their attorneys, if represented) separately during the mediation. If the mediator might do so, he/she should discuss this during the opening statement so that no one is alarmed if it later occurs. Since there may not be a separate session, the mediator should not spend too much time on the procedural aspects. Mediators often refer to this session as a caucus. Since most people do not regularly use that term, a mediator should gauge the disputants' sophistication with the process to decide whether it may be better to refer to it as a separate session.

- *Note-taking*: If the mediator plans to take notes, the mediator should let the disputants and attorneys know. It is generally a good idea to provide pen and paper for the disputants and encourage them to listen for new information and to take notes if necessary while the other is talking. This enables the parties to remember issues they want to discuss without having to interrupt each other.

- *Explaining the Confidentiality of the Process*: The mediator should be well versed in the level of confidentiality which applies to the mediation and review this with the disputants. Some mediators have a confidentiality agreement prepared for parties (and attorneys, if applicable) to sign prior to beginning a mediation so that everyone is clear on the level of confidentiality that attaches. Others provide an opportunity for parties (and their attorneys, if applicable) to discuss and agree upon the level of confidentiality they want. *See* Chapter 5 *infra*.

The following is an example of the portion of a mediator's opening statement that addresses the procedural aspects of the process.

Let me explain how this process will work today. When I finish speaking and have answered any questions you may have, we will begin. [I see that you both have attorneys with you. It has been my experience that mediation works best when the parties themselves actively participate in the process. Mr. Green, have you and your attorney discussed your respective participation? . . . Ms. Kodly, have you and your attorney discussed your respective participation?]

Since Mr. Green sought this mediation [or brought this case to the attention of the court], we will begin with him by having him describe his concerns. Ms. Kodly, you will then have an opportunity to share your concerns [which I understand will be through your attorney.] Please feel free to add additional information or concerns. At some point, I may find it useful to meet with each of you individually. If such a situation arises, I will explain the process in greater detail.

I have found it best if each of you treat the other with courtesy and respect during this mediation so that when one of you is speaking, I would ask that the other listen carefully. Is that guideline acceptable to each of you? I have provided you with paper and pen to jot down any new information you may hear, as well as any issue you wish to discuss and are afraid you may forget. I too may be taking some notes. This is merely to help me keep information straight.

At the end of this mediation, I will discard my notes and encourage you to do the same because the discussions we have here are confidential. [NOTE: this will need to be tailored to the specific circumstances under which the mediation is conducted, see Chapter 5, infra.]

  • *Asking the Parties if They Have Any Questions*: The parties have just
    received a lot of information to think about so it is important to pause
    and let them ask any questions about the information which has been
    provided.

———

After answering any questions or determining that the disputants have
none, the mediator should be ready to hear from them. Begin by asking the
party who brought the claim (or the party's attorney) to describe the events
that led to the mediation.

[2] ACCUMULATING INFORMATION

In order to assist parties in mediation, mediators need to learn what are
the issues that brought the parties to mediation, whether voluntarily, by
contract, or by order of the court in which they filed their dispute. In addition
to listening to parties' descriptions of the actual circumstances surrounding
their dispute, mediators observe the behavior of the parties toward one
another before, during, and after a mediation as a means of accumulating
useful information. People communicate through more than just the spoken
word. Nonverbal cues, posture, and tone of voice all convey a wealth of
information.

A mediator should try to establish an atmosphere in which the possibility
of constructive dialogue is enhanced. This is no small achievement, for
frequently the parties have let their concerns simmer, exchanged heated
words, and then avoided each other. Assisting the parties in communicating
with one another constitutes an important first step toward building a
resolution.

The mediator's role in the information gathering process combines structure
and patience. With the mediator's assistance, the parties may be able to reorient their perspectives from an adversarial posture to one of collaboration. The
mediator's role, while not that of a decision-maker, need not be passive. The
mediator listens for the concerns the parties express and the practical ways
in which they can be met. The mediator tries to help the parties reestablish
trust so that practical solutions do not evade them. The mediator's role is not
to endorse each person's perception as "right or wrong" but to acknowledge
their concerns as ones which in fact they possess and which constitute the
benchmarks of settlement possibilities. Since all parties are different and
bring different perceptions to a situation, the mediator should not assume all
parties fit in the same box. The mediator must listen carefully and appreciate
the unique strands which individuals will highlight if given the appropriate
forum for doing so.

[a] Pre-mediation Information/Case File

Determining whether to review pre-mediation information or the case file
is an individual mediator's decision. In some instances there will not be any

pre-mediation information, or in a court-ordered case, there may not be any time to review or access the court file prior to beginning the mediation. If such information is available, sometimes it may be useful to have some sense of what are the issues, in advance of the first meeting. If mediating a divorce, the mediator might want to be aware, in advance, of the length of the marriage and the number and ages of any children. In complex disputes in which attorneys are involved, mediators will often ask attorneys to submit documentation prior to the mediation, including potentially some of the pleadings, as well as a separate summary of how the party currently sees the issues to be addressed in mediation. If the mediator chooses to review pre-mediation information, the mediator should keep in mind that the information provided may only represent the issues from one disputant's perspective. Secondly, reliance on documents should not replace the opportunity for the disputants to describe in their own words (or their attorney's) what has brought them to mediation.

[b] The Disputants' Opening Statements

The disputants or their attorneys will articulate their concerns. The mediator must listen carefully. What they say, the manner in which the information is shared, and the order of presentation are all important pieces of information. The mediator should usually let each disputant take as much time as needed without interruption from the other party or the mediator.

When the first party is finished, the mediator should not ask the other to "respond," but rather should invite that party to describe and explain her issues and concerns. The second person to speak often feels defensive—the mediator's job is to put the parties at ease enough to share what is important to them.

Mediators should usually refrain from asking any questions until all the disputants and/or their attorneys have spoken. While it may be tempting to ask "just a quick question" before each disputant has spoken, one never knows how long the answer may be to even a quick question. Further, if the first person's opening statement was long, a significant amount of time may have elapsed from the point the mediation began. By the time the second or third disputant has an opportunity to speak, he or she may have already given up any hope of this being a fair process. Finally, the comments of the remaining parties usually help clarify matters, thereby answering questions before the mediator asks them.

After each party has spoken, the parties often will look to the mediator to identify the next step in the process. The mediator could then identify and summarize the issues as the parties have put them forth. To perform that important task requires a mediator to organize the information accurately and constructively. Taking good "mediator notes" can be most helpful for executing that task, and a discussion of their role and status is warranted.

[c] Notes

A mediator's notes serve three important purposes:
- identification of the issues which the disputants wish to address

- clarification of statements/issues for the mediator
- record of "movement" with regard to offers and solutions

The mediator's notes *should not* be a transcript of the mediation. Notes, by definition, are selective. Two practical dangers arising from taking too many notes are:

- If the disputants observe the mediator taking voluminous notes, they may become more cautious in what they say. If they are represented by counsel, questions may be raised about future use of those notes.

- In taking copious notes, the mediator must look at what is being written rather than devote eye contact, concern and attention to the person who is speaking. This undermines the personal rapport that the mediator wants to establish.

In general, mediators should trust their memories for the larger details. A mediator's notes are an organizational tool and should permit the mediator to recall a particular issue by a quick glance.

In addition to using notes as an organizational tool, notes can help mediators assure the disputants that they have been heard. This is particularly useful when one disputant is repeating a thought over and over. The mediator can read the areas of concern which the mediator has noted and then ask if there is anything other than what the mediator has already captured in the notes which the disputant wishes to discuss at the mediation. This approach assures the disputant that the mediator has heard the concerns and allows the disputant to add anything which has not yet been included. When attorneys present the issues, it is generally easier to identify clearly and concisely the legal areas of discussion; however, the mediator may need to delve deeper into some of the other interests of the disputants. For example, attorneys may focus on monetary issues and potential outcomes in court, while omitting other concerns that are very important to the parties.

It is also important in taking notes that the information be recorded in neutral, simple terms. It is probable that the disputants will be able to see the mediator's notes during the mediation. One of the problems in recording exact words is that the mediator is confirming that person's characterization of the issue. One of the reasons mediation is an effective dispute resolution technique is that the mediator can "see" the dispute differently than the disputants. For example, one person may describe activities as "noise," while the other may describe it as "music." A mediator needs to think of a neutral term to describe it which both can accept. For example, "drum playing." In general, a mediator's notes should include as few modifiers as possible.

The following paragraph summarizes the information that the parties shared with the mediator during their opening statements in a small claims action:

Upon meeting with two parties, the mediator learned from Mr. Watkins that he is a landlord and is suing Mr. Goodwin for back rent of $750; the lease allows tenants to keep only "small" pets; Mr. Goodwin has obtained a large dog; and Mr. Watkins has had frequent complaints from other tenants regarding Mr. Goodwin's late evening, early morning parties on the weekends.

Mr. Goodwin has responded that the rent has not been paid as the oven has been broken for two months; Mr. Watkins has not fixed the oven despite requests by Mr. Goodwin to do so; and he objects to Mr. Watkins' unannounced presence in his apartment several times in the past month.

Mr. Watkins	**Mr. Goodwin**
rent ($750)	oven (2 months)
dog	visits
parties	

Accumulating information and taking effective notes depends heavily upon the mediator's ability to listen. In the following excerpt, Joseph Stulberg details these required listening skills for the mediator.

[d]   Listening Skills

Joseph B. Stulberg, TAKING CHARGE/MANAGING CONFLICT (1987), pp. 70–73 *

Lexington Books

What constitutes effective listening skills? There is little in the literature of psychology or communication that illuminates this concept. Most texts simply exhort us to "listen more carefully," meaning that the listener must make every effort to *understand* what the speaker is saying. But there is a difference between *hearing* what someone says, *listening* to what she says, and *understanding* what she says.

If the mediator cannot *hear* what someone is saying, she simply asks her to speak louder, or asks others to reduce their noise, so that she can hear. This is a matter of *audibility*.

A mediator can *listen* to what someone is saying in a variety of ways: attentively, with a look of boredom, while doodling, while listening to music. Listening *effectively* to what someone is saying consists of more than just hearing sounds. One listens in order to *understand* the message the speaker is trying to communicate. To listen effectively is to capture the entire message that someone is sending. . . . Here are some guidelines that a mediator can follow to make certain that she receives all that is sent:

Concentrate: Minimize distracting activities. . . .

Monitor the rate: People cannot talk as fast as others can listen. A mediator should not use the overlapping time to daydream about something else.

Be patient: One cannot hear, let alone be certain she has captured what another is saying, if others are not given a chance to complete their statements.

Don't interrupt: One cannot listen while . . . talking.

Understand first, then evaluate: . . . A mediator cannot argue mentally with the speaker.

It is important for the mediator to listen effectively, but it is not enough. . . .There are ways for a mediator to check her understanding of what has been said, although she must always be sensitive to when and where she does it.

She can ask questions in order to clarify previous statements. She can attempt to summarize in her own words that was said. She can, in a separate session with the party, try to confirm her understanding of what the party said by identifying the emotion that the statement exhibits or the priority ranking she attaches to particular items. . . . *A mediator should never try to show her understanding of what was said by simply repeating back to the parties in their own words what they just said. . . .*

The mediator makes three serious mistakes if she adopts this style of so-called *reflexive listening* (actually, it is simply parroting). First, . . . if a [mediator] understands what was said, she should show it by summarizing the statements in her own words.

Second, from the moment a person begins to serve as mediator, she should try to reorient the way the parties view their situation. She starts to do this by always describing the dispute in less explosive, non-judgmental language than the parties have used to characterize their situation. . . .The mediator should not repeat the parent group's charges that the school district employs "lazy teachers"; instead, she should note that the parent group proposes to handle the issue of supervising the children at the school by assigning the responsibility to various neighborhood residents. Summarizing the parents' concerns in this way diffuses any personal attacks and forces the parties to focus their attention on the issues they must resolve—not on other people. . . .

Third, parties to a dispute have strong emotions. Despite what the mediator has told them about her neutrality, if one party hears the mediator repeat allegations, assertions of fact, or conclusions in the language of her adversary, then she will conclude, fairly or not, that the mediator believes everything the other has said. . . .

———

Listening is hard work. It appears easy because there is not much physical activity involved. But the parties will know whether the mediator is listening to them; the following signs confirm it:

- Effective and appropriate eye contact

- Appropriate facial gestures

- Appropriate affirmative head nods (Remember that the nod of the head can be interpreted as agreement or acknowledgment. A mediator should try to be consistent with any nods to avoid concerns regarding lack of impartiality)

- Avoidance of actions or gestures that suggest boredom (such as yawning and leaning on your hand)
- Asking clarifying questions
- Paraphrasing using neutral words
- Not interrupting the speaker
- Not talking too much
- Acknowledging and validating feelings and thoughts (having empathy)

[e] Questioning

Part of accumulating information may take place through the mediator's use of questions. Set out below are descriptions of the types of questions that are effective for a mediator to ask and the contexts in which asking them is most appropriate.

Clarifying: Commonly used to gather a clearer understanding or to confirm a piece of information. Clarifying questions are typically used at the beginning of mediation when the mediator is gathering information to understand the issues for discussion.

Examples:

Mr. Stockmeyer, can you explain in greater detail the injuries you suffered?

OR

Ms. Jones and Ms. Stoon, how would you like for that payment to be made and where?

Open: This question is designed to get or keep the disputants talking. This form of question should be used predominantly in the early stages of the mediation when the mediator is gathering information. Asking open questions gives the disputants the opportunity to share their experiences and shape the dialogue.

Examples:

Can you please elaborate on that statement?

The mediator usually will begin by asking broad questions which require explanations. As the session progresses, the mediator can ask narrower questions.

How do you see the situation being resolved?

Closed: These are questions which can be answered with merely a "yes" or "no" response. While this technique may extract some information, it should be used infrequently and with discretion because it does not elicit a complete response. The best use of closed questions is towards the end of a mediation or with disputants who volunteer a lot of information and the mediator is trying to limit their domination of the mediation.

Examples:

I have noted that your daughter Terry's religious upbringing and partici-pation are important concerns for you. Would you be satisfied with the proposal that she attend a religious camp this summer?

OR

Does this written agreement completely satisfy your original claim?

Justification: This type of question usually begins with "Why" and calls on someone to justify his/her position (e.g., past behavior, actions, feelings). Since this type of question tends to make people feel defensive and is often judgmental in nature, mediators should try to avoid using it. Often the question can be asked in another way to obtain the same useful information.

Example:

Instead of "Why did you fire Ms. Benk?" try, "What were the reasons for Ms. Benk's discharge?

Compound: This is typified by multiple questions being asked as one question. The problem with using a compound question is that it is confusing to the person who has been asked the question and thus leads to a confusing answer. As a result, mediators should try to avoid using these questions.

Example:

Were you wearing your seat belt and talking on your cell phone at the time of the accident?

Use of good questioning techniques can help the mediator learn and clarify information. More importantly it can help the parties understand more about the dispute from each other's perspective. A good exchange of information and joint problem solving can be fostered by the mediator's approach. A mediator should use questions to clarify, to help parties better understand their own interests and risks, to explore possibilities and to confirm movement or agreement. A mediator should not use questions merely to satisfy his or her own curiosity. Facilitative and evaluative mediators differ over whether a mediator should use questions to judge the situation. See Ch. 4, *infra*

[f] Non-Verbal Communication

Non-verbal communication is a vital part of our overall communication. Experts estimate that 55% of the information we gather is from non-verbal behavior; 38% from the tone and sound of the speaker's voice and only 7% from the actual words that the speaker uses. Paying attention to the silent cues and observing the communication between the parties will be valuable to the mediator. These cues help the mediator to identify such matters as the priorities, deeply held values, and areas that might be negotiable. See Ch. 4, *infra*.

Non-verbal cues will serve as guide posts and indicators, but a mediator should be careful not to make assumptions based on a single non-verbal action.

For example, traditionally, body language experts identified standing with one's arms crossed in front as a "closed" posture that indicates that individual's unwillingness to participate or hostility to the person or issue being discussed. Today, we understand that there might be many different reasons for assuming such a posture—e.g., one is cold, one is comfortable like that, one is missing a button and trying to cover it up, and on and on. Experts now say that we should look at the total package of behaviors that an individual exhibits and, more importantly, at changes in behaviors.

Non-verbal communication may not be obvious. As in all aspects of the mediation, the mediator must be careful not to assume too much. These issues should be explored with the party or parties if the mediator thinks that the party is signaling something or if cues from one of the parties or the party's demeanor does not match what the party is verbalizing. It may be appropriate to meet separately with the party to validate the feedback.

Mediators also need to be sensitive to their own non-verbal cues. A party may conclude that a mediator whose hands are folded is someone who is simply not interested in what the parties have to say, rather than someone who has simply achieved a comfortable physical position.

[3] AGENDA DEVELOPMENT

The parties have told their respective versions of the events that brought them to mediation. They probably have shared their reaction and evaluation of the other party's stated version of the events. The mediator should now lend a degree of structure to the discussion of the issues.

Characterizing the Issues

As opposed to the traditional way lawyers and law students think about "issues," in mediation an issue is some matter, practice, or action that enhances, frustrates, alters or in some way adversely affects some person's interests, goals or needs.

Mediation focuses on "negotiating issues," which are issues that people are capable of, and have the resources for, resolving. By definition, not all issues can be negotiated because the parties do not have all the resources necessary to resolve every problem for every person.

An example of an issue that is not a negotiating issue is "prejudice" or "bigotry." If one party has a prejudice or hatred against a particular group of people, mediation will not alter that party's deeply held attitudes and beliefs—no matter the length of the mediation session or the skill of the mediator. By contrast, the parties may be able to gain a greater understanding of how each views the situation. In addition, the parties may be able to discuss and reach agreements on particular behaviors that may be causing difficulties between them, behaviors which themselves are negotiable and may be rooted in, or shaped by, prejudicial attitudes. The specific incidents are negotiating issues, while the general attitudes of prejudice and bigotry are not.

As the parties and/or their attorneys speak, the mediator will listen carefully to what is said (and not said) and note the issues which the parties (or their counsel) have identified as needing to be discussed in order for them to resolve the dispute which brought them to mediation.

Unrepresented parties to a dispute will typically speak in plain English and not in the language commonly referred to as "legalese." Typically, they will relate a series of events and it will be up to the mediator to cull through the information to succinctly state what has been heard as the issues. It is important to realize the range of flexibility that the mediator possesses when characterizing the dispute.

Example: Fred Student housed his German Shepherd puppy at Al's House of Pets for 60 days over the summer and incurred a bill of $360. Fred has not made any payments on the bill and it is past due by six months. Fred has promised to drop off payments twice in the last two months to Al and has not done so.

What are the issues in this dispute?

A mediator, particularly one who is legally trained, might be tempted to characterize the issues as: "bad debt and broken promises." That is a mistake, for it simply invites parties to become defensive in arguing the merits of their claims. The more constructive approach is to characterize the issues as: "payment due and method of payment." By framing the issue in more neutral, future-oriented terms, the mediator reduces party defensiveness, invites party communication, and assists the parties to think creatively about possible resolutions.

When parties are represented in mediation, the statement of the issues will generally be in legalistic terms similar to how a cause of action would be presented to a court. A mediator's challenge in these circumstances is to help the parties (and their attorneys) identify the interests behind these issues, as well as, where appropriate, those non-legal issues which are of importance to them.

A mediator shapes both the way in which the parties talk with each other and the range of discussion. It may be tempting to limit the mediation discussion to the legal issues or four corners of the complaint if the mediation is of a case already filed in court. However, very often when people are embroiled in conflict, they get stuck. They keep talking about the same issues and ignoring the fact that previous difficulties may have an impact on the current dispute. Sometimes, the greatest assistance a mediator can provide is to help the parties expand their discussion. The common misconception about negotiation and mediation is that the most difficult disputes to resolve are those that involve a lot money and multiple issues. In fact, frequently the most difficult conflicts to resolve are those which involve a single issue and very little money; in these situations there is little room for the disputants to maneuver and there are few concessions to offer.

Priorities

The disputants and their attorneys will talk about many things. By definition, some will be more important to them than others. Assisting them in identifying what matters most and what matters least to them establishes an environment which invites negotiation. Note that disputants will often discuss what is most important to them first and then repeat it several times in different ways. Listening carefully may reveal the attachment an individual has to an issue, and tactful questioning can confirm the level of interest on a particular topic.

Structuring the Discussion

As human beings, each of us are limited by the fact that we can only talk about one thing at a time. Hence, the order in which issues are discussed is an important element of the process. Generally, the guiding principle when setting an agenda is that you want to order the discussion in a way that will assist parties to move toward resolution. Mediators who practice from a transformative perspective, however, would not view setting the agenda as the role of the mediator.

Some mediators will listen to the opening statements of the disputants with an ear towards identifying the "easy" issues. In the event that the parties and/or their attorneys do not chose a place to start their discussion, the mediator could then suggest one of these "easy" issues as a place to begin. The theory at work here is that individuals in dispute tend to feel frustrated and believe that their dispute will never be resolved—certainly not by talking with the other person. By helping disputants experience success rapidly, even if it is only a relatively minor matter, they become more optimistic and develop some momentum for productively discussing the more difficult issues.

By contrast, other mediators listen to the opening statements with the goal of identifying the core issue. Their theory is that by first bargaining on the issue that they view as central to the dispute, the smaller (and easier) issues then fall into place. Finding a good place to start will come with practice and often will be driven by the preferences of the individuals involved in the mediation and the specific circumstances of the mediation.

Here are some guides mediators may use to find a starting place and structure the discussions.

Categories: Often the issues can be divided according to various subject matters or principles. Typical categories are: economic matters and non-economic matters or financial and behavioral. Appropriate categories will vary according to the nature of the dispute. By dividing multiple issues into a limited number of categories, the mediator assists the parties in breaking down the dispute into manageable parts.

Nature of Remedies: Some concerns raised by the parties will invite remedies which are mutual, e.g., that both agree to do something for the other. Other concerns require one party to do something and the other party merely to accept it, e.g., one party pays the other party a sum of money. Often, mutual remedy issues are easier for the parties to discuss and agree to than are those for which one party has the burden of compliance.

Time: Sometimes the issues will break into categories according to time. For example, the disputants may wish to discuss the issues in chronological order (what happened first) or reverse chronological order (what happened last). In addition, sometimes an issue has a time constraint attached to it; the parties might find that discussion of those issues which are most constrained by time is constructive because there are outside interests pushing them towards resolution.

Relationship of the Party to the Issues: Some issues will be particularly difficult to resolve if the party or parties have a strong philosophical or personal attachment to the issue. It may be best to defer discussion of these matters until other issues are resolved and the parties have built some momentum towards resolution.

Logic: In some instances, issues will come up which are logically related to each other. In using this manner of organization, be careful not to focus unduly on past events instead of future possibilities.

While there are many ways to structure the agenda of discussion, the mediator must be prepared to take responsibility for setting an agenda based on what the parties have said if they do not do so for themselves. One of the greatest assets a mediator brings to the mediation is an ability to create structure and develop a process to assist the parties' communication. If the parties themselves or the mediator neglects to create an agenda, the possibility increases that the discussion will degenerate into impasse not because the parties necessarily disagree on all matters, but rather because no one focused on separating those items on which the parties agree from those about which they remain in substantial disagreement.

[4] GENERATING MOVEMENT

Even after an agenda for discussion has been agreed to and the first issue to discuss has been selected, the parties may still be stuck. At this point, the mediator's job is to assist the parties in thinking about their dispute in other ways to help them move forward. It is important to keep in mind that disputants and their attorneys may not want to resolve their dispute in mediation. They may believe it is in their (or their client's) best interest to pursue the traditional legal process, some other means of resolution, or no resolution at all. The mediator's job is not to make sure that every situation is resolved in mediation, but rather to help the parties consider their options and make an informed decision as to how to resolve their dispute.

In addition to considering the topics developed in Chapter 2, *supra*, on negotiation, there are additional ways a mediator may be helpful to the parties in generating movement. The following sections present some options to consider for keeping the mediation discussions moving.

[a] Procedural Items

Alternate discussion of issues. This is useful so that one party does not perceive him/herself as "winning" everything. A sure way for someone to become recalcitrant is if he/she believes that the other person is the only one who needs to make concessions.

Focus on the Future. It is helpful to remind parties that they cannot change what happened in the past, but they can decide how they want things to be in the future. As a means of comparison, the traditional litigation process focuses on the past, determining what happened, and who was wrong or right. In mediations involving an on-going relationship, what happened in the past need only be relevant in helping parties determine how they want to behave in the future.

Be positive. When disputants come to a mediation, they are often frustrated with the others, nervous about being in mediation, and stressed about having a dispute which has not been resolved. As mediator, you may be the only one who remembers that conflict can be positive—that it can offer an opportunity for the parties to learn from each other. By maintaining a positive atmosphere in the mediation, the mediator can help the parties view their dispute as a learning endeavor.

Use of Silence. Most people are not comfortable with silence. Silence can be very powerful in helping parties and their attorneys reflect on the effect of a particular proposal or statement. As mediator, do not be afraid of silence. In particular, use silence when one party or his or her attorney has made an offer or counteroffer. The mediator should not be the person who breaks the silence—give the other party or attorney an opportunity to respond.

Use of Humor. People become more flexible when they are laughing because laughter often reveals some comfort with oneself and the situation. However, humor should never be used at the expense of anyone involved in the mediation.

[b] Informational Items

Create Doubts. A great question for the mediator to pose to the parties and their attorneys is: "Is it possible . . .?" If the parties acknowledge that something is possible, even if they say it is unlikely, they already are less rigid in their position and may then be able to consider other options. A corollary to this technique is to challenge assumptions. Often we will assume the worst of people with whom we are in conflict. A mediator can be very helpful to the parties and their attorneys, by asking them to consider whether their assumptions may not be accurate.

Integrative Solutions. If the mediator helps the parties and their attorneys to identify their interests (not just their positions) and think creatively, they may be able to identify issues in which they both can achieve the "win-win" solution that they want. If one considers mediation as negotiation in the presence of a mediator, then the techniques and theory found in Chapter Two on negotiation will also be useful to a mediator.

Use of Facts. Often the disputants have not spoken for a significant period of time prior to the mediation, or perhaps ever. It is often helpful for the mediator to encourage the parties to listen for "new information" from the other and to consider that as a possible rationale for adopting a different "position."

Establish Priorities and Trade-Offs. Not everything that the parties or their attorneys present at mediation will be of equal importance to them. Helping them identify which items are most important will help them see that other items are less important. This may yield greater flexibility and ideas regarding items to "trade-off." While we often think that disputes arise when individuals disagree about what is most important, in actuality those differences may lead to an easy agreement. For example, if one person puts a high value on an issue such as full payment of the amount owed while the other puts a high value on a different issue, such as that there be no lump sum payment, these individuals may be able to reach an agreement which results in full payment over time and addresses both of their "high priority" issues.

Use Role Reversal. Helping parties and attorneys see the situation from the other person's perspective is often very helpful. This technique is most useful when meeting separately with the parties and they are able to react with greater honesty.

Point Out Possible Inconsistencies. A mediator should never embarrass or berate a party, attorney, or other person involved in the mediation, but sometimes a mediator can note gently that there may be inconsistencies within comments or proposals that have been made.

Identify Constraints on Others. Everyone operates under some constraints—be they resource, psychological or political. Proposed solutions must account for these constraints or the solution will not be acceptable. Assisting the disputants and their attorneys to see each other's constraints may be useful in helping them understand the dynamics at work in reaching an agreement and lead to greater creativity.

Be the Agent of Reality. The mediator should never force the parties to settle their dispute or any portion of it in mediation. The mediator may, however, help the parties to think through the consequences of not resolving the dispute in mediation (what is the party's BATNA and WATNA). The parties may want to consider monetary costs, time lost, relationship issues, and the uncertainty of a court outcome when evaluating the acceptability of the proposed negotiated settlement terms so that their decision to settle or not is as informed as possible.

[c] Relationship Issues

Appeal to Past Practices. Sometimes the parties will have had a prior good relationship. In such cases, it may be useful for the mediator to explore with the parties how they have resolved similar issues in the past. If the parties have no prior relationship (or no positive prior relationship), this will probably not be a useful technique.

Appeal to Commonly Held Standards and Principles. Sometimes both parties will express a common theme, for example, to be treated respectfully or that they are concerned about the "best interest of their child." While acknowledgment of this notion will not "solve" their issues, it is often helpful for the mediator to point out to the parties (and their attorneys) that they do agree on some matters. A corollary to this technique is to utilize "peer pressure" (what would the general public do in a situation) as a way of helping parties to identify commonly held standards.

These techniques can help trigger flexibility. But the mediator must remember that making progress is normally done incrementally. The mediator may select a place for the parties to begin their discussions, but quickly discover that resolving it is more complex or difficult than originally envisioned. The mediator can deploy several different approaches for generating movement (three different attempts is generally good because using more may make the parties feel inappropriately pressured) but then move on to another issue if the parties remain in disagreement. The mediator will return to that issue at some later point.

Sometimes the mediator will want to meet with the parties separately. This can be another effective way of generating movement. Because there are many issues to consider when using this technique, it warrants separate discussion.

[5] THE SEPARATE SESSION (CAUCUS)

At some point during the mediation session, the mediator, a party, or an attorney, may decide that it would be useful for the mediator to meet separately with each of the parties. A caucus may also be called for the mediators, in the event there are co-mediators, or for an attorney and client to meet alone. For the purpose of this section, we focus on the separate meetings a mediator conducts with the parties.

The extent to which caucuses are used varies tremendously. Some mediators believe that it is more desirable to use joint sessions, whenever possible, to allow the disputants to communicate directly with one another. They are reluctant to use caucuses for fear of breaking the flow of the joint session. Other mediators rely on the technique extensively, and only use joint sessions at the very beginning and perhaps end of a mediation. Some mediators do not declare an impasse unless they have had an opportunity to meet with the parties separately. As a generalization, evaluative mediators tend to be more enthusiastic about caucuses than are facilitative mediators. Similarly, attorney mediators tend to use caucus more frequently than non-attorney mediators. However, many mediators break with these generalizations and vary their use of caucus depending on the nature of the particular mediation. In any event, mediators' varied approaches to caucus are neither inherently right or wrong.

Regardless of their mediation style, it is agreed by all that a mediator should have a reason and a purpose in calling a caucus. The following sets out some reasons (using the acronym ESCAPE) why the mediator might decide to meet privately with each party.

[a] Rationale and Sequence of Separate Sessions

Explore settlement options: Sometimes the mediator will sense that the parties may be more open to discussing potential options if the other party is not present. In this situation, the mediator will usually begin with the party who appears to be willing to negotiate.

Signal warning signs: During the session, one party may exhibit behaviors which threaten any possibility of agreement. If this occurs, the mediator should meet first with the party who is exhibiting the behavior to discuss the mediator's observations.

Confirm movement: At the start of the session, one party may have indicated that the only acceptable resolution is for the other party to move. As the discussion progresses, the party appears to signal a change in that position, but the mediator is not sure and does not want to risk having the party get locked into not reconsidering the previous position. The mediator would meet first with the party who is indicating movement.

Address recalcitrant party: Every so often, one party will take a position early in the session and not move from it. It may become apparent to the mediator that the session will quickly conclude unless the other party is willing to meet the demand or the recalcitrant party is willing to consider movement. In such instances, the mediator should meet first with the "recalcitrant" party. As used here, the term "party" is not limited to named parties. A "recalcitrant party" may be an attorney or other representative.

Pause: At times, emotions can run high and the mediator may sense that the parties need a break to collect themselves, stop crying, or calm down. Separate meetings can provide this opportunity. The mediator should use his/ her judgment as to whether to meet first with the person who is upset or to meet first with the other party, thereby allowing the distraught individual an opportunity to calm down privately.

Evaluate: Finally, a caucus may be deemed necessary to evaluate the proposals that are currently being discussed. A private session affords the parties the opportunity to take a few moments to assess the impact of accepting or rejecting a potential resolution without the pressure of having the other party in the room. It also provides private time for reflection when the mediator is meeting with the other party. In situations in which there are multiple parties with shared interests or a party is represented, meeting alone enables them to consult with one another before making decisions. Overall, in this situation, the mediator can meet with either party first.

[b] Why Not Meet Separately

Some mediators follow a set sequence to their mediations. They start by making an opening statement, then asks each party to make their opening remarks, and then immediately call for caucus sessions. But there are important reasons why a mediator might decide not to meet separately with the parties, so the better practice is for the mediator to assess each situation and proceed accordingly. Set out below are reasons why the mediator might **not** want to meet separately with the parties:

It is unnecessary: If the parties are making progress and working together, there may be no need to stop them and meet separately. In fact, doing so might disrupt the momentum which has developed and have the effect of interrupting rather than assisting the process.

Low level of trust between the parties: Sometimes the parties have developed a very low level of trust between them. There will be no resolution to the dispute unless each party sees and hears from one another exactly why they accept particular settlement terms. Negotiating breakthroughs that happen while one party is out of the room will be viewed with suspicion and not accepted. In such circumstances, it might be best to keep the parties together.

Physical arrangements: Sometimes the physical set-up of the mediation does not lend itself to meeting separately with the parties. For example, if there is no place for the parties and their attorneys to wait while the mediator is meeting with the others, calling a caucus might not be prudent.

[c]   Principles of the Separate Session

Confidentiality. Many mediators take the approach that unless the caucusing party and attorney authorizes the mediator to share the content of what was said with the other party, the mediator must keep all information gained in a separate session private. Some other mediators take the reverse approach, which is that they are permitted to share all information they learn in caucus *except* where instructed otherwise by the caucusing party. A third approach would be to inform the parties at the beginning that nothing said in caucus would be considered confidential. Therefore they would be on notice not to share any information they were unwilling to tell the other party. While any of these approaches may be acceptable, depending on applicable ethical and procedural standards, it is crucial that the mediator adequately explain the nature of the confidentiality prior to asking the party to share information.

The mediator meets with each party every time a separate session is called. Meeting with each party every time a caucus is called serves two purposes. First, it reduces the level of suspicion about what happened during the caucus in which one party participated and the other did not. Second, it provides each party an opportunity to share information with the mediator. There are many reasons why parties may be reluctant to share full information in the presence of the other party; a caucus allows them to speak freely.

The mediator should have an identifiable reason for meeting separately with the parties. See Section [a] *infra*. Non-agreement between the parties and "not knowing what else to do" are not reasons to meet separately. It seems overly simple to point out that the parties will not be in agreement from the outset of mediation. However, one of the most common misuses of caucus occurs when the parties state in their opening statements that they do not agree, so the mediator immediately, or very soon after the mediation begins, calls for separate sessions. Many mediators believe that when the caucus is called so early in the process, it may become a summary of what the parties said in joint session rather than being of any real use. By calling an early caucus, the mediator has not provided the parties with the opportunity to negotiate for themselves, and thereby has not fostered joint problem solving. However, as noted above, some mediators (often those who use a more evaluative approach) do believe in the early use of caucus.

The amount of time a mediator spends with each party in caucus need not be identical. The mediator should promise *equal opportunity* to meet separately, *not equal time*. Although the mediator must provide the opportunity for each party to meet separately with the mediator, the length of their meetings need not be identical. In fact, it will rarely be equal. If after meeting with one party, the mediator discovers that there is no strategic reason for meeting with the other party, the mediator should still do so because the waiting party, or that party's attorney, may have a reason for wanting to meet with the mediator. The mediator would begin the second meeting by indicating that the mediator does not have anything he/she needs to ask or share but before reconvening, would willingly discuss anything the party or his/her attorney would like to share. Thus, the second meeting might last only a minute or two if the party (and his/her attorney) also have nothing to say. Nonetheless, since the mediator provided the opportunity to meet separately with the mediator and it was the party's decision to end the meeting, the mediator preserves the appearance of impartiality and the party will be less likely to be suspicious as to why the other caucus was so much longer. The party and attorney will be empowered to determine how long a caucus they desire.

[d]   The Mechanics of the Separate Session

When the time comes to meet separately, the mediator should:

- State the intention to meet separately with each party. The mediator should avoid using the term "caucus" if the term is not familiar to the disputants.

- Indicate the meeting sequence. If the parties are represented, the mediator will typically meet with the attorneys and their clients together. In some circumstances, the mediator might chose to meet with the attorneys without their clients. It would be highly unusual, for the mediator to meet with the represented parties without their counsel; however, typically a mediator would do so if such a meeting is requested by a party.

- Indicate the approximate length of the meeting. In mediations involving unrepresented individuals such as small claims mediation, a mediator should strive to keep separate meetings to no more than ten minutes apiece. In complex cases, or those in which the party is represented by an attorney, a caucus may last considerably longer. One reason the length is less problematic when a party is represented is that the "waiting time" will not seem as long if the party has someone with whom to talk and plan strategy when the mediator is meeting with the other participants.

- Excuse one party and counsel from the room in which the mediator will conduct the caucus.

When declaring the caucus, the mediator should provide directions as to the location of a suitable waiting area. The mediator might encourage the parties to use their waiting time to attend to personal matters or, in a structured fashion, assign them a task to complete. While time may go quickly for the mediator and the party inside the room, it can seem like an eternity to the party who is waiting outside. If the caucus is taking longer than initially predicted, the mediator should let the party and attorney waiting outside know that more time is required.

When alone with one party in the room, a mediator will often employ the following practices:

Record the time that the caucus began. The mediator may think that she will remember how long the meeting with each party has been, but time moves very quickly and it is important not to lose track of it—the party waiting won't!

Separate caucus notes from regular notes. The mediator can use either a separate piece of paper or the back of the joint information notes to record caucus insights. In any case, the mediator must record caucus information in such a way as to avoid inadvertently revealing confidential information.

Review the rules of confidentiality of the separate meeting and the purpose for meeting with the party. Remind the parties at the beginning and at the end of the each separate session of the level of confidentiality which attaches to information revealed and discussed in caucus. Often, caucus information is considered confidential unless the mediator has permission to share. The parties and their attorneys, however, can agree to a different level of confidentiality for caucuses. Therefore, it is critical that the degree of confidentiality be reviewed so that everyone is clear. This can be done jointly before the mediator excuses one of the parties or can be done individually with each party.

The language used by the mediator in caucus, as in full session, must remain neutral. Since the mediator is alone with one party, it is easy to get trapped into parroting the language used by that party or the attorney. Even though the other party is not in the room, the mediator must maintain neutrality, and the choice of language is one of the most obvious way to demonstrate that stance.

The reason for calling the caucus should shape the agenda. Before beginning a caucus, the mediator should have a clear sense of what to try to accomplish in the caucus; that enables the mediator to know how to both start and end the caucus. For example, if the caucus was called to evaluate settlement options, the mediator generally would start with a discussion of the issue that is most important to the parties (and attorneys) in evaluating those options. The mediator *need not* invite discussion of every issue in every caucus. The mediator should use caucus time strategically.

When the mediator has accomplished the reason for meeting separately, the mediator should conclude the meeting. Before doing so, the mediator may want to check with the party and the attorney to ascertain if there is anything else they would like to share. As the caucus ends, if confidentiality has been assured, the mediator must ask the party and the attorney if there is anything that the mediator is permitted to share with the other side. The party and attorney may give the mediator blanket authority to share everything discussed, permission to share some amount of information, or ask that nothing they shared be discussed. If the mediator believes that some information which has been identified as non-public may be beneficial to a settlement, the mediator may ask the party (and attorney) if they would be willing to share the information themselves. Alternatively, the mediator may ask for specific permission to share the information and explain to the party (and attorney) why it would be useful. In the end, whether the mediator agrees with the party and his/her attorney regarding non-disclosure, the mediator must respect the party's decision. Once the mediator's authority to share caucus information has been established, the mediator declares the caucus closed and escorts the party and attorney to the waiting area.

Second Caucus

To begin, the mediator should go get the other party and attorney in the waiting area and escort them to the mediation room. Once settled, the mediator begins the second meeting in the same fashion as the first (separate notes, record the time, and invite the party's and attorney's confidence). The difference is that the mediator has just spent time alone with the "other side" and presumably has gained some additional information or insight, and everyone knows it. The mediator must fight the temptation to immediately reveal information which was learned in caucus, even if the mediator has permission to do so. The mediator's role has not changed. After the first separate meeting, the mediator should not become an advocate for settlement options proposed by one side or compromise a party's position by immediately revealing that party's concerns and interests. The mediator's focus in the second caucus is to invite the second party and attorney to share their perspectives and concerns on the topics under review. It is also useful to remember the negotiation principles, such as "reactive devaluation," introduced in Chapter 2, *supra*, that may be at work in this situation.

A good technique to use in caucus is to ask questions as hypotheticals. For example, a mediator might ask "If the other party were willing to do X, would you be willing to do Y?" This allows the mediator to assume the scapegoat role if a suggestion is unacceptable. The party or attorney can reject the "hypothetical" without getting angry at the other side for proposing the idea. It also protects offers of movement made by one side.

The second caucus ends in identical manner to the first caucus by establishing with the party and attorney what information may be shared. Sometimes the mediator continues meeting with the parties in separate sessions, if additional developments or proposals regarding negotiating issues have occurred in caucus and they require clarification or exploration. Many mediators however, after meeting once with each party, reconvene all parties and counsel in joint session to continue the discussion.

Sometimes as a result of the information shared in separate sessions, the parties and attorneys will be in substantial agreement. Other times, the parties are still very far apart. Regardless of where the parties are on that continuum, the mediator should begin the joint session with some encouraging words. Specifically, the mediator should thank the parties and the attorneys for the opportunity to meet with them separately. If the parties are still far apart, indicate that is the case but that this does not mean that the session needs to end immediately. The parties and attorneys may want to add additional information or ideas.

If the parties are close together or even in substantial agreement, the mediator might continue (after thanking them) with a statement along the lines of, "As a result of my individual conversations with each of you, it appears that you may be close to reaching an agreement on the following issues, but the precise terms need to be worked out."

Even if the mediator is certain the parties and attorneys are at the same point, the mediator must decide how to reveal this potential consensus. Basically, there are three options:

(1)   The mediator announces the terms of the agreement: "After speaking with each of you, there appears to be agreement regarding the matter of rent arrears. Both Ms. Jones and Mr. Smith agree that payment by Mr. Smith to Ms. Jones of $250 will constitute complete satisfaction of the claim for rent arrears. Is that correct?"

(2)   The parties/attorneys reveal the agreement to each other: "Ms. Jones, will you please share with Mr. Smith and me your proposal for resolving the rent issue?"

(3)   Some combination of (1) and (2), above.

If the parties are unrepresented, it is usually preferable to allow the parties to reveal the agreement to each other since it is their agreement. This allows the parties to assume greater ownership over the agreement. However, if the parties are highly emotional or extremely angry at one another, or the agreement is very complicated, the mediator may choose to reveal some or all of the terms in the manner noted in (1), above. If the agreement is conveyed by the mediator, the mediator should check with each party after each term is revealed to ensure that there is agreement. At a minimum, the parties should at least be nodding their affirmation as the mediator speaks. If the parties are represented, the attorneys may want to take a more active role in discussing the settlement terms.

[6] CONCLUDING THE MEDIATION

It is the mediator's responsibility to end the session, whether or not the parties have settled their dispute. There are four ways in which a mediation session might end:

The parties do not reach any agreement. If the case was ordered by the court to mediation, the mediator will probably be required to file a report of "impasse" with the court. Most courts will accept a report from the mediator which states when the mediation occurred, who appeared at the mediation, and that no agreement was reached. While some judges may want to know why no agreement was reached, rules of confidentiality will often prevent mediators from providing this information. *See* Chapter 5, *infra,* for a more detailed discussion. If the case was mediated pursuant to an agreement of the parties, there is normally no need for the mediator to write a report.

The parties request to continue mediation after a specific period of time. This is usually requested when one or both of the parties want to resolve their dispute, but need additional time to gather information that has bearing on their decisions and actions. Typically, the mediator who began the mediation will complete the mediation.

The parties have a partial agreement on some issues and request a trial or other type of dispute resolution on those which they were unable to resolve. The parties may draft an agreement in which they identify both the settlement terms they have reached as well as the issues which remain unresolved but they have agreed to address in another forum. Any item included in the signed mediation agreement is typically not confidential, and thus, could be discussed with a judge or other dispute resolver.

The parties reach agreement on all the issues. When attorneys are present at mediation, typically one of the attorneys will draft the mediated agreement. If attorneys are not involved, the mediator will typically provide to the parties a document outlining their settlement terms. In some states, it is the mediator's ethical responsibility in a court-ordered case to ensure that the terms of agreement are memorialized (written and signed). However, the potentially critical issue of unauthorized practice of law (UPL) has been raised against some mediators who have drafted written agreements. *See* Chapter 7, *infra*, for a more detailed discussion. Regardless of who writes the final agreement, the parties often leave with a signed "Memorandum of Understanding."

[a] No Agreement

Some parties will decide not to resolve their dispute in mediation because they believe their case was not suitable for mediation, that they need more time to reflect, or that there are strategic reasons for wanting to take a case to trial or another form of dispute resolution. If the parties do not reach a consensus in mediation, the mediator should still try to end the session in an upbeat manner so that the parties will leave feeling positive about the time and energy they invested in their mediation effort. Many times, disputes which do not resolve at mediation do settle at some point before trial, with or without the further assistance of the mediator.

Before concluding, mediators typically do the following:

Review with the parties and attorneys any issues that were resolved and explore the possibility of a partial agreement outlining what issues have been resolved and which issues are still unresolved.

Encourage post-mediation communication between the parties by asking the parties or attorneys if they wish to exchange business cards or telephone numbers. Absent such an exchange, unrepresented parties often lack the ability to contact one another even if they wanted to reach out after the mediation.

Encourage the parties and attorneys to consider returning to mediation (with the same or different mediator) if they think it would be helpful.

End on a positive note. The mediator often accepts the scapegoat role by saying, "I regret that I was not able to assist you in resolving your dispute today," thereby encouraging the parties to have confidence that it is still within their capacity to end their controversy in a mutually satisfactory way.

[b] Agreement

Regardless of who writes the agreement (the parties attorneys or mediator), it must be done carefully and accurately, for the agreement most likely will become legally binding and enforceable. The parties also need to understand it and be able to refer back to it. If it is the result of a court-ordered mediation, a judge may have to review and enforce the agreement.

There are five basic elements of a written agreement:

> Who — Who are the parties
>
> What — What have the parties agreed to do
>
> Where — the place or location that an exchange will take place
>
> When — date of exchange; time limitations, be specific
>
> How — what form will the exchange take.

Research indicates that mediated agreements have higher compliance rates than orders that are issued by a judge. Mediators who encourage parties to define the steps in implementing the agreement often avoid misinterpretation of the agreement.

[i] Format of an Agreement

The written agreement should be clear and concise. Here are some guidelines:

Separate the different elements of the agreement, assign a number to each and list them sequentially. Do not write a long narrative.

Do not include "confessions."

Use the names of the parties, not legal jargon (e.g., complainant or respondent) and make certain the names are spelled correctly. The first time a name is referenced, write it out completely, then when referring to the parties later in the agreement, use just the first or last names (depending on the context of the dispute).

Write out dates rather than use the numerical equivalents (e.g., March 4, 2001 rather than 3/4/01). In addition, be precise; avoid using ambiguous phrases such as bi-weekly, monthly, at the end of the month, the end of the week, in the summer, etc.

When the agreement involves a monetary settlement, write out the dollar amount. This may appear very old fashioned, but it is easy to misread numbers or misplace a decimal. In addition, specify the place, method (e.g., by means of cash with receipt, bank check, money order, etc.) and timing of payments. If there is a payment schedule agreed to of less than five payments, write out each payment date and amount.

Keep the tone positive and prospective. A mediation agreement should not retell the dispute's history but be forward looking. A useful phrase to include is "in the future" particularly if a party has agreed to do (or not do) something in the future, but is unwilling to acknowledge that he or she did not (or did) do it in the past.

If unrepresented, the mediator should invite the parties to assist in writing the document by reading each element of the agreement as it is written. Ask them if the words used accurately captures their agreement. Pride of authorship belongs to the parties not the mediator.

When writing the terms of the agreement, the mediator should never change the substantive settlement terms the parties have adopted. If related issues come up during the drafting of the agreement which were not previously discussed, the mediator should raise the matter with the parties for their negotiation.

Just as the mediation must be conducted in a neutral manner, the agreement or memorandum of understanding must be written in a fair and balanced manner. It is useful to start with those items which are mutual obligations, alternating, where possible, whose name appears first in each sentence. The goal is for the agreement to reflect an appropriate sense of balance between the parties. If the mediation is successful, everyone should feel as though they achieved something from it, and the written agreement should reflect that fact.

[ii] Enforcement

One advantage of a mediated agreement is in compliance. Since the parties have worked out the settlement terms themselves, they are more likely to understand them, believe they are fair and workable, and feel compelled to honor them.

But what happens if the agreement is not fulfilled? If the case was mediated pursuant to a court order, the parties can often enforce their mediated agreement in the same manner as any court order. In order for the court to enforce the agreement, it must be clear and unambiguous. In addition, the court probably will only be able to enforce monetary terms. Settlement provisions such as, "The parties agree to treat each other respectfully in the future" are often helpful and fundamental in mediation agreements, but are not ones which a court can effectively enforce. An agreement may include them if the parties want them, but parties should understand that a court cannot enforce specific performance obligations such as that.

If the mediation is the result of a voluntary submission, the parties still have an enforceable agreement. If there is alleged non-compliance, then one party must take the additional step of filing a court case to enforce the mediation agreement as a contract.

If the parties are expressing a great deal of concern about enforcement, the mediator may want to explore with them whether there are issues which remain unresolved in the mediation. See Chapter 5, *infra*, for a more complete discussion of enforcement issues.

§ D OTHER FORMS OF MEDIATION

The facilitative, problem-solving approach to mediation is not universally adopted. The other two major schools of thought on mediation are transformative and evaluative. Read the following excerpts focusing on the differences and similarities between these approaches and what has been described above.

[1] TRANSFORMATIVE MEDIATION

The following excerpt from an article written by Robert A. Baruch Bush and Joseph P. Folger highlight the hallmarks of a transformative approach to mediation.

TRANSFORMATIVE MEDIATION AND THIRD-PARTY INTERVENTION: TEN HALLMARKS OF A TRANSFORMATIVE APPROACH TO PRACTICE

13 Mediation Q. 263, 266–275 (1996) ⁎

By Robert A. Baruch Bush and Joseph P. Folger

When mediators are effectively putting the transformative approach into practice, the ten patterns or habits of practice discussed below are evident in their work. . . . Each of the ten points describes, in part, what the work of a mediator implementing the transformative framework looks like. . .

Hallmark 1: *"The opening statement says it all"*: *Describing the mediator's role and objectives in terms based on empowerment and recognition.*

Mediators . . . following a transformative approach begin their interventions with a clear statement that their objective is to create a context that allows and helps the parties to (1) clarify their own goals, resources, options, and preferences and make clear decisions for themselves about their situation; and (2) consider and better understand the perspective of the other party, *if* they decide they want to do so.

. . . .

Hallmark 2: *"It's ultimately the parties' choice"*: *Leaving responsibility for outcomes with the parties.*

. . . An important hallmark of the transformative approach is that its practitioners consciously reject feelings of responsibility for generating agreements, solving the parties' problem, healing the parties, or bringing about reconciliation between them. Instead, third parties following a transformative framework sensitize themselves to feeling responsible for setting a context for, and supporting, the parties' own efforts at deliberation, decision making, communication, and perspective taking.

Thus, the mediator feels a keen sense of responsibility for recognizing and calling attention to opportunities for empowerment and recognition that might be missed by the parties themselves, and for helping the parties to take advantage of these opportunities as they see fit. In practice, calling attention to these opportunities means inviting the parties to slow down and consider the implications or questions that follow from a statement one of them has made. . . .

. . . .

When mediators firmly grasp the transformative framework, they recognize and feel strongly that *only the choices or changes that the parties freely make,* regarding what to do about their situation or how they see each other, will be of real or lasting value. . . .

Hallmark 3: *"The parties know best"*: *Consciously refusing to be judgmental about the parties' views and decisions.*

. . . The value placed on empowerment within the transformative framework motivates third parties who follow this approach to consciously avoid exercising judgment about the parties' views, options, and choices.

. . . .

The sign of transformative practice is that the third party's actions are responsive to the disputants' moves. A shift of power is not an outcome prompted or justified by third-party judgment; rather, it is one possible result of a series of moves that the parties themselves initiate, based on their own judgments.

Hallmark 4: *"The parties have what it takes":* *Taking an optimistic view of parties' competence and motives.*

. . . Third parties who successfully implement a transformative approach are consistently positive in their view of the disputants' fundamental competence, their ability to deal with their own situation on their own terms. Likewise, the third parties take a positive view of the disputants' motives, of the good faith and decency that underlie their behavior in the conflict situation, whatever the appearances may be. . . .

. . . .

This commitment to assuming the disputants' underlying competence and decency is actually quite critical to a transformative approach because it directly affects the steps the mediator will and will not take in practice. If a mediator believes that the parties are incapable of making good decisions about how to deal with their situation, the mediator will take over responsibility and act directively, instead of supporting the parties' own decision making. . . .

Hallmark 5: *"There are facts in the feelings":* *Allowing and being responsive to parties' expression of emotions.*

In transformative practice, third parties view the expression of emotions -anger, hurt, frustration, and so on -as an integral part of the conflict process. Intervenors therefore expect and allow the parties to express emotions, and they are prepared to work with these expressions of emotion as the conflict unfolds.

. . . .

. . . [W]hen parties express emotions, the mediator does not just wait until it is over and then go on with the issue discussion. Instead, the mediator asks the parties both to describe their feelings and, perhaps more important, to describe *the situations and events that gave rise to them.* These descriptions of the facts behind the feelings very often reveal specific points that the parties are struggling with, both to gain control over their situation and to understand and be understood by the other party. . . .

. . . .

Hallmark 6: *"Clarity emerges from confusion":* *Allowing for and exploring parties' uncertainty.*

Intervenors who understand the transformative framework expect that disputants will frequently be unclear and uncertain about the issues underlying their conflict, what they want from each other, and what would be the "right" choices for them. Indeed, the intervenors recognize that such unclarity presents important opportunities for empowerment. . . .

In practical terms, this means that the intervenor is willing to follow the disputants as they talk through and discover for themselves what is at stake, how they see the situation, what each believes the other party is up to, and what they see as viable options. . . .

Hallmark 7: *"The action is 'in the room'": Remaining focused on the here and now of the conflict interaction.*

In the transformative approach to practice, . . . the intervenors attend to the discussion that is going on "in the room," to each statement made by the disputants and to what is going on between them, rather than "backing up" to a broader view on the identification and solution of the problem facing the parties. The third party avoids looking at the unfolding conflict interaction through a problem-solution lens because doing so would make it hard to spot and capture opportunities for empowerment and recognition.

Instead, the mediator focuses on the specific statements (verbal and non-verbal) of the parties in the session about how they want to be seen, what is important to them, why these issues matter, what choices they want to make, and so on. The mediator uses this focus to spot precisely the points where parties are unclear, where choices are presented, where parties feel misunderstood, where each may have misunderstood the other—that is, the points where there is potential for empowerment and recognition. When the mediator spots such points, he or she attempts to slow down the discussion and to take time to work with the parties, together or separately, on clarification, decision making, communication, and perspective taking, that is, the processes of empowerment and recognition.

. . . .

Hallmark 8: *"Discussing the past has value to the present": Being responsive to parties' statements about past events.*

. . . Parties' comments about the past can be highly relevant to the present, in the unfolding conflict interaction. In talking about what happened, each disputant reveals important points about how he or she sees, and wants to be seen by, the other party. . . .

. . . .

[I]f third parties view the history of conflict as evil, as something that the session quickly must move beyond, then important opportunities for empowerment and recognition will almost certainly be missed. An important hallmark of transformative practice is a willingness to mine the past for its value to the present—in particular, for the opportunities such review offers parties to help clarify their choices and reconsider their views of one another.

Hallmark 9: *"Conflict can be a long-term affair": Viewing an intervention as one point in a larger sequence of conflict interaction.*

. . . [T]hird parties, following the transformative approach are more likely to believe that no single intervention can address all the dimensions of a conflict in their entirety. . . . This outlook is crucial in enabling the intervenor to avoid a directive stance aimed at only one measure of success: settlement.

Seeing the intervention as one point in a stream of conflict interaction also gives third parties an awareness of the *cycles* that conflict interaction is likely to go through. Third parties following a transformative approach expect disputants to move toward and away from each other (and possible agreement) as the conflict, and the intervention unfolds. . . .

Hallmark 10: *"Small steps count"*: *Feeling a sense of success when empowerment and recognition occur, even in small degrees.*

. . . Third parties committed to this approach are careful to mark for themselves (as well as for the parties) the micro-as well as the macro-accomplishments of sessions, and they do not define success solely in terms of the final agreements reached. Instead they see and value the links between parties' micro-accomplishments and their macrocommitments. . . .

QUESTIONS

(1) How are Test Design's list of Skills, Abilities and Other Attributes of a mediator, set out in Section B of this Chapter, *supra*, consistent with, and how are they different from, the transformative form of practice?

(2) If one subscribes to the transformative school of thought, how would the skills covered above differ (e.g. mediator's opening statement, setting the agenda, etc.)?

(3) What are the pros and cons for the parties in participating in a "transformative mediation?"

(4) Do you believe that the facilitative and transformative approaches are inconsistent with eachother?

[2]　EVALUATIVE MEDIATION

The following excerpt highlights some of the different approaches that might be employed by a mediator who practices from an evaluative framework. As you read this excerpt, consider whether this approach would be appropriate in all circumstances. For example, is attorney representation necessary if the mediator proceeds in an evaluative manner? Earlier in this chapter, Mr. Galton describes his linear model of mediation as follows:

> Mediator Introduction
>
> Lawyer's Opening Statements
>
> Collective Session
>
> Separate Caucuses
>
> Possible Additional Collective Sessions
>
> Possible Lawyers' Caucus
>
> Drafting the Agreement

Notice the focus on caucuses in an evaluative framework.

Eric Galton, MEDIATION: A TEXAS PRACTICE GUIDE
(1993), pp. 31-39, 42-46, 50-51 *

I will hasten to admit that I rarely hold a collective session immediately after the lawyers' opening statements. . . .

I would much prefer to allow . . . venting to occur in separate caucus outside the presence of the other side. . . .

As an experienced trial lawyer, I do not see mediation as ESP, voodoo, or a group therapy session. Anything told to me as a mediator in the privacy of the separate caucus is fine because I only hear it and it won't hurt my feelings. Further, despite the confidentiality of mediation, lawyers may be leery that their clients' candid statements in mediation may be used against them if the case does not resolve. For these reasons, I omit the collective session and move into the separate caucus except in the following situations:

1. When little or no discovery has been done. . . .

2. When the parties have a long-standing business relationship or friendship . . . [I]f the mediator is concerned that such direct exchange might be very destructive, she may elect to move the parties into separate caucus, get a sense of what will be communicated directly, help each party focus her thoughts, and then reunite the parties for a direct exchange after the initial separate caucus.

3. It may be appropriate to discuss the procedural posture of the case, what discovery is remaining to get the case ready for trial, the length of the trial, the likelihood of appeal, and the remaining costs. . . .

4. When an acknowledgment of the negotiation posture may be appropriate. . . .

5. When the party has a real interest in "public shaming" as a pre-condition to resolution. . . .

6. When a party needs to express grief. . . .

. . . [T]he separate caucus is the essence of mediation. . . . The mediator will separately caucus with each party several times. In complex cases, I may have nine or ten separate caucuses with each party.

While every mediation is different and the mediator may vary protocol in a particular case, the separate caucus usually has three general phases: the initial strength/weakness, objective evaluation caucus; the preliminary negotiation caucus; and the closing/resolution caucus.

The initial separate caucus with each party is typically the most lengthy phase of the mediation process. The mediator will usually visit with each party for at least 30 minutes. . . . The mediator has several goals in the initial caucus and it is indeed a highly critical phase of the process.

1. Bonding with the parties. . . .

The mediator bonds with the party not through any tactical plan, but by demonstrating that she has listened, is willing to listen, and is willing to

---

* Copyright © 1993 by Texas Lawyers Press. Reprinted with permission.

understand (not agree). The mediator bonds with the party by demonstrating preparedness, professionalism, neutrality, and compassion. . . .

2. Venting. . . .

In the separate caucus, venting occurs with no destructive consequences. But venting, beyond the relief it affords the party, also usually identifies many of the party's interests and needs. . . .

3. Identification of the decision-maker. . . . In civil litigation, the decision-maker or decision-makers may be any of the following:

(1)   The party only.

(2)   The lawyer only.

(3)   The party and the party's lawyer.

(4)   Someone not in the room.

. . . Most of the time, identification of the decision-maker is an easy task, but sometimes the determination is not so obvious. If uncertain, the mediator should ask who is going to make the decision.

. . . .

4. The lawyer as decision-maker. Undoubtedly, the dispute belongs to the party and not the lawyer. . . .

A mediator must *never* come between a lawyer and her client. . . . In instances in which the mediator perceives an attorney is placing her interest ahead of the client's interests, however, the mediator may wish to hold a private meeting with the client's counsel to discuss such issues openly and diplomatically.

5. When the lawyer and client are at odds. . . .

The mediator's role in such situations is *not* to dispense legal advice or to play the "second lawyer." Rather, by posing specific and appropriate questions, the mediator should attempt to focus the party on the objective realities of the case so that the party will see both the weaknesses and strengths of her position.

6. Identification of negotiating style. . . .

[T]he negotiating "pace" of the decision-makers is the critical issue. . . .

. . . .Some parties to a mediation want to get down to business quickly; other may want to settle in a bit before getting into serious negotiations. Certain parties need to be dragged into the negotiations. . . .

. . . .Good mediators, if they do not intuitively know each party's pace, ask. . . .

In separate caucus, the mediator (with authorization from each party to disclose) should openly discuss with each party these stylistic differences and encourage each party to respect the style of the other and not to become frustrated. . . .

. . . .

Another essential aspect of the initial caucus is a strength/weakness analysis. . . .

[M]ost litigants have little difficulty identifying their strong points. The mediator simply plays the role of devil's advocate by asking "what if," "what about," "do you think," or "why do you believe" questions.

. . . .

Based on my experience, parties often do not fully appreciate risk, the other side's position, or the defects in their case without the direct interaction the process affords. The neutral's strength/weakness questions are accepted and welcomed *because* she is a neutral and is not contaminated; that is, the neutral is not the other side.

. . . .

. . .In the first caucus, a mediator may take the following approach regarding monetary expectations:

1.   . . . what are your monetary expectations?

2.   Why do you have such monetary expectations?

3.   Are these expectations realistic?

4.   What are your monetary needs?

5.   What do you realistically expect . . . the other side to offer?

. . . .

The strength/weakness analysis, which is part of the initial caucus, occurs continuously . . . throughout all caucuses. . . .

. . . .

Some mediators may call a lawyer caucus at some point during the caucus phase of the proceeding.

. . . Most often, the mediator is provided a monetary proposal and is authorized to deliver the offer to the other party . . . [T]he benefit of such an approach is that the mediator, to some extent, deflects a negative reaction to an offer and encourages a party to continue on with the negotiation.

The liability with such an approach, however, is that a party does not get to see "up close and personal" the other party communicate the message. . . . A mediator in such a situation may call a lawyer caucus and have the lawyer delivering the message communicate it directly to the opposition. . . .

In other circumstances, a mediation advocate may wish to suggest a lawyer caucus in order to have a private meeting with the mediator. Typically, a mediation advocate may make such a request when she wishes to let the mediator know she is having a problem with her client. . . .A private meeting with the mediator permits the mediation advocate to explain fully those areas in which her client may need some additional reality checking. . . .

In Chapter 13 of his book, Mr. Galton reviews some impasse breaking and impasse avoidance techniques. Many are similar to the generating movement techniques suggested in the "facilitative" mediation discussion earlier in this chapter. The following are some of the more evaluative approaches a mediator might take:

- Re-review litigation costs. . . .
- Re-review risks (in caucus only)
- Solicit disagreement by the party's counsel. In a separate caucus, ask the party's counsel whether he seriously disagrees with an identified weakness in the other party's position. The party may need to hear that his lawyer disagrees with him. . . .
- Declare a goal unattainable (in caucus only). . . .
- Have the party's lawyer describe what will happen at trial (in caucus only). . . .

It should be noted that the manner in which these techniques are employed may result in a more or less directive outcome. For example, a mediator asking a party's attorney about the expected costs of litigation and risks at trial to accomplish a "re-review of litigation costs and re-review of risks" might fall within a facilitative framework. A mediator who provides his or her opinion regarding the strengths and weaknesses of the party's case or the expected results would also be re-reviewing litigation costs and risks, but it would be much more evaluative.

———

QUESTIONS

(1) How are the Test Design's list of Skills, Abilities and Other Attributes of a mediator consistent with, and how are they different from, the evaluative form of practice?

(2) If one subscribes to the evaluative school of thought, how would the skills covered above differ (e.g. mediator's opening statement, setting the agenda, etc.)?

(3) What are the pros and cons for the parties in participating in a mediation conducted by "an evaluative mediator"?

(4) Would an evaluative mediator need to incorporate different practices if one or more of the parties are unrepresented?

Chapter 4

MEDIATOR ROLES, ORIENTATIONS, AND STYLES

§ A INTRODUCTION

This chapter focuses on the mediator. It presents varying perspectives relating to the functions to be served by the mediator and his or her overall orientation toward the parties in mediation. Section B contains excerpts from theorists and commentators with different philosophical notions of the proper *role* to be served by the mediator. Section C views the mediator's role from a practice perspective by reviewing the overall *orientations* that have been recommended or identified by commentators on the mediation process. Section D presents an empirical perspective and reviews the *styles* of mediation that have been identified by researchers. You should consider carefully how these various *roles, orientations* and *styles* interrelate. Which ones are consistent with one another? Which are inconsistent?

§ B MEDIATOR ROLES

[1] ROLE CONCEPTIONS

In the following two excerpts, Lon Fuller and Robert A. Baruch Bush develop their conceptions of the mediator's role by first emphasizing the unique character of mediation. They then argue for a conception of the mediator's role that is most consistent with mediation's true character. Fuller sees mediation's "central quality" as "its capacity to reorient the parties toward each other." He thus views the mediator's role (or "function") as that of assisting the parties "to free themselves from the encumbrance of rules and of accepting, instead, a relationship of mutual respect, trust and understanding. . . ." Similarly, Bush examines "the special powers of mediation" in developing his "empowerment-and-recognition" conception of the mediator's role. He rejects two popular conceptions of the mediator's role—the "efficiency" conception and the "protection-of-rights" conception—because they are not in line with mediation's unique character.

MEDIATION—ITS FORMS AND FUNCTIONS

44 S. Cal. L. Rev. 305, 307-308, 315, 318, 325-326 (1971) *

By Lon L. Fuller

. . . [O]f mediation one is tempted to say that it is all process and no structure.

Casual treatments of the subject in the literature of sociology tend to assume that the object of mediation is to make the parties aware of the "social norms" applicable to their relationship and to persuade them to accommodate themselves to the "structure" imposed by these norms. From this point of view the difference between a judge and a mediator is simply that the judge orders the parties to conform themselves to the rules, while the mediator persuades them to do so. But mediation is commonly directed, not toward achieving conformity to norms, but toward the creation of the relevant norms themselves. This is true, for example, in the very common case where the mediator assists the parties in working out the terms of a contract defining their rights and duties toward one another. In such a case there is no pre-existing structure that can guide mediation; it is the mediational process that produces the structure.

It may be suggested that mediation is always, in any event, directed toward bringing about a more harmonious relationship between the parties, whether this be achieved through explicit agreement, through a reciprocal acceptance of the "social norms" relevant to their relationship, or simply because the parties have been helped to a new and more perceptive understanding of one another's problems. The fact that in ordinary usage the terms "mediation" and "conciliation" are largely interchangeable tends to reinforce this view of the matter.

. . . When we perceive how a mediator, claiming no "authority," can help the parties give order and coherence to their relationship, we may in the process come to realize that there are circumstances in which the parties can dispense with this aid, and that social order can often arise directly out of the interactions it seems to govern and direct.

. . . Where the bargaining process proceeds without the aid of a mediator the usual course pursued by experienced negotiators is something like this: the parties begin by simply talking about the various proposals, explaining in general terms why they want this and why they are opposed to that. During this exploratory or "sounding out" process, which proceeds without any clear-cut offers of settlement, each party conveys—sometimes explicitly, sometimes tacitly, sometimes intentionally, sometimes inadvertently—something about his relative evaluations of the various items under discussion. After these discussions have proceeded for some time, one party is likely to offer a "package deal," proposing in general terms a contract that will settle all the issues under discussion. This offer may be accepted by the other party or he may accept it subject to certain stipulated changes.

Now it is obvious that the process just described can often be greatly facilitated through the services of a skillful mediator. His assistance can speed the negotiations, reduce the likelihood of miscalculation, and generally help the parties to reach a sounder agreement, an adjustment of their divergent valuations that will produce something like an optimum yield of the gains of reciprocity. These things the mediator can accomplish by holding separate confidential meetings with the parties, where each party gives the mediator a relatively full and candid account of the internal posture of his own interests. Armed with this information, but without making a premature disclosure of its details, the mediator can then help to shape the negotiations in such a way that they will proceed most directly to their goal, with a minimum of waste and friction.

. . . [T]he central quality of mediation . . . [is] its capacity to reorient the parties toward each other, not by imposing rules on them, but by helping them to achieve a new and shared perception of their relationship, a perception that will redirect their attitudes and dispositions toward one another.

This quality of mediation becomes most visible when the proper function of the mediator turns out to be, not that of inducing the parties to accept formal rules for the governance of their future relations, but that of helping them to free themselves from the encumbrance of rules and of accepting, instead, a relationship of mutual respect, trust and understanding that will enable them to meet shared contingencies without the aid of formal prescriptions laid down in advance.

EFFICIENCY AND PROTECTION, OR EMPOWERMENT AND RECOGNITION?: THE MEDIATOR'S ROLE AND ETHICAL STANDARDS IN MEDIATION[*]

41 Fla. L. Rev. 253, 255-257, 259-273, 277-282 (1989)

Transformative

By Robert A. Baruch Bush

. . . [V]oices on all sides are calling for uniform standards for mediator qualifications and practice. The concern for standards is especially urgent not only because of the growth of voluntary mediation in recent years, but also because of a growing trend toward state legislation providing for mandatory, court-connected mediation of civil disputes.

. . . [T]he adoption of common standards, no matter how urgent, requires as a first step the acceptance of a common conception of the mediator's role on which to base such standards. Unfortunately, no such common conception exists today, nor has one even been sought before now. On the contrary, until now pluralism has reigned in mediation practice. Mediation has been seen by some as a vehicle for citizen empowerment; by others as a tool to relieve court congestion; and by still others as a means to provide "higher quality" justice in individual cases. These and other visions of mediation have coexisted and produced very different conceptions of the mediator's role. But no one conception had found general acceptance. Therefore, even if the public interest urgently demands common standards, we cannot reasonably meet this demand without first choosing which conception of the mediation process and the mediator's role should govern.

. . . [M]ediators occupy a unique role which they are ethically obligated to understand and fulfill.

. . . [U]nder the common definition of mediation, a neutral third party works with the disputing parties to help them reach a mutually acceptable resolution. This definition might itself appear to answer the question of what the mediator's role should be. However, this standard definitional language can be read in different ways, and it does not reflect in practice any common conception of the mediator's role in the process. On the contrary, as discussed above, many different conceptions exist. Among these, however, two call for special and critical discussion. Both the efficiency and protection-of-rights conceptions of the mediator's role are quite popular today; both have greatly influenced the operation of mediation programs and the articulation of mediation standards. Nevertheless, neither merits such popularity or influence. Despite their prevalence, both conceptions are deeply flawed, and for similar reasons.

The efficiency conception holds that the mediator's primary role, and the main value of the mediation process, is to remove litigation from the courts by facilitating settlement agreements in as many cases as possible. This reduces court congestion, frees scarce judicial time, and economizes on public and private expense. Sometimes this conception is framed more narrowly by saying that the mediator's role is simply to facilitate agreements. However, this characterization is usually only a surrogate for the efficiency conception, since the value of agreements in this view is that they represent conservation of public and private resources. Therefore the efficiency conception usually is accompanied by a focus on mediators' settlement rates and time-and-cost figures. This conception is advanced most commonly by judicial administrators and planners, and by the business-law community, as part of the search for "alternatives to the high costs of litigation."

By contrast, the protection-of-rights conception holds that the mediator's primary role, and the main value of the mediation process, is to safeguard the rights of the disputing parties and potentially affected third parties by imposing various checks for procedural and substantive fairness on an otherwise unconstrained bargaining process. This prevents settlement agreements from compromising important rights. Sometimes, this conception is expressed by saying that the mediator's role is to ensure that agreements are based on informed consent and that they are not fundamentally unfair to either side. This characterization, however, is really only a surrogate for the protection-of-rights conception, for the primary concern is avoiding unknowing waivers of legal rights, including the right to fundamental fairness inherent in legal doctrines such as unconscionability. Therefore, the protection-of-rights conception usually engenders a focus on mediator duties, especially on the duty to advise and urge parties to obtain independent legal counsel and the duty to terminate a mediation that threatens to produce an unreasonably unfair agreement. Advocates of disadvantaged groups and the trial practice segment of the bar are among those advocating this conception. It has heavily influenced most of the mediation practice codes proposed in recent years.

The efficiency and protection-of-rights conceptions, as described, might seem to be exaggerations of the views different groups actually hold. Perhaps efficiency advocates also really care about protection of rights, and vice versa, and the differences are only ones of emphasis. However, the question at hand is which conception should govern. When two conceptions clash, they cannot both govern; and in practice the efficiency and protection-of-rights conceptions are bound to conflict. A mediator focusing on reaching agreements, and doing so expeditiously, will inevitably be insensitive to protection of rights. Conversely, a mediator focusing on protecting rights will often hesitate about or even resist reaching an agreement, and certainly will be in no hurry to do so. It is no exaggeration to describe each conception as focusing on one role as the primary role of the mediator which, even if other roles are acknowledged, takes precedence and governs in practice.

Therefore, in their primary focus, the efficiency and protection-of-rights conceptions of the mediator's role are not only distinct, but poles apart. The efficiency conception sees mediation as a more economical alternative to trial in court, while the protection-of-rights conception sees mediation as a more principled alternative to the unconstrained bargaining of settlement negotiations. Despite their dissimilarity, however, two observations apply equally to both. First, both take an essentially negative view of mediation as the avoidance of something bad—expensive court involvement or unprincipled bargaining—rather than a positive view of mediation as the accomplishment of something good in itself. This negative approach sadly misses the positive essence of mediation, ... Second, both conceptions of the mediator's role are fundamentally and similarly flawed, in two critical respects.

The first flaw in both conceptions is that efficiency and protection of rights are both interests that third parties other than mediators can promote much more effectively than mediators themselves. Therefore, why give either of these jobs to mediators in the first place? If efficiency is the concern, an arbitrator can be more effective than a mediator in removing cases from court and disposing of them expeditiously and finally. The greater structure of the arbitration process, and the arbitrator's decisional authority, make speedy and final disposition much more likely in arbitration than in mediation. On the other hand, if protection of rights is the primary concern, a judge can do so far more effectively than a mediator. As many have observed, the informality and privacy of mediation, and its de-emphasis on substantive rules of decision, inevitably place rights and fairness at risk. By contrast, adjudication's emphasis on procedural formality, substantive rules, and neutral supervision of zealous advocates assures greater protection of rights and fairness than mediation could possibly afford. In short, if the concern is efficiency or protection of rights, mediation can be dismissed altogether as superfluous, because other processes can perform both these functions much more effectively.

One answer to this criticism is that mediation can accomplish something else of value that these other processes cannot. If so, however, then this value and not the two in question should define the mediator's role. . . . Another answer is that, while other processes can more effectively promote either efficiency *or* protection of rights, mediation somehow can combine both functions as those other processes cannot. As argued above, however, in practice these two functions are bound to conflict with one another. Thus, it is difficult to see how mediation, or any process, could effectively serve both.

In fact, this leads to the second flaw common to both the efficiency and protection-of-rights conceptions. Not only are mediators incapable of serving *both* these roles simultaneously, they actually are incapable of serving *either* of them separately. Indeed, the attempt to serve either will render the mediation process either useless or abusive.

If we adopt the efficiency conception, under which the mediator's primary role is simply to reach agreements as expeditiously as possible, the effect is to create a role devoid of any clear ethical constraints on mediator behavior. Mediators become little more than case-movers; the only performance standards are their agreement rates and time/cost figures. Such a conception creates perverse incentives; it opens the door to, and indeed encourages, manipulative and coercive mediator behavior, especially in a process unconstrained by procedural or substantive rules or fear of publicity. Mediation becomes the "forced march to settlement" that many of its critics have rightly decried. One might expect two possible outcomes from the adoption of such a role for the mediator: disputants with any presence of mind simply will balk, rendering the process useless; or disputants with less presence of mind will be intimidated, rendering the process abusive. The mediator either cannot or should not succeed in the role of efficient case-mover.

On the other hand, if we adopt the protection-of-rights conception, mediators cannot effectively serve this role without undermining their usefulness altogether. As Professor Stulberg has argued, mediators who try to protect substantive rights and guarantee that agreements are fair must adopt substantive positions that inevitably compromise their impartiality, either in actuality or in the parties' eyes.[31] Yet, impartiality is crucial to the mediator's many tasks. The mediator has to create an effective environment for bargaining, develop information, and persuade parties to explore different options, search for areas of agreement and exchange, and finally accept something different from their initial demands; and the ability to do all this depends on maintaining the trust and confidence of both parties in the mediator's complete impartiality. Thus, making protection of rights the mediator's primary and direct role prevents the mediator from serving many other crucial functions. The same is true if the mediator tries to protect rights indirectly, by urging the parties at every significant juncture in the process to consult independent outside counsel. Doing so undermines the mediator's ability to develop the sense of movement, rapprochement, and trust with and between the parties that is crucial to attaining mutually acceptable agreements.

In short, mediators can succeed in the protective role only by limiting their function to protection and nothing more, transforming mediation into simply

---

[31] *See* J. STULBERG, TAKING CHARGE/MANAGING CONFLICT 141-49 (1987); Stulberg at 87, 96–97 [J. Stulberg, *The Theory and Practice of Mediation: A Reply to Professor Susskind*, 6 VT L. REV. 85, 88–91 (1981)]; *see also* McCrory, *Environmental Mediation—Another Piece for the Puzzle*, 6 VT L. REV. 49, 80–81 (1981).

a kind of regulated negotiation process. Even then, the substantive positions a mediator takes may doom the negotiation process itself, as the party disfavored by the mediator's positions simply may balk at a "regulated" settlement. Alternatively, if parties succumb to the mediator's positions, which by nature are subjective and unreviewable, the result may be an agreement that simply substitutes the mediator's personal views of right and fairness for those of the parties. This may be just as abusive, in its way, as the agreement-oriented mediator's "forced march to settlement."

To summarize, the mediator cannot effectively and coherently fulfill the role envisioned by either the efficiency or the protection-of-rights conception. On the other hand, neutral third parties in other processes, such as arbitration and adjudication, *can* fulfill these roles. Therefore, neither the efficiency nor the protection-of-rights conception offers a sound basis for establishing uniform standards for mediator qualifications, training, and practice. For this reason, it is important to resist the tendency to gravitate toward either conception, both of which remain extremely influential despite their deficiencies. The only basis for resisting them, however, is the articulation of another conception of the mediator's role which is sounder, more fruitful, and more in touch with the positive essence of mediation. This is the . . . empowerment-and-recognition conception.

. . . The basis for a sounder conception of the mediator's role lies in examining what mediation *can* do that other processes cannot. In other words, what important powers or capacities are unique to mediation that are not found to the same degree, if at all, in other methods of dispute resolution? The mediator's role should then be to act in ways that fulfill these unique capacities.

. . . Thoughtful mediation theorists and practitioners have given much consideration to identifying mediation's unique powers. In their comments, two points consistently are expressed regarding the capacities of the mediation process.

The first special power of mediation, and what some call "[t]he overriding feature and . . . value of mediation," is that "it is a consensual process that seeks self-determined resolutions."[36] Mediation places the substantive outcome of the dispute within the control and determination of the parties themselves; it frees them from relying on or being subjected to the opinions and standards of outside "higher authorities," legal or otherwise. Further, mediation not only allows the parties to set their own standards for an acceptable solution, it also requires them to search for solutions that are within their own capacity to effectuate. In other words, the parties themselves set the standards, and the parties themselves marshall the actual resources to resolve the dispute. When agreement is reached, the parties have designed and implemented their own solution to the problem. Even when the parties do not reach an agreement, they experience the concrete possibility, to be more fully realized in other situations, that they can control their own circumstances. They discover that they need not be wholly dependent on outside institutions, legal or otherwise, to solve their problems. I call this the

---

[36] J. Folberg & A. Taylor at 245. [J. FOLBERG & A. TAYLOR: MEDIATION: A COMPREHENSIVE GUIDE TO RESOLVING CONFLICTS WITHOUT LITIGATION (1984)].

empowerment function of mediation: its capacity to encourage the parties to exercise autonomy, choice, and self-determination.

. . . Mediated outcomes empower parties by responding to them as unique individuals with particular problems, rather than as depersonalized representatives of general problems faced by classes of actors or by society as a whole.

The second special power of mediation was described classically by Professor Lon Fuller: "The central quality of mediation [is] its capacity to reorient the parties to each other . . . by helping them to achieve a new and shared perception of their relationship, a perception that will redirect their attitudes and dispositions toward one another."[43] What Fuller describes here is not just a technique to produce agreements, but an inherently valuable accomplishment uniquely attainable through mediation. Fuller sees mediation as evoking in each party recognition and acknowledgment of, and some degree of understanding and empathy for, the other party's situation, even though their interests and positions may remain opposed. Of course, such mutual recognition often will help produce concrete accommodations and an ultimate agreement. But even when it does not, evoking recognition is itself an accomplishment of enormous value: the value of escaping our alienated isolation and rediscovering our common humanity, even in the midst of bitter division. Professor Leonard Riskin observes accordingly that one of the great values of mediation is that it can "encourage the kind of dialogue that would help . . . [the disputants experience] a perspective of caring and interconnection."[45] Others also have stressed this special power of mediation to "humanize" us to one another, to translate between us, and to help us recognize each other as fellows even when we are in conflict. I call this the recognition function of mediation.

. . . Here, then, are the special powers of mediation: It can encourage personal empowerment and self-determination as alternatives to institutional dependency, and it can evoke recognition of common humanity in the face of bitter conflict. Both powers involve restoring to the individual a sense of his own value and that of his fellow man in the face of an increasingly alienating and isolating social context. These are valuable powers indeed. Further, they are unique to mediation. These are functions mediation can perform that other processes cannot.

As for evoking empathetic recognition of the other fellow, adjudication and arbitration at best treat such recognition as irrelevant. More often, they destroy the very possibility of empathy by encouraging strong, frequently extreme, adversarial behavior. While in negotiation, recognition may occur, but only haphazardly, for no one stands above the fray to encourage and help the parties rise above their own positions and acknowledge those of their opponents. As for empowerment, it is almost by definition impossible in

---

43 Fuller, *Mediation—ts Forms and Functions* at 325. [Lon L. Fuller, *Mediation—Its Forms and Functions*, 44 S. CAL. L. REV. 305 (1971)].

45 Riskin at 354 [Riskin, *Toward New Standards for the Neutral Lawyer in Mediation*, 26 ARIZ. L. REV. 329 (1984)]; *see also id.* at 332, 347-49, 352, 359 (referring to the value of caring and interconnection); Riskin, *supra* note 6, at 56–57 (relating mediation to the shift in public values from self-fulfillment to the ethic of commitment) [Riskin, *Mediation and Lawyers*, 43 OHIO ST. L.J. 29, 30–34 (1982)].

adjudication and arbitration. Both disempower the parties in differing degrees, whether by their authoritative and legalistic character, or by their heavy reliance on advice and representation by professional advocates. Although empowerment is more of a possibility in negotiation, the difficulty of reaching settlement in unassisted negotiations often frustrates this possibility, and negotiation through professional advocates again involves disempowerment in its own way.

Thus, what mediation can do that other processes cannot, is to encourage empowerment of the parties and evoke recognition between them. These are its unique and valuable capacities. The mediator's role is to act so as to fulfill these unique capacities. Accordingly, in general terms, the mediator's role is: (1) to encourage the empowerment of the parties—i.e., the exercise of their autonomy and self-determination in deciding whether and how to resolve their dispute; and (2) to promote the parties' mutual recognition of each other as human beings despite their adverse positions. I emphasize here that this role can and should be performed successfully whether or not the parties reach an agreement, and whether or not any agreement reached satisfies some external standard of right or fairness. In other words, it is not the mediator's job to guarantee a fair agreement, or *any* agreement at all; it *is* the mediator's job to guarantee the parties the fullest opportunity for self-determination and mutual acknowledgment. Mediators who ignore this job have not fulfilled their professional responsibilities, even if the parties reach an agreement. Conversely, mediators who do this job *have* fulfilled their responsibilities, even if the parties reach *no* agreement.

. . . The empowerment-and-recognition conception of the mediator's role relieves the mediator of any sense of obligation to produce agreements or to ensure against "unfair" agreements; for the definition of success in this role is neither reaching agreements nor protecting rights. However, the empowerment-and-recognition conception by no means frees mediators entirely from a sense of professional obligations; it merely redirects the concern. Now the mediator will feel obligated to do everything possible to ensure that the parties are empowered to exercise their autonomy and self-determination, and that on some level they acknowledge and recognize each other's common humanity. Yet this question still remains: How do mediators know whether they have fulfilled these obligations responsibly? In other words, what specific expectations should mediators strive to satisfy? . . .

Apart from the marshalling of information, the mediator should push for the parties to fully comprehend all the information before them, including the range of issues presented and each party's positions. Therefore, the mediator should summarize, clarify, question, and test for comprehension before allowing decisionmaking to proceed. On another level, and in light of the information marshalled, the mediator should push for the parties to fully identify and consider all possible options for resolving the issues, before they focus on specific options and actually make decisions.

Perhaps most important, as the process begins either producing the terms of an agreement or moving toward impasse, the mediator should push for the parties to consider and understand fully the consequences of *either* outcome, before they decide for or against agreement. Phrased in the negative, the mediator should make every effort to prevent the parties from either reaching *or* failing to reach an agreement on the basis of inaccurate or incomplete information or understanding, including failures of either side to understand the other's positions.

The empowerment role also defines the mediator's obligation with respect to law and legal advice. On one hand, the empowerment role is based on the premise that the law need not control the parties' decision regarding how to resolve the dispute; some recent legislation is quite clear about this. On the other hand, the empowerment role assumes the importance of ensuring that decisions are based on all available information. Clearly, information about the law may be relevant to the parties "as an indication of what is obtainable from the legal marketplace, . . . as an indication of societal standards, . . . [or] as an expression of underlying principles . . . which the parties might want to consider in approaching their own resolution."[73] Accordingly, the mediator's obligation here must be two-sided. The mediator should push for the parties to obtain and consider independent legal advice before committing themselves to an agreement. However, the mediator also should push for the parties not to abdicate their autonomous judgment and power of choice by mechanically deferring to legal experts and law, but rather to assess their own best interests independently, and make independent decisions in light of all considerations. These obligations should apply whether or not the mediator directly provides the parties with information about the law.

Turning now to the recognition role, fulfilling this role requires the mediator to make every effort to evoke mutual acknowledgment and recognition between the parties. Therefore, the mediator should first of all push for the parties to articulate their positions and the reasons behind them as clearly, forcefully, and yet as respectfully as possible. This will help ensure that each party's views are accessible and therefore able to evoke acknowledgment from the other. Second, as recognition rarely is automatic, the mediator should go further and affirmatively translate and explain each party's positions and reasons to the other, in terms most likely to evoke the other's recognition and empathy. Finally, the mediator should push for each party to hear and understand the other's position without feeling threatened, to the point where each can feel, and if possible somehow express, a measure of recognition of the other party's situation.

The above description of specific obligations flowing from the empowerment-and-recognition role is illustrative, not exhaustive. Yet it includes some of the most important elements of what we should expect mediators to do. One crucial element not mentioned above is the obligation of impartiality, which is necessary to fulfill both aspects of the empowerment-and-recognition role. What I mean by impartiality, however, goes beyond the usual connotation of disclosure of conflicts and neutrality regarding outcome. . . .

Mediators should be visibly evenhanded or two-sided in their pushing. In other words, they should direct their invitations, support, encouragements, challenges, and urgings toward each party in turn, and each should see clearly that the other is receiving similar treatment. If necessary, mediators should

---

[73] Center for Mediation in Law [CENTER FOR MEDIATION IN LAW, THE PLACE OF LAW IN MEDIATION (1983) (training materials)].

explicitly assure the parties that they intend to behave identically toward each side, and of course they should always fulfill this assurance. Mediators whose pushing is positive in character, and who adhere to the requirement of *active* impartiality, can serve for each side as translator to the other and also serve each side as devil's advocate for the other. And they can do so without ever losing the trust and confidence of both sides that is necessary to fulfilling both aspects of the mediator's role. I should note, however, that this may be much easier to do if the mediator does at least some of this pushing while meeting separately with each side, a point I return to below.

One other aspect of the obligation of active impartiality is also quite important in fulfilling both aspects of the empowerment-and-recognition role. The impartiality of mediators means not only that they are allied with neither side, but that because of a lack of personal investment, they have more distance and perspective on the parties' discussions. This position "above the fray" should not be a passive listening post. Rather, it should be the basis for what I call the mediator's job of narration. The mediator can impartially hear, and impartially report to the parties, many crucial parts of their own dialogue that they themselves may not have grasped fully or even heard because of their closeness to the situation. Offers, counteroffers, new options for resolution, actual agreements on issues, and statements of acknowledgment and recognition all are presented frequently in mediation sessions without one or both parties even realizing what has occurred. To fulfill both the empowerment and recognition functions, the mediator can and should be an actively impartial *narrator* who lets no relevant exchange between the parties go unheard or ignored.

To conclude this discussion, I must emphasize the fact that almost all the obligations I have described as flowing from the empowerment-and-recognition conception are affirmative obligations, not constraints or restrictions. The reason for this is, as suggested above, that this conception of the mediator's role stems from a positive view of mediation as *seeking* something good in itself, namely empowerment and recognition. The negative view of mediation as *avoidance* of trial or unprincipled bargaining, and the efficiency and protection-of-rights conceptions that derive from this view, tend to produce negative or restrictive definitions of the mediator's obligations (or none at all).

[2] MEDIATOR ACCOUNTABILITY

Should the mediator feel a sense of responsibility or accountability for the outcome of a mediation? Should the mediator seek to insure that the result is fair or just? Lawrence Susskind and Joseph Stulberg present us with a now classic debate over mediator accountability in the following excerpts. In focussing on the role of the environmental mediator, Susskind expresses concern not only for the rights of the disputants but also for those unrepresented at the table. Arguably, agreements made at an environmental mediation affect individuals not represented at the mediation, including future generations. Building on this protection-of-rights conception of the environmental mediator's role, Susskind argues that the mediator must feel responsible not only for the mediation *process*, but also for the *outcome* of the mediation. Stulberg challenges such a conception of the mediator's role. He argues that Susskind's notion that a mediator should be accountable for the fairness of the outcome of a mediation is inconsistent with the essential functions and qualities of a mediator, particularly that of mediator neutrality. He then presents his conception of the seven essential functions and three desirable qualities of a mediator.

ENVIRONMENTAL MEDIATION AND THE ACCOUNTABILITY PROBLEM

6 Vt. L. Rev. 1, 14-16, 18, 42, 47 (1981) [*]

By Lawrence Susskind

. . . One analysis of environmental mediation suggests nine steps that must be completed for mediation to be successful: (1) all the parties that have a stake in the outcome of a dispute must be identified; (2) the relevant interest groups must be appropriately represented; (3) fundamentally different values and assumptions must be confronted; (4) a sufficient number of possible solutions or options must be developed; (5) the boundaries and time horizon for analyzing impacts must be agreed upon; (6) the weighting, scaling, and amalgamation of judgments about costs and benefits must be undertaken jointly; (7) fair compensation and mitigatory actions must be negotiated; (8) the legality and financial feasibility of bargains that are made must be ensured, and (9) all parties must be held to their commitments. Although these steps will ensure a fair and efficient process, the success of a mediation effort must also be judged in terms of the fairness and stability of agreements that are reached. From this standpoint, a mediator should probably refuse to enter a dispute in which the power relationships among the parties are so unequal that a mutually acceptable agreement is unlikely to emerge. In addition, environmental mediators should probably withdraw from negotiations in which any of the parties seek an agreement that would not be just from the standpoint of another participant or from the standpoint of a party not at the bargaining table.

To achieve just and stable agreements, mediators may have to find ways of enhancing the relationships among the parties so they will be better able to reconcile future differences (that threaten implementation) on their own. Mediators may also have to build the basic negotiating capabilities of one or more of the parties to ensure more equal bargaining relationships.

Agreements are sometimes reached because one party with substantial power holds out for what it wants while other parties, with less leverage, realize that they can either accept a small gain or wind up with nothing at all. Under these circumstances, all sides may sign such agreements but with unequal degrees of enthusiasm. This result sends a message to the community-at-large that it is acceptable for the most powerful interests to pressure opponents into accepting less than completely fair outcomes. Mediators should avoid setting such precedents, if only because they undermine the chances

---

[*] Copyright © 1981 by Vermont Law Review. Reprinted with permission.

of attracting less powerful but obstructionist parties to the bargaining table in the future.

It is also quite possible that short-term solutions with which the parties to an environmental dispute are quite pleased can generate new and different problems for other groups outside the bargaining process. It would be irresponsible to ignore these problems if they are indeed foreseeable; if only because implementation may be obstructed by those outside groups later on.

The classic model of labor mediation places little emphasis on the mediator's role as a representative of diffuse, inarticulate, or hard-to-organize interests. All the appropriate parties to a labor-management dispute are presumed to be present at the bargaining table. Thus, the problems of protecting unrepresented segments of the society or reducing impacts on the community-at-large receive little, if any, attention. Joint net gains are presumed to be maximized through the interaction of the parties and their ability to know for themselves how best to achieve their objectives. No effort is made to bolster the claims or abilities of the weaker stakeholders. Precedent is not a concern; indeed, one of the presumed strengths of labor mediation is that parties are free to devise agreements of their own design. Finally, spillovers, externalities, and long-term impacts are, for the most part, ignored since the time frame for implementing most labor-management agreements is relatively short. The parties will usually face the same adversaries again in a few years which makes it easier for them to hold each other to their agreements.

Although procedural fairness and ethical behavior on the part of labor mediators and self-interest maximizing behavior on the part of the participants in labor-management negotiations are presumed to be sufficient to ensure just and stable agreements, these assumptions are inappropriate in the environmental field. Just and stable agreements in the environmental field require much closer attention to the interests of those unable to represent themselves. Joint net gains can be achieved only if the parties attempt to understand the complex ecological systems involved and to generate appropriate compromises that go beyond their self-interests. In short, self-interested negotiation must be replaced by "principled negotiation."

. . . [E]nvironmental mediators ought to accept responsibility for ensuring (1) that the interests of parties not directly involved in negotiations, but with a stake in the outcome, are adequately represented and protected; (2) that agreements are as fair and stable as possible, and (3) that agreements reached are interpreted as intended by the community-at-large and set constructive precedents.

. . . Environmental mediators, to the extent that they adopt the broader view of their responsibilities suggested in this article, will probably need to possess substantive knowledge about the environmental and regulatory issues at stake. Effective environmental mediation may require teams composed of some individuals with technical background, some specialized in problem-solving or group dynamics and some with political clout.

. . . An environmental mediator should be committed to procedural fairness—all parties should have an opportunity to be represented by individuals with the technical sophistication to bargain effectively on their behalf.

Environmental mediators should also be concerned that the agreements they help to reach are just and stable. To fulfill these responsibilities, environmental mediators will have to intervene more often and more forcefully than their counterparts in the labor-management field. Although such intervention may make it difficult to retain the appearance of neutrality and the trust of the active parties, environmental mediators cannot fulfill their responsibilities to the community-at-large if they remain passive.

THE THEORY AND PRACTICE OF MEDIATION: A REPLY TO PROFESSOR SUSSKIND

6 Vt. L. Rev. 85, 86–87, 91–97, 114, 115-116 (1981) [*]

By Joseph B. Stulberg

. . . The basis of this article is that Susskind's demand for a non-neutral intervenor is conceptually and pragmatically incompatible with the goals and purposes of mediation. The intervenor posture that Susskind advocates is not anchored by any principles or obligations of office. The intervenor's conduct, strategies or contribution to the dispute settlement process is, therefore, neither predictable nor consistent. It is precisely a mediator's commitment to neutrality which ensures responsible actions on the part of the mediator and permits mediation to be an effective, principled dispute settlement procedure.

Susskind maintains, in four distinct ways, that a mediator of environmental disputes should not be neutral. Environmental mediators ought to be concerned about:

1. The impacts of negotiated agreements on under-represented or unrepresentable groups in the community.

2. The possibility that joint net gains have not been maximized.

3. The long-term or spillover effects of the settlements they help to reach.

4. The precedents that they set and the precedents upon which agreements are based.

At a substantive level, Susskind argues that the mediator must ensure that the negotiated agreements are fair.

. . . What functions of office does the mediator have that enable him to fulfill that objective? A brief listing would include the following functions.

A mediator is a catalyst. Succinctly stated, the mediator's presence affects how the parties interact. His presence should lend a constructive posture to the discussions rather than cause further misunderstanding and polarization, although there are no guarantees that the latter condition will not result. It seems elementary, but many persons equate a mediator's neutrality with his being a non-entity at the negotiations. Nothing could be further from the truth. Susskind, borrowing from the writings of a distinguished mediator,

---

notes that the mediator performs some procedural functions and, if necessary, assumes an active role. Even the mediator's assumption of a procedural role, however, is an important action that, in itself, may be sufficient to reorient the parties towards an accommodation. Susskind implies that the procedural role is passive whereas an active role would include suggesting substantive resolutions to an issue. The active/passive distinction, however, seriously misrepresents the impact of the mediator's presence on the parties. Much as the chemical term, catalyst connotes the mediator's presence alone creates a special reaction between the parties. Any mediator, therefore, takes on a unique responsibility for the continued integrity of the discussions.

A mediator is also an educator. He must know the desires, aspirations, working procedures, political limitations, and business constraints of the parties. He must immerse himself in the dynamics of the controversy to enable him to explain (although not necessarily justify) the reasons for a party's specific proposal or its refusal to yield in its demands. He may have to explain, for example, the meaning of certain statutory provisions that bear on the dispute, the technology of machinery that is the focus of discussion, or simply the principles by which the negotiation process goes forward.

Third, the mediator must be a translator. The mediator's role is to convey each party's proposals in a language that is both faithful to the desired objectives of the party and formulated to insure the highest degree of receptivity by the listener. The proposal of an angry neighbor that the "young hoodlum" not play his stereo from 11:00 p.m. to 7:00 a.m. every day becomes, through the intervention and guidance of a mediator, a proposal to the youth that he be able to play his stereo on a daily basis from 7:00 a.m. to 11:00 p.m.

Fourth, the mediator may also expand the resources available to the parties. Persons are occasionally frustrated in their discussions because of a lack of information or support services. The mediator, by his personal presence and with the integrity of his office, can frequently gain access for the parties to needed personnel or data. This service can range from securing research or computer facilities to arranging meetings with the governor or President.

Fifth, the mediator often becomes the bearer of bad news. Concessions do not always come readily; parties frequently reject a proposal in whole or in part. The mediator can cushion the expected negative reaction to such a rejection by preparing the parties for it in private conversations. Negotiations are not sanitized. They can be extremely emotional. Persons can react honestly and indignantly, frequently launching personal attacks on those representatives refusing to display flexibility. Those who are the focus of such an attack will, quite understandably, react defensively. The mediator's function is to create a context in which such an emotional, cathartic response can occur without causing an escalation of hostilities or further polarization.

Sixth, the mediator is an agent of reality. Persons frequently become committed to advocating one and only one solution to a problem. There are a variety of explanations for this common phenomenon, ranging from pride of authorship in a proposal to the mistaken belief that compromising means acting without principles. The mediator is in the best position to inform a party, as directly and as candidly as possible, that its objective is simply not obtainable through those specific negotiations. He does not argue that the proposal is undesirable and therefore not obtainable. Rather, as an impartial participant in the discussions, he may suggest that the positions the party advances will not be realized, either because they are beyond the resource capacity of the other parties to fulfill or that, for reasons of administrative efficiency or matters of principle, the other parties will not concede. If the proposing party persists in its belief that the other parties will relent, the question is reduced to a perception of power. The mediator's role at that time is to force the proposing party to reassess the degree of power that it perceives it possesses.

The last function of a mediator is to be a scapegoat. No one ever enters into an agreement without thinking he might have done better had he waited a little longer or demanded a little more. A party can conveniently suggest to its constituents when it presents the settlement terms that the decision was forced upon it. In the context of negotiation and mediation, that focus of blame—the scapegoat—can be the mediator.

. . . One way to generate a list of the desirable qualities and abilities a mediator should possess is to adopt the posture of a potential party to a mediation session and analyze the type of person that it would want in the role. The following qualities and abilities would probably be included: capable of appreciating the dynamics of the environment in which the dispute is occurring, intelligent, effective listener, articulate, patient, non-judgmental, flexible, forceful and persuasive, imaginative, resourceful, a person of professional standing or reputation, reliable, capable of gaining access to necessary resources, non-defensive, person of integrity, humble, objective, and neutral with regard to the outcome. Three of these qualities merit further analysis.

It is very important that a mediator have the capacity to appreciate the dynamics of the environment in which the dispute is occurring. The objective of negotiation and mediation is to have parties agree to do something. Discussions are to result in action. The mediator must be able to appreciate the real world constraints, pressures, and frustrations under which the parties act. Only then can he establish the tempo of discussions and range of settlement possibilities in a manner commensurate with the urgency of the dispute. Parties with vital interests at stake will not be persuaded to reorient their perspectives towards one another by the intervenor who simply admonishes them to love one another.

Second, the mediator must be intelligent. The question remains, however, whether the mediator must be knowledgeable about the substantive area in dispute. In an environmental dispute involving nuclear reactor plants, what should the mediator know about the science of nuclear energy? This question, touched upon by Susskind, has been framed in ways that are seriously misleading. We do not know what constitutes technical knowledge nor in which subjects the mediator should have such knowledge. Should the mediator, for example, know about the science of nuclear energy, the science and economics of alternative energy resources, the legal regulatory process governing the licensing of nuclear plants, or the politics of energy development? Are all of those items of technical knowledge? If so, which type or types should the mediator possess?

That this question even surfaces reflects an insidious example of a straw man argument. Susskind correctly suggests that an environmental mediator needs to possess substantive knowledge about a dispute. His conclusion intimates, when combined with his suggestions that mediators traditionally assume primarily a passive role and are concerned predominately with procedural matters, that the traditional mediator need not possess equivalent substantive knowledge. Nothing could be further from the truth. The mediator of a labor-management negotiation session who is not familiar with the intricacies of budgets, work schedules, personnel practices, legal guidelines stipulating mandatory bargaining subjects, arbitration awards which interpret particular phrases of contract language and the like, is ineffective and even becomes a stumbling block to an agreement. Susskind's argument hints of the distinction between communication skills and substantive knowledge in a particular subject area.

From the perspective of the potential party to the mediation sessions the mediator should possess both process (communication) skills and content knowledge. The content knowledge a mediator should have depends on the specific type of dispute into which the mediator might intervene and what the parties believe will be the most useful to them. The parties at least want the mediator to be intelligent enough to become educated about the matters in dispute as the talks progress. The knowledgeable mediator can ask penetrating questions, be sensitive to when parties are erecting artificial constraints on their conduct, and avoid becoming an obstacle in the discussions of the more subtle nuances of the matters in dispute. The mediator does not possess such knowledge, however, for the purpose of serving as an expert who advises the parties as to the "right answers."

The third major characteristic is that a mediator must be neutral with regard to outcome. Parties negotiate because they lack the power to achieve their objectives unilaterally. They negotiate with those persons or representatives of groups whose cooperation they need to achieve their objective. If the mediator is neutral and remains so, then he and his office invite a bond of trust to develop between him and the parties. If the mediator's job is to assist the parties to reach a resolution, and his commitment to neutrality ensures confidentiality, then, in an important sense, the parties have nothing to lose and everything to gain by the mediator's intervention. In these two bases of assistance and neutrality there is no way the mediator could jeopardize or abridge the substantive interests of the respective parties.

How is this trust exemplified in practice? Suppose a party advocates certain proposals because of internal political divisions which might impede discussions. For tactical reasons, however, the party does not want to reveal these internal divisions to the other parties. A mediator to whom such information is entrusted can direct discussions so that such a dilemma can be overcome. The mediator's vigorous plea made in the presence of all parties to remove the proposal from further discussions, for example, might provide a safe, face-saving way for that party to drop its demand.

There is a variety of information that parties will entrust to a neutral mediator, including a statement of their priorities, acceptable trade-offs, and their desired timing for demonstrating movement and flexibility. All of these postures are aimed to achieve a resolution without fear that such information will be carelessly shared or that it will surface in public forums in a manner calculated to embarrass or exploit the parties into undesired movement. This type of trust is secured and reinforced only if the mediator is neutral, has no power to insist upon a particular outcome, and honors the confidences placed in him. If any of these characteristics is absent, then the parties must calculate what information they will share with the mediator, just as they do in communicating with any of the parties to the controversy.

. . . If we were to accept the obligations of office that Susskind ascribes to the environmental mediator with regard to insuring Pareto-optimal outcomes, then the environmental mediator is simply a person who uses his entry into the dispute to become a social conscience, environmental policeman, or social critic and who carries no other obligations to the process or the participants beyond assuring Pareto-optimality. It is, in its most benign form, an invitation to permit philosopher-kings to participate in the affairs of the citizenry.

. . . A final note is in order regarding the propriety of a mediator having a substantive commitment to a particular outcome or range of outcomes for a given dispute. It appears that the impetus for Susskind's prescription, that an environmental mediator not be neutral, emanates from the understandable reluctance to accord conclusive weight to the preferences of the parties in every conceivable situation. For example, if parties to a collective bargaining session agree to adopt a racially-discriminatory hiring policy, the mediator, Susskind would argue, should object. Although the stated principle is correct, the mediator's role is not thereby converted into that of an advocate, even if the parties find acceptable an arrangement that is contrary to important principles of public policy or morality.

How should the mediator respond to such a situation? The answer seems relatively straightforward. The mediator should press the parties to examine whether or not they believe that (1) they would be acting in compliance with the law or with principles they would be willing, as rational agents, to universalize; (2) their activities will be acceptable to their respective constituencies and not overturned by public authorities; and (3) in the short and long run, their proposed actions are not contrary to their own self-interest. If the parties listen to these arguments and still find the proposed course of action acceptable, then the mediator can simply decide as an individual that he does not want to lend his personal presence and reputation, or the prestige of the mediation process, to that agreement and he can withdraw. That judgment is one for the mediator *qua* moral agent, not mediator, to make. It is comparable to the dilemma faced by a soldier who is given an order to commit a morally heinous act.

It is certainly the case that each of us is not neutral with regard to everything. Each of us has preferences, interests, commitments to certain moral principles and to an evolving philosophy of life which, when challenged or transgressed, will prompt us into advocating and acting in a manner that is faithful to these dictates. There is clearly no reason to be apologetic or hesitant about defending or advocating such considered judgments. It is also true, however, that mediation as a dispute settlement procedure can be used in a variety of contexts, not all of which would meet approval with everyone's considered judgments. What is important is that one keep distinct his personal posture of judgment from the rule defined practice of the mediator and act accordingly.

————

Never pass on legal advice – stick w/ passing information

NOTES AND QUESTIONS

(1) Bush was obviously influenced by Fuller in developing his "empowerment and recognition" conception of the mediator's role. When Fuller was writing in the early 1970's, mediation was most widely used in the field of labor-management relations. Arguably, that field is less bound by rules of law and may therefore be more conducive to having the mediator eschew a protection of rights conception of the mediator's role and to assist the parties in creating their own norms during the mediation and defining their rights and duties toward one another. Does the rejection of a protection of rights conception become more difficult as mediation is used in substantive areas that are more traditionally defined by the parties' legal rights, particularly where such a dispute has become a court case and has been referred to a lawyer-mediator?

(2) How is the classic debate between Susskind and Stulberg over mediator accountability affected by the increased use of mediation by the courts and the entry of lawyers into the mediation field? In *Public Values and Private Justice: A Case for Mediator Accountability*, 4 Geo. J. Legal Ethics 503, 508–509, 521 (1991),[*] Judith Maute argues:

> The extent of mediator accountability for fairness varies by whether or not the mediator is a lawyer, and by whether the parties are independently represented by counsel.
>
> . . . Legal knowledge facilitates mediation. A dispute over respective rights and obligations is legal in nature. In such cases, the lawyer-mediator cannot ignore the law's relevance or one's legal knowledge. The lawyer-mediator cannot avoid the higher accountability to approximate or improve upon the likely result of litigation simply by concealing one's status as a lawyer. . . .
>
> When the parties are not independently represented, the lawyer-mediator represents them jointly in a limited capacity. When mediating a litigable dispute, the neutral lawyer is accountable to both the legal system and her clients. Discipline and malpractice liability should provide downside risks for failing to satisfy the obligation. Where the mediation substitutes for legal process, the neutral lawyer has a duty to protect the public value of fairness. The mediator should assure, therefore, that the parties have sufficient information to make informed decisions on whether to settle privately or proceed to court. The parties must understand their respective

---

legal positions and what might happen in court. Lacking such information, they cannot test a proposed agreement against their own sense of fairness, which is the key to successful mediation.

. . . Mediators intercede to facilitate an agreement the parties could not reach on their own. If it produces agreement, the mediation may substitute for public adjudication, often a desirable and appropriate end. When mediation intercedes to settle a legal dispute, additional safeguards are needed to protect for two important values at risk with private settlement: public values of fairness and authoritative public resolution of legal conflicts. The mediator is properly held to a higher standard of accountability. The process should enable both parties to obtain relevant information about the law and how it might apply to the instant facts. When disparities in power or knowledge disable a weaker party from effective bargaining, the mediator must intervene to avoid a patently unfair agreement at odds with the probable outcome of adjudication. . . .

Although a lawyer-mediator may possess general legal knowledge that may suggest to her that the unrepresented disputants are headed toward an agreement that would be an unlikely outcome if the dispute were adjudicated in court, how might the lawyer mediator assure herself during the mediation that her legal assessment is correct? That is, aside from the theoretical concerns that Bush and Stulberg would have with Maute's position, are there practical concerns?

In *Informed Consent in Mediation: A Guiding Principle for Truly Educated Decisionmaking*, 74 Notre Dame L. Rev. 775, 812 (1999),* Jacqueline Nolan-Haley argues for acceptance of a principle of informed consent in mediation that would promote fairness:

A robust theory of informed consent requires that parties be educated about mediation before they consent to participate in it, that their continued participation and negotiations be voluntary, and that they understand the outcomes to which they agree. Informed consent serves the values of autonomy, human dignity, and efficiency. It guards against coercion, ignorance, and incapacity that can impede the consensual underpinnings of the mediation process.

Nolan-Haley takes pains to point out that she is not advocating an adversarial model for mediation sessions nor, unlike Judith Maute, is she suggesting that mediation outcomes approximate likely adjudicated outcomes. Rather, she argues for a "sliding-scale model of informed consent disclosure," where mediators would owe a greater duty of informed consent disclosure to unrepresented parties than to those parties represented by counsel. Recognizing the value of neutrality in mediation, she considers the research of Cobb and Rifkin and others:

Perhaps the real question should be: when is absolute neutrality called for and when is a modified approach preferable? I argue that when court programs require unrepresented parties to enter the

---

mediation process, fairness demands that these parties know their legal options before making final decisions in mediation. A modified approach to mediator neutrality permits mediators to employ an *informative* decisionmaking model and give unrepresented parties such information. *Id.* at 837.

But how is this information to be supplied to the parties? Will the lawyer-mediator simply make a threshold decision that one or both parties need legal information and then suggest that they consult a lawyer? Although such an approach would be less likely to compromise a mediator's neutrality than having the mediator supply the information, is it realistic to expect that many unrepresented parties will be able to afford lawyers?

(3) Does Judith Maute's argument for mediator accountability go beyond that of Susskind? It certainly is contrary to traditional notions of mediator neutrality. Recall that a mediator's ability to "be neutral with regard to outcome" is high on the list of Stulberg's desirable qualities of a mediator. Recognizing the tension between accountability and neutrality, Maute offers the following viewpoint that is clearly premised on a protection of rights conception of the mediator's role: "When a mediated agreement avoids adjudication, traditional mediator neutrality undermines protection of the parties' legal rights." Maute, *supra* at 503. What does it mean to be neutral? Stulberg recognizes that mediators will have "preferences, interests, commitments to certain moral principles and to an evolving philosophy of life," but argues that a mediator must keep this "personal posture of judgment" distinct from his or her role as a neutral dispute resolver.

The complexity of the concept of mediator neutrality is demonstrated by Sara Cobb and Janet Rifkin in their study of mediator neutrality, *Practice and Paradox: Deconstructing Neutrality in Mediation*, Law & Soc. Inquiry 35, 37 (1991): ". . . [L]ike other folk concepts, neutrality is both 'transparent' *and* 'opaque': transparent because it operates on the basis of widely held assumptions about power and conflict, and opaque because it is exceedingly difficult to raise questions about the nature and practice of neutrality from *within* this consensus." Is neutrality then more of an aspirational goal of the mediator? Consider the following: "For ourselves we recommend a strictly neutral settlement strategy as an initial position. Deviating from this stance should be explicitly and deliberately chosen and justified. We are impressed with the difficulty of making such powerful value decisions for others. Should mediators attempt to do so, they should act openly and with the obligation to explain their judgment to the parties." Sydney E. Bernard, Joseph P. Folger, Helen R. Weingarten & Zena R. Zumeta, *The Neutral Mediator: Value Dilemmas in Divorce Mediation*, 4 Mediation Q. 61, 73 (1984).

(4) Susskind's notion of mediator accountability is premised to a large extent on the perceived need to protect the interests of unrepresented third parties to an environmental mediation by insuring that the outcome is fair to all relevant interests. Arguably, there are similar concerns in a divorce mediation, where interested third parties such as the children, grandparents and other relatives often are not represented at the table. Should a divorce mediator be concerned with the fairness of the outcome? In *Mediation and Therapy:*

An Alternative View, 10 Mediation Q. 21 (1992),* John M. Haynes, a prominent divorce mediator and mediation trainer, argues that while a therapist
or lawyer exercises power over both process and content when rendering professional services to a client, when acting as a mediator the therapist or lawyer
must separate his or her role as professional (therapist or lawyer) from his
or her role as mediator. He offers the following advice to divorce mediators:

> . . . [W]e actually assert power in controlling the process but deny
> power in relation to the content. The assumed contract in mediation
> is that the mediator will assist the clients to resolve specific prob-
> lems *on their own terms*. In divorce, these problems include the
> amount and duration of child and maintenance support, the appro-
> priate division of assets, and future parenting roles. *Id.* at 23.

> . . . [T]he mediator does exercise power when managing the pro-
> cess because true process neutrality can often benefit one side at
> the expense of the other. Families choose mediation because they
> want someone to regulate a dispute and provide an environment in
> which a self-determined solution can be found. The mediator cannot
> proclaim process neutrality. He or she cannot stand aside while one
> party verbally abuses the other, cannot permit secrecy, and must
> intervene to assure that all parties understand the issues and the
> data that determine the issues. . . . The mediator's neutrality is
> confined to the content of the agreement. He or she is not neutral
> on the process; indeed, he or she continually exercises power to
> control the process to assure a mutual problem definition, a neutral
> environment, and a joint decision that is mutually acceptable. *Id.*
> at 24.

Is the line Haynes draws between process neutrality and content (outcome)
neutrality a clear one? Keep this in mind as you consider the discussion of
mediator orientations in the following section.

§ C   MEDIATOR ORIENTATIONS

With the increased entry of lawyers into the mediation field, issues concerning the orientation of the mediator have become more salient. Because lawyer-
mediators possess substantive legal knowledge and often have considerable
litigation experience, there is a temptation to apply this knowledge and
experience during the mediation and offer the mediator's personal evaluation
of the case. Many have argued that an *evaluative* orientation is inconsistent
with the notion of the mediator as a communication facilitator and that the
mediator's orientation should be a strictly *facilitative* one. Moreover, with the
publication by Robert A. Baruch Bush and Joseph Folger of *The Promise of
Mediation: Responding to Conflict Through Empowerment and Recognition*,
there has been an increasingly strong interest in having the mediator adopt
a *transformative* orientation. Consider how the following descriptions and
arguments for these various orientations are consistent or inconsistent with
the mediator roles previously discussed.

---

[1]   FACILITATIVE VS. EVALUATIVE

The debate over the efficacy of a facilitative versus an evaluative mediator orientation has been sparked in large part by the publication of the "Riskin grid." In a 1994 article at 12 *Alternatives to the High Cost of Litigation* 111, Leonard Riskin sought to "propose a system for classifying mediator orientations." Riskin's system is based on the answers to two questions: "1. Does the mediator tend to define problems *narrowly* or *broadly*? 2. Does the mediator think she should *evaluate*—make assessments or predictions or proposals for agreements—or *facilitate* the parties' negotiation without evaluating?" Riskin explains this classification scheme in the following excerpt from his longer article on the same subject. Note that Riskin is not advocating either style, but simply seeking to describe the mediator orientations in current practice. The excerpt from the article by Lela Love presents her arguments against an evaluative orientation, and Donald Weckstein presents the counter-argument that mediator activism in the form of evaluation or other interventions may actually enhance party self-determination.

UNDERSTANDING MEDIATORS' ORIENTATIONS, STRATEGIES, AND TECHNIQUES: A GRID FOR THE PERPLEXED

1 Harv. Negot. L. Rev. 7, 24-32, 34-38 (1996) [*]

By Leonard L. Riskin

. . . Most mediators operate from a predominant, presumptive or default orientation (although, as explained later, many mediators move along continuums and among quadrants). For purposes of the following explication of mediator orientations, I will assume that the mediator is acting from such a predominant orientation. For this reason, and for convenience, I will refer to the "evaluative-narrow mediator" rather than the more precise, but more awkward, "mediator operating with an evaluative-narrow approach."

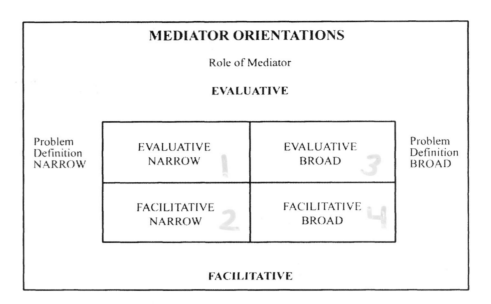

A mediator employs strategies—plans—to conduct a mediation. And a mediator uses techniques—particular moves or behavior—to effectuate those strategies. Here are selected strategies and techniques that typify each mediation orientation.

1. Evaluative-Narrow

A principal strategy of the evaluative-narrow approach is to help the parties understand the strengths and weaknesses of their positions and the likely outcome of litigation or whatever other process they will use if they do not reach a resolution in mediation. But the evaluative-narrow mediator stresses her own education at least as much as that of the parties. Before the mediation starts, the evaluative-narrow mediator will study relevant documents, such as pleadings, depositions, reports, and mediation briefs. At the outset of the mediation, such a mediator typically will ask the parties to present their cases, which normally means arguing their positions, in a joint session. Subsequently, most mediation activities take place in private caucuses in which the mediator will gather additional information and deploy evaluative techniques, such as the following, which are listed below from the least to the most evaluative.

  a.   *Assess the strengths and weaknesses of each side's case.* . . .

  b.   *Predict outcomes of court or other processes.* . . .

c. *Propose position-based compromise agreements.* . . .

d. *Urge or push the parties to settle or to accept a particular settlement proposal or range.* . . .

2. Facilitative-Narrow

The facilitative-narrow mediator shares the evaluative-narrow mediator's general strategy—to educate the parties about the strengths and weaknesses of their claims and the likely consequences of failing to settle. But he employs different techniques to carry out this strategy. He does not use his own assessments, predictions, or proposals. Nor does he apply pressure. He is less likely than the evaluative-narrow mediator to request or to study relevant documents. Instead, believing that the burden of decision-making should rest with the parties, the facilitative-narrow mediator might engage in any of the following activities.

a. *Ask questions.* . . .

b. *Help the parties develop their own narrow proposals.* . . .

c. *Help the parties exchange proposals.* . . .

d. *Help the parties evaluate proposals.* . . .

The facilitative nature of this mediation approach might also produce a degree of education or transformation. The process itself, which encourages the parties to develop their own understandings and outcomes, might educate the parties, or "empower" them by helping them to develop a sense of their own ability to deal with the problems and choices in life. The parties also might acknowledge or empathize with each other's situation. However, in a narrowly-focused mediation, even a facilitative one, the subject matter normally produces fewer opportunities for such developments than does a facilitative-broad mediation.

3. Evaluative-Broad

It is more difficult to describe the strategies and techniques of the evaluative-broad mediator. Mediations conducted with such an orientation vary tremendously in scope, often including many narrow, distributive issues. . . .

In addition, evaluative-broad mediators can be more-or-less evaluative, with the evaluative moves touching all or only some of the issues.

The evaluative-broad mediator's principal strategy is to learn about the circumstances and underlying interests of the parties and other affected individuals or groups, and then to use that knowledge to direct the parties toward an outcome that responds to such interests. To carry out this strategy, the evaluative-broad mediator will employ various techniques, including the following (listed from least to most evaluative).

a. *Educate herself about underlying interests.* . . .

b. *Predict impact (on interests) of not settling.* . . .

c. *Develop and offer broad (interest-based) proposals.* . . .

d. *Urge parties to accept the mediator's or another proposal.* . . .

If the mediator has concluded that the goal of the mediation should include changing the people involved, she might take measures to effectuate that goal, such as appealing to shared values, lecturing, or applying pressure.

4. Facilitative-Broad

The facilitative-broad mediator's principal strategy is to help the participants define the subject matter of the mediation in terms of underlying interests and to help them develop and choose their own solutions that respond to such interests. In addition, many facilitative-broad mediators will help participants find opportunities to educate or change themselves, their institutions, or their communities. To carry out such strategies, the facilitative-broad mediator may use techniques such as the following.

    a.   *Help parties understand underlying interests.* . . .

    b.   *Help parties develop and propose broad, interest-based options for settlement.* . . .

    c.   *Help parties evaluate proposals.* . . .

Figure 3 highlights the principal techniques associated with each orientation, arranged vertically with the most evaluative at the top and the most facilitative at the bottom. The horizontal axis shows the scope of the problems to be addressed, from the narrowest on the left to the broadest on the right.

Mediator Techniques
Role of the Mediator
Evaluative

	Problem Definition **NARROW**		Problem Definition **BROAD**
	Urges/pushes parties to accept narrow (position-based) settlement **Proposes** narrow (position-based) agreement **Predicts** court or other outcomes **Assesses** strengths and weaknesses of each side's case	**Urges/pushes parties** to accept broad (interest-based) settlement **Develops and proposes** broad (interest-based) agreement **Predicts** impact (on interests) of not settling **Educates self** about parties' interests	
	Helps parties evaluate proposals **Helps parties** develop & exchange narrow (position-based) proposals **Asks** about consequences of not settling **Asks** about likely court or other outcomes **Asks** about strengths and weaknesses of each side's case	**Helps parties** evaluate proposals **Helps parties** develop & exchange broad (interest-based) proposals **Helps parties** develop options that respond to interests **Help parties** understand interests	

Facilitative

D. Movement along the Continuums and Among the Quadrants: Limitations on the Descriptive Capabilities of the Grid

Like a map, the grid has a static quality that limits its utility in depicting the conduct of some mediators.

It is true that most mediators—whether they know it or not—generally conduct mediations with a presumptive or predominant orientation. Usually, this orientation is grounded in the mediator's personality, education, training, and experience. For example, most retired judges tend toward an extremely evaluative-narrow orientation, depicted in the far northwest corner of the grid. Many divorce mediators with backgrounds or strong interests in psychology or counseling—and who serve affluent or well-educated couples—lean toward a facilitative-broad approach. Sometimes, the expectations of a given program dictate an orientation; for example, narrow mediation tends to dominate many public programs with heavy caseloads.

Yet many mediators employ strategies and techniques that make it difficult to fit their practices neatly into a particular quadrant. First, some mediators deliberately try to avoid attachment to a particular orientation. Instead, they emphasize flexibility and attempt to develop their orientation in a given case based on the participants' needs or other circumstances in the mediation.

Second, for a variety of reasons, some mediators who have a predominant orientation do not always behave consistently with it. They occasionally deviate from their presumptive orientation in response to circumstances arising in the course of a mediation. In some cases, this substantially changes the scope of the mediation. A mediator with a facilitative-broad approach handling a personal injury claim, for instance, normally would give parties the opportunity to explore underlying interests. But if the parties showed no inclination in that direction, the mediator probably would move quickly to focus on narrower issues.

In other cases, a mediator might seek to foster her dominant approach using a technique normally associated with another quadrant. Thus, some mediators with predominantly facilitative-broad orientations might provide evaluations in order to achieve specific objectives consistent with their overall approach. Gary Friedman, an extremely facilitative-broad mediator, is a good example. When mediating divorces, Friedman typically follows the practice—standard among divorce mediators—of meeting with the parties alone, without their lawyers. In these sessions he routinely predicts judicial outcomes. He also emphasizes the principles underlying the relevant rules of law, and then encourages the parties to develop a resolution that makes sense for them and that meets their own notions of fairness. In essence, he evaluates in order to free the parties from the potentially narrowing effects of the law.

Frances Butler, who mediates child-custody disputes for a New Jersey court, provides another example. She uses a mixture of facilitative and evaluative techniques in the service of a broad, facilitative agenda: she asks questions (a facilitative technique) to help her understand the situation, then makes proposals (an evaluative technique), and then solicits the parties' input (a facilitative technique) in order to modify the proposals.

A narrow mediator who runs into an impasse might offer the parties a chance to broaden the problem by exploring underlying interests. This might lead to an interest-based agreement that would enable the parties to compromise on the distributive issue as part of a more comprehensive settlement. Similarly, a broad mediator might encourage the parties to narrow their focus if the broad approach seems unlikely to produce a satisfactory outcome.

For these reasons it is often difficult to categorize the orientation, strategies, or techniques of a given mediator in a particular case. . . .

NOTES AND QUESTIONS

(1) Some mediation practice books and materials are now distinguishing between facilitative and evaluative mediation and offering advice on when

these forms of mediation are most appropriate. For instance, Marjorie Corman Aaron discusses the many factors that should be considered by the mediator before providing the parties with an evaluation. M. C. Aaron, *Evaluation in Mediation,* in Mediating Legal Disputes 267–305 (Dwight Golann ed. 1996).

(2) Since its initial publication in 1994, the "Riskin grid" has provoked considerable commentary and controversy. In *"Evaluative" Mediation is an Oxymoron*, 14 Alternatives to High Cost of Litig. 31 (1996), Kimberlee Kovach and Lela Love argue that "evaluative mediation" is an oxymoron because anyone who engages in the activities Riskin describes as "evaluative" is not engaged in mediation. They do not argue that these "evaluative" activities are wrong or unhelpful, but rather that they should not be labeled mediation because they are inconsistent with the distinctive attributes of the mediation process. Kovach and Love would therefore draw a line that clearly distinguishes evaluation from mediation. On the other side, James Stark has argued that "case evaluation, performed competently, has a useful place in certain forms of mediation practice." James Stark, *The Ethics of Mediation Evaluation: Some Troublesome Questions and Tentative Proposals, From an Evaluative Lawyer Mediator*, 38 S. Tex. L. Rev. 769 (1997). John Bickerman takes the position that the parties often want and expect an evaluative mediator: "Without sacrificing neutrality, a mediator's neutral assessment can provide participants with a much-needed reality check. . . . Sophisticated parties ought to have the freedom to choose the mediation style that best suits their needs. . . ." John Bickerman, *Evaluative Mediator Responds*, 14 Alternatives to High Cost of Litig. 70, 70 (1996). Of course, Kovach and Love would respond that such an approach is fine—give the parties what they want, just don't call it mediation. Consider the arguments of Professors Love and Weckstein in the following excerpts.

(3) For a symposium addressing these issues see 2000 Journal of Dispute Resolution, issue 2.

THE TOP TEN REASONS WHY MEDIATORS SHOULD NOT EVALUATE

24 Fla. St. U. L. Rev. 937, 937-948 (1997) .*

By Lela P. Love

. . . The debate over whether mediators should "evaluate" revolves around the confusion over what constitutes evaluation and an "evaluative" mediator. . . .

An "evaluative" mediator gives advice, makes assessments, states opinions—including opinions on the likely court outcome, proposes a fair or workable resolution to an issue or the dispute, or presses the parties to accept a particular resolution. The ten reasons that follow demonstrate that those activities are inconsistent with the role of a mediator.

I.   THE ROLES AND RELATED TASKS OF EVALUATORS AND FACILITATORS ARE AT ODDS

Evaluating, assessing, and deciding for others is radically different than helping others evaluate, assess, and decide for themselves. Judges, arbitrators, neutral experts, and advisors are evaluators. Their role is to make decisions and give opinions. To do so, they use predetermined criteria to evaluate evidence and arguments presented by adverse parties. The tasks of evaluators include: finding "the facts" by properly weighing evidence; judging credibility and allocating the burden of proof; determining and applying the relevant law, rule, or custom to the particular situation; and making an award or rendering an opinion. The adverse parties have expressly asked the evaluator—judge, arbitrator, or expert—to decide the issue or resolve the conflict.

In contrast, the role of mediators is to assist disputing parties in making their own decisions and evaluating their own situations. A mediator "facilitate[s] communications, promotes understanding, focuses the parties on their interests, and seeks creative problem solving to enable the parties to reach their own agreement."[9] Mediators push disputing parties to question their assumptions, reconsider their positions, and listen to each other's perspectives, stories, and arguments. They urge the parties to consider relevant law, weigh their own values, principles, and priorities, and develop an optimal outcome. In so doing, mediators facilitate evaluation by the parties.

These differences between evaluators and facilitators mean that each uses different skills and techniques, and each requires different competencies, training norms, and ethical guidelines to perform their respective functions. Further, the evaluative tasks of determining facts, applying law or custom, and delivering an opinion not only divert the mediator away from facilitation, but also can compromise the mediator's neutrality—both in actuality and in the eyes of the parties—because the mediator will be favoring one side in his or her judgment.

Endeavors are more likely to succeed when the goal is clear and simple and not at war with other objectives. Any task, whether it is the performance of an Olympic athlete, the advocacy of an attorney, or the negotiation assistance provided by a mediator, requires a clear and bright focus and the development of appropriate strategies, skills, and power. In most cases, should the athlete or the attorney or the mediator divert their focus to another task, it will diminish their capacity to achieve their primary goal. "No one can serve two masters." Mediators cannot effectively facilitate when they are evaluating.

II.   EVALUATION PROMOTES POSITIONING AND POLARIZATION, WHICH ARE ANTITHETICAL TO THE GOALS OF MEDIATION . . .

III.   ETHICAL CODES CAUTION MEDIATORS—AND OTHER NEUTRALS—AGAINST ASSUMING ADDITIONAL ROLES . . .

IV.   IF MEDIATORS EVALUATE LEGAL CLAIMS AND DEFENSES, THEY MUST BE LAWYERS; ELIMINATING NONLAWYERS WILL WEAKEN THE FIELD . . .

---

9 John Feerick et al., *Standards of Professional Conduct in Alternative Dispute Resolution*, 1995 J. DISP. RESOL. 95 app. at 123.

IN PRAISE OF PARTY EMPOWERMENT—AND OF MEDIATOR ACTIVISM

33 Willamette L. Rev. 501 (1997), pp. 502–504, 532-535, 539-540, 547-550, 552-553, 559*

By Donald T. Weckstein

. . . I come to praise party empowerment, not to bury it! The success and effectiveness of mediation is dependent upon the free choice of disputants in determining how best to resolve their conflicts. . . . A coerced settlement is inconsistent with a legitimate mediation process, as is any resolution that lacks voluntary and informed consent of the disputants. A party who is unaware of important information or available alternatives to an offered settlement is prevented from exercising effective self-determination. . . .

This article attempts to answer questions concerning when, if ever, a mediator should give an opinion, evaluation, suggestion, recommendation, or prediction, or offer pertinent information or advice. . . . [T]his article contends that in several situations these interventions enhance rather than deny party self-determination.

The key to self-determination is informed consent. A disputant who is unaware of relevant facts or law that, if known, would influence that party's decision cannot engage in meaningful self-determination. A mediator generally should encourage parties to seek such information from other sources. However, if a party cannot or will not do so and looks to the mediator for guidance, it should not be considered improper for the mediator to serve as a source of pertinent information. Likewise, if the mediator's style is to offer that information unless the parties decline it, the mediator should be free to do so ethically. Self-determination extends to the disputants' willingness or unwillingness to be exposed to a mediator's educational efforts or evaluations. Accordingly, when consistent with the parties' expectations and the mediator's qualifications, activist intervention by the mediator should be encouraged rather than condemned. . . .

This Article attempts to demonstrate that educating disputants about relevant norms and information enhances, rather than undermines, party self-determination. It is difficult to imagine a conscientious mediator who would want or encourage disputants to make decisions concerning settlement in ignorance of important legal, technical, or other factual information. The decision of whether and how to use this information are determinations for the parties to make. If they choose to ignore it, it will be their intentional choice and not a default made in ignorance. Accordingly, the relevant inquiry should not be *whether* to inform the parties but *how* to inform them.

One option is for the mediator to volunteer "information" short of professional "advice. . . ."

Assuming the mediator is qualified by training and experience to give relevant information concerning wrongful discharge rights and remedies, at least two major problems must still be resolved: (1) Can the mediator give such information without sacrificing his or her impartiality? (2) Is there really a difference between offering such information and offering professional advice, assuming the later to be impermissible?

. . . If the mediator had anticipated the problem of the unrepresented status of the claimant, the mediator, at the outset of the mediation, and with concurrence of both parties, might have provided a brief summary of the applicable law. . . .

Even if the mediator had missed the opportunity to educate the parties in advance, information concerning legal norms still can be made available in the course of the mediation. One possibility is for the mediator to ask the parties at the beginning of each mediation whether they would object to the mediator informing them of relevant principles of law, as the need may arise.

Another practice, usable by the mediator . . . is to ask counsel for the respondent to briefly state his understanding of the main principles of the law . . . in the applicable jurisdiction. Because counsel knows that the mediator is familiar with the law, the presentation is not likely to be too one-sided. . . . A variation of this scenario would be for the mediator to ask the claimant to try to explain her understanding of the law in this area, and then ask respondent's counsel whether that also is his understanding. . . .

When one or more parties are represented by legal counsel, allowing a qualified mediator to offer legal information probably is more acceptable since counsel can correct any inaccuracy or imbalanced recital of relevant law. Nevertheless, some parties and mediators may still regard this type of mediator intervention as raising an *appearance* of partiality. . . .

Even if one party may benefit more than another in a particular matter, each party in every case has the opportunity to benefit from an activist mediator's offer of neutral, professionally competent information. There is no bias for or against either party, only a bias in favor of the integrity of the process so that all parties have the opportunity to be informed and, thus, empowered to engage in true self-determination. . . .

Mediator evaluations, although controversial, are little more than another way of making a suggestion or recommendation. When an evaluation is made in terms of how a court or arbitrator might evaluate all or part of a disputant's case, it is, in effect, a prediction. Predictions and evaluations go a step beyond a mediator's offer of abstract information. They speculate how a third-party decisionmaker or the mediator would apply that information.

. . . [P]redictions of likely arbitral outcomes are common and expected in labor grievance mediations. Predictions of how a court might determine issues in other proceedings also can be useful in overcoming impasses or establishing a framework for the parties to develop a resolution that meets their own notions of fairness. . . . While represented parties can receive that type of information from their legal counsel, a knowledgeable mediator's prediction provides more objective information with probably greater utility in the negotiations. . . .

Whether a mediator's prediction will be considered ethical likely will be influenced by one's preconceptions of the mediation process, the parties' expectations, the mediator's explanation of the nature of the prediction, and the way the particular jurisdiction treats other information-based interventions, such as professional evaluations and advice.

Since a predicted outcome that favors one party may raise questions of the mediator's impartiality in the eyes of others, the mediator is well-advised to phrase the prediction as one based on experience and study of relevant data, and not as a personal opinion. To avoid party misinterpretation, the mediator should explain that the prediction is only an estimate and the actual outcome may differ for various reasons, including, for example: (1) differences in the orientations and perceptions of judges, juries, and arbitrators; (2) the actual evidence offered and admitted in the adjudication; and (3) other environmental factors that might influence the tribunal. The mediator must emphasize that the prediction is not a directive or recommendation, and that the parties should reach their own agreement of a fair resolution, with or without reference to the prediction. . . .

Like predictions, other evaluations frequently relate to the strengths and weaknesses of a party's case . . . .

Mediation . . . initiates a facilitated negotiation process, during which a mediator's evaluation may become one of many factors used to aid the parties' self-determination of their dispute.

Evaluations, especially of a predictive nature, generally should be resorted to only after other more facilitative measures have failed to break an impasse. The manner in which the evaluation is presented may be critical to its reception by the parties. A "gestalt" impression of the value of a disputants' case, or general sense of how the mediator feels a court would determine the matter, is more likely to engender resistance from the party whose case is devalued, and to raise suspicions of partiality. A more effective—and acceptable—approach would be an issue-by-issue evaluation, particularly if combined with a decision analysis which seeks to establish probabilities of success at each step of a potential judicial proceeding. Normally, a mediator can minimize resistance to an evaluation by delivering it, with explanations, in caucus. If a decision analysis is used, however, the choices that would need to be made might be presented to all parties in a joint session, with the percentages of success and bottom-line settlement values worked out collaboratively by the mediator with each party in private caucuses.

Among the more controversial activistic interventions is the propriety of mediator evaluations or predictions raising questions of the fairness of proposed settlement offers. . . .

A mediator, like other professional practitioners, is obligated to subordinate his or her own interests to that of the parties served—subject only to the overriding interest of the profession's social function. Pursuant to this professional obligation, in certain circumstances, the mediator's role to assure the disputant's informed self-determination would ethically justify a greater degree of activistic intervention. Among the circumstances favoring enhanced interventions are: (1) when the parties request their use or appear to need or expect activist assistance from the mediator, and (2) when the dispute resolution context calls for accountability by the mediator to third parties or overriding legal principles. For example, activist intervention commonly would be justified if the mediator believed that the best interest of children of a divorcing couple were not being considered adequately.

As a general practice, perhaps incorporated in a standard of ethics, a mediator, at the outset of the mediation, should consult with the parties regarding their expectations and the mediator's usual style of mediation. Unless the parties indicate a preference for purely facilitative mediation or reject or limit the applications of specific types of activistic intervention, the mediator should be free to offer such interventions as he or she deems appropriate. . . .

[2] TRANSFORMATIVE MEDIATION

Recall that Baruch Bush had argued in the excerpt from his 1989 article, appearing above, that mediators should see their role as one of "empowerment and recognition." In his book with Joseph Folger, *The Promise of Mediation*, the empowerment and recognition role forms the basis for an argument that mediators should adopt a *transformative* orientation so that mediation can reach its full potential. A transformative mediation offers the parties opportunities for personal empowerment and encourages the parties to give and receive recognition of each other's interests, concerns, and needs. Bush and Folger distinguish transformative mediation from problem-solving mediation. They argue that the mediator's activities in a problem-solving mediation are too directed toward achieving the goal of an outcome that will satisfy the parties rather than providing the parties with opportunities for empowerment and recognition. Folger and Bush set forth the "hallmarks" of transformative mediation in their article, *Transformative Mediation and Third Party Intervention: Ten Hallmarks of a Transformative Approach to Practice*, 13 Mediation Q. 263 (1996). How does the transformative orientation compare to facilitative or evaluative? Is it consistent with one or both? [Read, or reread, the excerpt from Folger & Bush, Chapter 3, Section D *supra*.]

NOTES AND QUESTIONS

(1) The practice of transformative mediation got a boost in 1994 when the world's largest employer, the United States Postal Service, adopted transformative mediation for its REDRESS (Resolve Employment Disputes Reach Equitable Solutions Swiftly) program, in which postal service employees opt for mediation as an alternative to the Equal Employment Opportunity (EEO) complaint process. In *Upstream Effects from Mediation of Workplace Disputes: Some Preliminary Evidence from the USPS*, 48 Labor L.J. 601 (1997), Jonathan F. Anderson and Lisa Bingham report on a preliminary study of the REDRESS program in three pilot cities: "Ninety-two percent of supervisors and 41% of employees experienced recognition of the other's perspective. Over two-thirds of all participants felt increased empowerment over their situation. There is evidence that mediation is having a transformative effect on participants. . . ."

(2) For articles that discuss and analyze the themes and concepts of transformative mediation from various practice and theoretical perspectives, see *Transformative Approaches to Mediation*, Special Issue, Mediation Q., vol 13, no. 4, Summer 1996.

(3) For critical reviews of Bush and Folger's mediation model, see Carrie Menkel-Meadow, *The Many Ways of Mediation: The Transformation of Traditions, Ideologies, Paradigms, and Practices*, 11 Negotiation J. 217, 235–238 (1995); and Michael Williams, *Can't I Get No Satisfaction?: Thoughts on The Promise of Mediation*, 15 Mediation Q. 143 (1997).

§ D   MEDIATOR STYLES

A few empirical studies of mediators in operation have sought to identify and characterize the varying styles employed by individual mediators. Although the settings for these studies varied widely by type of dispute and locale, there are bases for comparison. In her book, *The Mediators* (1983), Deborah Kolb reported on a study of public sector labor mediators working for the Wisconsin Employee Relations Commission and the Federal Mediation and Conciliation Service. Kolb identified two distinct mediator styles—*dealmakers* and *orchestrators*. The state mediators tended to adopt a *dealmaker* style that placed a heavy reliance on caucusing and having the parties communicate through the mediator rather than directly with each other. One *dealmeaker* described the basic tactic used to strike a deal as "hammering." The federal mediators, on the other hand, tended to use an *orchestrator* style that emphasized flexibility and direct communication between the parties, putting the burden on the parties to come to an agreement. Susan Silbey and Sally Merry studied mediators in three Massachusetts-based community and family mediation programs. In their article, *Mediator Settlement Strategies*, 8 L. & Pol'y (1986), Silbey and Merry identified two modal styles of mediation, *bargaining* and *therapeutic*. The *bargaining* style tended to be more structured and controlling, employing caucuses and discouraging direct communication among the parties. It ignored emotions and concentrated on the bottom line. The *therapeutic* style, on the other hand, encouraged the parties to fully and freely express their feelings to one another. In the excerpt that follows, James Alfini surveys the styles of lawyer-mediators handling relatively high stakes civil cases in the Florida court-sponsored mediation program. He identifies three mediator styles: *trashing, bashing,* and *hashing it out.* The student should consider and compare these styles in light of the settings in which the mediators operated.

TRASHING, BASHING, AND HASHING IT OUT: IS THIS THE END OF "GOOD MEDIATION"? *

19 Fla. St. U. L. Rev. 47, 66-73 (1991)

By James J. Alfini

. . . Our interviews with the circuit mediators and lawyers revealed three distinct styles. These three approaches to the mediation process are characterized as (1) trashing, (2) bashing, and (3) hashing it out.

1. Trashing

The mediators who employ a trashing methodology spend much of the time "tearing apart" the cases of the parties. Indeed, one of these mediators suggested the "trasher" characterization: "I trash their cases. By tearing apart and then building their cases back up, I try to get them to a point where they will put realistic settlement figures on the table."

To facilitate uninhibited trashing of the parties' cases, the overall strategy employed by these mediators discourages direct party communication. Following the mediator's orientation and short (five to ten minutes) opening statements by each party's attorney, the mediator puts the parties in different rooms. The mediator then normally caucuses with the plaintiff's attorney and her client in an effort to get them to take a hard look at the strengths and weaknesses of their case. One plaintiff's lawyer described the initial caucus:

> The mediator will tell you how bad your case is . . . try to point out the shortcomings of the case to the parties and try to get the plaintiff to be realistic. They point out that juries aren't coming back with a lot of money anymore on these types of cases. They ask you tough questions to get you to see where you might have a liability problem or the doctor says you don't have a permanent injury so you may get nothing. They will try to get you to take a hard look at the deficiencies in your case that obviously I already know, but sometimes it enlightens the plaintiff to hear it from an impartial mediator.

Having torn down the case in this manner, the mediator will try to get the plaintiff and plaintiff's attorney to consider more "realistic" settlement

---

options. The mediator then gives the plaintiff's lawyer and her client an opportunity to confer, while the mediator shuttles off to caucus with the defense.

The defense caucus is similar to that conducted with the plaintiff, except that the mediator may present the defendant with a new settlement offer if the plaintiff caucus has resulted in one. A defense attorney described the caucus:

> During the defense caucus, the mediator will usually say, "Well you know they've asked for this figure and they think they have a strong case in this regard. Their figure is 'x.' They're willing to negotiate. They have told me that they'll take this amount which is obviously lower than the original demand"—if he has authority from the plaintiff to reveal that to you. If he doesn't, he won't say anything about that. He asks, "What do you think the case is worth? Why?"

> He'll then work through the case with us, pointing out outstanding medicals, lost wages and other special damages, then tallying them up and a certain percentage of pain and suffering and come up with a figure. And then they may discuss the strength of the case. I've had mediators say things to me in the caucus such as, "I was impressed by the plaintiff; I think they're going to be believable. Have you factored that into your evaluation of the case?"

If the trasher gets the defense to put a figure on the table that is closer to the plaintiff's current offer, the mediator will then shuttle back to the plaintiff.

Once the trasher has achieved the goal of getting both sides to put what she believes to be more realistic settlement figures on the table, she will shuttle back and forth trying to forge an agreement. If this is accomplished, the mediator may or may not bring the parties back together to work out the details of the agreement. One trasher explained that, once separated, he never brings the parties back together even at the final agreement stage.

On the whole, the attorneys appeared to accept, if not appreciate, the extreme caucusing methodology of the trasher. As one defense lawyer whose practice is limited to personal injury actions explained:

> We communicate through the mediator. Personal injury is a very emotional type of practice where emotions run high. What we find is that the personalities of the attorneys come into conflict, the personality of the carrier comes into conflict and the personality of the adjuster comes into conflict. So it's best to bring in a distance of parties. To walk back and forth and give some insight to each other.

Mediators who employ a trashing methodology tend to draw on their own experiences with the litigation process to get the parties to take a hard look at their cases. Indeed, all of the trashers that were interviewed are experienced trial lawyers. They call upon their own experiences not only to expose procedural and substantive weaknesses on both sides, but also to get the parties to consider the costs of litigation. One defense attorney explained that once the mediator points out the weaknesses and has the party assess the costs of litigation, the mediator will say, "'Do you guys really want to spend all this money to take this case to trial?' I see a lot of that which, for your typical insurance company, is a very fruitful approach." This same lawyer, however, saw this approach as less effective when representing government agencies: "It's not nearly as fruitful because governmental agencies, especially the sheriff, are such easy targets for lawsuits that nuisance value doesn't really exist. If we don't think we have done anything wrong, we generally fight to the bitter end even if we get clobbered."

If the trashing methodology is to be effective, the importance of having a mediator with litigation experience was underscored by this same attorney:

> I've had two occasions where we had a mediator that had never really litigated and had not dealt with the type of issues we were dealing with. In both cases, he, I felt, completely misperceived the issues and the possible exposure and liability. In one case, he thought we had horrible exposure and we really didn't, at least in my opinion. In the other case, he thought we had a great defense because there was a whole lot of things against us and we really needed to settle.

2. Bashing

Unlike the trashers, the mediators who use a bashing technique tend to spend little or no time engaging in the kind of case evaluation that is aimed at getting the parties to put "realistic" settlement figures on the table. Rather, they tend to focus initially on the settlement offers that the parties bring to mediation and spend most of the session bashing away at those initial offers in an attempt to get the parties to agree to a figure somewhere in between. Their mediation sessions thus tend to be shorter than those of the trashers, and they tend to prefer a longer initial joint session, permitting direct communication between the parties.

Most of the bashers interviewed were retired judges who draw on their judicial experience and use the prestige of their past judicial service to bash out an agreement. One of the retired judges explained that he emphasizes his judicial background during his opening statement to get them in the right frame of mind:

> I introduce myself and give them my background because I think that's very helpful to litigants to know they're before a retired judge with a lot of experience. . . . I tell them that even a poor settlement, in my judgment, is preferable to a long and possibly expensive trial together with all the uncertainties that attend a trial.

This mediator described the mediator's role as "one who guides," and explained why he believed that a retired judge makes an effective mediator: "If you're a retired judge you bring much more prestige to the mediation table than just an attorney because the people look at this attorney and say, 'I have an attorney; what do I need this guy for?' A 'judge' they listen to."

The notion that a mediator is "one who guides" suggests that the basher adopts a more directive mediator style than that employed by the trasher. The differences between the trasher and the basher in this regard were perhaps best revealed in their responses to a question we asked concerning the differences between mediation and a judicial settlement conference. The trashers tended to see the settlement conference judge as being much more aggressive than the mediator ("judges can lean on you, mediators I guess can, but they shouldn't"), while the bashers felt just the opposite. Another basher elaborated on his perception of the differences:

> The judge has to be very careful. Because if he expresses an opinion, the next thing he knows he's going to be asked to excuse himself because one side or the other will think he's taking sides. In mediation, you don't have to worry about that. You can say to the plaintiff, "there's no way the defendant is going to pay you that kind of money." You can say things as a mediator that you can't say as a judge.

As soon as the basher has gotten the parties to place settlement offers on the table, as one attorney explained, "there is a mad dash for the middle." One of the retired judges described a case he had mediated that morning:

> [T]he plaintiff wanted $75,000. The defendant told me he would pay $40,000. I went to the plaintiff and said to him, "They're not going to pay $75,000. What will you take?" He said, "I'll take $60,000." I told him I wasn't sure I could get $60,000 and asked if he would take $50,000 if I could get it. He agreed. I then went back to the defendant and told him I couldn't settle for $40,000, but "you might get the plaintiff to take $50,000" and asked if he would pay it. The answer was yes. Neither of them were bidding against themselves. I was the guy who was doing it, and that's the role of the mediator.

A defense attorney found this bidding process to be the most objectionable aspect of circuit mediation. He explained that it discouraged the responsible attorney from carefully evaluating her case beforehand and making an initial settlement offer that was both reasonable and realistic:

> [T]his is one of my real complaints about mediation . . . mediation is a game. . . . What mediation has done has said, "Look, if you do what you should do as a responsible attorney, what you do is establish a floor and when you get to the mediation, the mediator is going to expect you to move up." Otherwise, his position is going to be "wait a minute, you didn't come here with an open mind. You didn't come in a position to negotiate in good faith."

Another attorney found the bashing methodology totally inappropriate for complex, multiparty cases. The attorney offered as an example a groundwater contamination case in which he was involved. He said that the case involved a number of individual parties, insurance companies, and third party complaints against real estate companies. The mediation took place in a courtroom with a retired judge as the mediator. The mediator sat in the front of the courtroom and the attorneys and their clients sat together, theater style:

> We weren't even looking at one another. The mediator didn't have a clue as to what the case was all about. You'd think he would at least try to figure out who should meet with who and whether collateral issues could be dealt with. Just kind of organize the procedure.

But he didn't even do that. The mediator was absolutely worthless. It is the fact that the parties were forced to get together to talk that may force some settlements. It's hard to believe that it would be because of anything the mediator did.

Although the basher style is the most directive of the three circuit mediation styles, it apparently is preferred by some attorneys in circuits where it is the predominant style. A mediation program director in one of these circuits explained that she has received complaints from attorneys who felt that the mediator assigned to their case was "not pushy enough." They said that the attorneys had come to expect mediators who would "hammer some sense" into the other side.

3. Hashing It Out

The third circuit mediation style can best be described as one involving a hashing out of a settlement agreement because it places greater reliance on direct communication between the opposing attorneys and their clients. The hashers tend to take a much more flexible approach to the mediation process, varying their styles and using techniques such as caucusing selectively, depending on their assessment of the individual case and the needs and interests of the parties. When asked to describe the mediator's role in one sentence, a hasher responded, "Facilitator, orchestrator, referee, sounding board, scapegoat."

The hasher generally adopts a much less directive posture than the trashers and bashers, preferring that the parties speak directly with one another and hash out an agreement. However, if direct communication appears counterproductive, the hasher acts as a communication link. One explained,

> If the parties are at war, they communicate through me. If the lawyers are not crazy, they communicate with each other through me. If the lawyers are crazy, and the parties can talk with each other, they talk with each other. If nobody can talk, they communicate through me. My preference is that they communicate with each other.

When asked how he gets the parties to communicate, the mediator elaborated:

> I may caucus with them to find out if they can. . . . If they don't want to, I don't force them. If they want to communicate, I put them together and say, "OK, tell them what you told me, if you want to." Or if it's a really complex thing like a long list of demands, I don't want to have to memorize it because I'm liable to misstate something. I simply say, "you tell them." . . . I may warn the other side not to respond, just to hear what they have to say, maybe ask questions, but don't get defensive. Then I'll take them out. Then I'll get with the other side and say, "How do you want to respond to this? Do you want me to bring them in?"

In addition to this more flexible orchestration of the process, the hasher is also unwilling to keep the parties at the mediation session if they express a desire to leave, unlike the trashers and bashers. When asked what he would do if the parties expressed a desire to leave the mediation session prematurely, a hasher responded, "Mediation is essentially a voluntary process even though they're ordered to show up. . . . If they don't want to go through the process or negotiate, they're basically free to walk out." None of the bashers and trashers was willing to give the parties this much latitude. They all expressed the view that it was the mediator's prerogative to decide when the mediation session was over. As one basher explained, "It's my decision to either declare it an impasse and have everybody go home or to continue. It's not their decision. You have to reassert control."

The hashers also differed from the trashers and bashers in reporting a willingness to caucus separately with the attorneys or the clients if they believed it might facilitate settlement. One hasher explained:

> Sometimes, I talk to the parties and say, "Do you mind if I talk to your lawyers alone? I want to go through some procedural matters so that this thing will go a little smoother and a little faster." I ask the lawyers, "What do you want to do? How do you guys want to handle it?" Sometimes they say to me, "I really want you to talk to my clients. They're really unrealistic." I say OK and then figure out how to do it. I don't do it in an opening. I'll do it in a caucus. I'll get some tipoffs and leads by asking some questions of the counsel that leads me to do what I think he needs done. If his assessment is accurate.

Flexibility apparently is the hallmark of the hasher style of mediation. Although hashers prefer to adopt a style that encourages direct party communication to hash out an agreement, they are willing to employ trasher or basher methodologies if they believe it to be appropriate in a particular case.

NOTES AND QUESTIONS

(1) Does the identification of these various styles have relevance in the practice world? Consider the following from Thomas J. Stipanowich, *The Multi-Door Contract and Other Possibilities*, 13 Ohio St. J. Disp. Resol. 303, 371-372 (1998): *

> An example involving a leading architectural-engineering (A/E) firm illustrates the downside of indiscriminate emphasis on a hard-driven dollar settlement. Engaged in a two-party dispute with a major contractor, the firm sought mediation partly in hopes of enhancing communications with the other party. They chose a mediator who was a construction attorney with considerable mediation experience and many references. Unfortunately, the parties insufficiently explored the mediator's style and strategies and their appropriateness to the parties' goals. At the end of the day, the mediator had settled the dispute, but at a cost. According to the A/E firm's attorney, the only contact between the parties consisted of short

presentations before the mediator. The mediator quickly summarized the parties' respective positions and, having apparently reached his own conclusions about the bona fides, separated the disputants and spent the rest of the day "beating on the parties" to achieve a settlement. To the client's horror, no opportunity existed to enter into a mutual discussion or seek a consensus of any kind—only a "shuttlecock dickering" over dollars. Despite a dollar settlement, the client emerged with no intention to repeat the mediation experience.

If a leading A/E firm represented by sophisticated counsel has this kind of experience in mediation, one wonders what is happening in the great run of cases. Clearly, users and their attorneys need a good deal more education about the range of mediator styles and strategies, permitting meaningful inquiries of prospective neutrals.

Stipanowich's suggestion about educating the parties and their lawyers about mediator styles is a practical one, because it would allow them to ask prospective mediators meaningful questions about their styles prior to retaining the mediator's services. How might this suggestion be put into operation? Would this be best accomplished through mediation classes in law school? Through continuing legal education programs?

(2) Is one mediator style more effective than another if one measures effectiveness by either the percentage of mediations resulting in settlements or the parties' satisfaction with the mediation process? A few studies have attempted to correlate mediator style with effectiveness. In a study of labor mediators, Brett, Drieghe, and Shapiro identified two basic styles—*dealmaking* and *shuttle diplomacy*. Jeanne M. Brett, Rita Drieghe & Debra L. Shapiro, *Mediator Style and Mediation Effectiveness*, 1986 Negot. J. 277 (1986). Although they found that there were no significant differences in terms of the percentage of settlements associated with each style, they did find a correlation between styles and *types* of settlement. Settlement types ranged from compromise settlements to having the company grant the grievance. They concluded that the five labor mediators they studied "choose behaviors that they believe will facilitate the type of outcome they seek to achieve in a particular grievance." *Id.* at 281. In *The Settlement-Orientation vs. the Problem-Solving Style in Custody Mediation*, 50 J. Soc. Issues 67 (1994), Kenneth Kressel, Edward Frontera, Samuel Forlenza, Frances Butler, and Linda Fish analyzed mediator styles in 32 custody mediation cases and identified two contrasting styles, a *settlement-oriented* style and a *problem-solving* style. They concluded that although the *settlement-oriented* style was used in the majority of cases, the *problem-solving* style "produced a more structured and vigorous approach to conflict resolution during mediation, more frequent and durable settlements, and a generally more favorable attitude toward the mediation experience." *Id.* at 68.

(3) How influential is the type of dispute over the choice of mediator styles or strategies? One group of experienced mediators developed a settlement strategy model that located mediator strategies "along a continuum between two polar positions—neutrality and intervention." Sydney E. Bernard, Joseph P. Folger, Helen R. Weingarten & Zena R. Zumeta, *The Neutral Mediator:*

Value Dilemmas in Divorce Mediation, 4 Mediation Q. 61, 62 (1984). They then contrasted labor mediators and divorce mediators, arguing that labor mediators are much less likely than divorce mediators to adopt an interventionist settlement strategy. Is there a difference between mediator styles and mediator strategies? Does the word strategy suggest more of a conscious choice on the part of the mediator, while a mediator's style is more of an unconscious product of the mediator's background, personality, and training?

Chapter 5

LEGAL ISSUES IN MEDIATION

§ A INTRODUCTION

The purpose of this chapter is to present some of the more prominent legal issues that have arisen in the mediation process. Chief among these are issues relating to confidentiality, privilege, compelling mediators to testify, pre-dispute mediation clauses, the requirement of "mediation in good faith," and the enforceability of mediated agreements. While mediation is often touted as a flexible, non-legal process, unfettered by rigid procedures and rules, it is perhaps inevitable that with the more frequent use of mediation by legal professionals attempts would be made to make the mediation process more regularized and uniform. Thus, over the past decade, we have witnessed a burgeoning statutory and case law on mediation. Excerpts from these cases and draft provisions of the Uniform Mediation Act are reproduced in this chapter to illuminate salient legal issues. These materials are not exhaustive, however, of all legal issues in mediation. Some legal issues relate to topics that are covered elsewhere in this coursebook. For example, ethical issues facing the mediator such as conflicts of interest and the unauthorized practice of law as well as issues relating to mediator liability and immunity are explored in Chapter 7, *infra,* and legal issues concerning a lawyer's participation in mediation, including the lawyer's duty to inform a client of dispute resolution alternatives, are covered in Chapter 8, *infra.*

§ B CONFIDENTIALITY

Confidentiality is generally considered to be an essential ingredient in mediation. Policy concerns and legal issues arise, however, over the means that may be used to insure that the confidentiality of a mediation session is maintained. The materials in this section represent the various approaches to maintaining the confidentiality of mediation communications.

[1] POLICY

TOWARD CANDOR OR CHAOS: THE CASE OF CONFIDENTIALITY IN MEDIATION

12 Seton Hall Legis. J. 1, 1-3 (1988) [*]

By Michael L. Prigoff

Confidentiality is vital to mediation for a number of reasons. These reasons are discussed in detail below.

Effective mediation requires candor

A mediator, not having coercive power, helps parties reach agreement by identifying issues, exploring possible bases for agreement, encouraging parties to accommodate each others' interests, and uncovering the underlying causes of conflict. Mediators must be able to draw out baseline positions and interests, a task which would become impossible if the parties were constantly looking over their shoulders. Mediation often reveals deep-seated feelings on sensitive issues. Compromise negotiations often require the admission of facts which disputants would never otherwise concede. Confidentiality insures that parties will fully participate.

Fairness to the disputants requires confidentiality

The safeguards present in legal proceedings—qualified counsel and specific rules of evidence and procedure—are absent in mediation. In mediation, unlike the traditional justice system, parties often make communications without the expectation that they will later be bound by them. Subsequent use of information generated at these proceedings could be unfairly prejudicial, particularly if the parties' level of sophistication is unequal. Mediation could be used as a discovery device if mediation communications were admissible in subsequent judicial actions. This is especially true where a mediation program is affiliated with an entity of the legal system, such as a prosecutor's office.

The mediator must remain neutral in fact and in perception

The mediator's potential to be an adversary in subsequent legal proceedings would curtail the disputants' willingness to confide during mediation. Court testimony by a mediator, no matter how carefully presented, will inevitably be characterized so as to favor one side or the other. This would destroy a mediator's efficacy as an impartial broker.

---

[*] Copyright © 1988 by Seton Hall Legislative Journal. Reprinted with permission.

Privacy is an incentive for many to choose mediation

Whether it be protection of trade secrets or simply a disinclination to "air one's dirty laundry in the neighborhood," the option presented by the mediator to settle disputes quietly and informally is often a primary motivator for parties choosing this process.

Mediators, and mediation programs, need protection against distraction and harassment

Fledgling community programs need all of their limited resources for the "business at hand." Frequent subpoenas can encumber staff time, and dissuade volunteers from participating as mediators. Proper evaluation of programs requires adequate recordkeeping. Many programs, uncertain as to whether records would be protected absent statutory protection, routinely destroy them as a confidentiality device.

NATIONAL LABOR RELATIONS BOARD v. MACALUSO

United States Court of Appeals for the Ninth Circuit
618 F.2d 51 (1980)

Wallace, Circuit Judge:

The single issue presented in this National Labor Relations Board (NLRB) enforcement proceeding is whether the NLRB erred in disallowing the testimony of a Federal Mediation and Conciliation Service (FMCS) mediator as to a crucial fact occurring in his presence. We enforce the order.

I.

In early 1976 Retail Store Employees Union Local 1001 (Union) waged a successful campaign to organize the employees of Joseph Macaluso, Inc. (Company) at its four retail stores in Tacoma and Seattle, Washington. The Union was elected the collective bargaining representative of the Company's employees, was certified as such by the NLRB, and the Company and Union commenced negotiating a collective bargaining agreement. Several months of bargaining between Company and Union negotiators failed to produce an agreement, and the parties decided to enlist the assistance of a mediator from the FMCS. Mediator Douglas Hammond consequently attended the three meetings between the Company and Union from which arises the issue before us. . . .

During the spring and summer of 1976 the Company engaged in conduct which led the NLRB to charge it with unfair labor practices. Proceedings were held and the NLRB ruled that the Company had violated section 8(a)(1) of the National Labor Relations Act (NLRA) by threatening pro-union employees, and section 8(a)(3) of the NLRA by discharging an employee for union activity. At this unfair labor practice proceeding the NLRB also found that the Company and Union had finalized a collective bargaining agreement at the three meetings with Hammond, and that the Company had violated NLRA sections 8(a)(5) and (1) by failing to execute the written contract incorporating the final agreement negotiated with the Union. The NLRB ordered the Company to execute the contract and pay back-compensation with interest, and seeks enforcement of that order in this court. In response, the Company contends that the parties have never reached agreement, and certainly did not do so at the meetings with Hammond.

The testimony of the Union before the NLRB directly contradicted that of the Company. The two Union negotiators testified that during the first meeting with Hammond the parties succeeded in reducing to six the number of disputed issues, and that the second meeting began with Company acceptance of a Union proposal resolving five of those six remaining issues. The Union negotiators further testified that the sixth issue was resolved with the close of the second meeting, and that in response to a Union negotiator's statement "Well, I think that wraps it up," the Company president said, "Yes, I guess it does." The third meeting with Hammond, according to the Union, was held only hours before the Company's employees ratified the agreement, was called solely for the purpose of explaining the agreement to the Company accountant who had not attended the first two meetings, and was an amicable discussion involving no negotiation.

The Company testimony did not dispute that the first meeting reduced the number of unsettled issues to six, but its version of the last two meetings contrasts sharply with the Union's account. The Company representatives testified that the second meeting closed without the parties having reached any semblance of an agreement, and that the third meeting was not only inconclusive but stridently divisive. While the Union representatives testified that the third meeting was an amicable explanatory discussion, the Company negotiators both asserted that their refusal to give in to Union demands caused the Union negotiators to burst into anger, threaten lawsuits, and leave the room at the suggestion of Hammond. According to the Company, Hammond was thereafter unable to bring the parties together and the Union negotiators left the third meeting in anger.

In an effort to support its version of the facts, the Company requested that the administrative law judge (ALJ) subpoena Hammond and obtain his testimonial description of the last two bargaining sessions. The subpoena was granted, but was later revoked upon motion of the FMCS. Absent Hammond's tie-breaking testimony, the ALJ decided that the Union witnesses were more credible and ruled that an agreement had been reached. The Company's sole contention in response to this request for enforcement of the resulting order to execute the contract is that the ALJ and NLRB erred in revoking the subpoena of Hammond, the one person whose testimony could have resolved the factual dispute.

II.

Revocation of the subpoena was based upon a long-standing policy that mediators, if they are to maintain the appearance of neutrality essential to successful performance of their task, may not testify about the bargaining sessions they attend. Both the NLRB and the FMCS (as amicus curiae) defend that policy before us. We are thus presented with a question of first impression before our court: can the NLRB revoke the subpoena of a mediator capable of providing information crucial to resolution of a factual dispute solely for the purpose of preserving mediator effectiveness? . . . We must determine . . . whether preservation of mediator effectiveness by protection of mediator neutrality is a ground for revocation consistent with the power and duties of the NLRB under the NLRA.

The NLRB's revocation of Hammond's subpoena conflicts with the fundamental principle of Anglo-American law that the public is entitled to every person's evidence. . . . The facts before us present a classic illustration of the need for every person's evidence: the trier of fact is faced with directly conflicting testimony from two adverse sources, and a third objective source is capable of presenting evidence that would, in all probability, resolve the dispute by revealing the truth. Under such circumstances, the NLRB's revocation of Hammond's subpoena can be permitted only if denial of his testimony "has a public good transcending the normally predominant principle of utilizing all rational means for ascertaining truth." The public interest protected by revocation must be substantial if it is to cause us to "concede that the evidence in question has all the probative value that can be required, and yet exclude it because its admission would injure some other cause more than it would help the cause of truth, and because the avoidance of that injury is considered of more consequence than the possible harm to the cause of truth." 1 Wigmore, Evidence 296 (1940). We thus are required to balance two important interests, both critical in their own setting.

We conclude that the public interest in maintaining the perceived and actual impartiality of federal mediators does outweigh the benefits derivable from Hammond's testimony. This public interest was clearly stated by Congress when it created the FMCS: "It is the policy of the United States that (a) sound and stable industrial peace and the advancement of the general welfare, health, and safety of the Nation and of the best interests of employers and employees can most satisfactorily be secured by the settlement of issues between employers and employees through the processes of conference and collective bargaining between employers and the representatives of their employees; (b) the settlement of issues between employers and employees through collective bargaining may be advanced by making available full and adequate governmental facilities for conciliation, mediation, and voluntary arbitration to aid and encourage employers and the representatives of their employees to reach and maintain agreements concerning rates of pay, hours, and working conditions, and to make all reasonable efforts to settle their differences by mutual agreement reached through conferences and collective bargaining or by such methods as may be provided for in any applicable agreement for the settlement of disputes. . . ." 29 U.S.C. § 171. [F]ederal mediation has become a substantial contributor to industrial peace in the United States. The FMCS, as amicus curiae, has informed us that it participated in mediation of 23,450 labor disputes in fiscal year 1977, with approximately 325 federal mediators stationed in 80 field offices around the country. Any activity that would significantly decrease the effectiveness of this mediation service could threaten the industrial stability of the nation. The importance of Hammond's testimony in this case is not so great as to justify such a threat. Moreover, the loss of that testimony did not cripple the factfinding process. The ALJ resolved the dispute by making a credibility determination, a function routinely entrusted to triers of fact throughout our judicial system. . . .

Public policy and the successful effectuation of the Federal Mediation and Conciliation Service's mission require that commissioners and employees maintain a reputation for impartiality and integrity. Labor and management or other interested parties participating in mediation efforts must have the assurance and confidence that information disclosed to commissioners and other employees of the Service will not subsequently be divulged, voluntarily or because of compulsion, unless authorized by the Director of the Service. No officer, employee, or other person officially connected in any capacity with the Service, currently or formerly shall, . . . produce any material contained in the files of the Service, disclose any information acquired as part of the performance of his official duties or because of his official status, or testify on behalf of any party to any matter pending in any judicial, arbitral or administrative proceeding, without the prior approval of the Director. 29 C.F.R. § 1401.2(a), (b) (1979). . . . To execute successfully their function of assisting in the settlement of labor disputes, the conciliators must maintain a reputation for impartiality, and the parties to conciliation conferences must feel free to talk without any fear that the conciliator may subsequently make disclosures as a witness in some other proceeding, to the possible disadvantage of a party to the conference. If conciliators were permitted or required to testify about their activities, or if the production of notes or reports of their activities could be required, not even the strictest adherence to purely factual matters would prevent the evidence from favoring or seeming to favor one side or the other. The inevitable result would be that the usefulness of the (FMCS) in the settlement of future disputes would be seriously impaired, if not destroyed. The resultant injury to the public interest would clearly outweigh the benefit to be derived from making their testimony available in particular cases.

During oral argument the suggestion was made that we permit the mediator to testify, but limit his testimony to "objective facts." . . . We do not believe, however, that such a limitation would dispel the perception of partiality created by mediator testimony. In addition to the line-drawing problem of attempting to define what is and is not an "objective fact," a recitation of even the most objective type of facts would impair perceived neutrality, "for the party standing condemned by the thrust of such a statement would or at least might conclude that the (FMCS) was being unfair."

We conclude, therefore, that the complete exclusion of mediator testimony is necessary to the preservation of an effective system of labor mediation, and that labor mediation is essential to continued industrial stability, a public interest sufficiently great to outweigh the interest in obtaining every person's evidence. No party is required to use the FMCS; once having voluntarily agreed to do so, however, that party must be charged with acceptance of the restriction on the subsequent testimonial use of the mediator. We thus answer the question presented by this case in the affirmative: the NLRB can revoke the subpoena of a mediator capable of providing information crucial to resolution of a factual dispute solely for the purpose of preserving mediator effectiveness. Such revocation is consonant with the overall powers and duties of the NLRB, a body created to implement the NLRA goals of "promot(ing) the flow of commerce by removing certain recognized sources of industrial strife and unrest" and "encouraging practices fundamental to the friendly adjustment of industrial disputes. . . ." 29 U.S.C. §151.

NOTES AND QUESTIONS

(1) The Prigoff article and the *Macaluso* case focus on the policy reasons for protecting confidentiality in mediation. Are the policy reasons mentioned in the *Macaluso* opinion consistent with those enumerated by Prigoff?

(2) Would the court's decision in *Macaluso* have been easier if the parties had contracted for confidentiality through an agreement such as the one reprinted in the next section below?

(3) Note that *Macaluso* holds only that the *mediator* cannot be compelled to testify and does not impose a broader confidentiality restriction (the parties did testify). Does it make sense to prohibit the mediator from testifying but allow the parties to do so? Policy reasons?

[2] CONTRACT

Many mediators seek to establish confidentiality by having the parties sign a confidentiality agreement prior to the mediation session. A sample agreement is reproduced below. Beyond the potential legal benefits of having contracted for confidentiality, are there other advantages to having the parties sign an agreement? Does it assist in educating the parties about the importance of keeping mediation communications confidential?

CONFIDENTIALITY AGREEMENT OF RODNEY MAX

Reprinted in James J. Alfini and Eric Galton, ADR Personalties and Practice Tips (1998) at 236 ˙

This is an agreement by the parties to submit to mediation concerning _____. We understand that mediation is a voluntary process, which we may terminate at any time.

In order to promote communication among the parties, counsel and the mediator, and to facilitate settlement of the dispute, each of the undersigned agrees that all statements made during the course of the mediation are privileged settlement discussions, are made without prejudice to any party's legal position, and are inadmissible for any purpose in any legal proceeding. Any information disclosed by a party, or by a witness on behalf of a party, is confidential.

˙ Copyright © 1998 by American Bar Association. Reprinted with permission.

Each party agrees to make no attempt to compel the mediator's testimony, nor to compel the mediator to produce any documents provided by the other party to the mediator. In no event will the mediator disclose confidential information provided during the course of mediation, testify voluntarily on behalf of either party, or submit any type of report to any court in connection with this case. The mediator may find it helpful to meet with each party separately; in this event, the mediator will not reveal what is said by one participant to the other(s) without permission.

The parties and, if they desire, their representatives, are invited to attend mediation sessions. No one else may attend without the permission of the parties and the consent of the mediator.

We agree to pay fees at the rate of $_____ per hour for all time spent on this matter, plus any out-of-pocket costs. We have agreed to divide this fee equally between the parties.

We agree that the mediator has the discretion to terminate mediation at any time if mediator believes that the case is inappropriate for mediation or that an impasse has been reached.

Signature:_____
Representing: _____
Signature:_____
Representing: _____

_____

NOTE

Although many mediators have the parties sign confidentiality agreements, the courts may be somewhat timid if asked to enforce a confidentiality agreement. Enforcement is generally sought to preserve the confidentiality of a mediation communication, thus preventing the introduction of evidence that may be seen as crucial to deciding a particular case. However, such a result would go against the general policy that frowns on agreements to exclude evidence. Consider how this policy intersects with Rule 408 of the Federal Rules of Evidence, discussed in the next section.

[3] EVIDENTIARY EXCLUSIONS

[a] Introduction

As the court points out in *Macaluso, supra*, the mediator was "the one person whose testimony could have resolved the factual dispute." Yet, the court upheld the revocation of the subpoena of the mediator because "the complete exclusion of the mediator testimony is necessary to the preservation of an effective system of labor mediation." Thus, the court found that the strong policy reasons for preserving mediation confidentiality overrode the similarly strong policy that one is entitled to "every person's evidence." Similarly, Rule

408 of the Federal Rules of Evidence excludes from evidence certain communications made during settlement negotiations, effecting a strong policy of encouraging the settlement of court cases. As you read the materials below, consider how far Rule 408 protections extend. For example, would the testimony excluded by the *Macaluso* court have been excluded by Rule 408?

[b] Federal Rules of Evidence, Rule 408

"Evidence of (1) furnishing or offering or promising to furnish, or (2) accepting or offering or promising to accept, a valuable consideration in compromising or attempting to compromise a claim which was disputed as to either validity or amount, is not admissible to prove liability for or invalidity of the claim or its amount. Evidence of conduct or statements made in compromise negotiations is likewise not admissible. This rule does not require the exclusion of any evidence otherwise discoverable merely because it is presented in the course of compromise negotiations. This rule also does not require exclusion when the evidence is offered for another purpose, such as proving bias or prejudice of a witness, negativing a contention of undue delay, or proving an effort to obstruct a criminal investigation or prosecution."

CONFIDENTIALITY, PRIVILEGE AND RULE 408: THE PROTECTION OF MEDIATION PROCEEDINGS IN FEDERAL COURT

60 La. L. Rev. 91, 102–108 (1999)·

By Charles W. Ehrhardt

The policy of fostering free and frank discussions in negotiations which lead to settlement and compromise of actions prior to trial is recognized in Federal Rule of Evidence 408. Offering or accepting or promising to offer or accept a valuable consideration in compromising or attempting to compromise a claim is not admissible to prove liability for the claim. Rule 408 not only protects against the admission of offers of settlement and compromise but also prohibits the admission of statements or admissions of fact which are made during settlement discussions.

Many jurisdictions at common law limited the protection of the exclusionary rule only to the offers of settlement themselves and not to statements of fact or admissions of fault which were made during the settlement negotiations. However, the drafters of the Federal Rules rejected this distinction on the basis that such a limitation in Rule 408 would hamper "free communication between parties." There would be "an unjustifiable restraint upon efforts to negotiate settlements" and that continuing to recognize this distinction would be "a preference for the sophisticated, and a trap for the unwary."[40]

Two theories have provided a rationale for the rule that offers of settlement and compromise are inadmissible on the issue of liability for the underlying

[40] S. Rep. No. 93-1277 at 10 (1974).

claim. Wigmore's view is that an offer of compromise is not motivated from a belief that the adversary's claim is well-founded but rather a desire for peace. Therefore, he argues that the offer of compromise is not relevant because it does not signify an admission. There is no express or implied concession by a party when a offer is made.

Most modern commentators argue that the justification for the rule excluding offers of compromise is not relevance, but one of evidentiary privilege. This rationale recogizes the strong public policy favoring negotiated dispute resolution requires that offers of compromise be made without fear the offer will be used against the offeror.

The protections of Rule 408 to encourage free communication are available in all settlement and compromise negotiations. They include the traditional informal settlement discussions which occur between parties and counsel. The protection is applicable to all types of alternative dispute resolution, regardless of whether the jurisdiction additionally recognizes an additional protection for mediation; e.g. a local rule of a federal district court or a statute creating a privilege for mediation proceedings. Rule 408 applies regardless of whether some more specific protection is applicable. In other words, if a court determines that a testimonial mediation privilege will not be recognized or is not applicable, Rule 408 may still bar the evidence when it is offered at trial.

No specific statute or court-rule is necessary for Rule 408 to be applicable in mediation proceedings, regardless of whether the mediation is voluntary or court-ordered. Mediations involve statements made during attempts to settle or compromise a claim. However, some district court local rules as well as some states have specifically adopted a provision which applies Rule 408 to mediation proceedings, probably as a reminder to counsel and the parties.

B. Inapplicability

Rule 408 precludes the admission at trial of evidence of settlement negotiations which are offered to prove liability for the underlying claim. The second sentence of Rule 408 cautions that documents presented during settlement negotiations are not protected simply because they were so presented. In other words, the rule is not a shield behind which one can divulge pre-existing documents during settlement discussions or negotiations and have them protected from admissibility during trial.

The rule does not prohibit discovery of matters pertaining to the settlement negotiations. However, because a party is aware of the statements made by the opponent during the negotiations or the joint sessions, the availability of discovery is not as significant as it is when the party is unaware of the evidence. Although Rule 408 does not prohibit discovery of an opponent's communications regarding negotiation strategies, Rule 26(c) of the Rules of Civil Procedure as well as the attorney-client privilege and the work product doctrine may be applicable to protect these discussions.

Rule 408 is only applicable when the offer of compromise is offered to prove liability. The final sentence of Rule 408 provides that the rule does not require the exclusion of evidence relating to settlement offers when it is offered for another purpose, "such as proving bias or prejudice of a witness, negativing a contention of undue delay, or proving an effort to obstruct a criminal investigation or prosecution." This sentence illustrates some of the purposes for which the rule would not exclude evidence; it is not an exclusive listing.

1. Bias or Prejudice

If a witness testifies during a trial, the cross-examining counsel may attack the credibility by showing a relevant bias, prejudice or interest. Evidence of a settlement agreement involving the witness is admissible when it is relevant to show the bias of the witness when testifying in the instant case. The language of Rule 408 does not prohibit admission of the evidence since it is not offered to show the validity or invalidity of the underlying claim. The second sentence of Rule 408 specifically recognizes that evidence of the prior settlement may be admitted to show bias. The details of the settlement agreement are subject to a Rule 403 balancing, as are the details of other evidence being offered to attack credibility by showing bias.

2. Act or Wrong Committed During Settlement Negotiations

When the question is not the validity or invalidity of the underlying claim, but rather a material issue of an act which occurred during the negotiations, Rule 408 does not prohibit the admission of evidence. For example, when an alleged wrong is committed during the negotiations; e.g., libel, assault, breach of contract, or unfair labor practice, the evidence of statements made during negotiations is not being offered to prove the liability for the underlying claim and is not prohibited. Wrongful acts are not protected simply because they occurred during settlement discussion. The rule excluding settlement offers and discussions was not intended to be a shield for the commission of independent wrongs. So too, if a suit alleging that an insurance company failed to make a reasonable settlement within the policy limits, either the insured or the insurance company can offer evidence of the settlement offers that were made during the negotiations.

3. Impeachment

If a party testifies during the trial, a statement of fact made by the party during settlement negotiations may be offered as a prior inconsistent statement to impeach credibility. Applying the literal language of Rule 408, the evidence is not barred because the evidence of the prior statement is not offered to prove the validity or invalidity of its claim. This interpretation is bolstered by the policy that the rules of evidence should not be a shield to commit perjury. On the other hand, if a party's statements made during settlement negotiations are admissible to impeach whenever they are inconsistent with the party's trial testimony, the freedom of discussion in settlement negotiations will be inhibited. The few cases facing this issue are not in agreement. Most commentators assume that there are, at least, some cases where the interests of justice compel the introduction of prior inconsistent statements made during settlement discussions.

When Rule 408 is applied to evidence of statements by the parties or counsel during mediation proceedings, it does not prohibit discovery but does prohibit evidence which is offered at trial to prove liability or the absence of liability for the claim. However, when a statement of a party is offered to prove a material issue other than liability, the evidence is not excluded. For example, if it is asserted that a mediation agreement was the result of duress which occurred during the mediation proceeding, Rule 408 would not prohibit the testimony of the witnesses to what occurred. So too, if a mediation between a witness and a party resulted in a settlement which required the witness to testify in favor of the party in another action, Rule 408 does not bar the admission of the settlement agreement. In at least a few cases, statements made during a mediation may be admissible as prior inconsistent statements to impeach a witness who testifies during a trial to material facts which are inconsistent with what the party stated during the mediation. Even though Rule 408 does not protect certain statements made during mediation, a district court's local rule may protect confidentiality.

VERNON v. ACTON

Indiana Court of Appeals
693 N.E.2d 1345 (1998)

RILEY, Judge

The Vernons were involved in a car accident with Adam J. Acton (Acton) on May 9, 1995. The parties proceeded to a mediation with Paul Pettigrew on October 23, 1995; the mediation concluded that day. The Vernons filed a complaint for damages alleging negligence on December 5, 1995. Acton responded on February 29, 1996, and filed a counterclaim for breach of settlement agreement. The Vernons replied to the counterclaim on March 11, 1996. Acton then filed a motion to enforce settlement agreement and a motion for attorney's fees. Evidentiary hearings were conducted on August 13, 1996, and October 18, 1996. On November 26, 1996, the court entered its findings of fact and conclusions of law and judgment requiring the Vernons to accept the settlement and pay attorney's fees. The Vernons now bring this timely appeal. . . .

The Vernons contend that the trial court committed reversible error in the admission of certain evidence and the exclusion of other evidence. Pettigrew, the mediator, testified over the Vernons' objection that an agreement between the two parties was reached during the mediation and what the terms of that agreement were, but that it was never reduced to writing and signed by the parties. Additionally, David Young, the claims representative for Farmer's Insurance, was permitted to testify that a settlement agreement was reached during the mediation and the sum of that settlement. However, neither witness was permitted to testify as to what transpired during mediation beyond that information.

Both parties point to Ind. A.D.R. 2.11, about the confidentiality of mediation, to make their respective cases. However, A.D.R. 1.4 states that: "these rules shall apply in all civil and domestic relations litigation filed in all Circuit,

Superior, County, Municipal, and Probate Courts in the state." Ind. ADR 1.4; *Anderson v. Yorktown Classroom Teachers Ass'n, 677 N.E.2d 540, 542 (Ind. Ct. App. 1997)*. Because the complaint was not filed until December 5, 1995, after the mediation had taken place, the Indiana Rules of Alternative Dispute resolution do not apply in this case. See *Anderson, 677 N.E.2d at 542* (holding that the ADR rules were not invoked when the parties went to arbitration and no case had been filed with an Indiana state court).

Therefore, we must base our decision on Ind. Evidence Rule 408, which states:

> Evidence of (1) furnishing or offering or promising to furnish, or (2) accepting or offering or promising to accept a valuable consideration in compromising or attempting to compromise a claim, which was disputed as to either validity or amount, is not admissible to prove liability for or invalidity of the claim or its amount. Evidence of conduct or statements made in compromise negotiations is likewise not admissible. This rule does not require exclusion when the evidence is offered for another purpose, such as proving bias or prejudice of a witness, negating a contention of undue delay, or proving an effort to obstruct a criminal investigation or prosecution. Compromise negotiations encompass alternative dispute resolution.

Evid. R. 408. This rule does not require the exclusion of evidence when that evidence is offered for "another purpose." *Thomas v. Thomas, 674 N.E.2d 23, 26 (Ind. Ct. App. 1996)*, reh'g denied, trans. denied; *Hahn v. Ford Motor Co., 434 N.E.2d 943, 956 (Ind. Ct. App. 1982)*. The evidence admitted here is not about liability or invalidity of a claim, but to show whether or not a settlement agreement was reached. This is within the rules' contemplation of "another purpose" and therefore was properly admitted under Evid. R. 408. *Thomas, 674 N.E.2d at 26*.

Next, we must address whether the trial court properly excluded the testimony of Young at trial. The Vernons asked Young if he remembered a discussion that took place during the mediation; Young was not permitted to answer. (R. 225). Although this question was clearly soliciting evidence of statements made during the contract negotiations, the Vernons argue that they were not offering the evidence to show liability or validity of the claim, but to show whether or not a settlement agreement was reached. If the evidence addresses whether or not a settlement agreement was reached and not the merits of the negligence action, the trial court erred in excluding this testimony. Evid. R. 408; *Thomas, 674 N.E.2d at 26; Hahn, 434 N.E.2d at 956*.

However, this is not yet dispositive. "Reversible error may not be predicated upon an erroneous evidentiary ruling unless a substantial right of a party is affected."

When the trial court excludes evidence, the proponent must make an offer of proof to preserve the ruling for appellate review.

Here, although Vernon discussed the merits of his objection with the trial court judge, he never made an offer of proof on this point.

On appeal this court must determine whether the Vernons were prejudiced by the exclusion of Young's testimony. We cannot make that determination unless we have some idea what the testimony would have been; this is the purpose of an offer of proof. *Taylor v. State, 677 N.E.2d 56, 65 (Ind. Ct. App. 1997),* trans. denied. Because there was no offer of proof to aid us in our review, the trial court's error has not been sufficiently preserved.

The Vernons also contend that the parties contracted to keep any statements made during the mediation process confidential and inadmissable in court and that this contract should be honored by the court. Ind. Evidence Rule 402 states that "all relevant evidence is admissible, except as otherwise provided by the United States or Indiana constitutions, by statute not in conflict with these rules, by these rules or by other rules applicable in the courts of this State." Evid. R. 402. Evidence is relevant if it has a tendency to make the existence of any fact that is of consequence to the determination of the action more or less probable than it would be without the evidence. Ind. Evidence Rule 401. Whether or not Young and Pettigrew believed an agreement was reached through the mediation will aid in the determination of whether a settlement agreement was reached. The admitted testimony of Young and Pettigrew is relevant in this case. Furthermore, the evidence does not fall under one of the exceptions to the rule that all relevant evidence is admissible. Ind. Evidence Rule 403, 402.

As discussed above, the admission of evidence in connection with settlement negotiations is controlled by Evid. R. 408; when applicable, admission of evidence in connection to some form of alternative dispute resolution is controlled by the Indiana Rules of Alternative Dispute Resolution. Evid. R. 408; A.D.R. 1.4, 2.11, 3.4, 4.4, 5.6, 6.4, 7.3. In *Marchal*, the parties attempted to control the admission of evidence at trial pursuant to a mediation by stipulating that the mediator could testify at trial as to the contents of the mediation. *681 N.E.2d 1160.* We held that:

> neither parties, nor their attorneys, may enter into a stipulation which purports to bind the trial court with respect to a question of law; and any such stipulation is a nullity. A trial court commits reversible error when it enforces a stipulation, entered into by parties through their attorneys, which runs contrary to statutory provisions.

Id., at 1162. Although we recognize the parties' freedom to contract, here, the Indiana Rules of Evidence control evidence admitted during trial, not the agreement to mediate.

III. Sufficiency of the Evidence

Due to the fact that the trial court entered findings of fact and conclusions of law along with its judgment, the applicable standard of review is found in Ind. Trial Rule 52(A). "On appeal of claims tried by the court without a jury . . . the court on appeal shall not set aside the findings or judgment unless clearly erroneous . . ." T.R. 52(A).

The Vernons challenge the trial court's finding that "the essential terms of the Settlement Agreement and the respective obligations of each party are clear and unambiguous from the testimony before the Court." (R. 186). Whether a settlement agreement has been reached is a factual matter to be determined by the fact-finder. *Klebes v. Forest Lake Corp., 607 N.E.2d 978,*

982 (Ind. Ct. App. 1993), reh'g denied. There is testimony in the record from more than one witness about the terms of the settlement agreement entered into by the parties pursuant to mediation. From this testimony, the trial court judge could reasonably find that the terms of the settlement agreement are clear and unambiguous. The Vernons ask us to accept their version of the facts; however, as stated above, we will not reweigh the evidence or assess the credibility of the witnesses. *Hvidston, 591 N.E.2d at 568.*

The Vernons also challenge the sufficiency of the evidence of the court's conclusion that "plaintiffs have brought a frivolous, unreasonable and groundless action in light of the fact that settlement was reached prior to this lawsuit being filed." (R. 187). This determination was necessary for the court to award attorney fees to Acton pursuant to Ind. Code 34-1-32-1. For the purpose of this statute, a claim or defense is frivolous, unreasonable or groundless if:

> it is taken primarily for the purpose of harassment, if the attorney is unable to make a good faith and rational argument on the merits of the action, or if the lawyer is unable to support the action taken by a good faith and rational argument for an extension, modification, or reversal of existing law.

. . . In its findings of fact the trial court determined that pursuant to mediation the parties agreed to a full and final settlement of the Vernons' claim against Acton and that the terms of such agreement were clear and unambiguous. (R. 186). Since the claim had already been settled, the Vernons' complaint alleging the negligence of Acton in relation to the May 9, 1995, automobile accident was frivolous, unreasonable, and groundless. Therefore, we will not disturb the conclusion of the trial court.

CONCLUSION

The trial court did not err . . . in admitting evidence about whether an agreement was reached through mediation, and any error in excluding evidence was not preserved for our review. The evidence was sufficient to sustain the trial court's findings of fact and conclusions of law.

Affirmed.

NOTES AND QUESTIONS

(1) Professor Ehrhardt points out that Rule 408 is only applicable to communications that are offered to prove liability and discusses some of the other evidentiary purposes for which a particular communication would not be shielded by Rule 408. Professor Alan Kirtley describes these limitations as a "weakness" of Rule 408: "Since mediation discussions tend to be free flowing and often unguarded, revelations later serving as impeachment, bias or 'another purpose' evidence are likely. The 'another purpose' clause in the hands of creative counsel leaves little in mediation definitely exempt from disclosure." Kirtley also points out that Rule 408 offers no protection against

discovery of mediation discussions or against their admission in proceedings that are not governed by the rules of evidence such as administrative hearings and criminal cases. He thus concludes that Rule 408 is no substitute for a mediation privilege: "A mediation privilege should be of broad unambiguous scope, bar discovery, and exclude evidence in all types of proceedings." Alan Kirtley, *The Mediation Privilege's Transition from Theory to Implementation: Designing a Mediation Privilege Standard to Protect Mediation Participants, the Process and the Public Interest*, 1995 J. of Disp. Resol. 1, 11–14.

(2) The Vernons argued against the inclusion of mediation communications on two fronts: (1) the Indiana ADR Rules relating to confidentiality, and (2) a contract in which the parties agreed that all statements made during mediation would be confidential and inadmissable in court. As to both, the court ruled that the admission of evidence concerning settlement agreements is controlled by Rule 408 and ruled against the Vernons. Although the court's interpretation of the Indiana ADR Rules seems clear, why did the court refuse to give effect to the confidentiality agreement? Does it reflect a judicial bias against agreements to exclude evidence? If so, does this reinforce the argument for the kind of mediation privilege presented in the next section?

[4] PRIVILEGE

While the federal government and many states have enacted numerous laws to protect the confidentiality of mediation communications, this legislative activity has resulted in a hodgepodge of statutory formulations. To insure that confidentiality will be handled uniformly across all U.S. jurisdictions, the National Conference of Commissioners on Uniform State Laws (NCCUSL) and the American Bar Association (ABA) have undertaken the drafting of a Uniform Mediation Act. The drafting committee of the NCCUSL/ABA Uniform Mediation Act has chosen an evidentiary privilege as the means of assuring confidentiality. The relevant February 2001 draft provisions are reprinted below, preceded by Professor Alan Kirtley's article outlining the contours of an effective mediation privilege.

THE MEDIATION PRIVILEGE'S TRANSITION FROM THEORY TO IMPLEMENTATION: DESIGNING A MEDIATION PRIVILEGE STANDARD TO PROTECT MEDIATION PARTICIPANTS, THE PROCESS AND THE PUBLIC INTEREST

1995 J. Disp. Resol. 1, 20–35 *

By Alan Kirtley

With mediation so widely practiced in varying forms, the initial challenge is crafting a mediation privilege which is neither over-inclusive nor under-inclusive. The ideal statute would cover mediations where confidentiality is intended by the participants, the mediation is conducted by a qualified mediator and the privilege is justified as a matter of public policy. Most traditional privileges arise when a professional relationship is established: attorney-client, physician-patient or cleric-parishioner. Mediation is an emerging professional activity. Public licensure of mediators is a growing trend, but not the norm. As a result, it is premature in most jurisdictions to base the mediation privilege upon the formation of a professional relationship with a licensed or certified mediator. Other approaches have been necessary.

Narrow approaches extend the privilege only to mediations conducted under the auspices of a particular statute, court, mediation program, alternative dispute resolution procedures or mediators with specified qualifications and/or training. The advantage of such privilege statutes is clarity; specifically identifiable classes of mediations are protected. Policymakers are able to pinpoint specific mediations for protection, and in theory tailor the privilege's content to best serve a particular type of mediation: for example, family mediations or community disputes. The weakness of the narrow approach is that mediations equally warranting protection are not covered. For example, mediations conducted: 1) in a tort case where the parties and mediator desire privilege protection but the jurisdiction only has a privilege for marital dissolution cases, or 2) by a highly skilled mediator who, it is discovered after the mediation, fails to meet the training or experience requirements of the privilege statute. This approach also has the potential for confusion in states with several narrowly drawn mediation privilege statutes, rather than a general statute, if each provision has significantly varying terms.

In contrast to narrow approaches, other statutes have a broad reach. Laudably, these general rules extend the privilege across the entire field of mediation. Unfortunately, such statutes do so often without defining "mediation," or defining it so broadly so as to include any intervention by a third party. The unintended effect of such statutes may be application to a teacher attempting to settle a playground fight, a neighbor presiding over a family dispute or a bystander intervening in a dispute between drivers after a traffic accident. Recognizing these problems, certain provisions narrow the definition of mediation with qualifying adjectives: " 'mediation' is the *deliberate and knowing* use of a *neutral* third person." This effort to reduce over-inclusiveness with "self-referential" and vague modifying terms only opens up the privilege to *post hoc* challenges. The privilege would not apply if a party could later prove she did not realize or understand the nature of the process she had engaged in or could show that the mediator lacked impartiality or neutrality. Though well intentioned, the broad approach yields uncertainty and the potential for significant over-inclusiveness.

A third approach, found in a few statutes, is to activate the privilege when the mediation occurs pursuant to an order of court or agreement between the mediation parties. For example, the Washington statute triggers the privilege "if there is a court order to mediate, a written agreement between the parties to mediate, ..."[153] These statutes generally require written agreements to mediate to avoid the obvious proof problems of oral agreements. To activate the privilege, some of the statutes insist that the parties' agreement include

---

[153] WASH. REV. CODE 5.60.070(1) (Supp. 1994).

a recitation of statutory language or other language evidencing their intent that communications will be confidential. Such "magic language" requirements are unjustified traps for careless parties who nevertheless intended to invoke the privilege.

Requiring written agreements to mediate is not without its problems. For example, conciliation programs attempt to resolve disputes exclusively via telephone contacts with the parties and do not utilize written agreements to mediate. Also, in mediations where emotions are high, the trust level low and great reluctance to sign anything exists, such as in certain marital, labor or environmental disputes, requiring parties to sign an agreement at the beginning of the process may dampen or scuttle the mediation.

Of the three approaches examined, the Washington statute best minimizes both over-inclusiveness and under-inclusiveness. The Washington statute's broad availability is tempered by the court order/agreement to mediate requirement. Privilege protection is extended to disputes where most needed: parties in litigation and parties who unequivocally intended to mediate, both situations where the presence of a "professional" mediator is likely. By triggering its operation on the existence of a writing, the statute's application is unambiguous.

The Washington-type statute does have the potential for being under-inclusive. For example, those who mediate without a court order or written agreement do not access the privilege. Legally uninformed or careless parties and mediators are placed in peril. However, most mediators are cognizant of the importance of confidentially issues, and most regularly use written agreements to mediate. Moreover, policy-makers have options available to reduce the risks caused by the court order/mediation agreement requirement to particular mediation programs (dispute resolution centers) or subject matter areas (family law). They may eliminate the requirement for mediations conducted by specified programs or under particular statutes.

Once a mediation falls within the privilege, care must be taken to ensure that the entire process receives the privilege's protection (from the first intake call to the exit interview). Protection is especially needed for the sensitive information that is often disclosed by prospective mediation clients to program staff during intake interviews. Many statutes are vulnerable to narrow interpretation because they do not define the mediation process, define it vaguely with terms like "mediation," "resolution process," or limit the protection to information disclosed "during" or "in the course of" mediation or only when the mediator is present. Such statutes put into question the confidentiality of intake, inter-session and exit interview communications.

The Washington statute contains the phrase "any communication made or materials submitted in, or in connection with, the mediation proceeding."[170] The word "proceeding" encompasses the whole of the mediation process, similar to the word "case" in the litigation context. To add clarity some statutes specifically state that the mediation process commences with initial intake discussions, spans multiple sessions and ends only with resolution or termination.

---

[170] WASH. REV. CODE 5.60.070(1) (Supp. 1994).

B. Persons Covered by the Privilege

Mediators, mediation parties, the parties' lawyers and the staff of mediation organizations are involved in mediation. Others may be present during a mediation session: a party's family members or "support persons," staff members and outside consultants of an organizational party, "witnesses," mediator trainees and other observers. Once a mediation falls within the privilege there is no policy justification for allowing disclosure of information acquired during mediation by anyone. Everyone with access to mediation information should be "burdened" by the privilege.

Statutes vary in their effectiveness on this issue. Those that name no one risk an interpretation that the mediation privilege is limited to those in the "professional relationship," the parties and the mediator, leaving others present free to disclose or subject to subpoena. Other statutes which name only the parties, the mediator or both may limit the reach of the privilege to those named. The same result could occur with statutes that use the word "participants." Several statutes extend to all persons present. For example, the Washington statute places the burden of the privilege on "the mediator, a mediation organization, a party or any person present." By specifically listing all who may have access to information arising out of a mediation proceeding, the Washington statute ensures comprehensive protection against disclosure. It also eliminates the argument that confidentiality is waived by the presence of persons other than the mediator and the parties.

C. Later Proceedings in Which the Privilege Will Be Effective

Crafting a mediation privilege statute also involves considering the subsequent proceedings in which the privilege will apply. Traditionally, confidential information protected by a privilege is exempt from discovery and barred from evidence in civil and criminal actions. Mediation privilege provisions have taken differing approaches. Many are silent or list only "civil" cases. Other statutes extend the privilege to "civil and criminal," "any proceeding," "any subsequent legal proceeding," "judicial or administrative proceeding" or other proceedings.

Statutes referencing "civil and criminal" are consistent with existing privilege law and will undoubtedly be interpreted to extend to such actions. Judicial treatment is less certain for silent statutes and those using vague phrases: "any proceeding" and "any subsequent proceeding." However, if the state involved has a counterpart to Federal Evidence Rule 1101(c), then the rule of privilege will apply to "all stages of all actions, cases, and proceedings." Statutes limiting the privilege to civil cases may reflect a policy judgment that the criminal justice system's need for access to mediation information outweighs the benefit of preserving mediation confidentiality. A narrower policy consideration may be to protect the safety of those involved in mediation or threatened third parties. The latter concern is better addressed through specific exceptions to the mediation privilege. Mediation privileges which do not apply to criminal cases are inconsistent with traditional privileges and produce a chilling effect upon mediation discussions. Such statutes are particularly onerous in jurisdictions with programs for mediating criminal complaints. Such programs cannot operate unless the accused is assured mediation communications will be barred from the criminal trial. This reality was recognized by the Georgia Court of Appeals in *Byrd v. State*[200] , which, in the absence of a privilege statute, held that a mediation settlement agreement from a criminal diversion program was not admissible in the accused's subsequent criminal prosecution as an admission of guilt. In reaching this result, the Georgia Court of Appeals stated:

> By allowing this alternative dispute resolution effort to be evidenced in the subsequent criminal trial, the trial court's ruling eliminates its usefulness. For no criminal defendant will agree to 'work things out' and compromise his position if he knows that any inference of responsibility arising from what he says and does in the mediation process will be admissible as an admission of guilt in the criminal proceeding which will eventualize if mediation fails.

Even in mediations not directly involving a criminal complaint—family matters, neighborhood disputes and business situations—mediation discussions will be restricted if the parties learn that what they say or submit may be used later in a criminal courtroom.

Statutes, such as Washington's, which extend the privilege to "any judicial or administrative proceeding" properly protect mediation communications from use in criminal cases. They also recognize the prevalence of administrative justice in our contemporary legal system and the need to exclude privileged mediation communications from administrative hearings.

D. Holders of the Privilege

A critical task of any mediation privilege law is establishing who holds the right to assert or waive the privilege (i.e., a "holder" of the privilege). Holder status varies in the traditional privileges. With the attorney-client and physician-patient privileges the protection of the client/patient disclosure is paramount. Therefore, only the client/patient holds the privilege. In contrast, under the traditional rule husbands and wives are joint holders of the spousal privilege. Each spouse retains control over disclosures by the other.

With respect to the cleric-penitent privilege, statutes vary as to whether the penitent, the cleric, or both are holders of the privilege. In some jurisdictions the cleric may refuse to testify even if the penitent has waived the privilege in deference to the cleric's religious obligation not to discuss confidential communications.

The mediation process presents a unique context for the operation of an evidentiary privilege. Rather than the usual bilateral relationship in traditional privileges, mediation always involves at least three persons: the mediator and two parties. Additionally, two distinct relationships are at work simultaneously in a mediation: a professional relationship between the mediator and each of the parties, and a confidential relationship between the parties. Both relationships generate distinct interests in preserving confidentiality.

---

[200] 367 S.E.2d 300 (Ga. App. Ct. 1988).

Generally, the parties and the mediator share a common interest in maintaining the confidentiality of mediation communications. However, after a failed mediation, interests may diverge as to whether mediation communications ought to be disclosed. Each of the participants—the mediator or either of the parties—in different circumstances may wish to maintain confidentiality, or discover or introduce mediation information in a later proceeding. A mediation privilege must rationally reconcile these potentially competing interests in an unambiguous fashion.

Special care must be taken to protect the role of the mediator. Preserving confidences in order to maintain neutrality is elemental for mediators. As a result, mediators regularly refuse to be the "tie-breaking" witness in a subsequent proceeding, even when the parties so desire. Mediator testimony inevitably leads to one of the parties viewing the mediator as biased. Moreover, if mediator testimony becomes commonplace, the public is likely to form the undesirable perception that the particular mediator or the mediation process does not protect confidences. These important policy considerations were recognized by the Ninth Circuit Court of Appeals in *NLRB v. Macaluso, Inc.* The court stated:

> However useful the testimony of a conciliator might be . . . in any given case, . . . the conciliators must maintain a reputation for impartiality, and the parties to conciliation conferences must feel free to talk without any fear that the conciliator may subsequently make disclosures as a witness in some other proceeding, to the possible disadvantage of a party to the conference. If conciliators were permitted or required to testify about their activities, or if the production of notes or reports of their activities could be required, not even the strictest adherence to purely factual matters would prevent the evidence from favoring or seeming to favor one side or the other.[214]

Subjecting mediators and mediation organization records to subpoena disrupts the delivery of mediation services. This is particularly true for community dispute resolution centers which rely heavily on volunteers. Fighting off subpoenas, the usual response in these cases, is time consuming, costly and anxiety provoking. The limited situations in which a mediator may feel compelled to breach confidentiality irrespective of party preferences, such as to protect a vulnerable person or to prevent an injustice, can be accommodated through exceptions to the privilege. For these reasons, a mediation privilege statute should give the mediator holder status which is independent from that of the parties.

As with other aspects of the mediation privilege, statutes vary vastly as to their treatment of this important issue. Some statutes are silent as to who holds the privilege. Others assign the rights to assert and/or waive the privilege to the parties only, the mediator only, or the parties and the mediator as joint holders. A small group of statutes bifurcates the "holder" status by assigning separate rights to the parties and the mediator.

Silent Statutes: A silent statute can be expected to generate confusion in the tripartite setting of mediation. In one case, a silent statute has been interpreted to be non-waivable by the mediation parties.

---

[214] 618 F.2d 51, 55 (9th Cir. 1980).

Party-Holder Statutes: Statutes making parties exclusive holders of the mediation privilege are in accordance with traditional privilege law. Mediation parties as clients of the mediation professional exercise the privilege rights, as do clients and patients of attorneys and physicians under those privileges. Also, mediation parties exercise holder rights jointly because their special confidential relationship is analogous to the marital privilege. Party-holder statutes are also consistent with mediation ideology that lodges decision-making power with the parties. While the joint party-holder approach is appropriate with respect to *party* disclosures, the mediator is afforded no means to resist compelled testimony. Such statutes undervalue the critical interest of preserving perceptions of mediator neutrality for all parties in individual cases and the public at large.

Mediator-Only Holder Statutes: Statutes vesting "holder" rights exclusively in the mediator are consistent with the cleric-penitent privilege in a few jurisdictions, but an inversion of traditional privilege rights as to other privileges based on a professional relationship. The mediator is given sole authority to assert or waive the privilege. Mediation clients lose all control over disclosure decisions, even when all are agreeable to disclosure. Party preferences become legally irrelevant as to communications involving their privacy interests. Also, this type of statute invites undesirable lobbying of the mediator by a party wanting to disclose mediation communications. The mediator will make an enemy of one of the parties no matter what she does. The limited benefit of such statutes is that the parties cannot force *mediator* disclosures. Less restrictive alternatives exist to accomplish that result.

Joint-Holder Statutes: Statutes making the mediator and the parties joint holders of the privilege ostensibly balance the power to assert or waive the privilege. Mediators have the means to avoid compelled testimony; parties may assert the privilege against a mediator who has decided to disclose mediation information. However, joint-holder provisions have the potential for causing stalemate. While the mediator no longer holds absolute power under a joint-holder statute, she effectively has veto power over parties' disclosures. A mediator is unlikely to join in a waiver of the privilege to permit party disclosures if the result is that she may be called to testify. This statutory scheme also encourages parties to lobby the mediator. One party may seek a mediator's vote for disclosure as a means of convincing the other party to agree to waive confidentiality. Joint-holder provisions represent little improvement over other statutes examined to this point.

Bifurcated-Holder Statutes: Another approach to addressing the differing interests of the mediator and mediation parties with respect to disclosure of mediation information has been to bifurcate holder rights. Such statutes recognize that party disclosures should be solely within party control, free of mediator interference. Equally important, mediators are given the means to avoid compelled testimony. A few states have enacted statutes with bifurcated holder rights.

The Washington statute is an example of the bifurcated model. The privilege is waived as to *party* disclosures if all the parties agree in writing. The mediator has no control over *party* disclosures. *Mediator* disclosures, however, require the joint consent of the parties *and* the mediator. The effect of the statute is that a mediator may not disclose confidential mediation information without party approval, nor may the parties compel mediator testimony.

Bifurcated statutes fulfill the critically important function of protecting the mediator from being the forced "tie-breaker" witness. While parties may not compel mediator testimony under a bifurcated statute, their loss is limited. Parties who agree to disclosure may themselves testify freely as to what was said and done at the mediation. At the same time, each party as an independent holder of the privilege may block both *party* and *mediator* testimony. Bifurcated provisions properly balance the interests of preserving mediator neutrality and providing parties with significant control over the disclosure of mediation information.

UNIFORM MEDIATION ACT (FEBRUARY 2001 DRAFT)

National Conference of Commissioners on Uniform State Laws and the American Bar Association*

SECTION 3. DEFINITIONS. In this [Act]:

. . . .

(2) "Mediation" means a process in which a mediator facilitates communication and negotiation between parties to assist them in reaching a voluntary agreement regarding their dispute.

(3) "Mediation communication" means a statement, whether oral, in a record, verbal, or nonverbal, that is made during a mediation for purposes of considering, conducting, participating in, initiating, continuing, or reconvening a mediation or retaining a mediator.

(4) "Mediator" means an individual, of any profession or background, who conducts a mediation.

. . . .

(a) "Proceeding" means a legislative process, or a judicial, administrative, arbitral, or other adjudicative process, including related pre-and post-hearing motions, conferences, and discovery.

SECTION 4. SCOPE

(a) Except as otherwise provided in subsections (b) or (c), this [Act] applies to a mediation in which the parties agree in a record to mediate or are required by statute or referred by a court or governmental entity, or an arbitrator to mediate.

(b) This [Act] does not apply to a mediation:

(1) relating to the negotiation of or arising under the terms of a collective bargaining relationship;

(2) involving parties who are all minors which is conducted under the auspices of a primary or secondary school or correctional institution; or

(3) conducted by a judicial officer who might make a ruling on the case or who is not prohibited by court rule from communicating with an authority as provided in Section 8 (a).

(c) If the parties agree in advance that all or part of a mediation is not privileged, the privileges under Section 5 through 7 do not apply to the mediation or part agreed upon. The agreement must be in an authenticated record or reflected in the record of a proceeding. The parties must inform the mediator and any nonparty participants of the agreement.

SECTION 5. CONFIDENTIALITY OF MEDIATION COMMUNICATIONS; PRIVILEGE AGAINST DISCLOSURE; ADMISSIBILITY; DISCOVERY.

(a) A mediation communication is confidential, and, if privileged, is not subject to discovery or admissible in evidence in a proceeding.

(1) the communication is privileged under Section 5,

(2) the privilege is not waived or precluded under Section 7, and

(3) there is no exception that prevents disclosure of the communication under Section 8.

(b) In a proceeding the following rules apply:

(1) A party may refuse to disclose, and may prevent any other person from disclosing, a mediation communication.

(2) A mediator may refuse to disclose a mediation communication.

(3) A mediator may refuse to disclose a mediation communication of the mediator

(4) A nonparty participant may refuse to disclose, and may prevent any other person from disclosing, a mediation communication of the nonparty participant.

(c) Evidence that is otherwise admissible or subject to discovery does not become inadmissible or protected from discovery solely by reason of its use in a mediation.

SECTION 6. WAIVER AND PRECLUSION OF PRIVILEGE

(a) A privilege under Section 5 may be waived in a record, or it may be waived orally during a proceeding, if it is expressly waived by all mediation parties and:

(1) in the case of the privilege of a mediator, it is expressly waived by the mediator; and

(2) in the case of the privilege of a nonparty participant, it is expressly waived by the nonparty participant.

(b) A person who discloses or makes a representation about a mediation communication that prejudices another person in a proceeding is precluded from asserting the privilege under Section 5, to the extent necessary for the person prejudiced to respond to the representation or disclosure.

(c) A person who intentionally uses or attempts to use a mediation for the primary purpose of planning or concealing a crime or criminal activity, or committing a crime may not assert the privilege under Section 5.

(d) A person who violates a provision in Section 8(d) through (f) is not precluded by the violation from asserting the privilege under Section 5.

NOTES AND QUESTIONS

(1) Does the proposed Uniform Mediation Act (UMA) definition of mediation satisfy Professor Kirtley's over-inclusive/under-inclusive concern? Do the UMA confidentiality provisions extend to a broad range of subsequent proceedings? Are the right persons identified as the holders of the privilege? Are the waiver provisions sensible?

(2) Does the UMA privilege extend confidentiality protection to all the areas discussed by Professor Ehrhardt as not shielded by Rule 408?

(3) Although there currently is no federal statute recognizing a general mediation privilege, a number of federal acts provide for a mediation privilege in specific types of proceedings. Most prominently, Congress created a mediation privilege in the Administrative ADR Act that prohibits the disclosure of communications made during mediations under the Administrative Procedure Act. Even then, it is not clear that the federal courts will interpret these congressional acts as providing broad confidentiality protection. In *In re Grand Jury Subpoena*, 148 F.3d 487 (5th Cir 1998), the federal appeals court refused to uphold the district court's ruling that a federal mediation privilege protected against a federal grand jury subpoena for records of a mediation conducted under a state agricultural loan program. Although the relevant federal act (the Agricultural Credit Act) requires mediations to be "confidential," the Fifth Circuit ruled that it was not clear that Congress had intended to create a privilege that was so broad that it would protect mediation communications from a federal grand jury. In the following case, consider Magistrate Judge Kaplan's rationale for refusing to find that Congress had provided for a "mediator privilege" in the Alternative Dispute Resolution Act of 1998 that would extend to the mediation communications at issue in this case.

FEDERAL DEPOSIT INSURANCE CORPORATION v. WHITE

United States District Court for the Northern District of Texas
76 F. Supp. 2d 736 (1999)

JEFF KAPLAN, United States Magistrate Judge.

MEMORANDUM OPINION AND ORDER

Plaintiff Federal Deposit Insurance Corporation has filed a motion to enforce a settlement agreement entered into between the parties to this litigation at the conclusion of a post-trial mediation. Defendants John A. White and Donna A. White have filed a cross-motion to set aside the settlement agreement. For the reasons stated herein, plaintiff's motion is granted and defendants' motion is denied.

I.

The FDIC sued the Whites for violations of the Texas Uniform Fraudulent Transfer Act and civil conspiracy. Following a five-day trial, the jury returned a verdict in favor of the FDIC and against the Whites. The Court then ordered the case to mediation. Hesha Abrams was appointed to serve as the mediator. All parties and their attorneys were ordered to attend the mediation "and proceed in good faith in an effort to settle this case." The mediation was held on September 29, 1999. After a full day of negotiations, a settlement was reached and memorialized in a written agreement. The Court subsequently ordered the parties to submit the settlement papers and an agreed judgment by October 29, 1999.

One day before these documents were due, the Whites repudiated the settlement agreement. The Whites allege that, "throughout the mediation, they were threatened with criminal prosecution by the FDIC by and thru its representative, Andrew Emerson." As a result, the Whites contend that the settlement agreement was coerced and should be set aside. The FDIC maintains the agreement should be enforced according to its terms. Both parties were given an opportunity to brief the issues and present additional evidence and argument at a hearing on December 3, 1999. This matter is now ripe for determination.

II.

The Whites rely on their own affidavits and the testimony of their former attorneys in order to prove that the settlement agreement was coerced. These affidavits purport to detail the substance of certain comments made by the mediator and FDIC representatives during the mediation. The FDIC argues that this evidence is inadmissible because "mediation communications are privileged." (Plf. Motion to Strike P 4).

The applicability of evidentiary privileges in federal court is governed by Rule 501 of the Federal Rules of Evidence. This rule provides, in relevant part:

> Except as otherwise required by the Constitution of the United States or provided by Act of Congress or in rules prescribed by the Supreme Court pursuant to statutory authority, the privilege of a witness, person, government, State, or political subdivision thereof shall be governed by the principles of the common law as they may be interpreted by the courts of the United States in light of reason and experience.

FED. R. EVID. 501. The FDIC contends that Congress created a "mediator privilege" as part of the Alternative Dispute Resolution Act of 1998 ("ADRA"), Pub. L. No. 105–315, 112 Stat. 2993. The ADRA directs federal district courts to enact local rules requiring litigants in civil cases to "consider the use of an alternative dispute resolution process at an appropriate stage in the litigation." *Id.*, 112 Stat. 2994, § 4(a), *codified at 28 U.S.C. § 652*(a). Such local rules must "provide for the confidentiality of the alternative dispute resolution processes and prohibit disclosure of confidential dispute resolution communications." *Id.*, 112 Stat. 2995, § 4(d), *codified at 28 U.S.C. § 652*(d). In furtherance of this mandate, the Civil Justice Expense and Delay Reduction Plan for the Northern District of Texas has been amended to provide for the confidentiality of ADR procedures. The Plan now provides that:

> all communications made during ADR procedures are confidential and protected from disclosure and do not constitute a waiver of any existing privileges and immunities.

It is obvious that Congress sought to protect communications made during the course of mediation from unwarranted disclosure. "Confidentiality is critical to the mediation process because it promotes the free flow of information that may result in the settlement of a dispute." *In re Grand Jury Subpoena, 148 F.3d 487, 492 (5th Cir. 1998), cert. denied, 119 S. Ct. 1336 (1999), citing* K. Feinberg, *Mediation—A Preferred Method of Dispute Resolution*, 16 PEPP. L. REV. S5, S28-29 (1989). However, "confidential" does not necessarily mean "privileged." *Id., citing Nguyen Dan Yen v. Kissinger, 528 F.2d 1194, 1205 (9th Cir. 1975)*. Privileges are not lightly created and cannot be inferred absent a clear manifestation of Congressional intent. *United States v. Nixon, 418 U.S. 683, 710, 94 S. Ct. 3090, 3108, 41 L. Ed. 2d 1039 (1974)*. The Court does not read the ADRA or its sparse legislative history as creating an evidentiary privilege that would preclude a litigant from challenging the validity of a settlement agreement based on events that transpired at a mediation. Indeed, such a privilege would effectively bar a party from raising well-established common law defenses such as fraud, duress, coercion, and mutual mistake. It is unlikely that Congress intended such a draconian result under the guise of preserving the integrity of the mediation process. Certainly, the Court did not intend such a result by its order. *See also Fields-D'Arpino v. Restaurant Associates, Inc., 39 F. Supp. 2d 412, 418 (S.D.N.Y. 1999)* (ADRA does not make mediation communications privileged).

For these reasons, the FDIC's motion to strike is denied. The Court will allow the Whites and their former attorneys to testify about statements made at the mediation.

III.

John A. White and Donna A. White allege that they were threatened with criminal prosecution throughout the mediation. According to John White:

> On the date of the mediation, Attorney for the FDIC, Andrew Emerson, began the session with statements of not-so-subtle innuendos that I was in dire jeopardy of losing my freedom; however, if I would agree and pay the certain "agreed upon" amounts on time; that, while he could not promise me immunity, he would advise the Justice Department that the FDIC was only interested in the money being paid and not in me going to jail. Throughout the entire proceedings and particularly on the date of the mediation, I felt that it was being communicated to me by the representative of the

FDIC that if I did not agree to the settlement, the FDIC would take further action through the Justice Department in the form of criminal prosecution.

Donna White testified that she was frightened and intimidated by the prospect of going to jail. She stated that "time and time again, the mention of criminal prosecution was brought up" at the mediation. On one occasion, the mediator told Donna that "one of the worse case scenarios could be that I might be put into a position where I might be offered immunity from jail if I would testify against my husband." Donna said that she "felt coerced into signing the Settlement Agreement just to keep from going to jail." Rosa Orenstein, counsel for John White, confirmed that the issue of criminal prosecution was discussed at the mediation.

A.

The threat of criminal prosecution may constitute duress whether or not the threatened party is actually guilty of a crime. As one court stated:

> It was never contemplated in the law that either the actual or threatened use or misuse of criminal process, legal or illegal, should be resorted to for the purpose of compelling the payment of a mere debt, although it may be justly owing and due, or to coerce the making of contracts or agreements from which advantage is to be derived by the party employing such threats. Ample civil remedies are afforded in the law to enforce the payment of debts and the performance of contracts, but the criminal law and the machinery for its enforcement have a wholly different purpose, and cannot be employed to interfere with that wise and just policy of the law that all contracts and agreements shall be founded upon the exercise of the free will of the parties, which is the real essence of all contracts.

Greene v. Bates, 424 S.W.2d 5, 9 (Tex. Civ. App.—Houston [1st Dist.] 1968, no writ), *quoting Hartford Fire Insurance Co. v. Kirkpatrick, 111 Ala. 456, 20 So. 651, 654 (1896). See also* RESTATEMENT (FIRST) OF CONTRACTS § 493, cmt. c (1932). Of course, duress is an affirmative defense that must be proved by the party seeking to avoid an otherwise valid contract. *Greene, 424 S.W.2d at 8*. The critical inquiry is whether the party was induced to enter into the contract by the threat of criminal prosecution. *Id.*

B.

The evidence shows that the Whites were concerned about their potential criminal exposure long before mediation. And for good reason. David Groveman, in-house counsel for the FDIC, testified that a criminal referral had already been made before the case proceeded to trial in August 1999. Groveman told the Whites, though their attorneys, that "said referral once made is the province of the FBI and U.S. Attorney, not the FDIC." He reiterated this point several times both prior to and during the mediation. Still, Groveman maintained that the FDIC was only interested in getting paid. It was in this context that the mediator raised the issue of criminal liability. Although this subject was fully and openly discussed by the parties throughout the mediation, no overt or subtle threats were ever made by the FDIC or the mediator. In fact, it was *the Whites* who asked for a non-prosecution agreement during the course of settlement negotiations. They agreed to the settlement even after their request was rejected by the FDIC.

The Court finds that the settlement agreement between the FDIC and the Whites was not the result of duress or coercion. Accordingly, the agreement will be enforced as written. *See Bell v. Schexnayder*, 36 F.3d 447, 449 (5th Cir. 1994).

IV.

The written agreement signed by the parties at the conclusion of the mediation requires the Whites to execute certain documents in furtherance of the settlement. These include: (1) an agreed final judgment in this case; (2) an agreed judgment in John White's pending bankruptcy; and (3) a promissory note in the principal sum of $ 1 million with a graduated payment schedule. Copies of these documents are attached to the FDIC's motion to enforce the settlement agreement. John A. White and Donna A. White are hereby ordered to sign each document where indicated and return them to counsel for the FDIC by *December 30, 1999*. An agreed final judgment, signed by the parties and their attorneys, must be hand delivered to the chambers of Magistrate Judge Kaplan by January 7, 2000.

The failure to comply with this order will subject the offending party to monetary sanctions and a possible contempt citation.

[5] EXCEPTIONS

Recall that in the *Macaluso* case, *supra*, the mediator was "the one person whose testimony could have resolved the factual dispute." Yet, the court upheld the revocation of the subpoena of the mediator because "the complete exclusion of the mediator testimony is necessary to the preservation of an effective system of labor mediation." Should the court have carved out an exception to confidentiality and considered the mediator's testimony for the limited purpose of determining whether the Company and the Union had reached an agreement? As you read the Uniform Mediation Act provision dealing with exceptions to confidentiality and the related materials below, consider the policies that are served by each confidentiality exception and whether they are consistent with, or erode, the policies that protect the confidentiality of mediation communications.

THE MEDIATION PRIVILEGE'S TRANSITION FROM THEORY TO IMPLEMENTATION: DESIGNING A MEDIATION PRIVILEGE STANDARD TO PROTECT MEDIATION PARTICIPANTS, THE PROCESS AND THE PUBLIC INTEREST

1995 J. Disp. Resol. 1, 39–52 [*]

By Alan Kirtley

Mediation occurs after the events precipitating a dispute. During mediation preexisting facts, statements, documents and tangible objects are often presented. The availability of such information to the mediation process is critically important. A privilege rule covering such preexisting information encourages party candor. However, other policy considerations weigh in favor of not extending the privilege to otherwise discoverable facts and documents.

While the mediation process needs privilege protection to function effectively, the privilege should not permit mediation to become a blackhole into which parties can purposefully bury unhelpful evidence. For example, a party's admission during mediation that he falsified accounting records would be privileged, but his placing the records on the mediation table should not make the records privileged. Allowing discovery of preexisting facts and documents that are presented in mediation is consistent with traditional privilege and evidence law. The Washington statute contains a representative example of an exception for "otherwise discoverable" evidence found in several state privileges. These statutes follow the correct course by leaving the litigation discovery process undisturbed.

This approach however causes concern for unwary parties who tell or show "it all" during mediation. Such persons are unlikely to understand the distinction between privileged communications and the later discoverability of disclosed facts and preexisting documents. The concern is that unscrupulous parties will use mediation, where candor is urged and confidentiality promised, as an informal discovery devise. But barring discovery based on clues obtained during mediation would entwine former mediation parties in litigation to determine whether the source of the discovery lead came from or was independent of the mediation. The benefit is not worth the cost. Moreover, such a policy would be inconsistent with other privileges that do not protect facts, but only confidential communications. By carefully explaining the nuances of confidentiality, mediators can reduce the chances that mediation will become an informal discovery devise for unscrupulous parties. Nonetheless, mediation disputants and their counsel need to be aware of the consequences before divulging discovery tips during mediation discussions.

One form of otherwise discoverable mediation information merits privilege protection. In anticipation of mediation, parties may solicit preliminary appraisals, financial statements or expert opinions. This material is obtained to provide "ballpark" information for mediation negotiations. Washington and a few states maintain the privileged status for materials "prepared specifically for use in mediation and actually used in the mediation proceeding." Such statutes are consistent with the attorney-client privilege and the work-product doctrine. Only on very narrow grounds does the work-product doctrine allow discovery of the facts and opinions of consulting experts. Mediation's goals of encouraging informal, prompt and cost effective settlement are served if parties are not yoked with these preliminary estimates in later litigation.

b. Party Agreements and the Privilege

Parties usually begin a mediation by entering into a written agreement to mediate. Among other things, an agreement to mediate outlines the process, describes the mediator's role and sets forth the participants' understanding regarding confidentiality. Without an exemption to the privilege, such agreements remain confidential communications. This is despite the fact that mediation participants may need access to the agreement to mediate in order to demonstrate that the privilege was triggered, to evidence participation in a mandated mediation, to establish the terms of the mediator's undertaking or to prove a prior agreement to disclose otherwise privileged material. The Washington statute and a few other statutes have an exception for the agreement to mediate.

Settlement agreements present special considerations. Some parties are attracted to mediation out of the desire to preserve the privacy of their settlements. Yet, in certain cases, such as product liability and environmental cases, secret settlement agreements may do harm to third parties or the public at large. Also, parties may need access to their settlement agreement for enforcement purposes.

. . .

c. Subject Matter Exceptions

Among the most difficult policy choices in crafting the mediation privilege is deciding what particular classes of information should be excepted from the privilege in all instances. The process mirrors the analysis involved as to whether a mediation privilege is warranted. As to each type of information, the cost of the loss of evidence to the justice system must be weighted against the benefit of a broad-based mediation privilege.

A "laundry list" of subject matter exceptions has been enacted in various states or suggested. Examples include: (1) admission of threats to commit child abuse, a crime, a felony, physical/bodily harm, and damage to property; (2) information pertinent to a crime, an action claiming fraud or suits against the mediator; (3) information relating to the commission of a crime during mediation, and (4) use of mediation information for research purposes or non-identifiable reporting. In addition, some privilege statutes permit disclosure when mandated by another statute or a court. For purposes of the analysis that follows, the various exceptions have been organized in the categories of past criminal activity, ongoing or future crimes and threats of harm, and breakdowns in the mediation process and enforcement of mediated agreements.

i. Past Criminal Activity

[I have] argued that the mediation privilege ought to apply in all criminal cases. For the same reasons, admissions of past criminal activity made during mediation should not be excepted from the privilege . . . [E]xcepting admissions of past criminal activity would eliminate programs mediating criminal cases and stifle mediation communications in other types of disputes.

Admissions of past criminal activity do not necessarily present current or future risks of harm. Such an approach is consistent with the treatment of confidential disclosure of past criminal activity under traditional privileges. Undoubtedly, because of that body of law, most mediation privilege statutes do not exclude disclosures regarding past criminal activity. Mediation disclosures involving ongoing or future plans to do crime and threats of harm require separate analysis.

ii. Ongoing and Future Crime; Threats of Harm

The few mediation statutes providing for disclosure of criminal activity generally limit the exception to ongoing or future crime. Such exclusions are consistent with some views of the attorney-client privilege; society does not wish to allow individuals to seek out the assistance of a lawyer in planning or carrying out a crime. However, the other privileges generally do not have an exception for ongoing or future crimes. In mediation, where the context is a meeting of persons in conflict, there is substantial risk of retaliatory reporting of mediation information. For example, an exception that allows a party to report, and the mediator to be compelled to testify to, the other party's use of drugs, illegal gambling, welfare misreporting or not paying income taxes is not warranted. The risks such offenses present to individuals or society do not justify penalizing mediation candor. On the other hand, an exclusion aimed at "serious physical harm" is a justified policy choice.

Public policy favoring disclosure of otherwise privileged information is nowhere stronger than in the area of abuse of vulnerable persons such as children, the aged and persons with a disability. In most states statutes exist requiring the reporting of knowledge of abuse or neglect of vulnerable persons to a designated governmental agency, even if learned during a confidential interview. That position is consistent with the law governing traditional privileges where the risk of injury is serious. The interests of mediation confidentiality are not so unique as to justify a different result. It is not surprising that the most common exclusion in mediation privilege statutes is for information relating to child abuse. The same result is reached in states, including Washington, with an exception allowing for disclosure of information "when mandated by statute."

Few mediation privilege statutes allow for disclosure of threats of physical harm made during mediation. Most of these statutes limit the exception to credible threats of serious bodily harm or violence. Such exceptions allow a mediation participant who is so threatened to take protective measures. A more troublesome question arises when the threat is directed toward a non-participant of the mediation. Does the mediator have a duty to warn the third party or notify the police of the threat?

Applying the reasoning of *Tarasoff v. Regents of the University of California* [351] to the mediation process, mediators may have an independent duty to report threats against third persons. In that case, a psychologist and others were sued for failing to inform a third person of death threats made by the psychologist's client during confidential treatment sessions. The client killed the threatened person. The court held the risk of serious physical injury or death to an identifiable person created a duty for the professional to warn the intended victim. Important to the case was the fact that both the applicable psychotherapist-patient privilege and professional ethics standards permitted disclosure by the psychologist under the circumstances presented.

In response to *Tarasoff*-like risks in mediation, several mediation privilege statutes have an exception eliminating confidentiality for threats of serious physical harm. The absence of such an exception is a weakness of most mediation privilege statutes, including Washington's. A *Tarasoff* exception for mediation would eliminate the privilege "when the mediator or a party reasonably believes that disclosing the mediation communications or materials is necessary to prevent a mediation party from committing a crime likely to result in imminent death or substantial bodily injury to an identifiable person." Adding a *Tarasoff* exception would implicate few mediations, resolve the *Tarasoff* dilemma for mediators and potentially save lives.

iii. Breakdowns in the Mediation Process; Enforcement of Mediation Agreements

As with any dispute resolution mechanism, there will be breakdowns in the mediation process. Mediators may commit malpractice. Parties may fail to bargain in good faith. Mediation agreements may be tainted with fraud, or may be ambiguous or unfair. The mediation privilege should not provide a safe haven for participant wrongdoing or injustice. However, in allowing for disclosure of mediation information to deal with serious process breakdowns, care must be taken not to eviscerate the mediation privilege with exceptions that are too easily called upon.

A party claiming mediator misconduct must have access to mediation information and the mediator's testimony. A privilege that bars access to such information results in de facto immunity for malpracticing mediators. For that reason, and because the few claims of malpractice likely to arise will not greatly impact the operation of the privilege, a clear-cut exception to the privilege for mediator malpractice is appropriate. The Washington statute and a few other statutes address this obvious need. The Washington statute provides an exception to the privilege "in a subsequent action between the mediator and a party to the mediation arising out of the mediation." Exceptions for malpractice by mediators would be improved by explicit language permitting disclosure to mediator licensing authorities as well. Mediators also need access to mediation information to defend themselves against claims and

---

[351] 551 P.2d 334 ([Cal.] 1976).

charges, and to bring suit against parties, usually to collect agreed upon fees. Several exceptions accommodate such mediator needs for disclosure.

Good faith bargaining is the pathway to mediated settlements. However, providing an exception to the mediation privilege based on a claim of bad faith bargaining, short of fraud, is problematic. Most parties undertake mediation voluntarily. While such parties often negotiate under a mediator's entreaty to bargain in good faith, they may discontinue negotiations at will. When parties mediate voluntarily, mediation discussions should not be revealed based on a claim of bad faith negotiations. Negotiating in bad faith is often in the eyes of the beholder. Stonewalling or moving in small increments may be justified in particular mediations. Parties who become frustrated by their opponents' bargaining tactics have the option of withdrawing from the mediation and pursuing other means of resolving the dispute.

A different approach is justified when mediation parties come to the table involuntarily and under a statutory obligation to bargain in good faith, such as in labor mediation, farmer/creditor mediation and mandatory child custody mediation. In such cases, mediation communications are essential evidence to prove or defend against a claim of bad faith bargaining. Mediation communications should be available in contexts when parties have a statutory obligation to bargain in good faith, established standards of good faith bargaining exist and bargaining in bad faith is actionable. For example, in a school district/teachers' union mediation, if one side bargains in bad faith, mediation communications must be revealable to an administrative judge or court in order to obtain or oppose the requested relief. For that reason, some mediation privilege statutes eliminate confidentiality for claims of bad faith bargaining in mandatory mediations or simply exclude mediations in which negotiating in good faith is a legal obligation. While in this context parties should be free to introduce mediation communications to enforce good faith bargaining laws, the mediator should not be compelled to testify. It was on precisely that issue that the *Macaluso* and other court decisions provided the genesis of the mediation privilege.

Most would agree that mediation settlements tainted by fraud, obtained through duress or deemed unconscionable should not be enforceable. Yet relatively few mediation privilege statutes address these issues, and those that do mostly contain only fraud exceptions. This deviation from what might be expected may reflect the conclusion that fraud, duress and unconscionability are present in few mediations, and may reflect the concern that exceptions dealing with those ills will open the mediation privilege to widespread misuse by parties suffering from "bargainer's remorse." For example, a stated fraud exception to the privilege could be cited by those unwilling to abide by their mediation agreements, whether justified or not. Undoubtedly, states without fraud, duress or unconscionability exemptions, such as Washington, recognize that courts are likely to be willing to set aside the privilege when presented with viable contract defenses to the enforcement of a mediation settlement agreement. Once in court, mediation participants who wish to make out a case of fraud, for example, could seek *a priori* approval from the judge to present mediation information. By hearing the competing claims *in camera,* the court could preserve confidentiality unless disclosure was held to be necessary and appropriate. Since the parties will be able to present evidence related to fraud, duress or unconscionability, mediators should not be compelled to testify as the "tie-breaking" witness. A similar approach is appropriate when interpretive issues arise regarding the meaning of a settlement agreement.

UNIFORM MEDIATION ACT (FEBRUARY 2001 DRAFT)

National Conference of Commissioners on Uniform State Laws and the American Bar Association *

SECTION 7. EXCEPTIONS TO PRIVILEGE.

(a) There is no privilege against disclosure under Section 5 for a mediation communication which is:

(1) an agreement evidenced by a record authenticated by all parties to the agreement;

(2) available to the public [open records law] or that is made during a session of a mediation which is open to the public or is required by law to be open to the public;

(3) a threat to inflict bodily injury;

(4) intentionally used to plan, attempt to commit, or commit a crime, or conceal an ongoing crime or criminal activity;

(5) sought or offered to prove or disprove abuse, neglect, abandonment, or exploitation in a proceeding in which a public agency is protecting the interests of an individual protected by law; but this exception does not apply where a [child protection] case is referred to participate in mediation by a court and a public agency participates [, or a public agency participates in the child protection mediation];

(6) sought or offered to prove or disprove a claim or complaint of professional misconduct or malpractice filed against a mediator in a proceeding; or

(7) sought or offered to prove or disprove a claim or complaint of professional misconduct or malpractice filed against a party, nonparty participant, or a representative of a party based on conduct occurring during a mediation;

(b) There is no privilege under Section 5 if a court, administrative agency, or arbitration panel finds, after a hearing in camera, that the party seeking discovery or the proponent of the evidence has shown that the evidence is not otherwise available, that there is a need for the evidence that substantially outweighs the interest in protecting confidentiality and the mediation communication is sought or offered in:

(1) a court proceeding involving a felony; or

(2) a proceeding to prove a claim or defense under other law sufficient to reform or avoid liability on a contract arising out of the mediation.

(c) Notwithstanding subsections 7(a)(7) and 7(b)(2), a mediator may not be compelled to provide evidence of a mediation communication or testify in such proceedings.

(d) If a mediation communication is not privileged under an exception in subsection (a) or (b), only the portion of the communication necessary for the application of the exception for nondisclosure may be admitted. The admission of particular evidence for the limited purpose of an exception does not render that evidence, or any other mediation communication, admissible for any other purpose.

NOTES AND QUESTIONS

(1) Does the draft Uniform Mediation Act section dealing with exceptions to a mediation privilege provide for all of the exceptions delineated by Professor Kirtley? Would Kirtley agree with the wording of the UMA exception "a threat to inflict bodily injury"?

(2) In the following cases, courts wrestle with the application of mediation privilege exceptions. As you read these cases, consider how well each court considers the policy concerns raised by Professor Kirtley and the UMA provision.

OHIO EX REL. SCHNEIDER v. KREINER

Ohio Supreme Court
699 N.E.2d 83 (1998)

In 1988, relator, Tom Schneider ("Schneider"), married Theresa Schneider. They had two children. In 1994, the Schneiders divorced and entered into a shared parenting agreement. Subsequently, criminal charges were filed against Schneider for violating the agreement. The criminal case was referred to the Private Complaint Mediation Service ("Mediation Service"). The Mediation Service, established by the Hamilton County Municipal Court, mediates disputes between parties in certain municipal court cases.

During a mediation of this type, the mediator listens to the positions of both parties and then asks each party to agree on the issues and to recommend possible solutions. If an agreement is reached, the mediation concludes, but the parties do not sign a written agreement. However, the mediator may suggest that each party take notes regarding the requirements of the agreement. At the conclusion of the mediation, a "Statement of Voluntary Settlement" is signed by the parties and filed with the court. In addition, the mediator completes a "Preliminary Complaint Form." On the form, the mediator describes the allegations made by the plaintiff, denotes the relationship between the parties, and compiles information relating to the parties and the status of the dispute. The mediator also describes the disposition of the dispute under a section entitled "Hearing Disposition." Under another section, the mediator states what future action may be taken if the agreement is broken and, under a "Comments" section, may make personal observations about the mediation and the dispute. This form is not shown to the parties and, unlike the Statement of Voluntary Settlement, is not signed by them.

In December 1996, the Mediation Service mediated the case. Schneider and his former spouse agreed to perform and refrain from performing certain acts in exchange for the dismissal of the criminal charges against Schneider. The parties signed the Statement of Voluntary Settlement form indicating their agreement.

Subsequently, Schneider requested access to the entire mediation file from respondent, Cathleen Kreiner, director of the Mediation Service. Included in the file was a copy of the complaint form prepared by the mediator. Kreiner denied access to the file. Kreiner later offered to provide Schneider a copy of the Statement of Voluntary Settlement and a disposition report of the mediation service, both of which were filed in the office of the clerk of courts.

Schneider then filed a complaint requesting a writ of mandamus to compel Kreiner to provide him access to the complaint form. Schneider also requested attorney fees. This court granted an alternative writ and issued a schedule for the presentation of evidence and briefs.

This cause is now before the court for a consideration of Schneider's request for oral argument as well as the merits.

MOYER, CJ

For the reasons that follow, we deny relator's request for oral argument and his request for a writ of mandamus.

. . . .

II

Relator contends that he is entitled to a writ of mandamus under *R.C. 149.43.* We have construed *R.C. 149.43* " 'to ensure that governmental records be open and made available to the public * * * subject to only a few very limited and narrow exceptions.' " *State ex rel. The Plain Dealer v. Ohio Dept. of Ins. (1997), 80 Ohio St. 3d 513, 518, 687 N.E.2d 661, 668,* quoting *State ex rel. Williams v. Cleveland (1992), 64 Ohio St. 3d 544, 549, 597 N.E.2d 147, 151.*

Among those exceptions in effect at the time of relator's request was former *R.C. 149.43(A)(1)(k),* 146 Ohio Laws, Part III, 4661, which provided that public records do not include "records the release of which is prohibited by state or federal law." Respondent asserts that *R.C. 2317.023* exempts the requested complaint form from disclosure as a confidential mediation communication. We agree with the respondent.

R.C. 2317.023 provides:

"(A) As used in this section:

"(1) 'Mediation' means a nonbinding process for the resolution of a dispute in which both of the following apply:

"(a) A person who is not a party to the dispute serves as mediator to assist the parties to the dispute in negotiating contested issues.

"(b) A court, administrative agency, not-for-profit community mediation provider, or other public body appoints the mediator or refers the dispute to the mediator, or the parties, engage the mediator.

"(2) 'Mediation communication' means a communication made in the course of and relating to the subject matter of a mediation.

"(B) *A mediation communication is confidential. Except as provided in division (C) of this section, no person shall disclose a mediation communication in a civil proceeding or in an administrative proceeding.*" (Emphasis added.)

Pursuant to the statute, the initial question is whether the complaint form sought by Schneider is a "mediation communication" as defined by the statute. *R.C. 2317.023(A)(2)* defines a mediation communication as "a communication made in the course of and relating to the subject matter of the mediation." The document sought here is a complaint form completed by the mediator. The mediator, in completing the form, describes information relating to the parties and the nature of the dispute. Significantly, the mediator also describes the disposition of the dispute under a section entitled "Hearing Disposition," and may make personal observations about the dispute under a separate section.

Under the statutory definition, it is clear that this form is a mediation communication. It is made in the course of the mediation by the mediator. The mediator compiles information on the form and then describes the outcome. The form is also related to the subject matter of the mediation. The form contains information about the dispute between the parties. It also reflects the thoughts and impressions of the mediator as to the outcome of the mediation, whether and what action shall be taken in the event of breach of the agreement, and the mediator's own observations about the mediation.

R.C. 2317.023(B) states that "[a] mediation communication is confidential." The words of this statute are clear. Mediation communications are confidential and may not be disclosed. "An unambiguous statute means what it says." *Hakim v. Kosydar (1977), 49 Ohio St. 2d 161, 164, 3 Ohio Op. 3d 211, 213, 359 N.E.2d 1371, 1373.* We give words in statutes their plain and ordinary meaning unless otherwise defined. *Coventry Towers, Inc. v. Strongsville (1985), 18 Ohio St. 3d 120, 122, 18 Ohio B. Rep. 151, 152, 480 N.E.2d 412, 414.* Accordingly, having determined that the document sought by relator is a mediation communication, we are compelled by the words of the statute to conclude that the form is confidential and may not be disclosed, unless one of the exceptions enumerated in *R.C. 2317.023(C)* applies to the relator's cause.

Relator contends that the confidentiality requirement of *R.C. 2317.023(B)* does not apply because *R.C. 2317.023(C)(1)* and (4) preclude the application of *R.C. 2317.023(B)*. We disagree.

R.C. 2317.023(C) provides:

"Division (B) of this section does not apply in the following circumstances:

"(1) * * * To the disclosure by any person of a mediation communication made by a mediator if all parties to the mediation and the mediator consent to the disclosure;

"* * *

"(4) To the disclosure of a mediation communication if a court, after a hearing, determines that the disclosure does not circumvent Evidence Rule 408, that the disclosure is necessary in the particular case to prevent a manifest injustice, and that the necessity for disclosure is of sufficient magnitude to outweigh the importance of protecting the general requirement of confidentiality in mediation proceedings."

R.C. 2317.023(C)(1) does not prevent the application of *R.C. 2317.023(B)* to this cause. There is no evidence that either relator's former spouse or the mediator has consented to disclosure of the complaint form.

Similarly, *R.C. 2317.023(C)(4)* does not apply to allow disclosure of the complaint form compiled by the mediator. The plain language of *R.C. 2317.023(C)(4)* requires a hearing to determine whether this exception to confidentiality is applicable. The presence of a hearing requirement presupposes that the parties will argue the applicability of the exception at a hearing conducted solely for that purpose. There has been no such hearing or request for such a hearing in this cause.

Even applying the substantive provisions of this provision, the relator's arguments lack merit. Disclosure of the complaint form compiled by the mediator is not necessary to prevent a manifest injustice, nor is the necessity for disclosure of sufficient magnitude to outweigh the importance of protecting the general requirement of confidentiality. Relator's sole assertion for requesting the document is that he may face potential criminal charges if he does not comply with the agreement reached in mediation. However, the mere possibility that the relator may be involved in future litigation cannot possibly establish the presence of a manifest injustice, as required by the statutory exception. Such a conclusion does not comport with the common meaning of "manifest injustice," which is defined as a clear or openly unjust act. See Webster's Third New International Dictionary (1986) 1164, 1375. The plain meaning of the words of the statute requires more than a possibility of future litigation.

Likewise, the possibility of future litigation does not create a necessity for disclosure of a magnitude sufficient to outweigh the general requirement of confidentiality. Every agreement in mediation may be breached. Such a breach could result in future litigation. However, this possibility cannot outweigh the plain words of *R.C. 2317.023(B)*, which establish a requirement of confidentiality. By those words, the General Assembly has determined that confidentiality is a means to encourage the use of mediation and frankness within mediation sessions. Were we to agree with the relator's argument, we would severely undermine that determination by the General Assembly, as reflected in the clear words of the statute. Accordingly, *R.C. 2317.023(C)(4)* does not apply to relator's request.

Finally, relator asserts that *R.C. 2317.023(B)* does not apply to this cause because the statute was not effective at the time that the record was created, *i.e.*, when the mediation session occurred. *R.C. 2317.023* became effective on January 27, 1997, which was after the record was created but before relator requested the form and filed this mandamus action. 146 Ohio Laws, Part II, 4033.

This contention also is meritless. *R.C. 2317.023* was effective at the time of the request for the form. The date the form was created is not relevant for the purposes of *R.C. 149.43.* "Since the statute merely deals with record disclosure, not record keeping, only a prospective duty is imposed upon those maintaining public records." *State ex rel. Beacon Journal Publishing Co. v. Univ. of Akron (1980), 64 Ohio St. 2d 392, 396, 18 Ohio Op. 3d 534, 537, 415 N.E.2d 310, 313.*

Accordingly, there is no authority to overcome the confidentiality requirement of *R.C. 2317.023(B).* The complaint form sought by the relator is a mediation communication which is not subject to disclosure under *R.C. 149.43* because *R.C. 2317.023(B)* clearly provides for its confidentiality. Therefore, we deny the relator's request for a writ of mandamus, and his request for attorney fees is also denied.

Writ denied.

OLAM v. CONGRESS MORTGAGE COMPANY

United States District Court for the Northern District of California
68 F. Supp. 2d 1110 (1999)

WAYNE D. BRAZIL, United States Magistrate Judge.

The court addresses in this opinion several difficult issues about the relationship between a court-sponsored voluntary mediation and subsequent proceedings whose purpose is to determine whether the parties entered an enforceable agreement at the close of the mediation session.

As we explain below, the parties participated in a lengthy mediation that was hosted by this court's ADR Program Counsel—an employee of the court who is both a lawyer and an ADR professional. At the end of the mediation (after midnight), the parties signed a "Memorandum of Understanding" (MOU) that states that it is "intended as a binding document itself. . . ." Contending that the consent she apparently gave was not legally valid, plaintiff has taken the position that the MOU is not enforceable. She has not complied with its terms. Defendants have filed a motion to enforce the MOU as a binding contract.

One of the principal issues with which the court wrestles, below, is whether evidence about what occurred during the mediation proceedings, including testimony from the mediator, may be used to help resolve this dispute. Before we address the merits of these issues, we must decide whose law to apply (state or federal).

[The court discussed the factors surrounding the choice of federal or state (California) law, ultimately deciding to follow California law on the issue of mediator testimony]

Having decided, for reasons set forth below, that fairness required the court to take evidence from the mediator in this case, I elected to call the mediator to the witness stand after the other principal participants in the September 10, 1998, mediation had testified. But, importantly, I also decided to take the testimony from the mediator in closed proceedings, under seal. After hearing his testimony in this protected setting, and after considering all the other evidence adduced during the hearing, I was positioned to determine much more reliably whether, or to what extent, overriding fairness interests required me to use and publicly disclose testimony from the mediator in making my decision about whether the parties had entered an enforceable settlement contract.

PERTINENT CALIFORNIA PRIVILEGE LAW

The California legislature has crafted two sets of statutory provisions that must be addressed by courts considering whether they may use in a subsequent civil proceeding any evidence about what occurred or was said during a mediation.

Section 703.5 of the California Evidence Code states, in pertinent part: "No person presiding at any judicial or quasi-judicial proceeding, and no arbitrator or mediator, shall be competent to testify, in any subsequent civil proceeding, as to any statement, conduct, decision, or ruling, occurring at or in conjunction with the prior proceeding, except as to a statement or conduct that could [give rise to contempt, constitute a crime, trigger investigation by the State Bar or the Commission on Judicial Performance, or give rise to disqualification proceedings]."

We note, before proceeding, that by its express terms § 703.5 applies (as pertinent here) only to statements or decisions made, or conduct occurring, in connection with a mediation. Read literally, this statute would not apply to perceptions of participants' appearance, demeanor, or physical condition during a mediation. We also note, however, that compelling mediators to testify or otherwise offer evidence about *anything* that occurred or was perceived during a mediation threatens confidentiality expectations of the participants and imposes burdens on mediators—and that such threats and burdens tend, at least in some measure, to undermine interests that the California legislature likely sought to protect when it enacted this statute. In construing and applying this statute, we endeavor to honor the purposes that drive it.

The other directly pertinent provision from the California Evidence Code is § 1119. It states, in pertinent part: "Except as otherwise provided in this chapter: (a) No evidence of anything said or any admission made . . . in the course of, or pursuant to, a mediation . . . is admissible or subject to discovery, and disclosure of the evidence shall not be compelled, in any . . . noncriminal proceeding. . . . (b) No writing . . . prepared in the course of, or pursuant to, a mediation . . . is admissible or subject to discovery, and disclosure of the writing shall not be compelled in any . . . noncriminal proceeding. . . . (c) All communications . . . by and between participants in the course of a mediation . . . shall remain confidential."

Of the other provisions that expressly qualify the prohibitions set forth in section 1119, the most important for our purposes is § 1123. It states that "[a] written settlement agreement prepared in the course of, or pursuant to, a mediation, is not made inadmissible, or protected from disclosure . . . if the agreement is signed by the settling parties and . . . (b) The agreement provides that it is enforceable or binding or words to that effect."

As noted above, the "Memorandum of Understanding" that the parties executed at the end of the mediation session in this case states expressly that it "is intended as a binding document itself." No party contends that this MOU is inadmissible.

WAIVERS BY THE *PARTIES* (BUT *NOT* THE MEDIATOR) OF THEIR MEDIATION PRIVILEGE

As we noted earlier, the plaintiff and the defendants have expressly waived confidentiality protections conferred by the California statutes quoted above. Both the plaintiff and the defendants have indicated, clearly and on advice of counsel, that they want the court to consider evidence about what occurred during the mediation, including testimony directly from the mediator, as the court resolves the issues raised by defendants' motion to enforce the settlement agreement.

Faced with a document that on its face appears to be an enforceable settlement contract, and contending that her apparent consent was not legally valid because of serious temporary impairments in her mental, emotional, and physical condition, plaintiff's waiver reaches not only perceptions by other participants of her appearance, demeanor, condition, and conduct during the mediation, but also their recollections of what she said and what others said in her presence. Her waiver expressly covers testimony about such matters not only by opposing counsel and parties, but also by the mediator and by her then lawyer, Ms. Voisenat. It covers group sessions as well as private caucuses.

While not as complete, defendants' waivers also are substantial. Defendants have not relinquished their right to protect the confidentiality of communications between them and their counsel, or the private communications between the mediator and them or their lawyers. They have stipulated, however, that evidence may be admitted about perceptions and communications made during group sessions—and they have actively sought the testimony of the mediator about his perceptions in and recollections from both the group sessions and his private caucuses with plaintiff or Ms. Voisenat.

The plaintiff and the defendants have made the waivers discussed above on the record, through counsel (plaintiff has directly participated in the hearings in which her waivers have been made). In addition, the court described the waivers with particularity in its Order Re July 21, 1999 Status Conference, filed July 23, 1999. At the beginning of the evidentiary hearing the parties acknowledged and affirmed these waivers in writing by affixing their signatures below the relevant paragraphs on a copy of that July 23rd Order. These waivers are deemed sufficient under § 1122(a)(1) of the California Evidence Code to remove § 1119 as a barrier to admission of the evidence the court accepted during the evidentiary hearing.

THE MEDIATOR'S PRIVILEGE

California law confers on mediators a privilege that is independent of the privilege conferred on parties to a mediation. By declaring that, subject to exceptions not applicable here, mediators are incompetent to testify "as to any statement, conduct, decision, or ruling, occurring at or in conjunction with [the mediation]," section 703.5 of the Evidence Code has the effect of making a mediator the holder of an independent privilege. Section 1119 of the Evidence Code appears to have the same effect—as it prohibits courts from compelling disclosure of evidence about mediation communications and directs that all such communications "shall remain confidential." As the California Court of Appeal recently pointed out, "the Legislature intended that the confidentiality provision of section 1119 may be asserted by the mediator as well as by the participants in the mediation." It follows that, under California law, a waiver of the mediation privilege by the parties is not a sufficient basis for a court to permit or order a mediator to testify. Rather, an independent determination must be made before testimony from a mediator should be permitted or ordered.

In the case at bar, the mediator (Mr. Herman) was and is an employee of the federal court (a "staff neutral"). He hosted the mediation at the behest of the court and under this court's ADR rules. These facts are not sufficient to justify ordering him to testify about what occurred during the mediation—even when the parties have waived their mediation privilege and want the mediator to testify. Mr. Herman is a member of the California bar—and no doubt feels bound to honor the directives of California law. He also is a professional in mediation—and feels a moral obligation to preserve the essential integrity of the mediation process—an integrity to which he believes the promise of confidentiality is fundamental.

Out of respect for these feelings, the court chose not to put Mr. Herman in an awkward position where he might have felt he had to choose between being a loyal employee of the court, on the one hand, and, on the other, asserting the mediator's privilege under California law. Instead, the court announced that it would proceed on the assumption that Mr. Herman was respectfully and appropriately asserting the mediator's privilege and was formally objecting to being called to testify about anything said or done during the mediation.

Regardless of whether Mr. Herman invoked the mediator's privilege, the wording of section 703.5 can be understood as imposing an independent duty on the courts to determine whether testimony from a mediator should be accepted. Unlike some other privilege statutes, which expressly confer a right on the holder of the privilege to refuse to disclose protected communications, as well as the power to prevent others from disclosing such communications, section 703.5 is framed in terms of competence to testify. In its pertinent part, it declares that (subject to exceptions not applicable here) a mediator is not competent to testify "in any subsequent civil proceeding" about words uttered or conduct occurring during a mediation. This wording appears to have two consequences: it would not empower a mediator to prevent others from disclosing mediation communications, but it would require courts, on their own initiative, to determine whether it would be lawful to compel or permit a mediator to testify about matters occurring within a mediation.

So the issue of whether it was appropriate under California law in these circumstances to compel the mediator to testify was squarely raised both by the court's assuming that Mr. Herman invoked the applicable statutes and by the court's understanding of its independent duty to address this question.

Before turning to other elements of our analysis of this issue, it is important to emphasize one critical and undisputed fact: at the end of the mediation, the parties and their lawyers signed a document, typed clearly by the mediator, which appears on its face to contain the essential terms of an agreement, which expressly states that it "is intended as a binding document itself," and which affirms the parties' agreement that "the court will have continuing jurisdiction over the enforcement of this memorandum of understanding as well as the ultimate settlement agreement and any disputes arising therefrom. . . ."

The fact that the parties and their lawyers signed such a document at the end of the mediation permits California courts to proceed to consider, in a hearing to determine whether the parties entered an enforceable contract, whether to admit evidence about what was said and done during the mediation itself. If there were no signed writing, and the alleged contract was oral, California law would not permit courts to use evidence from the mediation itself to determine whether an enforceable agreement had been reached. *See, Ryan v. Garcia, 27 Cal. App. 4th 1006 (Third Dist. 1994)* (applying and interpreting what was then section 1152.5 of the California Evidence Code, a predecessor to the current version of section 1119 of that Code).

We turn to the issue of whether, under California law, we should compel the mediator to testify—despite the statutory prohibitions set forth in sections 703.5 and 1119 of the Evidence Code. The most important opinion by a California court in this arena is *Rinaker v. Superior Court, 62 Cal. App. 4th 155 (Third District 1998)*. In that case the Court of Appeal held that there may be circumstances in which a trial court, over vigorous objection by a party and by the mediator, could compel testimony from the mediator in a juvenile delinquency proceeding (deemed a "civil" matter under California law). The defendant in the delinquency proceeding wanted to call the mediator to try to impeach testimony that was expected from a prosecution witness. That witness and the delinquency defendant had earlier participated in a mediation—and the delinquency defendant believed that the complaining witness had made admissions to the mediator that would substantially undermine the credibility of the complaining witnesses testimony—and thus would materially strengthen the defense. In these circumstances, the *Rinaker* court held that the mediator could be compelled to testify if, after *in camera* consideration of what her testimony would be, the trial judge determined that her testimony might well promote significantly the public interest in preventing perjury and the defendant's fundamental right to a fair judicial process.

In essence, the *Rinaker* court instructs California trial judges to conduct a two-stage balancing analysis. The goal of the first stage balancing is to determine whether to compel the mediator to appear at an *in camera* proceeding to determine precisely what her testimony would be. In this first stage, the judge considers all the circumstances and weighs all the competing rights and interests, including the values that would be threatened not by public disclosure mediation communications, but by ordering the mediator to appear at an *in camera* proceeding to disclose only to the court and counsel, out of public view, what she would say the parties said during the mediation. At this juncture the goal is to determine whether the harm that would be done to the values that underlie the mediation privileges simply by ordering the mediator to participate in the *in camera* proceedings can be justified—by the prospect that her testimony might well make a singular and substantial contribution to protecting or advancing competing interests of comparable or greater magnitude.

The trial judge reaches the second stage of balancing analysis only if the product of the first stage is a decision to order the mediator to detail, *in camera,* what her testimony would be. A court that orders the *in camera* disclosure gains precise and reliable knowledge of what the mediator's testimony would be—and only with that knowledge is the court positioned to launch its second balancing analysis. In this second stage the court is to weigh and comparatively assess (1) the importance of the values and interests that would be harmed if the mediator was compelled to testify (perhaps subject to a sealing or protective order, if appropriate), (2) the magnitude of the harm that compelling the testimony would cause to those values and interests, (3) the importance of the rights or interests that would be jeopardized if the mediator's testimony was not accessible in the specific proceedings in question, and (4) how much the testimony would contribute toward protecting those rights or advancing those interests—an inquiry that includes, among other things, an assessment of whether there are alternative sources of evidence of comparable probative value.

So we turn now to a description of that balancing analysis.

As indicated in an earlier section, the product of the first stage of the analysis was my decision that it was necessary to determine (through sealed proceedings) what Mr. Herman's testimony would be. Reaching that determination involved the following considerations. First, I acknowledge squarely that a decision to require a mediator to give evidence, even *in camera* or under seal, about what occurred during a mediation threatens values underlying the mediation privileges. As the *Rinaker* court suggested, the California legislature adopted these privileges in the belief that without the promise of confidentiality it would be appreciably more difficult to achieve the goals of mediation programs. *Rinaker v. Superior Court, supra, 62 Cal. App. 4th at 165–166,* citing *Ryan v. Garcia, 27 Cal. App. 4th 1006, 1010 (Third Dist. 1994).* Construing an earlier version of the mediation privilege statute, the same court of appeal had opined a few years before that without assurances of confidentiality "some litigants [would be deterred] from participating freely and openly in mediation." That court also quoted approvingly the suggestion from a practice guide that "confidentiality is absolutely essential to mediation," in part because without it "parties would be reluctant to make the kinds of concessions and admission that pave the way to settlement."

While this court has no occasion or power to quarrel with these generally applicable pronouncements of state policy, we observe that they appear to have appreciably less force when, as here, the parties to the mediation have waived confidentiality protections, indeed have asked the court to compel the mediator to testify—so that justice can be done.

If a party to the mediation were objecting to compelling the mediator to testify we would be faced with a substantially more difficult analysis. But the absence of such an objection does not mean that ordering the mediator to disclose, even *in camera,* matters that occurred within the mediation does not pose some threat to values underlying the mediation privileges. As the *Rinaker* court pointed out, ordering mediators to participate in proceedings arising out of mediations imposes economic and psychic burdens that could make some people reluctant to agree to serve as a mediator, especially in programs where that service is pro bono or poorly compensated.

This is not a matter of time and money only. Good mediators are likely to feel violated by being compelled to give evidence that could be used against a party with whom they tried to establish a relationship of trust during a mediation. Good mediators are deeply committed to being and remaining neutral and non-judgmental, and to building and preserving relationships with parties. To force them to give evidence that hurts someone from whom they actively solicited trust (during the mediation) rips the fabric of their work and can threaten their sense of the center of their professional integrity. These are not inconsequential matters.

Like many other variables in this kind of analysis, however, the magnitude of these risks can vary with the circumstances. Here, for instance, all parties to the mediation want the mediator to testify about things that occurred during the mediation—so ordering the testimony would do less harm to the actual relationships developed than it would in a case where one of the parties to the mediation objected to the use of evidence from the mediator.

We acknowledge, however, that the possibility that a mediator might be forced to testify over objection could harm the capacity of mediators in general to create the environment of trust that they feel maximizes the likelihood that constructive communication will occur during the mediation session. But the level of harm to that interest likely varies, at least in some measure, with the perception within the community of mediators and litigants about how likely it is that any given mediation will be followed at some point by an order compelling the neutral to offer evidence about what occurred during the session. I know of no studies or statistics that purport to reflect how often courts or parties seek evidence from mediators—and I suspect that the incidence of this issue arising would not be identical across the broad spectrum of mediation programs and settings. What I can report is that this case represents the first time that I have been called upon to address these kinds of questions in the more than fifteen years that I have been responsible for ADR programs in this court. Nor am I aware of the issue arising before other judges here. Based on that experience, my partially educated guess is that the likelihood that a mediator or the parties in any given case need fear that the mediator would later be constrained to testify is extraordinarily small.

That conviction is reinforced by another consideration. As we pointed out above, under California law, and this court's view of sound public policy, there should be no occasion to consider whether to seek testimony from a mediator for purpose of determining whether the parties entered an enforceable settlement contract unless the mediation produced a writing (or competent record) that appears on its face to constitute an enforceable contract, signed or formally assented to by all the parties. Thus, it is only when there is such a writing or record, and when a party nonetheless seeks to escape its apparent effect, that courts applying California law would even consider calling for evidence from a mediator for purposes of determining whether the parties settled the case. Surely these circumstances will arise after only a tiny fraction of mediations.

The magnitude of the risk to values underlying the mediation privileges that can be created by ordering a mediator to testify also can vary with the nature of the testimony that is sought. Comparing the kind of testimony sought in *Rinaker* with the kind of testimony sought in the case at bar illustrates this point. In *Rinaker,* one party wanted to use the mediator's recollection about what another party said during the mediation to impeach subsequent trial testimony. So the mediator was to serve as a source of evidence about what words a party to the mediation uttered, what statements or admissions that party made.

As the Court of Appeal appeared to recognize, this kind of testimony could be particularly threatening to the spirit and methods that some people believe are important both to the philosophy and the success of some mediation processes. Under one approach to mediation, the primary goal is not to establish "the truth" or to determine reliably what the historical facts actually were. Rather, the goal is to go both deeper than and beyond history—to emphasize feelings, underlying interests, and a search for means for social repair or reorientation. In this kind of mediation, what happened between the parties in the past can be appreciably less important than why, than what needs drove what happened or were exposed or defined by what happened, than how the parties feel about it, and than what they can bring themselves to do to move on.

Moreover, the methods some mediators use to explore underlying interests and feelings and to build settlement bridges are in some instances intentionally distanced from the actual historical facts. In some mediations, the focus is on feelings rather than facts. The neutral may ask the parties to set aside pre-occupations with what happened as she tries to help the parties understand underlying motivations and needs and to remove emotional obstacles through exercises in venting. Some mediators use hypotheticals that are expressly and intentionally not presented as accurate reflections of reality—in order to help the parties explore their situation and the range of solution options that might be available. A mediator might encourage parties to "try on" certain ideas or feelings that the parties would contend have little connection with past conduct, to experiment with the effects on themselves and others of expressions of emotions or of openness to concessions or proposals that, outside the special environment of the mediation, the parties would not entertain or admit. All of this, as mediator Rinaker herself pointed out, can have precious little to do with historical accuracy or "truth."

Given these features of some mediations, it could be both threatening and unfair to hold a participant to the literal meaning of at least some of the words she uttered during the course of a mediation. And testimony from the mediator about what those words were during the mediation might constitute very unreliable (actively misleading) evidence about what the earlier historical facts were.

For these reasons, a court conducting the kind of balancing analysis called for by the *Rinaker* court should try to determine what kind of techniques and processes were used in the particular mediation in issue. The more like the processes just described, the more harm would be done by trying to use evidence about what was said or done during the mediation to help prove what the earlier historical facts really were. On the other hand, if the mediation process was closer to an adjudicate/evaluative model, with a clear focus (understood by all participants) on evidence, law, and traditional analysis of liability, damages, and settlement options, use of evidence from the mediation in subsequent civil proceedings might be less vulnerable to criticism for being unfair and unreliable.

Regardless of which approach or methods the mediator used, however, the kind of testimony sought from the mediator in this case poses less of a threat to fairness and reliability values than the kind of testimony that was sought from the mediator in *Rinaker*. During the first stage balancing analysis in the case at bar, the parties and I assumed that the testimony from the mediator that would be most consequential would focus not primarily on what Ms. Olam said during the mediation, but on how she acted and the mediator's perceptions of her physical, emotional, and mental condition. The purpose would not be to nail down and dissect her specific words, but to assess at a more general and impressionistic level her condition and capacities. That purpose might be achieved with relatively little disclosure of the content of her confidential communications. As conceded above, that does not mean that compelling the testimony by the mediator would pose no threat to values underlying the privileges—but that the degree of harm to those values would not be as great as it would be if the testimony was for the kinds of impeachment purposes that were proffered in *Rinaker*. And in a balancing analysis, probable degree of harm is an important consideration.

What we have been doing in the preceding paragraphs is attempting, as the first component of the first stage balancing analysis, to identify the interests that might be threatened by ordering the mediator, in the specific circumstances presented here, to testify under seal—and to assess the magnitude of the harm that ordering the testimony would likely do to those interests. Having assayed these matters, we turn to the other side of the balance. We will identify the interests that ordering the testimony (under seal, at least initially) might advance, assess the relative importance of those interests, and try to predict the magnitude of the contribution to achieving those interests that ordering the testimony would likely make (or the extent of the harm that we likely would do to those interests if we did not compel the testimony).

The interests that are likely to be advanced by compelling the mediator to testify in this case are of considerable importance. Moreover, as we shall see, some of those interests parallel and reinforce the objectives the legislature sought to advance by providing for confidentiality in mediation.

The first interest we identify is the interest in doing justice. Here is what we mean. For reasons described below, the mediator is positioned in this case to offer what could be crucial, certainly very probative, evidence about the central factual issues in this matter. There is a strong possibility that his testimony will greatly improve the court's ability to determine reliably what the pertinent historical facts actually were. Establishing reliably what the facts were is critical to doing justice (here, justice means this: applying the law correctly to the real historical facts). It is the fundamental duty of a public court in our society to do justice—to resolve disputes in accordance with the law when the parties don't. Confidence in our system of justice as a whole, in our government as a whole, turns in no small measure on confidence in the courts' ability to do justice in individual cases. So doing justice in individual cases is an interest of considerable magnitude.

When we put case-specific flesh on these abstract bones, we see that "doing justice" implicates interests of considerable importance to the parties—all of whom want the mediator to testify. From the plaintiff's perspective, the interests that the defendants' motion threatens could hardly be more fundamental. According to Ms. Olam, the mediation process was fundamentally unfair to her—and resulted in an apparent agreement whose terms are literally unconscionable and whose enforcement would render her homeless and virtually destitute. To her, doing justice in this setting means protecting her from these fundamental wrongs.

From the defendants' perspective, doing justice in this case means, among other things, bringing to a lawful close disputes with Ms. Olam that have been on-going for about seven years—disputes that the defendants believe have cost them, without justification, at least scores of thousands of dollars. The defendants believe that Ms. Olam has breached no fewer than three separate contractual commitments with them (not counting the agreement reached at the end of the mediation)—and that those breaches are the product of a calculated effort not only to avoid meeting legitimate obligations, but also to make unfair use, for years, of the defendants' money.

Defendants also believe that Ms. Olam has abused over the years several of her own counsel—as well as the judicial process and this court's ADR program (for which she has been charged nothing). Through their motion, the defendants ask the court to affirm that they acquired legal rights through the settlement agreement that the mediation produced. They also ask the court to enforce those rights, and thus to enable the defendants to avoid the burdens, expense, delay, and risks of going to trial in this matter. These also are matters of consequence.

And they are not the only interests that could be advanced by compelling the mediator to testify. According to the defendants' pre-hearing proffers, the mediator's testimony would establish clearly that the mediation process was fair and that the plaintiff's consent to the settlement agreement was legally viable. Thus the mediator's testimony, according to the defendants, would reassure the community and the court about the integrity of the mediation process that the court sponsored.

That testimony also would provide the court with the evidentiary confidence it needs to enforce the agreement. A publicly announced decision to enforce the settlement would, in turn, encourage parties who want to try to settle their cases to use the court's mediation program for that purpose. An order appropriately enforcing an agreement reached through the mediation also would encourage parties in the future to take mediations seriously, to understand that they represent real opportunities to reach closure and avoid trial, and to attend carefully to terms of agreements proposed in mediations. In these important ways, taking testimony from the mediator could strengthen the mediation program.

In sharp contrast, refusing to compel the mediator to testify might well deprive the court of the evidence it needs to rule reliably on the plaintiff's contentions—and thus might either cause the court to impose an unjust outcome on the plaintiff or disable the court from enforcing the settlement. In this setting, refusing to compel testimony from the mediator might end up being tantamount to denying the motion to enforce the agreement—because a crucial source of evidence about the plaintiff's condition and capacities would be missing. Following that course, defendants suggest, would do considerable harm not only to the court's mediation program but also to fundamental fairness. If parties believed that courts routinely would refuse to compel mediators to testify, and that the absence of evidence from mediators would enhance the viability of a contention that apparent consent to a settlement contract was not legally viable, cynical parties would be encouraged either to try to escape commitments they made during mediations or to use threats of such escapes to try to re-negotiate, after the mediation, more favorable terms—terms that they never would have been able to secure without this artificial and unfair leverage.

In sum, it is clear that refusing even to determine what the mediator's testimony would be, in the circumstances here presented, threatens values of great significance. But we would miss the main analytical chance if all we did was identify those values and proclaim their Importance. In fact, when the values implicated are obviously of great moment, there is a danger that the process of identifying them will generate unjustified momentum toward a conclusion that exaggerates the weight on this side of the scale. Thus we emphasize that the central question is not which values are implicated, but how much they would be advanced by compelling the testimony or how much they would be harmed by not compelling it.

We concluded, after analysis and before the hearing, that the mediator's testimony was sufficiently likely to make substantial contributions toward achieving the ends described above to justify compelling an exploration, under seal, of what his testimony would be. While we did not assume that there were no pressures or motivations that might affect the reliability of the mediator's testimony, it was obvious that the mediator was the only source of presumptively disinterested, neutral evidence. The only other witnesses with personal knowledge of the plaintiff's condition at the mediation were the parties and their lawyers—none of whom were disinterested. And given the foreseeable testimony about the way the mediation was structured (with lots of caucusing by the mediator with one side at a time), it was likely that the mediator would have had much more exposure to the plaintiff over the course of the lengthy mediation than any other witness save her lawyer.

But it also was foreseeable that substantial questions would be raised about the reliability of the testimony that Ms. Olam's former lawyer, Phyllis Voisenat, would give. We knew, when we conducted this first stage balancing, that Ms. Voisenat no longer represented Ms. Olam. We also knew that strains had developed in that relationship before it had ended, and that lawyer and client had felt that their ability to communicate with one another left a great deal to be desired. Moreover, Ms. Olam had suggested through her new lawyer (the fifth attorney to work with her in connection with her disputes with the defendants) that she might contend during the hearing that Ms. Voisenat, her former lawyer, had been one of the sources of unlawful pressure on her to sign the settlement agreement at the end of the mediation. And there were at least rumblings from the plaintiff's camp about a malpractice suit by Ms. Olam against Ms. Voisenat, who, understandably, expressed concerns about the possible use against her in such litigation of testimony she would give in these proceedings. For all these reasons, there was a substantial likelihood that plaintiff would raise serious questions about the accuracy of Ms. Voisenat's testimony and that, given all the circumstances, the court would not be sure how much it should rely on the evidence Ms. Voisenat would give.

We also could foresee that the circumstances in which the mediator would have interacted with Ms. Olam during the mediation held the promise of yielding perceptions of her mental, emotional and physical condition that would be especially well-grounded. Because we know how the court's mediators are trained, we could anticipate that Mr. Herman met with the plaintiff and her lawyer in private, away from the defendants and their counsel—thus freeing plaintiff from the emotional charges, defensiveness, stress, and "pressure to posture" that negotiating in the presence of "the enemy" can inspire. We also could expect (because we know how Mr. Herman trains other people to act as mediators) that in his private meetings with plaintiff and her lawyer Mr. Herman would try to create an environment that was as unthreatening and as comfortable for her as possible. And that environment would likely give him more reliable access to the plaintiff's real condition than any of the witnesses connected with the defense of the case could have had.

In short, there was a substantial likelihood that testimony from the mediator would be the most reliable and probative on the central issues raised by the plaintiff in response to the defendants' motion. And there was no likely alternative source of evidence on these issues that would be of comparable probative utility. So it appeared that testimony from the mediator would be crucial to the court's capacity to do its job—and that refusing to compel that testimony posed a serious threat to every value identified above. In this setting, California courts clearly would conclude the first stage balancing analysis by ordering the mediator to testify *in camera* or under seal—so that the court, aided by inputs from the parties, could make a refined and reliable judgment about whether to use that testimony to help resolve the substantive issues raised by the pending motion.

As noted earlier, we called the mediator to testify (under seal) after all other participants in the mediation had been examined and cross-examined—so that the lawyers (and the court) would be able to identify all the subjects and questions that they should cover with the mediator. With the record thus fully developed, we were well situated to determine whether using (and publicly disclosing) the mediator's testimony would make a contribution of sufficient magnitude to justify the level of harm that using and disclosing the testimony would likely cause, in the circumstances of this case, to the interests that inform the mediation privilege law in California. As our detailed account, later in this opinion, of the evidence from all sources demonstrates, it became clear that the mediator's testimony was essential to doing justice here—so we decided to use it and unseal it.

[The court went on to conclude, based in part on the mediatior's *in camera* testimony, that plaintiff had failed to present adequate evidence that the agreement she entered into was unenforceable.]

NOTES AND QUESTIONS

(1) Is the Ohio statute cited in *Schneider*, providing for a confidentiality exception "to prevent a manifest injustice," too broad? Does it give too much discretion to the courts in granting an exception?

(2) In taking the mediator's testimony "in closed proceedings, under seal" in the *Olam* case, was Judge Brazil, in effect, carving out a "manifest injustice" exception similar to that found in the Ohio statute? Judge Brazil's lengthy commentary on the need for confidentiality displays a sensitivity to important policy concerns. Was his decision to go forward with the mediator's testimony largely influenced by the fact that, as he states, he had been responsible for his court's ADR programs for 15 years and had never before encountered the issue? Was the fact that both parties agreed to waive confidentiality critical to his decision?

§ C AGREEMENTS TO MEDIATE AND STATUTORY REQUIREMENTS TO MEDIATE

What are the consequences of a party's unwillingness to mediate if he or she has a contractual agreement to mediate or is required to mediate pursuant to a federal or state statute? If it were arbitration rather than mediation that was in question, it is now well established that the courts will enforce arbitration provisions. The inclusion in contracts of clauses in which the parties agree to binding arbitration if a dispute among them should arise has become increasingly widespread over the past few decades. The courts have generally been willing to enforce these arbitration clauses unless the party resisting enforcement can show that the arbitration clause was fraudulently induced or otherwise invalid as a matter of contract law. Similarly, courts will enforce statutory requirements to arbitrate unless it can be shown that the statutory scheme places an unconstitutional burden on a party's right to a jury trial.

While contractual agreements to mediate and statutory requirements to mediate are now commonplace as well, their enforceability is more problematic than the enforcement of arbitration contracts and statutory mandates. Some have argued that a court's enforcement of an agreement or requirement to mediate would be futile, because, although parties may be forced to the mediation table, they cannot be forced to settle. Others have argued that public policy now favors mediation as a means of resolving disputes and that courts should further this policy by enforcing mediation requirements. As you read the following cases, consider the policy rationales presented by the courts as they confront issues over whether to enforce mediation agreements or statutory requirements to mediate.

ANNAPOLIS PROFESSIONAL FIREFIGHTERS LOCAL 1926 v. CITY OF ANNAPOLIS

Maryland Court of Special Appeals
642 A.2d 889 (1994)

Wilner, C.J.

The union representing firefighters employed by the City of Annapolis appeals from an order of the Circuit Court for Anne Arundel County declining to enter a preliminary injunction against the City and dismissing the union's complaint. The underlying dispute is whether lieutenants and captains in the fire department are supervisory personnel and, for that reason, ineligible for inclusion within the bargaining unit. The City now claims they are; the union asserts they are not. The issue before us is whether the court erred in refusing to enjoin the City from taking that issue to impasse and then unilaterally removing lieutenants and captains from the unit. Under the circumstances of this case, we hold that the court did not err. . . .

The State Mediation and Conciliation Service is a statutory unit within the State Division of Labor and Industry. The duties of the Service include the mediation of labor disputes and, where the parties agree, establishing arbitration boards to arbitrate such disputes. If mediation fails and a disputant refuses to arbitrate, the Service is authorized to conduct an investigation, decide "which disputant is mainly responsible or blameworthy for continuance of the dispute," and, over the signature of the Commissioner of Labor and Industry or the Chief Mediator, "publish in a daily newspaper a report that assigns responsibility or blame for the continuance of the dispute."

The City has had a collective bargaining agreement with the union for some period of time. During all of that time, the appropriate unit has included captains and lieutenants, notwithstanding the prohibition against mixing supervisory and nonsupervisory personnel in the same unit. Indeed, in the most recent (1990-93) agreement, the City expressly recognized the union as the sole and exclusive bargaining agent for "all eligible employees in the Annapolis Fire Department in the rank of firefighter through captain pursuant to the provisions of . . . Section 3.21.050 of the Annapolis City Code." At least implicit, if not explicit, in this is an historical recognition by the City that captains and lieutenants, despite the common perception of positions so designated, are not supervisory personnel.

The most recent contract between the City and the union became effective July 1, 1990 and was due to expire on June 30, 1993, subject to the provision in art. 27 of the contract that it would "automatically be renewed from year to year hereafter unless a successor to this agreement is executed by the parties hereto." Art. 27 also provided that, should either party desire to modify the agreement, it would have to notify the other party at least 120 days prior to June 30, 1993. Such notice would trigger the duty to negotiate the proposed changes. Article 28 provided:

> "If after a reasonable period of negotiations over the terms of an agreement, a dispute exists between the City and the Union, the parties may mutually agree that an impasse has been reached; except that if such dispute exists as of May 1, 1993 an impasse shall be deemed to have been reached. Whenever an impasse has been reached, the dispute shall be submitted to mediation. If the parties are unable to agree to a mediator the Division of Mediation and Conciliation shall be required to provide a mediator. The parties hereto agree, that should the mediator recommend the process of fact-finding, that process shall be used in an advisory manner."

Negotiations over a new contract began in April, 1993. During the negotiations, the City, for the first time, contended that captains and lieutenants were supervisory personnel and therefore ineligible for inclusion in the same bargaining unit as the rest of the firefighters. The Union rejected that contention but continued to negotiate other matters.

As the expiration date of the agreement approached, the City announced that it would extend the term of the existing agreement for two weeks to allow time for the parties to reach agreement on a new contract. Subsequently, the City made what it termed its "Final Proposal." In that offer, the City proposed that lieutenants could remain in the bargaining unit until October, 1993, while the question of their supervisory status would be referred to a third party for decision; captains, however, would be removed from the unit. The Union rejected that proposal and, subject to the automatic extension provision in art. 27, the collective bargaining agreement expired without a successor agreement having been reached. The City, giving no effect to the automatic extension provision in art. 27, then announced that the collective bargaining agreement had expired, that the parties were at an impasse, and that captains and lieutenants would thereafter be excluded from the bargaining unit. The City also explicitly withdrew its offer to have a third party determine the supervisory status of the lieutenants.

Initially, the Union filed a verified complaint of unfair labor practices with the Division of Labor and Industry. It complained about a number of things, including the City's removal of captains and lieutenants, noting that, of the 80 members of the unit, 22, or more than 25%, were captains or lieutenants. Indeed, the president and secretary of the union, who comprised two-thirds of the union's negotiating committee, were lieutenants. By unilaterally removing such personnel, the union claimed, the City was interfering with the employees' right of self-organization and refusing to negotiate in good faith.

On July 26, 1993, the Commissioner of the Division of Labor and Industry sent appellants a letter stating:

> "As you know, the Mediation and Conciliation Service was once a unit of the Division of Labor and Industry. Due to state budget cuts, the unit was abolished on July 1, 1991, and remains disbanded to date. Accordingly, the entity the City Ordinance authorizes to process the unfair labor practice charge does not exist."

The Commissioner also asserted that the Division would not assert jurisdiction over the charge as the ordinance did not impose an obligation on the State to do so and the Division lacked resources to devote to the matter.

The union then filed in the Circuit Court for Anne Arundel County a complaint for injunctive relief asserting, among other things, that it was "without an adequate administrative remedy or remedy at law to enforce their rights," that the unilateral removal of fire lieutenants and captains from the bargaining unit "voided their opportunity to participate through collective bargaining in the setting of their terms and conditions of employment," "caused grave harm to the organization and structure of the [union]," and "violated each and every plaintiff's rights to due process." Accordingly, in order to preserve the status quo, it requested a preliminary injunction to restrain the City from unilaterally removing lieutenants and captains from the bargaining unit. In a memorandum filed in support of the complaint, the union repeated the claims it had made in its unfair labor practice charge and asserted further that the unilateral removal violated the captains' and lieutenants' due process rights under the U.S. Constitution and the Maryland Declaration of Rights. . . .

After a hearing, the court entered an order denying the request for preliminary injunction and dismissing the complaint. In the order, the court declared, in relevant part:

> "1. There is no legal authority known to the Court which would support the issuance of an injunction against Defendant under the circumstances alleged in the Complaint;
>
> 2. As a result of the abolition of the State Mediation and Conciliation Service named in the City of Annapolis' collective bargaining ordinance, § 3.32.070 of the Annapolis City Code, Plaintiffs may seek relief from alleged unfair labor practices on the part of Defendant, including the issue of the exclusion of fire captains and fire lieutenants from the Annapolis Professional Firefighters' bargaining unit, by addressing their claims to the Annapolis City Council.

*   *   *   *   *   *

> 4. Injunctive relief is inappropriate because Plaintiffs have failed to establish that they will suffer immediate, irreparable injury which cannot be readily, adequately and completely compensated with money."

In this appeal, the union raises the single question, "Did the Court below err in failing to grant injunctive relief prohibiting the City of Annapolis from unilaterally excluding Fire Lieutenants and Fire Captains from the collective bargaining unit represented by [the union]?" . . . .

In enacting Chapter 3.32, and agreeing to art. 28 of the collective bargaining agreement, the City understood the obvious—that, in the course of collective bargaining, disputes could arise that the parties might not be able to resolve efficiently through unassisted bilateral negotiations. Two areas, or categories, of disputes were particularly recognized—an impasse in negotiating a new agreement and a claim of unfair labor practice. In both instances, a common and sensible way of resolving such disputes was chosen—referral to the State Mediation and Conciliation Service, a unit created by the Legislature for precisely this purpose. The agreement with the union was obviously subject to the ordinance and indeed made several references to it. The impasse provisions of art. 28, dealing with a breakdown in negotiating a new agreement, are entirely consistent with § 3.32.070 of the ordinance, calling for mediation of any dispute over an unfair labor practice charge.

What we have then is a legislative direction and a voluntary written agreement to submit the very kind of dispute that arose in this case to mediation, and, failing that, to neutral fact-finding. In *Anne Arundel County v. Fraternal Order, 313 Md. 98, 543 A.2d 841 (1988)*, a similar kind of dispute arose between the county and the police union—whether a detention center lieutenant could be included in the bargaining unit with lower level detention center employees. The issue before the Court was whether the county could be required to submit that dispute to arbitration under an arbitration clause in the collective bargaining agreement.

Recognizing that the agreement was not subject to the State Uniform Arbitration Act and assuming that no other statute authorized the arbitration clause, the Court overruled existing common law and held the clause valid under Maryland common law. At 107, it stated the new holding: "We believe that agreements to arbitrate future disputes generally should be enforceable even in the absence of a specific statutory provision." This was consistent with the Court's more general and often-expressed view that "arbitration is a favored method of dispute resolution." *Id.* at 105; also *Bd. of Educ. v. P.G. Co. Educators' Ass'n, 309 Md. 85, 522 A.2d 931 (1987)*. More specifically, the Court held that a determination "as to which representation unit is appropriate for a certain group of employees" was a proper subject for arbitration as it "merely permits the Union to bargain with the County on behalf of the employees."

Section 3.32.070 and art. 28 of the agreement are not, strictly, arbitration provisions. They look rather to mediation and, failing that, neutral fact-finding, which are and have long been equally well-recognized and beneficial methods of dispute resolution, especially in labor disputes. As we have observed, the Legislature blessed this mechanism in this very context as early as 1904. For disputes that are susceptible to it, mediation and neutral evaluation have become, throughout the nation and increasingly throughout this State, equally "favored methods of dispute resolution," and we can see no rational basis for not enforcing agreements to utilize such methods in much the same manner as agreements to arbitrate are enforced. . . .

We believe that, as a matter of Maryland common law, consistent with the liberal approach now taken to alternative dispute resolution agreements generally, a written agreement to submit either an existing or a future dispute to a form of alternative dispute resolution that is not otherwise against public policy will be enforced at least to the same extent that it would be enforced if the chosen method were arbitration.

What we then have is a dispute for which the parties have chosen a specific, enforceable dispute resolution process. The only "fly in the ointment" is that, because of lack of funding, the agency selected to mediate the dispute or, failing mediation, to engage in neutral fact-finding, has become nonoperational (though still provided for in the State Code) and therefore, as a practical matter, unavailable. The question is whether that unfortunate fact vitiates the chosen process entirely, thereby either leaving the parties without a remedy or requiring the courts to reenter an area from which they have largely, and wisely, been excluded for the past six decades.

There is no reason to vitiate the chosen process, and it makes no sense to do so. The Uniform Arbitration Act (Md. Code Cts. & Jud. Proc. art., § 3-211) requires that, if an arbitration agreement provides a method for the appointment of arbitrators, that method shall be followed, but that a court shall appoint one or more arbitrators if "the agreed method fails or for any reason cannot be followed." The statute further states that a court-appointed arbitrator "has all the powers of an arbitrator specifically named in the agreement."

Although this power, under the Act, is a statutory one, it is not foreign to or inconsistent with the general equitable jurisdiction of a circuit court. Equity courts have long had the power, for example, when specifically enforcing agreements, to appoint trustees to carry out their decrees when a party proves recalcitrant or when otherwise necessary to implement the agreement. . . .

Upon this analysis, it is clear that, had such a remedy been requested by the union, the court could have designated a substitute mediator/neutral fact-finder in light of the parties' inability or unwillingness to agree themselves upon a substitute for the nonfunctional State Mediation and Conciliation Service. Unfortunately, except to the extent included within the union's general prayer for relief, that request was not made. The only specific relief sought was an injunction, the effect of which would have been to retain captains and lieutenants within the bargaining unit until such time, if ever, that the county council, by amendment to the ordinance, declared such positions to be supervisory.

It is, of course, axiomatic that, except in compelling circumstances, the issuance or denial of an injunction rests within the sound discretion of the equity court, and that considerable latitude is afforded to trial judges in exercising that discretion.

In deciding whether the court here abused that discretion, we may take cognizance of both the general policy of the State to avoid injunctions in labor disputes and the fact that a better alternative was available in this particular case. As to the former, whether or not this particular dispute was formally subject to the anti-injunction provisions of Md. Code Labor & Empl. art., title 4, subt. 3, the issuance of such an injunction, given its practical effect, would certainly have been inconsistent with the general policy established by the Legislature in that part of the Code. We note, in that regard, § 4-302(b) expressing the policy of the State that "negotiation of terms and conditions of employment should result from voluntary agreement between employees and employer" and § 4-313 providing that, except where irreparable injury is threatened, a court may not grant injunctive relief in a labor dispute "if the plaintiff has failed to make every reasonable effort to settle the labor dispute . . . with the help of available dispute resolution mechanisms, governmental mediation, or voluntary arbitration."

As to the latter, for the reasons we have explained above, the union, and upon its request, the court, had a viable, less intrusive, and more appropriate alternative to the injunctive relief sought in this case. It is for these reasons that we shall affirm the judgment below, without prejudice to either party seeking further relief in the circuit court consistent with this Opinion.

Judgment Affirmed

KIRSCHENMAN v. SUPERIOR COURT OF CONTRA COSTA COUNTY

California Court of Appeal, First District
36 Cal. Rptr. 2d 166 (1994)

ANDERSON, P. J.

Petitioners (defendants below and their attorney) seek a writ to vacate an order sanctioning them for failing to personally attend a mediation session and *requiring* them to participate in further mediation. Plaintiffs, real parties in interest, respond by urging us to rule that once an attorney orally agrees to mediate a dispute neither that attorney nor the client may withdraw consent absent court approval upon a showing of good cause; we hold otherwise. We grant relief because (1) the court had no authority to mandate mediation; (2) there was no enforceable agreement to mediate; and (3) in any event, there was no failure to comply with the court's mediation order.

Petitioners are Wayne Kirschenman and Kirschenman Enterprises, Inc. (hereafter Kirschenman) and Attorney Robert D. Patterson who represents Kirschenman (one of 14 named defendants) in the underlying multiparty commercial litigation and related cross-actions. A status conference was held in the underlying case on April 15, 1994. Patterson appeared by telephone. The court asked the attorneys present if they were "interested in any kind of mediation on the case" and Patterson replied that he "would be willing to do that on behalf of Kirschenman." Thereafter the attorneys chose private mediation and the court announced that there would be another status conference in 60 days. There was no discussion of personal appearance at the mediation by the litigants or their counsel, no minute order was entered nor was any written order signed by the court.

By letter dated May 13, 1994, Attorney Patterson informed the court that plaintiffs' counsel and the defense attorneys located in Northern California were in the process of arranging to employ a mediator and that mediation was tentatively scheduled to occur in the early part of June. Patterson also stated that he had been informed by his client, Mr. Kirschenman, that Kirschenman would make no settlement of any kind. Patterson then asked to be excused from the mediation. The court denied the request. Thereupon, petitioners filed a mediation brief and paid their share of the mediation expenses. Neither Kirschenman nor Patterson appeared in person at the mediation session, which was held on June 6, 1994, but both did make themselves available by telephone.

Plaintiffs' counsel filed a motion for sanctions for failure of petitioners to participate in mediation. Petitioners opposed the motion pointing out that they had filed a brief, paid their portion of the mediation expenses, and had made themselves available by telephone for the mediation session. They also pointed out that neither the mediator nor any attorney had attempted to make telephone contact during the session. Nevertheless, respondent court granted the motion for sanctions in its entirety.

On June 17, 1994, a second status conference was held at which time the court announced that all parties were ordered to engage in further mediation before August 29, 1994. The court was asked by plaintiffs' counsel to clarify what it meant by "attendance" at mediation, and the court replied that it meant personal appearance by lawyers and either clients or their carriers, except for those out of state who were allowed to appear by telephone.

Upon application of petitioners for extraordinary relief, we stayed the order directing petitioners to participate in further mediation and the order imposing sanctions.

DISCUSSION

Our consideration of the order sanctioning petitioners for not attending the first mediation session in person and the order requiring petitioners to attend a further session commences with the proposition that the court had no statutory authority *to require* the parties to participate in mediation. Nor did respondent court initially purport to mandate mediation or any other form of alternative dispute resolution, but rather merely inquired of the attorneys attending the status conference if they were interested in mediation.

Thus, respondent court's authority to sanction petitioners and to make orders regarding mediation in this case rests on the court's authority to enforce the oral agreement of petitioners to participate in mediation. Plaintiffs cite to federal cases which have enforced *written* agreements for nonbinding alternative dispute resolution. (*See DeValk Lincoln Mercury, Inc. v. Ford Motor Co.* (7th Cir. 1987) 811 F.2d 326, 335; *AMF, Inc. v. Brunswick Corp.* (E.D.N.Y. 1985) 621 F. Supp. 456, 463.) Plaintiffs also refer to policy statements, such as that in Business and Professions Code section 465, subdivision (b), which encourage and support resolution of disputes by the use of alternatives to the courts. However, we note that even in the legislation to which plaintiffs refer, the parties are specifically not prohibited from revoking consent to participate in voluntary dispute resolution. (See Bus. & Prof. Code, § 467.7.)

Petitioners timely sought to withdraw from participation in mediation prior to the appointment of the mediator. They should have been permitted to do so.

Let a peremptory writ of mandate issue directing respondent court to vacate its order imposing sanctions and its order requiring petitioners to participate in further mediation. Petitioners are to recover costs of this writ proceeding.

PRODUCTION CREDIT ASSOCIATION v. SPRING WATER DAIRY FARM, INC.

Minnsesota Supreme Court
407 N.W.2d 88 (1987)

COYNE, J.

This appeal arises out of a claim and delivery (replevin) action to foreclose on personal property which secured a debt. The district court granted Production Credit Association of Worthington (PCA) the right to possession of the property, but then stayed its order to permit mediation under Minn. Stat. § 583.26 (1986). PCA petitioned the court of appeals, seeking a writ of prohibition. The court of appeals denied the petition. We accepted review in order to examine PCA's contention that mandatory mediation under the Farmer-Lender Mediation Act is not required when a creditor has begun its claim and delivery action before the effective date of the act. We affirm.

PCA, a corporation operating under the Farm Credit Act of 1971, and Spring Water Dairy Farm, Inc., a family farm corporation as defined in Minn. Stat. § 500.24, subd. 2 (1986), entered into a series of loan transactions. The debt was secured by perfected security interests in various kinds of property, including farm machinery and equipment, vehicles, crops, warehouse receipts and accounts from the disposition of collateral. In addition, Peter and Lois Henstra, the principal shareholders of Spring Water Dairy Farm, Inc., guaranteed payment of the corporate debt. Spring Water Dairy and the Henstras defaulted on the loan, the entire balance of which was due on September 30, 1982.

In January of 1984, PCA commenced a claim and delivery (replevin) action against Spring Water Dairy and the Henstras. Spring Water Dairy then filed a petition for bankruptcy, which was dismissed on October 28, 1985. In December of 1985 PCA reinstituted its claim and delivery action. Peter Henstra promptly filed a petition for bankruptcy.

During the pendency of the chapter 13 bankruptcy proceedings PCA sought an order in its replevin action for immediate possession of the property securing the Spring Water Dairy debt. On March 31, 1986, Henstra's bankruptcy petition was dismissed. Noting the failure of the earlier chapter 11 proceeding, the bankruptcy court declared that "the filing of the chapter 13 case was in bad faith and brought for the sole purpose of frustrating lawful attempts by [Henstra's] creditors to realize on their collateral under circumstances of long-standing and substantial default on underlying indebtedness." The bankruptcy court also castigated PCA for proceeding with its replevin action in violation of the automatic stay on debt enforcement invoked by the filing of the bankruptcy petition. On that same date the state district court granted PCA the right to possession of its personal property security, effective April 3, 1986, and permanently enjoined defendants and others from disposing of any Spring Water Dairy property in which PCA held a valid security interest. Defendants immediately served a "borrower's request for mediation," notifying PCA that defendants demanded mediation pursuant to Minn. Stat. § 583.26, subd. 2(c), which had become effective on March 22, 1986. Act of

March 21, 1986, ch. 398, art. 1, § 19, 1986 Minn. Laws 400, 411. On April 8, 1986, the district court stayed enforcement of the order granting PCA possession of its collateral for 90 days, or until a mediator certified that one of the parties acted in bad faith, if that should occur earlier, so that mediation could be had in accordance with the statute.

Following its earlier decision in *Laue v. Production Credit Association*, 390 N.W.2d 823 (Minn. App. 1986), the court of appeals denied PCA's petition for extraordinary relief from the stay of the order authorizing PCA to seize Spring Water Dairy's property. For the reasons set out below, that denial does not constitute an abuse of discretion.

PCA contends, first, that to require mediation before permitting a replevin or claim and delivery action pending on March 22, 1986, the effective date of Minn. Stat. §§ 583.20-.32 (1986) is to give the Farmer-Lender Mediation Act retroactive effect.

Minn. Stat. § 583.26, subd. 1, requires a creditor who wishes to start any one of several kinds of proceedings to enforce a debt against agricultural property to serve a mediation notice on the debtor and on the director of the agricultural extension service or his nominee. The creditor may not begin the proceeding until the parties have completed mediation, except as otherwise provided in the Act. A debtor who fails to respond by filing a mediation request with the director within 14 days after receipt of the notice waives the right to mediation under the Act, and the creditor may then proceed against the agricultural property. Minn. Stat. § 583.26, subd. 2(a) and (b). Both parties, however, seize on subdivision 2(c) of section 583.26 as authority for their respective positions. Subdivision 2(c) provides:

> If a debtor has not received a mediation notice and is subject to a proceeding of a creditor enforcing a debt against agricultural property * * * the debtor may file a mediation request with the director. The mediation request form must indicate that the debtor has not received a mediation notice.

PCA bases its argument on what it conceives as the overall plan of section 583.26, contending that subdivision 2(c) does not stand alone but is part of a sequence that begins before the commencement of a proceeding with the subdivision 1 requirement that "[a] creditor desiring to start a proceeding" serve a. mediation notice. The arrangement of a statute may be a persuasive indicator of legislative intent. PCA's concept of the overall plan of section 583.26 seems, however, to begin and end with a time frame that starts before the commencement of debt enforcement proceedings. Not only does the argument limit a section which sets out a comprehensive format for manda-tory mediation to a strict chronology, but it fails to take account of the other sections of the Farmer-Lender Mediation Act and of the other parts of section 583.26 as well.

While subdivision 1 contemplates future action, subdivision 2(c) is in the present tense—"If a debtor * * * *is* subject to a proceeding of a creditor" (emphasis supplied)—and sets out a procedure by which a debtor can initiate mediation. Like subdivision 2(c), subdivision 5(a) and 5(b) refer to pending proceedings: a creditor who receives a mediation meeting notice "may not continue proceedings," and "time periods under and affecting those procedures stop running" until after mediation is concluded.

We are of the opinion that the pending procedures to which subdivisions 2 and 5 refer include those pending at the effective date of the Farmer-Lender Mediation Act as well as those procedures subsequently instituted without prior service of a mediation notice. Dismissal is the customary remedy when an action is commenced in violation of a statute. Had the legislature intended to make mediation mandatory only with respect to proceedings initiated subsequent to the effective date of the act, subdivisions 2(c), 5(a), and 5(b) would have been unnecessary. Since service of a mediation notice is prerequisite to the commencement of a proceeding to enforce a debt, a debtor served with a summons and complaint but not with a mediation notice could obtain a dismissal of the action without specific statutory provision for dismissal. The intention to permit the debtor subject to a proceeding pending on the effective date of the Act to demand mediation seems the rational purpose for the inclusion of these provisions.

Furthermore, the legislative findings set out as a sort of preamble to the Farmer-Lender Mediation Act, Minn. Stat. § 583.21 (1986), support this position. Legislative findings are given some weight in the interpretation of statutes. Here the legislature expressed concern about the severe financial stress to which the agricultural sector is subjected:

> Thousands of this state's farmers are unable to meet current payments of interest and principal payable on mortgages and other loan and land contracts and are threatened with the loss of their farmland, equipment, crops, and livestock through mortgage and lien foreclosures, cancellation of contracts for deed, and other collection actions. The agricultural economic emergency requires an orderly process with state assistance to adjust agricultural indebtedness to prevent civil unrest and to preserve the general welfare and fiscal integrity of the state.

Minn. Stat. § 583.21. Those findings are as applicable to farmers subject to debt collection proceedings which were pending on March 22, 1986, as to farmers against whom such proceedings were instituted on March 23. The threat of loss of farmland, equipment, crops, and livestock is just as real, and somewhat more imminent, where proceedings to enforce the debt were already underway on March 22, 1986, and the necessity for orderly process is equally present.

Finally, we do not regard permitting a debtor to invoke mandatory mediation before the creditor takes possession of agricultural property as retroactive application of the Act even though debt enforcement proceedings were underway before the effective date of the Act. It is simply recognition of a legislative intendment to halt the process before agricultural property changes hands and to maintain the parties in their present respective positions until they have had an opportunity to adjust the indebtedness by mediation.

PCA also contends that the district court should have ruled, as a matter of law, that the defendants' conduct prior to their demand for mediation constituted bad faith which deprived them of any right to mediation. The trial court found substantial evidence of bad faith but quite correctly observed that the Act requires that a finding of bad faith be made by the mediator, not by the district court. Minn. Stat. § 583.27, subd. 1 (1986), requires the parties to engage in mediation in good faith and describes kinds of conduct which do not show good faith. All of the described misconduct is related in some way to the mediation process or to the mediation period.

If the mediator finds that the creditor has not participated in mediation in good faith, as good faith is defined in the Act, the debtor may require court supervised mandatory mediation with continued suspension of the creditor's remedies. If the court finds that the creditor has not participated in mediation in good faith, the creditor's remedies may be suspended for an additional period of 180 days. Minn. Stat. § 583.27, subds. 2 and 3. If the mediator finds that the debtor has not participated in good faith, the creditor may immediately proceed with the creditor's remedies. Minn. Stat. § 583.27, subd. 4.

It is apparent that the good faith requirement is intended to insure good faith participation in the mandatory mediation process without regard to the prior conduct unless that prior conduct has placed the actor in such a position that the actor cannot participate in mediation in good faith. But mediation is mandatory and it is the failure of the mediation process because of bad faith that justifies the mediator's determination of bad faith and invocation of the remedies provided by the Act.

Affirmed.

NOTES AND QUESTIONS

(1) Note that the court in *Annapolis Professional Firefighters* clearly stated that agreements to mediate should be enforced in the same way as agreements to arbitrate. Why did the court fail to discuss policy arguments (e.g., futility) against enforcement? Was it because the agreement to mediate had "teeth" in that the state statute required mediation as a precursor to a state investigation to assign blame for the continuation of the dispute? *See DeValk Lincoln Mercury, Inc. v. Ford Motor Co.,* 811 F.2d 326 (7th Cir. 1987), where compliance with a "mediation clause" in a commercial agreement was a condition precedent to pursuing other legal remedies.

(2) In refusing to enforce an oral agreement to mediate, did the court in *Kirschenman* effectively rule that parties may revoke their consent to participate in "voluntary dispute resolution" at any time? Was the imposition of sanctions by the trial court appropriate in light of the fact that the defendant and his attorney apparently were available by telephone? Under what circumstances should a court permit "attendance" by telephone?

(3) In *Production Credit Association*, the court refuses to find that the defendant violated the "good faith" requirement of the state statute. The court states that the statute requires that a finding of "bad faith" be made by the mediator and not the court. As you read through the materials in the next section, consider whether it is appropriate for a mediator to enforce a

mediation-in-good-faith requirement. Would mediator enforcement be consistent with a mediator's duty to be impartial and neutral, and to maintain and preserve the confidentiality of the proceedings?

Alfini doesn't like/except for very limited situation)

§ D MEDIATION IN "GOOD FAITH"

Although mediation is considered a consensual, voluntary process, is a party in a mediation under some obligation to treat the mediation with a certain degree of seriousness, particularly where the mediation is court-ordered? The preceding section explored the consequences of a party's refusal to participate in mediation when required to do so. What if the party participates in the mediation but does so half-heartedly or strategically—so much so that the party is arguably not making a "good faith" effort to settle the case? This section presents the arguments and policy concerns over imposing a "good faith" participation requirement in mediation.

DECKER v. LINDSAY

Texas Court of Civil Appeals
824 S.W.2d 247 (1992)

SAM H. BASS, J.

Issues

We are faced with two questions today: (1) Can a party be compelled to participate in an alternative dispute resolution (ADR) procedure despite its objections?, and (2) Have relators established their right to mandamus relief?

John and Mary Decker, relators, seek mandamus relief against respondent, Judge Tony Lindsay, who signed an order on October 18, 1991 referring their suit against Jordan Mintz, the real party in interest, to mediation under TEX. CIV. PRAC. & REM. CODE ANN. § 154.021(a).

The October 18, 1991, order requires the parties to agree on a mediation date "within the next 30 days," or by November 18, 1991. If no agreed date is scheduled, the order provides that the mediator will select a date within the next 60 days, or by December 18, 1991. The order also reads, "TO BE MEDIATED PRIOR TO TRIAL SETTING OF 1-20-92."

We are concerned primarily with the following provisions of Judge Lindsay's order:

Mediation is a *mandatory but non-binding settlement conference,* conducted with the assistance of the Mediator. . . .

Fees for the mediation are to be divided and borne equally by the parties unless agreed otherwise, shall be paid by the parties directly to the Mediator, and shall be taxed as costs. *Each party and counsel will be bound by the Rules for Mediation printed on the back of this Order.* . . .

Named parties shall be present during the entire mediation process. . . . *Counsel and parties shall proceed in a good faith effort to try to resolve this case.* . . .

Referral to mediation is not a substitute for trial, and the case will be tried if not settled.

(Emphasis added.)

Two of the Rules for Mediation, affixed to the order, are relevant to our discussion:

2. Agreement of the Parties. Whenever the parties have agreed to mediation they shall be deemed to have made these rules, as amended and in effect as of the date of the submission of the dispute, a part of their agreement to mediate.

. . . .

6. Commitment to Participate in Good Faith. While no one is asked to commit to settle their dispute in advance of mediation, all parties commit to participate in the proceedings in good faith with the intention to settle, if at all possible.

Mandamus issues only to correct a clear abuse of discretion or the violation of a duty imposed by law when there is no other adequate remedy by law. Mandamus relief may be afforded where the trial court's order is void. However, the order of the trial court must be one beyond the power of the court to enter; it is not enough that the order is merely erroneous. The relator bears the burden of establishing his entitlement to mandamus relief.

Relators assert Judge Lindsay's order is void and constitutes a clear abuse of discretion for the following reasons, which they also stated in their objection to mediation filed with the trial court: (1) the lawsuit arises out of a simple rear-end car collision, where the only issues are negligence, proximate cause, and damages; (2) trial is likely to last for only two days; (3) it is relators' opinion that mediation will not resolve the lawsuit, and they have not agreed to pay fees to the mediator; (4) mediation may cause relators to compromise their potential cause of action under the *Stowers* doctrine; (5) the law does not favor alternative dispute resolution where one of the litigants objects to it and when the litigants have been ordered to pay for it; and (6) court-ordered mediation, over the relators' objection and at their cost, violates their right to due process under the fifth and fourteenth amendments to the United States Constitution and article I, section 13 of the Texas Constitution and their right to open courts under article I, section 13 of the Texas Constitution.

The real party in interest disputes relators' contention that the lawsuit and its issues are simple. The real party in interest has raised the defense of unavoidable accident and asserts that the parties have wide-ranging disagreement over Mr. Decker's claimed economic and medical damages.

Relators contend that trial will last for only two days. Consequently, it will take only slightly more time than the mediation ordered. However, the proposed joint pretrial order, signed by counsel for the relators and counsel for the real party in interest, provides an estimated trial time of three to four days.

While relators assert that mediation will not resolve the lawsuit, the real party in interest suggests that in a day invested in mediation, where communication between the parties is facilitated, relators may change their evaluation of the lawsuit.

Under TEX. CIV. PRAC. & REM. CODE ANN. § 154.054(a) (Vernon Supp. 1992), the court may set a reasonable fee for the services of an impartial third party appointed to facilitate an ADR procedure. Unless otherwise agreed by the parties, the court must tax the fee as other costs of the suit. TEX. CIV. PRAC. & REM. CODE ANN. § 154.054(b) (Vernon Supp. 1992). No fee was ever set for the mediation in this case. On December 6, 1991, after this proceeding was filed, the mediator advised the parties that she waived her fee in the case.

We cannot say that Judge Lindsay abused her discretion in impliedly finding the first three reasons advanced by relators were not reasonable objections to court-ordered mediation. Mediation may be beneficial even if relators believe it will not resolve the lawsuit. The statute certainly allows a reasonable fee to be charged, and relators never challenged the reasonableness of the fee, but now the fee issue is moot.

Concerning relators' remaining objections, Texas law recognizes that an insurer has a duty to the insured to settle a lawsuit if a prudent person in the exercise of ordinary care would do so. *G.A. Stowers Furniture Co., 15 S.W.2d at 547;* If an ordinarily prudent person would have settled the lawsuit, and the insurer failed or refused to do so, it is liable to the insured for the amount of damages eventually recovered in excess of the policy limits. Relators assert that an insured, for example the real party in interest here, frequently assigns to the plaintiff his *Stowers* rights against his insurer, in return for a covenant that the plaintiff will not execute on the insured's personal assets. Therefore, relators contend that by ordering them to mediation, Judge Lindsay is interfering with their right to preserve a potential cause of action against the liability insurer of the real party in interest.

First, relators have no *Stowers* rights against the liability insurer of the real party in interest. *See American Centennial Ins. Co., 810 S.W.2d at 250-51.* Second, there has been no trial; there has been no judgment; there has been no assignment of the real party in interest's *Stowers* rights to relators; there has been no determination that a reasonably prudent person would have decided, at the time relators made their offer, to settle the litigation for the policy limits. A *Stowers* cause of action does not accrue until the judgment in the underlying case becomes final. We cannot say that Judge Lindsay abused her discretion in impliedly finding that court-ordered mediation would not cause relators to compromise a potential cause of action under *Stowers.*

Relators rely on *Simpson v. Canales, 806 S.W.2d 802 (Tex. 1991),* for their contention that the law does not favor alternative dispute resolution procedures where one of the parties objects to it and when the parties are compelled to pay for it. Relators' reliance on *Simpson* is misplaced. In *Simpson,* the supreme court found that the trial court abused its discretion in appointing a master to supervise all discovery because the "exceptional cases/good cause" criteria of TEX. R. CIV. P. 171 had not been met and the blanket reference of all discovery was unjustified. Although the supreme court commented that the parties had been ordered to pay for resolution of discovery issues by a master that other litigants obtained from the court without such expense, the matter of expense was not a basis for the court's decision.

Relators also argue that chapter 154 of the Texas Civil Practice and Remedies Code presents a "voluntary" procedure, and that mandatory referral to a paid mediator is not within its scope.

Section 154.002 expresses the general policy that "peaceable resolution of disputes" is to be encouraged through "voluntary settlement procedures." TEX. CIV. PRAC. & REM. CODE ANN. § 154.002 (Vernon Supp. 1992). Courts are admonished to carry out this policy. TEX. CIV. PRAC. & REM. CODE ANN. § 154.003 (Vernon Supp. 1992). A court cannot force the disputants to peaceably resolve their differences, but it can compel them to sit down with each other.

Section 154.021(a) authorizes a trial court on its motion to refer a dispute to an ADR procedure. However, if a party objects, and there is a reasonable basis for the objection, the court may not refer the dispute to an ADR procedure. TEX. CIV. PROC. & REM. CODE ANN. § 154.022(c). The corollary of this provision is that a court may refer the dispute to an ADR procedure if it finds there is no reasonable basis for the objection. A person appointed to facilitate an ADR procedure may not compel the parties to mediate (negotiate) or coerce the parties to enter into a settlement agreement. TEX. CIV. PRAC. & REM. CODE ANN. § 154.053(b) (Vernon Supp. 1992). A mediator may not impose his or her own judgment on the issues for that of the parties. TEX. CIV. PRAC. & REM. CODE ANN. § 154.023(b) (Vernon Supp. 1992).

Therefore, the policy of section 154.002 is consistent with a scheme where a court refers a dispute to an ADR procedure, requiring the parties to come together in court-ordered ADR procedures, but no one can compel the parties to negotiate or settle a dispute unless they voluntarily and mutually agree to do so. Any inconsistencies in chapter 154 can be resolved to give effect to a dominant legislative intent to compel referral, but not resolution.

However, Judge Lindsay's order does not comport with the scheme set forth in chapter 154. Her order, and the mediation rules that are a part of it, do more than require the parties to come together; they require them to "negotiate" in good faith and attempt to reach a settlement.

Finally, relators object to Judge Lindsay's order on the constitutional grounds of due process and open courts.

Relators' brief does not contain any argument or authorities supporting their contention that their due process rights under the fifth and fourteenth amendments to the United States Constitution and article I, section 13 of the Texas Constitution have been violated. Therefore, they have not demonstrated their entitlement to mandamus relief on this ground. They have not brought forth contentions that chapter 154 is in and of itself unconstitutional.

However, in one very important respect, Judge Lindsay's order violates the open courts provision. It requires relators attempt to negotiate a settlement of the dispute with the real party in interest in good faith, when they have clearly indicated they do not wish to do so, but prefer to go to trial. As we noted above, the order does more than refer the dispute to an ADR procedure; it requires negotiation. Chapter 154 contemplates mandatory referral only, not mandatory negotiation.

Having reviewed the arguments of relators, which do not attack the statute, but only the order of referral, and those of the real party in interest and the documents submitted to us, we conclude that Judge Lindsay's order is void insofar as it directs relators to negotiate in good faith a resolution of their dispute with the real party in interest through mediation, despite relators' objections.

We conditionally grant the petition for writ of mandamus, and order Judge Lindsay to vacate those portions of her order of October 18, 1991, that require the parties to participate in mediation proceedings in good faith with the intention of settling. We are confident that Judge Lindsay will act in accordance with this opinion. The writ will issue only in the event she fails to comply.

NOTES AND QUESTIONS

(1) Subsequent Texas appellate court decisions appear to be split over the question of whether to uphold a trial court's imposition of sanctions for failing to mediate in good faith. *Compare Texas Department of Transportation v. Pirtle*, 977 S.W.2d 657 (Tex. App. Ct. 1998) (upholding trial court's assessment of costs against a party that did not file a written objection to the court's mediation order but then refused to mediate in good faith) *with Texas Parks and Wildlife Department v. Davis*, 988 S.W.2d 370 (Tex. App. Ct. 1999) (overturning trial court's sanction and distinguishing *Pirtle* on the grounds that a written objection to the mediation had been filed).

(2) The following debate between Professor Kim Kovach and Dean Edward Sherman took place in the wake of the decision in *Decker v. Lindsay*.

LAWYER ETHICS IN MEDIATION: TIME FOR A REQUIREMENT OF GOOD FAITH IN MEDIATION

Winter 1997 Disp. Resol. Mag., pp. 9–13 [*]

By Kimberlee K. Kovach

If mediation is to survive as a truly different paradigm for dispute resolution, then we must design and implement a requirement of good faith participation in the process.

As a process that allows parties involved in a dispute to discuss their positions, interests and options for resolution, mediation relies upon communication to achieve greater understanding in an effort to reach mutually satisfactory resolutions. This is a major paradigm shift from the traditional adversary system. The rules and guidelines appropriate for an adversarial, third-party determined outcome, are, at best, inapplicable to a participatory, interest-based mutual problem-solving process.

Even though lawyers are often instructed about alternative dispute resolution procedures, their inclination in practice is to resume known behaviors, many of which are not conducive to a less or non-adversarial process. Research has demonstrated that even when lawyers desire to use a more collaborative problem-solving approach to negotiation, they find it difficult to do.

As the use of mediation has increased, it has become subsumed by the legal system and those who practice within it. Adversariness has continued, albeit inappropriately, within mediation. In this context of mediation, often missing are the positive attributes such as party participation, creativity and the all-gain collaborative approaches that contribute to satisfaction with the process.

As reluctant as I am to urge rules, especially where flexibility of the process is of paramount concern, if mediation is to survive at all as a distinct paradigm, then there must exist rules that guarantee that conduct by the participants is consistent with the goals and objectives of the process. Consequently, guidelines that direct and enforce behaviors favorable for mediation must be enacted and implemented, or the potential of the mediation paradigm will fail.

In this article, I first examine why such a requirement is necessary, despite some of the admitted difficulties with its implementation. I then attempt to describe what is meant by a "good faith" requirement. Methods of implementation are discussed, as well as potential consequences for the failure to adhere to such a requirement.

Why a Rule is Necessary

As a component of good faith and the wisdom of such a requirement is contemplated, consideration must be given to the absence of this element. Many times mediations are conducted with an assumption that good faith is to be present. Agreements to mediate include good faith participation and when describing mediation, both academic and practice-oriented literature include good faith as part of the process.

Yet conflict arose in Texas when an intermediary appellate court explicitly stated that good faith need not be present in mediation—or at least the court could not order it.[2] Thereafter, mediation was often treated as nothing more than another step in the litigation path to the courthouse. This view of mediation is coincidental with, and likely caused by, at least in part, the assimilation of mediation within the legal system.

Yet, if good faith participation was required, mediation would likely be a different process, one more consistent with earlier definitions, such as assisting parties in reaching a mutually satisfactory or acceptable resolution and assisting individuals in achieving a new perception of their relationship and attitudes.

The resolution of conflict within the United States legal system is still based largely upon the win-lose dichotomy as determined by a third party. Alternatively, underlying mediation, is the opportunity for the parties themselves, often in collaboration with each other, to reach the resolution. In an adversarial context, lawyers are quick to legalize a matter—and view it solely in terms of legal precepts and definitions. In mediation, a broad view of the

---

[2] See Decker v. Lindsay, 824 S.W.2d 247 (Tex. Ct. App. 1992).

problem may assist in creative solutions. In litigation, much time is spent trying to obtain information, and conversely withholding it until trial. Mediation is based upon sharing information, honest disclosure, and perhaps, good faith and fair dealing in the effort to achieve a mutually satisfactory solution.

Praise for ADR in general is often focused on benefits to the court, specifically settlement. But additional attributes of ADR have been acknowledged, many of which are more prevalent in mediation than the other processes. Assisted dialogue, cooperative and collaborative problem solving, reality testing, empowerment, flexibility and the search for mutually beneficial solutions are among special characteristics of ADR.

Query whether these attributes can exist at all in an environment where good faith is absent? For example, if in a mediation, one party fails to cooperate—perhaps failing to disclose information—how can the other be expected to cooperate? Or one side refuses to move or makes increments of increase or decrease so small as to insult the other, can it really be expected that the other side will make any move? Much of mediation is conducted in a litigation context, the habitat of the adversary; participants who come to mediation from an adversarial context, bring tactics that emphasize and continue adversariness. Consequently, where no effort to settle exists, the procedure is frustrated.

If process-debilitating techniques continue, the result will be mutation of the mediation process to accommodate adversarial conduct. In many ways, this has already happened. The notion of mediation as a novel paradigm for dispute resolution is being eroded, as lawyers view the process as merely another tool within the litigation arena to be used combatively.

Examples of dilatory uses of mediation abound. One is the scheduling of mediation for the sole purpose of discovery—that is, the use of mediation to assess the other side in terms of their potential effectiveness at trial or to wear down a litigant where one party is more financially able than the other.

Another is fraud or misrepresentation in mediations that leads one side to make an agreement they likely otherwise would not have, or actual deception during and as part of the mediation regarding who was present and their role, specifically a jury consultant.

Obstacles to Overcome

A number of obstacles stand in the path of implementation of a good faith requirement. Yet addressing and dealing with them seems no more difficult than allowing the mediation process to be mutated to another pretrial procedure, such as discovery.

For example, defining good faith has been problematic in a number of other situations where it is has been imposed. Yet such definitional difficulty was not preclusive. The courts have struggled with defining good faith, but that is often the nature of legal concepts. Indeed, mediation itself is a definitional dilemma.

Although one alternative to good faith has been suggested—that is, the concept of minimal meaningful participation or just participation—this too has been noted to be just as difficult to define with precision as the term good faith. In the end, struggling with a precise, usable definition of good faith may, in fact, lead to more in-depth scrutiny of mediation and its uses, particularly as implemented with legalized disputes, and perhaps it is like obscenity: you know it when you see it.

Some fear that implementation of a good faith requirement will necessitate compromise of the mediator's role, particularly with regard to confidentiality and neutrality. While good faith may remain somewhat subjective in determination, which may, at times, place a burden on the mediator, this could be no greater a burden than the mediator has to carry when parties abuse the process. Currently, mediators commonly disclose that a party has failed to appear for mediation. Reporting the absence of good faith can be seen as an extension of the obligation to inform the court of the parties' compliance with the order to mediation.

While subscribing to the concept of the mediator's role as one of facilitation, I also believe that the mediator has a professional duty to set parameters and be in control of the process. Making an assessment or determination of the good faith nature of the parties' participation falls within this role. Identification of specific guidelines and objective considerations would aid the mediator in deciding if the parties complied with the requirement.

Theorists and practitioners alike are adamant about the confidential nature of the mediation process; but like most things in life, nothing is absolute. Although the mediator should generally maintain the privacy of the parties, there are situations where an overriding interest, such as the life or safety of an individual takes precedence.

To be sure, where a good faith requirement exists, there should be a concurrent exception to any rule on confidentiality, since the communication during the mediation is essential evidence to address the claim of bad faith. Mediators will likely not be proponents of an exception to confidentiality, nor relish the idea of appearing in a court to testify about the mediation.

One option is to have the mediator merely "certify" whether good faith was present, or provide a written checklist about the parties' conduct; in Minnesota, the mediator files an affidavit. This does, however, confer a decisional role on the mediator that will affect neutrality. However, this is likely after the fact. Alternatively, the mediator might report to the court what specifically happened (or didn't) and allow the court to make the final determination of whether the conduct constituted bad faith. In both instances, the court would decide proper sanctions, if any.

With a limit on the ability of the mediator to testify, and guidelines about the allegations that must be substantiated, the exception to confidentiality can be narrowly drawn. Difficulties encountered in creating a very specific, narrow and limited exception for the reporting of violations of a good faith requirement will be outweighed by the benefits of such an obligation.

There is also fear that the establishment of a good faith requirement in mediation will trigger satellite litigation regarding the rule itself. It would be paradoxical indeed if a process designed to reduce litigation and ease the administration of justice created its own special brand of vexing and annoying motion practice. Specific guidelines for what constitutes good faith as well as rational sanctions for non-compliance are ways to reduce the potential, although satellite litigation is not wholly preventable and in fact is happening already in mediation in other contexts. However, the benefits of good faith participation in the majority of cases that participate positively in mediation outweigh the detriment of potential of satellite litigation.

Ethical Tensions

Good faith participation in mediation may also be viewed by lawyers as conflicting with established ethical duties. Lawyers remark that to meet and discuss a case with the opponent, let alone work together in reaching an agreement, is antithetical to one's zealous representation of the client. It is perceived as almost "wimpy" to sit down amicably with the "other side." Embracing the rule of zealous representation is often justification for rambo-like tactics, and consequently lawyers are hesitant to collaborate with others in a creative problem-solving effort.

Tulane Law School Dean Ed Sherman outlined the values of our civil litigation system with the assertion that these values should also accompany the use of alternatives within that system. This statement is likely premised upon the use of ADR as a method to achieve settlement within litigation, and therefore any settlement should be consistent with its context, the court. Although these values may be laudable within the legal system, I am not convinced that they are necessarily appropriate in the context of alternatives, particularly when inclusion may modify, if not destroy, the alternatives.

This is precisely the reason why we need new ethical duties established. Good faith in negotiation may very well conflict with the adversarial model of problem solving. But as we embark into the next century with new and alternative methods of lawyering, where neither the trial nor the courtroom is the paradigm for dispute resolution, we must, in the same way, enact modern rules of ethics.

A precise and specific definition of good faith must be determined prior to implementation of such a rule. Prior criticism of good faith directives is based on the lack of objective standards, and that a demonstration of good or bad faith is dependent on one's state of mind. Objective standards, that are not based upon the content of the proposals, are therefore necessary.

In my view, good faith relates to the *manner* of participation rather than its content. A good faith requirement is essentially strong encouragement for the parties and their counsel to use their best efforts during the mediation process. Good faith does not imply that parties are required to resolve their disputes, and certainly should not be used to coerce the parties to settle the matter on any particular economic basis.

Similarly, an allegation of bad faith should not be based upon the specific content of the negotiations. Economic aspects, the offers and responses, in and of themselves, may not create a bad faith claim. . . .

What a Good Faith Requirement Could Look Like

The following are mere suggestions which have not benefited from the wisdom of deliberation, discussion or comment.

Model Rule for Lawyers Requiring Good Faith Participation in the Mediation Process

Rule 1.7 GOOD FAITH IN MEDIATION

A lawyer representing a client in mediation shall participate in good faith.

(a) Prior to the mediation, the lawyer shall prepare by familiarizing herself with the matter, and discussing it with her client.

(b) At the mediation, the lawyer shall comply with all rules of court or statute governing the mediation process, and counsel her client to do likewise.

(c) During the mediation, the lawyer shall not convey information that is intentionally misleading or false to the mediator or other participants.

Statutory Basis for Good Faith Requirement

MEDIATION CODE

001. All parties and their counsel shall participant in mediation in good faith. "Good Faith" includes the following:

a. Compliance with the terms and provisions of [cite to state statute or other rule setting forth mediation; for example Texas Civil Practice and Remedies Code, §154. 001 et seq.].

b. Compliance with any specific court order referring the matter to mediation.

c. Compliance with the terms and provisions of all standing orders of the court and any local rules of the court.

d. Personal attendance at the mediation by all parties who are fully authorized to settle the dispute. This shall *not* be construed to include anyone present by telephone.

e. Preparation for the mediation by the parties and their representatives. This includes the exchange of any documents requested or as set forth in a rule, order, or request of the mediator.

f. Participation in meaningful discussions with the mediator and all other participants during the mediation.

g. Compliance with all contractual terms regarding mediation which the parties may have previously agreed to.

h. Following the rules set out by the mediator during the introductory phase of the process.

i. Remaining at the mediation until the mediator determines that the process is at an end or excuses the parties.

j. Engaging in direct communication and discussion between the parties to the dispute, as facilitated by the mediator.

k. Making no affirmative misrepresentations or misleading statements to the other parties or the mediator during the mediation.

l. In pending lawsuits, refrain from filing any new motions until the conclusion of the mediation.

002. "Good Faith" does not require the parties to settle the dispute. The proposals made at mediation, monetary or otherwise, in and of themselves do not constitute the presence or absence of good faith.

003. Determination of Good Faith

a. In court-annexed cases, the court shall make the final determination of whether good faith was present in the mediation.

b. Where a lawsuit has not been filed, the responsibility for finding a violation of the good faith duty rests upon the mediator, who shall use the elements of this statute and context of any contract between the parties as a basis for deliberation.

004. Consequences for the Failure to Mediate in Good Faith

If it is determined that a party or a representative of a party has failed to mediate in good faith, the following actions can be instituted at the discretion of the court or mediator:

a. The individual shall pay all fees, costs, and reasonable expenses incurred by the other participants.

b. The individual will pay the costs of another mediation.

c. The individual will be fined up to $5,000.00.

"GOOD FAITH" PARTICIPATION IN MEDIATION: ASPIRATIONAL, NOT MANDATORY

Winter 1997 Disp. Resol. Mag., pp. 14–16 *

By Edward F. Sherman

Professor Kim Kovach expresses in this magazine the understandable concern that, with increased use of mediation in disputes pending in the courts, it is becoming "subsumed by the legal system" as the lawyers involved resort to traditional adversary behavior. The solution she proposes is a "good faith" participation requirement enforced by sanctions and applicable in all mediations.

Right Goals, Wrong Remedy

I have no quarrel with the values and aspirations that Professor Kovach sets out for mediation. Mediation, relying "upon communication to achieve greater understanding in an effort to reach mutually satisfactory resolutions," is certainly aided by the candid and sincere participation of parties and lawyers. "Honest disclosure" of relevant information should be encouraged in the interests of promoting a mutually-acceptable settlement. Parties and lawyers should be urged to engage "in open and frank discussions" so as to

---

"set out one's position for others to better know and understand." The process clearly works best if they "demonstrate a willingness to listen and attempt to understand the position and interests of the other parties" and "to discuss positions in detail, and explain the rationale" for any proposal.

Where I disagree with Professor Kovach is that this level of communication should be mandated and enforced by sanctions in rules and court orders requiring "good faith" participation. Mediation is a voluntary, consensual process in which the parties are empowered to seek their own solutions with the aid of a mediator facilitator. Court rules adopted in recent years requiring parties to mediate are justified as only requiring participation in a nonbinding process that does not undermine their right not to settle. A requirement of "good faith" participation, which is inherently vague and subjective, unduly entrenches on the voluntariness of settlement and on parties' legitimate right to demand their day in court.

When a mediation is not court-ordered, the parties are free to agree to reasonable participation requirements that would be enforceable by an action for breach of contract. But where the mediation is ordered by a court, participation requirements should not unduly interfere with the parties' choice as to such forms of participation as how to present and argue their case, what information to reveal, whether to make offers or counteroffers, and whether to settle.

I have no trouble with setting out in advance the aspirations for proper participation in a court-ordered mediation. A court order (or the mediator in writing or orally) can properly describe the kind of participation that will enhance communication in the mediation. Mediators routinely seek to obtain a general commitment from the parties that they will make a fair and reasonable attempt to resolve the matter through mediation. Mediators also often urge the parties to be frank and candid and to listen to the other side with an open mind.

Analogies Don't Work

Insofar as these are only aspirations that the mediator encourages the parties to try to achieve, I see no problems. It is only when such vague aspirations are converted into legal mandates enforceable by sanctions that I think a "good faith" requirement is inconsistent with the objectives of mediation.

Court orders and rules sometimes require "good faith" participation, although that requirement has been found improper by a Texas appellate court. Federal Rule of Civil Procedure 16(f) provides for sanctions for failing "to participate in good faith" in a pretrial conference, but this has generally been invoked only for such objective behavior as failure to appear or prepare.

Similarly, the labor laws do impose a duty to bargain "in good faith." However, this is an inapt analogy for mediation because collective bargaining contemplates that the employer and bargaining representative will jointly set wages and working conditions and are therefore required to participate actively with an intention to reach agreement.

It is, of course, true that courts have found bad faith bargaining in such conduct as "Boulwarism" (adopting a "take it or leave it" position), "surface bargaining" (as in rejecting a proposal and tendering one's own without attempting to reconcile the differences), offering a proposal that is "predictably unacceptable," and failing to offer "concessions of value." It is also true that these examples of bad faith in collective bargaining are fairly conventional tactics sometimes used by negotiators in lawsuits.

Mediation, however, is an entirely different kind of process. It is essentially a process of assisted negotiation in which the parties are entitled to make concessions or to present offers that are unattractive or unacceptable to the other side. To deny them the right to take strong, or even extreme, positions— for example, that there is no liability, or that a certain sum is the only basis on which a settlement is possible—would deny them the legitimate right to have those issues determined by a trial. Because of the ultimate right to a jury trial, the level of accommodation to the other side that is and should be required in collective bargaining is not suitable for mediation.

Subjectivity of "Good Faith"

A number of Professor Kovach's factors for determining whether there is "good faith" participation reveal how subjective and vague that standard is. Consider:

- How would a court being asked to impose sanctions determine if a party "arrive[d] at the mediation prepared with knowledge of the case" having "taken into account the interests of the other parties"?

- What would a court have to review to determine whether a party "engag[ed] in open and frank discussions about the case" in a way that "set out one's position for others to better know and understand"?

- What would demonstrate a lack of "willingness to listen and attempt to understand the position and interests of the other parties" and "to discuss positions in detail, and explain the rationale why a specific proposal is all that will be offered, or why one is refused"?

Professor Kovach's proposed statute is not quite so expansive, but still defines "good faith" in such hard-to-determine terms as "engaging in direct communication and discussion" and making no "misleading statements."

Enforcement of a "good faith" participation requirement raises the possibility of satellite litigation, seeking sanctions that could severely undermine the economy and efficiency in mediation. As demonstrated by the history of Rule 11 sanctions, the potential for adversariness in sanctions litigation can easily cancel out any benefit from the deterrent effect of sanctions.

Confidentiality Problems

There are also serious confidentiality problems in litigating requests for sanctions. The parties and mediator may be called on to testify concerning communications made during the mediation. Courts would thus be faced with either rejecting confidentiality in bad faith participation cases (thereby undermining the need to encourage candor in mediations), or upholding confidentiality (thereby denying the parties access to crucial evidence on the participation issue).

Professor Kovach would create an exception to mediation confidentiality "since the communication during the mediation is essential evidence to address the claim of bad faith." This would open the door to calling the mediator and parties to testify as to much of what went on in the mediation, including what was said, what offers were made, what parties' reactions were, etc. Her suggestion that the "mediator might report to the court what specifically happened (or didn't)" would be an alarming breach of mediation confidentiality.

I have no trouble with requirements imposed by rules or court orders as to reasonably objective conduct. These would include providing the other party and mediator with a short statement of 1) the issues in dispute, 2) the party's position as to them, 3) the relief sought (including a particularized itemization of all damages claimed), and 4) any offers or counter-offers already made. An order might also require parties to provide in advance, or bring to the mediation, certain documents, such as current medical reports or specific business records deemed central to the issues. Finally, a requirement that the parties and counsel attend (including those who have reasonable authority to settle) has been upheld—although I disagree with Professor Kovach's proposed rule that attendance could never be satisfied by telephone.

Objective Conduct Standards

I have also suggested that a less subjective participation requirement might be the "minimal meaningful participation" necessary to insure that the process is not futile. Mediation is the least structured ADR process and requires the least amount of formal participation. In achieving its objective of getting the parties to communicate in the interests of settlement, it requires little more than that they briefly indicate their positions as to the relevant issues, listen to the other side and react to its positions.

Unlike "evaluative" and "trial run" ADR processes, a comprehensive presentation of the case is not necessarily required. Failure to address or to disclose information as to all issues may suggest weakness or lack of candor to the other party and thereby lower its willingness to make offers, but that is a strategic risk a party should be entitled to take. Although an objective of mediation is to identify the underlying interests of the parties in hope of finding a solution that satisfies both sides, the disguising of true interests and bottom lines cannot realistically be prohibited; the courts would be enmeshed in judging subjective negotiation behavior that could severely abridge litigant autonomy.

I am sympathetic to Professor Kovach's concern with devising standards of participation conduct that are consistent with the goals and objectives of mediation. But I think that, like the "professionalism" codes, the standards should be aspirational rather than mandatory and enforceable by sanctions.

NOTES AND QUESTIONS

(1) Professor Kovach's proposed statute places the responsibility on the court rather than the mediator, in court-annexed mediations, to "make the final determination of whether good faith was present in the mediation." Although placing responsibility on the court may initially overcome concerns over compromising confidentiality and mediator neutrality, how will a court make this determination absent input from the mediator?

(2) Consider how the courts made the good faith determination in the following two cases.

IN RE BOLDEN

District of Columbia Court of Appeals
719 A.2d 1253 (1998)

Farrell, *Associate Judge*:

In the course of a tax appeal, the Superior Court judge imposed a civil penalty—a fine of $200—on attorney A. Scott Bolden after Bolden, in the judge's words, "unilaterally [aborted]" a mediation session held under the Superior Court's Multi-Door Dispute Resolution ("Multi-Door") system. The judge's authority for the sanction was Super. Ct. Tax R. 13 (b), which states in relevant part:

> If counsel or an unrepresented party . . . fails to appear for *or participate in good faith* in any alternative dispute resolution session, the Court may dismiss the case with or without prejudice, or take such other action, including the award of attorney's fees and reasonable expenses, and the imposition of . . . *such other penalties and sanctions, as it deems appropriate.* [Emphasis added.]

See also Super. Ct. Civ. R. 16 (l), 16-II.

Underlying the judge's imposition of the fine was her determination that Bolden "did not have the agreement of all the parties when counsel aborted said mediation." We observe, however, that no judge is present at Multi-Door mediation sessions, nor was the record of the meeting in question here transcribed or taped. The District of Columbia, a party to the tax appeal, *was* present at the mediation and has conceded in its brief and oral argument to us that the record as constituted does not support the finding of an unconsented, "unilateral" termination of the mediation by Bolden. The judge apparently relied on statements such as the following in written submissions Bolden filed: "Petitioners' counsel decided not to go forward"; "Petitioners' counsel advised the respondent's [*i.e.*, the District's] counsel, the mediator, and the [Tax] Division representative of his decision to seek a new mediation schedule." We agree with Bolden that these are insufficient, without more, to support the finding of a unilateral termination. Elsewhere Bolden explained to the judge: "The respondents . . . did not object to rescheduling of the mediation. In fact, although respondents advised petitioners' counsel that they were ready to proceed [with the mediation], they also confirmed that they would not (and did not) take a position or object if petitioners' counsel made the appropriate representations to the Court regarding a *request* for rescheduling of the mediation." (Emphasis in original.) The District does not dispute this account.

While Tax Rule 13 (b) requires counsel to "participate in good faith in any alternative dispute resolution session," nothing in it suggests that there must be a formal, on-the-record consent to an adjournment pending a party's request for rescheduling by the court. That would impose undue formality on a process which, while mandatory when applicable, is meant to be flexible and to preserve the parties' ultimate control over their case. Moreover, Bolden's reason for wanting postponement is clearly relevant to whether he took part in good faith. Bolden represented, and the District has not disputed, that the reason he suggested rescheduling the mediation was the mediator's refusal upon objection by the District to allow his tax expert, who had become physically unavailable on short notice, to participate via telephone conference call. Correct though that ruling may have been, Bolden's consequent unwillingness to go forward until the expert was available is understandable—particularly since, as he also represented, the agreed purpose for this meeting had been to hear the expert's opinion. Although the judge opined that the expert's views and supporting information "could have been made available to counsel, prior to the mediation, for counsel's use during the mediation," the District rightly points out that this entails considerable surmise as to what sort of presentation would have been acceptable to the District and sufficient to make the mediation fruitful.

A trial judge's decision to impose a sanction under Tax Rule 13 (b), like similar decisions under Super. Ct. Civ. R. 16 (l) and 16-II, will be reviewed only for an abuse of discretion. Informed discretion, however, "requires that the trial court's determination be based upon and drawn from a firm factual foundation." We hold that this foundation is lacking for the judge's conclusion that Bolden acted in bad faith in causing adjournment of the mediation session. Accordingly, we vacate the sanction ordered by the trial judge.

NICK v. MORGAN'S FOODS, INC.

United States District Court for the Eastern District of Missouri
99 F. Supp. 2d 1056 (2000).

RODNEY W. SIPPEL, J.

Morgan's Foods, Inc. seeks reconsideration of this Court's order sanctioning it for its failure to participate in mediation in good faith.

In contravention of this Court's Order referring this matter to Alternative Dispute Resolution (ADR), Morgan's Foods failed to submit the required mediation memorandum and failed to send a corporate representative with authority to settle the case to the mediation. Not surprisingly, the mediator was unable to mediate a settlement. After being called upon to explain why it ignored the Court's Order regarding ADR, counsel for Morgan's Foods admitted that his client—on his advice—made a calculated decision to disregard some of the provisions of the ADR Referral Order. Based on Morgan's Foods' failure to comply with key provisions of the ADR Referral Order, the Court concluded that Morgan's Foods failed to participate in mediation in good faith and entered sanctions accordingly. Morgan's Foods now asks the Court to reconsider the imposition of sanctions. Because the Court remains convinced that Morgan's Foods and its counsel did not participate in good faith in the ADR process, its motion for reconsideration will be denied. Moreover, the Court will impose additional sanctions for the frivolous nature of this motion and Morgan's Foods' vexatious multiplication of these proceedings.

Background

Gee Gee Nick filed this lawsuit against Morgan's Foods alleging sexual harassment and retaliation in violation of Title VII of the Civil Rights Act of 1964. A scheduling conference pursuant to Federal Rule of Civil Procedure 16 (Rule 16) was held on May 20, 1999. At that time, the parties were asked if they wished to participate in the ADR process pursuant to E.D.Mo. L.R. 6.01 – 6.05. The matter was set for referral to ADR on August 1, 1999. The parties were to complete the ADR process and report back to the Court the results of the mediation by September 30, 1999.

The August 2, 1999 Order of Referral required the ADR process to be conducted in compliance with E.D.Mo. L.R. 6.01 – 6.05. The Order of Referral also specifically required:

(1) **Memoranda:** Not later than seven **(7) days** prior to the initial ADR conference, each party will **provide the neutral with a memorandum** presenting a summary of disputed facts and a narrative discussion of its position relative to both liability and damages. These memoranda shall be treated as **Confidential Communications** and shall not be filed in the public record of the case nor provided to any other party or counsel.

(2) **Identification of Corporate and/or Claims Representatives:** As a part of the written memoranda described in paragraph (1), counsel for corporate parties or insurers shall state the name and general job titles of the employee(s) or agent(s) of the corporation or insurance company who will attend ADR conferences and participate on behalf of the entity.

(3) **Authority of Neutral:** The neutral shall have authority to consult and conduct conferences and private caucuses with counsel, individual parties, corporate representatives and claims professionals, to suggest alternatives, analyze issues and positions, question perceptions, stimulate negotiations, and keep order.

(4) **Duty to Attend and Participate:** All parties, counsel of record, and corporate representatives or claims professionals **having authority to settle claims** shall attend all mediation conferences and **participate in good faith**. Early neutral evaluation conferences shall be attended by all counsel of record.

(5) Compliance with Deadlines: all deadlines must be complied with in a timely fashion and the appropriate forms filed with the Clerk of the District Court. If a deadline cannot be met, the designated lead counsel shall **file a motion requesting an extension of the deadline** prior to the expiration of that deadline. **Noncompliance of any deadline set herein by this Court may result in the imposition of sanctions to the appropriate party or parties.**

(emphasis added)

Prior to the mediation, counsel for Morgan's Foods indicated to Nick's counsel, but not the Court, that he did not feel that the mediation would be fruitful. Morgan's Foods' only request for relief directed to the Court was a request to hold the ADR conference on October 18, 1999. The Court allowed the parties to delay mediation until that date.

The parties appeared before the Court on another matter on October 15, 1999. At that time, the Court inquired into the parties' preparedness for the upcoming mediation. Counsel for Morgan's Foods assured the Court that his client was prepared to discuss settlement in good faith and that he would have a representative present with authority to settle.

The ADR conference was held on October 18, 1999. Present at the conference was Nick, Nick's court-appointed counsel, counsel for Morgan's Foods, the local regional manager of Morgan's Foods, and the neutral.

Nick provided the required memorandum to the neutral and attended the ADR conference with full authority to settle the case.

Morgan's Foods did not provide the memorandum to the neutral as was required by the Court's Order. Morgan's Foods also failed to have a representative attend the conference who had authority to settle. Morgan's Foods' corporate representative who attended the conference did not have any independent knowledge of the case, nor did she have authority to reconsider Morgan's Foods' position regarding settlement. The limit of Morgan's Foods' regional manager's authority was $ 500. Negotiation of any settlement amount above $ 500 had to be handled by Morgan's Foods' general counsel, who was not present at the ADR conference.

Not surprisingly, the ADR conference did not result in a settlement. Nick made an offer of settlement which was rejected without a counteroffer by Morgan's Foods. Nick made another offer to settle the case. Again, this offer was rejected without a counteroffer. The ADR conference was terminated shortly thereafter.

The neutral reported back to the Court after the close of the ADR conference. At that time, the neutral informed the Court of the level of Morgan's Foods' participation in the ADR process. On October 22, 1999, the Court issued an Order directing Morgan's Foods to show cause why it should not be sanctioned for its failure to participate in good faith in the Court ordered ADR process.

Morgan's Foods responded to the Court's Show Cause Order on October 29, 1999. In that response, Morgan's Foods asserted that the August 2, 1999 referral Order was merely a "guideline" provided to parties suggesting a manner in which they might participate in the ADR process. Morgan's Foods admitted that it made a calculated strategic decision not to comply with the "guideline" because Morgan's Foods felt compliance would be a waste of time.

In the meantime, Nick filed a Motion for Sanctions. Nick requested that Morgan's Foods be sanctioned for failing to participate in the ADR process in good faith. Nick requested an award of the costs and fees of her participation in the failed mediation.

The Court held a hearing on its Show Cause Order and Nick's Motion for Sanctions on December 1, 1999. Counsel for Morgan's Foods appeared at the hearing and reasserted the positions taken in Morgan's Foods' response to the Court's Show Cause Order. Counsel confirmed that the Morgan's Foods' corporate representative had only $ 500 of authority to settle the case. Counsel further confirmed that any decision to change the company's settlement position had to be made by Morgan's Foods' general counsel who was not present at the ADR conference but was available by telephone. Morgan's Foods' counsel also took full responsibility for the decision not to file the memorandum required by the August 2, 1999 referral order. Morgan's Foods continued to advance its argument that filing the required mediation memorandum would have been a waste of time and money.

After hearing argument by both sides, the Court made its ruling on the record. The Court found that Morgan's Foods failed to participate in good faith in the Court-ordered ADR process and sanctioned Morgan's Foods in an amount to include the total cost of the ADR conference fees and Nick's costs in preparing for and attending the conference. The Court also ordered counsel to obtain a copy of the hearing transcript, provide the transcript to his client, and return a letter to the Court confirming that Morgan's Foods had read the transcript.

Morgan's Foods filed a Motion for Reconsideration and Vacation of the Court's Order Granting Plaintiff's Motion for Sanctions on December 20, 1999. It is that motion for reconsideration which is before the Court.

Morgan's Foods has asked that the sanctions order be reconsidered for the following reasons:

1. This Court lacks the general authority to enter sanctions for a party's failure to comply with a Court Order;

2. The local rules really don't require that a mediation memorandum be prepared;

3. The local rules are merely "guidelines" which do not require compliance;

4. The ADR neutral's repeated request for a mediation memorandum could be ignored because the neutral's request was not a court order;

5. A defendant's verdict at trial would have vindicated their conduct in the ADR process;

6. The Court's order is really just a product of "understandable frustration [by the Court] that cases like this one which the Plaintiff foists upon this Court clog the Court's docket."

Analysis

The District Court Has Both Express and Inherent Power to Enforce The ADR Referral Order

While the Court's authority to order parties to participate in ADR in good faith and to enforce that order would seem to be beyond question, Morgan's Foods nevertheless doubts the Court's power. To address Morgan's Foods concerns, the Court will review the basis of its authority to order and enforce good faith participation in ADR.

The Court's authority to enforce its orders by imposing sanctions is founded upon the Federal Rules of Civil Procedure and a district court's inherent authority to manage the progress of litigation.

The District Court's Authority to Impose Sanctions Pursuant to Rule 16

Rule 16 of the Federal Rules of Civil Procedure addresses the use of pretrial conferences to formulate and narrow issues for trial and to discuss means for dispensing with the need for costly and unnecessary litigation.

Pretrial settlement of litigation has been advocated and used as a means to alleviate overcrowded dockets, and courts have practiced numerous and varied types of pretrial settlement techniques for many years.

Since 1983, Rule 16 has expressly provided that settlement of a case is one of several subjects which should be pursued and discussed vigorously during pretrial conferences. *G. Heileman Brewing Co. v. Joseph Oat Corporation, 871 F.2d 648, 651 (7th Cir. 1989).*

Rule 16 expressly gives the court the authority in its discretion, to order litigants to participate in pretrial proceedings, including hearings to facilitate settlement.

Rule 16 also explicitly addresses a judge's authority to issue sanctions for failure to comply with the court's pretrial orders.

> (f) Sanctions. In lieu of or in addition to any other sanction, the judge shall require the party or the attorney representing the party or both to pay the reasonable expenses incurred because of any noncompliance with this rule, including attorney's fees, unless the judge finds that the noncompliance was substantially justified or that other circumstances make an award of expenses unjust.

Fed. R. Civ. P. 16

The District Court's Authority to Impose Sanctions Pursuant to Its Inherent Authority to Control Litigation

Because Morgan's Foods questions this Court's authority to award sanctions in this case, it is worth noting that the Court's power to impose sanctions extends beyond those enumerated in the Federal Rules of Civil Procedure. As the Seventh Circuit observed in its opinion in G. Heilman Brewing Co., the concept that district courts exercise procedural authority outside the explicit language of the rules of civil procedure is not frequently documented, but valid nevertheless. *(871 F.2d at 651.)* The Federal Rules of Civil Procedure are not intended to be the exclusive authority for actions to be taken by district courts. *Link v. Wabash R.R., 370 U.S. 626, 8 L. Ed. 2d 734, 82 S. Ct. 1386 (1962).*

In *Link*, the Supreme Court noted that a district court's ability to take action in a procedural context may be grounded in "'inherent power,' governed not by rule or statute but by the control necessarily vested in courts to manage their own affairs so as to achieve the orderly and expeditious disposition of cases." *Id., at 630-31* (footnotes omitted).

> This authority likewise forms the basis for continued development of procedural techniques designed to make the operation of the court more efficient, to preserve the integrity of the judicial process, and to control courts' dockets. Because the rules form and shape certain aspects of a court's inherent powers, yet allow the continued exercise of that power where discretion should be available, the mere absence of language in the federal rules specifically authorizing or describing a particular judicial procedure should not, and does not, give rise to a negative implication of prohibition.

Id. at 629-30; see also, Fed. R. Civ. P. 83.

The Supreme Court has long held that "the inherent powers of federal courts are those which 'are necessary to the exercise of all others.'" *Roadway Express, Inc. v. Piper, 447 U.S. 752, 764, 65 L. Ed. 2d 488, 100 S. Ct. 2455, (1980).* See *Newman-Green, Inc. v. Alfonzo-Larrain R., 854 F.2d 916, 921-22 (7th Cir. 1988)* (en banc) (court discussing examples of specific procedures, such as the power to punish for contempt, power to sanction persons who file frivolous pleadings, power to determine whether there is jurisdiction); *Strandell v. Jackson County, 838 F.2d 884, 886 (7th Cir. 1988); Thompson v. Housing Auth. of Los Angeles, 782 F.2d 829, 831* (9th Cir.), cert. denied, *479 U.S. 829, 107 S. Ct. 112, 93 L. Ed. 2d 60 (1986); Halaco Eng'g Co. v. Costle, 843 F.2d 376, 380 (9th Cir. 1988)* (court stating that the Supreme Court has recognized that a district court has inherent authority to impose sanctions for discovery abuses which may not be a technical violation of discovery rules).

The foregoing cases clearly establish that a district court has express authority, under the Federal Rules of Civil Procedure and its inherent authority, to impose sanctions when a party violates the Federal Rules of Civil Procedure, the court's local rules, and the court's orders.

Good Faith Participation in ADR Does Not Require Settlement

The Court understands that ADR conferences and settlement negotiations can fail to achieve the settlement of a case for many reasons. The Federal Rules of Civil Procedure, this court's local rules and the specific court order in this case referring the case to ADR do not mandate settlement. Good faith participation in ADR does not require settlement. In fact, an ADR conference conducted in good faith can be helpful even if settlement is not reached. On the other hand, the rules and orders governing ADR are designed to prevent abuse of the opponent, which can and does occur when one side does not participate in good faith.

When a party agrees to participate in a mediation process in good faith, the Court is entitled to rely on that representation. Implicit in the concept of good faith participation is the assurance that the parties will participate in ADR in accordance with the Court's order. *Raad v. Wal-Mart Stores, Inc., 1998 U.S. Dist. LEXIS 11881, 1998 WL 272879,* at *6 (D. Neb. May 6, 1998).

Good Faith Participation in ADR Includes Providing the Neutral With a Mediation Memorandum

This Court's referral order required preparation of a memorandum seven days in advance of the ADR conference. The memorandum was required to contain:

a. A summary of the disputed facts;

b. A discussion of the party's position on liability and damages;

c. The name and general job title of the employee of the corporation who will attend and participate at the ADR conference. Failure to provide the information required in the memorandum undermines the ADR process.

Morgan's Foods has made it clear that it considered the memorandum requirement a waste of time. Morgan's Foods is right that its failure to prepare the required memorandum wasted valuable time. Unfortunately for Morgan's Foods, it is right for all of the wrong reasons. Morgan's Foods' failure to prepare the memorandum was a waste of plaintiff's time, plaintiff's counsels' time, the neutral's time and the Court's time.

Morgan's Foods' contention that a mediation memorandum is a waste of time is simply wrong. The memorandum would have permitted the neutral to prepare for the ADR conference. At a minimum the memorandum might have alerted the neutral that Morgan's Foods' corporate representative was not an appropriate participant in the ADR conference. It is even possible that Morgan's Foods' memorandum would have compelled the neutral to delay or even cancel the conference.

Morgan's Foods' calculated refusal to prepare a mediation memorandum was a direct violation of the Court's local rules and the Court's ADR Referral Order.

Good Faith Participation in ADR Requires the Participation of A Corporate Representative With Authority to Settle

Morgans' Foods also violated the Referral Order by failing to have an appropriate corporate representative attend the mediation.

The August 2, 1999 Referral Order specifically required attendance of a "corporate representative . . . having authority to settle claims." Presence of the corporate representative is the cornerstone of good faith participation.

The authority of a district court to require a duly-empowered corporate officer to attend a settlement conference is well settled. *Universal Cooperatives v. Tribal Co-Operative Marketing Development Federation of India, Ltd., 45 F.3d 1194, 1196 (8th Cir. 1995)* (citing *G. Heileman Brewing Co., Inc. v. Joseph Oat Co., 871 F.2d 648, 655 (7th Cir. 1989));* see also, *In re LaMarre, 494 F.2d 753, 756 (6th Cir. 1974)* (court stating that it is well within the scope of a district court's authority to compel the appearance of a party's insurer at a pretrial conference and to enforce the order).

At the risk of restating the obvious, the Court will review why attendance of a corporate representative with settlement authority is so important.

During the ADR conference, all parties have the opportunity to argue their respective positions. In the Court's experience, this is often the first time that parties, especially corporate representatives, hear about the difficulties they will face at trial. As a practical matter this may also be the first time that firmly held positions may be open to change. For ADR to work, the corporate representative must have the authority and discretion to change her opinion in light of the statements and arguments made by the neutral and opposing party.

Meaningful negotiations cannot occur if the only person with authority to actually change their mind and negotiate is not present. Availability by telephone is insufficient because the absent decision-maker does not have the full benefit of the ADR proceedings, the opposing party's arguments, and the neutral's input. The absent decision-maker needs to be present and hear first hand the good facts and the bad facts about their case. Instead, the absent decision-maker learns only what his or her attorney chooses to relate over the phone. This can be expected to be largely a recitation of what has been conveyed in previous discussions. Even when the attorney attempts to summarize the strengths of the other side's position, there are problems. First, the attorney has a credibility problem: the absent decision-maker wants to know why the attorney's confident opinion expressed earlier has now eroded. Second, the new information most likely is too much to absorb and analyze in a matter of minutes. Under this dynamic it becomes all too easy for the absent decision-maker to reject the attorney's new advice, reject the new information, and reject any effort to engage in meaningful negotiations. It is quite likely that the telephone call is viewed as a distraction from other business being conducted by the absent decision-maker. In that case the absent decision-maker will be preoccupied with some other matter demanding her attention at the time she is asked to evaluate new information in a telephone call. Confronted with distractions and inadequate time to evaluate the new information meaningfully, the absent decision-maker's easiest decision is to summarily reject any offer and get back to the business on her desk. Even a conscientious decision-maker cannot absorb the full impact of the ADR conference when they are not present for the discussion. The absent decision-maker cannot participate in good faith in the ADR conference without being present for the conference.

Unfortunately, as discussed in *Dvorak v. Shibata, 123 F.R.D. 608 (D. Neb. 1988)* occasionally parties may use the absence of the decision-maker as a weapon. Such parties "feign a good faith settlement posture by those in attendance at the conference, relying on the absent decision-maker to refuse to agree," thereby taking advantage of their opponent. *Id, at 610.*

In such cases the offending party is able to "gain information about [its] opponent's case, strategy, and settlement posture without sharing any of its own information." *Radd, 1998 WL 2722879, at *5* Instead of a negotiation session, the mediation becomes a stealth discovery session, to the unfair benefit of the party whose decision-maker is not in attendance. When that happens, the Court's referral to mediation has been callously misused. "Meanwhile, the opposing side has spent money and time preparing for a good-faith, candid discussion toward settlement. If the other party does not reciprocate, most if not all of that money and time has been wasted." *Id.*

In sum, when a corporate representative with the authority to reconsider that party's settlement position is not present, the whole purpose of the mediation is lost, and the result is an even greater expenditure of the parties' resources, both time and money, for nothing.

Conclusion

Morgan's Foods did not participate in good faith in the ADR process. The absence of good faith is evidenced not by the parties failure to reach settlement, but by Morgan's Foods' failure to comply with the Court's August 2, 1999 Referral Order. Morgan's Foods' failure to participate in the ADR process in good faith would not be vindicated by a defendant's verdict at trial. Whether the parties participated in good faith in the ADR process is measured by their actual conduct at the mediation, not by the hypothetical result of a subsequent trial.

Morgan's Foods' lack of good faith participation in the ADR process was calculated to save Morgan's Foods a few hours of time in preparing the mediation memorandum and to save its general counsel the expense and inconvenience of a trip to attend the mediation. The consequence of Morgan's Foods' lack of good faith participation in the ADR process, however, was the wasted expense of time and energy of the Court, the neutral, Nick, and her court-appointed counsel.

If Morgan's Foods did not feel that ADR could be fruitful and had no intention of participating in good faith, it had a duty to report its position to the Court and to request appropriate relief. Morgan's Foods did not do so and sanctions are appropriate to remedy the resulting waste of time and money.

As a final thought, I feel compelled to address Morgan's Foods' suggestion that the sanction order was the result of "understandable frustration that cases like the one Plaintiff foists upon this Court clog the Court's docket." Morgan's Foods suggests that my actions were motivated by frustration stemming from frivolous allegations in Nick's Complaint.

Morgan's Foods is well aware that each United States District Judge takes an oath to "administer justice without respect to persons, and do equal right to the poor and to the rich . . . and [to] faithfully and impartially discharge and perform all duties . . . under the Constitution and laws of the United States." *28 U.S.C. § 453.* That knowledge alone should have prevented Morgan's Foods from suggesting that the sanction order was merely the result of some misplaced temper tantrum. It should go without saying that this Court does not believe that allegations of sexual harassment on the job are frivolous.

It is unfortunate that when confronted with its willful violation of the Court's Order, Morgan's Foods refused to acknowledge the failings of its own behavior and instead attacked the Court. Admittedly the Court felt frustration at the way this case was handled, but that frustration stemmed completely from Morgan's Foods' flagrant and willful disregard of the Court's August 2, 1999 Order referring the matter to ADR.

Many of the arguments advanced by Morgan's Foods' motion are frivolous accomplishing nothing but increasing the cost of litigation. The Court therefore will impose additional sanctions to reflect the frivolous nature of this motion.

Accordingly,

IT IS HEREBY ORDERED that Defendant Morgan's Foods' Motion for Reconsideration [Doc. # 71] is DENIED.

IT IS FURTHER ORDERED that Defendant Morgan's Foods shall pay $ 1,390.63 to counsel for plaintiff as sanctions in this matter. Defendant's counsel shall pay $ 1,390.62 to counsel for plaintiff as sanctions in this matter. That amount includes $ 1,045.00 in attorney's fees for preparing and attending the mediation in this case, the $ 506.25 fee paid to the neutral for the cost of the ADR conference, and $ 1,230.00 in attorney's fees for preparing and arguing the motion for sanctions regarding Morgan's Foods' participation in the mediation.

IT IS FURTHER ORDERED that Defendant Morgan's Foods shall pay $ 30.00 to Plaintiff Gee Gee Nick for the costs she incurred in attending the mediation of this case. Defendant's counsel shall also pay $ 30.00 to Plaintiff Gee Gee Nick for the costs she incurred in attending the mediation of this case.

IT IS FURTHER ORDERED that Defendant Morgan's Foods shall pay $ 1,500.00 to the Clerk of the United States District Court, Eastern District of Missouri as sanctions in this matter. That amount reflects the savings realized by Morgan's Foods' by virtue of its failure to prepare the required mediation memorandum and its decision not to send Morgan's Foods' general counsel to attend the ADR conference. Defendant Morgan's Foods and its counsel shall each pay $ 1,250.00 to the Clerk of the United States District Court, Eastern District of Missouri as a sanction for vexatiously increasing the costs of this litigation by filing a frivolous Motion for Reconsideration which further demonstrated the lack of good faith in Morgan's Foods conduct in this case.

QUESTIONS

(1) Why was the *Nick* court more willing to find a violation of the good faith requirement than the *Bolden* court?

(2) How did the factors considered by the *Nick* and *Bolton* courts compare to those in Professor Kovach's proposed rule?

§ E ENFORCEABILITY OF MEDIATED AGREEMENTS

Which legal principles should a court apply when being asked to enforce a mediated agreement? In many jurisdictions, the answer to this question is unclear at present. In other jurisdictions, the courts or the state legislatures have decided that mediated agreements should be enforced in the same manner as a contract. Even in these jurisdictions, however, the enforceability issue may be complicated by the fact that there may be other relevant laws that contradict the mediation enforcement provisions. Enforceability may also implicate confidentiality concerns. If the parties are fighting over the interpretation of certain terms in the mediation agreement, relevant evidence over what the parties intended may be excluded because of confidentiality requirements. Indeed, the parties may even be disagreeing over whether an agreement was struck. Recall the *Macaluso* case excerpted in the first section of this chapter, where the court refused to hear testimony from the mediator even though the court stated that it would be the best evidence of the existence of a mediated agreement.

The cases in this section are illustrative of the range of policy concerns over whether and how to enforce a mediated agreement. The *Ames* case illustrates problems of statutory interpretation that may confront a court faced with an enforceability issue. While the *Silkey* case also has the court wrestling with an issue of statutory interpretation, there it revolves around the enforceability of an oral mediation agreement. Finally, the *Haghighi* litigation suggests that a legislature may create more problems than it solves when it seeks to address the enforcement issue head-on.

IN RE MARRIAGE OF AMES

Texas Court of Civil Appeals
860 S.W.2d 590 (1993)

H. Bryan Poff, Jr., J.

Appellant Raymond K. Ames appeals from the trial court's final decree granting him and his wife Nancy Jo Ames a divorce. In four points of error, Raymond contends the trial court erred in (1) not recognizing his repudiation of the mediated settlement agreement; (2) entering the decree of divorce without any evidence to support it; (3) modifying the settlement agreement; and (4) overruling his motion for new trial. We note that Raymond initially argues the settlement agreement is invalid; however, anticipating we might not agree, he alternatively argues that the agreement is inviolable and the court erred in modifying the agreement. His second argument compels us to reverse the judgment and remand the cause to the trial court.

Raymond filed suit to divorce his wife Nancy, appellee. Nancy answered Raymond's petition and filed a counter-petition for divorce. The parties were ordered to mediation which resulted in a community property settlement agreement reached on June 5, 1991. Both parties and their respective attorneys signed the settlement agreement. The record reflects that on June 20, 1991, Raymond attempted to withdraw his consent to the settlement agreement by means of a letter from his attorney to Nancy's attorney. On August 20, 1991,

Nancy filed a "Motion For Entry of Decree of Divorce" based on the June 5 settlement agreement. On November 27, 1991, the trial court entered a decree of divorce.

In the first of four points of error, Raymond contends that the trial court erred in entering its decree of divorce on the basis of the settlement agreement because he had repudiated the agreement. We disagree. In its order of mediation, the trial court stated that "this case is appropriate for mediation pursuant to Tex. Civ. Prac. & Rem. Code §§ 154.001 et. seq." Chapter 154 of the Texas Civil Practice and Remedies Code is entitled "Alternative Dispute Resolution Procedures." Section 154.071(a) states:

> If the parties reach a settlement and execute a written agreement disposing of the dispute, the agreement is enforceable in the same manner as any other written contract.

Tex. Civ. Prac. & Rem. Code Ann. § 154.071(a) (Vernon Supp. 1993). We interpret this statute to mean, inter alia, that a party who has reached a settlement agreement disposing of a dispute through alternative dispute resolution procedures may not unilaterally repudiate the agreement.

While parties may be compelled by a court to participate in mediation, Tex. Civ. Prac. & Rem. Code §§ 154.021, 154.023 (Vernon Supp. 1993), "[a] mediator may not impose his own judgment on the issues for that of the parties." Tex. Civ. Prac. & Rem. Code § 154.023(b) (Vernon Supp. 1993). Put another way, a court can compel disputants to sit down with each other but it cannot force them to peaceably resolve their differences. *Decker v. Lindsay, 824 S.W.2d 247, 250* (Tex.App.—Houston [1st Dist.] 1992, no writ). The job of a mediator is simply to facilitate communication between parties and thereby encourage reconciliation, settlement and understanding among them. Tex. Civ. Prac. & Rem. Code Ann. § 154.023(a). Hopefully, mediation will assist the parties in reaching a voluntary agreement that will serve to resolve their dispute and avoid the need for traditional litigation.

If voluntary agreements reached through mediation were nonbinding, many positive efforts to amicably settle differences would be for naught. If parties were free to repudiate their agreements, disputes would not be finally resolved and traditional litigation would recur. In order to effect the purposes of mediation and other alternative dispute resolution mechanisms, settlement agreements must be treated with the same dignity and respect accorded other contracts reached after arm's length negotiations. Again, no party to a dispute can be forced to settle the conflict outside of court; but if a voluntary agreement that disposes of the dispute is reached, the parties should be required to honor the agreement.

Raymond argues strenuously, however, that section 154.071(a) does not apply in this case. Raymond maintains that section 154.071(a) conflicts with Tex. Fam. Code Ann. § 3.631(a) (Vernon 1993), and that the Family Code provision is controlling. Section 3.631(a) states:

> To promote amicable settlement of disputes on the divorce or annul-
> ment of a marriage, the parties may enter into a written agreement
> concerning the division of all property and liabilities of the parties and

maintenance of either of them. The agreement may be revised or repudiated prior to rendition of the divorce or annulment unless it is binding under some other rule of law.

Raymond contends that section 3.613(a) controls over section 154.071(a) of the Texas Civil Practice and Remedies Code because section 3.613(a) deals with an agreement incident to divorce while section 154.071(a) concerns agreements in general. Raymond cites the well known rule that a specific statute should control over a general statute and thus concludes that section 3.613(a) is controlling.

We are not convinced, however, that the two statutes are in conflict. Even though section 3.613(a) is the more specific statute in this case, the Family Code provision expressly states that an agreement may be repudiated prior to rendition of the divorce "unless it is binding under some other rule of law." Pursuant to section 154.071(a) of the Practice and Remedies Code, the settlement agreement is binding. Raymond could not unilaterally repudiate the agreement. The trial court was empowered to consider the settlement agreement. Point of error one is overruled.

In his third point of error, Raymond, in the alternative, argues that if the agreement was not repudiated, the trial court erred in dividing the community property because the court's division differed significantly from the settlement agreement. Nancy contends that this argument is not properly before us because Raymond did not prepare and submit a proposed judgment to the court for signature as he was entitled to do under Tex. R. Civ. P. 305. While it is true that Raymond did not submit a proposed judgment, this does not preclude him from challenging the judgment entered by the court.

We agree with Raymond that there are several provisions of the divorce decree that are not found in the settlement agreement. First, while the settlement agreement is silent as to income tax liabilities, the divorce decree requires Raymond to pay all income tax liabilities of the parties through December 31, 1990. Second, the settlement agreement recites that Raymond will execute a $ 320,000 promissory note to Nancy; the divorce decree orders Raymond to execute the note and also orders him to pay a $ 320,000 money judgment. Third, the settlement agreement states that the stock of Raymond's company (Ridgmont Construction) is to be pledged as collateral for the promissory note if it will not impair Ridgmont's bonding capacity; the divorce decree contains no such conditional language.

Nancy contends that the divorce decree is "sufficiently representative of the agreement reached by the parties" to be upheld on appeal. We disagree. In *Vineyard v. Wilson*, 597 S.W.2d 21, 23 (Tex.Civ.App.—Dallas 1980, no writ), the court invalidated a judgment that did not embody the exact terms of the agreement on which it was based. "In order for a consent judgment to be valid, the parties must have definitely agreed to all the terms of the agreement. Nothing should be left for the court to provide." *Id.* In a judgment by consent, "the court has no power to supply terms, provisions, or essential details not previously agreed to by the parties." *Matthews v. Looney, 132 Tex. 313, 317, 123 S.W.2d 871, 872 (1939).* In fact, the court must accept the express terms of the agreement as binding "unless it finds that the agreement is not just and right." Tex. Fam. Code Ann. § 3.631(b) (Vernon 1993). The trial court made no such finding in this case. Therefore, the court was bound to accept the agreement. Because the trial court added terms to its decree of divorce that were not in the settlement agreement, the divorce decree cannot be allowed to stand. Point of error three is sustained.

In his second point of error, Raymond contends that the trial court erred in entering the decree of divorce because there is no evidence to support the decree. Clearly, the settlement agreement provides no evidence of the above-mentioned additional provisions of the decree. We also note that, contrary to the recitations in the decree of divorce, the parties never appeared before the trial judge at a hearing. The only evidence before the trial court was the settlement agreement. The record contains no evidence to support the court's modification of the agreement. The judgment and decree are therefore not supported by the evidence. Point of error two is sustained.

In his fourth point of error, Raymond contends that the trial court erred in refusing to grant his motion for new trial. We sustain this point of error. Inasmuch as one of the bases for a new trial was that "there are many provisions in the Decree of Divorce signed by the Court on November 27, 1991, contrary to or beyond the scope of, the agreement signed by the parties at the conclusion of the Mediation," a new trial should have been granted.

The judgment of the trial court is reversed and the cause is remanded to that court for proceedings not inconsistent with this opinion.

NOTES AND QUESTIONS

(1) Note that the relevant Texas ADR statute makes written settlement agreements "enforceable in the same manner as any other written contract," but a provision of the relevant family law statute provides that a settlement agreement "may be revised or repudiated prior to rendition of the divorce or annulment unless it is binding under other some other rule of law." Do you agree with the court's rationale in choosing the ADR provision over the family law provision? Texas appellate courts are split on this issue. *See Alvarez v. Reiser*, 958 S.W.2d 232 (11th Dist. Tex. App. Ct. 1997) (holding in accord with *Ames*), and *Cary v. Cary*, 894 S.W.2d 111 (1st Dist. Tex. App. Ct. 1995) (holding disagrees with *Ames*).

(2) The *Ames* divorce case involved a mediated property settlement. Should the law permit mediated agreements to be more open to repudiation if they involve the custody or support of minor children? See *Wayno v. Wayno*, 756 So. 2d 1024 (4th Dist. Fla. Ct. App. 2000), where a Florida appellate court upheld a trial court's order setting forth different child support and custody arrangements than had been agreed to by the parties in a mediated court-approved, settlement agreement.

SILKEY v. INVESTORS DIVERSIFIED SERVICES, INC.

Indiana Court of Appeals
690 N.E.2d 329 (1997)

RILEY, Judge

STATEMENT OF THE CASE

Appellants, Herschel J. Silkey and Wanda Louise Silkey (Silkeys), appeal from an order granting Appellees', Investors Diversified Services, Inc. (IDS) and Mark Powers (Powers) (collectively referred to as the Brokers), amended Motion to Enforce Mediation Agreement and Request for Sanctions.

We affirm.

ISSUES

The Silkeys present two issues for our review which we restate as:

I. Whether the trial court erred in determining that an oral agreement reached during a mediation session was a final and binding agreement?

II. Whether the trial court erred in determining that the verbal agreement reached during a mediation session complied with the Indiana Statute of Frauds, Ind. Code § 32-2-1-1.

FACTS AND PROCEDURAL HISTORY

In early 1983, the Silkeys received a capital gain of $ 650,000 from the sale of their farm land to a coal company. They sought investment assistance from Powers, who was a registered representative of IDS and possessed all the necessary securities licenses to qualify for that position. IDS is a securities dealer and brokerage firm with its principal offices located in Minneapolis, Minnesota, with an office located and doing business in Evansville, Indiana, and at other locations throughout the State of Indiana.

As a result of meetings and discussions, Powers recommended, and the Silkeys purchased, several investments, including a $100,000 investment in JMB Carlyle Real Estate Limited Partnership XII. This investment's performance did not meet the Silkeys' expectations, and on June 29, 1994, the Silkeys filed a complaint against IDS and Powers alleging misrepresentation, violations of the Indiana Securities Act, breach of fiduciary duty, and constructive fraud.

On August 16, 1995, the trial court ordered the parties to mediation. Mediation was held in Evansville, Indiana on January 17, 1996, five days before the scheduled trial date, with a mutually agreed-upon mediator. The mediator concluded the mediation with an oral recitation of the terms of the agreement and received verbal assent from all of the parties to the terms. This exchange was recorded on an audio tape. The tape was later transcribed by the mediator, and copies were sent to all parties. On January 18, 1996, the mediator filed with the trial court a Mediation Report which confirmed that a settlement had been reached, and the trial was removed from the court's calendar. On January 22, 1996, a typed transcription was sent to all parties by the mediator. On February 19, 1996, the Brokers forwarded to the Silkeys a Settlement Agreement and Mutual General Release (Agreement) which was prepared by counsel for the Brokers and signed by IDS and Powers. After receiving the Agreement, the Silkeys refused to sign it, and the Silkeys' counsel informed the Brokers of the repudiation. Subsequently, the Silkeys' counsel withdrew their representation, and the Silkeys obtained new counsel.

The Brokers filed a Motion to Enforce Agreement for Settlement on August 23, 1996. The trial court found that this was not a case where the parties were disputing whether the document accurately reflected the agreement, but rather the Silkeys were attempting to repudiate the agreement. The trial court concluded that an enforceable agreement was reached by the parties. The trial court ruled that the audio tape recording was a legally binding form of the agreement which set forth with reasonable certainty the terms and conditions and the parties' agreement to these terms and conditions. The trial court then directed that the terms of the audio tape recording be reduced to writing and that, when the writing fairly and accurately reflected the terms of the agreement, the parties would sign and file the agreement with the court.

DISCUSSION AND DECISION

I. Effect of the Oral Agreement

The central question in this case is what effect, if any, should be given to the oral agreement reached by the parties at the conclusion of the mediation. The Silkeys argue that the Rules of Alternative Dispute Resolution control the disposition of this question. The rules provide that:

(2) If an agreement is reached, it shall be reduced to writing and signed. The agreement shall then be filed with the court. If the agreement is complete on all issues, it shall be accompanied by a joint stipulation of disposition.

(3) After the agreement becomes an order of the court by joint stipulation, in the event of any breach or failure to perform under the agreement, the court, upon motion, may impose sanctions, including costs, interest, attorney fees, or other appropriate remedies including entry of judgment on the agreement.

A.D.R. 2.7(E) (1996).

The Silkeys acknowledge that an agreement was reached and that it was reduced to writing. Appellant's Brief at 20. They also acknowledge that they have rescinded their verbal assent to the terms of the agreement. *Id.* They argue that because this agreement was neither signed by them nor filed with the court, there was no contract or breach; therefore, they argue neither enforcement nor sanction is appropriate. *Id.* We disagree.

The Silkeys present their appeal as one of statutory interpretation; therefore, we begin with consideration of the A.D.R. rules. The Indiana Supreme Court has noted in the preamble to the A.D.R. rules that the rules were "adopted in order to bring some uniformity into alternative dispute resolution with the view that the interests of the parties can be preserved" in nontraditional settings. A.D.R. Preamble. Mediation is a process to "assist[] the litigants in reaching a mutually acceptable agreement." A.D.R. 2.1. Although a court may order parties to participate in mediation and require that participation be in good faith, it cannot order them to reach agreement. *Id.* The ultimate goal of mediation is to provide a forum in which parties might reach a mutually agreed resolution to their differences. The A.D.R. rules provide a uniform *process* for negotiation, but they do not change the law regarding settlement agreements or their enforcement. Nothing in the text of the A.D.R. rules for mediation suggests the Indiana Supreme Court intended to change the trial court's role in enforcing settlement agreements. Thus, although the *process* of the mediation is controlled by the A.D.R. rules, the enforcement of any valid agreement is within the authority of the trial court under the existing law in Indiana.

"The judicial policy of Indiana strongly favors settlement agreements." *Germania v. Thermasol, Ltd., 569 N.E.2d 730, 732 (Ind. Ct. App. 1991).* Courts retain the inherent power to enforce agreements entered into in settlement of litigation which is pending before them. *Id.* Settlement is always referable to the action in the court, and the carrying out of the agreement should be controlled by that court.

The Silkeys argue that because no written agreement was ever signed, no joint stipulation was ever entered, and therefore, no breach occurred which could allow the court to enforce the agreement. The Silkeys misunderstand the rule. The text to which the Silkeys refer does, in fact, explain the manner in which the parties will present their agreement to the trial court in order to have it *transformed by the court* into an *order* of joint stipulation. This promotes judicial efficiency by assuring that the parties do not appear before the court in a later dispute over the same issue or action. Thus, the rule provides a uniform procedure by which parties dispose of an action in accordance with the terms of their agreement.

The Silkeys argue that they were never compelled to agree and so should not be held to an agreement about which they have changed their minds. Such a rule would clearly create a disincentive for settlement. Additionally, it would allow mediation to serve not as an aid to litigation, but as a separate and additional impetus for litigation. Neither the A.D.R. rules nor the law support such an interpretation.

The Silkeys are correct that a party has full authority over whether to settle his case or proceed to trial. Having decided to accept a settlement, however, the party is bound to that decision. "In the absence of fraud or mistake a settlement is as binding and conclusive of the parties' rights and obligations as a judgment on the merits." The Silkeys do not allege fraud or mistake in reaching this settlement agreement; in fact, they do not question the terms of the agreement at all. Instead, they assert that they "no longer agree" to the terms of the settlement. This is not a sufficient ground to rescind a contract.

The Silkeys argue that the agreement was not final or binding because it is oral. A settlement agreement is not required to be in writing. Whether a party has consented to particular terms is a factual matter to be determined by the fact-finder.

The trial court found that the terms of the agreement were not in dispute. In reaching this decision, it relied on the parties' affidavits, pleadings, and memoranda of law. At the hearing on the matter, the trial court admitted the tape recording of the recitation of agreement over the Silkeys' objection. It does not appear from the trial court's written findings that it relied on the tape recording of the agreement in reaching its decision, nor was it required to do so because neither the content nor the authenticity of the tape was in question. In fact, as noted, the Silkeys raise the issue that the agreement reached in the mediation was preliminary for the first time on appeal. Having failed to raise this issue before the trial court, it is waived.

The evidence before the trial court clearly supports its finding that the parties entered an agreement at the close of the mediation session. The trial court had available to it a tape and a transcript which clearly indicated the parties had agreed in substance to the terms of the mediation. The Silkeys did not argue to the trial court that there were any changes or defects in the terms as they were reduced to writing by the Brokers. Having found that a settlement agreement had been reached, the trial court acted within its authority under the A.D.R. rules and the case law in Indiana in directing the parties to reduce their agreement to writing and sign and file it with the court.

II. Statute of Frauds

The second issue raised by the Silkeys is that the verbal agreement is not in compliance with the Statute of Frauds and is, thus, unenforceable. They make three arguments on this issue: first, that the terms did not constitute the entire agreement; second, that the audio tape is insufficient to meet the requirements of a writing in order to take the agreement outside the Statute of Frauds; and third, that the agreement cannot be performed within one year of its making.

The Statute of Frauds provides:

> No action shall be brought in any of the following cases: . . .

> Fifth: Upon any agreement that is not to be performed within one (1) year from the making thereof . . .

> Unless the promise, contract or agreement upon which such action shall be brought, or some memorandum or note thereof, shall be in writing, and signed by the party to be charged therewith, or by some person thereunto by him lawfully authorized . . .

Ind. Code § 32-2-1-1. The Silkeys argue that the Statute of Frauds is applicable to this agreement due to the fact that it will not be performed within one year. They argue that this agreement will not be fully performed until January 31, 2001. However, the agreement is not this definite. The terms of the agreement guarantee that the Silkeys would receive an initial payment of cash immediately and a guarantee of a distribution of an additional fixed sum *on or before* January 31, 2001. If the investment pays a dividend equivalent to this additional sum before January 31, 2001, there is no further obligation on the part of the Brokers. The fact that this agreement *may not* be performed within one year is insufficient alone to make it subject to the requirements of the Statute of Frauds:

> It must affirmatively appear by the terms of the contract, that its stipulations are not to be performed within a year after it is made, in order to bring it within the provisions of the statute of frauds. (sic) The Statute of Frauds has always been held to apply only to contracts which, *by the express stipulations of the parties,* were not to be performed within a year, and not to those which *might or might not,* upon a contingency, *be* performed within a year. The one year clause of the Statute of Frauds has no application to contracts which are *capable* of *being* performed *within* one year of the making thereof.

It is possible that the agreement could be fully performed within one year of its making if the underlying investment were to pay a distribution equal to or greater than the guarantee amount within the first year. There is no express stipulation between the parties that the agreement would not be performed within one year. Thus, the agreement falls outside the Statute of Frauds. Because the Statue of Frauds is not applicable to this settlement agreement due to the fact that it could be completed within one year, we need not address whether it meets the other requirements of the Statute of Frauds.

CONCLUSION

The trial court acted within its authority to enforce a settlement agreement in a case pending before it where the parties clearly agreed to the terms, but later attempted to rescind their assent. The oral settlement agreement is enforceable, and the parties may be ordered to reduce their agreement to writing and file it with the court. Additionally, because the oral agreement may be performed within one year and there is no express stipulation between the parties that it will not be performed, it is outside the Statute of Frauds.

Affirmed.

ALI HAGHIGHI v. RUSSIAN-AMERICAN BROADCASTING CO.

United States District Court for the District of Minnesota
945 F. Supp. 1233 (1996)

This matter was originally before the Court on September 27, 1996, upon plaintiff's motion for an order "declaring the settlement agreement of February 14, 1996, to be valid and enforceable and further declaring defendant to be in breach thereof." The Court treated plaintiff's motion as a motion to enforce a settlement agreement and scheduled an evidentiary hearing for November 25, 1996. *See Sheng v. Starkey Laboratories, Inc., 53 F.3d 192 (8th Cir. 1995).* The Court also requested that the parties submit supplemental briefs addressing whether mediator Gerald Laurie is a competent witness or is privileged from testifying at the evidentiary hearing, and the effect of Minn. Stat. § 572.35, subd. 1 on the enforceability of any settlement.

Defendant argues the settlement agreement alleged by plaintiff is defective as a matter of law because it fails to state that it is binding as required by Minn. Stat. § 572.35. Minn. Stat. § 572.35, subd. 1 states:

> A mediated settlement agreement is not binding unless it contains a provision stating that it is binding and a provision stating substantially that the parties were advised in writing that (a) the mediator has no duty to protect their interests or provide them with information about their legal rights; (b) signing a mediated settlement agreement may adversely affect their legal rights; and (c) they should consult an attorney before signing a mediated settlement agreement if they are uncertain of their rights.

On its face, the statute appears to preclude settlements unless the settlement document includes the four provisions listed in the statute. Such a reading of the statute, however, creates a trap for both the unwary and the wary. The Court does not believe the Minnesota Legislature intended this result, particularly in mediations where both parties are represented by counsel and are fully aware of the binding effect of a settlement agreement. Accordingly, the Court finds Minn. Stat. § 572.35 does not bar enforcement of the alleged settlement.

In addition, Defendant's then counsel failed to include this language in a settlement document he drafted, and which he claimed was legally sufficient to settle the parties' dispute. Thus, Defendant has waived any argument that either Minn. Stat. § 572.35, subd. 1 or the parties' Mediation Agreement require the settlement document to state it is binding. The evidentiary hearing scheduled for November 25, 1996 will go forward as scheduled. Plaintiff bears the burden of proving that a settlement agreement was reached.

Defendants also argue that a recent amendment to Minn. Stat. § 595.02 precludes either party from calling the mediator, Mr. Laurie, to testify at the evidentiary hearing. Minn. Stat. § 595.02, subd. 1a provides:

> No person presiding at any alternative dispute resolution proceeding established pursuant to law, court rule, or by an agreement to mediate, shall be competent to testify, in any subsequent civil proceeding or administrative hearing, as to any statement, conduct, decision, or ruling, occurring at or in conjunction with the prior proceeding, except as to any statement or conduct that could: (1) constitute a crime; (2) give rise to disqualification proceedings under the rules of professional conduct for attorneys; or (3) constitute professional misconduct.

Although it is unclear whether the statute creates a privilege or a rule of competency, in either case, the Federal Rules of Evidence require that "in civil actions and proceedings with respect to an element of a claim or defense as to which State law supplies the rule of decision," the competency or privilege of a witness "shall be determined in accordance with State law." See Fed. R. Evid. 501 and 601. Although the Court questions the appropriateness of such a limitation on testimony in circumstances where a dispute arises regarding the existence of a mediated settlement, the statute clearly supports Defendant's argument that Mr. Laurie may not testify. Therefore, neither party may call Mr. Laurie at the evidentiary hearing on November 25, 1996.

IT IS SO ORDERED.

ALI HAGHIGHI v. RUSSIAN-AMERICAN BROADCASTING CO.

Minnesota Supreme Court
577 N.W.2d 927 (1998)

BLATZ, Chief Justice.

This case comes to us on an Order of Certification issued by the United States Court of Appeals for the Eighth Circuit under the Uniform Certification of Questions of Law Act. The certified question asks:

> Whether a hand written document prepared by the parties' attorneys at the conclusion of a mediation session conducted pursuant to the Minnesota Civil Mediation Act and signed contemporaneously on each page by the respective parties attending the mediation session but which does not itself provide that the document is to be a binding agreement, is rendered unenforceable as a mediated settlement agreement by virtue of Minn. Stat. § 572.35, subd. 1?

We answer the question in the affirmative.

Defendant Russian-American Broadcasting Company, L.P. (RABC), provides ethnic programming, including Russian language radio and cable programming. Plaintiff Ali Haghighi, d/b/a International Radio Network (IRN), distributes foreign language radio programming on a subscriber basis. On March 23, 1993, RABC and IRN entered into a contract whereby RABC allowed IRN to rebroadcast its Russian language radio programming over IRN's subcarrier signal to subscribers in the Minneapolis/St. Paul area. Shortly thereafter, the contractual relationship between the parties began to deteriorate, and in July 1995, IRN initiated a breach of contract action against RABC. RABC filed an answer denying that it had breached the contract and a counterclaim seeking recovery of overdue payments that RABC alleged were owed by IRN under the contract. The parties agreed to mediate their dispute.

Before the mediation session, both parties signed a Mediation Agreement. Among other provisions, the Mediation Agreement fully incorporates the language of Minn. Stat. § 572.35, subd 1 (1996). The Mediation Agreement states in pertinent part:

> Minnesota Civil Mediation Act. Pursuant to the requirements of the Minnesota Civil Mediation Act, the mediator hereby advises the parties that: (a) the mediator has no duty to protect the parties' interests or provide them with information about their legal rights; (b) signing a mediated settlement agreement may adversely affect the parties' legal rights; (c) the parties should consult an attorney before signing a mediated settlement agreement if they are uncertain of their

rights; and (d) a written mediated settlement agreement is not binding unless it contains a provision that it is binding and a provision stating substantially that the parties were advised in writing of (a) through (c) above.

The mediation session took place on February 14, 1996, and lasted the entire day. RABC was represented by Russell Moro, its Chief of Staff, who had the authority to bind RABC. IRN was represented by its owner, Ali Haghighi. Both parties' attorneys were present as well—Kirk Reilly on behalf of RABC, and Robert Gust on behalf of IRN. The mediation was a typical shuttle format, with both parties in separate rooms while the mediator went back and forth between them, attempting to find common ground. After four or five hours of negotiation, the mediator brought the parties together and recited terms which he believed the parties agreed upon. Both the mediator and RABC's attorney, Kirk Reilly, suggested that the parties write the terms down before Moro left town.

Because Moro had a plane to catch, the parties did not type up a formal document. Instead, Reilly and Gust drafted a handwritten document together, with Reilly drafting the majority of the document. The finished product contained fourteen terms and consisted of three pages. Both attorneys reviewed the document and initialed each of the terms and revisions. Moro and Haghighi then signed each page. The document did not contain a provision stating that it was binding, as required by both the Mediation Agreement and the Minnesota Civil Mediation Act.

On August 28, 1996, IRN filed a summary judgment motion to declare the handwritten document enforceable as a settlement agreement. The district court treated IRN's motion as a motion to enforce a settlement agreement and scheduled an evidentiary hearing. Before the evidentiary hearing, the district court requested that the parties submit supplemental briefs addressing the impact of the Minnesota Civil Mediation Act, Minn. Stat. § 572.35, subd. 1, on the enforceability of any settlement agreement. On November 8, 1996, the district court issued an order stating that, although on its face Minn. Stat. § 572.35, subd. 1 appears to preclude enforcement of the handwritten document, the court did not believe that the legislature intended such a result in mediations "where both parties are represented by counsel and are fully aware of the binding effect of a settlement agreement." Accordingly, the district court concluded that Minn. Stat. § 572.35, subd. 1 did not bar enforcement of the handwritten document.

After holding an evidentiary hearing to determine whether the parties intended the handwritten document to represent a binding settlement agreement, the district court found that the objective words and conduct of the parties both during and after the mediation session demonstrated that both parties intended to be bound by the handwritten document and that the document represented a final and complete settlement of the case and an agreement as to all essential terms. Therefore, the district court concluded that IRN met its burden of proving that a settlement agreement existed and granted IRN's motion to enforce the handwritten document. RABC appealed, and the United States Court of Appeals for the Eighth Circuit certified to this court the question of whether Minn. Stat. § 572.35, subd. 1 renders the handwritten document unenforceable.

"A certified question is a matter of law and this court is free to independently review it on appeal." As a threshold issue, the certified question requires this court to assume the handwritten document was prepared at the conclusion of a mediation session conducted pursuant to the Minnesota Civil Mediation Act. Given these facts, we conclude that the handwritten document is rendered unenforceable by the plain language of Minn. Stat. § 572.35, subd. 1.

Canons of statutory interpretation provide that "when the words of a law in their application to an existing situation are clear and free from all ambiguity, the letter of the law shall not be disregarded under the pretext of pursuing the spirit." In accordance with this principle, this court has consistently stated that when a statute is free from ambiguity, we will not look beyond the express language of the statute.

There is no ambiguous language in the provision at hand. The statute clearly provides that a mediated settlement agreement will not be enforceable unless it contains a provision stating that it is binding. The handwritten document prepared by the parties did not contain such a provision. Given a strict, plain language reading, the statute precludes enforcement of the document.

However, IRN contends that such a reading would accomplish an absurd result in this case. When the literal meaning of the words of a statute produces an absurd result, we have recognized our obligation to look beyond the statutory language to other indicia of legislative intent. IRN argues that the legislature clearly intended to protect parties who are unrepresented at mediation and who might not be aware of the legal consequences of the proceedings. Thus, IRN argues that when parties are represented at mediation by attorneys, there is no need for the requirement that the mediation settlement contain a provision stating that it is binding. We disagree. Requiring that a settlement agreement contain a provision stating that it is binding, even when both parties are represented by attorneys, does not produce an absurd result. While IRN contends that the legislature intended this statute to protect only unrepresented parties, it is just as likely that the legislature intended that a settlement document state that it is binding in order to encourage parties to participate fully in a mediation session without the concern that anything written down could later be used against them. If the literal language of this statute yields an unintended result, it is up to the legislature to correct it. This court "will not supply that which the legislature purposefully omits or inadvertently overlooks."

The plain language of the Minnesota Civil Mediation Act requires that a mediated settlement agreement prepared at the conclusion of a mediation session conducted under this Act contain a provision stating that the settlement agreement is binding. Because the handwritten document does not contain such a provision, it is, therefore, unenforceable.

Certified question answered in the affirmative.

NOTES AND QUESTIONS

(1) Note that the federal district court in *Haghighi* ruled that the Minnesota statute prevents the mediator's testimony. However, the court questions the "appropriateness of such a limitation on testimony in circumstances where a dispute arises regarding the existence of a mediated settlement." Why?

(2) In response to the decision of the Minnesota Supreme Court, the Eighth Circuit reversed the federal district court's decision and remanded the case for further proceedings in light of the state court's decision on the certified question. *Ali Haghighi v. Russian-American Broadcasting Co.*, 173 F.3d 1086 (8th Circ. 1999). For a trenchant discussion and critique of the *Haghighi* litigation and the relevant Minnesota rule, see James R. Coben and Peter N. Thompson, *The Haghighi Trilogy and the Minnesota Civil Mediation Act: Exposing a Phantom Menace Casting a Pall Over the Development of ADR in Minnesota,* 20 Hamline J. Pub. L. & Pol'y 299 (1999).

Chapter 6
DIVERSITY, POWER, AND FAIRNESS

or remember risk of destroying impartiality

§ A INTRODUCTION

Because mediation promotes individual autonomy in the decision-making process, each person's values and aspirations assume a prominent role in how people discuss, develop, and shape their mediated outcomes. Having someone's individual characteristics play such a salient role creates both opportunities and dangers to which the mediator must be attuned. These matters, both pragmatic and theoretical, arise in three different ways.

First, individual differences require the mediator to be sensitive to how different backgrounds and values affect the manner in which individuals participate in the discussion process; a mediator must deploy her communication skills to ensure that mediated conversations foster maximum participation and understanding by all participants. These issues will be discussed in Section B. *Second,* parties, in light of their differences, command different resources and skills that affect how they negotiate; the danger is that mediation participants, through the dynamics of the bargaining process, might accept proposed settlement terms that exacerbate pre-existing inequalities, thereby raising the undesirable possibility that participating in mediation undermines rather than advances a person's fundamental interests. We will focus on these concerns in Section C. *Third,* since each party in mediation decides what priority to attach to various principles and norms to resolve their dispute, the possibility arises that settlement terms acceptable to individuals might clash with outcomes required by law. This dilemma, addressed in Section D, presents the basic question of how to structure the proper relationship between the mediation process and the rule of law.

'B

'C

'D

As you study the following excerpts, envision yourself in multiple roles: as a party, an advocate, a mediator or a professional who designs justice systems. Ask yourself: does the process as structured and implemented comport with our fundamental convictions about treating persons with dignity and respect?

§ B DIVERSITY, INDIVIDUAL DIFFERENCES AND THE RESOLUTION OF DISPUTES

We live in a diverse society. To facilitate effective communication and understanding among persons of differing backgrounds, a mediator must both discern the cognitive and affective meanings of the disputing parties' comments and behaviors and also make certain that each party understands the other's concerns and proposals. This begins at the very basic level of ensuring that parties comprehend what each mediation participant is saying. If persons speak different languages, then a mediator must secure a language interpreter so that everyone effectively engages in a discussion. Diversity differences, though, penetrate far more subtly.

We value things differently, and that leads to behavioral differences. In some cultures, for example, people show respect by not having direct eye-contact with their discussion counterparts, yet other individuals might interpret a person's not maintaining eye contact as a sign of disrespect. Similarly, a married man in some religious traditions will not shake hands with a female who is not his wife, while persons raised in other traditions view a person's refusal to shake one's hand as a deliberate act of disengagement or hostility. Persons from different cultures develop different habits and practices regarding what constitutes a comfortable physical distance between two persons who are conversing; if one person invades the other's space, deliberately or accidentally, one or more of those individuals can become uncomfortable. Similarly, the fact that some persons speak more loudly or quickly than others sometimes leads persons to conclude that the person speaking loudly is disrespectful, or that the fast-talking individual is being deceptive.

These examples, and the myriad of other situations one can envision, reflect how varying practices emanate from different, though not necessarily conflicting, values. What is the significance of such complexities for a mediator? The mediator must adopt procedural and conversational practices that enable all parties to feel that they are being treated with dignity and respect. The mediator, for instance, would try to place parties at the conference table at a distance comfortable for everyone; the mediator, if female, would not demand to shake the hand of a male party whose culture or religion forbade such conduct. The mediator would schedule meeting times in a manner that respected the participants' desire to celebrate particular holidays or religious events, or serve parties with food and beverages that reflected their differing cultures. By behaving in such a manner, the mediator displays fundamental sensitivity and respect to persons of varying backgrounds, and thereby enables all participants to feel included.

At the same time, a mediator cannot fall into the trap of interacting with disputants based on stereotypes. There is an important difference between one's being conscious of differences based on race, gender, ethnicity, or religion, and one's engaging in stereotyping; while membership in a particular group tends to create commonalities among group members, each individual adopts particular views, behaviors, and values in their own way. A mediator must be sensitive to blending a respect for group norms with awareness of how individual group members embrace or reject that norm. In this very fundamental way, a mediator must take seriously the belief that every case is different because each person is unique.

Diversity conflicts can also reflect clashes of fundamental values. Controversies regarding leadership succession in a family-operated business can pit one family member's belief about the priority of family cohesiveness against another person's desire to exercise autonomy by pursuing other life callings. Deep value conflicts emerge when a group's cultural values define gender roles in a manner that is sharply at odds with the dominant culture's public policy. Such a conflict occurs, for example, when parents instruct a medical doctor to perform what they see as a mild form of genital circumcision/mutilation on their young, female daughter in order to keep her pure for marriage, and the doctor, citing her medical code of conduct, refuses to perform the procedure. In such situations, encouraging persons to engage in discussions to search for a workable, acceptable resolution is challenging; some efforts will succeed while others fail. While no mediator should be deterred from trying to assist parties to such a dispute, the mediator must recognize that more is at stake than simply trying to deploy an effective technique to help parties respect alternative practices; rather, one party may be asking the other to alter a web of fundamental convictions. Exploring those matters with the parties requires the mediator to possess an intellectual acumen and sensitivity of the highest order. These controversies, in particular, also raise the question of whether the mediator's own background enables her to act in a neutral fashion, or be perceived and accepted by the parties as so acting.

In sum, there are multiple sources of differences among parties. To the extent possible, the mediator, wants to capitalize on the strengths of those differences in order to assist parties design and shape imaginative bargaining outcomes. The mediator works to make certain that parties understand one another's proposals and conduct in light of their respective life patterns and values; she wants to ensure that parties do not encounter impasse by drawing improper inferences about their bargaining counterpart's attitudes or behavior, particularly if those inferences are based on inaccurate stereotyping or ignorance of one another's cultural practices.

The first excerpt below from Michelle LaBaron Duryea and J. Bruce Grundison highlights at a general level how immigrants to a new culture (in this instance, Canada) might perceive and interact with citizens of the dominant culture. It poignantly references how making adjustments to living in a new culture creates challenges both within a family or cultural group unit as well as between that family/group unit and citizens and institutions of the dominant culture. Professor Kolb's excerpt on gender, raises the troublesome concern of whether persons of a particular gender may be systematically disadvantaged by participating in mediation.

CONFLICT AND CULTURE: RESEARCH IN FIVE COMMUNITIES IN VANCOUVER, BRITISH COLUMBIA.

By Michelle LeBaron Duryea and J. Bruce Grundison,

University of Victoria Institute for Dispute Resolution, 1993. pp. 28–42

[Ed. Note. Methodologically, the authors refer to the persons whom they interviewed at this stage of their research as "key informants."]

"IMMIGRANT SYNDROME"

While immigrant groups are diverse in many ways, they also have much in common. An interesting discussion was presented by a key informant commenting on the Latin American community who identified what he called the "immigrant syndrome." While his comments related to the Latin American community, there were themes that may apply to other immigrant groups.

In his framework, the immigrant syndrome has four components: the linguistic choke, the cultural choke, the social-familial choke, and the loss of identity choke. The linguistic choke occurs when individuals without skills to communicate with the dominant culture turn to their children to help them with their communication. This causes conflicts in the family because children realize that they can gain power in the family through linguistic aptitude. The linguistic choke also affects one's possibilities of gaining employment. Sometimes women are able to get jobs faster than men, not because they acquire the language faster, but because many jobs that women can find do not need sophisticated language skills. Cleaning is an example. Power in the spousal unit changes, and many marriages have broken up because of the independence that immigrant women can achieve in Canada.

The social-familial choke refers to the social and familial changes in the family structure. Many Latin Americans, for example, were well off in their countries of origin and left their countries because of political and civil wars. When they come to Canada many of these refugees are treated as "third class citizens." This change in status can cause problems in adaptation to Canadian ways.

A more subtle problem is called the cultural choke. When immigrants come to Canada they are faced with a value system different from the one they were accustomed to in their countries of origin. Depression is high among immigrants, many of whom never really overcome the losses they experience: many have lost their families, friends, and homes. In Canada they feel alone and lonely. Values about achievement are very different. Americans and Canadians value an individualistic focus on achievement whereas some cultures value a group focus on achievement.

The fourth component is the loss of identity choke. Latin American individuals, for example, may refer to themselves as Salvadoreans, Colombians, or Guatemalans, but in Canada they are collectively labeled as Hispanics or Latin Americans. Immigrants attempt to build a community by trying to adapt to the new social identity assigned to them by the dominant culture in Canada. Many refugees are in a state of mourning; they grieve the loss of their homes, families, and climate, and require counselling to help them with their feelings of depression and isolation.

CONFLICT ISSUES

INTRODUCTION

When asked about issues in their communities around which there may be conflict, individual key informants focused considerable attention on family conflict even though they were invited to comment on several categories of conflict.

One key informant, commenting on the emphasis on family conflict, said that conflicts within families often arise in immigrant communities in which there are many related people and potential interferers. Family conflict has been studied quite extensively already, said the key informant, with casework on families where ethnicity is the key variable being the most studied area even in analyses focusing on religion, language and education. Given the amount of work already devoted to family conflict, the informant cautioned that the family conflict category should not be allowed to dominate the research agenda.

FAMILY CONFLICTS

Key informants in all groups discussed conflicts arising from challenges to traditional family structures, such as generational and gender roles, which occur when immigrants adopt Canadian lifestyles. The role of the extended family is important in each community. Family unity is highly valued, and conflict can cause all family members to suffer: spouses, parents, children, teens, young adults, and older generations.

Key informants from the Chinese community indicated that disorder and imbalance in spousal roles may occur when spouses immigrate at different times. The following paraphrase from one key informant's comments describes some of the problems:

> Whoever comes to Canada first will automatically be dominant, because they will know better where to go and what to do. They will know society better and have better language skills. In one case, the woman came first. Then her husband came. He had to rely upon his wife all of the time. He felt lost as a man and as a professional; he did not have the same status here in Canada that he had in China. There were many arguments that came from this experience. If a woman is a professional worker in China and comes here after her husband, she will have problems of a similar nature to those described by this husband.

. . . .

Key informants from the Latin American community also reported shifts in power within the spousal unit as a result of changes in roles within the family. Women often gain authority because they are able to gain employment faster than men. They can get jobs where English language skills are not essential. While divorce is not encouraged in countries of origin, divorce rates are high among Latin Americans who move to Canada because of the independence that Latin American women are able to achieve in Canada.

In Canada, immigrant children gain power by learning to speak the language. Within the Latin American community, children are frequently required to interpret for the family. This role reversal contributes to the parents' sense of loss of status and control, and power struggles between parents and children can result.

Key informants reported that family problems in this community are very serious and need attention. Parent-teen conflict can become so severe that teens run away from home and begin to sell drugs to make money to survive. Key informants reported needing programs on effective parenting and parental rights. Families are highly valued in the Latin American culture, so if the family begins to disintegrate there is profound difficulty and loss for the family members, particularly the elder generations.

Changing parental roles may cause family conflicts within the Polish community, but in ways that differ from some of the other communities. One of our key informants suggested that Poland's egalitarian society prepares women to have careers which may take priority over those of their husbands. In Canada, however, many recent immigrants of Polish descent perceive that men hold most positions of power. Polish men may see their wives, many of whom at one time had professional careers, working as homemakers or in jobs with low social status. Here the men may begin to accept a subordinate social status for women. Other Polish informants suggest that women have better opportunities for advancement in Canada than they did in Poland. . . .

In the Polish community, children may experience their parents' frustration through physical abuse, but key informants indicated that intergenerational violence is less common than differences in values. Rules such as curfews may seem onerous to some children who compare their own parents to those of friends. Although spanking or slapping may have been common in Poland, children soon learn at school that such treatment can be illegal, and they may threaten to telephone the 9-1-1 emergency number if their parents touch them. Children may not openly shun their Polish heritage, but parents have difficulty teaching their children about Polish customs, manners, and language. Also, children usually master a new language rapidly and become more fluent in English than their parents. Combined with the difference in cultural values, this can be a recipe for continuing conflict.

Finally, key informants noted that Polish families sometimes immigrate in phases, with dynamics within the families changing as each member arrives. Prolonged separation causes some of the difficulties as the parents form new attachments and relationships outside their marriage bond. Other problems result from the different stages of adaptation through which family members go; the first to arrive will likely know more English than the later arrivals and will certainly know more about resources and services available in the new country. . . .

Intergenerational conflicts arise from differences in attitude about family values and traditions. Parents try to uphold traditional values; children retaliate. A key informant reported that sons are valued more than daughters, and preferential treatment for boys can cause conflicts among siblings. Domestic help is expected from the daughters, but not from sons. Challenges to traditional work ethics can cause intergenerational disputes within the family. Parents may value hard work, but younger children may not see any reasons for hard work.

Conflicts also occur between older children and grandparents who are accustomed to having decision-making authority within the family. In Canada, grandparents are not given this authority; . . . [this] can create tension and divisions in the family. Sometimes grandparents try to strengthen their own position by winning over a certain grandchild as an ally.

Older generations may also be exploited by family members who may ask them to care for the grandchildren or to give their pension to support the family. Stripped of the power and authority they used to have in the extended family structure in Vietnam, seniors may feel ignored and isolated, and there are very few programs aimed at helping them.

INTERGROUP CONFLICT

A number of the key informants were asked to assess the state of intergroup relations in British Columbia, having particular reference to the Lower Mainland, on a scale of 1 to 10, with 0 representing serenity and 10 an explosive state. While one Chinese key informant mentioned that intergroup relations are better now than when she was a youngster, all key informants said that there is room for improvement. With the exception of the key informants from the Polish community who rated British Columbia between 5 and 6 on the scale, all respondents assessed the volatility of intergroup relations as 7 or higher. Considerable emphasis was placed on the urgency of addressing this issue. Several key informants assessed the situation as potentially explosive. . . .

One key informant stated that while the dominant Canadian culture is polite and respectful, many Canadians hold stereotypical beliefs about different ethnocultural groups. For example, many Canadians do not know the differences that exist between the Latin American peoples and may assume that anyone speaking Spanish must be Mexican. Latin Americans may be stereotyped as lazy, loud, or violent. Misinterpretation of mannerisms or customs may encourage stereotyping. For example, police may think that a Hispanic individual is "shifty" if he does not make eye contact in the same manner as other Canadians.

The issue of stereotyping is illustrated further in the following section on conflict issues.

CONFLICTS INVOLVING POLICE

Key informants from immigrant communities indicate they have been subject to discrimination and stereotyping by police. For example, Latin American youths may be seen as "gang members" whether or not they actually have such affiliations.[2] Police may go to arrest a Latin American youth on an immigration matter and also arrest ten of his friends, subjecting them to strip searches and questioning.

Key informants from the Polish and Latin American groups reported they are accustomed to seeing the police as corrupt representatives of repression, so there is little room for trust or positive interaction. The process of understanding laws and developing trust of public authorities is hindered for Latin Americans because of negative experiences in their countries of origin and the lack of established community support in Canada. Perceived harassment of community youth perpetuates this distrust. Distrust of police has led in some

---

[2] Use of the term "gang" is problematic because of its connotations with extreme violence, lawlessness, and organized crime. Key informants suggested the use of the word "group," but we have retained "gang" out of fidelity to the original data. It should not be taken from this that gangs are necessarily involved in serious crime, nor that their mention here in any way implies a specific connection between ethnicity and gang membership.

cases to immigrants taking the law into their own hands, which causes further difficulties.

One key informant suggested there could be major trouble if there is no improvement in relationships between police and minorities. Gang-related and other organized criminal activity has been increasing, but youth gangs are not limited to immigrant communities. There is a clear need to train institutional staff in effective ways of resolving conflict and in dealing effectively with a diverse community.

Police departments in Victoria and Vancouver have been doing intercultural awareness training. The issue is sensitive because some training has been found to reinforce negative stereotypes. Recently, the Canadian Centre for Police Race Relations was opened in Ottawa. It will provide information about bias-free standards, policies, and procedures for the selection, recruitment, and performance of police officers. In addition, the centre will provide cross-cultural and anti-racism training for police officers, as well as developing effective liaison, consultation and out-reach mechanisms for police to use in dealing with diverse clients and communities.

Liaison between cultural groups and police is one step being taken to address key issues. In Vancouver an identified need is to have storefront police offices for specific groups. A group of British Columbia's Aboriginal people have been involved in creating such a service in Vancouver. They have been particularly concerned about issues of credibility and official recognition and have considered it important that the individual overseeing the project report directly to the government or to the Vancouver Police Department, not to an independent board. A similar centre has been set up for Chinese people to provide translation, referral, and response services that suit victim needs. In another initiative, police representatives have been communicating with their counterparts in Hong Kong to get a better understanding of some of the cultural variables involved in organized crime in the Chinese community. . . .

CONFLICTS INVOLVING ORGANIZATIONS

Because of unpleasant experiences in their countries of origin, many in the Latin American community mistrust authority figures such as police, government officials, and social service workers. Some individuals in the Latin American community have experienced political imprisonment and torture, including some refugee claimants from Guatemala and El Salvador. Many view authority as abusive and oppressive and are suspicious of the police and social service agencies.

Their backgrounds may lead them to mistrust interventions in the family by social workers. One key informant commented that the Ministry of Social Services ("MSS") is perceived as an "agency designed to destroy families." If children do not like the discipline from their parents they may call Social Services. Parents may be afraid. Some do not understand the authority and the role of the social workers. Others challenge social workers, feeding stereotypes that Latin American men are threatening and violent. The key informant said that better communication might be achieved by providing social workers with information about families' cultural values and providing parents with information about how the services can help them, including when and how a social worker can intervene to help with family problems.

Difficulties with communicating in English can hinder interventions. One reported example involved a Latin American woman who was placed in a transition house after deciding to leave her abusive husband. She felt isolated because her inability to speak English prevented her from communicating with others in the transition house. After a few weeks the woman returned to her husband because, despite the abuse, she could at least speak with him in Spanish.

Government organizations and agencies usually do not have workers available who speak Polish or understand the Polish culture. Polish immigrants may not get the services they require because either they cannot communicate their needs or they do not seek out help, fearing the English-speaking institutions. Furthermore, some Poles may be suspicious of volunteer organizations because they expect others to be motivated by the need to make money.

Members of the South Asian community reported conflicts with Workers' Compensation Board ("WCB"), Unemployment Insurance Commission ("UIC"), Insurance Corporation of British Columbia ("ICBC"), and MSS. Key informants said these organizations hold stereotypical beliefs that South Asians take undue advantage of their services. As a result, persons of South Asian descent may be considered "guilty until proven innocent" of "milking the system." South Asian clients of ICBC complain that they are not dealt with fairly and that their word may not have the same weight as that of an accident victim from the dominant culture.

One key informant indicated that immigrants bring with them assumptions about how to proceed with bureaucracies. In many cases they are accustomed to a big shadow economy. Some do not understand the workings of ICBC or WCB. Others may be unwilling to make use of the social assistance system. The key informant said that depending on the context of conflict, one person may attribute difficulties with an organization to racism, others to their understanding of how the bureaucracy works. South Asian immigrants have acquired a real distrust of bureaucracy in their countries of origin, a distrust which they bring to Canada. They may assume there is considerable elasticity regarding discretionary powers and may not realize the constraints placed on individual discretion within bureaucracies. They may search for the right button to press and become confused when this does not work. A person who knows how to deal with a bureaucracy such as ICBC is a valued individual in the community.

Conflicts with UIC often relate to transient workers employed in farm work, in which the South Asian population is disproportionately represented. Workers who move from one location to another may be denied UIC benefits because of government regulations.

In addition, South Asians may not see intervention into families by MSS as helpful. They may view social workers and other social service providers as akin to police. They resist the invasion of their family. One key informant indicated that no matter how specialized or respectful the bureaucracy becomes, South Asian families may still resist outside interference. . . .

SCHOOL CONFLICT

Different styles of teaching and classroom management are the source of conflicts between teachers and parents from certain cultural backgrounds. For example, Chinese and South Asian parents expect that teachers will use types of classroom discipline different from those techniques usually employed in Canadian schools. Teachers sometimes fail to use their authority correctly, some parents think. South Asian parents typically view any call for participation in parent-teacher conferences as negative because they are unfamiliar with this approach. Parents may be uncomfortable with the consultative model proposed by the British Columbia School Act, preferring to give teachers and the educational system full control.

Aside from the interference in family issues mentioned above, schools may be a source of conflict when the teachers attempt to communicate about problems the children have. One key informant suggested that presenting parents with several choices works much better than criticizing them or telling them outright what to do.

A number of South Asian key informants have reported that their children have not been treated fairly in school. Children have been shunned by their peers as a result of cultural stereotyping. Young boys who wear turbans, for example, have been teased by other children at school. In many cases the schools do not address this problem. This can lead to conflicts between the parents and the school as well as to conflicts between the child and the parents.

Incidents of name-calling discrimination against students of South Asian heritage have been attributed to biased press reports about ethnocultural groups. For instance, after a recent shooting in the South Asian community, the local press described several weapons confiscated by police from "Asian gangs" during the preceding month.[2] The timing and description of these reports did not assist in creating a positive public image of the South Asian community. One key informant questioned whether in other circumstances the press would report that there had been "another Caucasian shooting"; it had labelled the South Asian incident "another Sikh shooting."

NEIGHBOURHOOD AND HOUSING CONFLICTS

Latin American and South Asian key informants reported neighbourhood and housing conflicts. Landlord/tenant problems can arise from the different style and ingredients of cooking used by South Asians as well as from the number of adults living in single family dwellings. Community reaction to the extended family traditions of South Asians can lead to and can reinforce prejudices, stereotypes, and racist behavior. Members of the South Asian group also find that because of religious differences, they are not accepted by the dominant society. Many Sikh men feel discriminated against because of their turbans. . . .

---

[2] *See* Footnote 1, *supra.*

EMPLOYMENT CONFLICTS

Conflicts relating to employment were mentioned particularly by key informants from the Latin American community. This issue is particularly important to adult immigrants who have been trained in specific careers in their home countries. Doctors and lawyers find it hard to have their credentials accepted. Loss of one's status and one's career is difficult to bear. As well, the lack of Latin American lawyers, doctors, psychologists, and other professionals is a disadvantage for community members who need these services and may not be fluent in English.

Immigrants from Poland experience many conflicts about employment as well. Employment counsellors may advise some to lower their expectations and to accept jobs which require far less training than the often highly-educated immigrants have. Canadian officials in Poland who warmly accept immigration applications from professionals and assure the new immigrants that there will be jobs may raise people's expectations about life in Canada. The situation is further aggravated by lack of opportunities for advanced training in English, job retraining, and gradual integration into their chosen professions. . . .

NOTES AND QUESTIONS

(1) Assume that the perspectives of the key informants reported in the Duryea/Grundison study accurately portray similar experiences for immigrant persons living in the United States and that you are mediating a case in the United States in which one party is claiming unlawful termination from his/her employment. The defendant is a member of the majority culture. What discussion dynamics might the mediator anticipate if the plaintiff is (a) a male member of the majority culture? (b) a female immigrant from a Latin American country whose husband is unemployed? (c) a male son living with his parents and sister who recently immigrated from Poland? What might the mediator do to avoid engaging in inappropriate assumptions or stereotypes? If the mediator recognizes dynamics that are due to cultural interactions, how should it affect her handling of the situation?

(2) You are mediating a case involving a school teacher, guidance counselor, and a 7th grade student and his parents. The student has been reported as habitually tardy, if not truant, from school. Under state law, the school district must file charges in juvenile court against the student and parents if his unexcused absences continue. During the mediation conference, you learn the following information about the student and his parents: the student and parents immigrated to this country 12 months ago; the parents rely on their son to transport himself to school; the student's mother is employed but the father does not have steady work; the father speaks very little English while his son and spouse are more fluent; the mother leaves for work at 6:00 a.m. each weekday morning; the father believes that it is a mother's responsibility to raise the child, including making certain that he attends school regularly; the father, often depressed by his not having found regular work in the United

States, frequently socializes with male companions until the early morning hours and is often asleep when his wife leaves for work. School district participants state that both parents have a responsibility for making certain that their son attends school. What "diversity" challenges confront the mediator and parties? What options might exist for constructively addressing the situation?

(3) If a party's background makes her skeptical of persons who are authority figures, how can a mediator explain and execute her role in the dispute resolution process to engender trust? Does it make a difference if a mediator adopts an evaluative rather than facilitative orientation (*see* Chapter 4, *supra*)? Conversely, if a party's background leads her to rely on authority figures for establishing and enforcing basic norms, would it make a difference if a mediator adopts a facilitative rather than evaluative orientation?

(4) As noted in Chapter 1, *supra*, mediation's use during its Foundational Years was highly valued because it provided a forum for participants to discuss their interests and concerns that significantly affected the way in which they interacted with one another. This was especially important for addressing such matters as police-community relations, where the topics to be discussed did not constitute legal causes of action. This capacity for participants in mediation to address multiple matters, not just those that are appropriate topics in litigation, assumes added urgency when matters of diversity are involved, for persons can experience being harmed or aggrieved whether or not the legal system recognizes a cause of action.

One compelling example is the phenomenon of "hate speech." There is a significant tension in weighing the competing interests of free speech and the harm experienced by those individuals who are the objects of racist speech. For a compelling account of these tensions, see Mari J. Matsuda, *Public Response to Racist Speech: Considering the Victim's Story*, 87 Mich. L. Rev. 2320 (1989). Professor Matsuda's proposal for combating this type of speech is to develop both civil and criminal legal interventions to prohibit it, thereby providing incentives for persons to change their behavior. But is making the undesired conduct illegal the only, or best, way to minimize its presence? A different approach, using mediation, is described in Chapter 10 [H], *infra*. Universities have tried to combat racist speech on campus by students towards one another by developing speech codes. Some of these codes have been declared unconstitutional. *See Doe v. University of Michigan*, 721 F. Supp. 852 (E.D. Mich. 1989). Could various University stakeholders, with a mediator's assistance, develop a workable set of protocols that effectively address these matters? For a probing analysis of the deeper issues raised by this topic, see Catherine A. MacKinnon, *Only Words* (1993).

(5) For a perspective on how the mediator's own cultural background influences the manner in which he or she conducts a conversation, see Mary E. Pena-Gratereaux and Maria I. Jessop, *Mediation and Culture: Conversations with New York Mediators from Around the World*. Washington Heights-Inwood Coalition Mediation Program (2000).

HER PLACE AT THE TABLE: A CONSIDERATION OF GENDER ISSUES IN NEGOTIATION

By Deborah M. Kolb and Gloria C. Coolidge

(In) Negotiation Theory and Practice, 261-71 (William Breslin and Jeffrey Z. Rubin, Eds.) (The Harvard Program on Negotiation Books (1991)*

Our purpose here is to explore the ramifications of feminist theories of development and social organization to the exercise of power and the resolution of conflict in negotiated settings. . . . [W]e suggest that there are four themes that are most relevant to an understanding of some of the ways that women frame and conduct negotiations. These are:

— a relational view of others;

— an embedded view of agency;

— an understanding of control through empowerment; and

— problem-solving through dialogue.

HER VOICE IN NEGOTIATION

There are at least three reasons why the subject of an alternative voice in negotiation is not closed. First, our experience and those of others suggest that there are significant differences in the ways men and women are likely to approach negotiation and the styles they use in a search for agreement.

. . . [A]t least some women experience their gender as a factor in negotiation. The fact that research may not capture this experience may derive from the settings of the research (usually the laboratory) and the questions the research poses (which are usually aggregate behavioral indicators). Secondly, there is evidence that in real negotiations (as opposed to simulations), women do not fare that well. . . . If negotiation is a woman's place, we would expect women to excel, not be disadvantaged. There is a third reason. . . . [T]he prescriptions to get to win-win outcomes in negotiation offer ambiguous advice to the negotiator, whether male or female. The advice to focus on interests, not positions, and invent options for mutual gain emphasizes the relational dimension of negotiation. . . .

On the other hand, advice to separate people from problems and focus on objective criteria, gives a rationalized and objective cast to negotiation that may be quite different from the subjective and embedded forms of feminine understanding. . . . [I]n the press to provide prescription, it is the technical and rationalized analysis that increasingly dominates. Integrative bargaining, or joint-gain negotiation, while acknowledging the importance of empathetic relationships, suggests that the critical skills necessary to implement win-win outcomes are primarily technical and analytic.

. . . [T]he prescriptive voice of principled or joint gain negotiation, while there is much to applaud in its perspective, has a tendency to drown out alternative ways of seeing and doing things. We need to consider the structures and contexts in more nuanced ways. From our perspective we begin with gender and the themes that might comprise an alternative voice.

HER PLACE AT THE TABLE

Styles of Talk

The essence of negotiation is strategic communication. Parties want to learn about the alternatives available and the priority of interests of the other. At the same time, they want to communicate in ways that further their own aims, whether it is to elucidate their interests or obfuscate them, depending on strategy. Research on gender in communications suggests that women's distinctive communication style, which serves them well in other contexts, may be a liability in negotiation.

Women speak differently. Their assertions are qualified through the use of tag questions and modifiers. . . . [T]he female pattern of communication involves deference, relational thinking in argument, and indirection. The male pattern typically involves linear or legalistic argument, depersonalization and a more directional style. While women speak with many qualifiers to show flexibility and an opportunity for discussion, men use confident, self-enhancing terms. In negotiation, those forms of communication may be read as weakness or lack of clarity and may get in the way of focusing on the real issues in conflict. . . .

Similarly, women's modes of discourse do not signal influence. Women's speech is more conforming and less powerful. Women talk less and are easily interrupted while they, in turn, are less likely to interrupt. In mixed groups, they adopt a deferential posture and are less likely to openly advocate their positions. At the same time, there is a proclivity to be too revealing—to talk too much about their attitudes, beliefs, and concerns.

Given that the process of negotiation as it is customarily enacted calls for parties to be clear and communicate directly and authoritatively about their goals, feelings, interests, and problems, a deferential, self-effacing, and qualified style may be a significant detriment. It is also possible that such a stance can also be an asset in projecting a caring and understanding posture. The choice for women is to learn to become more conversant with negotiation skills but also adept in an alternative style of communication at the negotiating table, one that is more congruent with the task.

Expectations at the Table

. . . [E]vidence from research on women in organizations, particularly in management, suggest that it is not so easy for women to act forcefully and competitively without inviting criticism and questions about both her femininity and ability and threatening something of the accustomed social order.

When performance in decision making and negotiating tasks is judged equivalent by objective measures, men and women are rated differently by those involved, to the detriment of women. They are seen as less influential and receive less credit for what influence they may have exerted. As mediators they are judged less effective, even when the outcomes they achieved are superior.

At the same time, women are expected to do the emotional work in a group. In negotiation contexts, they often carry the burden for attending to relationships and the emotional needs of those involved. While such a burden might be consistent with a voice she might like to speak in, a woman who has trained herself to negotiate from a different premise might find that these expectations frequently constrain her ability to maneuver for herself or those she represents. Learning how to use their strengths and manage the dual impressions of femininity and strategic resolve are important aspects of negotiating tactics for women.

Relational View of Others

There seems to be two major ways that a relational view of self is potentially manifest in negotiation. The first is the conception a woman has of herself as a party negotiating. She conceives of her interests within a constellation of responsibilities and commitments already made. That is, she is always aware of how her actions in one context impact on other parts of her life and on other people significant to her.

The second implication is that relational ordering in negotiation may be a prerequisite for interaction. Relational ordering means creating a climate in which people can come to know each other, share (or do not share) values, and learn of each other's modes of interacting. Expressions of emotion and feeling and learning how the other experiences the situation are as important, if not more important, than the substance of the discourse. In other words, separating the people from the problem is the problem. Negotiation conducted in a woman's voice would, we predict, start from a different point and run a different course than either a purely principled or purely positional model.

Embedded View of Agency

Women understand events contextually both in terms of their impact on important ongoing relationships and as passing frames in evolving situations which grow out of a past and are still to be shaped in the future. The male imagination stereotypically focuses on individual achievement and is sparked by opportunities for distinctive activity that are bounded by task and structure. This exemplifies a self-contained concept of agency. An embedded form of agency emphasizes the fluidity between the boundaries of self and others. Thus, women are energized by their connections and so interpret and locate activities in a spatial and temporal context in which boundaries between self and others and between the task and its surroundings are overlapping and blurred.

If one operates from an embedded view of agency, any negotiation must be understood against the background from which it emerges. That means that there is the expectation that people in negotiation will act in a way that is consistent with their past and future behavior in other contexts. Negotiation is not, therefore, experienced as a separate game with its own set of rules but as part of the extended organization context in which it occurs.

Control Through Empowerment

Power is often conceived as the exertion of control over others through the use of strength, authority or expertise. It is usually defined as the ability to exert influence in order to obtain an outcome on one's own terms. Conceiving of power in this way leads to a dichotomous division between those who are powerful and those who are powerless. A model in which power is accrued for oneself at the expense of others may feel alien to some women and/or be seen by others as somehow incongruent with female roles. Anticipating that assertiveness may lead away from connection, women tend to emphasize the needs of the other person so as to allow that other to feel powerful. Her behavior may thus appear to be passive, inactive or depressed.

. . . An empowerment view which allows all parties to speak their interests and incorporates these into agreements that transcend the individualized and personalized notion of acquiring, using, and benefitting from the exercise of power is often dismissed as hopelessly naive. However, it is clear that there are situations (particularly those that involve ongoing and valued relationships) in which mutual empowerment is a much desired end.

Problem Solving Through Dialogue

Dialogue is central to a woman's model of problem solving. It is through communication and interaction with others that problems are framed, considered, and resolved. This kind of communication has specific characteristics that differentiate it from persuasion, argument, and debate. . . .

Problem solving through dialogue in negotiation suggests a special kind of joining and openness in negotiation. In place of a strategic planning model of negotiation, in which considerable effort is devoted to analyzing and second-guessing the possible interests and positions of the other, problem solving through dialogue involves the weaving of collective narratives that reflect newly-emerging understanding. There exists through this kind of interaction the potential for transformed understanding and outcomes. It is a stance of learning about the problem together and is built on the premise that you have a high regard for the other's interest and she has a high regard for yours. Such a framework suggests a rather different structure of negotiation than the "dance" of positions.

It also suggests a different process from that which is often descried as the essence of joint gain negotiation. The essence of negotiating for joint gains involves a search for those sets of agreements that satisfy interests which the parties are seen to value differently. The tactics entail the logical identification of these differences and the creative exploration of options which will satisfy them. Implied in this model is a view that goals and interests are relatively fixed and potentially known by the parties. The secret to making agreement lies in designing a process where goals and interests can be discovered and incorporated into an agreement. In problem solving through dialogue, the process is less structured and becomes the vehicle through which goals can emerge from mutual inquiry. The stance of those involved is one of flexibility and adaptiveness (distinguished from control) in response to potential uncertainty. This kind of sensing may lead to transformed understandings of problems and possible solutions

NOTES AND QUESTIONS

(1) If Kolb and others are correct in describing communication patterns among men and women as being significantly different, what impact, if any, should that have on the procedural guidelines by which mediators conduct conversation? For example, is the standard guideline of "no interruptions and only one person speaks at a time" a rule that systematically favors one gender? For the impact of storytelling on mediation dynamics, see Sara Cobb and Janet Rifkin, *Practice and Paradox: Deconstructing Neutrality in Mediation*, American Bar Foundation, 1991.

(2) Kolb's work was published more than a decade ago. Do you believe that her conclusions are still apt today?

(3) The salience of a party's individual characteristics arises most frequently in a mediation session as challenges posed to the mediator. The following hypothetical situations have been used when training new mediators:

Joseph B. Stulberg and Lela P. Love, COMMUNITY DISPUTE RESOLUTION TRAINING MANUAL, REVISED EDITION (1996, Michigan Supreme Court) *

1. You are Caucasian or Hispanic and mediating a case between an African-American male and female. Before you can complete your opening, the male gets up to leave, saying, "You can't help us because this involves heterosexual issues." How would you respond: if you are heterosexual? if you are homosexual? Assuming you give a satisfactory response to the first challenge, what if the challenge becomes, "You can't help us because you're white"? What should you do?

2. You are co-mediating a case with a co-mediator of the opposite gender. The parties are 2 men from Latin America, who direct all their comments and eye contact to the male co-mediator. What should you do?

3. You are mediating a case which involves parties from the Caribbean. One of the issues involves an incident in which the respondent stepped over the complainant's baby while the baby was playing in a narrow hallway. The baby was not touched, but the complainant became so angry at the respondent's conduct that she bashed

in the hood of the respondent's car with a bat. The complainant keeps saying, "he stepped over my baby's legs." You do not understand what concerns the complainant and she will not explain why stepping over the baby is such a serious matter. What should you do?

4. You are mediating a case in which racial or gender epithets are being flung across the table. A party (a) who is female is called a "w_____," (b) who is Asian-American is called "slant_____," or (c) who is African-American is called "n_____." What should you do?

5. You are mediating a case in which the complainant talks about fires being started in the apartment below her and illnesses and afflictions happening to occupants of the complainant's apartment. You suspect that the complainant may be accusing the respondent of practicing some sort of black magic. What should you do?

§ C POWER AND THE RESOLUTION OF CONFLICT

People and organizations possess power, and some have more than others. When persons or groups interact with one another, they start from different initial positions with respect to their capacity to influence what the other can or will do.

Power inequalities can arise at both an interpersonal level and institutional level. Whereas mediation advocates identify process informality as one of mediation's distinctive strengths, mediation critics assert that mediation's informality permits bargaining behavior to reinforce or exacerbate power disparities, thereby leading to undesirable results. To prevent such inequities, critics suggest one of two strategies: reshape the mediation process by incorporating rules and procedures that will reduce inequalities, or impose obligations on the mediator to ensure fair outcomes.

FAIRNESS AND FORMALITY: MINIMIZING THE RISK OF PREJUDICE IN ALTERNATIVE DISPUTE RESOLUTION

Wis. L. Rev. 1359, 1360–01, 1367–74, 1387–91, 1402–04 (1985) *

By Richard Delgado, Chris Dunn, Pamela Brown, Helena Lee, and David Hubbert

[W]e [raise] a concern that has seemingly been overlooked in the rush to deformalize—the concern that deformalization may increase the risk of class-based prejudice. ADR has been promoted, in large part, with the rhetoric of egalitarianism. Moreover, it is aimed at serving many groups whose members are particularly vulnerable to prejudice. Thus, if our criticism is correct— if rhetoric is untrue or if ADR injures some of those it is designed to help— society should proceed cautiously in channeling disputes to alternative mechanisms. . . .

II. PROCEDURAL SAFEGUARDS IN FORMAL ADJUDICATION

Virtually absent from previous discussions of ADR is consideration of the possibility that ADR might foster racial or ethnic bias in dispute resolution. Before turning . . . to that question, [we survey] the main elements of formal adjudication that operate to reduce prejudice at trials. . . .

The American legal system strives to provide litigants a fair trial: to this end, it has developed an array of rules. To secure their intended purpose, however, the rules must be applied even-handedly. That task falls, in the first instance, to the trial judge.

Both internal and external constraints are designed to keep a judge from exhibiting bias or prejudice. Internal constraints stem from a judge's professional position. Many judges are appointed for lengthy terms, in some cases for life, and are to that extent freed from having to be politically responsive in their decisions. Moreover, when a judge is appointed he or she agrees to apply an existing system of rules. The simple act of applying rules reduces bias. Furthermore, the repetitive nature of their caseloads disposes judges to perceive a case not in terms of the parties in dispute, but of the legal and factual issues presented—for example, as a pedestrian-intersection accident case, rather than one of a black victim suing a white driver. The doctrine of stare decisis is intended to produce consistent results in similar cases, and anomalous results can be subjected to appellate review.

External constraints also operate to control bias. The Code of Judicial Conduct requires judges to disqualify themselves from cases in which their impartiality is in question; it specifically requires disqualification if a judge feels any animus or prejudice towards a party. If a judge should disqualify himself or herself, but does not do so, recusal statutes enable parties to request a new judge. . . .

In addition to rules that limit prejudice by circumscribing the role of judge or jury, modern procedural systems contain rules that limit prejudice by prescribing the events that occur in the course of litigation. Some of these rules promote fairness and discourage prejudice more or less directly. Others promote fairness indirectly by equalizing the parties' knowledge or by requiring public trials. . . .

One group of rules lessens the scope for bias in adjudication by requiring notice of the suit to all parties and timely filing of pleadings, motions, and responses. Early notice enables defendants to move to eliminate duplicative lawsuits, possibly filed to harass, or suits that have no foundation in fact. The rules requiring pleadings and motions to be filed with the court and opposing counsel enable parties to learn about and respond promptly to significant events in the action. . . .

Other rules specify that pleadings need only give a brief, plain statement indicating the basis of a claim or defense and provide for liberal amendment. These rules encourage resolution of lawsuits on their merits, rather than on the basis of the traditional complex pleading rules that benefitted wealthy or experienced parties. The rules require that the complaint state the basis of the claim. That disclosure may warn a party and the court that the claim is groundless and motivated by prejudice, enabling appropriate action to be taken.

Another rule requires counsel to sign all papers filed in a case. The signature certifies that the attorney, after reasonable inquiry, believes that the paper is grounded in fact and either warranted by existing law or by a good faith argument for modification of current law. The attorney's signature also certifies that the paper is not filed for an improper purpose such as bias or prejudice.

. . . If scandalous or indecent matter, a possible indication of prejudice, appears in any paper filed, the rules provide for sanctions against the attorney who filed it, and that portion of the paper may be stricken. These provisions confine pleadings and other papers to material issues and punish those who inject matter for the purpose of embarrassing or harassing the adversary.

The use of pretrial orders also serves to reduce prejudice. A federal rule requires the parties to consider and define the issues for trial. Once agreement is reached, a pretrial order is entered which guides the course of trial. This order may only be modified to prevent manifest injustice. . . . If an extraneous issue, motivated by bias or prejudice, arises later it may be excluded based on the pretrial order.

The requirement that the court state its findings and opinions further limits bias. It puts judges's reasoning into the public record, allows for appellate review, and encourages judges to find the facts in an unbiased manner. Finally, the rules provide for a new trial if it can be shown that the proceedings were affected by prejudice, bias or improper influence of the jury.

Rules of evidence also serve to reduce prejudice. These rules are intended to facilitate introduction of all relevant evidence. . . . Evidence which is not relevant but rather is offered to induce prejudice should be excluded. Even when relevant, evidence may be excluded if its probative value is outweighed by the danger of prejudice, confusion of the issues, or misleading the jury.

. . . [M]odern rules of procedure and evidence contain numerous provisions that are intended to reduce prejudice in the trial system by defining the scope of the action, formalizing the presentation of evidence, and reducing strategic options for litigants and counsel. ADR, to date, has very few such safeguards; indeed, the absence of formal rules of procedure and evidence is often touted as an advantage-it enables ADR to be speedy, inexpensive, and flexible. ADR decisionmakers or other third parties are rarely professional, and there is rarely a decision making body similar to a jury. Rules of evidence are absent or open-ended; the inquiry is wide-ranging, probing, "therapeutic." The proceedings are often conducted out of the view of the public, in an intimate setting, and with little, if any, provision for review.

III. THEORIES OF PREJUDICE AND ADR

The selection of one mode or another or dispute resolution can do little, at least in the short run, to counter prejudice that stems from authoritarian personalities or historical currents. Prejudice that results from social-psychological factors is, however, relatively controllable. Much prejudice is environmental—people express it because the setting encourages or tolerates it. In some settings people feel free to vent hostile or denigrating attitudes towards members of minority groups; in others they do not.

Our review of social-psychological theories of prejudice indicates that prejudiced persons are least likely to act on their beliefs if the immediate environment confronts them with the discrepancy between their professed ideals and their personal hostilities against out-groups. According to social psychologists, once most persons realize that their attitudes and behavior deviate from what is expected, they will change or suppress them.

l. rev.

Given this human tendency to conform, American institutions have structured and defined situations to encourage appropriate behavior. Our judicial system, in particular, has incorporated societal norms of fairness and even-handedness into institutional expectations and rules of procedure at many points. These norms create a "public conscience and a standard for expected behavior that check *overt* signs of prejudice." They do this in a variety of ways. First, the formalities of a court trial—the flag, the black robes, the ritual—remind those present that the occasion calls for the higher, "public" values, rather than the lesser values embraced during moments of informality and intimacy. In a courtroom trial the American Creed, with its emphasis on fairness, equality, and respect for personhood, governs. Equality of status, or something approaching it, is preserved—each party is represented by an attorney and has a prescribed time and manner for speaking, putting on evidence, and questioning the other side. Equally important, formal adjudication avoids the unstructured, intimate interactions that, according to social scientists, foster prejudice. The rules of procedure maintain distance between the parties. Counsel for the parties do not address one another, but present the issue to the trier of fact. The rules preserve the formality of the setting by dictating in detail how this confrontation is to be conducted.

. . . .

V. PREJUDICE IN ADR-ASSESSING AND BALANCING THE RISKS

. . . [We] showed that the risk of prejudice is greatest when a member of an in-group confronts a member of an out-group; when that confrontation is direct, rather than through intermediaries; when there are few rules to constrain conduct; when the setting is closed and does not make clear that "public" values are to preponderate; and when the controversy concerns an intimate, personal matter rather than some impersonal question. . . .

It follows that ADR is most apt to incorporate prejudice when a person of low status and power confronts a person or institution of high status and power. In such situations, the party of high status is more likely than in other situations to attempt to call up prejudiced responses; at the same time, the individual of low status is less likely to press his or her claim energetically. The dangers increase when the mediator or other third party is a member of the superior group or class. . . .

ADR also poses heightened risks of prejudice when the issue to be adjudicated touches a sensitive or intimate area of life, for example, housing or culture-based conduct. Thus, many landlord-tenant, interneighbor, and intra-familial disputes are poor candidates for ADR. When the parties are of unequal status and the question litigated concerns a sensitive, intimate area, the risks of an outcome colored by prejudice are especially great. If, for reasons of economy or efficiency ADR must be resorted to in these situations, the likelihood of bias can be reduced by providing rules that clearly specify the scope of the proceedings and forbid irrelevant or intrusive inquiries, by requiring open proceedings, and by providing some form of higher review. The third party facilitator or decisionmaker should be a professional and be acceptable to both parties. Any party desiring one should be provided with an advocate, ideally an attorney, experienced with representation before the forum in question. To avoid atomization and lost opportunities to aggregate claims and inject public values into dispute resolution, ADR mechanisms should not be used in cases that have a broad societal dimension, but forward them to court for appropriate treatment.

Would measures like these destroy the very advantages of economy, simplicity, speed, and flexibility that make ADR attractive? Would such measures render ADR proceedings as expensive, time-consuming, formalistic, and inflexible as trials? These measures do increase the costs, but, on balance, those costs seem worth incurring. The ideal of equality before the law is too insistent a value to be compromised in the name of more mundane advantages. Continued growth of ADR consistent with goals of basic fairness will require two essential adjustments: (1) It will be necessary to identify those areas and types of ADR in which the dangers of prejudice are greatest and to direct those grievances to formal court adjudication; (2) In those areas in which the risk of prejudice exists, but is not so great as to require an absolute ban, checks and formalities must be built into ADR to ameliorate these risks as much as possible.

THE MEDIATION ALTERNATIVE: PROCESS DANGERS FOR WOMEN

100 Yale L.J. 1545, 1547–51, 1555–59, 1563–79, 1581–2, 1610 (1990) *

By Trina Grillo

The western concept of law is based on a patriarchal paradigm characterized by hierarchy, linear reasoning, the resolution of disputes through the application of abstract principles, and the ideal of the reasonable person. Its fundamental aspiration is objectivity, and to that end it separates public from private, form from substance, and process from policy. This objectivist paradigm is problematic in many circumstances, but never more so than in connection with a marital dissolution in which the custody of children is at issue, where the essential question for the court is what is to happen next in the family. The family court system, aspiring to the ideal of objectivity and operating as an adversary system, can be relied on neither to produce just results nor to treat those subject to it respectfully and humanely.

There is little doubt that divorce procedure needs to be reformed, but reformed how? Presumably, any alternative should be at least as just, and at least as humane, as the current system, particularly for those who are least powerful in society. Mediation has been put forward, with much fanfare, as such an alternative. The impetus of the mediation movement has been so strong that in some states couples disputing custody are required by statute or local rule to undergo a mandatory mediation process if they are unable to reach an agreement on their own. Mediation has been embraced for a number of reasons. First, it rejects an objectivist approach to conflict resolution, and promises to consider disputes in terms of relationships and responsibility. Second, the mediation process is, at least in theory, cooperative and voluntary, not coercive. The mediator does not make a decision; rather, each party speaks for himself. Together they reach an agreement that meets the parties' mutual needs. In this manner, the process is said to enable the parties to exercise self-determination and eliminate the hierarchy of dominance that characterizes the judge/litigant and lawyer/client relationships. Third, since in mediation there are no rules of evidence or legalistic notions of relevancy, decisions supposedly may be informed by context rather than by abstract principle. Finally, in theory at least, emotions are recognized and incorporated into the mediation process. This conception of mediation has led some commentators to characterize it as a feminist alternative to the patriarchally inspired adversary system. . . .

. . . [I] conclude that mandatory mediation provides neither a more just nor a more humane alternative to the adversarial system of adjudication of custody, and, therefore, does not fulfill its promises. In particular, quite apart from whether an acceptable result is reached, mandatory mediation can be destructive to many women and some men because it requires them to speak in a setting they have not chosen and often imposes a rigid orthodoxy as to how they should speak, make decisions, and be. This orthodoxy is imposed through subtle and not-so-subtle messages about appropriate conduct and about what may be said in mediation. It is an orthodoxy that often excludes the possibility of the parties' speaking with their authentic voices.

Moreover, people vary greatly in the extent to which their sense of self is "relational"—that is, defined in terms of connection to others. If two parties are forced to engage with one another, and one has a more relational sense of self than the other, that party may feel compelled to maintain her connection with the other, even to her own detriment. For this reason, the party with the more relational sense of self will be at a disadvantage in a mediated negotiation. Several prominent researchers have suggested that, as a general rule, women have a more relational sense of self than do men, although there is little agreement on what the origin of this difference might be. Thus, rather than being a feminist alternative to the adversary system, mediation has the potential actively to harm women.

Some of the dangers of mandatory mediation apply to voluntary mediation as well. Voluntary mediation should not be abandoned, but should be recognized as a powerful process which should be used carefully and thoughtfully.

problems w/ mandatory mediation

Entering into such a process with one who has known you intimately and who now seems to threaten your whole life and being has great creative, but also enormous destructive, power. Nonetheless, it should be recognized that when two people themselves decide to mediate and then physically appear at the mediation sessions, that decision and their continued presence serve as a rough indication that it is not too painful or too dangerous for one or both of them to go on. . . .

. . . .

II. THE BETRAYAL OF MEDIATION'S PROMISES

. . . .

Persons in the midst of a divorce often experience what seems to them a threat to their very survival. Their self-concepts, financial well-being, moral values, confidence in their parenting abilities, and feelings of being worthy of love are all at risk. They are profoundly concerned about whether they are meeting their obligations and continuing to be seen as virtuous persons and respectable members of society. They are especially vulnerable to the responses they receive from any professional with whom they must deal. Against this backdrop, mediation must be seen as a relatively high-risk process. To begin with, for most people it is a new setting. Its norms are generally not understood by the parties in advance, with the result that the parties are extremely sensitive to cues as to how they are supposed to act; they will look to the mediator to provide these cues. Mediators are often quite willing to give such cues, to establish the normative components of the mediation, and to sanction departures from the unwritten rules. The informal sanctions applied by a mediator can be especially powerful, quite apart from whatever actual authority he might have. These sanctions might be as simple as criticizing the client for not putting the children's needs first, or instructing her not to talk about a particular issue. That these informal sanctions might appear trivial does not mean they will not be as influential in changing behavior as sanctions that might on their face appear more severe; "the microsanctions of microlegal systems to which we are actually susceptible may be much more significant determinants of our behavior than conventional macrosanctions which loom portentously, but in all likelihood will never be applied to us."[41]

. . . .

Traditional western adjudication is often criticized for its reliance on abstract principles and rules rather than on subjective, contextualized experience. . . .

Of course, under the common law some context, in the form of the facts of an individual case, is also to be considered. The concern for the particular facts of a dispute has been characterized as a feminine search for context, while the pursuit of applicable legal principles has been viewed as a masculine search for certainty and abstract rules. To the extent that its issues are framed merely as questions of law, simply involving precedents and rights, the result

---

[41] Reisman, *Looking, Staring and Glaring: Microlegal Systems and Public Order*, 12 DEN. J. INT. L. & POL'Y 165, 177 (1983).

in a case may be insensitive to the particular facts of the dispute. The invocation of stare decisis to establish the broad rules of a decision also serves to minimize the importance of the factual context to the resolution of a particular case. Finally, a primary focus on questions of law masks many underlying social and political questions.

Where child custody is being determined, a system that ostensibly brings context—*this* mother, *this* father, *these* children—into the process of dispute resolution, and renders a decision based on the lives of those actually involved in the dispute rather than on the basis of a general rule, has much to offer. There is, however, a cost to this change in emphasis; for although the language of legal rights may divert public consciousness away from the real roots of anger, the assertion of rights may also clarify and elucidate those roots. The process of claiming rights, by itself, can be empowering for people who have not shared societal power. Thus the risk of mediation is that if principles are abandoned, and context is not effectively introduced, we end up with the worst of both worlds. . . .

A series of attempts has been made to make the court system more responsive to the actual situation of persons undergoing a divorce and to their children by deemphasizing claims of right and principle. The first of these attempts consisted of reduced reliance on the notion of fault. Before this change, the principles shaping the legal process of divorce were not difficult to discern. In the absence of flagrant misconduct on the part of the spouse, one was to stay in one's marriage. One was not to engage in adultery. A man was to support his wife and children. A mother was to be the primary caretaker of her children.

. . . .

With the advent of "no-fault" divorce, these rules changed, signaling an as yet undefined departure from the principles upon which they had been based. It is now typical for states to allow divorce on grounds that do not require fault by either spouse. For the most part, one spouse need only show that the marital relationship is irreparable. These changes have increased the individual autonomy of married persons and given husbands and wives freedom to extricate themselves from unhappy relationships. They have reduced the oppressiveness of principles which, although written into the law, did not fit the manner in which many persons choose to lead their lives.

But there have been other consequences of these changes. For example, results were once much more predictable than they are now, both in terms of the availability of support and the likelihood of the father's being able to obtain custody of the children. This lack of predictability generally harms the party who has the lesser amount of power in the relationship, or who is most risk averse. . . .

The chief means by which mediators eliminate the discussion of principles and fault is by making certain types of discussion "off-limits" in the mediation. Mediation experts Jay Folberg and Alison Taylor propose the following as one of the "shared propositions" upon which nearly all mediators agree:

Proposition 5. In mediation the past history of the participants is only important in relation to the present or as a basis for predicting future needs, intentions, abilities, and reactions to decisions. [74]

It is typical for mediators to insist that parties waste no time complaining about past conduct of their spouse, eschew blaming each other, and focus only on the future. For example, one of the two essential ground rules mediator Donald Saposnek suggests a mediator give to the parties is the following:

> There is little value in talking about the past, since it only leads to fighting and arguing, as I'm sure you both know. . . . Our focus will be on your children's needs for the future and on how you two can satisfy those needs. . . . [U]nless I specifically request it, we will talk about plans for the future. [75]

Thus, while one of the principal justifications for introducing mediation into the divorce process is that context will be substituted for abstract principles, in fact, by eliminating discussion of the past, context—in the sense of the relationship's history—is removed. The result is that we are left with neither principles nor context as a basis for decision making.

. . . .

Felstiner, Abel and Sarat note that some people are apparently able to tolerate substantial amounts of distress and injustice. [77] This "tolerance," they posit, comes from a failure to perceive that they have been injured. They describe a three-step process by which (1) injurious experiences are perceived (naming), (2) are transformed into grievances (blaming), and, (3) ultimately, become disputes (claiming). "Naming" involves saying to oneself that a particular experience has been injurious. The acquaintance who called me could barely go this far. "Blaming" occurs when a person attributes fault to another (rather than to an impersonal force, such as luck or the weather). One cannot arrive at "claiming," that is, the assertion of rights, without passing through "blaming." By making blaming off-limits, the process by which a dispute is fully developed—and rights are asserted—cannot be completed. Short-circuiting the blaming process may fall most heavily on those who are already at a disadvantage in society. Whether people "perceive an experience as an injury, blame someone else, claim redress, or get their claims accepted . . . [is a function of] their *social position* as well as their individual characteristics." [81]

The cultural commitment to access to justice has focused on the last stage of disputing—claiming. The more critical place at which inequality is manifested, however, is before experiences are transformed into disputes, that is, at the naming and blaming stages. One adverse consequence of deemphasizing discussion of principle and fault is that some persons may be discouraged from asserting their rights when they have been injured. Even more troubling, some persons may cease to perceive injuries when they have been injured, or will

---

[74] J. FOLBERG & A. TAYLOR, MEDIATION 14 (1984).

[75] D. SAPOSNEK, MEDIATING CHILD CUSTODY DISPUTES 70 (1983).

[77] *See* Felstiner, Abel & Sarat, *The Emergence and Transformation of Disputes: Naming, Blaming, Claiming . . .*, 15 L. & SOC'Y REV. 631, 633 (1980-81).

[81] Felstiner, Abel & Sarat, *supra* note 77, at 636.

perceive injuries but those injuries will remain inarticulable, because the language to name them will not be easily available. My acquaintance whose husband had an affair and left her did not trust her sense that she had been injured, treated in a way that human beings ought not to deal with each other. She did not have the support of a clear set of legal principles to help her define her injury; rather, she had been exposed to a discourse in which faultfinding was impermissible, so that she ended up unable to hold her husband responsible for his actions, and instead felt compelled to share his fault. To the extent that there is something to be gained by the assertion of rights, especially for women and minorities, this is unacceptable.

. . . .

Rights assertion cannot take place in a context in which discussion of fault and the past are not permitted, for recognition and assertion of rights are ordinarily based on some perceived past grievance, as well as on some notion of right and wrong. From the point of view of the courts, minimizing conflict is always a good thing: less litigation means less expenditure of court time and resources. From the point of view of the individual, however, conflict sometimes must occur. Conflict may mean that the individual has realized he has been injured, and that he is appropriately resisting the continuation of that injury. The perception of injury arises from a sense of entitlement, which in turn is "a function of the prevailing ideology, of which law is simply a component."[95] If mediation creates a sense of disentitlement, it will interfere with the perception and redress of injuries in cases where they have in fact occurred. . . .

Context is also destroyed by a commitment to formal equality, that is, to the notion that members of mediating couples are, to the extent possible, to be treated exactly alike, without regard for general social patterns and with limited attention to even the history of the particular couples. Thus, it becomes close to irrelevant in determining custody that the mother may have been home doing virtually all the caretaking of the children for years; she is to move into the labor market as quickly as possible. It is assumed that the father is equally competent to care for the children. In fact, it frequently is said that one cannot assume that a father will not be as competent a caretaker as the mother just because he has not shown any interest previously:

> Many women have told me, "He never did anything with the children. If he is given even part-time responsibility for them, he'll ignore them, he won't know what to do."
>
> Research has shown, however, that little correlation exists between men's involvement with the children before and after divorce. . . . When they gain independent responsibility for the children, many men who were relatively uninvolved during the marriage become loving and responsive parents after divorce.[98]

In mediation, insistence on this sort of formal equality results in a dismissal of the legitimate concerns of the parent who is, or considers herself to be, the more responsible parent. Such concerns are often minimized by characterizing

---

[95] Felstiner, Abel & Sarat, *supra* note 77, at 643.

[98] R. ADLER, SHARING THE CHILDREN 33 (1988).

them as evidence of some pathology on the part of the parent holding them. The insistence of a mother that a young child not be permitted to stay overnight with an alcoholic father who smokes in bed might be characterized as the mother needing to stay in control. Or the mediator might suggest that it is not legitimate for one party to assume that the other party will renege on her obligations, simply because she has done so in the past. . . . The point is not that mothers never inappropriately desire to stay in control, or that people who have not fulfilled their obligations once will continue to fail to do so, but rather that by defining the process as one in which both parties are situated equally, deep, heartfelt, and often accurate concerns either are not permitted to be expressed or are discounted.

Equating fairness in mediation with formal equality results in, at most, a crabbed and distorted fairness on a microlevel; it considers only the mediation context itself. There is no room in such an approach for a discussion of the fairness of institutionalized societal inequality. For example, women do not have the earning power that men have, and therefore are not in an economically equal position in the world. All too often mediators stress the need for women to become economically independent without taking into account the very real dollar differences between the male and female experience in the labor market. While gaining independence might appear to be desirable, most jobs available for women, especially those who have been out of the labor market, are low paying, repetitious, and demeaning. Studies show that women in such dead-end jobs do not experience the glories of independence, but rather show increased depression. . . .

The notion of equality, used so effectively to remove control of children from women by treating men as equally entitled to custody regardless of their prior childcare responsibilities, is not nearly so effective when it comes to requiring men to assume responsibility for their children should they choose not to. One rarely hears of joint custody's being used to mandate that a father participate in the raising of his child although many women might desire that help. But fathers who wish to participate even marginally in childrearing are given full rights, and even special privileges to enable them to do so. These privileges are paid for by the mother in terms of inconvenience and instability in her own life. Fathers who do not want to be concerned with raising their children need only pay support, and many do not even do that. Despite the presumption in favor of joint custody, it is assumed, by and large, that the mother will be available to care physically and emotionally for the children for as much or as little time as she is granted.

Western wage labor is based on the availability of an "ideal" worker with no childcare responsibilities. Joan Williams has written that in this system men are raised to believe they have the right and responsibility to perform as ideal workers. Women are raised to believe that they should be able to spend some time with their small children and, upon return to outside employment, must shape their work around the reality that they have continuing childcare responsibilities.

The laws governing custody are now, in theory, gender neutral. Mediators, however, are as likely as others in society to assume that women's work commitments are secondary to those of men, and to give more credence to the work obligations and ambitions of fathers. Women may be encouraged in mediation not to think of themselves as ideal workers so that they will be able to take on primary responsibility for the children.

The result of assuming that one parent will make herself available in this way is that disproportionately more attention is paid to ensuring the access of the parent without physical custody (usually the father) to his children than to meeting the needs of the parent who, in all likelihood, will bear the primary responsibility for these children.

Custody decrees frequently specify joint legal or physical custody, or both, when in fact the children are with one parent—generally the mother—as much or more than children who are living under a sole custody arrangement. The result of such a discrepancy under a joint custody arrangement is that the caretaking parent may be subject to the control of the noncaretaking parent without being relieved of any sizeable amount of day-to-day responsibility for the children. . . .

. . . .

Another criticism of the traditional adversary method of dispute resolution is that it does not provide a role for emotion. Decisions by adversarial parties are posited as rational, devoid of emotion, self-interested, and instrumental (result-oriented). Some proponents of mediation and other methods of alternative dispute resolution believe these characteristics should be retained in mediation to the extent they permit parties to serve their self-interests efficiently. Others have argued that mediation and other forms of alternative dispute resolution provide an opportunity to bring intuition and emotion into the legal process.[117] This latter group of proponents points out that family conflicts in particular often involve a combination of emotional and legal complaints, so that the "real" issues are often obscured in the adversarial setting. Thus, "there may be a great need for an open-ended, unstructured process that permits the disputants to air their true sentiments."

Although mediation is claimed to be a setting in which feelings can be expressed, certain sentiments are often simply not welcome. In particular, expressions of anger are frequently overtly discouraged. This discouragement of anger sends a message that anger is unacceptable, terrifying and dangerous. For a person who has only recently found her anger, this can be a perilous message indeed. This suppression of anger poses a stark contrast to the image of mediation as a process which allows participants to express their emotions.

Women undergoing a divorce, especially ones from nondominant cultural groups, are particularly likely to be harmed by having their anger actively discouraged during the dissolution process. Women have been socialized not to express anger, and have often had their anger labeled "bad." A woman in the throes of divorce may for the first time in her life have found a voice for her anger. As her early, undifferentiated, and sometimes inchoate expressions of anger emerge, the anger may seem as overwhelming to her as to persons outside of it. And yet this anger may turn out to be the source of her energy,

---

[117] See, e.g., S. GOLDBERG, E. GREEN & F. SANDER, DISPUTE RESOLUTION 313 (1985) ("Family disputes are also well suited to alternative forums because the conflicts often involve a complex interplay of emotional and legal complaints.").

strength, and growth in the months and years ahead. An injunction from a person in power to suppress that anger because it is not sufficiently modulated may amount to nothing less that an act of violence. . . .

People are necessarily angry at divorce, in two senses. First of all, anger is inevitable in ending a marriage; almost everyone who obtains a divorce becomes angry sooner or later. This anger may have many different causes: it may be a result of anticipated losses, wrongful treatment, or the myriad compromises of self that may have been made along the way to the marriage's end. Second, some anger is necessary for the disengagement which is essential to the completion of the divorce. It is thus critical that any system of marital dissolution take anger into consideration and establish a means by which it is permitted to enter into the divorce process. . . .

Some mediation literature suggests that mediators should proceed by discouraging the expression of anger. This literature evinces a profound lack of respect for the anger that divorcing spouses feel. For example, Donald Saposnek suggests that "[i]n many ways, the mediator must act as a parent figure to the parents, since their struggles are often not unlike those of siblings squabbling over joint possessions."[129] Saposnek's depiction of divorcing parents suggests that their struggles are devoid of content. He characterizes their anger and conflict as "squabbling" rather than as arising from substantively important conflicts or as a necessary and important step in the divorce process.

Saposnek suggests that the mediator ask questions of the parties that will imply to them that elaboration of their feelings during conflicts with each other is "irrelevant and counterproductive" and that the mediator is "interested in . . . ideas for solutions to these problems." Saposnek thus views the expression of feelings as antithetical to problem-solving; a mediator must choose one or the other . . .

Even when mediation literature does approve of bringing anger into the process, it often recommends doing so in a way that subtly undercuts the legitimacy of the anger. Mediators are encouraged, where necessary, to permit parties to "vent" their anger, after which the parties can move on to discuss settlement. This view does not take anger seriously enough. Because it treats expressed anger as having no long-range impact on the party who is exposed to it, it is not necessarily seen as objectionable to require one party to be present and endure the other party's "venting"—even where the party enduring the venting has been the subject of abuse in the marriage. The effects of exposure to anger in such a case can be devastating. If the privilege of expressing anger has not been distributed equally in the relationship prior to mediation, then the mediator should not grant that privilege equally during the mediation.

Second, and equally critically, the view of anger as something to be "vented" does not take anger seriously as a path to clarity and strength. Anger that is merely vented has lost its potential to teach, heal, and energize; it is ineffective anger, anger that "maintains rather than challenges" the status quo.

---

[129] D. Saposnek, Mediating Child Custody Disputes 176 (1983).

Not all writers suggest that anger be suppressed or vented in the service of eventual suppression. Some mediators, however, especially those in mandatory settings, do advocate that parties suppress their anger. The mediator's personal antagonism toward anger and conflict may lead her to urge clients to keep their angry feelings to themselves.

At the same time, there are other forces which may intensify this dynamic of suppression. Mediators working under time pressures recognize that it takes time to express anger, and its full expression might, indeed, jeopardize a quick settlement. More significantly, there are substantial societal taboos against the expression of anger by women, taboos which have particular force when the disputant is a woman of color. For a woman who has just found her anger, anger which has enabled her to free herself from an oppressive relationship and involve herself and her family in a divorce proceeding, the suppression of the very force that has driven her forward is a devastating message.

. . . .

CONCLUSION

Although mediation can be useful and empowering, it presents some serious process dangers that need to be addressed, rather than ignored. When mediation is imposed rather than voluntarily engaged in, its virtues are lost. More than lost: mediation becomes a wolf in sheep's clothing. It relies on force and disregards the context of the dispute, while masquerading as a gentler, more empowering alternative to adversarial litigation. Sadly, when mediation is mandatory it becomes like the patriarchal paradigm of law it is supposed to supplant. Seen in this light, mandatory mediation is especially harmful: its messages disproportionately affect those who are already subordinated in our society, those to whom society has already given the message, in far too many ways, that they are not leading proper lives.

Of course, subordinated people can go to court and lose; in fact, they usually do. But if mediation is to be introduced into the court system, it should provide a better alternative. It is not enough to say that the adversary system is so flawed that even a misguided, intrusive, and disempowering system of mediation should be embraced. If mediation as currently instituted constitutes a fundamentally flawed process in the way I have described, it is more, not less, disempowering than the adversary system—for it is then a process in which people are told they are being empowered, but in fact are being forced to acquiesce in their own oppression.

NOTES AND QUESTIONS

(1) Professor Delgado concludes that the risk of mediated outcomes being influenced by prejudice are especially great in many landlord-tenant, inter-neighbor, and intra-familial disputes. Yet, since mediation's Foundational years, these types of cases have been central in many mediation programs.

Does that suggest that Delgado's concern was misplaced? A related concern that Delgado's thesis references is whether persons participating in mediation are being accorded "second class" justice; the literature refers to this topic as "access to justice." For a thoughtful analysis of these issues as they relate to mediation's use, see Craig A. McEwen and Laura Williams, *Legal Policy and Access to Justice Through Courts and Mediation*, 13 Ohio St. J. on Disp. Resol. 865 (1998).

(2) If Delgado's concerns are well placed, what are their implications for the structure and practice of mediation? If one introduces into the mediation process the types of "formalities" that Delgado proposes, would that advance or undermine mediation's core values? What capacities or protections, if any, does the mediation process afford to minimize the adverse impact of prejudice influencing the dialogue and outcome?

(3) The late Trina Grillo was herself an active mediator. The concerns she discusses arise, she believed, with particular urgency when parties are mandated to use mediation. Do you agree that the impact of mediation on women would be substantially different depending on whether the process was mandatory or voluntary? Others believe that the force of Grillo's critique stems not from its conceptual account but rather from identifying, and properly criticizing, multiple examples of poor mediating. For a thoughtful response to Grillo's article, see Joshua D. Rosenberg, *In Defense of Mediation*, 33 Ariz. L. Rev. 467 (1991).

(4) Concerns about power imbalance are especially sharp when mediation is used in family contexts in which there is a history of spousal or child abuse. *See, e.g.*, Andree G. Gagnon, *Ending Mandatory Divorce Mediation for Battered Women*, 15 Harv. Women's L.J. 272 (1992). For a list and discussion of the criticisms leveled at mediation when used in this context, see Kathleen O'Connell Corcoran and James C. Melamed, *From Coercion to Empowerment: Spousal Abuse and Mediation*, 7 Mediation Q. 303 (1990).

(5) Other authors have conducted studies to determine whether females who are parties to a divorce proceeding do worse in mediation than in adjudication. Their results suggest that mediation, minimally, fares no worse than adversarial processes in generating outcomes that are perceived by both female and male participants to be equitable and fair. *See* Joan B. Kelly, *Mediated and Adversarial Divorce: Respondents' Perception of Their Processes and Outcomes*, Mediation Q., No. 24, Summer 1989, at pp. 71–88, and Jessica Pearson, *The Equity of Mediated Agreements*, 9 Mediation Q. 179 (1991). The Herman et al. study, excerpted below, reports mixed results as to gender and ethnicity, though in a different substantive setting.

AN EMPIRICAL STUDY OF THE EFFECTS OF RACE AND GENDER ON SMALL CLAIMS ADJUDICATION AND MEDIATION

Institute of Public Law, University of New Mexico, xiii–xxxii (January, 1993)·

By Michelle Hermann, Gary LaFree, Christine Rack and Mary Beth West.

I. INTRODUCTION

A basic tenet of conflict theory is that socio-cultural factors influence decision-making processes. Applying this theory to the judicial system, scholars have asked whether informal processes, such as alternative dispute resolution, are more susceptible than adjudication to bias. In theoretical work and studies involving controlled experimental conditions, several authors have studied the differences between courts and alternative dispute resolution mechanisms in this context. The basic conclusions from these studies have been that the adversarial procedure of adjudication counteracts decision-maker bias, and that the risks of prejudice are greatest in informal settings involving direct confrontation where few rules exist to constrain conduct.

In addition, studies during the past 10 to 15 years have described the composition of parties, cases and outcomes in small claims courts and have tested the hypotheses that mediation is superior to adjudication in generating positive attitudes among litigants of small claims, that mediation is superior in altering post-dispute behavior (i.e. in achieving compliance), and that the two types of dispute resolution lead to significantly different case outcomes.

We proposed empirically to test the conclusions of some of these studies in actual mediations and adjudications in the Bernalillo County Metropolitan Court in Albuquerque, New Mexico.[1] Our research hypotheses were as follows:

That women and minorities achieve less in both mediated and adjudicated small claims settlements than males and nonminorities achieve in similar cases.

That the disparity between outcomes achieved by women and minorities and the outcomes achieved by males and nonminorities is greater in mediated small claims settlements than in adjudicated decisions.

That disputes involving inherent power imbalances, such as landlord-tenant or creditor-lender disputes, are more subject to the effects of bias in small claims mediation.

That the participation of women or minority mediators or adjudicators in small claims disputes involving minority disputants reduces the effects of bias. . . .

· Copyright © 1993 by the University of New Mexico. Reprinted with permission.

[1] [Ed. note: The final study sample consisted of 603 cases, 323 of which were adjudicated and 280 mediated.]

IV. RESULTS

1. Ethnicity

. . . [W]e sought to test the hypothesis that both minority and female claimants would do more poorly in the study cases. Moreover, because mediation is a less formal, less visible, and less controlled forum than adjudication, we hypothesized that effects of ethnicity and gender would be greater for mediated than adjudicated cases. Looking at objective monetary outcomes, our results confirmed our hypothesis for ethnicity, but not for gender. Measures of subjective satisfaction, however, were more complex and showed different patterns.

As measured by the objective Vidmar outcome ratio, minority claimants consistently received less money than nonminorities in our study cases, while minority respondents consistently paid more. These effects were stronger for mediated than adjudicated cases. When case characteristics were added to the model, claimant and respondent ethnicity was no longer statistically significant in the adjudicated cases. It is notable, however, that the most influential case character factors (being represented by a lawyer and being involved in a collection case) were both ethnically and sociologically related. For example, monetary outcomes were higher for collection cases involving individual respondents in which the claimant was either a lawyer or was represented by a lawyer. Whites were more likely to be claimants in collection cases, as well as to be lawyers or be represented by lawyers. Thus, monetary outcomes in adjudicated cases were due primarily to case characteristics and, secondarily, to the ethnicity of participants, with strong interrelationships between the two. In contrast, ethnicity remained significantly more important for predicting outcomes of mediated cases, even with the addition of the case characteristic variables. Case characteristics (such as whether the case was a collection case, whether a counterclaim was involved, the size of the dispute, whether claimants and respondents were individuals or businesses and whether lawyers were involved) had relatively little effect on outcomes in mediation. The one exception to these results occurred when the mediated agreement created a payment plan. Payment plans did help to explain the differences between white and minority outcomes. White claimants were more likely to enter into payment plans than minority claimants and minority respondents were more likely to enter into payment plans than white respondents. Because payment plans typically exchange a long time to pay smaller incremental amounts for a larger total amount paid, they become a significant factor in increasing the amounts paid by minority respondents. The only additional characteristic of claimants and respondents which had a significant effect on monetary outcomes in either mediation or adjudication was education. Higher education worked to the disadvantage of the respondent in adjudicated cases and to the advantage of the claimant in mediated cases.

Having found that minority claimants received less and minority respondents paid more in mediation cases, we sought to explore whether these effects might be counteracted by the ethnicity of the mediators. Our results were quite startling, showing that having two minority mediators eliminated the negative impact on the size of monetary outcomes for minority claimants in mediation. The combination of one minority mediator and one white mediator, however, did not produce a similar result.

Our analysis of subjective outcome and procedural satisfaction by ethnicity produced interesting contrasts. In general, claimants were no more or less satisfied in mediation than in adjudication with regard to procedure, outcome or long-term outcome. Compared to claimants in adjudication, however, mediation claimants reported the outcome as being fairer and less biased. In contrast, respondents in mediation were far more satisfied with the procedure, outcome and long-term outcome, as well as with fairness. The tendency for claimant and respondent satisfaction to be inversely related in adjudication was not found in mediation.

Despite their tendency to achieve lower monetary awards as claimants and to pay more as respondents in mediation, minority claimants taken together were more likely than nonminority claimants to express satisfaction with mediation. Minority claimants and respondents were consistently more positive about mediation than they were about adjudication on all satisfaction and fairness measures. They also reported process satisfaction significantly more often than nonminorities in mediation.

Minority claimants were more likely to be satisfied with the procedure when the two mediators were also minorities.[2] In fact, white as well as minority claimants were more likely to report procedural satisfaction when the mediation involved a minority respondent and two minority mediators. . . .

2. Gender

The effects found for minority participants were generally not replicated when the data were analyzed for gender. Gender of claimant and respondent had no direct effect on monetary outcomes for either adjudicated or mediated cases. The only statistically reliable tendency we found was for female respondents to pay lower monetary outcomes in mediation than adjudication.

Looking at measures of satisfaction, we found that as claimants and respondents, compared to all other ethnic/gender groups, white women report relatively greater satisfaction with adjudicated outcomes. While white female respondents achieved significantly better (i.e. lower) monetary outcomes than the other three groups in mediation, they also reported the lowest rates of satisfaction. Furthermore, compared to other mediation respondents, white women were less likely to see the mediation process as fair and unbiased. Minority women, on the other hand, reported higher satisfaction with mediation, despite their tendency to receive less as claimants and to pay more as respondents.

Female mediators had a significantly greater likelihood of having their disputants reach agreement in mediation. Mediations with two male mediators had the lowest agreement rate. Mediations with mixed gender pairs fell in the middle. Testing for disputant/mediator gender interactions, we found that female claimants were less likely to express procedural satisfaction and

---

[2] [Ed. note. The mediation format used in the New Mexico program assigned two persons to act as co-mediators for each case.]

reported a lack of fairness more often in cases where the two mediators were women. Conversely, respondents in those cases with a female claimant and two female mediators were somewhat more likely to report satisfaction with the outcome.

Both claimant and respondent groups in mediation were more likely to respond favorably to the procedure with a mixed gender pair of mediators.

3. Long-term Satisfaction and Compliance.

The higher frequency of respondent satisfaction in mediation remained unchanged over time. Approximately six months after initial interviews, mediation respondents still reported higher levels of satisfaction than adjudication respondents. . . .

Although we found few effects by ethnicity or gender, minority claimants tended to report higher long-term satisfaction levels in mediation than nonminority claimants. Women respondents in general, and minority women in particular, were more likely to comply with mediated agreements and non-monetary obligations. In contrast, white men were most likely to comply with court rulings.

V. DISCUSSION

It is apparent that among the rich variety of data we gathered about mediation and adjudication of small claims cases in Albuquerque, New Mexico, two findings are especially provocative. One is the finding that white women tend to do as well or better than others in mediation, yet are less satisfied with the outcome. The other is the finding that ethnic minorities achieve relatively poorer monetary outcomes than do whites, especially in mediation, yet are more satisfied with the outcome.

The findings for women are interesting from at least two perspectives. First, many scholars have argued that mediation is unfair to women because they are likely to achieve poorer outcomes in the process. Our study shows this fear to be unfounded, at least in the types of small claims dispute that we have examined here. . . .

Second, the gender findings are interesting because they show that white women are relatively less satisfied with the outcome of mediation and perceive it to be less fair, even though they achieve objectively more positive results. An examination of the open-ended responses of women in mediation shows a significant number who expressed anger. A number of white women also reported that they thought that the mediation process was unfair or biased. Surprisingly, unfairness was reported by female claimants and respondents most frequently when there were two female mediators. . . .

The data involving minorities raise substantial concerns about the fairness of the mediation process. This study demonstrates that the fears of scholars who have postulated that the invisible, informal, nonreviewable forum of mediation produces worse results for minority disputants may be well founded. What is particularly telling is that the presence of two minority mediators largely erases the disadvantage, so that the outcomes of minority disputants in mediation becomes nearly equal to those achieved by white disputants.

What is far less clear about these unequal results is what causes them and what their implications are for mediation. . . .

NOTES AND QUESTIONS

(1) One of the difficulties with research in this area is definitional: what is meant by a "successful" outcome in mediation and can each element be quantitatively measured? In the Herman study, outcome comparisons relate to elements of legally defined issues and remedies. But if a Respondent apologized to a claimant for improper or insensitive behavior and that apology led the Claimant to agree to a lower financial settlement, does that mean that the Claimant did "worse" than someone who received more money? How would an evaluator capture that sense of "fairness" that was so important to a party?

(2) Does the Herman finding regarding the favorable impact of a minority mediator team on mediated outcomes constitute evidence to support Delgado's claim that parties alter their behavior to conform to what is expected of them in the social context? If so, does that suggest, contrary to Delgado's conclusion, that nonminority claimants might behave constructively when participating in a mediation with parties of differing ethnicities, races, or religions?

(3) Some authors argue that it is the mediator's responsibility to address and rectify power imbalances. *See, e.g.,* Jacqueline M. Nolan-Haley, *Informed Consent in Mediation: A Guiding Principle for Truly Educated Decision Making*, 74 Notre Dame L. Rev. 775 (1999). One California statute converts this sentiment into a statutory duty for a mediator: "Mediation of cases involving custody and visitation concerning children shall be governed by uniform standards of practice adopted by the Judicial Council. The standards of practice shall include, but not be limited to, all of the following . . . *the conducting of negotiations in such a way as to equalize power relationships between the parties.*" Cal. Fam. Code § 3162(b)(3) (West Supp. 1998) (emphasis added). Scott Hughes, in his article entitled *Elizabeth's Story*, 8 Geo. J. Legal Ethics 553 (1995), combines a superb narrative of his client's divorce mediation experience with a penetrating analysis of the dangers of using mediation in a matrimonial dissolution setting when there are both explicit and subtle power disparities among the divorcing partners.

(4) In the Test Design Project, referenced in Chapter 3, *supra*, experienced mediators, arbitrators and other third-party neutrals created a list of basic competencies and skills required of a mediator. Would a person so qualified reduce the critic's fear concerning the adverse impact of the mediation process or persons who have been denied equal treatment because of race, ethnicity, gender, or historical origin or is the source of their concern exclusively structural?

§ D FAIRNESS: MEDIATION AND THE RULE OF LAW

Mediation advocates thoughtfully argue that mediation's primary strength is that it empowers participants to decide for themselves what priority to accord to conflicting legal, business, prudential, and personal principles. For many individuals, knowing the answer to the question: "what am I legally entitled or obligated to do?" does not conclusively answer the question: "what should I do to resolve this dispute?" The dialogue over what role public rules play in the dispute resolution process raises fundamental jurisprudential and policy questions.

To justify the use of mediation philosophically requires an account of how the rule of law is compatible with supporting mediation's commitment to promoting participant decision-making. Legal Positivists, most eloquently through the writings of H.L.A. Hart, offer a simple, compelling distinction: what the law is can differ from what the law ought to be. So, if mediation participants develop settlement terms that constitute, from their perspective, their shared vision of what ought to be, should their resolution be supported if it conflicts with what the law requires? Does it matter if the disputants have equal power and resources? Probing such questions quickly requires one to examine deep theories of legal obligation, legal legitimacy, and the concept of change in a democratic society. Investigating such questions enriches policy analysis, but important questions about mediation's use often cannot await their answers.

Mediation is a process that enables parties to engage in dialogue in a protected, private setting. Professor Fiss, in his celebrated article, maintains that privatizing justice through negotiated settlement erodes important public values; he argues, fundamentally, that having parties approve of settlement terms should not be the decisive standard for determining if the controversy has been resolved. In defense of mediation, Professor Menkel-Meadow takes issue with Fiss by highlighting competing considerations between those who advocate settlement and those supporting adjudication.

AGAINST SETTLEMENT

93 Yale L.J. 1073, 1075–80, 1082–3, 1085–87 (1984) [*]

By Owen Fiss

[I]n my view, . . . the case for settlement rests on questionable premises. I do not believe that settlement as a generic practice is preferable to judgment. . . . [I]t should be treated instead as a highly problematic technique for streamlining dockets. Settlement is for me the civil analogue of plea bargaining: Consent is often coerced; the bargain may be struck by someone without authority; the absence of a trial and judgment renders subsequent judicial involvement troublesome; and although dockets are trimmed, justice may not be done.

THE IMBALANCE OF POWER.

. . . [S]ettlement is . . . a function of the resources available to each party to finance the litigation, and those resources are frequently distributed unequally. . . .

The disparities in resources between the parties can influence the settlement in three ways. First, the poorer party may be less able to amass and analyze the information needed to predict the outcome of the litigation, and thus be disadvantaged in the bargaining process. Second, he may need the damages he seeks immediately and thus be induced to settle as a way of accelerating payment, even though he realizes he would get less now than he might if he awaited judgment. All plaintiffs want their damages immediately, but an indigent plaintiff may be exploited by a rich defendant because his need is so great that the defendant can force him to accept a sum that is less than the ordinary present value of the judgment. Third, the poorer party might be forced to settle because he does not have the resources to finance the litigation, to cover either his own projected expenses, such as his lawyer's time, or the expenses his opponent can impose through the manipulation of procedural mechanisms such as discovery. It might seem that settlement benefits the plaintiff by allowing him to avoid the costs of litigation, but this is not so. The defendant can anticipate the plaintiff's costs if the case were to be tried fully and decrease his offer by that amount. The indigent plaintiff is a victim of the costs of litigation even if he settles.

. . . [O]f course, imbalances of power can distort judgment as well: Resources influence the quality of presentation, which in turn has an important bearing on who wins and the terms of victory. We count, however, on the guiding presence of the judge, who can employ a number of measures to lessen the impact of distributional inequalities. He can, for example, supplement the parties' presentations by asking questions, calling his own witnesses, and inviting other persons and institutions to participate as amici. These measures are likely to make only a small contribution toward moderating the influence of distributional inequalities, but should not be ignored for that reason. Not even these small steps are possible with settlement. There is, moreover, a critical difference between a process like settlement, which is based on bargaining and accepts inequalities of wealth as an integral and legitimate component of the process, and a process like judgment, which knowingly struggles against those inequalities. Judgment aspires to an autonomy from distributional inequalities, and it gathers much of its appeal from this aspiration.

THE ABSENCE OF AUTHORITATIVE CONSENT.

The argument for settlement presupposes that the contestants are individuals. These individuals speak for themselves and should be bound by the rules they generate. In many situations, however, individuals are ensnared in contractual relationships that impair their autonomy. Lawyers or insurance companies might, for example, agree to settlements that are in their interests but are not in the best interests of their clients, and to which their clients would not agree if the choice were still theirs. But a deeper and more intractable problem arises from the fact that many parties are not individuals but rather organizations or groups. We do not know who is entitled to speak for these entities and to give the consent upon which so much of the appeal of settlement depends.

Some organizations, such as corporations or unions, have formal procedures for identifying the persons who are authorized to speak for them. But these procedures are imperfect. They are designed to facilitate transactions between the organization and outsiders, rather than to insure that the members of the organization in fact agree with a particular decision. Nor do they eliminate conflicts of interests. The chief executive officer of a corporation may settle a suit to prevent embarrassing disclosures about his managerial policies, but such disclosures might well be in the interest of the shareholders. The president of a union may agree to a settlement as a way of preserving his power within the organization; for that very reason, he may not risk the dangers entailed in consulting the rank and file or in subjecting the settlement to ratification by the membership.

. . . [T]hese problems become even more pronounced when we turn from organizations and consider the fact that much contemporary litigation involves even more nebulous social entities, namely, groups. Some of these groups, such as ethnic or racial minorities, inmates of prisons, or residents of institutions for mentally retarded people, may have an identity or existence that transcends the lawsuit, but they do not have any formal organizational structure and therefor lack any procedures for generating authoritative consent. . . .

Going to judgment does not altogether eliminate the risk of unauthorized action, any more than it eliminates the distortions arising from disparities in resources. The case presented by the representative of a group or an organization admittedly will influence the outcome of the suit, and that outcome will bind those who might also be bound by a settlement. On the other hand, judgment does not ask as much from the so-called representatives. There is a conceptual and normative distance between what the representatives do and say and what the court eventually decides, because the judge tests those statements and actions against independent procedural and substantive standards. The authority of judgment arises from the law, not from the statements or actions of the putative representatives, and thus we allow judgment to bind persons not directly involved in the litigation even when we are reluctant to have settlement do so.

THE LACK OF FOUNDATION FOR CONTINUING JUDICIAL INVOLVEMENT.

. . . [D]ispute-resolution . . . trivializes the remedial dimensions of lawsuits and mistakenly assumes judgment to be the end of the process. It supposes that the judge's duty is to declare which neighbor is right and which wrong, and that this declaration will end the judge's involvement. . . . Often, however, judgment is not the end of a lawsuit but only the beginning. The involvement of the court may continue almost indefinitely. In these cases, settlement cannot provide an adequate basis for that necessary continuing involvement, and thus is no substitute for judgment.

The parties may sometimes be locked in combat with one another and view the lawsuit as only one phase in a long continuing struggle. The entry of judgment will then not end the struggle, but rather change its terms and the balance of power. One of the parties will invariably return to the court and again ask for its assistance, not so much because conditions have changed, but because the conditions that preceded the lawsuit have unfortunately not changed. This often occurs in domestic-relations case, where the divorce decree represents only the opening salvo in an endless series of skirmishes over custody and support.

The structural reform cases that play such a prominent role on the federal docket provide another occasion for continuing judicial involvement. In these cases, courts seek to safeguard public values by restructuring large-scale bureaucratic organizations. The task is enormous, and our knowledge of how to restructure on-going bureaucratic organizations is limited. As a consequence, courts must oversee and manage the remedial process for a long-time—maybe forever. This, I fear, is true of most school desegregation cases, some of which have been pending for twenty or thirty years. It is also true of antitrust cases that seek divestiture or reorganization of an industry.

The drive for settlement knows no bounds and can result in a consent decree even in the kinds of cases I have just mentioned, that is, even when a court finds itself embroiled in a continuing struggle between the parties or must reform a bureaucratic organization. The parties may be ignorant of the difficulties ahead or optimistic about the future, or they may simply believe that they can get more favorable terms through a bargained-for agreement. Soon, however, the inevitable happens: One party returns to court and asks the judge to modify the decree, either to make it more effective or less stringent. But the judge is at a loss: He has no basis for assessing the request. He cannot, to use Cardozo's somewhat melodramatic formula, easily decide whether the "dangers, once substantial, have become attenuated to a shadow," because, by definition, he never knew the dangers.

JUSTICE RATHER THAN PEACE.

The dispute resolution story makes settlement appear as a perfect substitute for judgment . . . by trivializing the remedial dimensions of a lawsuit, and also by reducing the social function of the lawsuit to one of resolving private disputes: In that story, settlement appears to achieve exactly the same purpose as judgment—peace between the parties—but at considerably less expense to society. . . .

In my view, however, the purpose of adjudication should be understood in broader terms. Adjudication uses public resources, and employs not strangers chosen by the parties but public officials chosen by a process in which the public participates. These officials, like members of the legislative and executive branches, possess a power that has been defined and conferred by public law, not private agreement. Their job is not to maximize the ends of private parties, nor simply to secure the peace, but to explicate and give force to the values embodied in authoritative texts such as the Constitution and statutes: to interpret those values and to bring reality into accord with them. This duty is not discharged when the parties settle.

In our political system, courts are reactive institutions. They do not search out interpretive occasions, but instead wait for others to bring matters to their attention. They also rely for the most part on others to investigate and present the law and facts. A settlement will thereby deprive a court of the occasion, and perhaps even the ability, to render an interpretation. A court cannot proceed (or not proceed very far) in the face of a settlement. To be against settlement is not to urge that parties be "forced" to litigate, since that would interfere with their autonomy and distort the adjudicative process; the parties will be inclined to make the court believe that their bargain is justice. To be against settlement is only to suggest that when the parties settle, society gets less than what appears, and for a price it does not know it is paying. Parties might settle while leaving justice undone. The settlement of a school suit might secure the peace, but not racial equality. Although the parties are prepared to live under the terms they bargained for, and although such peaceful coexistence may be a necessary precondition for justice, and itself a state of affairs to be valued, it is not justice itself. To settle for something means to accept less than some ideal. . . .

THE REAL DIVIDE.

To all this, one can readily imagine a simple response by way of confession and avoidance: We are not talking about those lawsuits. Advocates of ADR might insist that my account of adjudication, in contrast to the one implied by the dispute-resolution story, focuses on a rather narrow category of lawsuits. They could argue that while settlement may have only the most limited appeal with respect to those cases, I have not spoken to the "typical" case. My response is twofold.

First, even as a purely quantitative matter, I doubt that the number of cases I am referring to is trivial. My universe includes those cases in which there are significant distributional inequalities; those in which it is difficult to generate authoritative consent because organizations of social groups are parties or because the power to settle is vested in autonomous agents; those in which the court must continue to supervise the parties after judgment; and those in which justice needs to be done, or to put it more modestly, where there is a genuine social need for an authoritative interpretation of law. I imagine that the number of cases that satisfy one of these four criteria is considerable; in contrast to the kind of case portrayed in the dispute-resolution story, they probably dominate the docket of a modern court system.

Second, it demands a certain kind of myopia to be concerned only with the number of cases, as though all cases are equal simply because the clerk of the court assigns each a single docket number. All cases are not equal. The Los Angeles desegregation case, to take one example, is not equal to the allegedly more typical suit involving a property dispute or an automobile accident. The desegregation suit consumes more resources, affects more people, and provokes far greater challenges to the judicial power. The settlement movement must introduce a qualitative perspective; it must speak to these more "significant" cases, and demonstrate the propriety of settling them. Otherwise it will soon be seen as an irrelevance, dealing with trivia rather than responding to the very conditions that give the movement its greatest sway and saliency.

NOTES AND QUESTIONS

(1) Do commentators such as Professors Fiss and Delgado make the mistake that Legal Positivists accuse lawyers of making by assuming that what is legal is also morally desirable? Does the legal/morally desirable distinction help explain how mediation can constitute an important engine of social change? In reflecting on these questions, revisit Chapter One's account of mediation's use in its Foundational years and examine the types of controversies to which it was put to use.

(2) Professor Fiss certainly is correct to note that persons with power may have no incentive to talk to others if they believe their interests are secured. In such settings, the use of the legal system to challenge existing arrangements is an important element for triggering change. For example, without the Ohio Supreme Court declaring that the state's system for funding public elementary and secondary education was unconstitutional, there appears to be no compelling incentive for residents of wealthier school districts to support reallocating their tax dollars to financially-poorer districts. *See DeRolph v. Ohio*, 89 Ohio St. 3d 1, 728 N.E.2d 993 (Oh. Sup. Ct. 2000). Yet, once parties are in litigation, participating in mediated negotiations might create opportunities for creative problem-solving. The simultaneous interplay of multiple dispute resolution processes, which is the realistic context for most dispute resolution efforts, creates significant challenges for the respective participants. For a more thorough discussion of the interrelationship between law and mediation, see Chapter 8, *infra*.

(3) The sharp distinction that Hart draws between law and morals has been rigorously challenged in the eloquent jurisprudential writings of Professor Ronald Dworkin; see especially his account in *Taking Rights Seriously*, Chapters 2, 3, and 5, and in his *Law's Empire*.

(4) During the course of a mediation conference involving a claim by the landlord for rent arrears, the mediator learns that the landlord is renting the basement area of his home in violation of the zoning ordinance governing single-family homes in that neighborhood; the mediator also learns that the tenant is an illegal immigrant. Both parties develop mutually acceptable settlement terms to pay the arrears and continue the tenancy. What should the mediator do? For a discussion of similar dilemmas, see the portion of Chapter 7, *infra*, dealing with Mediator Ethics.

WHOSE DISPUTE IS IT ANYWAY? A PHILOSOPHICAL AND DEMOCRATIC DEFENSE OF SETTLEMENT (IN SOME CASES)

83 Geo. L.J. 2663, 2663–71, 2692 (1995) *

By Carrie Menkel-Meadow

In the last decade or so, a polarized debate about how disputes should be resolved has demonstrated to me once again the difficulties of simplistic and adversarial arguments. Owen Fiss has argued "Against Settlement"; Trina Grillo and others have argued against mediation (in divorce cases and other family matters involving women); Richard Delgado and others have questioned whether informal processes are unfair to disempowered and subordinated groups; Judith Resnik has criticized the (federal) courts' unwillingness to do their basic job of adjudication; Stephen Yeazell has suggested that too much settlement localizes, decentralizes, and delegalizes dispute resolution and the making of public law; Kevin C. McMunigal has argued that too much settlement will make bad advocates; and David Luban and Jules Coleman, among other philosophers, have criticized the moral value of the compromises that are thought to constitute legal settlements. On the other side, vigorous proponents of alternative dispute resolution, including negotiation, mediation, and various hybrids of these forms of preadjudication settlement, criticize the economic and emotional waste of adversarial processes and the cost, inefficiency, and political difficulties of adjudication, as well as its draconian unfairness in some cases.

In my view, this debate, while useful for explicitly framing the underlying values that support our legal system, has not effectively dealt with the realities of modern legal, political, and personal disputes. For me, the question is not "for or against" settlement (since settlement has become the "norm" for our system), but *when, how, and under what circumstances* should cases be settled? When do our legal system, our citizenry, and the parties in particular disputes need formal legal adjudication, and when are their respective interests served by settlement, *whether public or private?*

As several recent commentators have noted, the role of settlement in our legal system has increased: some think because it is actively promoted by such developments as the Civil Justice Reform Act; others by simple caseload pressures, and still others because of the desirability of party-initiated or consented-to agreements to resolve disputes. While court administrators, judges, and some lawyers suggest that we must continue to mine the advantages of settlement for caseload reduction, or equity among claimants, especially in mass torts or class action settings, many legal scholars continue to

---

express concern with the use of settlement as a device for resolving our legal disputes.

The difficulty with the debate about settlement vs. adjudication is that there are many more than two processes, as well as other variables that affect the processes, to consider. The diverse interests of the participants in the dispute, the legal system, and society may not be the same. Issues of fairness, legitimacy, economic efficiency, privacy, publicity, emotional catharsis or empathy, access, equity among disputants, and lawmaking may differ in importance for different actors in the system, and they may vary by case—this is the strength of our common law system.

. . . David Luban argues that settlement is problematic because it reduces public participation in the business of dispute resolution and, consequently, reduces production of rules and precedents—in short, settlement leads to an "erosion of the public realm." Settlement works in favor of "private peace" and in opposition to "public justice." Luban, like other critics of settlement, suggests that the legal system is designed to engage us (and our judges, lawyers, and litigants) in the public discourse of lawmaking and policy debate that concerns itself with justice and self-defined societal values—in our case, democratic deliberation. By judging and enunciating rules, judges set baselines for political endowments and entitlements and alternately close and open debates by reviewing facts and articulating the rules and values that underlie particular legal positions. Settlements, on the other hand, represent cruder "compromises" of raw bargaining skill and extrajudicial power imbalances (economics, legal skill, and repeat play experience). Luban acknowledges that we can no longer imagine a "world without settlement." We need it simply to muddle through the hundreds of thousands of disputes our modern society produces. Unlike Fiss, he acknowledges that not all disputes are occasions for "structural transformation" or public elucidation of basic values. And, as he suggests realistically, "too many cases will make bad law." With an increase of cases, and trial and appeals courts making more and more law, there are likely to be irreconcilable inconsistencies in decisional law, producing a virtual "tower of Babel" of legal precedents.

Thus Luban shifts the focus to a consideration of *when and how* settlements should take place. His ultimate focus is on the need to keep settlements public and to decry the loss to democratic discourse when too many settlements are kept secret. Luban argues that secret settlements deprive us not only of "result" information, but the "facts" of discovery, necessarily "privatizing" information to which a democratic society should have access. He suggests that those who continue to favor secret settlements prefer the "problem-solving" (dispute resolution) conception of our legal system to "public production of rules and precedents" or the "public goods and discourse" function. Thus Luban is willing to tolerate settlement, but only if it is open to the "sunshine" laws and serves "at least some of the public values of adjudication," by keeping the settlement process and its information open to the public.

In this essay, I hope to explore some of the same questions that Professor Luban has framed for us—how can we decide which settlements to be for and which to be against? In other words, how can we tell good settlements from bad ones, and when should we prefer adjudication to settlement? Like others who have written on this subject, both recently and in the past, I do not think there are easy answers to this question; but more problematically, I want to suggest that it will be very difficult for us to specify in advance criteria for allocation to particular processes. In the words of current academic cachet, much depends on the context—of disputes, of disputants, and of the system being considered. I will here complexify and problematize Luban's seemingly easy proposition—that democratic discourse requires full disclosure of legal dispute information. In this essay, I will make a case for settlement by arguing that there are philosophical, as well as instrumental, democratic, ethical, and human justifications for settlements (at least in some cases).

Those who criticize settlement suffer from what I have called, in other contexts, "litigation romanticism," with empirically unverified assumptions about what courts can or will do. More important, those who privilege adjudication focus almost exclusively on structural and institutional values and often give short shrift to those who are actually involved in the litigation. I fear, but am not sure, that this debate can be reduced to those who care more about the people actually engaged in disputes versus those who care more about institutional and structural arrangements. I prefer to think that we need both adjudication and settlement. These processes can affect each other in positive, as well as negative ways, but in my view, settlement should not be seen as "second best" or "worst case" when adjudication fails. Settlement can be justified on its own moral grounds—there are important values, consistent with the fundamental values of our legal and political systems, that support the legitimacy of settlements of some, if not most, legal disputes. Those values include consent, participation, empowerment, dignity, respect, empathy and emotional catharsis, privacy, efficiency, quality solutions, equity, access, and yes, even justice.

Though some have argued that compromise itself can be morally justified, I will here argue, as well, that compromise is not always necessary for settlement and that in fact, some settlements, by not requiring compromise, may produce better solutions than litigation. In particular, my own arguments for settlements (of particular kinds) have been often misstated or oversimplified, for the purpose of argument, so that they begin to strike me as strawpersons and cause me to question whether we are really able to understand each other when we "sharpen" the argument by "narrowing" it.

To summarize, it seems to me that the key questions implicated in the ongoing debate about settlement vs. adjudication are:

1. In a party-initiated legal system, when is it legitimate for the parties to settle their dispute themselves, or with what assistance from a court in which they have sought some legal-system support or service?

2. When is "consent" to a settlement legitimate and "real," and by what standards should we (courts and academic critics) judge and permit such consent?

3. When, in a party-initiated legal system, should party consent be "trumped" by other values—in other words, when should public, institutional, and structural needs and values override parties' desire to settle or courts' incentives to promote settlement? In short, when

is the need for "public adjudication" or as Luban suggests, "public settlement" more important (to whom?) than what the parties may themselves desire?

. . .

I have here tried to make the following arguments on behalf of the "best" aspects of settlement:

1. Settlements that are in fact consensual represent the goals of democratic and party-initiated legal regimes by allowing the parties themselves to choose processes and outcomes for dispute resolution.

2. Settlements permit a broader range of possible solutions that may be more responsive to both party and system needs.

3. What some consider to be the worst of settlement, that is, compromise, may actually represent a moral commitment to equality, precision in justice, accommodation, and peaceful coexistence of conflicting interests.

4. Settlements may be based on important nonlegal principles or interests, which may, in any given case, be as important or more important to the parties than "legal" considerations. Laws made in the aggregate may not always be appropriate in particular cases, and thus settlement can be seen as yet another "principled" supplement to our common law system.

5. Settlement processes may be more humanely "real," democratic, participatory, and cathartic than more formalized processes, permitting in their best moments, transformative and educational opportunities for parties in dispute as well as for others.

6. Some settlement processes may be better adapted for the multiplex, multiparty issues that require solutions in our modern society than the binary form of plaintiff-defendant adjudication.

7. Despite the continuing and important debates about discovery and information exchange in the litigation process, some settlement processes (mediation and some forms of neutral case evaluation and scheduling) may actually provide both more and better (not just legally relevant) information for problem-solving, as well as "education" of the litigants.

8. When used appropriately, settlement may actually increase access to justice, not only by allowing more disputants to claim in different ways, but also by allowing greater varieties of case resolutions.

NOTES AND QUESTIONS

(1) Professor Menkel-Meadow criticizes Fiss and others for maintaining a romanticized vision of the adjudication process; she believes that party-facilitated settlements (mediation) can often secure more desirable outcomes

than those obtained through adjudication. Do you agree? By contrast, can one criticize Menkel-Meadow for offering a romanticized vision of mediation? The excerpt appearing in Chapter 10[I], *infra*, by Lela P. Love and Cheryl B. McDonald entitled *A Tale of Two Cities: Day Labor and Conflict Resolution for Communities in Crisis* provides a concrete setting in which competing visions of fairness collide.

(2) Commentators observe that many mediated negotiations are conducted "in the shadow of the law," such that failure to reach settlement might result in one party continuing to pursue her litigation options. Do the benefits of settlement dissipate if the negotiating context is divorced from this litigation fallback?

(3) Menkel-Meadow asserts that encouraging party settlement reflects one goal of democratic legal regimes. Do you agree? Does her account of the "best" aspects of settlement satisfactorily meet the concerns raised by commentators such as Delgado and Grillo that power inequities are reinforced through mediated negotiations, rather than rectified?

(4) Since its Foundational Years, disputing parties have turned to mediation as an important tool to resolve controversies involving significant social issues. Recently, mediation has been used extensively to help resolve environmental controversies involving multiple stakeholders. *See, e.g.,* the excerpt by Janet C. Neuman in Section 10[J], *infra*. Many such initiatives are reported in *Consensus*, a regular publication focusing on what professionals refer to as "policy disputes."

(5) Empirical research on the question of how party perceptions concerning outcome fairness affect compliance with the mediated outcome has yielded somewhat mixed results. *See* Craig A. McEwen and Richard M. Maiman, *Mediation in Small Claims Court: Achieving Compliance Through Consent*, 19 L. & Soc'y Rev. 11 (1984); Neil Vidmar, *The Small Claims Court: A Reconceptualization of Disputes and an Empirical Investigation*, 18 L. & Soc'y Rev. 515 (1984); Craig A. McEwen and Richard M. Maiman, *The Relative Significance of Disputing Forum and Dispute Characteristics for Outcome and Compliance*, 20 L. & Soc'y Rev. 439 (1986); Neil Vidmar, *Assessing the Effects of Case Characteristics and Settlement Forum on Dispute Outcomes and Compliance*, 21 L. & Soc'y Rev. 155 (1987); Rosselle Wissler, *Mediation and Adjudication in the Small Claims Court: The Effects of Process and Case Characteristics*, 29 L. & Soc'y Rev. 323 (1995).

Chapter 7

MEDIATOR CERTIFICATION AND ETHICS

§ A INTRODUCTION

The materials in this chapter deal with the related issues of who should be allowed to mediate, how their performances should be evaluated, and what standards should govern their behaviors. Section [B] contains commentary on qualifying mediators, examples of certification standards, and commentary on the considerations of creating a licensure or certification scheme. Section [C] presents two sample mediator codes of conduct. Section [D] covers the intersection between the legal community and mediation focusing specifically on the regulation of attorneys serving as mediators and the potential for allegations of the "unauthorized practice of law" for non-attorney mediators. As you read this chapter, consider how the context of the mediation will affect certification goals. Also consider the impact that the mediator roles, styles and orientations covered in Chapter 4, *supra*, have on what is considered to be ethical behavior.

§ B MEDIATOR QUALIFICATIONS

[1] CERTIFICATION

Along with the increased reliance on mediation as a means for resolving disputes has come an increased concern over the qualifications of mediators. While the debate continues today, even as far back as 1987, when the Society of Professionals in Dispute Resolution (SPIDR) formed the first Commission on Qualifications, the question, "What qualifies someone to be a dispute resolver?" was considered to be "a hardy perennial of debate in the dispute resolution field." The concern that legislatures, courts and government agencies, rather than those in the field, would develop standards for mediators was an articulated reason for establishing the Commission. Interestingly, more than a decade later, the same debates and arguments are prevalent.

In fact, this first Commission developed three central principles for consideration in establishing qualifications which are still referred to today.

[handwritten notes in margin:]

Critique
• internal inconsistency
• vague

Joint Standards p.376
— ABA §on med.
— AAA
— SPIDR

REPORT OF THE SOCIETY OF PROFESSIONALS IN DISPUTE RESOLUTION (SPIDR) COMMISSION ON QUALIFICATIONS, DISPUTE RESOLUTION FORUM

*Society of Professionals in Dispute Resolution, Washington D.C. 1989 3-4**

Executive Summary

The role of the SPIDR Commission on Qualifications [was] to examine the question of qualifications of mediators and arbitrators. Established by the Board of the Society of Professionals in Dispute Resolution, the Commission [was] composed of individuals representing a broad variety of backgrounds and experience. While recommendations may have general applicability, the primary focus of the Commission's inquiry [was] on those areas of alternative dispute resolution in which legislatures and other public bodies are now seeking to establish criteria that define who can serve as a mediator. . . .

The most commonly discussed purposes of setting criteria for individuals to practice as neutrals are (1) to protect the consumer and (2) to protect the integrity of various dispute resolution processes. Concerns also have been raised, particularly about mandatory standards or certification, including: (1) creating inappropriate barriers to entry into the field, thus, (2) hampering the innovative quality of the profession, and (3) limiting the broad dissemination of peacemaking skills in society. . . .

In determining how best to promote competence and quality in the practice of dispute resolution, the Commission considered several policy options. These included reliance on the free market, disclosure requirements, public and consumer education, "after the fact" controls such as malpractice actions, rosters, ethical codes, mandatory standards for neutrals and for programs, and improvements in training, including enhanced opportunities for apprenticeships.

After weighing these options, the Commission adopted three central principles, which recognize the need to strike an appropriate balance between competing concerns:

- that no single entity (rather, a variety of organizations) should establish qualifications for neutrals;

- that the greater the degree of choice the parties have over the dispute resolution process, program or neutral, the less mandatory the qualification requirements should be; and

- that qualification criteria should be based on performance, rather than paper credentials.

No Single Entity

This principle recognizes that the knowledge and techniques needed to practice competently may vary by context, process, issue, or institutional setting and that the establishment of uniform criteria for all neutrals could restrict the development of different approaches to dispute resolution and narrow entry into the field. Therefore, no single entity should be relied on to certify general dispute resolution competence. Moreover, entities seeking to establish criteria should be guided by groups that include representatives of consumers and experts in the field.

Degree of Choice

This principle rests on the assumption that the need for protection against incompetence rises as the parties' ability to protect themselves by freely choosing or rejecting particular dispute resolution processes, programs, or neutrals diminishes. As a consequence, SPIDR recommends:

1. When parties have free choice of the process, program, and neutral, no standards or qualifications should be established that would prevent any person from providing dispute resolution services, as long as there is full disclosure of the neutral's relevant training and experience, the fees and expenses to be charged, and any financial or personal interests or prior relationship with the parties that might affect the neutral's impartiality.

2. Where public or private entities operate programs that offer no choice of process, program, or neutral, an appropriate public entity should set standards of qualifications for such programs and for neutrals . . . and make such standards and qualifications available to the parties.

3. When parties have some, but not a complete, choice of process, program, or neutral, each program offering such services should establish clear selection and evaluation criteria and make such information available to the parties, together with its rules governing confidentiality, the means by which complaints may be lodged, and all relevant "full disclosure" information concerning the neutral selected by the particular case.

Performance-Based Qualifications

The Commission has found no evidence that formal degrees, which obviously limit entry into the dispute resolution field, are necessary to competent performance as a neutral. There is impressive evidence that individuals lacking such credentials make excellent dispute resolvers and that well designed training programs, which stress the specific skills and techniques of mediation and arbitration, are of critical importance in attaining competence. As a consequence, SPIDR recommends:

Qualifications based on performance: Academic degrees should not be a prerequisite for service as a neutral. Rather, qualification criteria, whether mandated by public bodies or adopted voluntarily by private agencies, should be based on performance, emphasizing the knowledge and particular skills necessary for competent practice.

Performance-based testing: Policy makers should adopt mediation and arbitration performance criteria . . . and incorporate performance-based testing into training and apprenticeship programs.

Qualifications for Trainers: To enhance the quality of training for neutrals, those offering such training should establish qualifications for their trainers, which emphasize knowledge of and competency to practice in the area for which the training is offered, the ability to teach others, and the ability to evaluate the performance of others in simulated settings.

Continuing Education: To ensure continued competency in this new and changing field, dispute resolution programs, entities that sponsor neutrals, and the neutrals themselves have a continuing obligation to maintain and improve acquired knowledge and skills through additional training, practice, and study.

In 1988, the Florida Supreme Court adopted qualifications for individuals wishing to be certified as mediators in three court-connected settings: county (cases below $15,000, including small claims), family (dissolution of marriage and child related issues), and circuit (civil cases above $15,000). A fourth area of certification, dependency (abuse and neglect cases), was added in 1998. The qualifications are as follows:

Florida Rules for Certified and Court-Appointed Mediators

Part I. Mediator Qualifications

Rule 10.100 General Qualifications

(a) County Court Mediators. For certification a mediator of county court matters must be certified as a circuit court or family mediator or:

   (1) complete a minimum of 20 hours in a training program certified by the supreme court;

   (2) observe a minimum of 4 county court mediation conferences conducted by a court-certified mediator and conduct 4 county court mediation conferences under the supervision and observation of a court-certified mediator; and

   (3) be of good moral character.

(b) Family Mediators. For certification a mediator of family and dissolution of marriage issues must:

   (1) complete a minimum of 40 hours in a family mediation training program certified by the supreme court;

   (2) have a master's degree or doctorate in social work, mental health, or behavioral or social sciences; be a physician certified to practice adult or child psychiatry; or be an attorney or a certified public accountant licensed to practice in any United States jurisdiction; and

have at least 4 years practical experience in one of the aforementioned fields or have 8 years family mediation experience with a minimum of 10 mediations per year;

(3) observe 2 family mediations conducted by a certified family mediator and conduct 2 family mediations under the supervision and observation of a certified family mediator; and

(4) be of good moral character.

(c) Circuit Court Mediators. For certification a mediator of circuit court matters, other than family matters, must:

(1) complete a minimum of 40 hours in a circuit court mediation training program certified by the supreme court;

(2) be a member in good standing of The Florida Bar with at least 5 years of Florida practice and be an active member of The Florida Bar within 1 year of application for certification; or be a retired trial judge from any United States jurisdiction who was a member in good standing of the bar in the state in which the judge presided for at least 5 years immediately preceding the year certification is sought;

(3) observe 2 circuit court mediations conducted by a certified circuit mediator and conduct 2 circuit mediations under the supervision and observation of a certified circuit court mediator; and

(4) be of good moral character.

(d) Dependency Mediators. For certification a mediator of dependency matters, as defined in Florida Rules for Juvenile Procedure 8.290(a), must:

(1) complete a supreme court certified dependency mediation training program as follows:

(A) 40 hours if the applicant is not a certified family mediator or is a certified family mediator who has not mediated at least 4 dependency cases; or

(B) 20 hours if the applicant is a certified family mediator who has mediated at least 4 dependency cases; and

(2) have a master's degree or doctorate in social work, mental health, behavioral sciences or social sciences; or be a physician licensed to practice adult or child psychiatry or pediatrics; or be an attorney licensed to practice in any United States jurisdiction; and

(3) have 4 years experience in family and/or dependency issues or be a licensed mental health professional with at least 4 years practical experience or be a supreme court certified family or circuit mediator with a minimum of 20 mediations; and

(4) observe 4 dependency mediations conducted by a certified dependency mediator and conduct 2 dependency mediations under the supervision and observation of a certified dependency mediator; and

(5) be of good moral character.

(e) Special Conditions. Mediators who have been duly certified as circuit court or family mediators before July 1, 1990, shall be deemed qualified as circuit court or family mediators pursuant to these rules. Certified family mediators who have mediated a minimum of 4 dependency cases prior to July 1, 1997, shall be granted temporary certification and may continue to mediate dependency matters for no more than 1 year from the time that a training program pursuant to subdivision (d)(1)(B) is certified by the supreme court. Such mediators shall be deemed qualified to apply for certification as dependency mediators upon successful completion of the requirements of subdivision (d)(1)(B) and (d)(5) of this rule.

The mediation community voiced a number of concerns over the Florida Standards. Most specifically, mediation professionals were concerned about the implications of an institution setting standards and were particularly concerned about the differentiation of qualifications for different types of mediators. Up until Florida issued its rules, mediation was thought of more generically—that is, a skilled mediator could mediate anything.

At the 1988 annual conference of the Society of Professionals in Dispute Resolution, then president of the organization, George Nicolau, gave a speech in which he used the Florida rule as a means to address the qualifications issue and emphasize the importance of the work of the Commission on Qualifications which he had appointed. The speech was reprinted in the *BNA Alternative Dispute Resolution Report Special Report Entitled: SPIDR Commission on Qualifications Presents Report at Annual Meeting* (2 ADRR 392 (1988)). He began by citing the history of the labor-management arena (in which mediators are qualified based on the perceptions of the parties and reputation of the mediator) and community mediation (in which programs select the mediators based on the program's sense of personal qualities the mediator should possess and then provide training). He noted the difference between the labor-management context, in which participation was more or less voluntary, and the community programs, in which the parties had "virtually no choice about being there—and as a result, no choice of the process in which they were to participate, no choice of the program that was going to mediate their dispute, and no choice of the neutral who was going to do the mediating." In the community setting, he noted, that "if the selection process is flawed, if the training is inadequate, if the program heads are more concerned with numbers than quality, the parties can do little or nothing about it. They remain at the mercy of persons masquerading as mediators and, more often than not, damage is done."

Nicolau was concerned about the Florida Supreme Court's adoption of qualifications for court-connected mediators. While acknowledging the necessity of establishing some criteria to assist the public and protect them from "charlatans and incompetents," he observed that the "easy response to this concern is Florida's." He went on to state that "reliance on qualifications criteria based mainly of academic credentials is patently exclusionary. Moreover . . . such a response is clearly contrary to what our collective experience has already taught us."

Sharon Press, then Assistant Director of the Florida Dispute Resolution Center, wrote a response to Nicolau's speech which was also published in the *BNA Alternative Dispute Resolution Report In Response: Florida Explains Court Rules In Face of Continuing Controversy* (2 **ADRR** 434 (1988)). Press began her response by placing the Florida qualifications in context, specifically explaining the difference between private mediation (in which individuals are free to opt for mediation and select any mediator they wish) and court-ordered mediation (in which the parties are ordered to attend mediation and may not know who to select as the mediator). Press noted that given the compulsory nature of the program, both the legislature and the Florida Supreme Court felt obligated "to ensure that these expanded judicial services are fruitful and that the mediators receiving the referrals are competent and held in high esteem by the litigants." She noted further that since Florida did not adopt a title act or seek to "license" mediators anyone remains free to call themselves a mediator, reflecting the conventional wisdom that the market place will ensure that competent mediators remain in business.

Focusing on the intent of the Supreme Court to ensure competence, Press cited two conclusions reflected in the qualifications rules: "1) since the various types of mediation are structured differently, different skills are required for each; and (2) educational background and experience alone are not accurate indicators of whether someone will be a good mediator." Specifically, the rules require "(1) different minimum educational and experiential standards based on the type of mediation and (2) certain minimum hours of training regardless of [one's] educational background or experience."

She went on to describe a typical circuit mediation for which the certification rules required that the mediator be either a Florida attorney or a retired judge, noting that "not only are the parties' lawyers present, they are the primary negotiators." Further, she explained that the typical session "revolves around discussion of legal arguments, the potential weaknesses of the case, and how the attorneys really think the case will do at trial. As a result of the importance to the mediation of legal reasoning and knowledge of Florida law, the threshold educational background and experience required for this type of mediation is being a former judge or member of the Florida Bar."

Press ended by reiterating Florida's commitment to the use of mediation and the court's obligation to ensure that individuals who are required to attend a mediation do so with a qualified mediator. She also indicated a willingness on the part of the Court to monitor the program. In fact, two years later, upon recommendation of the Florida Supreme Court Committee on Mediation and Arbitration Rules, the Court amended the rules of civil procedure to provide that the parties who have been ordered to mediation may choose their own mediator if they do so within ten days from the order of referral. Within that initial ten days, the parties are free to select anyone whom they can agree upon, certified or not. If the parties are unable to agree, then the court is required to appoint a certified mediator. *See* Rule 1.720(f), Florida

Rules of Civil Procedure, which was later joined by Rule 12.740, Florida Family Law Rules, and Rule 8.290(e)(2), Florida Rules of Juvenile Procedure.

NOTES AND QUESTIONS

(1) Does the rule change completely address the concerns raised by Nicolau relating to mediator qualifications tied to unrelated academic requirements?

(2) Effective January 1, 2000, the Virginia Department of Dispute Resolution revised their standards which were originally adopted in 1993 to "address a concern that the current certification categories of General and Family do not ensure that individuals with those certifications are qualified to mediate cases at the Circuit Court level." The revisions establish four categories of certification: General District Court, Juvenile and Domestic Relations District Court, Circuit Court-Civil, and Circuit Court-Family. The qualifications are solely based on training, observations, and co-mediations, with different standards set for each. The revisions also contained a reciprocity section addressing out–of–state mediators seeking certification in Virginia.

(3) The SPIDR Commission's last Report called for other public and private organizations not only to implement the recommendations but also to further develop performance-based criteria in different sectors and to design appropriate enforcement mechanisms. In the years following the work of the First SPIDR Commission, additional work has been done in developing performance based testing, ethical standards, disciplinary procedures, and credentialing of mediators; however, the reliance on "paper credentials" as a means of determining qualifications still persists. Why is that? Is the reliance on paper credentials predictable in light of the greater burden that would be placed on official bodies to develop and implement performance based standards? Keep these questions in mind as you read the following materials.

In 1995 and 1996, California debated Senate Bill 873 and Senate Bill 1428, respectively, which called for voluntary certification of basic mediation skills for mediators. The lessons learned through this experience were captured in a symposium issue of the University of San Francisco Law Review. Although neither bill passed, the issues raised through their debate, is a useful case study to review the principles and concerns surrounding certification and licensure of mediators.

MEDIATOR CERTIFICATION: WHY AND HOW

30 U.S.F. L. Rev., 757, 760–762, 767–773 (1996) *

By Donald T. Weckstein

I. Is There a Need for Certification of Mediators?

A. Certification vs. Licensing

Although the terms are often confused, and sometimes employed interchangeably, as used in this Article and in SB 1428, certification is a form of regulation short of licensing. No one may hold themselves out to practice a licensed occupation unless they possess the requisite license. . . . Certification in a particular field ordinarily is not a requisite to practice, but affords recognition that the certified person has met specified standards which noncertified practitioners may not have met. . . .

Unlike the *specialty* certifications within the licensed fields of medicine, law, and cosmetology, SB 1428 provided for certification of *basic* mediation skills which are believed to be applicable to all models, styles, and substantive fields of mediation practice. . . .

. . . .

What purposes, then, are served by certification which would not be more effectively served by licensing? Both licensing and certification offer protection to consumers by seeking to identify those who have met standards relevant to the practice of the profession or other occupation. Licensing, however, is anti-competitive. It creates a practice monopoly which tends to artificially limit the availability of services and foster high prices for services rendered. Licensing is also elitist. It imposes barriers to entry which may exclude potentially competent persons who happen to be poor, non-conforming, or unable to obtain the requisite training due to lack of time, financial resources, or proximity to a training facility.

Accordingly, licensing is best reserved for those occupations which cannot be competently practiced without extensive education and/or skills, and where the consumer is unlikely to be able to deter incompetent or unethical services until after serious or irreparable damage has been inflicted. . . . The case has not been, and probably cannot be, convincingly made for mediators. As stated in the SPIDR Qualification Commission's 1995 report:

> it is inappropriate for a government entity to formally license dispute resolution practitioners [because] licensure risks establishing arbitrary standards that could unnecessarily limit party choice of practitioners and limit access to the field by competent individuals . . . could work toward domination of the field by an exclusive group . . . [and] could inappropriately "freeze" the standards in a fluid field. . . .

. . . .

SB 1428 expressly disclaimed any intent to provide for the licensure of mediators in California. Accordingly, under legislation similar to SB 1428, a mediator could choose to make the necessary investments to obtain certification, or forego that marketing advantage and rely upon existing reputation, contacts, or other characteristics to maintain a mediation practice. Parties also would be free to choose a person who had never mediated but in whom they had confidence due to personal contacts or a reputation earned in another occupation such as government service, law, clergy, or counseling.

Nevertheless, aspects of licensing could conceivably result from mediator certification legislation. For example, a court may determine that it will refer cases only to a certified mediator, thus essentially licensing only certified mediators to mediate the rich source of judicially referred matters. Any regulatory scheme should take account of these potential uses of mediator certification and seek to guard against anti-competitiveness and elitism not justified by compelling public interests.

. . . .

C. The Case for Certifying Mediators

Potential public interests supporting state regulation of mediation include: (1) the protection of the public from the consequences of incompetent or unethical mediation services; (2) the prevention of existing professions from monopolizing the practice of mediation; (3) the reduction in court congestion through the encouragement of judges to refer legal actions to presumably qualified mediators; and (4) the promotion of mediation by (a) discouraging its practice by those who would besmirch its reputation, (b) channeling mediation business to those who have met established standards of training and practice, and (c) enhancing the credibility of the practice of mediation by facilitating its claim to professional status. . . .

1. The Need to Protect the Public

. . . .

Because a mediator does not make decisions which bind the parties, but rather works with the disputants to help them voluntarily resolve their differences, ineffective mediation usually results in no more than a lost opportunity to resolve a conflict, while leaving other dispute resolution options, including litigation open. This may result in increased costs, time, stress, and animosity, but it generally does not cause serious, irreparable damage. Nevertheless, some disputants have alleged that, but for the persuasiveness or pressure of a mediator, they would not have entered into an agreement which was highly unfavorable or costly. Certification can accomplish some degree of quality control to help minimize these losses. Unethical or overbearing practices by mediators might not be adequately addressed by a "just say no" approach, but could be mitigated by other measures short of licensing. Education, discipline, and public exposure could be part of a certification program, and potential controls could be provided by the threat of damage suits and professional organizational efforts, as well as by the impact of the economic market.

. . . .

2. The Need for a Certification Program That Is Inclusive Rather Than Exclusive

Of more urgency and persuasiveness is the concern that if a jurisdiction does not adopt a performance-based certification program responsive to both providers and disputants, certification of mediators on more narrow and less rational grounds will be achieved by one or more trade groups. . . .

The Russell Bill [SB 1428] wisely endorsed a number of "Dispute Resolution Principles". . . Among these principles are that disputants have the right to jointly select any neutral person or any organization to mediate for them and a "mediator shall not be required to possess any specific degree or license, nor shall possession of a specific degree or license bar a person from serving as a mediator." . . . [S]tudies and observations of mediator performance have found little or no correlation between educational background or professional licenses and successful mediation practice.

. . . .

3. The Ability to Reduce Court Congestion

. . . Since upwards of ninety percent of cases filed in court settle before or during trial, it is more likely that mediation (and other ADR referral programs) influence the time, rather than the rate, of settlement. . . .

4. The Desirability of Encouraging the Use of Mediation

. . . .

. . . [T]here are legitimate reasons for encouraging the courts and potential litigants or other disputants to consider mediation as a viable dispute resolution option. The existence of a well-designed certification program can help provide such an incentive by identifying those mediators who have met relevant standards of training, experience, and performance. These qualifications thus give some degree of comfort to less informed persons who might otherwise try to avoid the process or effectively default the mediator's selection to a party with more sophistication in the use of the process. . . .

SENATE BILL 1428 (as proposed 1996)

464.   (a) On and after July 1, 1997, a person shall not hold himself or herself out as a "certified mediator" unless he or she is certified by a mediator certifying organization pursuant to this chapter.

(b) To obtain certification as a mediator, a person shall do both of the following:

(1) Complete an application to become a candidate for certification as a mediator.

(2) Satisfy the training and experience requirements specified in this chapter.

464.1   (a) (1) The following entities may issue a mediation certificate which certifies that the recipient meets the standards of education, training, and experience required under this chapter.

    (A) A dispute resolution program established under Chapter 8 (commencing with section 465).

    (B) An accredited university or college.

    (C) Any other organization or person which, as of January 1, 1995, was domiciled in the State of California, has offered a mediation training program at least twice a year for two years, and provides a minimum of 25 hours of lecture and discussion and 33 hours of training that meets the standards specified in this chapter.

(2) The department shall issue a cease and desist order to any organization or person that issues mediation certificates that does not comply with the provisions of this chapter.

(b) (1) Any organization or person that was not domiciled in the State of California on or before January 1, 1995, prior to providing the type of education, training, and experience specified in this chapter, shall submit an application to the Department of Consumer Affairs, together with a fee to cover the department costs. Upon approval of the department, the organization may issue mediation certificates.

(2) The application shall contain a description of the mediation training provided by the organization or person and shall specify the criteria used by the organization or person in selecting its trainers. The criteria shall include, but not be limited to, the following:

    (A) The kinds of training programs in which the trainers participated in a range of fields including, but not limited to, court, commercial, community, and divorce.

    (B) Two years experience as a mediator trainer in a basic mediation skills course as attested to by written student evaluations, written course curriculum, written recommendations by two other mediator trainers, and a written evaluation document that includes assessment criteria.

    (C) The training and experience the trainers have had including the length of time they have practiced and the number and hours of mediated cases they have completed. Fifty hours of actual mediation experience may be substituted for a lack of experience as a trainer.

464.2   (a) A person may file an application with a mediator certifying organization to obtain certification as a mediator. The application shall include a statement concerning the applicant's training and experience.

(b) On the basis of an analysis of the information contained in the application by the mediator certifying organization, an applicant shall be assigned to one of the following three tracks:

  (1) The first track consists of applicants with no previous training or experience in mediation. Track 1 applicants shall complete 25 hours of training as outlined in Section 464.3, 18 hours of real practical experience, 15 hours of real or simulated practical experience from an approved provider as required by Section 464.1 and a personal assessment evaluation as described in Section 464.5.

  (2) The second track consists of applicants who have had 25 hours of approved training but have less than 33 hours of real or simulated practical experience, and have not completed a personal assessment evaluation as described in Section 464.5. Track 2 applicants shall complete 18 hours of real practical experience, 15 hours of real or simulated practical experience from an approved provider as required by Section 464.1 and a personal assessment evaluation as described in Section 464.5.

  (3) The third track consists of applicants who have 25 hours of training and 33 hours of real practical experience and are eligible to participate in a personal assessment and evaluation consistent with the requirements of the personal assessment evaluation as described in Section 464.5. If applicants in the third track have 25 hours of training and 50 hours of real practical experience in the last two years, a personal assessment evaluation as described in Section 464.5 is not required.

(c) An applicant's previous mediation training and experience shall be included in the application and shall specify the date and time the training was completed, when the experience was acquired, and the number and hours of mediations completed. Any previous training and experience shall be subject to written verification by the mediator certifying organization while observing confidentiality requirements.

(d) On the basis of an analysis of the applicant's application, the mediator certifying organization shall place the applicant in one of the three tracks and shall prescribe the training and experience that the person is required to receive, if any, to be eligible to participate in a personal assessment evaluation as described in Section 464.5.

. . . .

464.3 To obtain certification as a mediator, a person shall undergo training, which shall include, but not limited to, 25 hours of lecture and discussion on all of the following topics:

(a) The history of dispute resolution as a problem solving technique and its relationship to the traditional justice system.

(b) The structure, design, practice and theory of dispute resolution proceedings and services, including the varying roles, functions, and responsibilities of neutral persons, and the distinction between binding and nonbinding dispute resolution and between directive and facilitative processes.

(c) Communication skills and techniques, including developing opening statements, building trust, gathering facts, framing issues, taking notes, empowerment tactics, and effective listening and clarification skills. Face-to-face as well as over-the-telephone communication skills shall also be addressed.

(d) Problem identification, and disagreement management skills, including instruction in the establishment of priorities and areas of agreement and disagreement and the management of special problems that threaten the process.

(e) Understanding power imbalances, confronting unrealistic expectations being an effective agent of reality, making responsible evaluations, abstaining from giving legal advice, ensuring informed consent, and maintaining standards of fairness, and impartiality, and the importance of confidentiality.

(f) Techniques for achieving agreement or settlement, including instruction in creating a climate conducive to resolution, identifying options, reaching consensus, and working toward agreement.

(g) General review of fact patterns present in typical disputes, including landlord tenant, customer merchant, neighbor, and commercial cases.

(h) Administrative and intake skills relating to dispute resolution services, including completion of paperwork involved in the handling and tracking cases.

(i) The role and participation of attorneys and witnesses in dispute resolution proceedings.

(j) A code of ethics . . .

(k) An understanding of the cultural context, the diversity of stakeholders, respect for the different values and goals of the parties, and racial bias.

464.4 To obtain certification as a mediator, a person shall complete at least 33 hours of mediation experience, at least 18 of which shall include real practical experience in mediation. The balance of those hours may include real practical experience or role playing of simulated disputes, observation of actual intake and case management procedures, and mediation sessions that are supervised by a dispute resolution program organization. The applicant shall also complete a personal assessment evaluation as described in Section 464.5. In this regard, the program or organization shall develop an evaluative form to use for this purpose. . . .

464.5 (a) Prior to receiving a mediator's certificate, an applicant shall participate in one or more personal assessment evaluations as described in Section 464.5 by a supervisor or mentor that assess the specific skills and techniques utilized by the applicant.

(b) The personal assessment evaluation shall include at least one real mediation, conducted by the applicant, under the observation of a trained evaluator who is an experienced mediator.

(c) In evaluating the applicant's performance, each supervisor or mentor shall advise the applicant on how well he or she addresses the following issues:

   (1) Explaining and administering the process;

   (2) Facilitating the flow of communication;

   (3) Empowerment of the parties;

   (4) Active listening;

   (5) Ethical behavior;

   (6) Organization of issues;

   (7) Conflict analysis;

   (8) Developing options with the parties;

   (9) Managing negotiation;

   (10) Strategy planning;

   (11) Use of neutral language.

[handwritten margin note: performance based eval.]

464.6 Upon completion of the requirements for certification as a mediator, the mediation certification organization shall issue a certificate and a distinguishable stamp that includes the abbreviation "CM."

Keep the language of the Florida qualifications, *supra*, in mind as you read the next excerpt.

MEDIATOR CERTIFICATION: SHOULD CALIFORNIA ENACT LEGISLATION?

30 U.S.F. L. Rev. 617, 619-621, 627-632. (1996) [*]

By Robert C. Barrett

I. The Proposed Legislation

. . . .

SB 1428's centerpiece was the establishment of a voluntary certification program for mediators based on widely accepted training, experience, and performance criteria. The Bill would have prohibited a person, after the effective date of July 1, 1997, from holding himself or herself out as a "certified mediator" unless he or she was certified by a mediator certifying organization pursuant to the Bill's requirements. The necessary training consisted of a minimum of twenty-five hours of lecture and discussion about a specified list of eleven topics. . . .

The experience standards included a minimum of thirty-three hours of real or simulated experience, with at least eighteen hours of experience in real mediation. The Bill also would have required that the applicant "participate in one or more personal assessment evaluations . . . by a supervisor or mentor conducted by the mediator certification organization that assesses the specific skills and techniques utilized by the applicant." Under SB 1428, personal assessment evaluations would have involved either real or simulated mediations, however, at least one real mediation was to be "conducted by the applicant, under the observation of a trained evaluator who is an experienced mediator."

SB 1428 also contained a number of declarations of policy that have gained widespread acceptance among mediators. Included among them were the avoidance of licensure or "other state regulator agency involvement in the regulation of mediator" in California and the enactment of five basic "rights" of participants in mediation. These rights included: voluntary participation, confidentiality, informed consent based on full disclosure, joint selection of the mediator by the parties, and the parties' retention of decisionmaking power. Also included in this section of the Bill was the provision that a mediator need not be required to possess any specific degree or license, and the statement that possession of a specific degree or license would not bar a person from serving as a mediator.

The Bill contained a "grandfather" provision allowing those with twenty-five hours of training and fifty hours of "real practical experience in the last two years" to obtain certification without a personal assessment evaluation. The Bill also contained a statement encouraging, but not requiring, certified mediators "to maintain at least eight hours of mediation-related continuing education per year." Significantly, there was no provision for monitoring nor for "decertifying" mediators.

Under the Bill, mediator certifying organizations would have included programs receiving DRPA funding, accredited universities and colleges, and other California organizations or persons that as of January 1, 1995, offered mediation training at least twice a year for two years. Other organizations or persons could have become qualified to issue mediator certificates by applying to the Department of Consumer Affairs and meeting specified standards.

Finally, the Bill would have required persons who collect a fee for mediation services—whether or not certified—to furnish information about relevant training and experience, personal or business relationships with any of the parties, financial interests that would have a bearing on the case, fees and expenses to be charged, a code of ethics to which the mediator subscribes, any personal biases that would affect the mediator's performance, and any prior disciplinary action by any profession . . .

III. Continuing Concerns About Future Legislation

Despite the several improvements made in SB 1428, a number of concerns remain. This part discusses some of the most often mentioned points, and future legislation should attempt to address these issues.

A. The Lack of a Demonstrated Need for the Legislation

Those who opposed SB 1428 point to the lack of complaints against mediators to date, and the lack of demonstrated problems that consumers have had with mediators. . . .

. . . .

Despite the lack of demonstrated problems, and the frequently voiced opinion that legislation is not needed, there is widespread recognition that the rapid growth of the mediation field has increased the likelihood of inexperienced practitioners "hanging out a shingle" and, if able to attract clients, being in a position to harm unsuspecting parties through incompetent practice. Proponents of the Bill, pointing to the increasing volume of mediation legislation, argued that sooner or later the pressures to regulate the field would lead to passage of a bill; they still contend that it would be preferable to have a thoughtful and comprehensive legislative package enacted this year in order to head off that eventuality.

. . . .

B. A Basic Certificate May Appear More Significant Than It Really Is

While it may be useful to specify basic skills and to indicate by means of a certification process that a mediator has sufficient training and has acquired sufficient experience to exhibit those skills, it should be recognized that consumers may place undue reliance on the possession of a certificate. First, mediators may not always specify who issued their certificate and in precisely what kinds of cases the certificate indicates competence. more importantly, consumers are not likely to have the knowledge or opportunity to ask mediators exactly what earning a certificate entailed and what it represents. Finally, a consumer should not be encouraged to rely upon a certificate issued years earlier as evidence that the certifying organization will "stand behind" the integrity or competence of the mediator in actual practice later. Thus, the possession of a certificate, by itself, may result in misleading consumers into thinking that a mediator is thereby more likely to be qualified in a particular case than a mediator without a certificate.

. . . .

C. The Lack of Monitoring, Enforcement, and Complaint-Handling or Decertification Process

Closely related to a basic assumption of SB 1428, that the information conveyed by a certificate to a consumer would have been used appropriately, is the assumption that a certificate would have had continuing meaning. SB 1428, however, contained no provision for updating or renewing certificates over time, or for monitoring of mediator performance once a certificate is issued. Further, it contained no verification procedure to ensure that mediators would in fact have continued to meet the minimum standards contained in the Bill or would have maintained the minimum level of eight hours of continuing education per year that the Bill encouraged. Finally, there was no process for decertifying a mediator against whom well-founded complaints were registered or who in other ways had not continued to demonstrate minimum performance standards.

. . . .

D. The Grandfather Provisions Were Too Loose To Be Effective

SB 1428 provided that "[i]f applicants in the third track [those with the requisite hours of training and experience] have 25 hours of training and 50 hours of real practical experience in the last two years, a personal assessment evaluation. . . is not required." There was no specific requirement that the twenty-five hours of training would cover all the topics listed in the Bill. Moreover, in practical terms it would be nearly impossible to check the *content* of training courses, as compared to their *hourly length*. The result would have been that many existing mediators, including lawyers, retired judges, and others whose skills may have been developed years ago, would have been able to obtain certificates without completing a comprehensive training course. Moreover, there could be assurance that the grandfathered mediator had taken any training dealing with mediator ethics and various cultural and racial contexts in which dispute procedures might be used. This would have undermined the beneficial purposes of insistence on training.

. . . .

E. Potential for the Voluntary Program To Become Mandatory in Practical Effect

This concern is based on the potential that what was described in the legislation as a voluntary program would likely become mandatory in the future. As courts begin alternative dispute resolution programs, they will need to set qualifications standards; the easiest route to take in such an environment is to adopt an already-established program and make it mandatory. . . . The risk here is that if the certification program turns out to have flaws, which may have been overlooked because the program was voluntary, the flaws already have been institutionalized when the program becomes mandatory.

F. The Lack of Funding for an Ongoing Oversight Effort

. . . [T]he Bill contained nothing to assure that there would be continued oversight. No standards were included, and no funding was provided nor responsibility assigned to make sure the Bill was implemented successfully.

NOTES AND QUESTIONS

(1) Would the proposed California Legislation have accomplished the purposes identified by Donald Weckstein? Do you agree with Robert Barrett's critique of the proposed legislation?

(2) A further challenge engendered by a certification process is how to ensure mediator competence while preserving diversity. Ellen Waldman's article, *The Challenge of Certification: How to Ensure Mediator Competence While Preserving Diversity,"* addresses this knotty issue in the context of SB 1428. 30 U.S.F. L. Rev. 723, 724-725 (1996). In this article, she raised the following criticism of the proposed legislation:

> [T]he proposed Bill's overall sensitivity to the diverse professional mix which mediators bring to their work was laudable. However, the Bill displayed less sensitivity to the variety of mediator approaches prevalent in the field. SB 1428 failed to make clear that mediator training and performance evaluations must be implemented in ways that encourage the full panoply of regnant mediator styles. In so doing, the Bill threatened to establish credentialing machinery which constricted rather than enriched mediation practice. *

You should reflect back on the materials in Chapter 4, Mediator Roles, Styles and Orientations, *supra*, when considering the operationalization of a credentialing scheme. Is there a risk that mediators preferring a particular mediator style or orientation will dominate the certification process, leading to an undesirable homogenization of the mediation field? Waldman framed her criticism of the legislation in terms of diversity of style. Is there a similar concern regarding cultural, ethnic, and racial diversity?

[2] EVALUATION

ON EVALUATING MEDIATORS

6 Negotiation J. 23-30, 35-36 (1990) *

By Christopher Honeyman

The following is an attempt to come to grips with the problems involved in evaluating mediators. It is not intended to be a definitive statement, but rather as a basis for discussion. Because mediation encompasses such a vast range of activity under such varied circumstances, any attempt to apply the same criteria across the board is immediately suspect. Therefore, I have chosen to direct these observations primarily to situations in which an organized program is responsible for providing competent mediators to assist parties on a "case" basis. . .

. . . .

At present, mediators tend to be poorly evaluated or even, in effect, not evaluated at all. . . .

. . . .

. . . Conventional practice tends to identify three criteria by which a mediator's performance can be judged: rate of settlement of disputes, opinions of the parties, and general reputation among the mediator's peers. Each of these has obvious flaws.

Reliance on settlement rates (compared with those of mediators in similar situations) immediately raises the objection that since no two cases are the same, the mediators cannot be fairly compared. . . .

Even when a mediator's caseload is large, and its distribution random, the use of settlement rates to determine competence begs the question of what *kind* of settlement the mediator has helped the parties to reach. . . . "More" does not always mean "better."

. . . .

Reliance on the parties' opinions introduces other problems. Certainly people do develop strong opinions about particular mediators, but they are often unfamiliar with what may properly be expected of a mediator. . . . Another drawback to relying on parties' opinions lies in the fact that parties to disputes are unlikely, on any routine basis to devote the time and effort required to give careful answers to detailed questionnaires. Also, they are not privy to what may have happened in a mediator's caucus meeting with another party, so that their point of view is necessarily limited. And they are, of course, partisan; a mediator who has effectively dislodged a recalcitrant party from a beloved position, and thereby helped to settle the dispute, may not be thanked for those efforts.

. . . .

Meanwhile, a sterling reputation remains a kind of Holy Grail . . . Not only does it take a long time and many cases to arrive at professional reputation of any consequence in this line of work—in which the "product" simply isn't as clear or public as, say, an architect's—but most of us harbor doubts about the actual competence of one or another highly touted "expert" we've seen at close quarters. This particular form of skepticism assumes special significance in a field in which manipulation of people's perceptions is arguably a common tactic.

. . . [A] mediator's basic talents can usefully be distinguished as five different types of skill: investigation, empathy, invention, persuasion and distraction. . . .

One of the key problems in evaluation is the difficulty of convincing the mediator and others that the opinions rendered represent something more than a raw application of the evaluator's biases—a problem that has its roots in disagreements over the proper role of a mediator. (Individuals even within the same program may differ, for example, on the degree to which a mediator should try to help out the weaker or less skilled party.)

. . . .

The following evaluation scales are an attempt to draw distinctions between various skills that are relevant in at least some kinds of mediation. Though each skill is assessed according to numerical rankings that coincide with apparently concrete descriptions of what constitutes good work, these are mere devices and are therefore in some sense misleading. Please note: *The implied values must be rewritten for each type of mediation practice.* For that reason, I have deliberately avoided placing any relative weight among the scales. That emphasis will be unique to each mediation program. . . .

. . . .

Seven Parameters of Effectiveness. . . .

Investigation: Effectiveness in identifying and seeking out relevant information pertinent to the case. . . .

Empathy: Conspicuous awareness and consideration of the needs of others. . . .

Inventiveness and problem-solving: Pursuit of collaborative solutions, and generation of ideas and proposals consistent with case facts and workable for opposing parties. (Some programs and individual mediators believe that substantive ideas and proposals should only emanate from the parties. . . . Those working with this restriction may therefore wish to consider rewriting this scale to focus on the mediator's skill at *creating an environment* within which the parties can create the substantive proposals needed. . . .)

Persuasion and presentation skills: Effectiveness of verbal expression, gesture, and "body language" (e.g., eye contact) in communicating with parties. (With persuasion, again, there is a sharp difference of opinion between programs operating in different areas as to what degree or kind of activity is desirable. Some programs may wish to rephrase this scale in terms of the mediator's ability to create an environment conducive to the parties' attempts to alter each other's and their own preconceived opinions.) . . .

Distraction: Effectiveness at reducing tensions at appropriate times by temporarily diverting parties' attention. . . .

Managing the Interaction: Effectiveness in developing strategy, managing the process, coping with conflicts between clients and professional representatives. . . .

Substantive Knowledge: Expertise in the issues and type of dispute. (It is not established that substantive knowledge is an essential part of a mediator's background. Like the parties, an experienced mediator could tend to overlook the existence of certain assumptions that are no longer valid; someone not burdened with ingrained ideas may be able to bring a fresh approach . . .)

. . . .

Evaluating mediators is a complex process, but not an impossible one. While no single solution is likely to be found, a set of options is emerging. Any new refinement, admittedly, brings with it new difficulties, and the options laid out here are themselves complex to administer. An adroit program management may be able to put together relatively quickly a workable, efficient, and fair approach to evaluation that is tailored to its own circumstances. But most likely, the process of developing evaluation tools will require sustained effort, justified partly by recognition that only trial and error will eventually produce a result keyed to the program's, the parties', and the mediators' diverse needs.

Nevertheless, it should be apparent that avoidance of the problems is no longer an acceptable strategy. In an era when rational standards for judging the elements of mediators' effectiveness are becoming more refined, and when mediation itself is becoming an increasingly common option for resolving all kinds of disputes, retaining public confidence in any program will demand that the program devote time and effort to evaluating and strengthening its most important resources.

NOTES AND QUESTIONS

(1) In 1995, The Test Design Project, a diverse group of mediators who worked together for five years to develop tools for selecting, training and evaluating mediators, published "Performance-Based Assessment: A Methodology, for use in selecting, training and evaluating mediators" as the culmination of their of work on this topic. As part of the Test Design Project's work, they partnered with the American Institutes for Research (AIR) and the Human Resources Research Organization (HumRRO) to perform a feasibility study to determine whether it was possible to create a standardized, validated "bank" of test components. The feasibility study, completed in 1993, included family, commercial and community mediation. This study provided preliminary evidence of a significant degree of commonality of the core skills involved in practice in all three areas.

(2) The most recent incarnation of this activity is through the mediator skills project at the University of Georgia and the Academy of Family Mediators who are developing a voluntary certification system for mediators. The project began by looking empirically at mediation styles and skills, including such antecedent factors as demographics, personality characteristics, and previous professional training. From the empirical data, the project self-describes as striving to create "easily administered, objective screening tools program administrators can use to select prospective trainees and . . . veteran mediators." Although some individual programs have incorporated performance-based mediator qualifications tests (e.g., the San Diego Mediation Center and a pilot project of the Suffolk County Superior Court in Massachusetts), as of the end of 2000, there have been no state-wide or national efforts put in place. Why would it be easier to implement a performance-based scheme for a private center or association than for a court system?

(3) Transformative mediators have expressed grave concern with the performance-based testing models currently being developed which do not recognize their practice as competent mediation. For example, in the Interim

Guidelines for Selecting Mediators, in the section on assessing "Generating Agreements," the mediator would be given the lowest score if the mediator "did not initiate suggestions; required considerable help from the parties." From a transformative viewpoint, initiation of suggestions and not "following" the parties would be the mark of bad practice. How might this tension be managed?

§ C   MEDIATOR STANDARDS OF CONDUCT

Another approach to address the issue of mediator competence has been to develop codes of conduct and disciplinary procedures. In 1986, Hawaii became the first state to adopt such a code, entitled "Standards for Private and Public Mediators in the State of Hawaii." In recent years, several states have followed suit; some, such as Florida, are in their second incarnation of such standards. In addition, several professional associations have adopted standards of conduct for their members, including the development of "joint standards" by the American Bar Association Section on Dispute Resolution, the American Arbitration Association, and the Society of Professionals in Dispute Resolution.

In theory, mediator standards of conduct should address the ethical issues which arise for mediators. In 1992, Professor Robert A. Baruch Bush published his study of ethical dilemmas, *The Dilemmas of Mediation Practice: A Study of Ethical Dilemmas and Policy Implications*, National Institute for Dispute Resolution, which was the result of interviews he conducted with practicing community, divorce and civil mediators. He identified two major problems with the standards that existed to date, specifically,

> First, the codes and standards promulgated thus far almost always suffer from internal inconsistency. That is, where the mediator is confronted in a dilemma with the need to choose between two values, like fairness and self-determination, the codes typically contain provisions that, read together tell her *to choose both*. For example, they tell her to protect and to leave alone, when she can't possibly do both. . . .

> The second problem . . . is, the codes and standards are framed at a level of generality that is not responsive to the mediator's need to know how to apply the principles in specific situations. They lack concreteness . . . [y]et clearly, given the kinds of problems mediators encounter, specific guidance is what they most need. . . .*

The following section includes excerpts from the Florida Rules for Certified and Court-Appointed Mediators and the Joint Standards. You should review these with an eye towards noting similarities, differences and implicit/explicit definitions of the role of the mediator. In addition, since these standards were written and adopted after Professor Bush's study, did they address the problems he identified?

---

[1] COURT PROGRAMS

FLORIDA RULES FOR CERTIFIED AND COURT-APPOINTED MEDIATORS, AS AMENDED APRIL 1, 2000

Rule 10.200. Scope and Purpose

These Rules provide ethical standards of conduct for certified and court-appointed mediators. They are intended to both guide mediators in the performance of their services and instill public confidence in the mediation process. The public's use, understanding, and satisfaction with mediation can only be achieved if mediators embrace the highest ethical principles. Whether the parties involved in a mediation choose to resolve their dispute is secondary in importance to whether the mediator conducts the mediation in accordance with these ethical standards.

Committee Notes

2000 Revision: In early 1991, the Florida Supreme Court Standing Committee on Mediation and Arbitration Rules was commissioned by the Chief Justice to research, draft and present for adoption both a comprehensive set of ethical standards for Florida mediators and procedural rules for their enforcement. . . .

The Subcommittee on Ethical Standards began its task by searching the nation for other states or private dispute resolution organizations who had completed any significant work in defining the ethical responsibilities of professional mediators. . . . In May of 1992, The "Florida Rules for Certified and Court Appointed Mediators" became effective.

In the years following the adoption of those ethical rules, the Committee observed their impact on the mediation profession. By 1998, several other states and dispute resolution organizations initiated research into ethical standards for mediation which also became instructive to the Committee. In addition, Florida's Mediator Qualifications Advisory Panel, created to field ethical questions from practicing mediators, gained a wealth of pragmatic experience in the application of ethical concepts to actual practice that became available to the Committee. Finally, The Florida Mediator Qualifications Board, the disciplinary body for mediators, developed specific data from actual grievances filed against mediators over the past several years, which also added to the available body of knowledge. . . .

Upon reviewing the 1992 ethical Rules, it immediately became apparent to the Committee that reorganization, renumbering, and more descriptive titles would make the Rules more useful. For that reason, the Rules were reorganized into four substantive groups which recognized a mediator's ethical responsibilities to the "parties," the "process," the "profession" and the "courts." . . .

Finally, the Committee sought to apply what had been learned. The 2000 revisions are the result of that effort.

Rule 10.210. Mediation Defined

Mediation is a process whereby a neutral and impartial third person acts to encourage and facilitate the resolution of a dispute without prescribing what it should be. It is an informal and non-adversarial process intended to help disputing parties reach a mutually acceptable agreement.

Rule 10.220. Mediator's Role

The role of the mediator is to reduce obstacles to communication, assist in the identification of issues and exploration of alternatives, and otherwise facilitate voluntary agreements resolving the dispute. The ultimate decision-making authority, however, rests solely with the parties.

Rule 10.230. Mediation Concepts

Mediation is based on concepts of communication, negotiation, facilitation, and problem-solving that emphasize:

(1) self determination;

(2) the needs and interests of the parties;

(3) fairness;

(4) procedural flexibility;

(5) confidentiality; and

(6) full disclosure.

Rule 10.300. Mediator's Responsibility to the Parties

The purpose of mediation is to provide a forum for consensual dispute resolution by the parties. It is not an adjudicatory procedure. Accordingly, a mediator's responsibility to the parties includes honoring their right of self-determination; acting with impartiality; and avoiding coercion, improper influence, and conflicts of interest. A mediator is also responsible for maintaining an appropriate demeanor, preserving confidentiality, and promoting the awareness by the parties of the interests of non-participating persons. A mediator's business practices should reflect fairness, integrity and impartiality.

. . . .

Rule 10.310. Self-Determination

(a) Decision-making. Decisions made during a mediation are to be made by the parties. A mediator shall not make substantive decisions for any party. A mediator is responsible for assisting the parties in reaching informed and voluntary decisions while protecting their right of self-determination.

(b) Coercion Prohibited. A mediator shall not coerce or improperly influence any party to make a decision or unwillingly participate in a mediation.

(c) Misrepresentation Prohibited. A mediator shall not intentionally or knowingly misrepresent any material fact or circumstance in the course of conducting a mediation.

(d) Postponement or Cancellation. If, for any reason, a party is unable to freely exercise self-determination, a mediator shall cancel or postpone a mediation.

Committee Notes

2000 Revision: Mediation is a process to facilitate consensual agreement between parties in conflict and to assist them in voluntarily resolving their dispute. It is critical that the parties' right to self-determination (a free and informed choice to agree or not to agree) is preserved during all phases of mediation. A mediator must not substitute the judgment of the mediator for the judgment of the parties, coerce or compel a party to make a decision, knowingly allow a participant to make a decision based on misrepresented facts or circumstances, or in any other way impair or interfere with the parties' right of self-determination.

While mediation techniques and practice styles may vary from mediator to mediator and mediation to mediation, a line is crossed and ethical standards are violated when any conduct of the mediator serves to compromise the parties' basic right to agree or not to agree. Special care should be taken to preserve the party's right to self-determination if the mediator provides input to the mediation process. (See Rule 10.370).

On occasion, a mediator may be requested by the parties to serve as a decision-maker. If the mediator decides to serve in such a capacity, compliance with this request results in a change in the dispute resolution process impacting self-determination, impartiality, confidentiality, and other ethical standards. Before providing decision-making services, therefore, the mediator shall ensure that all parties understand and consent to those changes. (See Rules 10.330 and 10.340).

Under subsection (d), postponement or cancellation of a mediation is necessary if the mediator reasonably believes the threat of domestic violence, existence of substance abuse, physical threat or undue psychological dominance are present and existing factors which would impair any party's ability to freely and willingly enter into an informed agreement.

Rule 10.320.   Nonparticipating Persons

A mediator shall promote awareness by the parties of the interests of persons affected by actual or potential agreements who are not represented at mediation.

Committee Notes

2000 Revision: Mediated agreements will often impact persons or entities not participating in the process. Examples include lienholders, governmental agencies, shareholders, and related commercial entities. In family and dependency mediations, the interests of children, grandparents or other related persons are also often affected. A mediator is responsible for making the parties aware of the potential interests of such non-participating persons.

In raising awareness of the interests of non-participating persons, however, the mediator should still respect the rights of the parties to make their own decisions. Further, raising awareness of possible interests of related entities should not involve advocacy or judgments as to the merits of those interests. In family mediations, for example, a mediator should make the parents aware of the children's interests without interfering with self-determination or advocating a particular position.

Rule 10.330.   Impartiality

(a)   Generally. A mediator shall maintain impartiality throughout the mediation process. Impartiality means freedom from favoritism or bias in word, action, or appearance, and includes a commitment to assist all parties, as opposed to any one individual.

(b)   Withdrawal for Partiality. A mediator shall withdraw from mediation if the mediator is no longer impartial.

(c)   Gifts and Solicitation. A mediator shall neither give nor accept a gift, favor, loan, or other item of value in any mediation process. During the mediation process, a mediator shall not solicit or otherwise attempt to procure future professional services.

Committee Notes

2000 Revision: A mediator has an affirmative obligation to maintain impartiality throughout the entire mediation process. The duty to maintain impartiality arises immediately upon learning of a potential engagement for providing mediation services. A mediator shall not accept or continue any engagement for mediation services in which the ability to maintain impartiality is reasonably impaired or compromised. As soon as practical, a mediator shall make reasonable inquiry as to the identity of the parties or other circumstances which could compromise the mediator's impartiality.

During the mediation, a mediator shall maintain impartiality even while raising questions regarding the reality, fairness, equity, durability and feasibility of proposed options for settlement. In the event circumstances arise during a mediation that would reasonably be construed to impair or compromise a mediator's impartiality, the mediator is obligated to withdraw.

Subsection (c) does not preclude a mediator from giving or accepting de minimis gifts or incidental items provided to facilitate the mediation.

Rule 10.340.   Conflicts of Interest

(a)   Generally. A mediator shall not mediate a matter that presents a clear or undisclosed conflict of interest. A conflict of interest arises when any relationship between the mediator and the mediation participants or the subject matter of the dispute compromises or appears to compromise the mediator's impartiality.

(b)   Burden of Disclosure. The burden of disclosure of any potential conflict of interest rests on the mediator. Disclosure shall be made as soon as practical after the mediator becomes aware of the interest or relationship giving rise to the potential conflict of interest.

(c)   Effect of Disclosure. After appropriate disclosure, the mediator may serve if all parties agree. However, if a conflict of interest clearly impairs a mediator's impartiality, the mediator shall withdraw regardless of the express agreement of the parties.

(d) Conflict During Mediation. A mediator shall not create a conflict of interest during the mediation. During a mediation, a mediator shall not provide any services that are not directly related to the mediation process.

Committee Notes

2000 Revision: Potential conflicts of interests which require disclosure include the fact of a mediator's membership on a related board of directors, full or part time service by the mediator as a representative, advocate, or consultant to a mediation participant, present stock or bond ownership by the mediator in a corporate mediation participant, or any other form of managerial, financial, or family interest by the mediator in any mediation participant involved in a mediation. A mediator who is a member of a law firm or other professional organization is obliged to disclose any past or present client relationship that firm or organization may have with any party involved in a mediation.

The duty to disclose thus includes information relating to a mediator's ongoing financial or professional relationship with any of the parties, counsel, or related entities. Disclosure is required with respect to any significant past, present, or promised future relationship with any party involved in a proposed mediation. While impartiality is not necessarily compromised, full disclosure and a reasonable opportunity for the parties to react are essential.

Disclosure of relationships or circumstances which would create the potential for a conflict of interest should be made at the earliest possible opportunity and under circumstances which will allow the parties to freely exercise their right of self determination as to both the selection of the mediator and participation in the mediation process.

A conflict of interest which clearly impairs a mediator's impartiality is not resolved by mere disclosure to, or waiver by, the parties. Such conflicts occur when circumstances or relationships involving the mediator cannot be reasonably regarded as allowing the mediator to maintain impartiality.

To maintain an appropriate level of impartiality and to avoid creating conflicts of interest, a mediator's professional input to a mediation proceeding must be confined to the services necessary to provide the parties a process to reach a self-determined agreement. Under subsection (d), a mediator is accordingly prohibited from utilizing a mediation to supply any other services which do not directly relate to the conduct of the mediation itself. By way of example, a mediator would therefore be prohibited from providing accounting, psychiatric or legal services, psychological or social counseling, therapy, or business consultations of any sort during the mediation process.

Mediators establish personal relationships with many representatives, attorneys, mediators, and other members of various professional associations. There should be no attempt to be secretive about such friendships or acquaintances, but disclosure is not necessary unless some feature of a particular relationship might reasonably appear to impair impartiality.

Rule 10.350.   Demeanor

A mediator shall be patient, dignified and courteous during the mediation process.

Rule 10.360.   Confidentiality

(a)   Scope. A mediator shall maintain confidentiality of all information revealed during mediation except where disclosure is required by law.

(b)   Caucus. Information obtained during caucus may not be revealed by the mediator to any other mediation participant without the consent of the disclosing party.

(c)   Record Keeping. A mediator shall maintain confidentiality in the storage and disposal of records and shall not disclose any identifying information when materials are used for research, training, or statistical compilations.

Rule 10.370.   Professional Advice Or Opinions

✱ controversial ✱

(a)   Providing Information. Consistent with standards of impartiality and preserving party self-determination, a mediator may provide information that the mediator is qualified by training or experience to provide.

more facilitative than evaluative

(b)   Independent Legal Advice. When a mediator believes a party does not understand or appreciate how an agreement may adversely affect legal rights or obligations, the mediator shall advise the party of the right to seek independent legal counsel.

(c)   Personal or Professional Opinion. A mediator shall not offer a personal or professional opinion intended to coerce the parties, decide the dispute, or direct a resolution of any issue. Consistent with standards of impartiality and preserving party self-determination however, a mediator may point out possible outcomes of the case and discuss the merits of a claim or defense. A mediator shall not offer a personal or professional opinion as to how the court in which the case has been filed will resolve the dispute.

✱ vague balancing test

Committee Notes

OK quest

"Have you thought about how you are going to prove that defense?"

"Do you have witnesses?"

2000 Revision (previously Committee Note to 1992 adoption of former rule 10.090): Mediators who are attorneys should note Florida Bar Committee on Professional Ethics, formal opinion 86-8 at 1239, which states that the lawyer-mediator should "explain the risks of proceeding without independent counsel and advise the parties to consult counsel during the course of the mediation and before signing any settlement agreement that he might prepare for them."

1999 Revision: The primary role of the mediator is to facilitate a process which will provide the parties an opportunity to resolve all or part of a dispute by agreement if they choose to do so. A mediator may assist in that endeavor by providing relevant information or helping the parties obtain such information from other sources. A mediator may also raise issues and discuss strengths and weaknesses of positions underlying the dispute.

Finally, a mediator may help the parties evaluate resolution options and draft settlement proposals. In providing these services however, it is imperative that the mediator maintain impartiality and avoid any activity which would have the effect of overriding the parties' rights of self-determination. While mediators may call upon their own qualifications and experience to supply information and options, the parties must be given the opportunity to freely decide upon any agreement. Mediators shall not utilize their opinions to decide any aspect of the dispute or to coerce the parties or their representatives to accept any resolution option.

While a mediator has no duty to specifically advise a party as to the legal ramifications or consequences of a proposed agreement, there is a duty for the mediator to advise the parties of the importance of understanding such matters and giving them the opportunity to seek such advice if they desire.

Rule 10.380.   Fees and Expenses

(a) Generally. A mediator holds a position of trust. Fees charged for mediation services shall be reasonable and consistent with the nature of the case.

(b) Guiding Principles in Determining Fees. A mediator shall be guided by the following general principles in determining fees:

   (1) Any charges for mediation services based on time shall not exceed actual time spent or allocated.

   (2) Charges for costs shall be for those actually incurred.

   (3) All fees and costs shall be appropriately divided between the parties.

   (4) When time or expenses involve two or more mediations on the same day or trip, the time and expense charges shall be prorated appropriately.

(c) Written Explanation of Fees. A mediator shall give the parties or their counsel a written explanation of any fees and costs prior to mediation. The explanation shall include:

   (1) the basis for and amount of any charges for services to be rendered, including minimum fees and travel time;

   (2) the amount charged for the postponement or cancellation of mediation sessions and the circumstances under which such charges will be assessed or waived;

   (3) the basis and amount of charges for any other items; and

   (4) the parties' pro rata share of mediation fees and costs if previously determined by the court or agreed to by the parties.

(d) Maintenance of Records. A mediator shall maintain records necessary to support charges for services and expenses and upon request shall make an accounting to the parties, their counsel, or the court.

(e) Remuneration for Referrals. No commissions, rebates, or similar remuneration shall be given or received by a mediator for a mediation referral.

[handwritten margin note: may destroy impartiality]

(f) Contingency Fees Prohibited. A mediator shall not charge a contingent fee or base a fee on the outcome of the process.

Rule 10.400. Mediator's Responsibility to the Mediation Process.

A mediator is responsible for safeguarding the mediation process. The benefits of the process are best achieved if the mediation is conducted in an informed, balanced and timely fashion. A mediator is responsible for confirming that mediation is an appropriate dispute resolution process under the circumstances of each case.

. . . .

Rule 10.410. Balanced Process

A mediator shall conduct mediation sessions in an even-handed, balanced manner. A mediator shall promote mutual respect among the mediation participants throughout the mediation process and encourage the participants to conduct themselves in a collaborative, non-coercive, and non-adversarial manner. *[handwritten: Alf: not resp. to outcome ; only process]*

Committee Notes

2000 Revision: A mediator should be aware that the presence or threat of domestic violence or abuse among the parties can endanger the parties, the mediator, and others. Domestic violence and abuse can undermine the exercise of self-determination and the ability to reach a voluntary and mutually acceptable agreement.

Rule 10.420. Conduct of Mediation

(a) Orientation Session. Upon commencement of the mediation session, a mediator shall describe the mediation process and the role of the mediator, and shall inform the mediation participants that:

    (1) mediation is a consensual process;

    (2) the mediator is an impartial facilitator without authority to impose a resolution or adjudicate any aspect of the dispute; and

    (3) communications made during the process are confidential, except where disclosure is required by law.

(b) Adjournment or Termination. A mediator shall:

    (1) adjourn the mediation upon agreement of the parties;

    (2) adjourn or terminate any mediation which, if continued, would result in unreasonable emotional or monetary costs to the parties;

    (3) adjourn or terminate the mediation if the mediator believes the case is unsuitable for mediation or any party is unable or unwilling to participate meaningfully in the process;

    (4) terminate a mediation entailing fraud, duress, the absence of bargaining ability, or unconscionability; and

(5)   terminate any mediation if the physical safety of any person is endangered by the continuation of mediation.

(c)   Closure. The mediator shall cause the terms of any agreement reached to be memorialized appropriately and discuss with the parties and counsel the process for formalization and implementation of the agreement.

Committee Notes

2000 Revision. In defining the role of the mediator during the course of an opening session, a mediator should ensure that the participants fully understand the nature of the process and the limits on the mediator's authority. [see rule 10.370(c)]. It is also appropriate for the mediator to inform the parties that mediators are ethically precluded from providing non-mediation services to any party [see rule 10.340(d)].

Florida Rule[s] . . . require that any mediated agreement be reduced to writing. Mediators have an obligation to ensure these rules are complied with, but are not required to write the agreement themselves.

Rule 10.430.   Scheduling Mediation

A mediator shall schedule a mediation in a manner that provides adequate time for the parties to fully exercise their right of self-determination. A mediator shall perform mediation services in a timely fashion, avoiding delays whenever possible.

Rule 10.500.   Mediator's Responsibility to the Courts

A mediator is accountable to the referring court with ultimate authority over the case. Any interaction discharging this responsibility however, shall be conducted in a manner consistent with these ethical rules.

. . . .

Rule 10.510.   Information to the Court

A mediator shall be candid, accurate, and fully responsive to the court concerning the mediator's qualifications, availability, and other administrative matters.

Rule 10.520.   Compliance with Authority

A mediator shall comply with all statutes, court rules, local court rules, and administrative orders relevant to the practice of mediation.

Rule 10.530.   Improper Influence

A mediator shall refrain from any activity that has the appearance of improperly influencing a court to secure an appointment to a case.

Committee Notes

2000 Revision: Giving gifts to court personnel in exchange for case assignments is improper. *De minimus* gifts generally distributed as part of an overall business development plan are excepted. [see also rule 10.330]

10.600.   Mediator's Responsibility to The Mediation Profession

A mediator shall preserve the quality of the profession. A mediator is responsible for maintaining professional competence and forthright business practices, fostering good relationships, assisting new mediators, and generally supporting the advancement of mediation.

. . . .

Rule 10.610.   Advertising

A mediator shall not engage in marketing practices which contain false or misleading information. A mediator shall ensure that any advertisements of the mediator's qualifications, services to be rendered, or the mediation process are accurate and honest. A mediator shall not make claims of achieving specific outcomes or promises implying favoritism for the purpose of obtaining business.

Rule 10.620.   Integrity and Impartiality

A mediator shall not accept any engagement, provide any service, or perform any act that would compromise the mediator's integrity or impartiality.

Rule 10.630.   Professional Competence

A mediator shall acquire and maintain professional competence in mediation. A mediator shall regularly participate in educational activities promoting professional growth.

Rule 10.640.   Skill and Experience

A mediator shall decline an appointment, withdraw, or request appropriate assistance when the facts and circumstances of the case are beyond the mediator's skill or experience.

Rule 10.650.   Concurrent Standards

Other ethical standards to which a mediator may be professionally bound are not abrogated by these rules. In the course of performing mediation services however, these rules prevail over any conflicting ethical standards to which a mediator may otherwise be bound.

Rule 10.660.   Relationships with Other Mediators

A mediator shall respect the professional relationships of another mediator.

Rule 10.670.   Relationship with Other Professionals

A mediator shall respect the role of other professional disciplines in the mediation process and shall promote cooperation between mediators and other professionals.

Rule 10.680.   Prohibited Agreements

With the exception of an agreement conferring benefits upon retirement, a mediator shall not restrict or limit another mediator's practice following termination of a professional relationship.

Committee Notes

2000 Revision. Rule 10.680 is intended to discourage covenants not to compete or other practice restrictions arising upon the termination of a relationship with another mediator or mediation firm. In situations where a retirement program is being contractually funded or supported by a surviving mediator or mediation firm, however, reasonable restraints on competition are acceptable.

Rule 10.690   Advancement of Mediation

(a)   Pro Bono Service. Mediators have a responsibility to provide competent services to persons seeking their assistance, including those unable to pay for services. A mediator should provide mediation services pro bono or at a reduced rate of compensation whenever appropriate.

(b)   New Mediator Training. An experienced mediator should cooperate in training new mediators, including serving as a mentor.

(c)   Support of Mediation. A mediator should support the advancement of mediation by encouraging and participating in research, evaluation, or other forms of professional development and public education.

[2]   GENERAL STANDARDS

STANDARDS OF CONDUCT FOR MEDIATORS (1994)

American Arbitration Association, American Bar Association Section on Dispute Resolution, Society of Professionals in Dispute Resolution *

The initiative for these standards came from three professional groups: The American Arbitration Association (AAA), the American Bar Association Section on Dispute Resolution (ABA), and the Society of Professionals in Dispute Resolution (SPIDR).

The purpose of this initiative was to develop a set of standards to serve as a general framework for the practice of mediation. . . . The standards are intended to apply to all types of mediation. . . .

Preface

The model standards of conduct for mediators are intended to perform three major functions: to serve as a guide for the conduct of mediators; to inform the mediating parties; and to promote public confidence in mediation as a process for resolving disputes. The standards draw on existing codes of conduct for mediators and take into account issues and problems that have surfaced in mediation practice. . . .

---

* Copyright © 1994 by the American Arbitration Association, American Bar Association, and the Society of Professionals in Dispute Resolution. Reprinted with permission.

I. Self-Determination: A Mediator Shall Recognize that Mediation is Based on the Principle of Self-Determination by the Parties.

Self-determination is the fundamental principle of mediation. It requires that the mediation process rely upon the ability of the parties to reach a voluntary, uncoerced agreement. Any party may withdraw from mediation at any time.

Comments:

> The mediator may provide information about the process, raise issues, and help parties explore options. The primary role of the mediator is to facilitate a voluntary resolution of a dispute. Parties shall be given the opportunity to consider all proposed options.

> A mediator cannot personally ensure that each party has made a fully informed choice to reach a particular agreement, but it is good practice for the mediator to make the parties aware of the importance of consulting other professionals, where appropriate, to help them make informed decisions.

II. Impartiality: A Mediator Shall Conduct the Mediation in an Impartial Manner.

The concept of mediator impartiality is central to the mediation process. A mediator shall mediate only those matters in which she or he can remain impartial and even-handed. If at any time the mediator is unable to conduct the process in an impartial manner, the mediator is obligated to withdraw.

Comments:

> A mediator shall avoid conduct that gives the appearance of partiality toward one of the parties. The quality of the mediation process is enhanced when the parties have confidence in the impartiality of the mediator.

> When mediators are appointed by a court or institution, the appointing agency shall make reasonable efforts to ensure that mediators serve impartially.

> A mediator should guard against partiality or prejudice based on the parties' personal characteristics, background or performance at the mediation.

III. Conflicts of Interest: A Mediator Shall Disclose all Actual and Potential Conflicts of Interest Reasonably Known to the Mediator. After Disclosure, the Mediator Shall Decline to Mediate Unless all Parties Choose to Retain the Mediator. The Need to Protect Against Conflicts of Interest Also Governs Conduct that Occurs During and After the Mediation.

A conflict of interest is a dealing or relationship that might create an impression of possible bias. The basic approach to questions of conflict of interest is consistent with the concept of self-determination. The mediator has a responsibility to disclose all actual and potential conflicts that are reasonably known to the mediator and could reasonably be seen as raising a question about impartiality. If all parties agree to mediate after being informed of conflicts, the mediator may proceed with the mediation. If, however, the conflict of interests casts serious doubt on the integrity of the process, the mediator shall decline to proceed.

A mediator must avoid the appearance of conflict of interest both during and after the mediation. Without the consent of all parties, a mediator shall not subsequently establish a professional relationship with one of the parties in a related matter, or in an unrelated matter under circumstances which would raise legitimate questions about the integrity of the mediation process.

fear of lawyers cozying up to certain parties

Comments:

> A mediator shall avoid conflicts of interest in recommending the services of other professionals. A mediator may make reference to professional referral services or associations which maintain rosters of qualified professionals.

> Potential conflicts of interest may arise between the administrators of mediation programs and mediators and there may be strong pressures on the mediator to settle a particular case or cases, The mediator's commitment must be to the parties and the process. Pressures from outside of the mediation process should never influence the mediator to coerce the parties to settle.

IV. Competence: A Mediator Shall Mediate Only When the Mediator Has the Necessary Qualifications to Satisfy the Reasonable Expectation of the Parties.

Any person may be selected as a mediator, provided that the parties are satisfied with the mediator's qualifications. Training and experience in mediation, however, are often necessary for effective mediation. A person who offers herself or himself as available to serve as a mediator gives parties and the public the expectation that she or he has the competency to mediate effectively. In court-connected or other forms of mandated mediation, it is essential that mediators assigned to the parties have the requisite training and experience.

Comments:

> Mediators should have available for the parties information regarding their relevant training, education and experience.

> The requirements for appearing on a list of mediators must be made public and available to interested persons.

> When mediators are appointed by a court or institution, the appointing agency shall make reasonable efforts to ensure that each mediator is qualified for the particular mediation.

V. Confidentiality: A Mediator Shall Maintain the Reasonable Expectations of the Parties with Regard to Confidentiality.

The reasonable expectations of the parties with regard to confidentiality shall be met by the mediator. The parties' expectations of confidentiality depend on the circumstances of the mediation and any agreements they may make. The mediator shall not disclose any matter that a party expects to be confidential unless given permission by all parties or unless required by law of other public policy.

Comments:

> The parties may make their own rules with respect to confidentiality, or the accepted practice of an individual mediator or institution may dictate a particular set of expectations. Since the parties' expectations regarding confidentiality are important, the mediator should discuss these expectations with the parties.

> If the mediator holds private sessions with a party, the nature of these sessions with regard to confidentiality should be discussed prior to undertaking such sessions.

> In order to protect the integrity of the mediation, a mediator should avoid communicating information about how the parties acted in the mediation process, the merits of the case, or settlement offers. The mediator may report, if required, whether parties appeared at a scheduled mediation.

> Where the parties have agreed that all or a portion of the information disclosed during a mediation is confidential, the parties' agreement should be respected by the mediator.

> Confidentiality should not be construed to limit or prohibit the effective monitoring, research, or evaluation, of mediation programs by responsible persons. Under appropriate circumstances, researchers may be permitted to obtain access to statistical data and, with the permission of the parties to individual case files, observations of live mediations, and interviews with participants.

VI. Quality of the Process: A Mediator Shall Conduct the Mediation Fairly, Diligently, and in a Manner Consistent with the Principle of Self-Determination by the Parties.

A mediator shall work to ensure a quality process and to encourage mutual respect among the parties. A quality process requires a commitment by the mediator to diligence and procedural fairness. There should be adequate opportunity for each party in the mediation to participate in the discussions. The parties decide when and under what conditions they will reach an agreement or terminate a mediation.

Comments:

> A mediator may agree to mediate only when he or she is prepared to commit the attention essential to an effective mediation.

> Mediators should only accept cases when they can satisfy the reasonable expectations of the parties concerning the timing of the process. A

mediator should not allow a mediation to be unduly delayed by the parties or their representatives.

The presence or absence of persons at a mediation depends on the agreement of the parties and mediator. The parties and mediator may agree that others may be excluded from particular sessions or from the entire mediation process.

The primary purpose of a mediator is to facilitate the parties' voluntary agreement. The role of mediator differs substantially from other professional-client relationships. Mixing the role of a mediator and the role of a professional advising a client is problematic, and mediators must strive to distinguish between the roles. A mediator should therefore refrain from providing professional advice. Where appropriate, a mediator should recommend that parties seek professional advice, or consider resolving their dispute through arbitration, counseling, neutral evaluation, or other processes. A mediator who undertakes, at the request of the parties, an additional dispute resolution role in the same matter assumes increased responsibilities and obligations that may be governed by the standards of other professions.

A mediator shall withdraw from a mediation when incapable of serving or then unable to remain impartial.

A mediator shall withdraw from the mediation or postpone a session if the mediation is being used to further illegal conduct, or if a party is unable to participate due to drug, alcohol, or other physical or mental incapacity.

Mediators should not permit their behavior in the mediation process to be guided by a desire for a high settlement rate.

VII. Advertising and Solicitation: A Mediator Shall be Truthful in Advertising and Solicitation for Mediation.

Advertising or any other communication with the public concerning services offered or regarding the education, training, and expertise of the mediator shall be truthful. Mediators shall refrain from promises and guarantees of results.

Comments:

It is imperative that communication with the public educate and instill confidence in the process.

In an advertisement or other communication to the public, a mediator may make reference to meeting state, national or private organization qualifications only if the entity referred to has a procedure for qualifying mediators and the mediator has been duly granted the requisite status.

VIII. Fees: A Mediator Shall Fully Disclose and Explain the Basis of Compensation, Fees, and Charges to the Parties.

The parties should be provided sufficient information about fees at the outset of a mediation to determine if they wish to retain the services of a mediator. If a mediator charges fees, the fees shall be reasonable, considering, among other things, the mediation service, the type and complexity of the matter, the expertise of the mediator, the time required, and the rates customary in the community. The better practice in reaching an understanding about fees is to set down the arrangements in a written agreement.

Comments:

A mediator who withdraws from a mediation should return any unearned fee to the parties.

A mediator should not enter into a fee arrangement which is contingent upon the result of the mediation or amount of the settlement.

Co-mediators who share a fee should hold to standards of reasonableness in determining the allocation of fees.

A mediator should not accept a fee for referral of a matter to another mediator or to any other person.

IX. Obligations to the Mediation Process: Mediators have a duty to Improve the Practice of Mediation.

Comments:

Mediators are regarded as knowledgeable in the process of mediation. They have an obligation to use their knowledge to help educate the public about mediation; to make mediation accessible to those who would like to use it; to correct abuses; and to improve their professional skills and abilities.

NOTES AND QUESTIONS

(1) Compare the AAA/ABA/SPIDR "Joint" Standards of Conduct to the Florida Standards and the Draft Standards of Practice for Family and Divorce Mediation reprinted in the Appendix to this book. What was the purpose behind each of these standards of conduct? What impact does the purpose have on their respective content? What implicit and explicit definitions of mediation are contained in each set of rules? Were any particular styles of mediation specifically excluded? Are the standards internally consistent as to what is the appropriate role of the mediator? Are the standards substantively different in any areas?

(2) In conjunction with the adoption of its standards of conduct in 1992, Florida adopted a disciplinary procedure to enforce the standards. The AAA/ABA/SPIDR standards were not drafted with an enforcement scheme in mind. What influence does the presence or absence of an enforcement scheme have on the standards? What would you expect to be some of the difficulties in attempting to enforce the Florida Standards of Conduct? The rules as originally adopted contained the following *subjective* provision:

Rule 10.070

(a)   (2) : A mediator shall withdraw from mediation if the mediator believes the mediator can no longer be impartial.

The 2000 revision changed the provision to this *objective* standard:

Rule 10.330   (b) Withdrawal for Partiality. A mediator shall withdraw from mediation if the mediator is no longer impartial.

(3) Before the Florida Supreme Court Committee on Mediation and Arbitration Rules submitted its proposed revisions to the Florida Supreme Court, several versions of revisions were circulated for comments. The following are the original two options for what became rule 10.370 Professional Advice or Opinions. How does the rule as amended differ from both initial options and what are the implications of the changes? Which option(s), including the one which was adopted, would appeal to evaluative mediators? To facilitative mediators? Which option would you prefer? Why?

Professional Advice or Opinions

Option One

1.   General Prohibition; Exception. A mediator shall not provide professional advice or opinions. However, a mediator may provide information about the process, draft proposals, point out possible outcomes of a case and help parties explore options.

2.   Independent Legal Advice. If a mediator determines that a party does not understand how an agreement affects legal rights or obligation, the mediator shall advise the party of the right to seek independent advice.

Option Two

1.   Limitation on Information or Advice. A mediator may provide information or advice that the mediator is qualified by training or experience to provide. However, in providing professional advice or information, a mediator shall not violate impartiality or self-determination of the parties.

2.   Independent Legal Advice. If a mediator determines that a party does not understand how an agreement affects legal rights or obligations, the mediator shall advise the party of the right to seek independent advice.

Committee Note [which would have been included with either option]

The primary role of the mediator is to facilitate a process which will provide the parties an opportunity to reach an agreement if they choose to do so. A mediator may assist the parties in that endeavor by providing information or expanding available resources to obtain information, by raising issues and offering opinions about the strengths and weaknesses of underlying positions, by suggesting and helping the parties explore resolution options, and by helping draft settlement proposals, In providing these services however, it is imperative that the mediator maintain impartiality and avoid any activity which would have the effect of overriding the parties' rights of self-determination.

While mediators may call upon their own qualifications and training to supply information and advice, the parties must be given the opportunity to consider and choose from the full range of options available to them. Mediators shall not adjudicate, substitute their advice or opinions for the true will of the parties, or in any way coerce or compel the parties to unwillingly resolve their dispute or accept any particular resolution option.

While a mediator has no duty to specifically advise a party as to the legal ramifications or consequences of a proposed agreement, there is a duty for the mediator to advise the parties of the importance of understanding such matters and giving them the opportunity to seek such advice if they desire.

(4) Florida has created a Mediator Advisory Ethics Committee (formerly called the Mediator Qualifications Advisory Panel/MQAP) to which mediators can address questions on the standards of conduct. The panel reviews the written request for advice and responds with a written opinion. The opinions are published in the *Resolution Report* published by the Florida Dispute Resolution Center which is mailed to all individuals who have completed a Florida Supreme Court certified mediation training program. They also can be found on line at www.flcourts.org/Courts/newsite/index.html

One opinion which created some controversy was issued in response to questions raised by a county mediator concerning the issue of giving advice. The original questions, along with the MQAP's response, follow. All rule references are to the Florida Rules for Certified and Court-Appointed Mediators unless otherwise specified.

Case Scenario

Douglas Stern, an authorized agent for Tough Financing, Inc., has brought an action in small claims court against Mary Naive for failure to make monthly payments as agreed in a contract and note executed several months ago. Both the contract and the note are standard documents used by the consumer lending company throughout the State of Florida. The claim is for $1250. At a pre-trial session, Mary admits to owing the money. The judge asks the defendant if there is a reason why he should not award a judgment to the plaintiff. Mary responds that she would like to work out a payment schedule, so the judge orders a session of mediation.

At the mediation session, Al Nicely, the mediator, scans the agreements and learns that Mary has obligated herself to pay interest at the rate of 29.5% per year if the payments are in arrears. The mediator also learns that Doug Stern told Ms. Naive in the hallway before the court session that she should avoid a judgment because it would hurt her credit. Mr. Nicely is aware that interest on judgments accrue at the rate of 8% per year. Ms. Naive states that she can afford to make payments of $110 per month, and the plaintiff quickly accepts the offer.

Question 95-002A

Would it be permissible for the mediator to ask: *Are you aware that the monthly payments do not cover the interest as it is accruing and you will be paying on this loan forever?*

Question 95-002B

Would it be permissible for the mediator to ask: *Ms. Naive, are you aware that if a judgment were entered against you, the interest would be reduced from 29.5% to 8%?*

Questions 95-002C

Would a mediator be interfering with a contractual relationship by pointing out the above to the defendant?

Question 95-002D

While it is known that a mediator should not advise, can a question be asked even if the framing of the question tends to advise or inform one or both of the parties involved?

Opinion 95-002A

The mediator's role as defined in rule 10.020(b) includes identifying issues, reducing obstacles to communication, and maximizing alternatives to help parties reach a voluntary agreement. In so doing, however, the mediator must maintain impartiality and refrain from giving legal advice.

In question 95-002A, the mediator asks one party to verify knowledge of inaccurate information Thus, the mediator's question is false, leading and inappropriate. Based on the figures in the case scenario, the respondent will not pay on the loan forever if she decides to pay the amount in the proposed offer. Raising this question would, if done intentionally or knowingly, constitute a violation of Rule 10.060(c) by misrepresenting material facts in the course of conducting a mediation. However, even in the event that the mediator were faced with information which demonstrated that the party would be paying on a loan forever, the question as framed would violate rule 10.070(a)(1), which requires that mediators maintain impartiality while raising questions for the parties to consider as to the fairness and equity of settlement proposals.

Opinion 95-002B

While the mediator's inquiry is indeed in question form, it is designed to advise the party about her legal options, a role that is appropriate for an attorney, but inappropriate for a mediator. Providing such advice in the form of a question does not lessen the impropriety of the act; as such, the mediator violates rule 10.090(a) & (b) by providing information the mediator is not qualified by training to provide and by failing to advise the participant to seek independent legal counsel.

Opinion 95-002C

As submitted, question 95-002C asks the advisory panel to give legal advice; this is beyond the jurisdiction of the panel.

Opinion 95-002D

It is improper for a mediator to provide legal advice by any method within the scope of a mediation, whether such advice be by statement, question or any other form of communication.

The mediator, while fulfilling the role of reality tester, must be aware of, and consciously avoid crossing the line between partiality and impartiality, neutrality and non-neutrality. The mediator may, however, often obtain the desired information if the question is framed more generally. It appears to the panel that the mediator wishes to be certain that the party is aware of the alternatives available for satisfaction of the debt—fulfillment of the contracted payments or payment through a judgment. It is the opinion of the panel that the mediator can obtain that information by asking the following: "Is interest levied on a judgment? Do either of you know?" These two questions set the stage for the parties to provide information to the mediator and to each other without placing the mediator in the position of providing that information. In so doing, the mediator assists in maximizing the exploration of alternatives, and adheres to the principles of fairness, full disclosure, self determination, and the needs and interests of the participants [Rule 10.020(d)(1), (2) and (5)], while honoring the commitment to all parties to move toward an agreement [Rule 10.070(a)].

Professor Jeffrey W. Stempel took issue with the MQAP's opinion in *Beyond Formalism and False Dichotomies: The Need for Institutionalizing a Flexible Concept of the Mediator's Role*, 24 Fla. St. U. L. Rev. 949 (1997).* * Specifically, he stated:

> Although the issues of interpreting the law and the Rules are reasonably close, I believe the Panel opinion was in error and took an excessively restrictive view of mediator discretion under Florida law. The statute prohibits a mediator's giving of "legal advice," an admittedly malleable term, but hardly one that requires the expansive definition placed upon it by the Panel. As a law professor, like most lawyers, I am frequently asked about legal problems by students and friends. Although I have yet to agree to represent any

of them (and could not do so in Florida without obtaining pro hac vice admission because I am a member of the Minnesota bar), I feel compelled as a teacher or friend to at least alert them to the apparent legal issues and to inform them of sources of information, potential counsel, and so on. Am I practicing law? Not at all (although some older vintage lawyers might assert it). Am I giving legal advice? Only in the broadest sense. . . .

. . . [T]he Panel's broad definition of "legal advice" by a mediator is defensible but extreme. It serves the text of the statute but not its purpose. The purpose of the prohibition, of course is to prevent the mediator from choosing sides, playing favorites, interfering with party-lawyer relations, or impeding voluntary resolution through needless, legalistic Monday-morning quarterbacking. As long as the mediator is not frustrating the purpose of the state through these or similar tactics, the Panel (and the Florida dispute resolution establishment) should accord the statutory limit on "legal advice" the sort of constrained, common-sense view that we as lawyers would employ when determining whether our communications rise to the level of providing representation or services. Alerting disputants to potential pitfalls and fairness concerns, even if done through very specific questions and comments (rather than the general questions endorsed by the Panel) should not be roundly forbidden as impermissible legal advice.

Consider the questions Professor Stempel raises as you read the next section on Mediation and the Legal System.

(5) Consider how each of the standards address the concept of self-determination. In an upcoming article in the Harvard Negotiation Law Review, Professor Nancy Welsh explores the way courts are modifying the meaning of this concept and analyzes the implications for mediation in the court context. She concludes her article by suggesting that the best way to protect party self-determination is by modifying the presumption that a mediated settlement agreement is immediately binding: *

[S]elf determination is *not* part of the lexicon regarding the enforcement of negotiated settlement agreements, and the standards currently used to determine whether parties exercised their "free will" in reaching a negotiated agreement are likely to fall short in protecting the fundamental principle of self-determination. Therefore, we may be *required to embrace and advocate for* a protection that holds court-connected mediation to a higher standard than traditional negotiation. The protection that I believe will be most effective is the imposition of a three-day non-waivable cooling off period before mediated settlement agreements (whether oral or written) become binding . . .

. . . .

. . .If self-determination—not settlement—is the fundamental principle underlying mediation, the benefits provided by this cooling off proposal clearly outweigh the possible risks. First, a cooling off period . . . is relatively straight forward, easily-administrable, and unlikely to invite litigation and/or intrusions upon the confidentiality of mediation.

Much more importantly, however, this option would reward mediators who view their role as primarily facilitative and penalize mediators who use techniques designed to force an agreement.

———————

What do you think of Professor Welsh's proposal?

§ D   MEDIATION AND THE LEGAL SYSTEM

IS MEDIATION THE PRACTICE OF LAW?

14 Alternatives 57 (May 1996) *

By Carrie Menkel-Meadow

One of the hottest questions in ADR ethics is whether mediating a case is the "practice of law."

. . . .

How we answer the question . . . will determine the standards by which we judge the work—whether we rely on legal ethics codes, or those of "coordinate" professions. . .

If mediation is the practice of law (or as Geoffrey Hazard has argued, it is the "ancillary" practice of law), we must refer to lawyers' ethics codes. Trouble is, they provide little, if any, guidance about issues like: confidentiality (among parties and with mediators), conflicts of interests, fees, and unauthorized practice (in co-mediating, for example, with a non-lawyer). . . .

The risk, as with many ethical issues, is that the desired solution to one problem determines the conclusion. Most of us in the field are concerned about access to mediation— expanding the pool of capable mediators, and the choices for consumers of mediation services. Therefore, we would like to define mediation broadly, so that it doesn't involve the practice of law. To that end, we argue that mediation in its "pure" form of facilitation does not involve law, but communication and other skills.

One example of this approach is a proposal by the District of Columbia Bar to clarify and revise the local ethics rule dealing with the unauthorized practice of law. The proposed amendment expressly exempts mediation because, "ADR services are not given in circumstances where there is a client relationship of trust and reliance and it is common practice for providers of ADR services explicitly to advise participants that they are not providing the services of legal counsel," Proposed Clarification and Revision of District of Columbia Court of Appeals Rule 49 Concerning the Unauthorized Practice of Law, Rule 49 Committee of the District of Columbia Bar.

Lawyer-Client Relationship

This approach to the issue, one of the more popular ones, treats the absence of a lawyer-client relationship as the governing test. It allows a broad range of individuals to mediate, including non-lawyers and lawyers who are not members of the local or state bar.

[handwritten margin note: Thinks this is Super-ficial test]

Another route to the same result is to simply define away the problem. A report two years ago to the Tennessee Supreme Court Commission on Dispute Resolution by the state Board of Professional Responsibility illustrates this approach. It recommends a rule of professional responsibility that says: "A neutral shall give legal opinions to a party only in the presence of all parties, providing, however, that a prediction of litigation outcomes by a lawyer acting as a dispute resolution neutral shall not for purposes of this section constitute the provision of a legal opinion."

. . . .

For people concerned about standards and quality control in mediation, here's the problem: to the extent that mediators, especially those who work within court programs or by court referral, "predict" court results or "evaluate" the merits of the case (on either factual or legal grounds), they are giving legal advice.

Mediators, courts and rules may disclaim responsibility for any information mediators give out, or treat it as not given by an agent, fiduciary, or "counsel." But as a practical matter, parties and others may rely on what the mediator tells them, in assessing their alternatives, suggesting other options, and agreeing to settlements.

Reliance on the Mediator

. . . .

The current trend . . . is to grant quasi-judicial immunity to at least court-based third party neutrals. . . . However, that means parties have virtually no recourse against a third-party neutral when they rely on a mediator's information or advice that is unfair, unjust, or just plain wrong. . . .

Ideally, we should analyze the work of third-party neutrals to see what they do, and then attempt to develop the appropriate regulatory models. I disagree with the argument that mediators can give neutral, unbiased "legal information" that is not the practice of law. . . .

. . . .

While some ADR experts pin their analysis on "client representation," I prefer to look at reliance. . . .

When mediators engage in some prediction or application of legal standards to concrete facts—and especially when they draft settlement agreements, I think they are "practicing" law. That means neutrals who are not trained as lawyers need to be wary of evaluative mediation. They still have other options as mediators: they can limit their role to facilitation, co-mediate with lawyers, or ask the parties to release them from liability for bad legal advice. Non-lawyer mediators might still be subject to the . . . regulation against unauthorized practice of law. . . .

Giving legal predictions and evaluations is law work, whether or not there is a lawyer-client relationship. Within these boundaries, we need rules that permit qualified people without legal training to mediate. . . .

Still there's clearly a quality control problem. Just because a mediator has a law degree— or even an up-to-date license to practice—does not mean that he or she will give accurate legal advice, prediction or evaluation. . . .

LAWYERS WHO MEDIATE ARE NOT PRACTICING LAW

14 Alternatives 74 (June 1996) *

By Bruce Meyerson

Generally speaking, to practice law, one must have a client. Assuming that mediators clarify with parties that no attorney-client relationship exists, engaging in a legal discussion would not be the practice of law. Specifically, in order for a mediator's conduct in advising parties about the legal aspects of a particular dispute to be considered the practice of law, the party to the mediation must view the mediator as her lawyer and therefore assume that she is receiving legal advice for her personal benefit. If the parties are represented by counsel, or if the mediator has carefully clarified that the unrepresented parties do not view the mediator as their lawyer, I cannot imagine a situation where parties to the mediation will be confused about the mediator's role and mistakenly assume that the mediator is functioning as a lawyer. . .

If . . . mediators are practicing law any time they give evaluations or predict outcomes, a number of undesirable consequences will follow. First, lawyer-mediators would be subject to all of the duties and obligations under the Model Rules, and presumably would owe these duties to the parties in the mediation. Although it is possible that a lawyer can function as a neutral mediator on behalf of clients in certain limited circumstances, Ethics Rule 2.2, in most instances the role of a mediator is fundamentally incompatible with an attorney's role in representing a client. For example, a mediator is supposed to be impartial and evenhanded during the mediation. On the other hand, a lawyer representing a client owes that client a duty of undivided loyalty. Most certainly, this obligation is inconsistent with the neutral duties owed to all of the parties in mediation. . . .

Second, a conclusion that mediation is the practice of law would raise the specter that thousands of professionals in other disciplines are engaged in the unauthorized practice of law. Surely, this is casting the "practice of law" net too widely.

Third, if mediation is the practice of law, judges presiding over settlement conferences would be breaking ethical rules in many jurisdictions. That could happen in states that prohibit judges from practicing law while they serve on the bench. Under these rules, judges would be practicing law when, in an attempt to settle a case, they discuss the legal merits of a case with disputing parties. A judge engaged in this common settlement technique would be engaged in unethical conduct. . . .

Clearly, we need a framework for regulating mediation. But we can develop that framework without labeling mediation as the practice of law.

NOTES AND QUESTIONS

(1) The Department of Dispute Resolution Services of the Supreme Court of Virginia adopted Guidelines on Mediation and the Unauthorized Practice of Law (UPL) in response to a UPL case filed in Virginia as an effort to "provide guidance and protection" particularly to the non-attorney mediator population. The Guidelines have sparked considerable debate on both sides of the issue. Concerns raised include that the guidelines are overly restrictive and "rob mediation of its fluidity and flexibility." In the June 2000 edition of *Alternatives*, Geetha Ravindra, director of the Department of Dispute Resolution Services explained the committee's actions in the following excerpt.[*]

[The UPL committee] recognized by definition, the mediation process is not the practice of law. There are activities, however, that mediators engage in during the mediation process, that may constitute the practice of law. The committee aspired to identify a test by which activities could be measured to assess whether they fall within the definition of the practice of law. . . .

As a result, the guidelines try to identify the extent to which evaluation may be provided in mediation without UPL concerns and when evaluation more clearly falls into the category of the practice of law. The guidelines . . . allow mediators to offer evaluation of, for example, strengths and

[*] Copyright © 2000-**CPR Institute for Dispute Resolution**, 366 Madison Avenue, New York, NY 10017-3122; (212) 949-6490. This article from June, 2000 edition of Alternatives, published by the CPR Institute, is reprinted with permission. The **CPR Institute** is a nonprofit initiative of 500 general counsel of major corporations, leading law firms and prominent legal academics whose mission is to install alternative dispute resolution (ADR) into the mainstream of legal practice. Copyright © 2000 by Geetha Ravindra. Reprinted with permission.

weaknesses of a case, assess the value and cost of settlement alternatives, or barriers to settlement.

The committee believed that mediators should not predict the specific resolution of legal issues because such activity is part of a lawyer's function as advisor and counselor and could give rise to an implicit lawyer/client relationship . . . [however] neutrals may be able to provide a range of possible outcomes under this definition.

(2) What are the arguments supporting and opposing the statement that mediation is the practice of law? Is there a relationship between style of practice and the validity of such a statement?

PUBLIC VALUES AND PRIVATE JUSTICE: A CASE FOR MEDIATOR ACCOUNTABILITY

4 Geo. J. of Legal Ethics 503, 503–505, 508–510, 514–521, 530–531, 534 (1991) *

By Judith Maute

When a mediated agreement avoids adjudication, traditional mediator neutrality undermines protection of the parties' rights.

As . . . officers of the legal system, lawyers have special responsibility for the quality of justice. . . .

. . . [N]agging questions of mediator accountability and ethics persist. The questions concern how to protect important values served in adjudication while facilitating private settlement. . . .

. . . .

. . . [W]hen mediated settlement supplants public adjudication, the mediator is accountable for procedurally fair process and minimally fair substantive outcome. Procedural intervention to insure access to relevant information and independent advice is consistent with neutrality. . . . As to substantive fairness, the probable litigated outcome should serve as a reference point; the parties are free to find a solution that better serves their personal values and concerns. The mediator, however, should refuse to finalize an agreement when one party takes undue advantage of the other, when the agreement is so unfair that it would be a miscarriage of justice, or when the mediator believes it would not receive court approval. Completed agreements failing this standard should be vulnerable to rescission for a limited period of time on request of a party or during public review. If rescission is not possible, the disadvantaged party should have recourse against a mediator for malpractice.

. . . .

A lawyer-mediator practices law in the sense of using legal knowledge to solve problems. Legal knowledge facilitates mediation. A dispute over respective rights and obligations is legal in nature. In such cases, the lawyer-mediator cannot ignore the law's relevance or one's legal knowledge. The lawyer-mediator cannot avoid the higher accountability to approximate or improve upon the likely result of litigation simply by concealing one's status as a lawyer. . . .

. . . .

. . . When the parties are not independently represented, the lawyer-mediator represents them jointly in a limited capacity. When mediating a litigable dispute, the neutral lawyer is accountable to both the legal system and her clients. . . . Where the mediation substitutes for legal process, the neutral lawyer has a duty to protect the public value of fairness. The mediator should assure, therefore, that the parties have sufficient information to make informed decisions on whether to settle privately or proceed to court. The parties must understand their respective legal positions and what might happen in court. Lacking such information, they cannot test a proposed agreement against their own sense of fairness, which is the key to successful mediation.

Considerable debate surrounds ethical restrictions on mediation. . . . Rule 2.2 of the ABA Model Rules regulates lawyers serving as "intermediaries," but not necessarily those serving as mediators. Although the Rule text superficially appears to fit, the non-binding comments to Rule 2.2 states it "does not apply to a lawyer acting as arbitrator or mediator between or among parties who are not clients of the lawyer. . . ."[28]

. . . .

The ABA should adopt a new rule governing only mediation. Proposed Rule 2.4 would apply when a lawyer undertakes to mediate a dispute between parties not previously represented by the lawyer. . . .

Proposed Model Rule 2.4
Mediator

(a) A lawyer may act as mediator to resolve a legal dispute between parties, separately represented or not, subject to the following conditions:

  1 the lawyer reasonably believes that the mediation can be undertaken impartially.

  2 the lawyer reasonably believes the dispute is suitable for mediation and the parties are able to participate effectively and to make adequately informed decisions.

  3 the parties are reasonably informed about the mediation process, including the advantages and risks involved and potential effect on the attorney-client privilege, and each party consents to participate.

(b) When the parties are not separately represented, the mediator should provide them with sufficient information about the law and its possible application so that each party can make adequately

---

[28] Model Rules Rule 2.2 comment 2.

informed decisions. Explanation of the applicable law shall occur in the presence of both parties to the mediation.

(c)   When the parties are not separately represented, the mediator may prepare a written agreement resolving the dispute subject to the following conditions:

 (1)   the terms approximate a likely adjudicated outcome, or the parties are adequately informed and voluntarily agree to different terms;

 (2)   the parties are informed of their right to seek independent legal advice, and urged to do so when the agreement addresses important legal rights;

 (3)   the lawyer may not knowingly finalize an agreement reasonably believed to be illegal, grossly inequitable, or based on false information.

(d)   The lawyer shall not communicate privately with any party regarding the substance of the mediation without obtaining the consent of all parties to the mediation. The content of private meetings is confidential and may not be disclosed to the parties without express consent of the party making the confidential disclosure.

(e)   The lawyer shall withdraw and terminate the mediation on the request of a party or if any of the conditions stated in paragraph (a) is no longer satisfied. The lawyer may terminate the mediation if it is determined that mediation is no longer appropriate. Upon withdrawal, the lawyer shall not continue to act on behalf of any of the parties in the matter that was the subject of the mediation.

. . . .

The amount of legal knowledge and preparation required can vary with the context. If serving as a volunteer in court-annexed programs to facilitate settlement of small disputes, the mediator's general knowledge of the substantive law will probably suffice. If, however, the lawyer is specially retained by parties to mediate their dispute, she is properly held to a higher standard of familiarity with the applicable law.

The limited scope of representation highlights the importance of the clients' control over the objectives of representation. . . .

The extent of obligations assumed will vary, depending on whether the parties engage independent counsel during the mediation or to review the proposed final agreement. If neither party is separately represented, the mediator represents them both in a limited capacity, and Proposed Rule 2.4 applies in full.

. . . One must consider realistically whether the parties' divergent interests are sufficient to warrant independent counsel, and whether retaining separate lawyers is feasible. If not, the mediator's role as neutral lawyer may be the parties' only chance for legal assistance to find an acceptable solution.

Proposed Rule 2.4 articulates the neutral lawyer's obligations. . . . The mediator must clarify her non-partisan role. A neutral lawyer should provide legal information jointly to the parties in a non-adversarial fashion. . . . I propose . . . a standard that the agreement approximate or improve upon the probable outcome of litigation. This incorporates the relevant substantive law and difficulties of proof, while acknowledging that personal preferences may result in an optimal private settlement at odds with probable legal outcome. . . .

Imagine, for example, a divorce mediation in which one spouse is willing to give the other a generous settlement so that she or he can quickly re-marry and alleviate guilt feelings associated with the dissolution. The mediator should accurately explain the applicable law and its probable application to their situation. The agreement should state the parties are adequately informed about the relevant law, briefly allude to the personal preferences responsible for the variance from the probable legal outcome and that they voluntarily enter the agreement because of their personal preferences.

. . . .

Only subsection (d) and the screening obligations in proposed Rule 2.4(a) would apply where parties are independently represented, Here the mediator is accountable for procedural, and not substantive, fairness. The mediator must assure a fair process, free of abusive behavior that coerces settlement favoring the stronger party. Less accountability is warranted because the parties retain a mediator only to facilitate negotiation, and expect no legal information. Here, there is no representation; civil liability should ensue only for failing to ensure the process is fair. This standard should apply whether or not the mediator is a lawyer.

Other Model rules also apply to mediation by lawyers, regardless of whether the parties are independently represented. *Model Rules* Rule 1.9 governs when a lawyer may assume a representation adverse to a former client. If a matter is substantially related to the former representation, so that confidences are likely shared, the lawyer may not assume the new representation without client consent. Before a lawyer can mediate a dispute involving a former client, informed consent is required from all parties to the mediation. Proposed Rule 2.4(d) makes explicit this principle for the neutral lawyer. Should the mediation fail, the lawyer must terminate all involvement with the dispute. Neither party should run the risk that the mediator will later serve as a partisan for the other.

Model Rules Rule 1.10 provides for imputed disqualification of the lawyer's firm. . . . Principles of limited representation and peripheral involvement should limit the risk of wholesale imputed disqualification. As a practical matter, the neutral lawyer has an extremely limited opportunity to obtain any confidential information. . . .

Additional minor amendments are warranted. *Model Rules* Rule 1.5 generally regulates lawyers' fees; proposed subsection (d) prohibits contingent fees in criminal defense and divorce representations. Mediation should be included in Rule 1.5(d). . . . To allow development of interdisciplinary mediation teams, some provision should be made regarding fee-splitting with non-lawyers and aiding in the unauthorized practice of law. . . .

For non-lawyer mediators, accountability raises delicate unauthorized practice issues. . . .

. . . .

Private mediation of legal disputes outside litigation can affect important legal rights. A party cannot evaluate the fairness of an option without minimally adequate information about the law. Mediation that does not assure each party has such information is likely to reinforce existing disparities in knowledge, resources and power. Unauthorized practice rules prohibit non-lawyers from giving legal advice and drafting legal documents. Therein lies the dilemma. . . . Restrictions against lawyers assisting another's unautho-rized practice should be narrowly construed. . . . Lawyers should be encour-aged to prepare brochures or video-tapes and to act as legal advisors to mediation teams without risking discipline for siding in the unauthorized practice of law. . . .

. . . Essentially private disputes bearing little relation to law are not of concern For routine, low-stakes consumer cases and other minor problems unlikely to be litigated, brochures may suffice. . . .

By contrast, divorce mediation requires that the parties have more precise legal information on such issues as the normal terms of separation, support, child visitation and taxes. Public concerns warrant greater lawyer involvement. . . .

. . . [T]he rules should be revised to accommodate lay mediation. Clearer ethical rules will enhance development of mediation programs which strike the proper balance between the values favoring private settlement and those concerned with protecting legitimate legal claims. Further, lawyers who medi-ate need clear guidance on the applicable law so they can better serve their mediation clients. Parties are more capable of making informed settlement choices if lawyers are encouraged to provide legal information for use in mediation.

. . . .

. . . When mediation intercedes to settle a legal dispute, additional safe-guards are needed to protect for two important values at risk with private settlement: public values of fairness and authoritative public resolution of legal conflicts. The mediator is properly held to a higher standard of account-ability. The process should enable both parties to obtain relevant information about the law and how it might apply to the instant facts, When disparities in power or knowledge disable a weaker party from effective bargaining, the mediator must intervene to avoid a patently unfair agreement at odds with the probable outcome of adjudication. Finally, these mediated agreements should receive meaningful public review to confirm they are within legal bounds and do not subvert important public values.

. . . .

. . . When access to court is short-circuited, the mediator should be account-able for the quality of private justice and its effect on public interests.

. . . .

A proposed agreement falling outside the range of acceptable outcomes war-rants further intervention. A mediator should not finalize an agreement which she believes to be illegal, grossly inequitable or based on false information.

The parties should be told of the problem and have remedies suggested to them. Mediator withdrawal remains the ultimate weapon to prevent an unfair agreement.

NOTE AND QUESTIONS

(1) Recent efforts to address the role of the lawyer/neutral have recently been initiated by CPR Institute for Dispute Resolution–Georgetown Commission on Ethics and Standards in ADR, which circulated a draft new Model Rule for comment in mid-1999, and the ABA Commission on Evaluation of the Rules of Professional Conduct ("Ethics 2000"). The CPR Commission focuses specifically on the ethical responsibilities of lawyers serving as third-party neutrals and does not address the ethical requirements of non-lawyers performing these duties or the ethical duties of lawyers acting in alternative dispute resolution proceedings as representatives or advocates. The rationale for focusing on lawyer/neutrals is the unique ethical problems which may arise—for example, confusion over the nature of the lawyer's role.

(2) Do you believe Maute's proposal is consistent with mediation as defined in the various ethical rules discussed earlier?

(3) Has Maute adequately dealt with the question of whether aspects of mediation practice may contribute to unauthorized practice of law charges?

Chapter 8

MEDIATION AND THE LAWYER

§ A INTRODUCTION

This chapter examines the relationship between litigation and mediation, and focuses on some of the special roles that lawyers play in mediation. Although people sometimes think about litigation and mediation as two entirely distinct processes, the reality is that many disputes are both litigated and mediated, sometimes virtually simultaneously. This mixing of processes affects the work of lawyers as both advocates and mediators. Section B will focus on the interrelationship between litigation and mediation. Section C focuses on the role that is and should be played by attorneys as representatives of their clients in the mediation process. It includes an examination of relevant ethical issues. Finally, Section D examines issues facing attorneys who hope to maintain "dual careers" as both litigators and mediators.

§ B THE RELATIONSHIP BETWEEN MEDIATION AND LITIGATION

Mediation and litigation are often intertwined. For example, when a case that has already been filed in court is ordered to mediation or taken to mediation voluntarily, the two processes are inevitably entangled. As the lawyers and clients engage in mediation, they must consider the implications of their mediation efforts for existing or potential future litigation. If an agreement is not reached in mediation, what is the likelihood of success in litigation? What disclosures should or should not be made during the mediation in light of the pending litigation? If an agreement *is* reached in mediation, what is gained or lost in terms of the litigation? As well, lawyers and clients must consider implications of the litigation for the mediation. Specifically, what discovery should or should not be sought in the litigation in light of the pending mediation? At what stage of the litigation does it make most sense to mediate? Should the attorney file certain motions in order to further the chances of resolving the dispute in mediation, or would it be better to delay filing such motions, for fear of wasting time or angering the opposition?

Mediation and litigation may also influence one another when a dispute that has not been filed in court is mediated. Here, although the disputants are not presently in court, they may recognize that litigation is a real possibility if the dispute is not successfully resolved through mediation or other alternative dispute resolution mechanisms. Thus, as the parties are mediating they may often be considering results that might be obtained in court, discovery that might be sought in litigation, or how information exchanged in mediation might be used in court.

As these two processes take place, it is inevitable that they will begin to influence one another. In the following excerpt, John Lande discusses the potential impact of this overlap, and suggests that we may begin to see development of a new "litimediation" culture. As you read the excerpt, consider whether you believe it is inevitable that mediation and litigation will blur into one another. Is it desirable or possible to retain the uniqueness of each process? For a related and classic discussion of the linkage between litigation and negotiation, see Robert H. Mnookin & Lewis Kornhauser, *Bargaining in the Shadow of the Law: The Case of Divorce*, 88 Yale L.J. 950 (1979).

HOW WILL LAWYERING AND MEDIATION TRANSFORM EACH OTHER?

24 Fla. St. U. L. Rev. 839, 839–41, 845–47, 879–90 (1997) *

By John Lande

In the past two decades, the use of mediation in legal disputes has increased dramatically. State legislatures have enacted statutes authorizing, and in some cases mandating, courts to order cases to mediation. In some areas, the use of mediation in litigation is so routine and accepted that lawyers do not wait to be ordered into mediation, but initiate mediation themselves. Indeed, in some places, mediation has become so much a part of the litigation process that lawyers may refrain from direct, unmediated negotiations, anticipating that they will conduct their negotiations in mediation. As court planners perceive growth in the volume and complexity of their caseloads and that their resources do not keep pace with that growth, it seems likely that many courts will find it increasingly attractive to order large numbers of cases to mediation. Where mediation becomes routinely integrated into litigation practice, we can expect that this will significantly alter both lawyers' practices in legal representation and mediators' practices in offering and providing mediation services. I describe this new dispute resolution environment as a "litimediation" culture, in which it becomes taken for granted that mediation is the normal way to end litigation.

. . . There was a time not long ago in the modern ADR era when the use of mediation in legal cases was extremely rare. It was so rare that some early mediating practitioners themselves did not have a name for the procedure. In a relatively short time, mediation has become so widely accepted that it is now enshrined in many statutes and generally viewed positively by lawyers, who are especially important actors in our adversarial legal system. Indeed, even though some statutes only authorize, but do not mandate, use of mediation, some courts routinely order most cases on their dockets to mediation. In areas where mediation has become a regular part of the litigation process, key actors in the legal system (such as judges, court administrators, and lawyers) may take it for granted that settlement negotiations will primarily take place in mediation. Shifting from a predominant culture of "litigotiation" that Professor Marc Galanter described a decade ago,[22] we may

---

* Copyright © 1997 by the Florida State University Law Review. Reprinted with permission.

[22] Galanter used the term "litigotiation" to refer to the strategic pursuit of settlement through mobilizing the court process. Thus, lawyers, and to some extent principals, pursue litigation with

be developing what might be called "liti-mediation" cultures in some areas where it has become taken for granted that mediation is the normal way of ending litigation.

In recent years, liti-mediation culture has expanded from what some might consider the isolated "backwaters" of low-status cases in areas like family law and small-claims court into the "heartland" of litigation, including legal disputes of virtually every kind. Thus, a well-developed liti-mediation culture requires a market with both a substantial variety and volume of mediators to provide a range of acceptable mediation services. Full-fledged liti-mediation cultures are especially likely to develop in larger urban areas where there are greater caseload pressures and difficulties in reaching resolution because of more tenuous relationships between lawyers and the clients themselves. Under these conditions, the pool of mediators is likely to be relatively large and characterized by relatively distant and professional (rather than close and personal) relationships with the various actors in a case.

. . . As mediation becomes a routine step in contested litigation, we can expect that mediation and litigation procedures will co-evolve, i.e., the dynamics of litigation will influence the practice of mediation and vice versa. Some obvious possibilities are that routine use of mediation in litigation could reduce the level of adversarial behavior in litigation generally, and the incorporation of mediation into the litigation process could increase the level of adversarialness in mediation.

. . . As mediation becomes more common, and especially where the courts are authorized to order cases into mediation, most lawyers will feel the need to be able to advise clients about the use of mediation, select appropriate mediators, and competently represent their clients in mediation. Indeed, the institutionalization of mediation may lead to establishment of an ethical duty to advise clients about mediation and even malpractice liability for failing to do so. Nonetheless, I suspect that informal social pressure and (actual or perceived) court mandates will influence lawyers to routinely incorporate mediation into their practices much more than the threat of professional discipline or liability. As lawyers perceive that participation in mediation is normal or even the "in thing," they are likely to take it for granted as a normal feature of the legal process.

Institutionalization of mediation is likely to result in significant redefinitions of the relationships between principals, lawyers, and mediators. Over time, lawyers and mediators in the same professional community are likely to establish distinctive reputations and ongoing relationships with each other. As the lawyers are likely to be repeat players, mediators may well see lawyers as their (the mediators') clients rather than the principals, with whom the mediators are much less likely to have repeat business. This alliance between mediators and lawyers—and mediators' great stake in their goodwill with the lawyers in their community—is likely to be reinforced if the lawyers (rather than the principals) typically do the shopping for mediators. When the lawyers in a case (or their major clients) are roughly comparable in their repeat-player

---

the private expectation of ultimately reaching settlement, but use the litigation process to gain strategic advantage in negotiation. See Marc Galanter, *Worlds of Deals: Using Negotiation to Teach About Legal Process*, 34 J. LEGAL EDUC. 268, 268 (1984).

status, the mediator would presumably be equally dependent on both lawyers and would generally not have an incentive to favor one side or another. When one side is a repeat player (such as an insurance company or a lawyer who uses mediation frequently) and the other side is not, the mediation process could consciously or unconsciously be affected by an ongoing relationship between a mediator and a lawyer.

Local norms about whether lawyers normally attend mediation sessions and, if so, how they participate may radically affect the constellation of relationships and the dynamics of the process. In some places, lawyers routinely attend mediation sessions; in other places, lawyers rarely attend. If lawyers do attend the mediation, they may affect the process dramatically. In some situations, the lawyers take a dominant role in which they do most of the talking, typically making their sides' opening statements and often responding to offers (presumably, though not necessarily, based on prior authorizations). In other situations, the lawyers are permitted only to observe and consult with their clients, but not speak for them.

Some mediators explicitly define their expectations about the lawyers' role in the mediator' opening statement. The lawyers' role is often reflected in, and affected by, the seating arrangements. The individuals seated directly next to the mediators often act as the primary spokespeople for their side. If the principals sit next to the mediator, this often signals that the lawyers are expected to act primarily as advisors to their clients rather than as advocates with the mediator and other side. Some mediators emphasize limitations on the lawyers' advisory role by insisting that the lawyers sit behind their clients rather than sitting at the table. If principals are represented by counsel but their lawyers do not attend mediation sessions, the lawyers typically review any agreement that is reached in mediation and may or may not talk with the mediators by phone.

The complicated sets of relationships between mediators, lawyers, and principals may cause confusion about the nature of the relationships and thus about what behaviors are appropriate. For example, are the principals primarily the mediators' clients, primarily the lawyers' clients, or both equally? The significance of this issue is illustrated in a simulated mediation of a personal injury case from a training video featuring a prominent Florida mediator and trainer. After the plaintiff's lawyer completed the opening statement, the mediator turned to the lawyer and, referring to the plaintiff, asked, "Would you mind if I ask her a question or two?" The question implied that the principal was primarily the lawyer's—not the mediator's—client and that the mediator could not address the principal directly without the lawyer's consent.

Should the mediator normally assume that lawyers accurately present their clients' perspectives or should mediators periodically confirm the principals' positions themselves? If principals do not appear comfortable with their lawyers' statements, would it be an improper interference in the lawyer-client relationship to suggest that the lawyers confer with their clients or to ask the principals (perhaps in caucus) to confirm their positions? These quandaries reflect an ambiguity in the relationships between mediators, lawyers, and principals. If mediators are more assertive, they risk alienating the lawyers and perhaps the principals as well. If mediators do not pursue these issues, they clearly reduce the quality of the principals' consent by failing to examine the issues carefully. Although these problems can be addressed by mediators, especially by setting expectations in the opening statements, they reflect serious potential threats to the authority of both mediators and lawyers. If mediators assume that lawyers may legitimately use an adversarial approach to mediation, even a mediator's questions to a principal may be perceived as inappropriately interfering with the lawyer's strategy. In these situations, mediators may feel quite reluctant to probe a principal's thinking in much depth.

Consider further that the question "Would you mind if I ask her a question or two?" mirrors a typical interaction in litigation in which one attorney displays respect to an *opposing attorney*. Of course, rather than being the principal's adversary, the mediator is supposed to *help* the principals. Given the fact that some mediators use strong directive tactics to pressure principals, it may well be necessary and appropriate for lawyers to protect the principals from the mediator. On the other hand, lawyers sometimes look to the mediators to provide precisely that kind of pressure on the lawyers' own clients that the lawyers feel unable or unwilling to effectively exert themselves. It is not uncommon for lawyers to believe that their clients are taking unreasonable positions but feel that they (the lawyers) cannot argue too strongly with their clients without losing the clients' confidence. Indeed, McEwen et al. reported that more than half the Maine lawyers they interviewed spontaneously identified a benefit of mediation as having mediators "challenge clients to relinquish unrealistic positions and claims," thus reinforcing the lawyers' own advice.[215]

This discussion shows how the participation of lawyers in mediation can complicate and confuse the relationships between lawyers, mediators, and principals. Given mediators' dependence on lawyers as regular sources of future business, it should not be surprising if mediators especially cater to lawyers' interests, possibly superseding the principals' interests. Indeed, mediators and lawyers may find that they share an interest in pressuring principals to settle, especially in those liti-mediation cultures where the dominant norm favors settlement per se as the primary goal of mediation.

. . . .

Institutionalization of mediation as a normal step in litigation may affect the pattern and pace of litigation. Under the mandatory divorce mediation statute in Maine, mediation has become an expected settlement event, forcing the lawyers and principals to seriously focus on the issues. McEwen and his colleagues found that the mandated mediation in Maine encouraged the lawyers and principals to settle earlier than they otherwise would have.[218] Conceivably, institutionalization of mediation could also delay settlement, depending on local judicial or legal norms about timing of settlement

---

[215] See Craig A. McEwen et al., *Bring in the Lawyers: Challenging the Dominant Approaches to Ensuring Fairness in Divorce Mediation*, 79 MINN. L. REV. 1317, 1370 (1995); see also Craig A. McEwen et al., *Lawyers, Mediation, and the Management of Divorce Practice*, 28 L. & SOC'Y REV. 149, 163-66 (1994).

[218] McEwen et al., *Bring in the Lawyers* at 1387.

negotiations. If lawyers expect that they will eventually settle the cases in mediation, they may hold off conducting direct negotiations early in litigation.

There is a split of opinion in the mediation community over the best time to conduct mediation. Some argue that mediation is most appropriate early in litigation (or better yet, before litigation), when principals have not yet hardened their positions and invested a great deal in litigation expenses. Others argue that mediation is not appropriate until late in litigation because principals can make informed decisions only after completing discovery. Whatever the local norms for the timing of mediation, where it becomes institutionalized, it is likely to be a (if not *the*) central settlement event around which other litigation activities revolve.

The involvement of lawyers in mediation may affect the timing of the process in several ways, generally adding time pressure to the mediation process. When lawyers attend mediation, the scheduling of mediation sessions may be more difficult because it obviously requires coordination of at least two additional schedules. Because lawyers often have tight schedules, the time available for mediation may be quite constrained. For example, in the dependency mediation clinic at my school, it is not unusual for lawyers to arrive late, have hearings or other appointments scheduled for a time soon after the mediation is set to begin, and be interrupted during mediation sessions by calls on their pagers and cellular phones. Given the pace of their schedules, they may want to settle cases as fast as possible, and they often express impatience if the principals, including their own clients, talk "too much." If the lawyers do not consider the parties' relationship concerns to be relevant or important, these issues may not be raised at all or discussed in much depth. When the principals are paying their lawyers on an hourly basis (often in addition to half of the mediator's fees), the principals may also feel a financial pressure to avoid dealing with issues that are not legally relevant and thus "get the mediation over" as quickly as they can.

Given all these time pressures, everyone involved may be reluctant to consider scheduling additional mediation sessions and thus may try to complete a settlement in a single meeting. When mediation takes place shortly before a scheduled trial date, it may be difficult or impossible to schedule a second session even if all the participants agree that it would be productive. The regular presence of lawyers may thus lead to a norm of mediations conducted in a single, possibly rushed session. Indeed, that is what McEwen and his colleagues observed in divorce mediation in Maine, where mediation usually involves a single mediation session lasting two to three hours.[225] By contrast, Jessica Pearson and Nancy Thoennes found that in public and private divorce mediation programs that lawyers did not attend, the mediations involved an average of 3.4 to 6.2 sessions, totaling an average of 6.3 to 8.7 hours, respectively.[226] It is possible that the difference in the amount of time in mediation is a function of whether discovery had been completed prior to mediation. Given the view of many lawyers that mediation is appropriate only after discovery has been completed, it is possible that mediations with

---

[225] McEwen et al., *Lawyers, Mediation and the Management of Divorce Practice* at 154.

[226] See Jessica Pearson & Nancy Thoennes, *Divorce Mediation Research Results, in* DIVORCE MEDIATION: THEORY AND PRACTICE (Jay Folberg & Ann Milne eds., 1988) at 429, 432.

lawyers attending are more likely to occur with discovery largely completed. Obviously, if discovery had not been completed prior to mediation, one would expect that it would take additional time in mediation to collect and analyze the relevant information. Nonetheless, the participation of lawyers is likely to add time pressure in mediation for the reasons described above.

Regular participation of lawyers in mediation sessions may also affect the negotiation dynamics in mediation, possibly encouraging use of positional dynamics of offer and counteroffer rather than a joint problem-solving effort to seek mutual gains by analyzing the principals' underlying interests. In a survey of 515 lawyers and fifty-five judges in New Jersey, Professor Jonathan Hyman and his colleagues found that, on average, the respondents estimated that about seventy percent of their cases were settled using positional methods, even though about sixty percent of the respondents said that problem-solving methods should be used more often. Hyman et al. suggest that problem-solving may be used less than lawyers would like due to fear that opponents will take advantage of them, perceived opportunities to gain advantage through positional methods, or simply habitual use of positional tactics.[229] Thus, it would not be surprising if lawyers bring an habitual positional mindset into mediation, especially if the mediator is also a lawyer or retired judge. Mediators who also have that mindset may feel inhibited about asking questions to avoid interfering with each side's positional strategy . . . .

As Professors David Lax and James Sebenius point out, lawyers' fears of losing strategic advantage through problem-solving tactics reflect real risks entailed in such an approach.[231] Lax and Sebenius also show, however, that using a mediator may reduce these risks by providing a neutral third party who can receive and analyze information in confidence.[232] Mediation can thus offer a useful forum for lawyers who want to use a problem-solving approach to negotiation. Indeed, McEwen et al.'s study suggests that mandatory divorce mediation in Maine may have offered just such opportunities and that most lawyers generally accepted them. The researchers found that lawyers generally adopt a norm of "the reasonable lawyer," who, rather than exacerbating conflict, typically tries to reduce it by "limit[ing] client expectations, resist[ing] identifying emotionally with the client, avoid[ing] substantially inflated demands, understand[ing] the likely legal outcome, assert[ing] the client's interests, respond[ing] to new information, and seek[ing] to reach a divorce settlement."[233] This finding, though at odds with many popular conceptions of lawyer behavior, is consistent with many other analyses of lawyers' settlement orientations, even outside of mediation. Being "reasonable," however, is not the same thing as using a problem-solving approach. Indeed, being "reasonable" may involve lawyers pressuring their own clients to give up demands and expectations (perhaps correctly) perceived as unreasonable,

---

[229] JONATHAN M. HYMAN ET AL., CIVIL SETTLEMENT: STYLES OF NEGOTIATION IN DISPUTE RESOLUTION (1995) at 166.

[231] See DAVID A. LAX & JAMES K. SEBENIUS, THE MANAGER AS NEGOTIATOR: BARGAINING FOR COOPERATION AND COMPETITIVE GAIN (1986) at 29-45.

[232] See id. at 172-78; see also Robert H. Mnookin, *Why Negotiations Fail: An Exploration of Barriers to the Resolution of Conflict*, 8 OHIO ST. J. ON DISP. RESOL. 235, 248-49 (1993).

[233] McEwen et al., *Bring in the Lawyers* at 1365.

rather than searching for options addressing the underlying interests of the principals. McEwen et al.'s data suggests that Maine lawyers may be more likely to address the concerns of both principals than lawyers in New Hampshire, where mediation practice is much less common. When asked about their primary goals in negotiating divorce cases (not limited to cases in mediation), 39.5% of Maine lawyers reported the goal of reaching "settlements fair to both parties," compared with 28.3% of New Hampshire lawyers, whereas only 15.8% of Maine lawyers reported the goal of "getting as much as possible for [their] client," compared with 33.3% of New Hampshire lawyers.[238] This may indicate that Maine lawyers are more likely to use problem-solving tactics, especially in mediation. Nonetheless, Hyman et al.'s data described above suggests that we should be cautious about assuming a tight link between lawyers' aspirations and actual problem-solving behavior.

As we have seen, the participation of lawyers in mediation may have quite different effects on the use of adversarial and problemsolving processes in mediation. On one hand, their participation may contribute to thorough and careful problem solving. On the other hand, their participation may inhibit such a process by incorporating traditional adversarial approaches into mediation.

QUESTIONS

(1) What does Professor Lande mean by the phrase "liti-mediation"? Do you find the concept useful?

(2) What do you predict will be the impact of the blending of litigation and mediation cultures?

(3) Would it be desirable to keep mediation more distinct from litigation? Would it be possible?

§ C LAWYERS' ROLE AS REPRESENTATIVE IN MEDIATION

Many issues surround the participation of lawyers, as representatives, in mediation. It is today well recognized that lawyers do and should perform many roles other than, or in addition to, representing clients in litigation. For example, the Preamble to the ABA Rules of Professional Conduct state:

> As a representative of clients, a lawyer performs various functions. As advisor, a lawyer provides a client with an informed understanding of the client's legal rights and obligations and explains their practical implications. As advocate, a lawyer zealously asserts the client's position under the rules of the adversary system. As negotiator, a lawyer seeks a result advantageous to the client but consistent with requirements of honest dealing with others. As intermediary between clients, a lawyer seeks to reconcile their divergent interests as an advisor and,

---

[238] McEwen et al., *Lawyers, Mediation, and the Management of Divorce Practice* at 178-79.

to a limited extent, as a spokesperson for each client. A lawyer acts as evaluator by examining a client's legal affairs and reporting about them to the client or to others.

Rule 2.1 goes on to explain that "In rendering advice, a lawyer may refer not only to law but to other considerations such as moral, economic, social and political factors, that may be relevant to the client's situation."

Given lawyers' responsibility to provide wise counsel, some have argued that lawyers have a duty, at least in some contexts, to inform their clients about mediation. The readings excerpted in Section 1 present several different perspectives on this issue, and also discuss the extent to which states have chosen to impose such a duty.

Once it has been decided that a particular dispute will be mediated, various issues arise regarding the appropriate role of the lawyer-representative in the mediation. One preliminary question is whether lawyers even ought to participation in a mediation at all. Some have argued that mediation works best when attorneys are absent from the mediation. Assuming a lawyer is going to participate in a mediation, other issues arise. What role should a lawyer play in selecting a mediator? When lawyers represent clients in mediation, is it appropriate for them to advocate on their clients' behalf? How should lawyers conduct themselves in the mediation? Should the rules' constraints on lying by lawyers be any different in mediation than they are in litigation or settlement negotiations? These questions are each addressed by the readings that follow.

[1] LAWYERS' DUTY TO ADVISE THEIR CLIENTS ABOUT MEDIATION

Opinions differ as to whether lawyers do or should have an ethical duty to advise their clients about mediation. In 1990 Professor Frank Sander and attorney Michael Prigoff engaged in a debate in the pages of the *A.B.A. Journal* regarding whether attorneys should have such a duty as to mediation or other forms of ADR. Professor Sander argued that the duty may already exist, and, if not, should be imposed. Mr. Prigoff agreed that it is often desirable, as a matter of good lawyering, to inform clients of ADR options, but suggested that it would be unwise to create an ethical duty requiring such conversations. Today, while the debate continues, several jurisdictions have adopted laws or rules either requiring or suggesting that attorneys discuss mediation or other ADR options with their clients. Some jurisdictions or commentators would require attorneys to inform their clients of particular ADR options only when the opposing attorney has suggested ADR or where ADR has been made available by the court. Writing in 1998, Professors Rogers and McEwen urge that further research still needs to be done before making it mandatory for attorneys to advise their clients about mediation. Professor Schmitz contends that not only the duty to inform one's client about ADR but also to inform oneself about ADR is already contained in the Code of Professional Responsibility.

AT ISSUE: PROFESSIONAL RESPONSIBILITY—SHOULD THERE BE A DUTY TO ADVISE OF ADR OPTIONS? YES: AN AID TO CLIENTS

A.B.A. J., Nov. 1990, at 50 [*]

By Frank E.A. Sander

Last year I put the question of mandating a duty to advise clients on alternative dispute resolution options to the students in my Legal Profession class.

Most of them answered that such a requirement already was implicit in the 1983 Model Rules of Professional Conduct, citing particularly Rule 1.4(b) ("A lawyer shall explain a matter to the extent reasonably necessary to permit the client to make informed decisions . . .") as well as some comparable provisions of the older Code of Professional Responsibility. So maybe the main argument against adopting such a requirement is that it is unnecessary.

But although many lawyers already are explaining the potential risks and benefits of dispute resolution options to their clients, many others are not. Why? For one thing, many lawyers are unfamiliar with the subject. Such unfamiliarity causes growing problems as more and more courts advocate ADR options. . . .

Every practitioner should have some knowledge of ADR options and the ability to convey that information to clients. An explicit requirement obviously is the best way to make sure lawyers become proficient in the field.

Some lawyers may be uncomfortable with involving a client with what they perceive as strategy. But if, as we repeatedly assert, our mission is to help clients find the best way to handle their disputes—not merely by litigation but also by a variety of other available techniques—why shouldn't it be part of our explicit professional obligation to canvass those options with clients?

How would we feel about a doctor who suggested surgery without exploring other possible choices?

Perhaps a number of lawyers are not now fulfilling this responsibility because of fear—because of the nagging thought that to do so may hurt them financially.

. . . .

Some attorneys also insist that their clients want to win rather than settle or mediate, but it is the client who should make that decision after being fully informed of all the available options. We might be surprised by the choices some clients will make when they are candidly told the costs and benefits of pursuing various courses.

How might such an obligation be implemented? There are many possible approaches. Attorneys could be required to hand out a brochure that describes the most common alternatives and to discuss these options with their clients and opponents. Then, as part of the attorneys' pretrial submissions, they could be required to certify compliance with that obligation. Such an approach is about to be initiated in Jackson County, Mo.

Another alternative is to have the lawyer write a letter canvassing the possible options, and then have this letter signed by the client, much as is now done with contingent fee agreements.

In the final analysis, the question may come down not to whether to recognize such an obligation, but who should do it. For surely if lawyers themselves do not take this step, others will do it for them. . . . [O]ne can readily envision a court holding a lawyer liable for malpractice because he failed to apprise his client of possibly cheaper, faster and less polarizing ways of achieving his objectives than via litigation.

AT ISSUE: PROFESSIONAL RESPONSIBILITY—SHOULD THERE BE A DUTY TO ADVISE OF ADR OPTIONS? NO: AN UNREASONABLE BURDEN

A.B.A. J., Nov. 1990, at 51 [*]

By Michael L. Prigoff

I agree with Professor Sander that we as lawyers have a professional obligation to advise our clients of all relevant information and options about the objectives of the representation, including disputes. In many cases, among these issues may be various dispute resolution methodologies.

However, I vigorously oppose what I suspect the real issue is: "Should an obligation to advise clients of dispute resolution options be a basis for professional discipline or malpractice liability?"

The argument for a disciplinary or malpractice standard is purely functional and bears no relation to traditional ethics or malpractice analysis. The rationale seems to be that ADR is "good"; not enough clients are aware of it; the best way to inform clients is to have their lawyers do it; the most efficient way to motivate lawyers to do so is to penalize them if they don't. Q.E.D. [which was to be demonstrated].

Let's look at the concept in practice. A comes into my office and asks me to sue B on a note. Even with such a simple factual pattern, there are a myriad of tactical decisions possible, even without considering ADR methodologies: Do we attempt settlement before suit? Do we file in state or federal court, and in which jurisdiction? Do we ask for a jury, and so forth.

If, instead of explaining each of these options to clients and letting them make these choices (which do not involve "the objectives of the representation," RPC 1.2(a)), I make the choices for them, is there anything that would be a basis for professional discipline or malpractice liability? I think not.

. . . .

For some clients and for some disputes, ADR options may prove more satisfactory. Yet our knowledge of which clients and which disputes are likely to benefit is woefully inadequate. Moreover, the real availability of many of these options is illusory, given their voluntary nature and the unwillingness of many parties to explore such options.

In my practice, I discuss ADR options in depth with every litigation client. Yet, despite these efforts to encourage the use of ADR, the vast majority of clients prefer to pursue conventional litigation. Clients favor our firm's approach, which stresses our role as dispute resolvers utilizing all available tools. But when the choices are made, they invariably opt for traditional litigation, which is why they sought our assistance in the first place.

What differences would the proposed obligation make in our approach? For one, we would feel constrained to provide written information about "available" options to each litigation client to protect against the allegation that we hadn't complied with the anticipated rule or standard. This, together with the time required to properly explain all options in every dispute, would add some cost to each representation, which would be more of a factor in smaller disputes.

Much as the ethical requirement of a written fee agreement for every matter is absurd in some circumstances, so would the proposed requirement be counterproductive to the goal of providing more satisfactory dispute resolution at an affordable price.

While the bar and public should be better informed about ADR, the proposal to make this responsibility a matter of professional discipline or malpractice liability is overkill and unfair micromanagement of the practice of law. In the real world of clients and lawyers, it unfairly burdens the bar and will prove counterproductive to the goals sought by ADR, at least with respect to smaller disputes.

EMPLOYING THE LAW TO INCREASE THE USE OF MEDIATION AND TO ENCOURAGE DIRECT AND EARLY NEGOTIATIONS

13 Ohio St. J. on Disp. Resol. 831, 862-63 (1998) [*]

By Nancy H. Rogers & Craig A. McEwen

Professor Frank Sander has argued that lawyers ought to have a duty to advise clients about the use of dispute resolution options. Sander argues, "[I]f . . . our mission is to help clients find the best way to handle their disputes . . . why shouldn't it be part of our explicit professional obligation to canvass those options with clients?"

An initial question is whether an attorney duty, if advisable, should be in professional responsibility rules rather than in uniform or model provisions for a statute or court rule. Colorado has imposed such a duty through its code

---

of ethics for attorneys,[181] and Michigan and Kansas through ethical provisions require lawyers to pass on the suggestion of use of alternative dispute resolution if raised by opposing counsel.[182] In Texas and Ohio, lawyers are exhorted to advise clients about dispute resolution options in lawyer creeds.[183]

Although the lawyer duties in Colorado, Texas, Michigan and Kansas were imposed through codes of ethics or interpretations of those codes, in two jurisdictions the provisions regarding lawyers' advice to clients were part of a court rule or statute. New Jersey lawyers are required by Supreme Court rule to inform clients of dispute resolution.[184] An Arkansas statute "encourages" lawyers to advise clients about dispute resolution processes.[185]

The more important question is not the placement of such duties in ethical provisions versus rules or statutes, but rather their advisability as a means to increase use of mediation. . . .

[C]orporate research . . . tells the story of lawyers who had been directed to consider mediation in their cases but who typically found a reason why mediation would not be appropriate. Those who ultimately began to recommend mediation regularly did so only after incentives regarding discovery were changed, after experience attending mediation sessions and after change in their office legal community. This research does not provide a strong endorsement for lawyer duties. It seems wise to await more research documenting changes in the bar in Colorado, Arkansas and elsewhere under their new provisions for attorneys before concluding that duties for lawyers to advise about mediation should be a part of the uniform or model mediation statute.

GIVING MEANING TO THE SECOND GENERATION OF ADR EDUCATION: ATTORNEYS' DUTY TO LEARN ABOUT ADR AND WHAT THEY MUST LEARN

1999 J. Disp. Resol. 29, 33–35 [*]

By Suzanne J. Schmitz

The codes of professional responsibility that govern attorneys establish a duty to know and understand alternative dispute resolution. Some jurisdictions have made that duty explicit, but even where it is not explicit, the codes imply such a duty.

---

[181] See *Colorado Adopts Ethics Rule*, 10 ALTERNATIVES TO HIGH COST LITIG. 70, 70 (1992).

[182] See Kansas Bar Association Ethics Advisory Committee, Opinion No. 94-1 (1994); State Bar of Michigan Standing Committee on Professional and Judicial Ethics, Opinion No. RI-255 (1996).

[183] See *Texas Supreme Court Lawyer's Creed; A Lawyer's Creed*, 70 OHIO ST. B. ASS'N RPTR. xli (1997).

[184] See N.J. SUP. CT. R. 1:40-1 (West 1998).

[185] See ARK. CODE ANN.' 16-7-101 (Michie 1997).

[*] Copyright © 1999 by the Curators of the University of Missouri. Reprinted with permission of the Journal of Dispute Resolution.

The lawyer owes the client the duty of competence. This duty encompasses the possession of legal skills and knowledge of court rules, such as those governing ADR. The attorney is also obligated to "abide by a client's decision concerning the objectives of representation, . . . and [to] consult with the client as to the means by which they are to be pursued."[35] The lawyer "should defer to the client regarding such questions as the expense to be incurred[. . .]."[36] Another of the attorney's duties is to "make reasonable efforts to expedite litigation consistent with the interests of the client"[37] The lawyer's duty as a counselor requires the lawyer to "render candid advice. In rendering advice, a lawyer may refer not only to law but to other considerations such as moral, economic, social and political factors, that may be relevant to the client's situation."[38]

These ethical obligations, when read as a whole, make clear the lawyer's duty to advise about, and thus to be informed about, ADR. Where local court rules adopt ADR programs or require counsel to report on the advisability of ADR, counsel must understand ADR processes in order to fulfill the ethical duty of competence. In order to address client concerns about cost-savings and speedy resolutions, lawyers must advise about ADR. For example, in Colorado and Hawaii, in matters involving or expected to involve litigation, the lawyer "should advise a client of alternative forms of dispute resolution which might reasonably be pursued to attempt to resolve the legal dispute or to reach the legal objective sought."[40] Georgia provides that "a lawyer as advisor has a duty to advise the client as to various forms of dispute resolution. When a matter is likely to involve litigation, a lawyer has a duty to inform the client of forms of dispute resolution which might constitute reasonable alternatives to litigation."[41]

To ensure that lawyers meaningfully counsel the client, Georgia requires lawyers to complete course work in ADR. Many states offer programs in ADR as part of their continuing education programs or incorporate ADR processes into programs on related topics. Further, lawyers are imposing on themselves a duty to counsel clients about ADR, and thus, to be informed about ADR. One example of such a duty appears in the Lawyer's Creed of Professionalism, which states that "in appropriate cases I will counsel my client with respect to mediation, arbitration and other alternative means of resolving disputes," and "I will endeavor to achieve my client's lawful objectives in business transactions and in litigation as expeditiously and economically as possible."[44]

---

[35] A.B.A. ANNOTATED MODEL RULES OF PROFESSIONAL CONDUCT Rule 1.2(a) (1996).

[36] Id. at Rule 1.2(a) cmt. 1.

[37] Id. at Rule 4.1.

[38] Id. at Rule 2.1.

[40] HAW. RULES OF PROFESSIONAL CONDUCT Rule 2.1 (1998); see also COLO. RULES OF PROFESSIONAL CONDUCT Rule 2.1 (1998); Kan. Bar Assoc. Ethics/Advisory Comm., Op. 94-01 (April 15, 1994); Mich. Comm. On Ethics, Op. RI-255 (April 3, 1996); Pa. Comm. On Legal Ethics and Prof. Resp., Op. 90-125 (Jan. 1, 1991) (ethics opinions regarding the lawyer's obligation to advise about offers to use ADR).

[41] GA. CODE OF PROFESSIONAL RESPONSIBILITY Canon 7-5 (1996).

[44] Lawyer's Creed of Professionalism, 1988 A.B.A. SEC. TORT & INS. PRACS. ANN. MEETING A(2) and (3).

Many commentators support the argument that the attorney must advise the client about ADR. The lawyer, like the physician, must inform the client of all the choices available so that the client may make an informed choice.

NOTES AND QUESTIONS

(1) Do attorneys currently have a duty to inform their clients of the availability of mediation in particular? Under what circumstances? What, if any, sanction can be applied against attorneys who fail to fulfill such a duty? What does your own jurisdiction require?

(2) One commentator has argued that attorneys have a duty to inform their clients about mediation where it might save them money. Stuart M. Widman, *Attorneys' Ethical Duties to Know and Advise Clients About Alternative Dispute Resolution*, Prof. Law. 18 (1993 symposium issue). What do you think of this argument?

(3) In your view, *should* there be a duty for attorneys to inform their clients of the availability of mediation as an alternative to negotiation or litigation? If so, when should such a duty arise? In all cases? Only if opposing counsel has offered to try to resolve the dispute through mediation? In what body of law should such a duty be contained? (Court rule? Statute? Code of Ethics?) For an argument that "[t]he ABA should amend the Model Rules to require lawyers to present the option of pursuing ADR to the client," see Robert F. Cochran Jr., *ADR, the ABA, and Client Control: A Proposal that the Model Rules Require Lawyers to Present ADR Options to Clients*, 41 S. Tex. L. Rev. 183, 200 (1999). *See also* Marshall J. Breger, *Should an Attorney be Required to Advise a Client of ADR Options?*, 13 Geo. J. Legal Ethics 427, 460 (arguing that the ABA should adopt a rule providing that "[a] lawyer has a duty to inform his client about the availability and applicability of alternative dispute resolution procedures that are reasonably appropriate under the circumstances").

(4) One commentator has suggested that attorneys who do not adequately inform their clients regarding mediation or other ADR options might be subject to malpractice claims. Robert F. Cochran, Jr., *Legal Representation and the Next Steps Toward Client Control: Attorney Malpractice for Failure to Allow the Client to Control Negotiation and Pursue Alternatives to Litigation*, 47 Wash. & Lee L. Rev. 819 (1990). Do you think such actions would have a high likelihood of success? Why or why not?

(5) In your view, do attorneys currently have a duty to learn about mediation or other forms of ADR? If they have such a duty, where is it currently enunciated?

(6) Do you believe attorneys *should* have a duty to inform themselves about mediation?

(7) For an article discussing lawyers' duty to discuss ADR in the family law context, see Nicole Pedone, *Lawyer's Duty to Discuss Alternative Dispute*

Resolution: In the Best Interest of Children, 36 Fam. & Conciliation Cts. Rev. 65 (1998).

[2]   DOES THE PARTICIPATION OF LAWYERS BENEFIT OR HARM THE MEDIATION PROCESS?

As an empirical matter, the extent to which attorneys attend and participate in mediation varies substantially by jurisdiction as well as by type of mediation. Lawyers are generally less likely to participate as advocates in family mediation than they are in non-family civil litigation. However, due to both cultural differences and divergences in statutes and court rules, there is substantial variation in both categories from jurisdiction to jurisdiction. In Maine, attorneys typically accompany their clients to family mediations, whereas in Missouri they do not.

Mediators and commentators debate the question of whether the participation of attorney/advocates in the mediation process is helpful or harmful to reaching a satisfactory resolution to the dispute. Some argue that attorneys undercut the process, because their adversarial perspective is inherently inconsistent with what ought to be the problem-solving or win-win approach of mediation. Pursuant to this perspective, a number of states have permitted mediators to prohibit lawyers from participating in mediation in certain contexts. *See e.g.,* Mont. Code Ann. § 40-4-302(3)(divorce), S.D. Codified Laws § 25-4-59 (divorce). In contrast, several other states provide that a mediator may not exclude counsel from participating in the mediation. *See, e.g.,* Neb. Rev. Stat. § 42-810, N.D. Cent. Code § 14-09.1-05, Wis. Stat. § 655.58(5).

Where attorneys are permitted to participate in the mediation, some commentators, such as Mark Rutherford, have suggested that to the extent the attorney participates at all, he or she should do so non-adversarially. Such a non-adversarial attorney would help to ensure that the agreement is fair, but not help his or her client secure any advantage.

On the other hand, some have argued that the presence and active participation of attorneys is beneficial to the mediation process. Craig A. McEwen, Nancy H. Rogers, and Richard J. Maiman suggest that it is important for lawyers to participate in mediation to protect the rights and interests of their clients. Ronald J. Gilson and Robert H. Mnookin further suggest that lawyers may actually help their clients reach a mutually acceptable agreement that might not otherwise have been achievable due to lack of trust, cooperation, and other factors.

LAWYERS AND DIVORCE MEDIATION: DESIGNING THE ROLE OF "OUTSIDE COUNSEL"

Mediation Q. 17, 18, 23-27, 31-32 (June 1986) *

By Mark C. Rutherford

For centuries now, attorneys have participated in a legal system that pits one party against another. Our judicial system relies on this adversarial process in order to bring about just and informed decisions. Synonyms for the word "lawyer" (for example, prosecutor, advocate) reflect not only this competitive atmosphere, but the resulting derogatory attitude society has taken toward the lawyer (for example, shyster, ambulance chaser, mouthpiece). . . .

In light of these shortcomings, mediation has emerged as a viable and promising alternative to litigation. It is a system that allows the disputants to be more personally involved in shaping their own remedy, rather than having one imposed on them by a tribunal whose understanding and creative options are sometimes hampered by restrictive procedures.

. . . .

There are three basic phases where outside counsel * can participate in the mediation process: (1) the pre-mediation referral process; (2) acting as an expert adviser in ongoing mediation consultations; and (3) review of the final mediated agreement, which may include drafting a legally binding marital agreement and representing the client(s) in court. . . .

. . . .

The most active role for outside counsel in the mediation process . . . is that of a zealous advocate of his or her client's interests. In every community there are attorneys who believe the highest achievement of the practitioner's art is the ruthless pursuit of a client's divorce case. . . . But this attitude . . . is in direct conflict with the objectives of divorce mediation. . . . This may instill unreasonable expectations in the couple, initiate unnecessarily divisive bargaining, prolong the mediation process, and increase animosity that may reduce the prospects for adherence to the agreement reached. . . .

Such problems can be avoided by abandoning the adversarial premise when dealing with divorce mediation. The adversarial process is designed to enable a neutral tribunal to rely on each party's counsel's zealous preparation and presentation of facts and law, in order to make informed decisions. This whole system revolves around the premise that a decision needs to be made by a neutral tribunal. Since the advent of no-fault divorce, this concept is not required when mediation is used to dissolve a marriage. Mediation is not a zero sum process; rather, it should focus on a compromised result. There is no need for pleadings and presentations to disinterested neutral tribunals. It is up to the couple to negotiate and make decisions.

* [Ed. note: "Outside counsel" is the phrase Mr. Rutherford uses to describe an independently retained attorney.]

By giving outside counsel the responsibility for ensuring that the parties are fully informed, the ABA Standards have acquiesced to the adversarial process. When each participant is advised from an adversarial perspective, the mediator becomes an extra party in an adversarial negotiation between the couple's outside counsels, thereby hampering the negotiations and increasing costs. . . .

. . . .

For mediation to succeed as a profession and to reach its highest objectives, advocacy has no place in any part of the process. For outside counsel to advocate a client's interests contradicts the very essence of mediation and can produce inequitable results.

. . . .

For mediation to be effective . . . total neutrality is essential. The foundation of the mediation model is for the mediator to be a neutral intermediary rather than an advocate for either party. . . . The next step is the recognition that the function of outside counsel is an extension of the process that the mediating attorney is performing, and in order to have a successful relationship between these two lawyering roles, it is necessary for both to respect the need for neutrality in mediation. In essence, there are two non-adversarial lawyering components in divorce mediation: the mediating attorney, and outside counsel. . . .

. . . .

. . . When an agreement has been obtained, the parties can request their outside counsel to evaluate and make corrective suggestions, not from an adversarial standpoint, but from a mediation orientation based on a standard of fairness and maximization, similar to a consulting opinion. . . . [T]he outside counsel can function as a check and balance system to assure the correctness of the mediated agreement. . . .

The other function of outside counsel is advisory. If qualified, the outside counsel can function as a specialist furnishing second opinions during the mediation. For example, the couple may have complex tax consequences concerning their separation, and as a tax specialist the outside counsel can advise the couple how to "maximize" their financial interests from a mediation orientation rather than from an adversarial one. . . .

. . . .

Dual representation by outside counsel of a couple who have mediated a settlement agreement is compatible with the spirit of the approach presented here.

BRING IN THE LAWYERS: CHALLENGING THE DOMINANT APPROACHES TO ENSURING FAIRNESS IN DIVORCE MEDIATION

79 Minn. L. Rev. 1317, 1319, 1322, 1376-77, 1394-95 (1995) [*]

By Craig A. McEwen, Nancy H. Rodgers, & Richard J. Maiman

Mandatory divorce mediation is under attack. According to some critical commentators, divorce mediation reinforces bargaining imbalances between parties and places women at a disadvantage. . . .

Mediation proponents respond that mandatory mediation can produce results as fair as or more fair than those achieved through a traditional divorce system, and they praise mediation's benefits as compared to litigation. To insure fairness, however, proponents sometimes advocate regulation. . . .

. . . .

. . . [W]e argue that the debate about fairness in divorce mediation, as well as the resulting legal schemes based on either the "regulatory" or "voluntary participation" approaches, results from the view that one must choose between a "lawyered" process ending in the courtroom, and an informal, problem-solving process involving parties but not lawyers in the mediation room. In our view, this dichotomy has unnecessarily narrowed the policy choices underlying mediation schemes, because it assumes that lawyers either cause conflict or act as mouthpieces for clients with a cause; that the divorce process is one in which, absent mediation (where lawyers do not appear), aggressive lawyers contest custody cases at hearings; and that mediators either protect parties' interests or pressure them toward a particular (and sometimes unjust) settlement.

We challenge these assumptions and the two approaches in statutes and court rules that follow from them—the "regulatory" and the "voluntary participation" approaches. We argue that the mediation scheme in Maine, where attorneys participate regularly and vigorously in mandated divorce mediation, provides a third avenue—one we call the "lawyer-participant" approach. Research evidence about this third approach undermines the assumptions that have confined the debate about fairness. . . .

. . . .

Most fairness concerns evaporate if lawyers attend mediation sessions with the parties or if the parties opt out of the process when unrepresented. Less intrusive regulations, such as judicial review of agreements, prohibition of settlement pressures, and provisions for unrepresented parties, may moderate the remaining fairness issues. The detailed rules of the "regulatory approach" largely become unnecessary to preserve fairness if lawyers are present.

By encouraging lawyer presence and permitting modification of the mediation ground rules, this scheme is more flexible and certain in responding to

---

the problems of bargaining imbalances and mediator pressures. Especially given the unpredictability and changing situational character of these challenges to fairness, the presence of lawyers in the process can assure necessary help in those unpredictable circumstances. The Maine research shows that with lawyers present as advisors and potentially as spokespersons, the risks of unfairness decline, even in the most unbalanced situations. By permitting adjustment of the mediation process (for example, allowing shuttle mediation), mediation can be tailored to fit particular relationships and issues in each case.

Lawyers prevent or moderate the effects of a face to face encounter with an abuser, thus diminishing the likelihood of unfairness in domestic violence cases. Maine lawyers attending mediation sessions with their clients report arranging separate sessions, time-outs, and other measures to protect their clients. Past violence, which may be a key factor in determining whether the parties will submit to an unfair settlement or will be forced into a frightening situation, becomes less of a bargaining factor if the parties attend with their lawyers. Lawyers can advise clients to avoid settlements that will allow further opportunities for abuse, or that are unlikely to be obeyed, or that are bad deals. Lawyers can also advise their clients to terminate mediation sessions. . . .

Issue limitations also become unnecessary if lawyers attend and can advise on economic trade-offs and legal issues. There is no more danger in combining the issues in mediation than exists if disposition of all issues occurs outside of mediation.

So, too, an assumption that lawyers will be absent underlies reliance on mediator qualifications as a means to ensure fairness. Absent lawyers, mediators must have at least some of the skills and knowledge that lawyers would otherwise provide. In fact, Maine divorce lawyers acknowledge that they sometimes get poor mediators. In these cases, the lawyers simply take charge and use the sessions as four-way negotiation sessions. Although mediator qualifications involving advanced educational degrees may help increase settlements or party confidence, they are unnecessary to protect against unfairness under the "lawyer-participant" approach, because mediators need not substitute their knowledge for that of lawyers. Lawyers can intervene (as discussed above) to compensate for inferior mediators and can request their removal.

Mediator duties to appraise [sic] parties of various legal rights, to terminate mediation, and to moderate bargaining imbalances also rest on the assumption that lawyers are absent in mediation. Obviously, requirements for post-mediation review of settlements by lawyers rest on the assumption that the lawyer does not take part in the give-and-take of negotiations.

In other words, lawyer participation reduces substantially the need for regulation. . . .

. . . .

Critics and proponents of mandatory divorce mediation recognize potential for unfairness in its use. They should also realize that the remedy is that lawyers should participate, along with their clients, in mandatory divorce mediation. Alternative approaches—the "voluntary participation" and "regulatory" approaches—are ineffective and costly. Furthermore, the assumptions underlying these dominant approaches are myths.

With lawyers present and participating, the concern for fairness no longer justifies heavy regulation or confining mediation to voluntary participants. Lawyer participation in the mediation sessions permits intervention on behalf of clients and buffers pressures to settle. Lawyers may also counsel clients to moderate extreme demands. In addition, once lawyers become accustomed to mediation, lawyer involvement in mandated mediation does not appear to prevent the meaningful participation of parties or inhibit emotional expression between spouses.

With mediation covering a broad scope of issues and with lawyers in attendance, the parties probably will pay more for lawyers and less for mediators. Overall costs, however, will probably remain unchanged because settlements are more likely to be comprehensive and less likely to fall victim to negative reviews by a non-participating lawyer. In addition, mediation with lawyers may reduce discovery costs. What the parties will get is likely to be a fair process in which lawyers intervene to protect against pressures from the other party, the process, or the mediator. They are also likely to get a more spontaneous mediation, unfettered by a web of regulation or defensive mediators. They will enjoy, as compared with parties in a system without mandatory mediation, a greater likelihood of having the opportunity to express themselves and to listen to discussions regarding matters of utmost concern. About one-half the time, they can expect to secure a settlement earlier in the process than would otherwise be the case.

Bringing the lawyers into mandatory mediation will permit the repeal of numerous statutes and a reduction in court rules. Furthermore, it will ease fairness concerns as a reason not to compel participation in mediation. The revised regulatory approach preserves the widespread use and flexibility of the mediation process without undue risk of unfairness.

DISPUTING THROUGH AGENTS: COOPERATION AND CONFLICT BETWEEN LAWYERS IN LITIGATION

*94 Colum. L. Rev. 509, 510–14, 522–23, 527–28, 530, 564–66 (1994)**

By Ronald J. Gilson & Robert H. Mnookin

Do lawyers facilitate dispute resolution or do they instead exacerbate conflict and pose a barrier to the efficient resolution of disputes? A distinctive characteristic of our formal mechanisms of conflict resolution is that clients carry on their disputes through lawyers. . . .

. . . Today, the dominant popular view is that lawyers magnify the inherent divisiveness of dispute resolution. According to this vision, litigators rarely cooperate to resolve disputes efficiently. . . .

. . . .

. . . We suggest that, in contrast to clients who are unlikely to litigate against one another ever again, lawyers are repeat players who have the opportunity to establish reputations. At the core of our story is the potential for disputing parties to avoid the prisoner's dilemma inherent in much litigation by selecting cooperative lawyers whose reputations credibly commit each party to a cooperative strategy.

. . . .

. . . The prisoner's dilemma provides a useful heuristic to illuminate a common characteristic of dispute settlement through litigation. In many disputes, each litigant may feel compelled to make a contentious move either to exploit, or to avoid exploitation by, the other side. Yet, the combination of contentious moves by both results in a less efficient outcome than if the litigants had been able to cooperate.

. . . .

. . . We are now ready to introduce individual lawyers into the clients' prisoner's dilemma model of litigation. Assuming the particular litigation game has the payoff structure of a prisoner's dilemma, each client would prefer mutual cooperation to mutual defection. However, each lacks the means credibly to commit to her good intentions. . . . [W]e show how disputing through lawyers may provide a means to make such a commitment: Lawyers, acting as agents, have the potential to solve the game theoretic problem of mutual defection. . . .

. . . .

Assume that both clients must litigate through a lawyer (an assumption that, for a change, *is* descriptively accurate). Further suppose that there exists a class of sole practitioners who have reputations for cooperation which assure that, once retained, they will conduct the litigation in a cooperative fashion. Three final assumptions define our "pre-litigation game." First, clients disclose their choice of lawyer—and thus, whether they have chosen a cooperative lawyer—prior to the beginning of the litigation game. Second, if one client chooses a cooperative lawyer and her opponent does not, the client choosing a cooperative lawyer can change her mind without cost before the litigation game begins. Third, after the litigation game begins, clients cannot change lawyers.

Under these assumptions, disputing through lawyers provides an escape from the prisoner's dilemma. As we have defined the pre-litigation game, each client's dominant strategy is to choose a cooperative lawyer because the choice of a cooperative lawyer binds each client to a cooperative strategy. If client A chooses a cooperative lawyer and client B also chooses a cooperative lawyer, both clients receive the higher cooperative payoff. Alternatively, if client B does not choose a cooperative lawyer, client A is no worse off having initially chosen to cooperate. In that event, client A replaces her cooperative lawyer with a gladiator and is in the same position as if she had chosen a gladiator in the first instance. Thus, her dominant strategy is to choose a cooperative lawyer and to switch if her opponent does not adopt a parallel strategy. Of course, client B confronts the same choices and has the same dominant strategy. The result is a cooperative equilibrium because the introduction of lawyers has transformed the prisoner's dilemma payoff structure into a game in which the only choices are mutual cooperation or mutual defection. Mutual cooperation obviously has the higher payoff for each party.

. . . .

The employment of lawyers with identifiable reputations does have the potential to facilitate cooperation between clients in litigation. However, the use of agents to make credible the commitment to cooperate itself poses two potential agency problems. First, the two lawyer-agents may "conspire" to maximize their incomes at the expense of their clients through noncooperative behavior that prolongs the litigation and increases legal fees. . . . Second, a client may subvert a lawyer with a reputation for cooperation. . . . For a lawyer with a limited number of clients, a particular client may be so important that the threat of withdrawn patronage may induce the lawyer to risk his cooperative reputation by behaving noncooperatively. In other words, there may be circumstances in which incentives may induce a lawyer to abandon his cooperative reputation.

. . . .

Problems of self-interest and client pressure hinder the use of sole practitioners as cooperative agents. Using law firms as reputational repositories has the potential to mitigate these problems. But, as with sole practitioners, the game theory-agency theory dialectic also plagues the use of law firms to overcome the problem of credible commitment. Solving the cooperation problem through the use of an organization as primary agent simply exposes a different set of agency problems that arise between the organization and its own agents—the individual lawyers composing the firm.

. . . .

Our story weaves together three principal ideas: (a) the prisoner's dilemma offers a suggestive and powerful metaphor for some aspects of litigation; (b) a lawyer's reputation may serve to bond a client's cooperation in the litigation process, thereby resolving the prisoner's dilemma; and (c) principal-agent conflicts (whether between lawyers and clients, or between lawyers and their firms) create incentives that sometimes facilitate cooperation in litigation but that, at other times, undermine cooperation. Our message is that the relationship between opposing lawyers and their capacity to establish credible reputations for cooperation have profound implications for dispute resolution: if the payoff structure establishes cooperation as the most desirable strategy and supportive institutional structures exist, lawyers may be able to damp conflict, reduce transaction costs, and facilitate dispute resolution.

Our story rests fundamentally on the idea that lawyers develop reputations, and that the reputation for being a cooperative problem-solver may be a valuable asset. When opposing lawyers know and trust each other, we believe there often will be substantial opportunities for both parties to benefit by reducing transaction costs. Our analysis, however, is limited by the absence of data. To be sure, we offer examples of professional settings—commercial litigation and family law practice—where behavior is consistent with our framework. But further empirical research, devoted to understanding what lawyers really do, might usefully explore a variety of empirical questions relating to the idea of reputational markets for lawyers.

. . . .

Theory suggests that a reputational market would operate most effectively when the size of the legal community is comparatively small. The actions of lawyers can then be well publicized, and lawyers can expect to face each other repeatedly in the future. Thus our analysis at least suggests why small-town lawyers may be less prone to exacerbate disputes with one another than are big-city lawyers, and also why one might expect to see a greater degree of cooperation within certain specialties than within the general community of attorneys. These questions suggest opportunities for empirical research to see whether there are significant differences among the levels of cooperation in various communities, and to what extent one can explain these differences by the existence (or nonexistence) of reputation markets.

. . . .

We began our inquiry by asking whether lawyers facilitate dispute resolution or instead exacerbate conflict. Common sense and anecdotal observation together suggest that lawyers sometimes help and sometimes hurt. Our goal has been to provide a theoretical framework to understand better when conflict and cooperation occur and how we can facilitate greater cooperation. The analysis presented represents an early reconnaissance mission that suggests for ourselves (and we hope for others) the value of further exploration—both theoretical and empirical.

NOTES AND QUESTIONS

(1) The The February 2001 Interim Draft UMA provides, in Section 9, that "An attorney or other individual designated by a party may accompany that party and participate in a mediation. A waiver of such participation given prior to the mediation may be rescinded." Do you favor adoption of such a provision? Why or why not?

(2) What do you perceive as the potential drawbacks, if any, of having attorneys participate in mediations as advocates?

(3) What do you perceive as the potential advantages, if any, of having attorneys participate in mediations as advocates? How do the advantages touted by Rogers and McEwen compare to those offered by Gilson and Mnookin? For a more complete explication of Professor Mnookin's views on how lawyers can assist in the settlement process, see Robert H. Mnookin, Scott R. Peppet, & Andrew S. Tulumello, *Beyond Winning: Negotiating to Create Value in Deals and Disputes* (2000).

(4) Should states be permitted to require disputants to mediate their disputes without the assistance of an attorney? Would such a restriction raise any constitutional concerns?

[3] LAWYERS' ROLE IN SELECTING A MEDIATOR

While in some court settings the mediator is simply assigned by the court, often disputants are given the opportunity to select their own neutral. First, when mediation is conducted pre-suit, or voluntarily, the disputants have complete discretion to select a mediator. Second, even when mediation is court ordered, many jurisdictions allow disputants to choose the mediator, rather than simply assigning a mediator from court staff or off of a roster. *See* Mo. Sup. Ct. Rule 17.03 (allowing court to appoint neutral when parties cannot agree); Fla. R. Civ. P. 1.720(f)(1) (providing parties with 10-day period in which to appoint mediator of own choosing).

The reality, for better or for worse, is that attorneys rather than their clients typically make the selection of a mediator when this discretion is left to the disputant. That is, in those many situations in which disputants are authorized to select their own mediator, and when they are represented by counsel, they often delegate this responsibility to their attorneys. Some attorneys may simply make a selection without consulting their clients. When clients are consulted, they often elect to leave the selection of the mediator up to their attorneys. Clients may believe that their attorneys are likely to be more qualified than they are in identifying both the traits that are desirable in a mediator and those individuals that possess such traits.

The fact that attorneys, rather than clients, are typically responsible for selecting the mediator likely has a significant impact on which persons tend to be called upon most frequently to be mediators. For example, because attorneys tend to focus on the legal aspects of disputes they are likely to believe that it is important for a mediator to be knowledgeable regarding the relevant law. They will often select an attorney and quite possibly a retired judge as a mediator. Attorneys will typically pick someone they know, such as a former attorney with whom or against whom they have litigated. Perhaps if clients held more responsibility for selecting mediators, they would be more likely to select persons who were knowledgeable in areas such as psychology, communications, science, or accounting, but who were not necessarily attorneys. Greater client participation in the selection process might also increase the diversity among mediators in terms of race, gender, and ethnicity. Today, most of the mediators who handle large civil cases are white men.

The following reading by David Geronemus outlines the factors attorneys ought to consider when they select a mediator. In doing so, Mr. Geronemus relies significantly on Professor Riskin's four-quadrant grid, which divides mediators along the dimensions of evaluative to facilitative and broad to narrow. *See* Chapter 4, Section 4[B], *supra.* Emphasizing that the "grid" is a good starting point for the selection of a mediator, Mr. Geronemus suggests that attorneys should also consider a variety of other factors relating to expertise, style and philosophy. He argues that attorneys ought to think through their decision carefully, in each case, based on their perceptions of what barriers are precluding the case from settling. A mediator who might be right for one dispute would not be right for another. Moreover, there may be many situations in which interpersonal skills are more important than legal knowledge.

The second reading, by Professor Jean Sternlight, briefly describes the professional responsibility literature on how attorneys and clients ought to divide decisionmaking responsibilities. After reading the material presented by Professor Sternlight, consider whether, as a matter of ethics, attorneys have a duty to consult with their clients regarding the selection of mediators.

MEDIATION OF LEGAL MALPRACTICE CASES: PREVENTION AND RESOLUTION

609 PLI/Lit 847, 860-66 Practising Law Institute Litigation and Administrative Practice Course Handbook Series Litigation PLI Order No. H0-003Q (June, 1999)*

By David Geronemus

The issue of choosing the right mediator might best be phrased as finding the mediator who is most likely to be successful in helping to resolve the dispute. There are certain clear prerequisites. Obviously any mediator should be neutral and respected by both sides. In this regard, consider how one should react to a mediator proposed by an opponent—especially one that the opponent has used before. Although some litigants reflexively reject a mediator the other side has used before, it is interesting to note that such a mediator presumably has the respect of the opposition. If the mediator agrees with you on the merits of the case, it will be difficult for your opponents to walk away from the mediator's advice. Thus, it is often worth investing the time to determine whether you can become comfortable with the mediator's neutrality. If so, he or she may well be a serious candidate for your mediation. This analysis also leads to the proposition that picking a mediator because you believe he or she may be sympathetic to you on the merits can be hazardous. Even if you are able to convince the other side to use your candidate, unless the other side perceives the mediator as neutral and fair throughout the process, he or she will be able to have little impact.

The mediation process that you participate in will vary enormously depending on the mediator you choose. In picking a mediator, it is important to begin with a general understanding of the range of available options.

One useful way of classifying mediators is to consider whether they rely principally on "evaluative" techniques or on "facilitative" techniques. See L. Riskin, *Mediator Orientations, Strategies and Techniques,* 12 Alternatives 111 (1994). [Ed. note: For the more complete article, see Leonard L. Riskin, *Understanding Mediators' Orientations, Strategies, And Techniques: a Grid For The Perplexed*, 1 Harv. Negotiation L. Rev. 7 (1996) (*See* Chapter 4, Section 4[B], *supra.*)]. Briefly stated, a purely evaluative mediator focuses on the strengths and weaknesses of the parties' cases, while a purely facilitative mediator will not offer an opinion on these issues, focusing his or her attention on clarifying communications and issues, defusing emotion, and curing any information deficiencies that may retard settlement. In addition, mediators

---

differ in whether they focus only on parties' legal rights or whether they also attempt to find creative solutions that satisfy the parties' underlying needs or interests. *Id*.

Even within these broad categories, mediators differ widely in their approaches. For example, some evaluative mediators tend to offer their views of the case early in the proceedings; others view evaluation as one of many impasse breaking techniques, and will offer evaluative feedback only as necessary to break an impasse—typically in the latter stages of the mediation. Indeed, this distinction can be crucially important to the success of the process, since the "right" evaluation at the wrong time can cause one of the parties to decide that the process is not worth pursuing. In addition, if a mediator evaluates the case before the parties have negotiated to impasse, there is always the risk that the evaluation will itself become a barrier to settlement. For example, assume that the opening positions before a mediation are $2 million demanded and $25,000 offered. Unbeknownst to the enthusiastically evaluative mediator, the plaintiff is really willing to settle for $250,000, not much more than the defendant would be willing to pay. I suspect that if the mediator produces an early evaluation of say $500,000, the mediator will have gone a long way towards making the case more difficult to settle. On the other hand consider what might occur if the mediator withheld the evaluation until the parties had negotiated to impasse at say $275,000 demanded and $200,000 offered. A well-reasoned statement by the mediator that the defendant should add to her offer may well be effective in breaking the impasse.

Mediators also differ in the extent to which they will want to work with the parties in structuring the process and in the kind of process that they prefer. For example, some mediators will want to work with the parties as soon as they are retained to discuss what kind of process makes sense. Others leave the process structure entirely to the parties. Some mediators will talk to the parties or counsel prior to the mediation to gain an understanding of the problems and opportunities that they may face at the mediation; others rely on the impressions that they gain in the mediation. Some mediators rely extensively on joint sessions, others do most of their work in private caucuses. And, of course, mediators differ in the substantive legal expertise that they bring to the process. Finally, some mediators have worn a judge's robes; others have not.

These differences among mediators lead to two points about choosing the right mediator for a case. First, given the extent of these differences, at least for cases with relatively high stakes, it is important to spend time learning in some detail about prospective mediators. Relying on a mediator's general reputation for having a high settlement rate, being a distinguished and fair member of the legal community, or being a highly skilled mediator is a useful start, but operates at too great a level of generality to provide the best answers. Talking with parties who have used the mediator before is one useful tool in learning in detail about a mediator's approach. Another approach that is underutilized is a joint interview of the mediator by both parties. Most mediators are in my experience willing to be interviewed about significant cases. There is probably no better way to learn about the approach that a mediator will take than to ask him or her about it. Indeed, to at least some extent lawyers will want to determine whether the prospective mediator has the right personality to interact in a productive way with the parties to the dispute, and to a great extent an interview provides a useful forum to find out.

Second, the choice of the mediator ought to be made with reference to the barriers to the settlement of the case and to your goals in the dispute. For example, if restoration of a damaged relationship is an important goal, it will be important to choose a mediator with strong interpersonal skills. By contrast, if there are widely divergent views of the merits that are making it difficult to settle the case, a mediator with strong evaluative skills will be important. Of course, in many cases both strong evaluative and facilitative skills will be required. And, the extent to which the mediation will require evaluation should determine the extent to which the mediator need have at least some specialized substantive experience.

Following these guidelines should enhance your chances of choosing the best possible mediator for your dispute. Making sure that you design the right sort of mediation process—preferably in conjunction with the mediator—is an equally important next step in utilizing mediation effectively.

LAWYER'S REPRESENTATION OF CLIENTS IN MEDIATION: USING ECONOMICS AND PSYCHOLOGY TO STRUCTURE ADVOCACY IN A NONADVERSARIAL SETTING

14 Ohio St. J. on Disp. Resol. 269, 349–52 (1999) [*]

By Jean R. Sternlight

A vast professional responsibility literature discusses the appropriate division of responsibilities in a case between lawyer and client. This literature attempts to fill in the gaps left by the rather vague strictures of both the Model Rules of Professional Conduct and the Model Code of Professional Responsibility. While both sets of rules essentially require the lawyer to defer to her client on major matters (ends) while allowing the lawyer leeway on tactical choices (means), [see Rule 1.2(a) of the Model Rules of Professional Conduct and Ethical Canon 707 of the Model Code of Professional Responsibility], this distinction leaves plenty of room for argument. One school of thought, which some have called "traditional," contends that expert attorneys should behave very directively toward their typically passive clients. The other model, which some have called "participatory," urges that because many strategic decisions involve important choices on ultimate objectives, attorneys need to work closely and consultatively with their clients. As Professor David Luban has observed:

> [The ends-means rule] assumes a sharp dichotomy between ends and means, according to which a certain result (acquittal, a favorable

settlement, *etc.*) is all that the client desires, while the legal tactics and arguments are merely routes to that result. No doubt this is true in many cases, but it need not be: the client may want to win acquittal *by* asserting a certain right, because it vindicates him in a way that matters to him; or he may wish to obtain a settlement without using a certain tactic, because he disapproves of the tactic. In that case, what the lawyer takes to be mere means are really part of the client's ends.[269]

In short, current rules, codes, cases, and commentary provide some guidance but do not provide crystal clear guidance on how, in general, lawyers and clients ought to divide decisionmaking responsibilities.

Nor do existing ethical provisions or commentary provide clear guidance on the specific question of how lawyers and their clients ought to divide negotiation and mediation responsibilities. While it is well recognized that lawyers have an obligation to convey settlement offers to their clients and to allow their clients to make the decision as to whether or not to accept a particular offer, few decisions or commentators have addressed the further questions of how lawyer and client should divide responsibilities beyond that bare minimum. One exception is Professor Robert Cochran, who has argued eloquently that lawyers ought to be required to consult with their clients extensively both as to the nature of the negotiation and as to whether a dispute would best be handled through litigation or rather through some form of alternative dispute resolution.[271] Cochran argues that such consultation is desirable to preserve parties' individual autonomy, to ensure better results, and to protect against attorney conflicts of interest.

NOTES AND QUESTIONS

(1) Do you believe that attorneys have an ethical obligation to consult with their clients regarding the choice of a mediator? Should attorneys have such an obligation?

(2) As a matter of "good practice," should attorneys consult with their clients regarding the choice of a mediator?

(3) Whether alone or in consultation with a client, what criteria should an attorney use in selecting a mediator for a particular dispute?

(4) Once they have decided on the relevant criteria for selecting a mediator, how do an attorney and client actually find a mediator who meets these criteria? Many not-for-profit and for-profit organizations, including the American Arbitration Association, the CPR Institute for Dispute Resolution and

---

[269] David Luban, *Paternalism and the Legal Profession*, 1981 Wis. L. Rev. 454, 459 n.9; see also Robert F. Cochran, Jr., *Legal Representation and the Next Steps Toward Client Control: Attorney Malpractice for the Failure to Allow the Client to Control Negotiation and Pursue Alternatives to Litigation*, 47 Wash. & Lee L. Rev. 819, 827-828 (1990); Mark Spiegel, *Lawyering and Client Decisionmaking: Informed Consent and the Legal Profession*, 128 U. Pa. L. Rev. 41, 57 (1979). [Ed. note: parentheticals omitted].

[271] See Cochran, *supra* note 269, at 823-24.

JAMS, maintain lists of mediators and will provide information about the mediators on their list. As well, some courts or administrative agencies provide training and/or "certify" mediators in their jurisdiction. Such organizations may also make available information about the mediators on their lists. Increasingly such information may be available through the internet, as well as on paper.

[4] SHOULD LAWYERS BE ADVOCATES FOR THEIR CLIENTS IN MEDIATION?

Should the attorney act as an "advocate" for the client, or is advocacy inappropriate in the nonadversarial mediation setting? These questions are controversial among mediators, attorneys, and academics. Some fear that adversarial attorneys will (if they haven't already) turn mediation into just another form of litigation. Recall Professor Lande's point, in the first excerpt in this chapter, that in a "litimediation" culture, the "incorporation of mediation into the litigation process could increase the level of adversarialness in mediation." Also recall Mark Rutherford's concerns, regarding how adversarial lawyering may undercut the benefits of mediation. *See* Section 2[C], *supra*. If the fear that adversarial lawyers may destroy mediation is well-founded, does it have a solution? Must we eliminate advocacy in order to limit adversarialness? Below, Professors Carrie Menkel-Meadow and Jean Sternlight offer their views.

ETHICS IN ALTERNATIVE DISPUTE RESOLUTION: NEW ISSUES, NO ANSWERS FROM THE ADVERSARY CONCEPTION OF LAWYERS' RESPONSIBILITIES

38 S. Tex. L. Rev. 407, 408–10, 426–28 (May, 1997)[*]

By Carrie Menkel-Meadow

While one strand of ADR (the one with which I identify—"qualitative"—better processes and solutions) has always associated itself with pursuing "the good" and the "just," the other strand of ADR (quantitative, efficiency concerned, cost-reducing, docket clearing) has produced institutionalized forms of dispute resolution in the courts and in private contracts. To the extent that ADR has become institutionalized and more routine, it is now practiced by many different people, pursuing many different goals. Demonstrating another form of irony is a recent continuing education program that advertised itself as "How to Win in ADR!" Thus, lawyers as "advocates," as well as "problem-solvers" and parties now come to the wide variety of dispute resolution processes with a whole host of different intentions and behaviors, many of which may be inconsistent with the original aims of some forms of ADR. As skillful advocates try to manipulate ADR processes in order to achieve their conventional party maximization goals, the rules of behavior demanded in ADR become both less clear and in some respects even more important.

. . . .

The first and most important dilemma is one that has plagued me throughout my career as a lawyer—scholar—practitioner: the powerful heuristic of the adversary model and its concrete expressions in legal dispute resolution as a paradigm which does not aid, indeed, makes more difficult, the resolution of "ethical" dilemmas when one seeks to use other processes. To put it at its most concrete, as I have asserted in debate with many legal ethicists, the Model Rules of Professional Conduct (still based on an adversarial conception of the advocate's, including "counselor's", role) is not responsive to the needs, duties, and responsibilities of one seeking to be a "non-adversarial" problem-solver and the Code of Judicial Conduct, while perhaps helpful for arbitrators, is not responsive to the particular needs, duties, and responsibilities of the now wide variation in third-party neutral practices. Rules premised on adversarial and advocacy systems, with legal decision-makers, simply do not respond to processes which are intended to be conducted differently (in forms of communication, in sharing of information, in problem analysis and resolution) and to produce different outcomes (not necessarily win-loss, but some more complex and variegated solutions to legal and social problems).

. . . .

While we continue to debate whether ADR is a good or bad idea (supplanting or supplementing more formal judicial systems) it is important to note that the behaviors, skills and tasks of parties and their representatives may be called on in different ways in these alternative processes. The zealous advocate who jealously guards (and does not share) information, who does not reveal adverse facts (and in some cases, adverse law) to the other side, who seeks to maximize gain for his client, may be successful in arbitrations and some forms of mini-trials and summary jury trials.

However, the zealous advocate will likely prove a failure in mediation, where creativity, focus on the opposing sides' interests, and a broadening, not narrowing of issues, may be more valued skills. Indeed, in the second generation of ADR training which now focuses on training the representatives how to "be" in a mediation or other ADR setting, there is recognition that certain aspects of the conventional adversarial role may, in fact, be disadvantageous for effective behavior and the achievement of Pareto optimal solutions in settlement contexts. Such principles as "reactive devaluation" in which one side simply discounts proposals from the other side because the proposals come from the other side, teach us that we will have to relearn how to process and prepare information in a settlement-oriented setting.

Some have suggested the settlement function is sufficiently different from the adversarial function requiring different individuals, with different personalities and orientations as well as ethics. Thus, as courts struggle with such legal issues as what it means to attend a settlement proceeding "in good faith," representatives of parties (which is the term I prefer to the term "advocates") have to consider how to become effective in a different forum. A different orientation to the client and to the "adversary" may be essential in the kind of creative option generation and problem-solving that is essential in a mediation setting.

LAWYER'S REPRESENTATION OF CLIENTS IN MEDIATION: USING ECONOMICS AND PSYCHOLOGY TO STRUCTURE ADVOCACY IN A NONADVERSARIAL SETTING

14 Ohio St. J. on Disp. Resol. 269, 291–97 (1999) [*]

By Jean R. Sternlight

Attorney advocacy, properly defined, is entirely consistent with and supportive of mediation. While many commentators have attacked attorneys' use of advocacy in the mediation process, . . . the problem is not advocacy per se, but rather certain kinds of advocacy or adversarial behavior employed under particular circumstances. However, some attorney behavior should be proscribed in mediation (as it is in litigation), and some attorneys have a lot to learn regarding how best to advocate for their clients in a mediation.

If advocacy is defined broadly as supporting or pleading the cause of another, there is no inconsistency between advocacy and mediation. Permitting an attorney to act as an advocate for her client simply allows that attorney to speak and make arguments on her client's behalf and to help her client achieve her goals. The purpose of mediation is to reach an agreement which is acceptable to and desired by all parties. To reach such an agreement, both parties may wish to share their views as to their likely success in court as well as to engage in problem-solving. While some parties may be comfortable participating pro se, others may prefer to be aided by an attorney. If a party can advocate for her own interests, this Author sees no reason why her representative should not also be permitted to "advocate" on her behalf.

Nor is it clear why "adversarial" behavior, at least broadly defined, is necessarily inconsistent with mediation. To the extent that acting adversarially means advocating only on behalf of one's own client and not on behalf of any other party or on behalf of the process or system, the conduct is easy to reconcile with mediation. The problem-solving that works well in mediation does not require sacrifice of one's self-interest, but rather allows parties to search for solutions that are mutually beneficial.

Therefore, it is not at all clear to this Author why an attorney, hired by a party, should work toward achieving mediation results that, while helpful to others or supportive of a peaceful solution, do not serve the wishes of the client. Of course, if a client chooses to direct her attorney to work toward an agreement that benefits all parties equally, rather than one that benefits the client most, she should be able to do so, but it is not clear why a client should be obliged to have her attorney represent interests other than her own. Certainly a client should not be required to have the attorney she has retained act contrary to her interests. Were we to entirely forbid attorneys from advocating on behalf of their clients, to require them to be neutral between their own clients and others or to require them to disclose all that they know

---

about their clients' interests and positions, many people would no doubt decide not to retain attorneys to help them in mediation.

Still, it is appropriate to place certain restraints on attorney and client advocacy and adversarial behavior in mediation, just as we have placed limits on such conduct in litigation. In litigation we require that attorneys and clients have an adequate basis for positions taken in pleadings, we require attorneys to disclose the existence of relevant binding precedent to a tribunal, and we limit attorneys' ability to lie on behalf of their clients. These and other constraints may be appropriate in the mediation context as well.

Nor does this endorsement of advocacy mean that attorneys are relegated to being mere "hired guns." A vast professional responsibility literature contains many works urging that attorneys do and should have their own sense of morality, and it is entirely appropriate for attorneys to attempt to convince their clients that a particular course of action is unwise or immoral. Acceptance of such a view does not require abandonment of the principle that attorneys should serve as advocates for their clients.

Yet, while attorneys may appropriately advocate for their clients in mediation, it is certainly true that those attorneys who attempt to employ traditional "zealous" litigation tools when representing their clients in mediation may frequently (but not always) fail either to fulfill their clients' wishes or to serve their clients' interests. Those who would hoard information, rely solely on legal rather than emotional arguments, or refuse to let their clients speak freely will often have little success in mediation. This is not because attorneys ought not to advocate for their clients, but rather because attorneys ought not to advocate *poorly* on behalf of their clients. . . .

The distinction between whether attorneys may advocate on behalf of their clients in mediation and how they may do so is not merely semantic. Once it is recognized that advocacy is permitted the question becomes when and how attorneys should best represent their clients in mediation. Attorneys need much more specific guidance on how to behave in mediations than the simple edict "thou shalt not advocate" or the equally simple "thou shalt advocate."

QUESTIONS

(1) Is advocacy the same as adversarialness? If not, how do they differ? For an argument that lawyers should advocate for their clients by learning to work effectively with mediators, see James K.L. Lawrence, *Mediation Advocacy: Partnering with the Mediators*, 15 Ohio St. J. on Disp. Res. 425 (2000).

(2) Is adversarialness appropriate in mediation? Is attorney advocacy appropriate in mediation?

(3). Is an attorney who does not "advocate" for a client in mediation failing adequately to represent the client? Is such failure a violation of the attorney's ethical responsibilities?

(4) Do we need a new set of ethics rules to cover the role of the attorney in mediation and other forms of ADR?

(5) Is it feasible to have one set of ethics rules that govern litigation and another set that govern mediation or other forms of ADR, when these processes may take place simultaneously?

[5] LAWYERS' ROLE AS REPRESENTATIVE OF CLIENTS IN MEDIATION

Virtually all commentators agree that good preparation by both attorney and client is essential for a productive and effective mediation. Too frequently attorneys either fail to do any advance planning or else prepare for the mediation as they might prepare for a court appearance or deposition. Instead, lawyers should prepare themselves and their clients for a very different kind of process that combines aspects of both litigation and negotiation. In order to be an effective advocate, the lawyer should become familiar with the law and facts of the case, work with one client to decide on a theme and strategy for the mediation, and decide which if any exhibits or demonstrations shall be used at the mediation. However, because the point of a mediation is not to "win" but rather to reach a mutually acceptable settlement, the attorney must also become familiar with the underlying needs and interests of the client, anticipate the projected interests of the opposing party, begin to brainstorm regarding possible solutions, consider settlement ranges and limits, and map out a settlement strategy. One of the most essential aspects of an attorney's preparation for mediation should be preparation of the client for the mediation. It is crucial that the client understand the purpose of a mediation, how it differs from litigation, what the different stages of the mediation will be, and what roles the client and the client's attorney will play in the mediation.

Commentators differ, however, as to the respective roles both attorney and client should play when an attorney accompanies the client to a mediation. Should the attorney essentially sit by silently, and let the client do most of the talking? Or, should the attorney dominate the mediation as attorneys typically dominate litigation proceedings, essentially asking the client to be a silent observer at the mediation?

In the following readings, Tom Arnold first offers attorneys twenty practical tips on how lawyers ought to prepare for and handle a mediation. Then, Jean Sternlight draws upon social science literature regarding barriers to negotiation to examine the respective roles attorneys and clients ought to take in a mediation. She suggests that in many, but not all, mediations, attorneys should allow and encourage their clients to play a very active role in the process, and that attorneys should not typically dominate a mediation as they would litigation.

20 COMMON ERRORS IN MEDIATION ADVOCACY

13 Alternatives to the High Cost of Litig. 69 (May, 1995) *

By Tom Arnold

Trial lawyers who are unaccustomed to being mediation advocates often miss important arguments. Here are 20 common errors, and ways to correct them.

Problem 1: Wrong client in the room

CEOs settle more cases than vice presidents, house counsel or other agents. Why? For one thing, they don't need to worry about criticism back at the office. Any lesser agent, even with explicit "authority," typically must please a constituency which was not a participant in the give and take of the mediation. That makes it hard to settle cases.

A client's personality also can be a factor. A "Rambo," who is aggressive, critical, unforgiving, or self-righteous doesn't tend to be conciliatory. The best peace-makers show creativity, and tolerance for the mistakes of others. Of course, it also helps to know the subject.

Problem 2: Wrong lawyer in the room

Many capable trial lawyers are so confident that they can persuade a jury of anything (after all, they've done it before), that they discount the importance of preserving relationships, as well as the exorbitant costs and emotional drain of litigation. They can smell a "win" in the court room, and so approach mediation with a measure of ambivalence.

Transaction lawyers, in contrast, tend to be better mediation counsel. At a minimum, parties should look for sensitive, flexible, understanding people who will do their homework, no matter their job experience. Good preparation makes for more and better settlements. A lawyer who won't prepare is the wrong lawyer.

Problem 3: Wrong mediator in the room

Some mediators are generous about lending their conference rooms but bring nothing to the table. Some of them determine their view of the case and urge the parties to accept that view without exploring likely win-win alternatives.

The best mediators can work within a range of styles that Leonard L. Riskin developed in a recent issue of Alternatives (September 1994 at p. 111). As Mr. Riskin described them, these styles fall along a continuum, from being totally facilitative, to offering an evaluation of the case. Ideally, mediators should

---

fit the mediation style to the case and the parties before them, often moving from style to style as a mediation progresses.

Masters of the process can render valuable services whether or not they have substantive expertise. When do the parties need an expert? When they want an evaluative mediator, or someone who can cast meaningful lights and shadows on the merits of the case and alternative settlements.

It may not always be possible to know and evaluate a mediator and fit the choice of mediator to your case. But the wrong mediator may fail to get a settlement another mediator might have finessed.

Problem 4: Wrong case

Almost every type of case, from antitrust or patent infringement to unfair competition and employment disputes, is a likely candidate for mediation. Occasionally, cases don't fit the mold, not because of the substance of the dispute, but because one or both parties want to set a precedent.

For example, a franchisor that needs a legal precedent construing a key clause that is found in 3,000 franchise agreements might not want to submit the case to mediation. Likewise, an infringement suit early in the life of an uncertain patent might be better resolved in court; getting the Federal Circuit stamp of validity could generate industry respect not obtainable from ADR.

Problem 5: Omitting client preparation

Lawyers should educate their clients about the process. Clients need to know the answers to the types of questions the mediator is likely to ask. At the same time, they need to understand that the other party (rather than the mediator) should be the focus of each side's presentation.

In addition, lawyers should interview clients about the client's and the adversary's "best alternative to negotiated agreement," and "worst alternative to negotiated agreement," terms coined by William Ury and Roger Fisher in their book, *Getting to Yes*. A party should accept any offer better than his perceived BATNA and reject any offer seen as worse than his perceived WATNA. So the BATNAs and WATNAs are critical frames of reference for accepting offers and for determining what offers to propose to the other parties. A weak or false understanding of either party's BATNA or WATNA obstructs settlements and begets bad settlements.

Other topics to cover with the client:

- the difference between their interests and their legal positions;
- the variety of options that might settle the case;
- the strengths and weaknesses of their case;
- objective independent standards of evaluation;
- the importance of apology and empathy.

Problem 6: Not letting a client open for herself

At least as often as not, letting the properly coached client do most, or even all, of the opening and tell the story in her own words works much better than lengthy openings by the lawyer.

To prepare for mediation, rehearse answers to the following questions, which the mediator is likely to ask:

— How do you feel about this dispute—Or about the other party?

— What do you really want in the resolution of this dispute?

— What are your expectations from a trial? Are they realistic?

— What are the weaknesses in your case?

— What law or fact in your case would you like to change?

— What scares you most?

— What would it feel like to be in your adversary's shoes?

— What specific evidence do you have to support each element of your case?

— What will the jury charge and interrogatories probably be?

— What is the probability of a verdict your way on liability?

— What is the range of damages you think a jury would return in this case if it found liability?

— What are the likely settlement structures, from among the following possibilities: Terms, dollars, injunction, services, performance, product, recision [sic], apology, costs, attorney fees, releases.

— What constituency pressures burden the other party? Which ones burden you?

Problem 7: Addressing the mediator instead of the other side

Most lawyers open the mediation with a statement directed at the mediator, comparable to opening statements to a judge or jury. Highly adversarial in tone, it overlooks the interests of the other side that gave rise to the dispute.

Why is this strategy a mistake? The "judge or jury" you should be trying to persuade in a mediation is not the mediator, but the adversary. If you want to make the other party sympathetic to your cause, don't hurt him.

For the same reason, plenary sessions should demonstrate your client's humanity, respect, warmth, apologies and sympathy. Stay away from inflammatory issues, which are better addressed by the mediator in private caucuses with the other side.

Problem 8: Making the lawyer the center of the process

Unless the client is highly unappealing or inarticulate, the client should be the center of the process. The company representative for the other side may not have attended depositions, so is unaware of the impact your client could have on a judge or jury if the mediation fails. People pay more attention to appealing plaintiffs, so show them off.

Prepare the client to speak and be spoken to by the mediator and the adversary. He should be able to explain why he feels the way he does, why he is or is not responsible, and why any damages he *caused* are great or only peanuts. But he should also extend empathy to the other party.

Problem 9: Failure to use advocacy tools effectively

You'll want to prepare your materials for maximum persuasive impact. Exhibits, charts, and copies of relevant cases or contracts with key phrases highlighted can be valuable visual aids. A 90-second video showing key witnesses in depositions making important admissions, followed by a readable size copy of an important document with some relevant language underlined, can pack a punch.

Problem 10: Timing mistakes

Get and give critical discovery, but don't spend exorbitant time or sums in discovery and trial prep before seeking mediation.

Mediation can identify what's truly necessary discovery and avoid unnecessary discovery. One of my own war stories: With a mediation under way and both parties relying on their perception of the views of a certain vice president, I leaned over, picked up the phone, called the vice president, introduced myself as the mediator, and asked whether he could give us a deposition the following morning. "No," said he, "I've got a Board meeting at 10:00."

"How about 7:30 a.m., with a one-hour limit?" I asked. "It really is pretty important that this decision not be delayed." The parties took the deposition and settled the case before the 10:00 board meeting.

Problem 11: Failure to listen to the other side

Many lawyers and clients seem incapable of giving open-minded attention to what the other side is saying. That could cost a settlement.

Problem 12: Failure to identify perceptions and motivations

Seek first to understand, only then to be understood. Messrs. Fisher and Ury suggest you brainstorm to determine the other party's motivations and perceptions. Prepare a chart summarizing how your adversary sees the issues (see chart below).

Part of preparing for mediation is understanding your adversary's perceptions and motivations, perhaps even listing them in chart form. Here is an example, taken from a recent technology dispute.

Plaintiff's Perceptions	Defendant's Perceptions
Defendant entered the business because of my sound analysis of the market, my good judgment and convictions about the technology.	I entered the business based on my own independent analysis of the market and the appropriate technology that was different from Plaintiff's
Defendant's business plan was based upon confidential information that I provided. He never would have considered it, but for me.	I interviewed nearly 100 market participants before arriving at my market plan, using my own judgment.
Defendant used me by pretending to be interested in doing business with me.	Plaintiff misled me with exaggerated claims that turned out to be false.
Defendant made a low-ball offer for my valuable technology. Another company paid me my asking price.	I made Plaintiff a fair offer; I later paid less for alternative technology that was better.

Problem 13: Hurting, humiliating, threatening, or commanding

Don't poison the well from which you must drink to get a settlement. That means you don't hurt, humiliate or ridicule the other folks. Avoid pejoratives like "malingerer," "fraud," "cheat," "crook," or "liar." You can be strong on what your evidence will be and still be a decent human being.

All settlements are based upon trust to some degree. If you anger the other side, they won't trust you. This inhibits settlement.

The same can be said for threats, like a threat to get the other lawyer's license revoked for pursuing such a frivolous cause, or for his grossly inaccurate pleadings.

Ultimatums destroy the process, and destroy credibility. Yes, there is a time in mediation to walk out—whether or not you plan to return. But a series of ultimatums, or even one ultimatum, most often is very counterproductive.

Problem 14: The backwards step

A party who offered to pay $300,000 before the mediation, and comes to the mediation table willing to offer only $200,000, injures its own credibility and engenders bad feelings from the other side. Without some clear and dramatic reasons for the reduction in the offer, it can be hard to overcome the damage done.

The backwards step is a powerful card to play at the right time—a walk away without yet walking out. But powerful devices are also dangerous. There are few productive occasions to use this one, and they tend to come late in a mediation. A rule of thumb: unless you're an expert negotiator, don't do it.

Problem 15: Too many people

Advisors—people to whom the decision-maker must display respect and courtesy, people who feel that since they are there they must put in their two bits worth—all delay a mediation immeasurably. A caucus that with only one lawyer and vice president would take 20 minutes, with five people could take an hour and 20 minutes. What could have been a one-day mediation stretches to two or three.

This is one context in which I use the "one martini lunch." Once I think that everyone present understands all the issues, I will send principals who have been respectful out to negotiate alone. Most come back with an expression of oral settlement within three hours. Of course, the next step is to brush up on details they overlooked, draw up a written agreement and get it signed. But usually those finishing touches don't ruin the deal.

Problem 16: Closing too fast

A party who opens at $1 million, and moves immediately to $500,000, gives the impression of having more to give. Rightly or wrongly, the other side probably will not accept the $500,000 offer because they expect more give.

By contrast, moving from $1 million to $750,000, $600,000, $575,000, $560,000, $550,000, sends no message of yield below $500,000, and may induce a $500,000 proposal that can be accepted.

 The "dance" is part of communication. Skip the dance, lose the communication, and risk losing settlement at your own figure.

Problem 17: Failure to truly close

Unless parties have strong reasons to "sleep on" their agreement, to further evaluate the deal, or to check on possibly forgotten details, it is better to get some sort of enforceable contract written and signed before the parties separate. Too often, when left to think overnight and draft tomorrow, the parties think of new ideas that delay or prevent closing.

Problem 18: Breaching a confidentiality

Sometimes parties to a mediation unthinkingly, or irresponsibly, disclose in open court information revealed confidentially in a mediation.

When information is highly sensitive, consider keeping it confidential with the mediator. Or if revealed to the adversary in a mediation where the case did not settle, consider moving before the trial begins for an order in limine to bind both sides to the confidentiality agreement.

Problem 19: Lack of patience and perseverance

The mediation "dance" takes time. Good mediation advocates have patience and perseverance.

Problem 20: Misunderstanding conflict

A dispute is a problem to be solved together, not a combat to be won.

WHAT'S A LAWYER TO DO IN MEDIATION?

18 Alternatives to the High Cost of Litig. 1 (July/August 2000) * *

By Jean R. Sternlight

What are lawyers supposed to do when they represent their clients in mediation? Should they act the same way many do in a deposition or trial, where they instruct the client not to volunteer information, and to carefully follow the attorney's lead? At the other extreme, should an attorney who is representing a client in a mediation even bother attending? If he or she does attend, should he or she largely sit silently, and let the client do the talking and run the show? Lawyers around the country are answering these questions in very different ways. The differences appear to stem not only from variations in individual philosophy but also from the culture of the local litigation and ADR community.

Surprisingly little has been written about what the role of the lawyer either is or should be in representing mediation clients. While vast literature now describes, critiques, and praises various aspects of the mediation process, most of this literature focuses on either the mediator or the mediation process. The few works that offer comprehensive suggestions on how attorneys can best represent their clients in mediation can be divided into two major categories: (i) those arguing that the attorney should play virtually no role in the mediation, and (ii) those arguing that the attorney should participate very actively in the mediation in order to adequately advocate for the client and also protect the client from potential harm.

A lawyer's skills can positively contribute to a successful mediation provided that counsel is attuned to how best to represent his or her client in mediation. Social sciences, particularly economics, psychology, and agency theory, offer many insights to an attorney who is trying to decide how to handle a mediation. Attorneys who are cognizant of these insights can, in consultation with their clients, help structure a mediation that is geared to overcome barriers to a mutually advantageous settlement. In many, but not all instances, it will be critical for the client to play an active role in the mediation in order to reach a mutually desirable agreement.

---

* [Ed. note: For a more complete version of this discussion, see Jean R. Sternlight, *Lawyers' Representation of Clients in Mediation: Using Economics and Psychology to Structure Advocacy in a Nonadversarial Setting*, 14 OHIO ST. J. ON DISP. RESOL. 269 (1999).]

Drawing on the psychological phenomena and strategic issues that arise in the lawyer-client relationship, set forth below are a few well-grounded tips for counsel representing a client in mediation.

. . . .

Counsel should always keep in mind some of the basic insights offered by economists and psychologists who have studied the question of why disputes often fail to settle (or take a long time to settle), even where an early settlement is seemingly desirable for all. One key factor is the psychological differences in the way attorneys and clients view the world. Empirical studies have demonstrated that most people are affected by a series of phenomena that cause them to act in a less than an objective, reasoned manner when they attempt to resolve disputes. To provide a few examples, people tend to be over optimistic as to their chances of success; they are more willing to gamble regarding perceived losses than perceived gains; and they prefer settlements that appear to be "just."

Also influential is the different way an attorney dissects a dispute as compared to a client. Parties are frequently interested not merely in monetary outcomes but also in "venting," receiving or giving an apology, or achieving vengeance or publicity. Studies have shown that lawyers, as compared to their clients, tend to be far more objective in their settlement approach. Lawyers often focus on a settlement's bottom-line dollar value rather than process issues or surrounding emotional concerns.

These differences between lawyers and their clients can impede desirable settlements. Attorneys, rooted in their hyper-rational world, may not realize the importance of non-monetary benefits or processes such as venting or apologizing. They may think they are aiding their clients by pushing them to be objective, but the client might have preferred terms that appealed to his or her nonobjective, emotional wishes.

. . . .

When attorneys attempt to settle their clients' disputes without using mediation, the clients remain very much in the background. While the attorney is ethically required to obtain the client's approval for any settlement, the attorney typically negotiates the deal on her own, merely consulting the client occasionally. The client is not present for the negotiation and therefore doesn't hear firsthand what the other side's position is; to hear the other side's anger; to assess the arguments of the opposing attorney; to explain the importance of non-monetary relief; to voice his feelings; or to give or receive an apology.

By contrast, in a mediation the client potentially can do each of these things and more, thereby enabling a settlement that would not otherwise have been possible. Mediation can permit the client to communicate directly with the opposing party and its attorney, and eliminate the erroneous transmissions that inevitably occur when one person acts as the agent for another.

Usually mediation can serve this beneficial purpose only where clients are permitted to play an active role in the mediation. If a client, while attending the mediation, does not express his or her own views in his or her own voice, neither the client nor the opposing party will secure many of the mediation's

encourages client participation

potential benefits. Where the attorneys "take over" the mediation and silence their own clients, they remove one of the mediation's primary potential benefits and convert the mediation back into a negotiation among attorneys.

Thus, in many instances it will be wise for an attorney to permit the client to participate vigorously, both by giving an opening statement and by speaking freely in other parts of the mediation. This participation will help the clients on both sides to communicate more directly, and to avoid some of the problems caused by differences between clients and their attorneys. For similar reasons, it also often will be desirable to permit much of the mediation to occur as a joint session, rather than moving immediately to caucus.

. . . .

In preparing for a mediation an attorney should try to think about why the case has not already settled. What might be some of the barriers? Perhaps the opposing party is blocking settlement because it has unrealistic expectations due to a lack of factual or legal information, or maybe the opposing party has unmet non-monetary goals. Maybe it is the opposing party's attorney who is blocking settlement, based on the attorney's lack of information or unmet monetary or non-monetary goals. Many times an attorney may realize that it is his or her own client's unrealistic expectations or unmet monetary or non-monetary needs that are preventing agreement. Occasionally an attorney may even have the insight that it is his or her own concerns that are the problem.

Once an attorney begins to understand why the dispute is not settling, the attorney often can see that clients' active participation in mediation might prove helpful. For example, if the opposing party or opposing attorney is blocking settlement because either has unrealistically high expectations regarding how the facts will play at trial, a client may be well qualified to teach the opposing party that the case is not as strong as the opposing party thought. Where the client tells his or her story compellingly and convincingly in the mediation, the opposing client and attorney may learn their case is not as strong as they believed.

Similarly, where the opposing client has unmet non-monetary needs, it may be critical for an attorney to have his or her client participate actively. The client is far better suited than the attorney to provide a meaningful apology. Where the opposing party needs to "vent" his anger or concerns, he or she may need to do so against a live opposing client, and not merely an attorney. A client also may be better than the attorney at helping to think up creative "win/win" solutions based on the disputants' mutual needs and interests.

Turning to blockages due to a client's misperceptions, active client participation on both sides can be critical in bringing a dose of reality to the client. Finally, allowing a client to participate actively can alleviate stresses due to the client's perception that an attorney may be acting out of self interest. These few examples illustrate that clients' active participation can be critical.

. . . .

There are situations in which attorneys would do their clients a real disservice by failing to attend or failing to participate actively. For example, sometimes the parties' failure to settle a dispute may be attributable not to lack of emotional or informational exchange between the parties, but rather to one party's misguided view of the law. Here, the most useful mediation may be one in which the opposing attorney or mediator finds a way to educate the misguided client—or attorney—as to his likelihood of success. As well, some clients' basic personality or circumstances may be such that it is important for their attorney to play the role of protector. It would typically be unwise to design a family mediation to encourage active participation by both a perpetrator and a victim of domestic violence.

. . . .

In sum, while there is no single recipe for mediation success, insights drawn from economics, psychology and agency theory reveal that active client participation is often critical to achieve the full benefits of mediation. Attorneys who consistently dominate the mediation, treating it like just another deposition or trial, or even allow their clients not to attend, often are doing their clients a disservice. Instead, drawing on the tools offered by social science, attorneys should attempt to assess what steps they and their clients should take to overcome whatever barriers may exist to a desirable settlement. Often this analysis will reveal that attorneys should foster rather than inhibit active client participation in mediation.

NOTES AND QUESTIONS

(1) Several books focus explicitly on how lawyers should represent their clients in mediation. *See* Eric Galton, *Representing Clients in Mediation* (1994), and John W. Cooley, *Mediation Advocacy* (1996). For a useful article see James K. L. Lawrence, *Mediation Advocacy: Partnering with the Mediator*, 15 Ohio St. J. on Disp. Res. 425 (2000).

(2) How do you believe lawyers and their clients should divide responsibilities in a mediation? If you believe the determination should vary from case to case, what factors do you believe are important to consider?

(3) What are some of the "barriers" that might preclude opposing parties from reaching a settlement? How might mediation help overcome each of these barriers?

(4) Do you believe that the degree of participation of lawyer or client in a mediation has any impact on whether the mediation ultimately results in a settlement? Why or why not?

(5) As between the attorney and the client, who should decide on the respective degrees of participation in a mediation? Are ethical rules relevant to the consideration of this question?

[6] MAY LAWYERS LIE IN MEDIATION?

Existing ethical rules restrain lawyers from lying in litigation or negotiation. ABA Model Rule 3.3 prohibits a lawyer, *inter alia*, from knowingly "mak[ing] a false statement of material fact or law to a tribunal" or "fail[ing] to disclose a material fact to a tribunal when disclosure is necessary to avoid assisting a criminal or fraudulent act by the client," or "fail[ing] to disclose to the tribunal legal authority in the controlling jurisdiction known to the lawyer to be directly adverse to the position of the client and not disclosed by opposing counsel." ABA Model Rule 4.1 prohibits a lawyer, in the course of representation, from "mak[ing] a false statement of material fact or law" or "fail[ing] to disclose a material fact to a third party when disclosure is necessary to avoid assisting a criminal or fraudulent act . . . ." However, the Official Comment notes that, under generally accepted negotiation conventions, statements as to price, value or a party's intentions regarding settlement would not typically be regarded as statements of material fact.

Which of these Rules do or should apply in the mediation context? Should a mediator be treated as a tribunal, to whom an attorney would be obliged to disclose adverse precedent? Should we impose greater obligations of truthfulness on lawyers who represent their clients in mediation than we impose in other litigation or settlement contexts? In the following excerpt, John W. Cooley discusses these questions.

MEDIATION MAGIC: ITS USE AND ABUSE

29 Loy. U. Chi. L.J. 1, 101-103 (1997) .

By John W. Cooley

Very little has been written about the ethical standards for lawyers who represent clients in mediation, much less the standards of truthfulness which should guide them. Nothing in the ABA Model Rules of Professional Conduct specifically addresses lawyer truthfulness in mediation. In mediation, of course, the advocate's duty of truthfulness has to be measured not only in relation to "others" but also to a special kind of "other"—a neutral who is sometimes a judge or a former judge. Thus, two questions emerge: (1) Do the ethical standards for truthfulness in negotiation . . . also govern the advocate's truthfulness vis-a-vis the opponents in mediation? and (2) Do those ethical standards also govern the advocate's truthfulness vis-a-vis a neutral (lawyer, nonlawyer, or judge) in mediation?

First, because the Model Rules are silent on the truthfulness standards for mediation advocates vis-a-vis their opponents, one would seem to be safe in concluding that the rules regarding truthfulness in negotiation apply. However, one could make a persuasive argument that a heightened standard of truthfulness by advocates in mediation should apply because of the "deception synergy" syndrome resulting from a third-party neutral's involvement. Practical experience shows that the accuracy of communication deteriorates on successive transmissions between and among individuals. Distortions tend to become magnified on continued transmissions. Also, available behavioral research concerning mediator's strategies and tactics reveals that mediators tend to embellish information, translate it, and sometimes distort it to meet the momentary needs of their efforts to achieve a settlement.[696] To help

---

[696] See Jennifer Gerarda Brown & Ian Ayres, *Economic Rationales for Mediation*, 80 Va. L. Rev. 323, 327-28 (1994).

protect against "deception synergy" perhaps more truthfulness should be required from mediation advocates and mediators. The practicality of such a proposal, however, is questionable. Can one reasonably expect advocates to behave any differently in mediation than they do in negotiation? Would such distinctions of truthfulness be impossible to define and even less possible to enforce? It seems likely. Thus, it appears that the standards governing advocates' truthfulness in negotiation vis-a-vis each other would also govern their conduct in mediation.

Second, with respect to truthfulness standards for mediation advocates vis-a-vis the mediator, apparently the only available guidance having even a modicum of applicability appears to be Model Rule 3.3, "Candor Toward the Tribunal." . . .

It is arguable, of course, that Rule 3.3 applies only to court tribunals which adjudicate matters in a public forum—and not to mediators, special masters, part-time judges, former judges, or others who conduct settlement conferences. If that is the intent of this rule, the Model Rules do not specifically say so. Nowhere do they define "tribunal." It is not even clear whether Rule 3.3 applies to a lawyer's conduct before a *private* tribunal consisting of an arbitrator or arbitrators, although it reasonably could. If such rules apply in arbitration, would they also apply in a med-arb or binding mediation?[703] Although it is true that the Comments to the above-quoted Rule 3.3 make no reference to settlement conference or mediation, it is also true that they do not explicitly exclude settlement either conferences or mediation from its coverage.

Other Model Rules further obfuscate the scope of the coverage of Model Rule 3.3. For example, Comments to Rule 3.9, "Advocate in Nonadjudicative Proceedings," make reference to courts and not tribunals, but for *administrative* tribunal. Thus, the question becomes: is "court" different in meaning than the unmodified term "tribunal"? Comment [1] to Rule 1.12, "Former Judge or Arbitrator," defines "adjudicative officer" as including "such officials as judges pro tempore, referees, special masters, hearing officers and other parajudicial officers, and also lawyers who serve as part-time judges." Is the term "tribunal" then broader than "adjudicative officer"? That is, does the unmodified term "tribunal" include both "adjudicative" and "nonadjudicative" officers? If so, would mediators or settlement officers fall within the scope of "nonadjudicative" officers, thus making Rule 3.3 applicable to mediators? For those readers who believe this analysis is an exercise in tautology, they may be correct. The objective of this analysis is to make two important points: (1) the current Model Rules are currently thoroughly deficient in providing guidance to mediation advocates on what their truthfulness behavior should be vis-a-vis mediators (whether or not the mediators are judges, former judges, or court-appointed neutrals); and (2) if Model Rule 3.3 were deemed to apply to mediation advocates, it would significantly enhance the standards of advocates' truthfulness-to-mediator responsibilities, most probably to the point that no advocate would find it sensible to participate in the mediation process.

---

[703] Ed. note: Cooley defines "binding mediation" as a process in which "the mediator makes a binding decision at a figure within the mediated bracket."

QUESTIONS

(1) John Cooley questions whether "a heightened standard of truthfulness by advocates in mediation should apply because of the 'deception synergy' syndrome resulting from a third-party neutral's involvement." What do you think? Would it be feasible to impose a higher burden of truthfulness in mediation than in negotiation? Would such a distinction be defensible? Would it deter mediation? Perhaps we need to impose a higher obligation of truthfulness in *both* mediation and negotiation? *See* James J. Alfini, *Settlement Ethics & Lawyering in ADR Proceedings: A Proposal to Revise Rule 4.1*, 19 N. Ill. U. L. Rev. 255 (1999) (arguing for a higher burden of truthfulness in negotiation).

(2) Do you agree with John Cooley that applying Model Rule 3.3 to mediation advocates would significantly deter advocates from participating in the mediation process? What other advantages or disadvantages do you see to applying Rule 3.3 to mediation advocates? For an argument that a lawyer owes the same duty of candor to all mediators, regardless of their background, as to a judge, see Bruce E. Meyerson, *Telling the Truth in Mediation: Mediator Owed Duty of Candor*, 4 No. 2 Disp. Resol. Mag. 17 (1997).

(3) In *In re Fee*, 898 P.2d 975, 980 (Ariz. 1995), the Arizona Supreme Court held that attorneys violated their duty of candor to a tribunal by failing to disclose their complete fee agreement to a judge acting as settlement judge or mediator. If the mediator had not been a judge, should the case have been decided differently?

§ D   SPECIAL ETHICAL AND PRACTICAL ISSUES FACING THE LAWYER-MEDIATOR

Many lawyer-mediators attempt to maintain their law practices, while also spending a percentage of their time serving as a neutrals. For some, continuing a law practice may be a short term necessity as they attempt to build their mediation business. Other lawyer-mediators enjoy pursuing both practices simultaneously, and believe that they are supportive of one another. A New Jersey ethical opinion explains the potential benefits of this combination for both lawyer-mediator and client.

. . .

> The emergence of ADR has presented attorneys with new and varied ways in which to serve their clients. No longer are attorneys limited to the traditional role of advocate in civil litigation. They may now represent their clients in ADR proceedings, assist their clients in establishing dispute resolution programs and negotiate contracts requiring ADR. Not surprising, they are in ever increasing numbers serving as arbitrators or mediators in ADR programs.

Attorneys engaged in ADR activities consider themselves professionals in dispute resolution. They report that their activities: (a) negotiating; (b) advocating in mediation, arbitration, or litigation settings; or (c) when no conflicts of interest arise, serving as third party neutrals, have been of great benefit to their client community. Their experience in ADR has also provided them with a theoretical as well as practical perspective they might not otherwise have gained and has influenced their 'transitional' adversarial practice, just as their litigation practice has informed and strengthened their ADR practice.

Joint Opinion. Opinion 657, Advisory Committee on Professional Ethics. Opinion 18, New Jersey Supreme Court Committee on Attorney Advertising, Alternative Dispute Resolution, 1994 WL 792644, at 2, 3 (N.J. Comm. Atty. Advt.) (April 4, 1994).

The attempt to combine work as an advocate with work as a neutral raises many interesting ethical and practical issues. Some of these issues have already been addressed in Chapter 7, Section [D], *supra*. One of the most pressing concerns is whether the attempt to maintain a dual practice raises special issues regarding conflicts of interest.

In addition, those who attempt to combine practice as a neutral with practice as an advocate must also consider whether lawyer and non-lawyer mediators can share profits, and how advertisements and solicitation should handled. As the law in this area is still developing, significant differences often exist between various states. The lawyer-mediator must research the extant law and ethical opinions in her own state to be sure she is behaving properly. Finally, combination of advocate and neutral practices also raise some interesting business concerns.

[1]   CONFLICT OF INTEREST ISSUES FACING THE LAWYER-MEDIATOR

Lawyer-mediators must worry about the possibility of conflicts of interest stemming from their dual practice. Once an attorney has served as a mediator in a dispute involving two clients, is the attorney forever precluded from representing either client as an advocate? Alternatively, may an attorney attempt to mediate a dispute between two parties where she has, in the past, represented one or both parties? Is an attorney barred from mediating or litigating due to past representation by other members of her firm? Is the firm barred from litigating all disputes involving a particular company because a member of the firm mediated a dispute involving that company? In the excerpts that follow, these important issues are explored and their implications are examined. First, Loretta W. Moore discusses some of the general questions surrounding conflicts of interests and disclosures encountered by lawyer-mediators. Second, a look at the experiences of the Florida firm Cobb Cole & Bell illustrates how these problematic issues forced a firm that previously included both litigators and lawyer-mediators to break up into multiple entities.

LAWYER MEDIATORS: MEETING THE ETHICAL CHALLENGES

30 Fam. L.Q. 679, 694–700 (1996) ˙

By Loretta W. Moore

IV. Conflicts of Interest and Disclosures

Model Rule 1.7 prohibits a lawyer from representing a client if the representation of that client will be directly adverse to another client or if the representation of a client may be materially limited by the lawyer's responsibilities to another client or third person. Model Rule 1.9 precludes a lawyer who has formerly represented a client from representing another person in the same or substantially related matter in which that person's interests are materially adverse to the interests of the former client without that client's consent. Model Rule 1.10 imputes disqualification of a lawyer by reason of Model Rules 1.7, 1.9 or 2.2 to the lawyer's law firm.

Mediation Standard III [of the AAA, SPIDR, ABA Standards of Conduct for Mediators (1996), *see* Section 7[C][2], *supra*] requires a mediator to disclose all actual and potential conflicts of interest reasonably known to the mediator. What disclosures are necessary? The Mediation Standard defines a conflict of interest as a "dealing or relationship that might create an impression of possible bias." A mediator who has a prior or current lawyer/client, consulting, or personal relationship with any disputing party or a party's lawyer must disclose the nature of such current or prior relationship to all other disputing parties at the mediation session. A mediator is likewise compelled to disclose any potential conflict of interest as soon as the mediator becomes aware of the relationship or a possible conflict of interest.

A. Disputes Involving Former or Current Clients

There is an attempt in the Model Rules to address the problem of a lawyer serving as an intermediary between existing clients. Rule 2.2 provides that a lawyer may serve as an intermediary in the form of a mediation between clients, if:

> (1) the lawyer consults with each client concerning the . . . advantages and risks involved, and the effect on the attorney-client privileges, and obtains each client's consent . . .; (2) the lawyer reasonably believes that the matter can be resolved on terms compatible with the clients' best interests [with] each client . . . able to make adequately informed decisions . . .; and (3) the lawyer reasonably believes that the common representation can be undertaken impartially and without improper effect on other responsibilities the lawyer has to any of the clients.

There is disagreement whether Rule 2.2 adequately covers the lawyer-mediator because it assumes prior representation of both clients, thus imposing higher standards than may be necessary in the ordinary case. Recognizing the apparent conflicts mediating between clients can present to a lawyer, most standards of conduct for mediators prohibit mediation by a lawyer who concurrently represents any of the mediating parties. Some jurisdictions preclude a lawyer-mediator from mediating a matter involving a party whom the lawyer-mediator currently represents in *any* matter. Other jurisdictions preclude a lawyer-mediator from mediating a matter involving a party who is a client in a related matter. . . .

B. Disputes Involving Business or Personal Associates

Generally, prior service as a mediator involving a party or a lawyer for a party is not viewed as legal representation or consultation. Nonetheless, the best policy is to avoid being secretive about prior professional associations or friendships with any of the individuals involved in the mediation session. A lawyer-mediator who is a member of a law firm is obliged to disclose to mediation participants any legal representation of any of the disputing parties by the mediator or a member of the mediator's law firm. The disclosure duty is continuing. It is best that the consent of the parties be obtained in writing. If the mediator believes that the relationship or interest would affect the mediator's impartiality, then the mediator should withdraw from the mediation.

C. Disputes Subsequent to the Mediation

Most jurisdictions bar mediators from representing a party in a matter "substantially related" to the mediated matter. Other jurisdictions prohibit the mediator from representing either party in any subsequent dispute between the same parties. It is considered unethical for a mediator to use the mediation process to solicit future business from one of the parties. With the exception of the tension between Model Rule 2.2 and mediation standards noted above, Model Rules 1.7, 1.9 and 1.10 governing the conduct of lawyers are consistent with the mediation standards regarding disclosures and conflict of interest. Lawyer-mediators should refer to applicable Model Rules and mediation standards to assure compliance.

D. Disqualifying the Law Firm

Several courts in nonfamily law cases have dealt with the issue of a mediator's subsequent representation of a disputing party. In *Poly Software International, Inc. v. Su*, [880 F. Supp. 1487 (D. Utah 1995)], the defendant moved to disqualify the plaintiff's lawyer and his firm on the ground that the lawyer had served as a mediator in previous litigation when plaintiff and defendant were business partners. The court looked at Model Rule 1.12 which prohibits former judges or arbitrators from representing anyone in connection with a matter in which they participated as a judge or arbitrator. After examining the role of a mediator as a neutral facilitator, the court compared the characteristics of a mediator with a judge, noting:

> These characteristics of mediation demonstrate that it differs significantly from more formal adversarial proceedings. . . . Most importantly, the mediator is not merely charged with being impartial, but

with receiving and preserving confidences in much the same manner as the client's attorney. In fact, the success of mediation depends largely on the willingness of the parties to freely disclose their intentions, desires and the strengths of their case; and upon the ability of the mediator to maintain a neutral position while carefully preserving the confidences that have been revealed.

The court reasoned that it is the mediator's assumed role of a confidant that distinguishes a mediator from an adjudicator. The court concluded that the appropriate ethical rule for mediators differs slightly from Model Rule 1.12 in that it precludes the mediator from representing anyone in connection with the same or a "substantially factually related" matter to that mediated unless all parties to the mediation consent after disclosure. While the court did not want to throw the disqualification net too wide to discourage attorneys from serving as mediators, it also did not want to discourage mediating parties from freely disclosing their position in mediation, if they knew that the mediator could someday serve as an attorney on the opposing side in a substantially related matter. In the court's view, the "substantially factually related" standard balanced these competing interests. *Poly Software* also imputed disqualification of members of the mediator's firm, extending the application of Model Rule 1.10(a) to lawyer-mediators. [*Id.* at 1495.]

A classic question regarding conflict of interest arising from prior mediation occurred in the New York case of *Bauerle v. Bauerle*, [615 N.Y.S.2d 954 (App. Div. 1994), *aff'd* 616 N.Y.S.2d 275 (App. Div. 1994)], involving a dissolution of marriage. The husband had consulted lawyer X regarding the filing of a divorce. Lawyer X recommended that the husband and wife consider mediation, referring them to lawyer-mediator Y, a member of the same law firm. Both lawyers X and Y were active members of the family law bar. The law firm's mediation center constituted an integral part of the firm's service to clients. The mediator scheduled an initial session with the parties which lasted two hours. The mediation subsequently broke off. The wife initiated divorce proceedings and moved to disqualify lawyer X and his law firm from representing the husband. The issue was whether the initial orientation session conducted by the mediator constituted mediation. The New York appellate court held that there was no appearance of impropriety or conflict of interest which required disqualifying X. The majority's short opinion found that because mediation never commenced, there was no prior attorney-client relationship between the law firm and the wife and that there was no disclosure of confidential information. The lawyer-mediator did not begin mediation because the parties had declined to provide written authorization to mediate and there was no discussion of any specific issues with the parties.

Two dissenting justices read the facts quite differently and concluded that lawyer X and the law firm should be disqualified. [616 N.Y.S.2d 275 (App. Div. 1994).] In the dissenters' version of the facts, the initial session included an explanation of the mediation process, a detailed discussion of the child support guidelines, ownership of the marital residence, marital debts, and the employment status of the parties and their income. The parties also discussed child support, spousal maintenance, possession of the marital residence, and distribution of several items of personal property.

Both the majority and dissent agreed that a lawyer-mediator may not subsequently represent a spouse in a domestic mediation in a divorce proceeding. . . .

. . . .

The majority misplaced reliance on the fact that the lawyer-mediator had never represented either party on a prior occasion. The bigger question that the majority left unanswered is whether a law partner to a lawyer-mediator can subsequently represent either party to a mediation in a related matter. In the dissent's view, whenever the disclosure of any material facts takes place, the lawyer-mediator, any of his law partners, and the law firm should be presumptively disqualified from representing either of the parties in a matter that was the subject of the mediation. Realistically, there are too many opportunities for members of a law firm to access confidential information imparted to the lawyer-mediator by the parties. . . .

E. Failure to Disclose a Conflict-of-Interest

Failure to disclose conflicts of interest may not only constitute unethical behavior subjecting a lawyer-mediator to professional disciplinary action but may expose her to civil liability as well. In a California decision [*Howard v. Drapkin*, 271 Cal. Rptr. 893 (Ct. App. 1990)], a psychologist was hired by the parents as a neutral third party to evaluate facts and circumstances surrounding a child's accusation of being sexually abused by the father. Sometime following a private evaluation session, the mother sued the neutral alleging, among other things, professional negligence and fraud, and that the neutral had failed to disclose that she had a prior professional relationship with the father and a close personal friendship with the wife of one of the partners in the law firm which represented the father in the underlying action. In this case, the neutral escaped liability as the California court extended common-law quasi-judicial immunity to neutral third parties for their conduct in performing dispute resolution services which are connected to the judicial process and involve mediation or other similar resolution of pending disputes. In other jurisdictions, mediators may not be protected by quasi-judicial or statutory immunity. The better course of action is for a mediator to be open regarding professional associations and friendships.

WITH CONFLICTS AT ISSUE, FLORIDA FIRM AND ITS FORMER PARTNERS RESTRUCTURE ADR—AGAIN,

15 Alternatives to the High Cost of Litig. 131, 137 (October 1997) *

A Florida law firm that spun off an alternative dispute resolution practice into three separate companies early this year to avoid conflicts apparently didn't go far enough. In the face of a court challenge putting the setup at issue—which the firm ultimately won—the three companies have been reorganized. In addition, the principal ADR company's name has been changed to eliminate a lingering perception of its affiliation to the law firm.

Daytona Beach, Fla.-based Cobb Cole & Bell on Jan. 1 established the three corporations to provide ADR and administrative services. . . .

. . . .

The novel setup didn't last long. In June, CCB Mediation officially changed its name to Upchurch Watson White & Fraxedas, after its top mediators. A second company focusing on ADR training established in the original transaction was folded into Upchurch Watson. And, at press time, the third company, CC&B Enterprises Inc., which provided administrative services to the law firm and the two ADR firms, and was intended to service other clients, was being reabsorbed by Cobb Cole.

The problem with the original structure arose from the exact source that the setup was intended to address, the appearance of conflicts between mediators and litigators. Soon after the spinoff, attorneys for the city of Vero Beach, Fla., asked that Cobb Cole be disqualified from representing Vero Beach's adversary in a litigation matter. The city had not used the firm as its counsel, but it had hired two of its attorneys as mediators in three cases, before the reorganization.

When a suit against Vero Beach was filed early this year in a Sunshine Laws case, the city moved to have Cobb Cole, which was representing the plaintiff, disqualified from the case. In July, Cobb Cole defeated the motion. The decision was upheld by a Florida appellate court on Aug. 28, and the firm retained representation in the matter.

But Cobb Cole, as well as CCB Mediation and the other companies, began the second restructuring soon after Vero Beach filed the disqualification motion late last winter. "The primary reason for the spinoff was to avoid downstream conflicts," says John J. Upchurch, a former Cobb Cole partner and former president of CCB Mediation, explaining that "the use of CCB Mediation Inc. simply didn't convey to the legal community that we were a distinct organization." Upchurch is now president of Upchurch Watson.

After Vero Beach's disqualification motion, Upchurch says that the law firm partners and the ADR firms' officers "decided it would be more effective and cause less strain if we were each responsible for our own administration and management." He adds that "in the glare of an actual case or controversy, we realized that to an independent finder of fact that it might not appear to be as sharp a separation" as the original transaction intended. . . .

Cobb Cole partner Jonathan D. Kaney says that the firm is satisfied that it wasn't disqualified in the litigation matter, and that the original arrangement withstood the court's scrutiny, even if it didn't last. The court "found for us and concluded as a matter of law there was no attorney-client relationship" created by the mediations, says Kaney, adding that the court also found that the firm and ADR companies "perfected the division."

Adds Cobb Cole managing partner Samuel P. Bell III, the case "merely confirmed the thinking that brought about the initial separation. . . . The basic issue is this need for separation. I think it has been confirmed and I believe it will be the future for everyone. I don't think there is any way people will be able to [have] an ADR operation inside a law firm."

In his July 17 opinion, Indian River County Circuit Judge Charles E. Smith found that the former Cobb Cole "mediation counsel," John S. Neely Jr., had followed Florida's professional conduct standard rule 10.80 on mediator confidentiality with regard to the Vero Beach cases he had handled. Smith also concluded that Neely and C. Welborn Daniel, another former Cobb Cole mediation counsel, were not a part of Cobb Cole after the Jan. 1 reorganization.

Furthermore, Smith concluded that even if it was assumed that Vero Beach was a Cobb Cole client, there was no violation of conduct rules because the new litigation matter wasn't the same or substantially related to the mediation cases, and no lawyer remained in Cobb Cole that had material information from those matters. (*Zorc v. City of Vero Beach*, Case No. 95-0250 CA 16 (Indian River County Ct. July 17, 1997)). On Aug. 28, Florida's Fourth District Court of Appeals affirmed Smith's ruling without an opinion. *Zorc v. City of Vero Beach*, Case No. 97-00465 (Fla. 4th Dist. Ct. App. Aug. 28, 1997). . . .

NOTES AND QUESTIONS

(1) What steps would you recommend that an individual or a firm seeking to combine mediation and litigation practices take to avoid potential conflicts of interest?

(2) What rationale might be offered for why a person who had previously mediated a dispute involving a particular client should not be permitted to represent that client in future litigation?

(3) What rationale might be offered for why a person who had previously represented a particular client in litigation should not be permitted to serve as mediator in a dispute involving that client?

(4) In *McEnany v. West Del. County Community School Dist.*, 844 F. Supp. 523, 533 (N.D. Iowa 1994), the court refused to void a settlement reached in mediation on grounds of bias, even though the mediator was an attorney with a firm that had done various kinds of legal work for one of the parties for over ten years. The court emphasized that the mediator himself had neither done nor had particular knowledge of the work, and that he had disclosed the relationship prior to commencing the mediation. What do you think of the result?

(5) In your view, what should the rules be regarding possible conflicts of interest involving lawyer-mediators? Should clients have the right to waive a conflict of interest?

(6) Should mediatiors be governed by the same conflict of interest rules that also govern judges who preside over settlement conferences? In *Cho v. Superior Ct.*, 45 Cal. Rptr. 2d 863 (Cal. App. 1996), the court held that a firm was disqualified from continuing to represent its client because the judge who had presided over the case and received confidences during several settlement conferences had subsequently retired and joined the firm. The court stated that the disqualification was necessary because "[n]o amount of assurances

or screening procedures, no 'cone of silence,' could ever convince the opposing party that the confidences would not be used to its disadvantage." *Id*. at 870.

(7) Conflict of interest rules that are developed to govern lawyer-mediators may also have an impact on other legal practices. In *Fields-D'Arpino v. Restaurant Assocs., Inc.*, 39 F. Supp. 2d 412 (S.D.N.Y. 1999), the court examined a situation in which the firm representing the defendant designated an attorney at the firm to meet with the plaintiff and try to settle the case. Calling this process "mediation," the court held that the defense firm must be disqualified given a New York ethical rule stating that "[a] lawyer who has undertaken to act as an impartial . . . mediator should not thereafter represent in the dispute any of the parties involved." *Id*. at 414 (citing N. Y. Code of Prof. Resp. EC 5-20).

(8) For a discussion of potential legal malpractice issues facing lawyer-mediators, see David Plimpton, *Liability Pitfalls May be Waiting for Lawyer-Neutrals*, 18 Alternatives to High Cost of Litig. 65 (April 2000).

[2] FEE SHARING ISSUES FACING THE LAWYER-MEDIATOR

Citing rules prohibiting lawyers and nonlawyers from sharing legal fees, several jurisdictions have wrestled with the question of whether or how lawyers and nonlawyers may join together in a practice to offer mediation services. A Florida Opinion provides that "any nonlawyer mediators employed by the inquirer's law firm may not have an ownership interest in either the law firm or the mediation department. To do so would implicate rules prohibiting sharing fees with nonlawyers, partnership with nonlawyers, and assisting in the unauthorized practice of law" (Florida Ethics Opinion 94-6, April 30, 1995). A Rhode Island Opinion also seems to preclude such an arrangement, emphasizing that a lawyer who provides mediation services will nonetheless be perceived as an attorney, and stating that the rule "avoids the possibility of a non-lawyer's interference with a lawyer's independent professional judgment and avoids encouraging non-lawyers from engaging in the unauthorized practice of law." (Rhode Island Opinion 95-1, Report No. 558, March 6, 1995). On the other hand, a Vermont Opinion states that so long as the partnership between lawyer and non-lawyer does not include the "practice of law," in that legal advice will not be offered by the attorney or any members of the attorney's firm, lawyer and non-lawyer mediators may join together to form a business. (Vermont Ethics Opinion No. 93-5, *undated*).

QUESTIONS

(1) Why do ethical rules generally prohibit fee-sharing between lawyers and nonlawyers?

(2) Given the purpose of the rule prohibiting fee-sharing between lawyers and nonlawyers, does it make sense to prohibit lawyers and nonlawyers from

sharing fees in a mediation practice? Does the distinction drawn in the Vermont opinion above make sense?

[3] ADVERTISING AND SOLICITATION ISSUES FACING LAWYER-MEDIATORS

Lawyers face very strict rules on advertisement and solicitation. Do these same rules apply to lawyers who choose to practice mediation exclusively or in combination with their advocacy practice? Opinions differ. Most jurisdictions provide that lawyers who mediate are nonetheless governed by the strict rules relating to attorney advertising. Thus, a Kansas Opinion states that the same restrictive advertising rules apply, even though "mediation may be a new addition to the 'forms' of practice. . . ." (Kan. Formal and Informal Op. No. 95-02, May 26, 1995). A New York opinion similarly states that even if mediation is not technically considered the "practice of law," a "lawyer's role as a neutral mediator may include rendering advice about legal questions or preparing a separation agreement. . . ." It further notes that even where a mediator "serves as a mediator outside of the law office, gives no legal advice or opinions, and does not draw up an agreement," participants would be aware of the fact that the mediator was an attorney. Therefore, opined the committee, lawyer-mediators should be proscribed from participating in a referral service that might mistakenly be thought by clients to be a disinterested agency. (N.Y. St. B. Ass'n Committee on Prof. Ethics, Op. 678, (42-95) Jan. 10, 1996). By contrast, an Illinois Opinion states that "[i]f the advertising and promotional material for the mediation business does not amount to advertising for the lawyer's law practice, it is not subject to the rules on lawyer advertising." (Ill. Op. No. 92-05, 10/92).

On the other hand, most jurisdictions seem to be fairly permissive in letting lawyers tout their mediation background in promotional materials. Thus, Kansas, South Carolina, and Tennesee have each stated that lawyers may indicate they are certified mediators on their letterhead, so long as the statement is truthful. (Kan. Op. 95-02, May 26, 1995), (SC Bar Advisory Op. 96-29), (Tenn. Ethics Op. 98-F-142(a), Dec. 11, 1998). However, several jurisdictions have carefully examined precisely how the mediator's status may be defined, so as to avoid misleading the public. In Tennessee, a lawyer-mediator may state that she is a "Rule 31 Listed Mediator" but not an "Approved Rule 31 Mediator," because the latter does not indicate what body issued the approval. (Tenn. Ethics Op. 98-F-142(a), Dec. 11, 1998). Similarly, in Florida, an opinion proscribes the mediation department of a law firm from using the trade name "Sunshine Mediation," as it would be misleading unless applied to the entire law practice. (Fla. Ethics Op. 94-6, April 30, 1995). A second Florida ethics opinion, MQAP 99-013, prohibited a law firm from listing Circuit Court Mediation as a specialty, where only one member of the two-person firm was a certified mediator.

NOTES AND QUESTIONS

(1) What are the rationales for restricting advertising and solicitation by attorneys?

(2) Do these rationales apply when a lawyer offers services as a mediator?

(3) Restrictions on advertisements by mediators may sometimes be more stringent than those applied to non-mediator attorneys. A Florida ethics opinion, MQAP 95-007, provided that a mediator was precluded from advertising that the mediator would provide "a dispassionate evaluation by a neutral party," reasoning that this activity was not consistent with Florida's definition of mediation. Could an attorney be prohibited from advertising that he or she would provide "a dispassionate evaluation"?

[4] BUSINESS CONCERNS FACING THE LAWYER-MEDIATOR

The attempt to integrate mediation and litigation practices has raised practical concerns for some attorneys, particularly when they are part of a larger firm that focuses on litigation. For a variety of reasons, lawyers often bring less money into the firm when functioning as mediators than as litigators. First, lawyer-mediators often charge a lower hourly rate when operating in their mediator capacity than they do when performing traditional litigation functions. Moreover, lawyer-mediators typically do not need the services of associate attorneys or paralegals to assist them and, consequently, the firm loses the ability to bill for work performed by these additional personnel. At the same time, mediators require only a fraction of the overhead that is often required by litigators. They don't usually require assistance from messengers and typically need little, if any, secretarial support. However, attorney-mediators may have a greater than normal need for conference room time. The bottom line is that it may be difficult for attorneys who decide they want to spend substantial time as mediators to work out an equitable financial arrangement with their own firms. These sorts of pressures, as well as others, may sometimes lead lawyer-mediators to leave their firms and go into practice on their own.

Chapter 9

THE INSTITUTIONALIZATION OF MEDIATION

Good or Bad ?
Both !

§ A INTRODUCTION

This chapter will focus on the institutionalization of mediation. Although, as discussed in Chapter 1, *supra*, mediation can trace its roots to community programs, today mediation is closely tied to numerous major societal institutions. Mediation is now established as part of many federal and state court programs, is employed by many federal and state agencies, is embraced by many corporations, and is used in schools, prisons and other settings. By 1994, every state, plus the District of Columbia and Puerto Rico, had enacted at least one statute relating to the use of mediation.

While such institutionalization has certainly helped to increase the use of mediation dramatically, there may also be some drawbacks to this trend. As you read this chapter, consider the positive outcomes achieved through institutionalization, as well as the potential negative consequences of what happens when a flexible process is placed in a structured environment. Certainly, institutionalization raises some new issues that require substantial thought.

In this chapter, particular attention will be given to the institutionalization of mediation within the court context. Section [B] will highlight the development of mediation as an institution. Section [C] will examine specific examples of court-based mediation, including an exploration of the policy choices to be made and results from empirical research on mediation in the court context. Section [D] will describe other institutional uses of mediation, including administrative agencies, and Section [E] will present critiques of institutionalization.

§ B DEVELOPMENT OF INSTITUTIONALIZATION

The modern movement towards institutionalization of ADR in general and mediation in particular traces its roots to the Pound Conference in 1976 in which judges, court administrators and legal scholars gathered together to discuss the public's pervasive dissatisfaction with the administration of justice. At that conference, Professor Frank E.A. Sander delivered a paper in which he described a courthouse of the future where parties could go for a variety of services to assist them in resolving their disputes. His vision, which was subsequently coined the "multi-door" courthouse, was premised on ✳ funding not only for judges but also for intake specialists, mediators, arbitrators, and other dispute resolvers. The Washington D.C. courts adopted this model.

For a variety of reasons, however, mediation as an institution has not grown exclusively in that direction. Institutions also rely heavily on volunteers and private providers to serve mediation programs. The primary reason is that a multi-door courthouse concept is very expensive for the sponsoring institution. A secondary reason is that while the concept of an intake specialist is reasonable in the abstract, in reality sorting cases has proven to be very difficult and complex. Despite a number of studies which have been conducted, researchers have not identified conclusive objective criteria that can be used to reliably determine which cases are most likely to benefit from each process. The individuals and the attorneys involved in the case, the amount in controversy, the status of negotiations, and the state of the law will all have an impact on the case dynamics. Thus, courts have shied away from the multi-door concept in part because the analysis needed to sort cases is extremely subtle.

In the following excerpt, Professor Frank E.A. Sander reflects on the history of the mediation movement and speculates on the future of mediation in light of institutionalization.

THE FUTURE OF ADR

2000 J. of Disp. Resol. 3, 3–8 (2000) [*]

By Frank E.A. Sander

Because I've been fortunate to observe the ADR scene for much of its recent development, I'm often asked my views of where we stand now. My somewhat flip answer is, "On Monday, Wednesday and Friday, I think we've made amazing progress. On Tuesday, Thursday and Saturday, ADR seems more like a grain of sand on the adversary system beach.". . .

What are some of the signs that the glass is half full? What are the things that give me optimism . . .? First, in 1998, the Congress of the United States enacted the Dispute Resolution Act which directs each federal district to establish an ADR program by local rule [28 U.S.C. sections 651-658 (Supp. IV 1998)]. There is also comparable state legislation in a large number of states, sometimes mandating referral of specific cases to ADR or authorizing judges to do so in their discretion.

Second, dispute resolution clauses, sometimes quite sophisticated, are increasingly being used in contracts of all kinds.

Third, some businesses and law firms systematically canvass cases for ADR potential. . . .

Fourth, the CPR Institute for Dispute Resolution, an impressive New York organization of representatives from 800 leading businesses and law firms, is dedicated to the goal of educating its members and others concerning better ways of resolving disputes. Its CPR pledge commits signers to explore ADR before resorting to court. . . .

Fifth, a number of states now require that lawyers discuss ADR options with clients or to certify on the pleadings that they have done so. . . .

Sixth, for disputes in the public sector, the Administrative Dispute Resolution Act of 1996 requires federal agencies to consider the use of ADR and to appoint an ADR specialist. And there have been some Executive Orders issued by the President to stimulate similar action in the U.S. Department of Justice.

Seventh, about half the states now have state offices of dispute resolution that seek to facilitate the resolution of public disputes by providing technical assistance or recommending competent dispute resolvers.

Eighth, virtually every law school as well as many schools of business and planning now offer one or more ADR courses. . . .

So those are a few of the positive indicators. What are the downsides and remaining challenges?

Let me pause briefly for a little historic summary. I think there have been three periods in the approximately twenty-five years of the modern ADR development. Obviously, we didn't invent mediation. . . . But, by common agreement, it was about 1975 that the current interest in ADR began. The first period . . . was about 1975 to 1982. I call it, "Let a thousand flowers bloom." There were many experiments. . . .

The second period, about 1982 to 1990 . . . I call "Cautions and caveats:" Concerns about where we're heading, attempts to sort out the wheat from the chaff. . . .

The third period, starting about 1990, is what I call "Institutionalization." The question there is: How do we weave ADR into the dispute resolution fabric so that ADR options are systematically considered at various points along the life of a dispute rather than putting the onus on the party who wants to use ADR, which will often be construed as a sign of weakness? . . .

What are the present obstacles and impediments to institutionalization, and what are some of the hopeful signs? When you look at the situation from the disputant's perspective there is often a lack of knowledge of ADR. . . . [T]he prevailing assumption that the court is *the* place to resolve disputes is a major part of the problem.

Second, there is a lack of readily available public dispute resolution options—the absence of a public facility like a comprehensive justice center where someone can go to have access to mediation or arbitration—a place where the sign over the door says, "This is where disputes get handled. The experts here will help you decide which is the best process for your case. . . .

What if we look at the situation from the perspective of lawyers? What are the impediments there? . . .

The fact is that in ADR [lawyers] lose control, particularly in flexible procedures like mediation. . . . So lawyers are sometimes reluctant to get involved with an unfamiliar, threatening procedure.

There are also economic incentives for lawyers to stay with litigation. . . .

There are also other perverse incentives. For example, in some companies a settlement is charged to the budget of that division, but litigation costs are

[handwritten margin note: problem — very few good studies of cost effectiveness]

not charged to a department. So in that company there's an incentive to litigate rather than settle a case. Attorney compensation also sometimes takes account of successful wins but not of money-saving settlements.

Finally, there is a public policy impediment, and that is the lack of adequate cost-benefit studies. . . . [I]t's very difficult to document the specific money savings of pursuing a case through mediation rather than court adjudication. We have some anecdotal data, but when you think about it, that kind of research is incredibly difficult to do. For example, one claim for mediation is that in cases of continuing relationships, it's often a more lasting solution. That is, it prevents future disputes because you get at the underlying concerns and it teaches the parties how to resolve disputes more effectively by themselves in the future. That means you have to have a longitudinal study, spanning over many years in order to document that kind of thing, quite aside from the difficult questions of how you measure the peace of mind that comes from an absence of future lawsuits. . . .

. . . .

Let me end up with some promising future directions for overcoming these impediments and advancing the cause of institutionalization. In the short run, we need to strengthen some of the institutionalization devices such as . . . the duty of a lawyer to apprize a client about ADR options as part of professional consultation, coupled with early court consideration of ADR possibilities, and judicial power to refer cases to appropriate ADR processes. All these institutionalization devices have an important indirect effect. They not only teach clients about these possibilities, but they also get lawyers up to par. . . .

. . . This is also why I favor mandatory mediation at the present time. There are some hot arguments in the literature with some people saying, "Mediation means voluntarily agreeing to a result. How can you force somebody to voluntarily agree to a result?" I think that confuses coercion *into* mediation with coercion *in* mediation. If you have coercion *in* mediation, it is not mediation. . . .[W]e have evidence that the process is very powerful, that it works for people who use it, but for some of the reasons I mentioned earlier, people don't seem to be using the process sufficiently voluntarily. So my view about mandatory mediation is about the same as affirmative action—that is, it's not the right permanent answer, but it is a useful temporary expedient to make up for inadequate past practices.

My basic view is that it is for the court, not the parties, to allocate the precious public resource that is the court. The courts and the legislature should decide how much use you should make of courts and in what kind of cases, not the parties or their lawyers. . . .

In the long run we need more education of lawyers and clients. . . .

Second, I am concerned about the long-term professional issues that are raised by ADR. At the moment we have a lot of people who have been trained in ADR, but there is insufficient paying work for them. . . . There are many places where ADR is done by volunteers, and that's a good thing. . . . But I get concerned about developing career paths by which talented graduates of . . . law schools can become self-purporting ADR professionals. . . .

Increasingly over this period of twenty-five years, more and more people have made careers out of ADR, but it's still extremely difficult and there's no simple way to do it. . . . That's not a good way of developing a new profession. . . .

§ C INSTITUTIONALIZATION OF MEDIATION IN THE COURT CONTEXT

Not surprisingly, courts have provided the most intense institutional use of mediation. In a few jurisdictions, judges are required to order mediation in certain types of cases (e.g., divorce actions in which children are involved). Judges in many other state and federal courts have the discretion to refer (or order) parties to mediation in many or all civil cases. In other courts, the judge may suggest or recommend mediation or conduct a judicial settlement conference using mediation techniques.

The following section presents excerpts regarding court-connected mediation. The first two readings look at the development of mediation in the courts. In the first excerpt, Professor Baruch Bush details an imaginary conversation with a judge who has been given an opportunity to order cases to mediation. Through this conversation, Professor Bush highlights the underlying philosophical decision-making which must take place before one embarks on institutional use of mediation. In the second excerpt, Sharon Press describes the institutionalization of mediation via a state-wide office and the various decisions that arise in that arena. In the second set of excerpts, specific mandatory mediation programs are analyzed empirically. Nancy Welsh and Barbara McAdoo evaluate the Minnesota court mediation scheme through the eyes of attorneys, and John McCrory evaluates the Maine court mediation program through the eyes of the litigants. Finally, a summary of the Rand Corporation's evaluation of the federal court mediation programs is included along with two responses to the report.

[1] POLICY DEVELOPMENT

MEDIATION AND ADJUDICATION, DISPUTE RESOLUTION AND IDEOLOGY: AN IMAGINARY CONVERSATION

3 J. Contemp. Legal Issues 1, 1–10, 14–15, 18–21, 23–24 (1989) [*]

By Robert A. Baruch Bush

This essay started out as an informal talk to a number of dispute resolution colleagues concerning what I believe is a neglected and important perspective on our field. My goal here is to bring some attention to that perspective, at two levels. First, I want to show that there is an underlying ideological dimension to the ongoing controversy over adjudication and mediation that accounts for a lot of the heat, if not the light, that goes on in the discussion of these and other dispute resolution processes. Second, I want to dig a bit deeper than I think most of us have dug so far to try to say what that ideological dimension is. . . .

Instead of approaching these goals through a formal or abstract analysis, however, I intend to pursue them through imagining a story or conversation which, as it were, gives voices to the different positions taken in the controversy over mediation and adjudication. I invite the reader to listen and respond to this conversation. . . .

The setting for the conversation is as follows. A judge has been empowered by a state statute to refer cases from his civil docket to mediation. The statute says that he can, in his discretion, refer any and all cases; the decision is his, and the parties cannot refuse mediation without showing good cause. The judge can send all his cases to mediation on a blanket basis, or certain categories of cases, or individual cases on a case by case basis, whichever he decides. This is what the statute empowers him to do, and the Supreme Court has set up rules enabling him and other judges to do it. The problem is that the judge is uncertain how to exercise this new power. . . .

So, he picks six representative cases from his civil docket: a divorce case with a custody question, a complex commercial litigation, a landlord-tenant case, a discrimination suit, a consumer case, and a personal injury litigation. He sends copies of the case files, with names deleted, to four individuals who are friends or associates: his law clerk, his court administrator, his former law professor, and a practicing mediator. . . . The judge asks each of them for their advice. . . .

He is a bit startled when he gets back the results of this survey, because he gets four completely different recommendations. From the law professor, he gets the recommendation that he should send *no* cases to mediation; all the cases should stay in court. The law clerk . . . says that the discrimination case, the consumer case, and the personal injury case should be kept in court, but the divorce, the landlord-tenant, and the commercial cases should go to mediation. The court administrator says he should send them all to mediation, *unless* both parties to the dispute object; if both parties object, he shouldn't refer them to mediation, whatever the type of case. Finally, the mediator tells him that he should send all the cases to mediation, whether or not the parties object.

The judge is puzzled by this set of responses. . . .

[So] he calls all four advisors and says, "I'd like you to argue this out in front of me. I want to hear what you have to say in the presence of one another. . . . "

So, the four advisors come together with the judge. . . . The court administrator goes first. ". . . As far as I'm concerned, the most important goal we have here is saving time and money. . . . The courts are heavily backlogged, delay is epidemic, and adding new judges and courtrooms appears fiscally— and politically—impossible. Settlements are the only solution. . . . [S]ince *all* cases have some potential to settle," she continues, "and we don't know which ones will and which ones won't, it makes sense to refer them all to mediation, unless we have a clear indication in advance that there's no real settlement possibility. . . . That's the reason for my recommendation. Refer to mediation, unless it's clear that there's opposition on both sides to settlement."

The law clerk then is called upon. He says, ". . . In my view, the main goal is not saving time and money, regardless of what the legislature may have had in mind. There are goals of dispute resolution that are much more important.

". . . [P]rotecting individual rights and ensuring some kind of substantive fairness to both sides in the resolution of the dispute are the most important goals. And where rights and substantive fairness are most important, adjudication in court is the best tool we have to accomplish those goals. However, there are cases where rights and fairness are not the only or the most important goals. For example, if there is an ongoing relationship between the parties, preserving that relationship may be very important both to the parties and to the public. In that case, mediation would be desirable, because preserving relationships is something that mediation does better than the adjudication process. Therefore, I think that you can distinguish between cases on the basis of the ongoing relationship factor. When you have such a relationship, refer to mediation; otherwise, keep the case in court. . . . "

Next is the mediator's turn. "I both agree and disagree with the administrator and the law clerk. . . . Sometimes the best solution will be one that saves the parties time and money; sometimes it will be one that preserves the relationship. Sometimes it will be one that does neither of these. That will all depend on many details of the case.

"But whatever the details, there is plenty of evidence that in terms of achieving the best results for the individual case in question, mediation is a process that has tremendous advantages over adjudication. The process is flexible, issues can be framed more effectively and discussed more fully, a greater variety of possible solutions can be considered, and unique, innovative and integrative solutions are possible, even likely. Therefore, mediation ought to be tried *first* in all cases because the potential to arrive at superior substantive results is always greater in mediation than in adjudication. If mediation doesn't work, . . . then the parties can go back to court. . . ."

Finally the law professor speaks. "Your Honor," he begins, "I'm sorry I have to disagree. But all of your other friends have missed the point. . . . A court is a public institution, and the goal of a court as a public institution is not to save time and money; nor is it to help private parties secure private benefits in individual cases. Your goal as a public institution is to promote important public values. That ought to be your primary concern: the promotion and the securing of important public values through the dispute resolution process. . . .

"I submit to you, your Honor, that the most important public values at stake in dispute resolution are basically four. . . .[T]he public values a court must concern itself with are: protection of fundamental individual rights, provision of social justice, promotion of economic welfare, and creation of social solidarity.

". . . [T]he rule-based, public adjudication process is an excellent—an unparalleled—instrument for accomplishing these values. Mediation, on the other hand, weakens and undermines every single one of these values. . . .

"This brings me to the heart of my argument, . . . [f]irst, we can't sacrifice public values of this statute solely to save time and money. . . . [T]o adopt a public policy saying that values like rights protection and social justice are less important than saving money and judicial economy would be inexcusable. Second, there's no way of neatly dividing up cases on the basis that some involve these public values and others do not. . . . All six of the kinds of cases that you submitted to us involve one or more of these public values. . . . Therefore, . . . 'channeling' of different cases to different processes is undesirable.

"Finally, you cannot, as the mediator suggested, consider the value of better results for the parties in the individual case superior to these *public* values. . . . As a matter of public policy, we cannot put private benefit over the public good. Therefore, your Honor, I say all of these cases should remain in court, unless perhaps a petition is submitted by both parties to adjourn pending voluntarily initiated settlement discussions or mediation."

. . . .

Before the judge has a chance to adjourn and consider the arguments more thoroughly, however, the mediator asks the judge for one more minute. . . . "When I say mediation ought to be used in all these cases, my reason is also based on promoting *public* values, public values which are important to *all* of the cases you sent us, public values different from and *more* important than the ones that the professor mentioned. In other words, like the professor's argument for adjudication, my argument for mediation is also a public values argument, but it is based on a different view of public values than the view he presented.

"Now my problem is that it is hard to articulate clearly what these different public values are. I think they're evoked or implied by concepts like reconciliation, social harmony, community, interconnection, relationship, and the like. Mediation does produce superior results, as I argued earlier. But it also involves a non-adversarial process that is less traumatic, more humane, and far more capable of healing and reconciliation than adjudication. Those are the kinds of concerns that make me feel that these cases ought to be handled in mediation, not for private benefit reasons and not for expediency reasons, but because of these reconciliatory public values promoted by mediation."

. . . .

Let us pause for a minute from this story. The conversation to this point should be familiar to many readers as a parallel to the state of the adjudication/mediation debate today. . . .

Given the state of the debate right now, what are the prospects for the immediate future in the use of adjudication and mediation? What are judges like the one in the story likely to do? I think there are three possible scenarios. First—and most likely, despite the good intentions of the judge in our story— expediency and private interest may rule. Mediation will be used widely, and perhaps indiscriminately, to reduce court caseload and to satisfy private disputants' individual needs. Second, and less likely, . . . the public values argument could lead to rejection of mediation generally and retrenchment back to adjudication in court as the primary way of resolving disputes. . . . Third, and least likely, if a clear and persuasive public value argument can be articulated on behalf of mediation, then in all likelihood mediation will spread more widely—but perhaps in a different form than the private-benefit/expediency version.

The present debate over adjudication and mediation therefore has two dimensions. One is the public-value versus private-benefit/expediency dimension. . . . [I]t is a clash over whether the public good *matters,* not what the public good *is.* . . . The second dimension is the public-value versus public-value dimension, and it is reflected in the conflict . . . here, between the professor and the mediator. . . . In this dimension, *both* adjudication and mediation represent public values, and the question is which public values are more important. This is a clash over what the public good *is,* a clash of social vision or ideology. . . . This is the dimension of the debate . . . to which the conversation above is about to proceed.

. . . .

The judge repeats his question to the mediator: "What exactly is this public value underlying mediation . . .?"

. . . .

". . . Simply put, it is the value of providing a moral and political education for citizens, in responsibility for themselves and respect for others. In a democracy, your Honor, that must be considered a crucial public value and it must be considered a public function. . . . It cannot be accomplished in adjudication. . . . In my view, this civic education value is more important than the values the professor is concerned about. . . . And, . . . even if the parties had reached no agreement in mediation, that education could still have occurred anyway. The case could then have gone back to court where those other values could have been dealt with as secondary matters.

"Finally, I just want to clarify an important connection between my argument here and our earlier discussion. On reflection, I've realized that the 'superior results' argument. . . is also based, at least in part, on the public value I'm talking about here. . .[T]he 'superiority' of results we speak of is not only, or primarily, that the results better serve the individual interests of the parties—a private benefit—but that they express each individual's considered choice to respect and accommodate the other to some degree—a democratic public value. . . ."

. . . .

Let us take another pause. What we have now in the story is a parallel of yet another debate that we see in a much larger field. . . .

Once the public-value argument for mediation is fully stated and set against the public-value argument for adjudication, it becomes clear that the adjudication/mediation debate derives from a much deeper debate between the liberal/individualist and the communitarian/relationalist visions of society. . . .

. . . .

To return to and conclude our conversation, . . . what additional advice does this reading suggest we might want to offer the judge in our story? In answer to this question, I want to exercise a little poetic license and jump into the conversation myself, to speak directly to this judge.

Based on what we have heard from the others so far, I would say, "Judge, you're asking what kind of choice you should make, as between keeping cases in court and referring them to mediation. But it's clear to me and I hope it's clear to you that you have a deeper choice to make here: a choice between different social visions. If you accept the prevailing individualist vision, Judge, then you should reject mediation completely, or limit it very severely, to ensure that public values like those advocated by the professor are not undermined. . . . On the other hand, if you accept the relational vision, then you should not merely use mediation; you should expand it to ensure the accomplishment of the most important public values under that vision. Therefore, you should refer all your cases to mediation, but with an important proviso. . . .

"But whatever you do, . . . as a public servant you should not use mediation at all, if you're going to use it simply as a tool for saving time and satisfying private litigants' individual interests. Because this will undermine *both* of the contending visions. . . .

". . . [M]ediation—as the mediator presented it to you—is either being co-opted or rejected entirely. No real attention has been given to the relational vision, and the potential of mediation as a transformative instrument, a means of civic education.

. . . .

"This sort of approach . . . —preference for mediation over adjudication across the board—means changing completely the terms of reference in this discussion. It means regarding mediation as a *primary* dispute resolution process, not an 'alternative' dispute resolution process. . . .

Finally, . . . if you are going to explore this vision of mediation, it means making sure that mediation as practiced is in fact an opportunity for self-determination and self-transcendence on the part of the parties, and not simply a tool of expediency. . . .

". . . Am I suggesting *mandatory* mediation for every case, absent good cause for exemption. . .? . . . [Y]es, I advise you to use your mandatory mediation power fully; but in any event, do whatever you consider appropriate to encourage mediation in every case.

". . . If you're not prepared . . . to make sure mediation really provides an opportunity for self-determination and self-transcendence—then my advice to you is very different. Forget mediation. . . . Salvage what you can of the individualist vision. Improve the courts . . . .

"Some people may ask: If I support mediation, then why should I *care* what the reasons are for expanding it? . . . Let's expand it first, and worry later about clarifying the reasons. . . . I disagree. . . . I am afraid that publicly sponsored, court-connected mediation oriented towards efficiency and private benefits alone, would crowd out other versions and reduce the chance for the educational vision to develop."

. . . .

That is what I would say to the judge—for now, at least. And that is where I close this installment of the conversation. And I throw it open to you, reader.

For other voices are surely needed to continue this conversation. After all this, what would *you* say?

BUILDING AND MAINTAINING A STATEWIDE MEDIATION PROGRAM: A VIEW FROM THE FIELD

81 Ky. L.J. 1029, 1029–1036, 1040–1041 (1992-93) ⸳

pragmatic view

By Sharon Press

As more and more states are seeking to improve the judicial system through increased use of alternative dispute resolution mechanisms, a number of issues surrounding how to establish a court-connected mediation program are repeatedly encountered. The format most often selected is the establishment of statewide mediation offices. . . .

Program Initiation Decisions

. . . .

. . . [E]stablishment of a statewide program has many advantages including: uniformity from jurisdiction to jurisdiction; known expectations; accessibility to mediation for all litigants; and economies of scale in the provision of technical assistance.

Merely reaching a consensus on establishment of a statewide program, however, does not adequately address all of the issues. The definition of "statewide" can vary greatly. . . . For example, a statewide program may involve, on the most complete side, the creation of a state office to oversee the program with site offices and state employees in each local jurisdiction. It may also provide for the creation of a state office that is responsible for both the oversight of the entire program and the provision of technical assistance for the local jurisdictions where the staff is county funded. Finally, a statewide program may simply involve the adoption of a state statute or court rule that allows the trial courts to order cases to mediation without provision of staff on either the state or local level.

Obviously, each model has its advantages and disadvantages. From a purely fiscal standpoint, the establishment of both state funded central and local mediation offices is very costly. . . . In addition, there are some benefits to private and public sector cooperation, such as the potential ability of the marketplace to regulate the field. On the other hand, merely providing the statutory mechanism for sending cases to mediation, without creating a central office to assist the oversight of the program, may be an inappropriate delegation of court authority and could result in an inadequate method of overseeing the provision of justice.

⸳ Copyright © 1993 by the University of Kentucky Law Journal. Reprinted with permission.

Statewide Office Models

As an initial matter, it must be determined what the office should look like in terms of staffing and to whom the central office should report. . . . The office can be coordinated via the executive branch, the legislative branch, the judicial branch, within the state university system, or some combination thereof. . . .

. . . At a minimum, the office should provide information and technical assistance to the local mediation programs during both the establishment phase and in the long-term development of the programs. The office should also act as the central location for the collection of statistics for the dual purposes of monitoring the program and making suggestions for improvement and modifications in the existing program. . . .

State Rules/Statutes

A statewide mediation program can be established by means of a state statute or court rule, although the relative authority vested in the judicial and legislative branches of government varies from state to state and must be assessed accordingly. In addition, the courts traditionally have been deemed to have broad discretion to make rules concerning those items deemed to be procedural, while the legislature retains the right to pass laws in all substantive areas.

. . . The primary advantage of using both state statutes and court rules is that doubt regarding the program's legitimacy is reduced, and through its rules the court is provided with the flexibility of making internal modifications. . . .

Once the method of adoption is determined, the specific language must be considered. In particular, a decision must be reached regarding the degree of specificity that will be covered in the state law and rules and how much flexibility, if any, will be permitted at the local level. The dilemma is in ascertaining a balance between uniformity and predictability throughout the state versus the ability of the program to accommodate the needs of the individual circuits and counties. . . .

Funding

. . . While most frequently the state office will be funded by the entity of which it is a part, it can be funded through a local program, by, for example, the collection of filing and mediator certification fees. Often the state program will collect all fees centrally and then redistribute funds to the local programs.

Other sources of funds for the individual programs include: local and state bar associations; individual practitioners; filing fee additions; grants; and party-assessed mediation fees. The source of funds needs to be considered both in terms of initial seed money and identification of sources for long-term commitments. Important questions to consider . . . are:

(1) How much money is available initially and is it enough to adequately and appropriately sustain a program?

(2) What is the reliability of receiving continued funding?

(3) Are there any restrictions attached to the grant of funds? . . . Are constraints placed on the continued receipt of the funds?

(4) How secure is the money? Is it tied to the political climate or the influence of a single individual? . . .

. . . The primary advantage of a filing fee addition is that it provides a steady, reliable source of revenue. . . . Additionally, in order to change the traditional view of the court system to recognize that litigation is just one service the courts can offer, adoption of a filing fee to fund alternative processes becomes both an appropriate and desirable source of funding.

There are, however, difficulties with this source of funding. . . . As filing fees continue to increase, concern has been raised that the filing fees alone might become an unreasonable bar of access to the court system. . . .

Goals of the Program

Identification of the goals of the program and establishing consensus around these goals is a crucial part in the successful development of a state program. The answers to funding, organizational, procedural and evaluation questions become much clearer once the goals are established. These possible goals include:

(1) to decrease the court's docket;

(2) to speed the pace of cases to resolution;

(3) to decrease the cost of resolving conflict through the courts for both the litigants and the court system;

(4) to decrease the demand on judges;

(5) to increase litigant satisfaction with the court system;

(6) to provide for a better means of justice;

(7) to lower recidivism;

(8) to improve relationships between the existing parties.

While these goals are not mutually exclusive . . . it should be noted that not all of these goals are compatible and the program must clearly specify what it is seeking to achieve. . . .

If the articulated goal of the program is to quickly produce an abundance of settlement, the mediators may inappropriately become directive in an effort to assist the program in meeting this goal. Dependence on this goal may also be in direct conflict with the goals of providing parties with the opportunity to exercise self-determination or to improve the relationship between the parties.

. . . .

Scope of Program

Establishment of a statewide program can be for all types or limited types of cases. . . .

The state might also consider whether all resources will be devoted to establishment of a mediation program or if mediation will be just one of the options available to the parties. . . . Providing more options to the parties and the court would encourage use of the most appropriate type. On the other hand, development of a single approach, such as mediation, would allow the courts to focus its energy and resources. . . .

QUESTIONS

(1) Professor Bush intentionally presents the ideological debate as an either/or choice over which set of public values one adopts. Might they be integrated? If so, how?

(2) Do you agree with Professor Bush that a person who adopts an individualist vision should reject mediation completely or limit it severely?

(3) If one were to adopt the relational vision, how should the program be organized based on the questions raised in the Press article?

[2] PRACTICE IMPLICATIONS/EMPIRICAL EVALUATIONS

DOES ADR REALLY HAVE A PLACE ON THE LAWYER'S PHILOSOPHICAL MAP?

18 Hamline J. Pub. L. & Pol'y 376, 376–377, 380–388, 390–393 (1997)*

By Barbara McAdoo and Nancy Welsh

For nearly two decades proponents of alternative dispute resolution (ADR) have touted the advantages of institutionalizing ADR within the courts. The anticipated benefits have included: quicker settlements, better settlements, resolution which is less expensive for the courts and litigants, and greater litigant satisfaction with both the procedure and the outcome. Many state and federal courts have listened. Indeed, in nearly every state, at least one local state and/or federal court has incorporated ADR in some manner. In Minnesota, with the promulgation of Rule 114 of the Minnesota General Rules of Practice, the Minnesota Supreme Court has chosen to institutionalize ADR in district courts throughout the state.

Is ADR delivering all of its intended benefits in these court-annexed programs? It appears that ADR processes, especially mediation, do consistently result in increased litigant satisfaction. Recent studies, however, do not always appear to support the claims that ADR produces substantially quicker settlements or reduced expenses for litigants or the courts. . . .

One particular striking feature of Rule 114 is its approach to encouraging the use of ADR. During its deliberations from 1987 to 1989, the [Minnesota] ADR Task Force struggled mightily with the question of whether or not to make ADR mandatory in all civil cases. The experience of other jurisdictions was instructive. In those jurisdictions where ADR was totally voluntary, parties used ADR rarely or not at all. In jurisdictions that made ADR of certain classes of cases mandatory, there was not always a good "match" between a case and the ADR process used to attempt resolution of the case. Therefore, the ADR Task Force recommended a rule which would require attorneys to consider ADR in every civil case, discuss ADR with their client(s) and opposing counsel, and advise the court regarding their conclusions about ADR, including the selection of a process, a neutral and the timing of an ADR process. The ADR Task Force recommended that attorneys and clients have great discretion and creative freedom in selecting an ADR process. Also, in order to ensure that attorneys and clients considered ADR seriously, the ADR Task Force also recommended that judges be given the ultimate discretion to order parties into non-binding ADR against their will. These recommendations of the ADR Task Force ultimately became part of the enabling legislation and Rule 114.

The ADR Task Force (and the subsequent ADR Implementation Committee) also recognized that Minnesota required an infrastructure to support the creative and appropriate application of Rule 114; a state-wide pool of qualified ADR neutrals who understood and could provide the ADR processes listed in the rule; an informed bar which had access to the pool of ADR neutrals; and an informed and pro-active judiciary. Thus, Rule 114 ultimately established specific training and continuing education requirements for ADR neutrals providing services under Rule 114; a written "Roster of Qualified Neutrals," to be distributed to all courts and available to all attorneys; and a "grandparenting" provision for ADR neutrals who already had substantial experience with ADR. The rule also established a seven person ADR Review Board, which was given the responsibility to develop the exact format of the written roster and determine the criteria to be used in deciding whether an individual could be "grandparented" onto the roster, without meeting the training requirements specified in the rule. . . .

In December 1994, the Minnesota Supreme Court expanded the authority of the ADR Review Board, in part to address evaluation issues. . . . In turn, the ADR Review Board engaged a consultant to help develop a work plan and identify a number of possible evaluation projects. This article reports on the data gathered from Hennepin County lawyers. . . . The research involved in-depth interviews with twenty-three civil litigators throughout Minnesota to collect data about how lawyers use ADR in relation to discovery, negotiation and trial; how lawyers decide which ADR process to use for a given case; and what kinds and numbers of settlements are occurring in ADR processes. This data was used to develop a questionnaire ("the Rule 114 questionnaire") to gather quantitative data. . . .

The Rule 114 questionnaire was sent to 1000 lawyers in Minnesota and the response rate was 74.8%. Hennepin County accounted for 446 responses or 59.6% of those responding. . . .

The overwhelming majority of Hennepin County attorneys—87.7%—indicated they had used an ADR process for their civil cases in Minnesota State Court in the past two years. . . . The responses to a . . . specific set of questions about the use of different ADR processes before and after the effective date of Rule 114 reported a striking increase in the use of mediation, but this was not true for other ADR processes. . . . In a court system in which ADR was introduced a little over a decade ago, over 90% of its lawyers now would, at a minimum, "sometimes" use ADR! This can not all be attributed directly to Rule 114, but it does suggest that the forced introduction to ADR in Hennepin County—culminating in the Rule 114 requirements—has led to a change in the way law is practiced. . . .

What follows are some preliminary conclusions, drawn from attorney perceptions of ADR, based on the lawyer interviews and the Rule 114 questionnaire, with editorial comments from the authors:

1. Although Hennepin County attorneys have indicated increased willingness to use ADR, a significant number still use ADR because they feel coerced into it. . . .

2. Discovery on cases sent to mediation is generally conducted about the same way as before Rule 114 was enacted. . . . When asked why mediation is not reducing the volume of discovery, 67.2% of those responding answered, "case circumstances usually require full discovery before the case is ready for mediation."

Comment: If discovery practices are barely changing, it is hard to claim that Rule 114 really has changed the way lawyers practice law. . . .

3. Attorneys' primary motivation for the use of ADR is to "save litigation expenses." . . . Significantly, lawyers largely overlooked some of the most salient, *non monetary* benefits of mediation. . . .

Comment: [Lawyers'] focus on the bottom line misses some of the potential qualitative benefits of ADR, particularly mediation. . . . In a sense, attorneys may be missing ADR's potential to help them provide more responsive "customer service" to their clients which should result in "better" results as well as increased client loyalty and referrals.

4. One third of Hennepin County attorneys reported that civil settlement rates increased during the past two years; almost two-thirds of those attributed this to "clients more interested in settling and staying out of court" or "increased use of ADR." Terms of settlement (i.e., *money*) however, were relatively unchanged. . . .

. . . .

. . . The preliminary data from the lawyer interviews as well as data from the Rule 114 questionnaire supports the view that lawyers choose mediators who fit the more "evaluative" profile. In particular:

1. Lawyers want lawyers as mediators.

2. Lawyers want litigators as mediators.

3. Most importantly, lawyers want mediators to have substantive experience in the field of law related the case. . . .

. . . [A]ttorneys increasingly are the gatekeepers to ADR processes. Based on the data described here, attorneys' perceptions and values influence the ability of ADR to deliver on its potential benefits. . . . Discovery practices could be curtailed; attorneys could negotiate to conduct only crucial discovery before the ADR event. Attorneys could plan more carefully with their clients in order to discern viable settlement options, including non-monetary elements. In short, attorneys could enlarge their "philosophical map."

Will ADR continue to result in greater litigant satisfaction with both the process and the outcome? . . . It is worrisome . . . that so few attorneys seem to value increased client satisfaction, increased client control of the outcome, and improved party relationships. If these potential benefits do not find their places on the lawyers' philosophical map, it is likely that the mediation model will continue to adapt to fit within the traditional legal culture and will look more and more like the traditional settlement conference mode. . . . Attorneys need to understand that providing responsive, quality service to their clients can mean more than applying the law to the facts and getting a settlement. Clients also have underlying interests that need to be acknowledged, as well as a need for involvement and control within the dispute resolution process. If lawyers permit it, ADR can help with this. . . .

. . . [I]f the lawyer's philosophical map fails to embrace a *client-centered* dispute resolution process, neither lawyers not their clients will ever benefit fully from ADR.

MANDATED MEDIATION OF CIVIL CASES IN STATE COURTS: A LITIGANT'S PERSPECTIVE ON PROGRAM MODEL CHOICES

14 Ohio St. J. on Disp. Resol. 813, 814–815, 817–819, 821–836, 842–843, 847, 849–851 (1999)*

By John P. McCrory

Due to the diversity of cases on state courts' civil dockets and the variations in approaches to using mediation, ranging from purely voluntary to mandatory, it is awkward and sometimes unproductive to deal with this topic generically. In the Article, I have confined the discussion to mandatory programs for cases on the general civil docket, excluding domestic relations and small claims cases. . . .

State legislatures and courts have been more guarded regarding the use of mediation for civil cases. Litigants are normally represented by attorneys and the cases fall within the mainstream of the litigation practice. Reasons offered for the reluctance of judges and lawyers to embrace mediation include the following: fear that it will alter the traditional attorney-client relationship, perhaps shifting a measure of responsibility for case control to the client; concern that mediation may lessen the need for traditional fee-generating work, such as extensive discovery prior to settlement negotiations; lawyers may be apprehensive about negotiating in the presence of their clients; and judges and lawyers lack experience with and understanding of mediation. Another proffered explanation is that "lawyers learn to be conservative about settlement by training and by fear of malpractice or ethical violation." . . .

Cases on the general civil docket that are the most likely candidates for mediation include negligence suits, commercial contract disputes, construction disputes, and real estate disputes, with personal injury cases likely to be the most prevalent. Lawyers representing parties may be inclined to handle cases in the traditional way when preparing for settlement negotiations or trial, including extensive discovery. Thus, the use of mediation for civil cases encroaches upon the traditional domain of lawyers to a greater degree than does small claims and domestic relations mediation. . . .

The considerations discussed above demonstrate that we cannot generalize about the implementation of mediation programs in state courts, any more than we can generalize about the mediation process. . . .

The planning process for a mediation program should focus on the segment of the docket that it will serve. . . .

Identifying the interests of litigants in civil case mediation programs to facilitate an inquiry as to how those interests can best be addressed is the central theme of this Article. While all participants in a planning process may be well intentioned, they are likely to focus on their own primary interests. Judges and court administrators, concerned with limited court resources and removing cases from over-crowded dockets, may wish to maximize the number of cases that are referred to mediation. Lawyers may be concerned about how programs will affect the way they practice law and the economics of practice. Litigants, on the other hand, may be most concerned with the quality of mediation services provided, to ensure that the time and money spent participating in mandated mediation will maximize chances for fair and efficient settlement.

. . . .

When courts mandate mediation, one of the first questions asked is: Who will pay the cost of administering the program and the cost of the mediation services? One view is that courts should not mandate an ADR process and then require that the litigants pay the cost of providing the services. The SPIDR Law and Policy Committee recommended that: "Funding for mandatory dispute resolution programs should be provided on a basis comparable to funding for trials." While arguments that courts or legislatures should provide funding to cover the cost of mandated mediation services has an obvious justification and appeal, as a practical matter, there are more important concerns for civil case litigants.

The cost of mediation services is likely to be only a fraction of the total costs to litigants participating in mandated mediation. . . .

Assuming that the user fee for court-mandated mediation is reasonable, a more important consideration for litigants is the quality of the program and the services provided. . . . For many courts, there is tension between providing quality mediation services and finding resources that can be devoted to a mediation program. In many states, it is unlikely that legislatures will be willing to, or courts will be able to, fully fund high quality court-mandated programs. . . .

Preoccupation with demands for providing mediation services without a user fee may be unproductive and may divert attention from the more important question of how a high-quality program can be established with reasonable and affordable user fees. As a practical matter, planners may be left to decide which of the various program models has the greatest potential for providing a high-quality program with the least possible burden on the litigants who are mandated to mediation. . . . From a consumer standpoint, quality should be a paramount program planning objective.

. . . .

When planning a court-based civil mediation program, several things should be remembered. First, the parties will normally have attorneys and litigation will have been started. To some extent, positions and expectations will be fixed. Second, commencement of litigation places a dispute in an arena that is the domain of lawyers who are likely to employ traditional litigation tools and strategies. Finally, the types of cases referred to mediation will vary and the needs of the parties, in terms of the assistance they need from a mediator to resolve their differences, will also vary.

There is concern in some quarters that the institutionalization of mediation in the courts will diminish party self-determination, result in mediation that is evaluative, and cause coerced settlements. . . . A flexible approach to the role of mediators in civil mediation will best serve the interests of litigants.

. . . .

The focus should . . . be on early settlement. The longer a case remains in the litigation process, the less likely the chances of achieving the time-and cost-saving goals of the mediation program. Delay may also inhibit the settlement efforts because of the parties' financial and psychological investment in a case. Early settlement does not mean uninformed settlement. The appropriate time for mediation will vary on a case-by-case basis and, for that reason, rigid approaches to scheduling mediation have been criticized. There must be a thoughtful balance between the parties' legitimate need for information and scheduling mediation at sessions at times when settlement efficiency can be maximized. . . .

The parties' need for information is often equated to the need for discovery. . . . Some cases will not require discovery, which may mean that mediation can be scheduled very early in the life of the case. In cases in which the need for discovery is modest, that need may be satisfied by an information exchange during mediation. In more complex cases, in which discovery is a significant factor, there is evidence that lawyers who are experienced in mediation are comfortable participating with limited discovery. The foregoing suggests possibilities for scheduling mediation at an early date without prejudicing the parties' need for information that is required for an informed and fair settlement.

The SPIDR Law and Policy Committee recommended that mandatory mediation should be used only when high-quality programs permit party participation. Many courts require that parties be present at the mediation sessions, but attendance alone does not ensure effective participation. Providing parties with an opportunity to speak and be key participants n a relaxed and informal atmosphere should be a program objective.

. . . .

Mediation program planners should be concerned about the "ADR literacy" of the attorneys who will represent litigants that are referred to mediation and should take steps to ensure that the clients are adequately prepared for and involved in the process. . . .

[I]f the objectives of mediation are to be realized, planners should focus on the nature and quality of party participation. . . . Realistically, lawyers will have primary responsibility for the level and quality of their clients' participation. This does not diminish the role of courts and mediators to monitor the quality of party involvement. . . .

Mediation is not a quick fix. Time is required for a mediator to gain a sufficient understanding of a dispute to be helpful to the parties. Time is needed for the parties to fully air their perspectives in an unhurried atmosphere. Finally, time is required to develop and explore acceptable options for settlement. If insufficient time is allotted, parties may believe they were not heard and understood, that settlement options were not clear, or that they were required to mediate in a coercive atmosphere.

. . . Planning should recognize the need for adequate time in mediation for all referred cases, including flexibility to accommodate complex cases that have extraordinary time requirements.

A key factor in the quality and success of a court-based program is the panel of mediators that is selected to provide mediation services. Where mediation is mandated, the court has a special responsibility to ensure that the mediators to whom cases are referred are competent. In addition, it is important that the mediator panel is the following:

- diverse in gender, race, and ethnicity;
- diverse with respect to mediation styles;
- diverse with respect to subject matter familiarity;
- of sufficient size to provide equal access to all referred or eligible cases; and
- experienced.

. . . .

Some commentators contend that the opportunity for party choice in selecting the mediator should be maximized. . . . It permits parties to select a mediator whom they believe to be right for their particular dispute and it gives them a greater stake and degree of confidence in the mediation process. While these concerns are important, there are competing considerations. Experience has shown that when litigants are free to choose any mediator from a court panel, a relatively small number of panel members do most of the work. . . .

From a consumer perspective, the following two competing factors must be balanced: the opportunity for party choice in the assignment of mediators and the overall experience and competence of the mediator panel. . . .

In some states there is concern and uncertainty regarding the relationship, and perhaps tension, between court-based mediation and private sector mediation providers. . . . From the litigants' standpoint, program planners should define the relationship to the public sector in a way that will maximize access to qualified mediators. . . .

. . . [F]rom a consumer's perspective, when mandatory court-based programs are put in place, the sponsors have an obligation to ensure that the litigants' time, money, and efforts are not wasted. . . .

The philosophy of a mediation program and its image in the eyes of litigants and their lawyers will be an important factor in determining its success. Fundamentally, there is an option between two models, diversion and integration. A diversion model might resemble small claims mediation in which the court says, go to mediation and do not return unless you cannot settle. . . .

The second model, integration, envisions incorporating mediation into case management and coordinating its use with other events, such as discovery. . . . Mediation should have a clear relationship to other procedures and be timed to maximize its effectiveness. . . .

The major distinguishing features in comparing program models are the source of mediators and their relationship to the court. The options are the following: court employees, referral to community mediation centers, volunteer court panels, court panels of private practitioners who work for a fixed fee, and private practitioners selected and paid by the parties. Planners should consider how the selection of a particular model will influence a court's ability to effectively do the following:

- integrate mediation into case handling procedures and
- monitor the quality and consistency of mediation services. . . .

NOTES AND QUESTIONS

(1) In light of the study done by McAdoo and Welsh, do you think that mediation is changing attorneys' mindsets? If not, how will this affect the nature of mediation in the future? Can you recommend any steps to help make attorneys more client-centered? Would continuing legal education help?

(2) McCrory asserts that the general civil docket is the most complex environment for implementing a mediation program. Do you agree? Why or why not?

(3) *See* John Lande, *Getting the Faith: Why Business Lawyers and Executives Believe in Mediation*, Harv. Negot. L. Rev. 137 (2000),* for another view on

---

the insitutionalization of mediation via the corporate legal community. Lande based his article on interviews conducted with "inside counsel, outside counsel, and non-lawyer executives." One of the outcomes of his survey was this understanding regarding institutionalization:

. . . Observations and accounts of the process of "getting the faith" in mediation also support the explanation of an institutionalization process. There seems to be a general pattern in which attorneys initially resist new mediation programs, and then, in relatively short order, become some of the biggest proponents for mediation use. Indeed, it has become something of a ritual at continuing legal education programs for "converts" to mediation to give testimonials about how they initially balked at using mediation, but how they are now satisfied believers who use it as often as possible and appropriate. Clearly, these "conversions" are based on experience, which presumably provides opportunities for comparison of litigation with and without mediation. However, the sharp shifts in avowed belief from skeptic to strong proponent suggest that the conversions are more a function of a change in perceived legitimacy of dispute resolution procedures than careful calculation of advantages and disadvantages. Obviously, the purpose of such public testimonials at professional gatherings is to legitimize mediation in order that others may make similar conversions in belief and practice.

Over time, repeated exposure to public and private testimonials, as well as the mediation process itself, transforms mediation from an innovation into a routine part of the disputing practice that becomes taken for granted as the (currently) normal way of doing things. After the mediation innovation has become institutionalized for a time, it becomes difficult to conceive of alternative arrangements, and even those who initially resisted the innovation are likely to resist changing a new status quo. . . .

AN EVALUATION OF MEDIATION AND EARLY NEUTRAL EVALUATION UNDER THE CIVIL JUSTICE REFORM ACT

RAND Corporation, xxvii, xxxiv–xxxv (1996)[*]

By James S. Kakalik, Terence Dunworth, Laural A. Hill, Daniel McCaffrey, Marian Oshiro, Nicholas M. Pace, Mary E. Vaiana

Summary

The Civil Justice Reform Act (CJRA) of 1990 emerged from a multi-year debate about ways to reduce delay and litigation costs in federal courts. The legislation required each federal district court to develop a case management plan to reduce costs and delay. The legislation also created a pilot program to test six principles of case management and required an independent evaluation to assess the effects of these principle and of other related case management techniques. The Judicial Conference and the Administrative Office of the U.S. Courts asked RAND's Institute for Civil Justice to conduct the evaluation in the ten pilot and ten comparison districts.

. . . .

This study's objective is to assess the implementation, costs, and effects of mediation and neutral evaluation programs for civil cases in the six CJRA pilot and comparison federal district courts that had mediation or neutral evaluation programs in 1992-93 involving a sufficient number of cases to permit detailed evaluation. . . .

Our evaluation provided no strong statistical evidence that the mediation or neutral evaluation programs, as implemented in the six districts studied, significantly affected time to disposition, litigation costs, or attorney views of fairness or satisfaction with case management. The low completion rate for our litigant surveys does not allow us to confidently make statistical inferences from the litigant data. Our only statistically significant finding is that the ADR programs appear to increase the likelihood of a monetary settlement.

We conclude that the mediation and neutral evaluation programs as implemented in these six districts are not a panacea for perceived problems of costs and delay, but neither do they appear to be detrimental. We have no justification for a strong policy recommendation because we found no major program effects, either positive or negative. . . .

Since the time when the cases in our study were referred to ADR, a number of the study districts have changed the timing and method of the referral, the number and type of cases deemed appropriate for inclusion, or the length and timing of the ADR session itself. Perhaps more important, mediators and evaluators have had time to acquire experience in conducting the sessions, and judicial officers have become more familiar with the types of cases that would be helped by a discretionary referral or by a firm suggestion to the parties to volunteer. The evolution and fine tuning of these ADR programs is an ongoing process.

The release of the RAND report had a major impact on the dispute resolution stage. Of particular concern were articles in the legal press which interpreted the report to say that it demonstrated empirically that court ADR did not work. The following are excerpts from two responses to the report. The first was written by Sanford Jaffe and Linda Stamato from the Center for Negotiation and Conflict Resolution at Rutgers University. Both are mediators who specialize in complex cases. The second response is a statement issued under the auspices of the CPR Judicial Project by 32 federal judges, scholars and counsel. Additional federal and state judges, legislators and other ADR policy makers joined the statement.

NO SHORT CUTS TO JUSTICE

15 Alternatives 67, 67–69 (May 1997) *

By Sanford M. Jaffee and Linda Stamato

The results, to put it mildly, are deflating to many in and around the dispute resolution community, especially to those who believe in ADR as the solution for problems of cost and delay. The results, frankly, also are disappointing—but not surprisingly so—because of the expectation, even hyperbole, that frequently and, in our view, inappropriately, often is associated with dispute resolution. The findings challenge on a subjective level as well, for they seem to contradict practitioners' direct experience and court officials who believe their programs lead them to reach different conclusions. . . .

. . . Rand's recommendations to the Judicial Conference are cautious and limited. . . .

So, what are we to make of this report? What do we do with it? First of all, resist two things: one, the temptation to focus attention too critically on the study and, two, the urge to make policy and/or budgetary decisions solely on the basis of its findings. Instead, consider the report and the data generated for what it is—a veritable treasure trove of information about a variety of court programs, valuable for a number of reasons, that, among others, may help to provide perspective on more realistic (and meaningful) objectives that those of direct cost and delay.

. . . .

There is no question that ADR has become part of the justice system in a very short period of time. Considering that reform in the courts is generally a long and difficult process, we should not be surprised, then, that some ADR programs are not structured or implemented well. Education and training are sometimes short-changed too, which probably is predictable when social reform, particularly civil justice reform, is attempted too quickly and on such a scale.

. . . .

If the case for ADR cannot (yet) be supported from a system-wide perspective on a time-and cost-savings basis, are there only policy justifications for having such programs? In our judgment, there are several, but one clearly overarches: Citizens should have access to a variety of processes for the resolution of their disputes; they should have access to options that complement traditional adjudication that, along with ADR are integral parts of the civil justice system.

What are some of the implications of this approach? The possibilities include:

- A shift in emphasis to policies that will improve existing programs so that the goal of providing access to a dispute resolution process that parties want, producing remedies they need, is met. Rather than focusing on programs to minimize the choice, emphasize providing more choice for parties and attorneys and structure programs in ways that attract users because they value their potential. . . .

- A shift in focus—from an assessment and research perspective—from cost and delay to "quality" issues, both in terms of process and outcome. . . .

CONCERNS AND RECOMMENDATIONS

15 Alternatives 6, 72-73 (May 1997) *

Scope and Limitations of the Rand Research

The Rand ADR findings must be understood in the specific context of the six programs studied. The four mediation programs and two neutral evaluation programs examined were neither exemplary not representative of the 51 mediation and 14 neutral evaluation programs now operating in the federal district courts. The six ADR programs were selected for study only because they were statutory pilot programs and had sufficient ADR caseloads to permit analysis. Moreover, the programs studied were new and examined early, before or as program refinements were underway. In several of the courts studied, substantial revisions to the ADR program were made after Rand data were collected.

     . . . .

The ADR programs studied also varied vastly in quality. Several had significant design flaws, later corrected, at the time they were studied. Indeed, one of the four mediation programs violated most of what is known about building successful court ADR programs. The court required no training for its lawyer-mediators, excluded settlement empowered clients and insurers from the mediations, and held short and often perfunctory mediation sessions.

Nor was the study environment optimal. Almost all the study courts changed their programs midstream to correct earlier missteps or implemented so many case-management innovations simultaneously that researchers could not effectively control for ADR effects. Comparable comparison cases were also difficult to find in programs where the tough-to-settle cases were routinely referred to mediation.

Other Pertinent Research

While Rand's cost and delay finding are consistent with some earlier research, other recent studies of well-designed court ADR programs have found significant reductions in case processing time and litigant costs. For example, current data form the Western District of Missouri's mediation program, called the Early Assessment Program, report EAP cases terminating 29% faster than control group cases, and savings per case of $10,000 based on attorney estimates. And importantly, the Federal Judicial Center's recent report to the U.S. Judicial Conference Committee on Court Administration and Case Management documents significant cost and time savings in the Missouri court and in the ADR programs in the Northern District of California. . . .

Quality and Justice Values

. . .Most significantly, the Rand researchers underscore the critical importance of careful program definition, structure and implementation, as well as sufficient resources and staffing to deliver quality ADR services in the courts. Policy makers should also assess other values informing ADR use in the public justice system, such as its capacity to increase public satisfaction with and confidence in the courts.

Recommendations to the U.S. Judicial Conference and Congress

. . .First, policy makers should evaluate the success or failure of ADR development in the federal courts under the Civil Justice Reform Act on the basis of full and fair understanding of the available empirical data and other research. . . .

Second, while we await final word on ADR's impact on cost and delay, we know that well-designed and well-implemented court ADR programs offer litigants better quality solutions to litigation and may increase public confidence in and satisfaction with our courts. Mixed cost and delay data should not overshadow these important justice values. Indeed, further and difference kinds of research in these areas is required.

Third, high-quality ADR programs need sustained support, professional staffing, and other resources to achieve long-term success and public legitimacy.

NOTES

(1) In 1994, the National Center for State Courts conducted a National Symposium on Court Connected Dispute Resolution Research under a cooperative agreement with the State Justice Institute (SJI). SJI had a history of funding such research for a number of years and was desirous of determining what was now known as a result of the research and even more importantly, determining where further evaluation and research were still needed. The research that had been conducted to date was collected and published in the *National Symposium on Court-Connected Dispute Resolution Research: A Report on Current Research Findings—Implications for Courts and Future Research Needs* (NCSC Publication No. R-152). The National Center for State Courts reported that the following themes emerged, which highlight the challenges of this type of research:

- . . . courts need to know more about the dynamics of the litigation process and attorneys' expectations about how ADR fits into that scheme. . . .

- courts need more reliable findings on the benefits of ADR. . . . [f]uture studies should use more consistent sets of measures in order to develop more comparable sets of findings across jurisdictions.

- . . . courts need significantly greater knowledge about the most effective methods for training, qualifying, and selecting ADR providers.

- innovative measures of participant satisfaction should be developed because most individual litigants are one-time users of the justice system and thus have no reference for comparing the dispute resolution process they experienced with other processes. In addition, research on satisfaction should address a broader array of factors and identify those that contribute to greater satisfaction with the dispute resolution process and its outcomes.

- courts need better access not only to research findings, but also to practical guides for implementing, operating and evaluating ADR programs.

(2) What type of studies or research do you think are needed?

§ D INSTITUTIONALIZATION IN OTHER CONTEXTS

While it is true that the courts have been in the forefront of the move to institutionalize mediation, they have not been the only player. Institutional uses of mediation can be found in schools—from primary and pre-school through high school and universities—as peer mediation programs or for resolution of school related conflicts such as truancy or for alleged breaches of the student code of conduct. *See* Chapter 10 Section G, *infra*. Federal and state agencies have also been using mediation and creating institutional mediation opportunities. In 1990, Congress passed the first Administrative Dispute Resolution Act ("ADRA" Public Law 101-552, 104 Stat. 2736, 5 U.S.C. 581 *et seq.* (1990)). This statute required each Federal agency to "adopt a policy that addresses the use of alternative means of dispute resolution," "designate a senior official to be the dispute resolution specialist of the agency," and "review each of its standard agreements for contracts, grants . . . [to] encourage the use of alternative means of dispute resolution." In 1996, the ADRA was reenacted and was made a permanent law without an expiration date. In 1998, an Interagency ADR Working Group was created. Chaired by Attorney General Janet Reno, the mission of the group was to "facilitate, encourage, and provide coordination for agencies."

In addition, Presidential executive orders have been issued. In 1991, President Goerge P. Bush entered an order for government counsel to be trained in dispute resolution techniques [Exec. Order No. 12,778, 56 Fed. Reg. 55,195 (1991)]. President Clinton followed up with his own executive order which endorsed the use of ADR and reiterated that litigation counsel be trained in ADR techniques. Specifically, it stated: "Where the benefits of Alternative Dispute Resolution . . . may be derived, and after consultation with the agency referring the matter, litigation counsel should suggest the use of an appropriate ADR technique to the parties. . . . " [Exec. Order No. 12,988, 61 Fed. Reg. 4719 (1996)].

The employee grievance arena has also proven to be particularly conducive to mediation. Here, the conflict is often between individuals who have an on-going relationship which will often benefit from a private, informal process of resolution. The following excerpt is from a General Accounting Office (GAO) Report entitled "Employers' Experiences with ADR in the Workplace." The GAO identified five private companies (Brown & Root, Hughes Electronics, Polaroid, Rockwell, and TRW) and five federal agencies (Department of Agriculture, State Department, US Postal Service, Air Force, and Walter Reed Army Medical Center) as case illustrations. The excerpt includes a portion of the letter summarizing the report as well as portions of the case descriptions.

ALTERNATIVE DISPUTE RESOLUTION: EMPLOYERS' EXPERIENCES WITH ADR IN THE WORKPLACE

(Letter Report, 8/12/97, GAO/GGD-97-157) 7-8, 9–11, 15, 17, 22–23, 26–27, 38, 40–41, 46–48, 61, 69, 71–72, 77, 79–80

By Michael Brostek

[T]he use of ADR in the private and federal sectors was spurred in the early 1990s by a dramatic increase in the number of discrimination complaints, along with the costs, time, and frustration involved in attempting to resolve them. Several new laws and regulatory changes made companies and agencies even more likely to develop ADR processes. Moreover, in some quarters—such as EEOC—a recognition emerged that the interest-based approach that is the basis for some ADR techniques can be a constructive alternative to adversarial, position-based processes.

. . . .

The increase in discrimination complaints in the early 1990s can be attributed to several factors, according to EEOC, dispute resolution experts, and officials of organizations that we studied. They said that downsizing efforts resulted in a surge of complaints in both the private and federal sectors. In addition, the Americans with Disabilities Act of 1990 established new grounds for employment-related complaints by the disabled. . . . At each of the five federal agencies we studied as case illustrations, officials said the increase in complaints at their agencies was driven partly by the availability of monetary awards in addition to the previously available forms of relief. Officials at four federal agencies said it was typical for a complainant to request compensatory damages, regardless of the severity of the allegation.

. . . .

EEOC, among others, has noted the potential value of the interest-based approach to dispute resolution in reducing the number of formal discrimination complaints. Reflecting on the high number of discrimination complaints among federal employees, an EEOC study recently concluded that ". . . there may be a sizable number of disputes in the 1614 process [so named for the regulations governing the process—29 C.F.R. Part 1614] which may not involve discrimination issues at all. They reflect, rather, basic communications problems in the workplace. Such issues may be brought into the EEO process as a result of a perception that there is no other forum available to air general workplace concerns. There is little question that these types of issues would be especially conducive to resolution through an interest-based approach."

. . . .

Most of the organizations we studied had data to show that their ADR processes, especially mediation, resolved a high proportion of disputes, thereby helping them avoid formal redress processes and litigation. Objective data were not generally available on the time and cost savings achieved by avoiding formal redress and litigation, nor on how the costs of dispute resolution involving ADR compared with the costs of more traditional methods. For the most part, however, managers believed that avoiding formal redress and litigation saved their organizations time and money. The organizations also reported that user satisfaction—another indicator of effectiveness or the lack of it—was generally high. . . .

. . . .

Among three of the four federal agencies we studied with experience in mediation, the limited data available suggested that mediation was more useful than the traditional processes for resolving discrimination complaints. For example, data from the Postal Service's Southern California EEO Processing Center showed that from fiscal year 1988 to fiscal year 1996, about 94 percent of the informal cases that were mediated were settled, compared with 57 percent of those that went through traditional counseling.

. . . .

Mediation was the most widely used technique among the organizations we studied. Most of the organizations reported using both internal and external mediators. Among the private firms, for example, Brown & Root and Polaroid reported they used their own employee volunteers as mediators most of the time. However, employees at these companies could ask for a mediator from an external source (such as the American Arbitration Association). Among the federal agencies, the Air Force selected mediators according to the issues involved—its practice is to assign mediators to the kinds of cases in which they specialized—and gave some consideration to the preference of the parties involved. The mediator could be an EEO counselor trained in mediation or an external mediator from another Air Force installation, another federal agency, a contractor, or a "shared neutrals" program. A shared neutrals program, such as the Seattle Interagency ADR Consortium is a cooperative venture in which federal agencies create a pool of mediators who are available to agencies that do not have their own mediators or that want a mediator from outside the agency.

Variation existed in the types of issues that were subject to mediation and in the point at which an employee could elect to use it. Two of the three private sector companies that reported they regularly used mediation—Brown & Root and Polaroid—offered mediation for a wide array of issues and at any point in the dispute resolution process. The other company, TRW, usually offered external mediation as a step before arbitration. Among the federal agencies, the Walter Reed Army Medical Center was alone in having established mediation for a wide array of disputes. The others generally reported confining the use of mediation to discrimination and to a point very early in the discrimination complaint process. This point occurred after an employee had contacted his or her agency's EEO office (the first step in the federal discrimination complaint process) but before the employee had filed a formal complaint. Among the agencies we studied, mediation was offered at this point as an alternative to the counseling that is required by the regulations governing the discrimination complaint process.

. . . .

The organizations we studied each cited lessons learned in planning, implementing, and evaluating their ADR programs. These lessons were varied, but many of them centered on ensuring that the appropriate ADR methods were used and that they fulfilled their potential.

Six of the organizations reported emphasizing the need for visible support of ADR by top management, citing the difficulty of marketing and sustaining ADR efforts in its absence. . . .

Six of the organizations said they learned that dispute resolution efforts have a greater likelihood of success if they occur early in a dispute before positions have solidified and underlying interests have been obscured. . . .

Two federal agencies—Walter Reed and Agriculture—said they learned that special care must be given to balancing the desire to settle and close cases against the need for fairness to employees and managers alike. . . .

Five organizations reported finding that ADR served a purpose merely by giving employees an opportunity to be heard. Employees, they said, got something worthwhile merely out of having their "day in court." Further, four organizations also reported finding that by following the outcomes of ADR processes, management became more aware of the causes of workplace disputes, of the organizational policies or decisions that led to complaints, and of systemic concerns that had not otherwise been apparent. . . .

. . . .

CASE ILLUSTRATION: BROWN & ROOT, INC.

Brown & Root, Inc., headquartered in Houston, Texas, provides construction, engineering, and maintenance services worldwide. Together, its two business units employ about 27,000 people in the United States, all of whom are covered by the company's alternative dispute resolution (ADR) program. The program, implemented in June 1993, includes an ombudsman-like role, mediation, and arbitration as well as a toll-free hotline for employee assistance.

A Brown & Root employee unable to resolve a dispute through the chain of command can contact the dispute resolution program administrator or an ombudsman—at Brown & Root referred to as an advisor. The advisor (or the program administrator) is to provide independent and confidential assistance to the employee, which can include such things as simply listening to the problem, answering questions, acting as a go-between, getting the facts, coaching the employee on how to independently resolve the problem, and providing referrals to other company resources. The advisors are trained mediators and often provide informal mediation. Should the dispute remain unresolved at this point, the employee can opt for in-house mediation, provided by trained employee volunteers.

The next two steps—external mediation and arbitration—are generally used only for issues involving statutorily protected rights. The employee pays a $50 processing fee to take his or her dispute to external mediation or arbitration; Brown & Root pays additional costs.

An unusual feature of Brown & Root's dispute resolution program is its Legal Consultation Plan that provides financial assistance to help employees obtain their own attorneys to assist them in their employment disputes. The employees pay a $25 deductible (for each dispute); the plan then pays 90 percent of the attorney fees, up to a maximum benefit of $2,500 annually.

According to Brown & Root's dispute resolution program brochure, its program is intended as the exclusive means for the final resolution of employment disputes and is mandatory for all employees. . . .

. . . .

. . . As of December 1996, 155 cases had been mediated, with a resolution rate of 90 percent. . . .

According to information provided by the company, in the dispute resolution program's first 3 years, the overall cost of dealing with employment conflicts, including the total cost of the program (the program's current annual budget is about $500,000) is less than half of what the company used to spend on legal fees for employment-related litigations. Legal fees alone are down about 90 percent (for the first 3 years of the program). Settlement costs have remained about the same since the program's inception, although there have been more settlements under the new program. In addition to the operating costs of Brown & Root's dispute resolution program, the company invested about $250,000 in development costs, including outside consultant fees, legal fees, and the cost of mailing literature about the program.

Another indicator of the program's success, according to the company's Associate General Counsel, is that the number of employment-related lawsuits has been reduced to nearly zero, and the number of cases filed with the Equal Employment Opportunity Commission or similar state entities has been reduced by half.

Brown & Root employees appear to be satisfied with the program. According to a speech by the Associate General Counsel, confidential anonymous surveys of the users of the dispute resolution program reported satisfaction with its procedures.

According to the company's Associate General Counsel for Human Resources, Brown & Root has learned several lessons about what makes a dispute resolution program effective. One lesson learned is that management's unwavering commitment and constant attention are prerequisites to the growth of an effective program. Brown & Root said, for example, that the general counsel's active role and organizational stature were crucial in launching the program and in maintaining its success. Also, Brown & Root said it learned that the effectiveness of a program is directly related to a company's investment in training and to its frequency of communication.

Also crucial to creating a program that will be widely accepted, in Brown & Root's experience, is ensuring the users' involvement in designing the program. The company said it learned that most employees prefer a collaborative dispute resolution process to an adjudicatory one.

The company also said it learned that mediation settlements and arbitration awards can alert management to problems within the organization. Upward communication by the dispute resolution program administrator has had a like effect.

Finally, Brown & Root said it learned the program has not been subjected to overwhelming use by chronic complainers, and the legal consultation plan has not been a financial burden. As of December 1996, 149 employees had received about $169,000 under the legal consultation program.

. . . .

CASE ILLUSTRATION: POLAROID CORPORATION

The Polaroid Corporation, headquartered in Cambridge, MA, employs 6,500 nonunion workers in manufacturing imaging products. Polaroid has long offered alternative dispute resolution (ADR) techniques as part of its traditional dispute resolution process. Since the 1950s, Polaroid has offered all grievants a hearing before a panel of three company officers; and nonmanagerial employees have had access to arbitration. In January 1995, Polaroid added mediation, peer panels, an ombudsman program, and a program to help grievants take part in the dispute resolution process.

A Polaroid employee is encouraged to use mediation at any stage of a grievance or appeal. The employee may choose from among 60 in-house mediators or, if the employee prefers, an external mediator. If the matter is not resolved earlier in the dispute resolution process, the employee can request a hearing before a panel of three company officers or a peer panel. . . . Arbitration is the final step for nonmanagerial employees appealing disciplinary or discharge actions. An arbitrator may award the employee the same remedies as a court, including monetary damages. Although Polaroid expects its employees to use the company's dispute resolution processes, an employee who is unable to resolve a grievance to his or her satisfaction through those processes can take the matter to court.

. . . .

With one exception, Polaroid pays all ADR program costs. An employee who takes his or her case to arbitration must pay $100 toward expenses. If the employee prevails in an arbitration hearing, Polaroid refunds the $100 payment.

. . . .

Management officials noted that most cases in Polaroid's dispute resolution program are resolved before they reach the panel or arbitration levels. . . .

. . . .

Polaroid officials also spoke highly of the company's experience with mediation, which was used extensively in grievances associated with downsizing. They told us that mediation techniques expedited the grievance process and, at a minimum, made settlements more likely by clarifying the issues.

. . . .

Although it revamped its dispute resolution system in 1995, Polaroid is considering further revisions to decrease the resolution time for serious cases—such as firings, which currently take 12 to 18 months—to a maximum of 14 weeks. The policy under consideration would require mediation to be used, reduce the number of grievance steps below the panel and arbitration levels, and impose stricter process time deadlines.

Polaroid learned two important lessons, according to the former Senior Corporate Counsel. The first was that most disputes could be resolved through informal processes. The second lesson was that one outgrowth of progressive dispute resolution processes is the enhancement of personnel management. She said that since Polaroid provided the processes and the climate for employees to raise issues and concerns, supervisors and managers have become more accountable for adhering to company policies. And because a cluster of grievances can indicate a problem in a work unit or dissatisfaction with a company policy, the system helps keep management aware of systemic or organizational concerns.

. . . .

CASE ILLUSTRATION: U.S. AIR FORCE

The U.S. Air Force, with facilities worldwide, employed more than 571,000 personnel in fiscal year 1996, including about 183,000 civilians. In the Air Force, the alternative dispute resolution (ADR) method that is emphasized is mediation, which has been used in personnel issues since 1990, particularly in civilian employee equal employment opportunity (EEO) cases. The Air Force has trained its EEO counselors in mediation to foster its use.

Civilian employees who believe they have been discriminated against can contact an EEO counselor who, if unable to resolve a particular matter, may suggest mediation. Both parties—employee and supervisor—must agree to mediation, which can occur at any point in the dispute. The Air Force's goal is to provide mediation within 4 weeks of a request for its use, according to the deputy dispute resolution specialist.

A mediator is selected depending on the issues involved (the Air Force prefers to match a mediator to a case with issues in which he or she specializes) and, to a limited extent, on the preferences of the parties. The mediator could be the counselor whom the employee initially contacted; another counselor not involved in the case; or an external mediator from another

Air Force installation, the Department of Defense's shared neutrals program, another federal agency, or a contract mediator. In addition to the disputants, the mediator must arrange for an Air Force official, who is authorized to agree to settlement terms, to directly participate in, or at least be kept informed of, the mediation proceedings in order to approve any proposed settlement terms. If a matter is resolved, the parties sign a settlement agreement, which is subject to a higher-level review before becoming final.

. . . .

In implementing the program, the Air Force continued training EEO counselors in mediation; at the time of our study, over 1,000 Air Force personnel (most of whom had dealt with employment disputes) had been trained, according to the General Counsel's memorandum. . . . To help less experienced mediators further develop their skills and to promote ADR use, the Air Force established the Mediator Mentoring Program, under which trained but inexperienced mediators apprentice with highly skilled and experienced mediators.

. . . .

In fiscal year 1996, the Air Force reported using ADR in 1,807 EEO cases, resolving 1,339 (74 percent) of them. It also reported that the amount of time it takes to resolve cases has declined. The average number of days to settle formal EEO complaints decreased from 329 to 136 between fiscal years 1992 and 1995. The General Counsel said that this is explained, in part, by the use of ADR. During this period, the average time to close formal complaints (including through a settlement) declined from 401 to 201 days. The Air Force also reported significant time savings in resolving informal EEO complaints.

In her memorandum, the Air Force General Counsel said that the ADR program has achieved important results in a relatively short period of time because of (1) strong support from senior management, (2) the fact that at least one employee has worked full-time on implementing ADR initiatives, (3) training and awareness briefings, and (4) financial support for ADR initiatives.

. . . Among the lessons learned was that early use of ADR enhances the potential for resolving the dispute in a way that satisfies the parties' underlying interests, whereas when time drags on without a resolution, people tend to "dig in their heels" and fight for their position. Another lesson was that mediation helps overcome disputes arising from poor communication, which is at the root of many disputes. Mediators also reported learning the importance of preparation, including explaining the mediation process to the parties; becoming generally familiar with the nature of the dispute; encouraging the disputants to review the facts of the dispute before mediation begins; and coordinating with appropriate officials (e.g., one authorized to agree to settlement terms). They also learned that not every case is appropriate for mediation, such as cases involving "chronic complainers" and those in which complainants have an inflated sense of what they might be entitled to receive. However, Air Force officials emphasized that even in such cases, if mediation might be helpful, it should be tried. The officials told us that other cases that are not appropriate for mediation are those involving fraud or those that are the subject of an Inspector General investigation. Further, the mediators reported that written agreements build trust, cooperation, and understanding.

Finally, Air Force officials noted that providing mediation training to the Air Force's EEO counselors was worthwhile. Although not all counselors became skilled in or comfortable with the mediation process, the training helped many of them do a better job of resolving EEO matters, whether they used mediation or more traditional counseling methods.

CASE ILLUSTRATION: U.S. POSTAL SERVICE

The U.S. Postal Service, an independent governmental establishment headquartered in Washington, D.C., is the nation's largest civilian employer with more than 800,000 workers. Although most employees are covered under collective bargaining agreements under which they can file equal employment opportunity (EEO)-related grievances, they can simultaneously file complaints under the EEO complaint system for federal employees. Mediation was introduced in 1986 in the EEO complaint program in Santa Ana, now within the Postal Services' Southern California EEO Processing Center. In 1994, the Postal Service piloted a headquarters-sponsored EEO complaint mediation program[69] in its North Florida District. At the time of our study, there were 20 pilot mediation sites.

Postal Service workers who believe that they have been discriminated against can contact the EEO office where they receive information about mediation and a form to make a request. Mediation is offered in lieu of the customary counseling in the informal phase of an EEO complaint. If a senior complaint processing specialist approves mediation, it is to be scheduled within approximately 2 weeks of the request. The Postal Service representative at mediation is to have settlement authority or have access to an official with that authority. If the parties achieve resolution, they are to sign a settlement agreement.

. . . .

A variety of factors led to the Postal Service's growing use of mediation, according to Postal Service officials. The grass roots program in Santa Ana was suggested by an EEO specialist experienced in mediation. In 1992, General Counsel and human resources staff at Postal Service headquarters began developing an agency wide alternative dispute resolution (ADR) policy in voluntary compliance with the Administrative Dispute Resolution Act of 1990 and to take advantage of federal employee EEO complaint system regulations encouraging ADR use. The first pilot under the agencywide initiative was in the North Florida District, its selection spurred by a need to comply with a consent decree resulting from a lawsuit. The Postal Service expanded EEO complaint mediation to other sites because of the high number of complaints and the sense that many complaints are rooted in personality conflicts that should be resolved in some other forum, according to the Manager, EEO Compliance and Appeals.

---

[69] The Postal Service's program is known as REDRESS (Resolve Employment Disputes, Reach Equitable Solutions Swiftly).

. . . .

Officials told us that support for expanding the ADR program camefrom the Postal Service's quality improvement program known as "Customer Perfect," which provided top-level policy endorsement, funding, and publicity. Under this program, they said that the Postal Service has provided conflict management and ADR training to about 1,100 managers and supervisors. It also held two week-long conferences to help managers from the cities with pilot programs design an ADR program and develop an implementation plan. Further, it trained staff as mediators in each location, developed a video and brochure about the program, and provided on-site program development assistance. Headquarters program staff have conducted numerous briefings at locations across the nation. The Postal Service has also worked with the unions to get their support.

Finally, the Postal Service's program implementation plans include a comprehensive evaluation of user satisfaction and cost effectiveness of mediation at the pilot locations. The evaluation is being conducted by an assistant professor at Indiana University's School of Public and Environmental Affairs as a research project at no cost; the Postal Service is paying for administrative support. . . .

As of June 1997, the Postal Service's evaluation was still under way. However, data reported from North Florida and Southern California show that mediation resolved a higher proportion of complaints in the informal stage than did the traditional process. Resolution rates were 74 percent (139 of 188 cases between October 1994 and December 1996) in North Florida and 94 percent (1,605 of 1,714 cases between October 1988 and September 1996) in Southern California. In the Southern California EEO Processing Center, for example, only 57 percent of cases that went through traditional counseling were resolved. In the North Florida program's first year, the "flow-through" rate (the rate of informal complaints becoming formal complaints) dropped from 43 to 22 percent, according to the ADR Counsel.

Postal Service surveys of employees and supervisors in North Florida who had used mediation and of those in a comparison group (in other locations) who had used the traditional process showed user satisfaction with mediation far exceeded user satisfaction with the traditional process. For example, 90 percent of mediation users said the process was fair compared with 41 percent of the comparison group. Seventy-two percent of the mediation users were satisfied with the outcomes compared with 40 percent of the comparison group.

Mediation was not very time consuming. In the Southern California EEO Processing Center, the typical mediation required about 90 minutes; cases in North Florida averaged 197 minutes.

Foremost among the lessons the Postal Service learned is the importance of top-level support in establishing and sustaining a program, according to Postal Service officials. . . .

Postal officials said that keys to a program's growth are demonstrable results and early successes. The ongoing evaluation should be particularly helpful in this regard. Because starting a mediation program requires a Postal

Service district to pay start-up costs, officials said they learned that some managers need convincing data to decide whether mediation is a worthwhile investment.

Officials said they also learned that the user-friendly dispute resolution program increased the number of informal complaints. However, based on North Florida's experience, a lower proportion of informal complaints turned into formal complaints, and the overall number of formal complaints declined. Postal Service officials attribute this reduction to employees' (especially supervisors)having developed conflict management competencies after having gone through mediation, some on several occasions. Officials also said that it is important to intervene promptly in a dispute while the issue is fresh in the disputants' minds and their positions have not hardened.

CASE ILLUSTRATION: U. S. DEPARTMENT OF STATE

. . . [the State Department Office of Equal Employment Opportunity and Civil Rights] S/EEOCR, has used mediation and dispute resolution boards to deal with EEO complaints. It uses mediation in the informal phase of an EEO complaint. Employees are provided information about mediation by counselors and when they visit the S/EEOCR office. Participating in mediation is voluntary for the employee but mandatory for management. In addition to the employee and the supervisor, a management representative with the authority to approve a settlement is party to the mediation. During the pilot, State has used internal mediators and mediators from a Washington, D.C.-based shared neutrals program. If the matter is resolved, the parties sign an agreement that is reviewed and monitored by S/EEOCR. . . .

. . . .

. . . Between May 1995 and December 1996, mediation was used in nine cases, achieving closure in three of them (one case was still in process at the time). [The Associate Director] attributed this low utilization to complainants' aversion to the process as well as State's failure to give ADR higher priority. . . .

The Associate Director, S/EEOCR said . . . outside mediators carry more credibility than internal mediators and that the shared neutrals program is not only a source of mediators but a way of matching a mediator's experiences and demographics to that of the parties and the issues. Further, he said he learned mediation training alone does not equip a person to mediate EEO cases. The position also requires a person with the right temperament and an understanding of EEO issues.

A February 1996 State briefing memorandum discussed other lessons about mediation. One lesson was a recognition of the need to remove management from direct involvement in the mediation process and instead appoint management representatives who have been briefed on ADR. Another lesson was to exclude as possibilities for mediation any cases that set precedent or involve large monetary settlements, significant investigation, a violation of criminal law, or issues dealing with security. . . .

CASE ILLUSTRATION: SEATTLE INTERAGENCY ADR CONSORTIUM

The Seattle Federal Executive Board's Interagency Alternative Dispute Resolution (ADR) Consortium is a "shared neutrals" program that began providing services in April 1993. The interagency group, comprised mostly of volunteer federal employees, offers low-or no-cost mediation services to more than 25 participating federal agencies in the Seattle, WA, area. The consortium uses the co-mediation model (two mediators working in tandem on each case) to deal with various types of employment-related disputes, including discrimination complaints, interpersonal conflicts, and grievances filed by collective bargaining unit members. . . .

Between May 1993 and February 1997, the consortium mediated 171 cases, settling 153 (89 percent) of them. Data on the nature of settlements were being analyzed at the time of our study, according to the consortium member responsible for the effort.

User satisfaction with the process and with the mediators is also high, according to the consortium's surveys of users. Of evaluations received from 75 users (survey results were not broken out by successful and unsuccessful mediations), 84 percent reported that their overall level of satisfaction with the mediation process was good to excellent, while 73 percent of the respondents who reached agreement said that their level of satisfaction with the agreement was good to excellent.

The co-chairman attributes the consortium's success to the training, development, and evaluation process for the volunteer mediators and to the evaluations completed after each mediation. The post mediation evaluations have been valuable in making improvements to the program, according to the co-chairman. . . .

Another lesson learned, according to the consortium co-chairman, was that some benefits derive even in cases not resolved through the consortium mediation. In these cases, issues in dispute often become clarified, which may help bring about later resolution. . . .

Initially, the consortium's mediation services were underutilized. However, through marketing efforts and as consortium successes became known by word-of-mouth, use of the consortium's services has increased to a point at which the pool of volunteer mediators is now being used to its limits. . . .

NOTES AND QUESTIONS

(1) Why have discrimination complaints been more readily subject to mediation? Are there are any negatives to this trend?

(2) What similarities and differences are there between the institutionalization of legal disputes through the court system and through government agencies or private companies?

(3) The REDRESS mediation program operates within the transformative framework. See Chapter 3. For a review of the initial evaluation of this program see *Mediating Employment Disputes: Perception of REDRESS at the United States Postal Service*, 20 Rev. Pub. Personnel Admin. 20 (Spring 1997).

(4) *See* Bruce Stiftel and Neil Sipe, *Mediation of Environmental Enforcement: Overcoming Inertia*, 1992 J. Disp. Resol. 303, for another example of institutional use of mediation. The article describes a pilot mediation program for environmental enforcement initiated by the Florida Department of Environmental Regulation (DER) in which DER could nominate for mediation enforcement cases in which at least one party was a government agency and settlement was possible. Enforcement cases could involve air quality, dredge and fill, domestic waste, groundwater, hazardous waste, industrial waste, drinking water, storm water, toxic materials. The authors conclude that the cases described "underscore the importance of mediators as providing a constituency for settlement in cases experiencing the inertia of non-settlement." In particular, they note that "when the mediator actively pursued the case, progress followed. When the mediator did not actively pursue the case, progress occurred only if outside deadlines forced action by the parties."

(5) For a complete description of the U.S. Equal Employment Opportunity Commission's mediation program, see http:/www.eeoc.gov/mediate.

§ E CRITIQUES OF INSTITUTIONALIZATION

The trend towards institutionalization of mediation has not been accepted universally or without criticism. In the following section, various authors highlight the potential "dark side" to institutionalization. Professor Menkel-Meadow raises questions about the potential co-option of the flexible mediation process when it becomes institutionalized in the rule-bound legal system; Professor Alfini moderates a panel discussion regarding the impact institutionalization has on the parties, the attorneys, and the court; and Sharon Press reflects on the challenges of institutionalization from the perspective of administering a state-wide court-connected mediation program. Finally, Barbara Phillips speculates on the future of mediation in light of institutionalization.

PURSUING SETTLEMENT IN AN ADVERSARY CULTURE: A TALE OF INNOVATION CO-OPTED OR "THE LAW OF ADR"

19 Fla. St. U. L. Rev. 1, 1–3, 5, 7–8, 10–11, 13, 16–17, 25, 30-44 (1991) [*]

By Carrie Menkel-Meadow

In this Article I tell a tale of legal innovation co-opted. Put another way, this is a story of the persistence and strength of our adversary system in the face of attempts to change and reform some legal institutions and practices.

In sociological terms, it is an ironic tale of the unintended consequences of social change and legal reform. A field that was developed, in part, to release us from some—if not all—of the limitations and rigidities of law and formal legal institutions has now developed a law of its own. With burgeoning developments in the use of nonadjudicative methods of dispute resolution in the courts and elsewhere issues about alternative dispute resolution (ADR) increasingly have been "taken to court." As a result, we are beginning to see the development of case and statutory law and, dare I say, a "common law" or "jurisprudence" of ADR.

. . . .

. . . In this Article I explore the larger institutional issues presented when lawyers, judges, and parties to a conflict come together to resolve disputes using new forms within old structures. As a proponent of a particular version of ADR—the pursuit of "quality" solution—I am somewhat troubled by how a critical challenge to the status quo has been blunted, indeed co-opted, by the very forces I had hoped would be changed by some ADR forms and practices. In short, courts try to use various forms of ADR to reduce caseloads and increase court efficiency at the possible cost of realizing better justice. Lawyers may use ADR not for the accomplishment of a "better" result, but as another weapon in the adversarial arsenal to manipulate time, methods of discovery, and rules of procedure for perceived client advantage. Legal challenges cause ADR "issues" to be decided by courts. An important question that must be confronted is whether forcing ADR to adapt to a legal culture or environment may be counterproductive to the transformations proponents of ADR would like to see in our disputing practices.

. . . .

. . . The major question I wish to explore here is whether, in a more likely scenario, the power of our adversarial system will co-opt and transform the innovations designed to redress some, if not all, of our legal ills. Can legal institutions be changed if lawyers and judges persist in acting from traditional and conventional conceptions of their roles and values?

. . . .

. . . [O]utcomes derived from our adversarial judicial system or the negotiation that occurs in its shadows are inadequate for solving many human problems. Our legal system produces binary win-lose results in adjudication. It also produces unreflective compromise—"split the difference" results in negotiated settlements that may not satisfy the underlying needs or interests of the parties. Human problems become stylized and simplified because they must take a particular legal form for the stating of a claim. Furthermore, the "limited remedial imagination" of courts in providing outcomes restricts what possible solutions the parties could develop. Some of us have argued that alternative forms of dispute resolution, or new conceptualizations of old processes, could lead to outcomes that were efficient in the Pareto-optimal sense of making both parties better off without worsening the position of the other. In addition, the processes themselves would be better because they would provide a greater opportunity for party participation and recognition of party goals. Thus, the "quality" school includes both elements of process and substantive justice claims. Some of the arguments here have been supported by the jurisprudential and anthropological work of those studying the different structures that human beings have developed in response to different disputing functions.

. . . .

The crucial point here is that different constituencies have pursued settlement or ADR for vastly different reasons—cheaper and faster is not necessarily the same thing as better. Those different reasons have led to very different institutionalized forms of ADR. Confusion about the purposes behind a particular form of innovation has led to important policy decisions and legal rulings which have given expression to different values underlying particular forms of ADR.

Partly because of the institutionalization of ADR, some of its earlier proponents, including anthropologist Laura Nader, now oppose ADR because it does not foster communitarian and self-determination goals. Instead, it is used to restrict access to the courts for some groups, just at the time when these less powerful groups have achieved some legal rights. Indeed, some critics have argued that ADR actually hurts those who are less powerful in our society—like women or racial and ethnic minorities—by leaving them unprotected by formal rules and procedures in situations where informality permits the expression of power and domination that is unmediated by legal restraints. In other criticisms, proceduralists have argued that various forms of ADR compromise our legal system by privatizing law making, shifting judicial roles, compromising important legal and political rights and principles, and failing to grant parties the benefits of hundreds of years of procedural protections afforded by our civil and criminal justice rules.

. . . .

. . . As ADR becomes institutionalized within the court system, one can ask whether advocacy is one of many tools of dispute resolution, or whether alternative forms of dispute resolution will be captured by the dominant culture of adversarial advocacy. If the processes of adversarial adjudication and "facilitated" settlement are joined in the same institutions, what are the implications for each process? More importantly, what are the implications for justice?

. . . .

In addition to private and public forums for dispute resolution, ADR has been institutionalized in the professional organizations and associations it has spawned. . . .

What has this "institutionalization" meant? Has the growth and expansion of alternative dispute resolution institutions changed the consciousness of whose job it is to solve legal problems?

In my view, the qualified answer to these questions is no. This is illustrated by the cases which are now beginning to deal with some of the difficult legal issues raised by the uses of ADR. As we survey some of these developments, I suggest that attempts to innovate have been partly, if not totally, "captured" and co-opted by the uses to which advocates have put these new procedures.

At the same time, advocates "attacking" or "manipulating" ADR may tell us something about its limits and abuses in the court system and alert us to the regulatory boundaries that may be necessary to keep each process working within its proper sphere.

. . . .

As ADR has been increasingly used by courts and by private institutions of dispute resolution, it has been increasingly "legalized"—made the subject of legal regulation, in both private and public rules systems. Skillful lawyers are raising legitimate claims and regarding the constitutionality of some of the aspects of ADR—such as infringements of the right to a jury trial, separation of powers, due process, and equal protection. . . .

. . . .

From another quarter, where the claims are usually brought by non-parties to the litigation, one of the major critiques of the development of ADR techniques has been that **ADR privatizes disputing.** To the extent that mandatory settlement conferences, mediation, and summary jury trials result in settlements before a full public trial, they may rob the public of important information. Some critics charge that with so much private settlement there will not be enough public debate, or enough cases going through the traditional adversary system, to produce good law.

. . . .

Public access and first amendment issues are only a few of the constitutional challenges that have been leveled against ADR. Invoking a first amendment claim, both litigants and the public may seek to open settlement processes that were designed to permit confidential and open exploration of options and possibilities for settlement.

I will not pursue in great detail the claims about the constitutionality of ADR because they have been well canvassed by others. As ADR proceeds in its various forms through the courts, advocates have raised issues about violations of the right to jury trial, due process, equal protection, and separation of powers. Most of these claims have failed, and it is clear that with certain protections like nonbinding results, rights to de novo hearings, and limited penalties, ADR can constitutionally be conducted in the courts. Thus, in the constitutional arena the key issue is how the particular ADR programs are structured. Nonbinding settlement devices have virtually all been sustained against constitutional challenges. Binding procedures, or those that tax too greatly the choice of process (such as cost or fee shifting penalties), are likely to be more problematic. Constitutional challenges are not likely to eliminate or abolish ADR in the courts, though they may have some role in shaping the particular forms that are used.

. . . .

The use of settlement activity in the courts should be understood as the clash of two cultures. To the extent that settlement activity seeks to promote consensual agreement through the analysis of the point of view of the other side, it requires some different skills and a very different mind-set from those litigators usually employ. Thus, the issue is whether judges and lawyers in the courts can learn to reorient their cultures and behaviors when trying to settle cases or whether those seeking settlement continue to do so from an adversarial perspective. To the extent that we cannot identify different behaviors in each sphere, we may see the corruption of both processes. If one of the purposes of the legal system is to specify legal entitlements from which settlements may be measured, or from which the parties may depart if they so choose, then having the adjudicators engage in too much mediative conduct may compromise the ability of judges to engage in both fact-finding and rule-making. If courts fail to provide sufficient baselines in their judgments, we will have difficulties determining if particular settlements are wise or truly consensual. There is danger in the possibility that good settlement practice will be marred by over-zealous advocacy or by over-zealous desire to close cases that may require either full adjudication or a public hearing.

Below I review some of the dilemmas presented by the clash of these cultures—settlement in an adversary culture—and suggest some ideas for consideration and small reforms for adoption, I do not see easy or facile answers to these dilemmas. I do not think we will develop a magic taxonomy of case types that will permit easy allocation of cases to one form of processing or another in part because of the dynamism of the legal system and its actors. Some cases may change in the course of attempted resolution and some lawyers, judges, and parties may develop new ideas and behavioral repertoires during the course of litigation in particular cases. We can continue to monitor the uses to which settlement is put within the court system and to develop some measures, controls, and standards for evaluating whether we are achieving what we want. Innovations in dispute resolution give us an opportunity to explore the limits of our preferences and conceptions about the proper roles of dispute resolvers. At the same time, the use of alternatives to adjudication within the court system raises new issues where the cultures begin to blur.

As Marguerite Millhauser has written, there is an unspoken resistance to alternative dispute resolution that derives in part from the tendency instilled by our adversarial training to distrust alternative forms of consciousness, such as a focus on solving the problem rather than winning the case. Some of this can be seen in the somewhat conflicting case law developments alluded to above. Some are settlement-promoting, while others are concerned about the limits of forcing settlement and our right to proceed [as adversaries] to trial if we want. But as these cases travel through the courts, it is clear that lawyers are approaching settlement [as adversaries]. They are ready to raise legal, technical, and procedural claims about how cases are being processed, and they are questioning whether settlement comes at the expense of other legal entitlements.

Similarly, there is some evidence that at least some lawyers persist in appearing at various ADR sessions wearing their adversarial suits. A recent professional workshop on alternative dispute resolution was titled "How to 'Win' at ADR." The Michigan courts have "co-opted" the language of ADR by calling their case processing program mediation; in fact, it is a hybrid form of case evaluation and arbitration.

To the extent that "qualitative" ADR consists of an opening of mind and consciousness to formulate a different style or approach to legal representation, the appearance of litigators at mandatory settlement proceedings may taint the quality of the process that ensues. Some firms have gone so far as to recognize that dispute resolution may require different forms of expertise and various personality types. Such firms have developed specialized departments, while others have instituted programs to teach traditional lawyers to conceive of their dispute resolution processes differently. The use of ADR may require some skills other than advocacy. For lawyers and judges who have been taught to argue, criticize, and persuade, rather than to listen, synthesize, and empathize, some changes in behavior will be necessary. Adversarial practices may be problematic in settlement not only because of the obvious risk of stalemate and hostility, but also because extreme positions most often produce unprincipled compromise even if a settlement agreement is reached. This confirms the criticisms of those who see settlement as an unprincipled process. Good settlement practice may be difficult to adapt to traditional adversarial forms.

In an important sense, the ADR movement represents a case study in the difficulties of legal reform when undertaken by different groups within the legal system. At the beginning were the *conceptualizers*—academics and judicial activists who developed both the critique of the adversary system and, in some cases, the design of alternative systems of dispute resolution. The *implementers* developed the concrete forms these innovations took when they moved into the legal system. Some of the *conceptualizers*—Frank Sander and several of the judges—were also *implementers*. In addition, other judges and judicial administrators principally concerned about case load management, and about the quality of solutions or decisions, became *implementers*. Support for the implementation of these ADR programs came from the principal foundation and government funding sources, as well as from groups of change-oriented practicing lawyers who have played an important catalytic role in supporting and using some of the first alternative procedures.

Finally, the *constituents* of these ADR systems—lawyers and their clients as consumers—were "acted upon," sometimes somewhat consensually, by the force of court rules or judicial encouragement. We are just beginning to see some of their reactions in the litigation developing from ADR innovation and in evaluation research.

Each of these groups of actors within the ADR legal reform movement inhabit different cultural worlds—academia, the judiciary, law practice, the business world, and everyday life. Each group uses, transforms, and "colonizes" the work of the others. The research of academics is ignored or simplified; judges move cases along and adopt the language of case management rather than justice; lawyers "infect" clients with a desire for adversarial advantage, or in other cases clients do the same to lawyers; and professionals argue about credentialing and standards for the new profession.

Each of these actors in the dispute resolution arena may be serving different masters. As the ideas are institutionalized, they develop into new and different forms of dealing with problems. Those who work in the field have attempted to create environments for dialogues among and between these constituencies. Some of these meetings have been productive and have fostered "cross-class" understanding. Just as often, however, such meetings leave people confirmed in their views that their particular paradigm is most accurate. Others do not understand the particular reality that some may face—whether it be the crush of caseloads or the lack of "justice" in settlements.

In my view, productive discourse about ADR will have to transcend the language of these cultural differences. Academics, and particularly those who theorize about jurisprudential concerns, need to root their views in the practicalities of our empirical world. Occasionally, judges and legal practitioners need to step back and review the larger jurisprudential and policy issues implicated in "quick-fix" reforms. Practitioners and clients need to consider new forms of practice and process while diminishing their adversarial ways of thinking. A professional life should be one of re-examination, growth, and change. If we are really looking for new ways to process disputes—both to increase case-processing efficiency and to promote better quality solutions—then we have to be willing to look critically at the innovations and their effects from all quarters. I believe that social innovation and transformation are possible here—the issues are whether conventional mind-sets will "infect" these innovations on the one hand, or whether the "cure" will be worse than the disease on the other.

In a sense, we are at a second stage in the development of alternative dispute resolution innovations. The bloom on the rose has faded as some experiments have been tried and now present their own problems or dilemmas. Some of us still aim for consciousness transformation and institutionalized forms of ADR and what can be done to make them work. Many of the issues raised by these developments require policy judgments for which we have an inadequate empirical data base; others require us to make normative choices based on what we value in a procedural system. If ADR is to meet the basic levels of fairness, then the following questions must be collected to prevent ADR from becoming totally swallowed by the adversarial system:

1. To what extent will courts lose their legitimacy as courts if too many other forms of case-processing are performed within their walls? If the "other" processes are not considered legitimate within public institutions, they will be legally challenged and transformed so that they will no longer be "alternatives," but only watered-down versions of court adjudication. These watered-down versions may be violative of the legal rights and rules our courts are intended to safeguard. Are theorists, practitioners, and citizens capable of changing our views of what courts should do?

2. Should some case types be excluded from alternative treatment?

3. What are the purposes for using particular forms of alternative dispute resolution? . . . If the goals and purposes of particular ADR institutions are clarified now, future problems based on overly abstract goals may be avoided.

4. What forms of ADR should be institutionalized? Not all ADR devices are the same. There is a tendency in the literature and in the rhetoric to homogenize widely different approaches to dispute resolution. A more thorough and careful consideration of each of the devices might lead to different conclusions about the utility and legitimacy of these devices. . . .

5. What are the politics of ADR? Does ADR serve the interests of particular groups? This is not an easy question to answer. Many have

argued that "minor" disputes have been siphoned out of the public legal system, while "major" disputes have continued to receive the benefits of the traditional court system. Large corporations are also removing their cases from the court system. Through the increased use of private ADR, the economics of dispute resolution are more subtle. Some may be "forced" out while others choose to opt out. What will this mean for payment and subsidies of dispute resolution? Will "free market" forces decide the fate of ADR? Who will control decision-making about ADR—judges, lawyers, clients, or legislators? If those with the largest stake in the system exit, who will supply the impetus and resources for court and rule reform? At the level of institutional decision-making, are these issues for individual judges, for the Congress, or for the United States Supreme Court to decide?

6. What are the cultural forces producing these legal changes at these particular times? Has the larger culture around us changed since particular legal innovations were adopted? If attempts to incorporate party participation in disputing were made in the "participatory" 1960s and 1970s, then does the 1980s era of privatization of public services dictate other considerations in the use of ADR? How has the rhetoric of quality justice been transformed into a rhetoric of quantity and case processing?

7. How are different forms of ADR actually functioning?. . .

. . . In order for ADR to develop in a way that enhances our trust in the American legal system, several important reforms should accompany our experimentation.

First some forms of ADR should remain mandatory, but not binding. . . .

Second, if some settlement processes are to be made mandatory, certain essential legal protections may have to flow from those processes. If they do not, then processes may have to be chosen consensually or voluntarily. . . .

Third, if settlement processes are to be conducted within the courts, they should be facilitated by those who will not be the ultimate triers of fact. Because I believe that good settlement practice frequently depends on the revelation of facts that would be inadmissible in court, the facilitator of settlement cannot be the same person who will ultimately find facts or decide the outcome of the case. . . .

Fourth, settlement facilitators must be trained to conduct settlement proceedings, particularly those that depart from conventional adjudication models. . . .

Fifth, we must provide the evidence for systematic evaluation of alternative dispute resolution devices. To accomplish this goal, I recommend the recording of proceedings, as well as more sophisticated data collection at the court level. . . .

Sixth, different forms of ADR should be unbundled and separately evaluated. . . .

Finally, categorical judgments about particular processes are likely to be unhelpful. Mediation or summary jury trials *per se* do not violate our procedural rules or jurisprudential norms. More often, the issue is whether a particular process is carried out sensitively or "coercively." . . .

QUESTIONS

(1) Professor Menkel-Meadow uses the term "ADR" in her article. Are the concerns she raised generic to alternative processes? Are mediation and arbitration equally susceptible to the concerns?

(2) Professor Sander delivered his more optimistic speech about the future of ADR and mediation, excerpted in Section [B] of this chapter, several years after Professor Menkel-Meadow wrote her article. Has the co-optation of mediation that she and others feared occurred?

(3) Professor Menkel-Meadow is uncomfortable with adversary behavior in mediation. Is there a difference between advocacy and adversary behavior? Can a lawyer be a good advocate for a client without engaging in adversary behavior?

WHAT HAPPENS WHEN MEDIATION IS INSTITUTIONALIZED?: TO THE PARTIES, PRACTITIONERS, AND HOST INSTITUTIONS

9 Ohio St. J. on Disp. Resol. 307, 307–314, 316–319, 321–324, 327–329, 331–332 (1994) *

By James Alfini, John Barkai, Robert Baruch Bush, Michele Hermann, Jonathan Hyman, Kimberlee Kovach, Carol Liebman, Sharon Press & Leonard Riskin

. . . .

Dean James Alfini: . . . The general question we'll be addressing today is: What are the real and potential effects of this institutionalization of mediation? In particular, we'll concern ourselves with the impact of institutionalization on: First, the mediation process. Second, the parties to the dispute, or the case in court. Third, the lawyers and the legal profession generally. Fourth will be the courts. . . .

Let's put the discussion in a hypothetical context. . . .

The Chief Justice of the State of Fiss . . . is very interested in bringing mediation into the court system, particularly into the trial court system. . . . Our panel is a consulting team that has been brought into the State of Fiss with the purpose of advising these policy makers on these important matters. . . .

Let's start with the concerns of the professional mediator in the State of Fiss. As you can imagine, their general concern is whether, once the court system—particularly lawyers and judges—get their mitts on this new process, mediation as they know it—good mediation—will come to an end. Whether lawyers and judges will, in fact, bastardize the process.

. . . .

Professor Baruch Bush: . . . The thing to be concerned about as mediation becomes institutionalized—not just through connections with the courts. . .—is that what tends to happen is the hardening of mediation practice into . . . the technocratic face rather than the humanistic face.

Let me be a little more specific, because there are a number of different things we can consider institutionalization. Courts' and lawyers' involvement is one. This tends to mean that the advancement of settlement and agreement is set up as an all important goal of mediation because disposition of cases matters very much to courts. Also, legal standards become imported into the definition of what constitutes a good agreement in mediation, as opposed to purely the parties' preferences. . . .

On the other hand, there are forces of institutionalization within the profession itself that tend to move the field toward the technocratic model. . . .

. . . .

. . . A growing body of research on practice suggests, that despite the image of mediation as reflecting self-determination and a more humanistic face, actual practice follows more of a problem-solving or technocratic approach, a directive approach to the process. . . . [T]hat kind of directive model of practice seems to be quite predominate, as opposed to an approach that focuses more on self-determination, choice-making, communication, perspective-taking—concepts that originated the field of mediation. . . . [T]his dimension has tended to get less emphasis the more the process crystallizes.

. . . Mediation had, and has, the potential to offer something truly different, something truly alternative. However, if that's going to happen, this trend towards crystallization into the technocratic model must be avoided.

. . . I think mediators themselves are the best source of control on this trend. . . .

Professor Carol Liebman: . . .

The California and New York experiences teach critical lessons about institutionalizing ADR. The higher the volume, the more routinized and dehumanized the process is likely to become, the more important the doorkeeper to the multi-door courthouse becomes and the harder that door keeping job is. . . .

It is difficult to maintain quality when you get mediators—sometimes paid, sometimes getting expenses, sometimes volunteers—who are doing a number of these every day, with little or no supervision. . . . If what you want is a quick fix, faster/cheaper mediation and that's all you want, mediation can be a very serious problem in terms of cutting off peoples' rights and pushing them out of the system without their getting a fair process—whether it's a fair hearing or a fair mediation.

Professor Michele Hermann: . . . [M]y first thought is that the impact of institutionalization is going to be driven by the motivation of the courts that institutionalize.

My second thought picks up on something that both Baruch and Carol mentioned, and that is that we seem to be assuming that this is going to happen in the context of the multi-door courthouse. What is most important in structuring the institutionalization of ADR in general is an appropriate dispute diagnosis system at the beginning. There are lots of cases . . . that are just fine with technocratic, distributive, directive sorts of settlement processes. Those are disputes where exclusively money is an issue, where there is no prior relationship or post relationship between or among the parties—a classic example is personal injury automobile cases. . . .

. . . [I]f you have a good dispute diagnosis then you can offer different choices to different kinds of cases.

. . . .

Dean Alfini: . . . What's going to be the impact of institutionalized mediation on the parties themselves? . . .

Professor Hermann: . . . .

In the mediation literature, women have been predicted to do worse in mediation. . . . [O]ur study [in the small claims court in Albuquerque, New Mexico] in mediation found that women did better in mediation than they did in adjudication. And women did better than men. The flip side in terms of satisfaction was that women liked mediation less than they liked adjudication and were most likely to describe the mediation process as being unfair when their case was co-mediated by two women. . . .

In terms of disputants of color, who in our sample were eighty seven percent self-described Hispanic, the minority disputants did somewhat worse in adjudication than did white disputants, but not enough to be really statistically significant. In mediation, they did dramatically worse than did white disputants. . . . But if both of the mediators were mediators of color then the outcome was no longer distinguishable from the outcome of white disputants. . . . [I]n terms of satisfaction, both claimants and respondents of color were more enthusiastic about mediation than they were about adjudication, and were more enthusiastic . . . than were white people in mediation.

. . . .

Ms. Sharon Press: . . . [I]n Florida, . . . what we knew before we got started was that approximately ninety-six percent of all cases settled and did not go on to trial. . . . What we've seen is a difference in *how* those cases settle. Traditionally the way cases settled—those ninety-six percent—is that the two or more lawyers who are representing the parties get together outside their clients and discuss settlement, and they come up with a settlement and that settlement is then presented to the clients. The clients don't have as much input or as much understanding as to why the case is settled the way it is settled. The difference in an institutionalized system like Florida is that the parties are mandated to participate in those settlement discussions. . . . I think that helps people to understand what's going on and I think it leads to better settlements as well.

We also know that people didn't choose to go to mediation, at least initially, when they didn't understand what the process was about. . . . Now that we have five or six years of institutionalized mediation experience, the courts need to mandate mediation in fewer cases. In more and more cases, the parties are saying to their lawyers they would like to use mediation. . . . So in that way, having an institutionalized system—at least initially in mandating it— you educate the parties and spread mediation in a way that is much faster than if you went through a slow learning curve of just letting people seep through the system.

. . . .

The final point that I have is slightly outside of the court system. . . . By participating in a mediation—whether it is mandated or not—I think that there is a spillover effect to people involved in it, that they learn that there are ways to resolve disputes. This was dramatically shown to me when I worked in a high school mediation program—a different kind of institution but an institution nonetheless. The students that came in as the disputants learned a process, learned a way of thinking about disputes that they may not have thought about before. And what we saw was that many of them wanted to become mediators . . . . [U]nless you have wide-spread institutionalization or the placing of this process in institutions, you don't have that kind of spillover. . . .

. . . .

Professor John Barkai:. . . Michele's impressive and useful research raises the question, "What is 'culturally appropriate' mediation?" . . . My experience is that different cultures use different forms of mediation. In Asia, mediation is often referred to as "conciliation." Asian conciliation, in either a business or personal setting, typically includes the seeking of an opinion from a wise and respected person within the community whom Westerners might call a mediator. . . . [Asians] do not seek or expect something that looks like American community mediation which seeks to enhance communication, empower the parties, and uncover underlying interests. . . . All of this leads me to the conclusion that if a mediator is working with disputants from other cultures, the mediator might want to ask, "What kind of mediation assistance would you like to have?"

. . . .

Professor Bush: . . . One possible explanation for some of the sort of paradoxical results that Michele got . . . is that perhaps people *don't* care mostly about money. . . .

. . .

. . .It could be that the reason why women liked mediation less was that it wasn't outcome that mattered to them most, it was how the process worked, how they were treated. So even though they got favorable outcomes, they *disliked* mediation because something else mattered more to them. And for the disputants of color, it was the same thing. Even though they got unfavorable outcomes, they *liked* mediation because something else mattered more.

Dean Alfini: . . . Professor Hyman, you've been doing research on settlement conferences recently. Does that research suggest how mediation or its institutionalization might have an impact on lawyers and the legal profession generally?

Professor Jonathan Hyman: . . . .

I think the key to a lot of these questions is the depth and sophistication of the understanding of lawyers, themselves, about the mediation process. If they see mediation in a kind of mechanical light—trying to speed up a series of offers and demands and exchange of concessions—if they see mediation as the way to advance that kind of dispute resolution process, which is the one they're mostly familiar with, then I don't think that institutionalizing mediation is going to have much effect for things other than small claims. . . .

. . . .When we did a survey of civil litigators in New Jersey—these are non-matrimonial civil cases claiming over $5000—we asked them about two kinds of settlement practices. . . . We received five hundred responses to our questionnaire, and surveyed most of the lawyers who were on the trial lists over a period of time throughout New Jersey. They reported to us that at least seventy percent of the cases that they knew about in their experience were settled by the positional method, not by the problem-solving method. But sixty percent of the respondents wanted more of the problem-solving method. And almost half wanted less of the positional method.

. . . This would tie in closely with what mediation can do; it's this kind of situation in which a mediator can be very helpful.

. . . .

[T]here's a substantial risk that the lawyers are going to swallow whatever system you adopt. They're going to keep replicating the same things they do now, and they'll take control of it. But there's an opportunity for letting lawyers participate in expanding the use of problem-solving methods and finding ways that they can do that. . . .

. . . .

Dean Alfini: . . . Texas, again, has been introducing more and more court-sponsored programs into their judicial system. The final set of concerns that we have, have to do with the impact on the courts. . . . What's the likelihood of the impact on the courts?

Professor Kovach: . . . It depends on what I think the state is willing to do on the front end. I think it also depends on identifying the specific goals, which was brought out earlier. . . . [T]he courts that did not take the time at the front end to become educated about the mediation process, educated about referral, and things like that, ended up spending more time on a case because of objections on the referral process, on the selection of the mediator, or fee issues, etc. . . . And it also then depends . . . if you have the resources. . . . What has turned out in the latest round of plans is that once the resources dried up, ADR plans and mediation plans have been the first to be dropped out of those plans.

Professor Barkai: As we try to forecast the future of mediation in the courts, I think that we are failing to look at the incentives and disincentives ADR holds for lawyers. The practice of law is a business, and lawyers are trying to figure out how ADR will impact their practice. The fee structure significantly impacts incentives for using ADR. There is not mush economic incentive for a lawyer on an hourly-fee to engage in mediation, court-annexed arbitration, or any form of ADR before almost all pretrial discovery is complete. Although ADR may mean reducing costs for clients, it also means reducing income for lawyers. There is an obvious conflict of interest there.

. . . .

Professor Bush: . . . [A]s "institutionalization" proceeds, I would argue for not placing transformation off the end of the spectrum. Instead, I think that we need to de-mystify that term, and talk about the possibility, and value, of change on a much more incremental, much more "micro" level. It's too soon to rigidify things and say, "this is possible and this is not," even when we're talking about courts, lawyers and "purely monetary disputes." It is certainly true, there are cases where people don't want to have somebody assist them in approaching conflict as a sort of change process. If so, then that shouldn't happen; that should be clearly a choice of the parties. On the other hand, if this kind of approach in not even available, because institutionalization has made it difficult or impossible for this to occur in mediation, then that's a limitation of choice of a different kind. And I don't think that's a wise idea to do that at this stage of our development.

. . . .

Professor Hyman: Well it seems from what we've been talking about here that you shouldn't rely on any institutions to make changes; that changes have to come from the bottom up—from the people on a more micro level. The proper role of the courts seems to be more in making those kinds of changes possible, understanding them, welcoming them, providing room for them, encouraging them, but not trying to institutionalize them. . . .

INSTITUTIONALIZATION: SAVIOR OR SABOTEUR OF MEDIATION?

24 Fla. St. U. L. Rev. 903, 904–913, 917 (1997) *

By Sharon Press

[O]ne of the most exciting and challenging developments for practitioners in the past ten years has been the increased institutionalization of ADR particularly in relation to mediation within the court system. Spreading ADR processes has been a goal many who are committed to the field have pursued with great vigor. As the old cliche reminds us, however, "be careful what you wish for." The growth and development of mediation and other dispute resolution processes in institutional settings, while certainly producing more

---

exposure and interest in these processes, has also brought with it a host of concerns I believe worthy of thought and discussion. . . .

. . .For purposes of this article, I use the term "institutionalization" to refer to any entity (governmental or otherwise) which, as an entity, adopts ADR procedures as a part of doing business. Some examples include schools that develop peer mediation programs, courts that establish rules to govern referral to ADR procedures, and government agencies that incorporate ADR processes in developing rules and regulations. My discussion will focus primarily on the institutionalization of court mediation programs, with examples drawn from Florida's experience because that is what I know best; however, I believe that many of the same opportunities and concerns raised are readily transferable to other institutions. To me, Florida's experience with court-connected mediation can serve as a case study for how and why bureaucracies develop.

Institutionally, Florida entered the ADR movement in the mid 1970s with the establishment of "citizen dispute settlement" (CDS) centers. The CDS centers are similar to the neighborhood justice centers of other jurisdictions and handle disputes (mostly minor criminal, neighborhood-type disputes) that are voluntarily brought by the individuals involved in the disputes. The model pursued for the Florida CDS centers, after the initial ones came into being, centered around local development with strong support form the Office of the State Courts Administrator (OSCA) and the Chief Justice of the Florida Supreme Court. . . .

Some argued that this development was not in keeping with the primary goal of the CDS movement, which was to empower those in the local community to resolve issues for themselves. On the other hand, these programs would not have spread as quickly or completely had it not been for the Florida Supreme Court's support. The research conducted by OSCA provided the data to show that the programs worked, the organizational manuals provided the step-by-step information on how to establish programs, and the training manuals and guidelines provided some measure of consistency and quality control that led to confidence in the program. Looking around the nation, one finds that programs have flourished primarily in those states in which the courts provided an institutional home, established institutional frameworks, and promoted the use of these processes. I believe there is a direct correlation. In Florida, the CDS programs thrived when the supreme court focused attention on the program. When attention shifted from the CDS programs toward the court programs, no new programs were established and many of those that were in existence expanded to include court cases. Within a few years, the bulk of the CDS centers' cases had shifted away from communities and towards courts. This shift is not surprising, based upon the difficulty CDS or neighborhood justice centers have in generating cases. Because the number of cases that a community center actually mediates is significantly lower than the number of cases that are scheduled (due to the inherent difficulty in getting both parties to attend a completely voluntary process), the centers face a continuing challenge, resulting in disappointingly low caseloads.

As part of its effort for the future, the Florida Supreme Court appears to be refocusing attention on neighborhood justice centers, and we once again are beginning to see an increase in the caseload numbers and a renewed commitment to the concept of neighborhood/community justice. . . .

If we start from the premise that mediation and other alternative processes provide a positive means of resolving disputes, then it seems to follow that providing for the more rapid spread and more comprehensive use of these processes would also be a positive step. As practitioners, we have longed for more cases to be referred to mediation so more disputants can benefit from the empowerment possibilities of mediated disputes (and also so there is enough work for us to pursue our chosen field). Institutionalization certainly focuses attention on the processes, and it can be very instrumental in promoting its uses; yet increased institutionalization is not without its downside. . . .

While the heightened awareness of mediation alternatives and the increased use of mediation is a very positive and exciting development in the evolution of our justice system, the natural consequences of this rapid, institutional development have also concerned me. Since 1987, Florida has experienced tremendous growth in the number of rules and laws surrounding the mediation program. From an administrative perspective, each additional rule has been necessary and important in the maturation of the program. Overall, however, I remain concerned about the ultimate effect that additional rules will have on the mediation process, i.e., what will happen when a flexible process, like mediation, is incorporated into the traditional court process. Which process changes?

A description of some of the recent revisions and additions to the Florida Statutes and the Florida Rules of Civil Procedure serves as an ideal way to illustrate this dilemma. In 1988, the Florida Supreme Court adopted qualifications for court mediators. To promote use of the qualifications and add to the comfort level of the judges and lawyers who would ultimately be the users of the process, the court relied heavily on previous experience and "paper credentials." The national mediation community was outraged by the development of mediator qualification requirements by an institution. Nevertheless, if an institution takes the step to order parties who file in court to participate in mediation prior to (or hopefully instead of) obtaining a trial before a judge, doesn't it logically follow that the court has an affirmative obligation to ensure that the individual to whom the case is referred has some expertise? To take it a step further, wouldn't it be irresponsible, if not negligent, for the courts *not* to develop some method of determining who should mediate for the courts and who should not? I do not see easy answers to these questions. While I am sympathetic to the view that the qualifications originally established by the Florida Supreme Court are not perfect, I do believe that the establishment of mediation as an alternative within the court system brought with it the obligation to provide some means for individuals ordered to mediation to have confidence in their mediator. I also believe, based on discussions I have had over the years with judges and attorneys, that mediation would not have succeeded in the court system if the early mediators in large cases were not attorneys.

This is not to say that the obligation of the court or institution that establishes the program ends with its initial rules and its ability to gain acceptance for the program. On the contrary, I am a strong proponent of the notion that if a court undertakes to institutionalize mediation, it has an ongoing obligation to routinely and systematically review the governing policies, rules, and procedures with an eye toward continual revision. To me, this is a crucial step in preventing the ossification of a flexible process.

In keeping with this continuing obligation, Florida has two standing supreme court committees on mediation and arbitration: the Supreme Court Committee on Mediation and Arbitration Training . . . and the Supreme Court Committee on Mediation and Arbitration Rules. . . .

In 1990, Florida revised its rules to provide for greater party control over the selection of a mediator. This rule revision opened the door for parties to select a mediator within the first ten days of referral to mediation. During this time, any mediator could be selected, including one not certified by the Florida Supreme Court. These revisions are an example of a critical step in the evolutionary process of an institutionalized mediation program, namely the obligation to introduce flexibility and choice into the process as it becomes more accepted.

This rule revision, while illustrative, was only one of the recommendations submitted to the supreme court in the three petitions that have been filed since the committee's appointment in 1989. In addition, the Florida Legislature has revised the statute governing mediation and arbitration several times since its adoption in 1987.

One of the legislative changes adopted provides for "judicial immunity in the same manner and to the same extent as a judge." . . . The passage of this legislation created a situation that led to the need for the next major set of rules, namely, the Florida Rules for Certified and Court-Appointed Mediators, which contain the standards of conduct and rules of discipline for supreme court-certified and court-appointed mediators.

The original legislation establishing the comprehensive mediation program contained a provision that the Florida Supreme Court would establish minimum standards and procedures for professional conduct and discipline. However, the adoption of the immunity for mediators provided the real impetus to adopt standards and a disciplinary procedure. Absent such adoption, parties to court-ordered mediation had no redress for inappropriate mediator behavior. . . .

With such a backdrop, one can readily appreciate the need for the development of standards of conduct. In 1992, the Florida Supreme Court adopted such a code of conduct and a means for enforcing the standards. . . . I remain concerned about the impact that these standards will have on the process. I come back again to the overriding concern that mediation is a flexible process and that adoption of a code of conduct will somehow rigidify the process. If the standards are written broadly to allow for the subtle nuances of an individual situation, might they then offer no real guidance to mediators in discharging their duties? If they are written very specifically, might they then inhibit a mediator's ability to handle each situation creatively?

A concrete example of how the standards might change the practice of mediation in an unintended manner is in the simple practice relating to the retention of notes. Because communication in court-connected mediation is privileged and cannot be disclosed absent a waiver of the privilege by all parties to the mediation, mediators typically do not retain notes from concluded mediation sessions. In fact, in the past, most trainers recommended to student mediators that they not retain notes. Will the adoption of a standard of conduct and the potential for a grievance being filed cause mediators not only to keep notes of their sessions, but also to request that parties sign off on statements that say they were fully capable of participating or that they were aware of their legal rights and were still desirous of pursing this mediated agreement? I wonder whether changes in these procedures will cause a greater underlying change in the way mediation is conducted. Will it lead to more party refusals to mediate? If so, maybe those were cases that should not have been mediated in any event.

After more than four years of experience under the mediator code of conduct and grievance system, we are starting to see some trends. . . . [A]n analysis of the grievances filed shows common concerns, namely the failure of the mediator either to allow the parties to exercise self determination, to act impartially, or to refrain from providing professional advice. A summary of the grievances that have been filed is published in the DRC newsletter . . . for educational purposes. The hope is that this formal (institutional) process of handling grievances will enable mediators to better understand their role in the process and prevent inadvertent inappropriate behavior.

. . . .

. . . I believe that the institutionalization of mediation programs has served a worthwhile purpose. It is only with institutionalization that we are able to achieve the increased attention and high level of debate around these issues. I have seen first hand . . . how helpful—and transforming—these programs can be. I know that most people are still not very sophisticated in thinking through their options for resolving disputes. In the school setting, students frequently view their options as limited to ignoring the situation, telling a teacher or other authority, or fighting it out. For adults, the choices are surprisingly similar: ignoring the conflict, appealing to the authority of the courts, or fighting it out. . . . Institutionalization provides necessary legitimacy and widespread utilization to a process that is only useful if one knows about it. One can only make informed decisions about whether to use mediation if one is aware that the process exists.

MEDIATION: DID WE GET IT WRONG?

33 Willamette L. Rev. 649, 655–656, 679, 689, 691-693, 701 (1997) [*]

By Barbara A. Phillips

The intense debate about mediation and other Appropriate Dispute Resolution forms comes at a time when immense changes are taking place in the relationship between courts and the public. ADR is not the main force driving these changes, but is merely a stream contributing to the broad river of change in how conflict is managed in our culture.

. . . .

Mediation is, in one sense, old as well as new. Our tendency to resolve dispute privately is part of our country's heritage, and is a central aspect of our Anglo-American legal system. From the remote antecedents of our legal system, there is evidence of procedures that gave disputants some control over their destiny. In Anglo-Saxon England, from the seventh to the mid-eleventh centuries, the third-party decision makers often persuaded the losing party to come to terms with the winning party, promoting their reconciliation. This occurred after "winner-take-all judgments" were announced to the parties, but *before* these judgments were finalized by oath-swearing. Reparation amounts for personal injury were made expressly subject to negotiation.

Some judges and those concerned with judicial ADR programs, facing pressure from various quarters to reform the handling of cases have asked whether invoking mediation might impede access to the courts and weaken the effectiveness of applicable law. This is a fair question. To answer it we must look at our society's concepts of justice, power, and balance.

. . . .

What does justice mean in the context of mediation? The law is only one factor parties consider in evaluating settlement options. If mediation is about self-determination, and if the affected parties reach an accommodation that works for them (absent a lack of capacity or other taint), why would a court question it?

Perhaps we are looking for justice in the wrong place. We do not speak of justice in referring to what people do to or for *themselves*. Justice has a meaning only in a more public context—when people are "done unto" or acted upon, particularly when the one acted upon is required to submit. Protection of the mediation process is far more relevant than the justice of the mediated agreement in the eyes of a third party.

As relevant to institutionally fostered mediation, justice means that mediation to which the parties are committed must not only be seen as fair and just, but must be so in fact. But this is no invitation for courts to control the process or the providers, for fairness and justice lie in the eyes of the users. As they are given options and choices about the appropriate dispute resolution process and the provider, justice in this sense will happen automatically.

. . . .

The challenge to courts is to *foster* mediation by managing the court's own panels, by allowing recourse to the private sector and loosely monitoring the results of its utilization, and by keeping up an open dialogue on the subject with counsel and, at times, litigants and providers.

By keeping in mind the goal of providing disputants with resources to secure quality outcomes to their disputes, courts can get the best results possible. Litigation has its place, and mediation is no substitute for it. Improved calendar management through mediation is often an incidental side-effect, but it is not the *purpose* of referring matters to mediation. The purpose is to facilitate quality resolution at reasonable cost. There is value in getting to know mediation on its own terms, rather than trying to reshape it in the image of it jurisprudential relatives—arbitration and judicial settlement conferencing.

. . . .

Courts can accomplish more by *allowing* things to happen rather than by *causing* them to happen. If that sounds weak, it is because we are using the wrong paradigm—the *Power Over* paradigm rather than the *Power With* paradigm. A rules review is a good place to start, determining whether the rule being invoked is appropriate to the case and serve the purpose of fostering development of a healthy, diverse, ethical, and professional resource for disputants.

. . . .

[A] key issue is whether mediation programs should be voluntary or mandatory. Most voluntary programs are not effective in teaching lawyers and courts enough about mediation so that they will use it. Lawyers often are not familiar enough with the mediation process to make informed judgments. There is substantial evidence that utilization does not occur without mandatory referrals. . . .

A powerful alternative to either approach is a mandatory program with *options*, such as Florida's private mediator selection. There, courts mandate mediation but allow the parties to select their own mediator. Oregon law provides a similar choice in its opt-out provisions. . . .

. . . .

Requiring mediation is similar to a screening checkup to determine whether trial is necessary. A good mediation *will* show which cases require litigation. If the cost is modest relative to the dispute's other costs and the parties' ability to pay, and the time involved is short, mediation is no more taxing than spending half a day sitting in court waiting for the matter to be heard.

. . . .

The answer to the question "Mediation: Did We Get It Wrong?" is "not yet." The trend is strongly toward acceptance of a facilitative model of mediation that can make good on mediation's potential. Some leading providers such as JAMS/Endispute, who in the past have been heavily invested in the judicial model of evaluative mediation are now teaching the facilitative approach. On an individual basis, this is inevitable. Absent official barriers, people who become more skilled mediators tend to expand their skills into the more challenging and more subtle types of practice. They learn that strong process management can co-exist with a deferential facilitative approach to mediation so that, to the fullest extent, the parties are afforded their right to self-determination.

Chapter 10

MEDIATION IN MANY CONTEXTS

§ A INTRODUCTION

This chapter introduces most of the major types of disputes for which mediation has been used, and explores many of the issues that arise in these various contexts. Nonetheless, the goal of this chapter is not to cover *all* of the many applications of mediation, but to impart a sense of the incredible breadth of the field. Moving, very generally, from the more simple applications of mediation to the more complex, the chapter will cover applications of mediation to resolve disputes involving small claims cases, family breakups, business deals, labor and employment disagreements, violations of criminal law, schoolchildren, health care, and public policy issues. The final two readings discuss uses of a form of mediation by native Hawaiians and Navajo native Americans. As you read about these varied types of mediation, consider both the similarities and differences that you see in how mediation is used in these contexts. Think for example about the role of the mediator, the participation of attorneys, and the role of the disputants. Do you think mediators should be required to have special training or credentials to work in any of these areas? Also consider any particular issues that you see arising in a given context. Is mediation well suited to resolve disputes in each of these areas? Are special protections needed?

§ B SMALL CLAIMS MEDIATION

THE USE OF MEDIATION IN SMALL CLAIMS COURTS

9 Ohio St. J. on Disp. Resol. 55, 61-64, 80-81 (1993) *

By Susan E. Raitt, Jay Folberg, Joshua Rosenberg & Robert Barrett

Numerous factors have led to the development of mediation programs in small claims courts over the past decade. First, there are the cost savings for the courts themselves. Mediators can "clearly reduce the amount of judge time the court must assign to small claims calendars" by settling a substantial percentage of trial-ready cases. Additionally, although in some instances there may be a paid mediation coordinator in the court, most mediation programs use volunteer mediators, resulting in a cost-effective alternative to judges or pro-tems.

---

* Copyright © 1993 by the Ohio State Journal on Dispute Resolution. Reprinted with permission.

Second, mediation benefits the disputants. "Because mediation is less confrontational and less formal, it can provide a forum where parties will be more relaxed and have a greater opportunity to explain her or his side of the case."[37] In explaining their positions to a third party neutral, the parties can vent their pent-up feelings. This psychological release often pinpoints the principal obstacle to settlement—the emotional component underlying the conflict. Once feelings about the conflict are expressed, the pathway to settlement is often open. Mediation may also provide a means for a defendant or plaintiff to negotiate a more satisfactory settlement than might be obtained in a court where a judgment is more likely to be a "win-lose" situation. Mediation promotes bargaining, and the mediator can help the parties invent options for mutual gain by making concessions on less important issues to gain ground on issues they view as most important.

Mediation may be able to help smooth out the potential one-sidedness of cases filed by more "sophisticated" businesses. The perception is that businesses that file large numbers of small claims cases have become very professional in the way they adjudicate small claims cases, whether they use a collection agency or their own collections office staff.

One of the reasons that businesses substitute mediation and arbitration for litigation is to promote settlement of commercial disputes without destroying continuing business relationships. This reasoning applies to businesses of all sizes as well as to individuals.

. . . .

It is also hoped that by increasing the use of mediation in small claims cases, the collectability of judgments may be enhanced. Even though plaintiffs win a large percentage of cases, many judgments are never collected. The inability to collect on judgments may be more frustrating to plaintiffs than all of the procedures proceeding the judgment. "If mediation can lead to a more satisfactory settlement, one that is more likely to be collected, plaintiffs who would expect to win at trial stand to benefit from mediation as well."[45]

. . . .

. . . [T]he small claims court was established as an alternative dispute resolution forum in the early part of this century. "Small claims court procedures are less expensive, faster, and less formal than the regular civil litigation process. It is very interesting, therefore, that [many] jurisdictions now have some form of mediation program for small claims cases."[46] Approximately twenty states use some form of alternative dispute resolution in their small claims court system. Most of these courts are using or experimenting with mediators to reduce the number of trials.

---

[37] John A. Goerdt, State Justice Institute, Small Claims and Traffic Courts: Case Management Procedures, Case Characteristics, and Outcomes in Urban Jurisdictions, at 23 (1992).

[45] Id. at 25.

[46] Id. at 23-24.

1. Categories of Small Claims Mediation Programs

. . . .

a. Sponsorship

Programs can be divided generally into two categories: i) court-based programs where mediation is done as "an arm of the court" and ii) programs that operate independently but receive referrals from the court.

b. Timing

The timing of mediation generally falls into one of three categories: i) prior to filing, ii) after filing of a claim but before the date set for a judicial hearing, and iii) on the date set for hearing, just prior to the hearing.

c. Location

Programs may be held i) at the courthouse or ii) in other facilities, including community rooms, mediation center conference facilities, church meeting rooms, law schools, or other non-court locations.

d. Choice

In most small claims mediation programs, participation is voluntary, but in some jurisdictions, the courts have made mediation mandatory; in such cases, whether a claim is settled remains, of course, voluntary.

e. Disposition

Most mediation programs, particularly those that are court-connected, have a procedure for making any settlement agreement a judgment of the court; in other programs, settlements rely on the mutuality of promises and the good faith of the parties to assure compliance.

f. Qualifications

There are a variety of ways to assure that mediators will be qualified. None of the programs surveyed required that all mediators be attorneys, and most drew their mediators from the community population. Mediators generally received training lasting between twenty and forty hours, although some programs had more formal requirements.

g. Length

Most programs reported that mediation sessions averaged about one hour in length, although some cases might take as little as twenty minutes and others up to three hours to reach a resolution.

Overall, mediation programs in the small claims court appear to be quite successful in settling a substantial percentage of contested cases before trial. In a national survey, it was reported that small claims mediation programs successfully settled from fifty percent to about ninety-five percent of the mediated cases. The USF Report indicated that, in California, while the rate at which responding ADR programs resolve the cases brought before them varies from twenty-five percent to ninety-five percent, it is generally about eighty percent.

To some extent, at least in the California study, higher resolution rates correlate with the time spent on each case, which varies from thirty minutes (in the court with a twenty-five percent success rate) to two or three hours (in the two courts reporting a success rate of ninety-five percent). The average time per case is under two hours. This indicates that successful mediation programs are more labor-intensive than the relatively short hearings in adjudication of small claims. In many mediation programs the labor comes exclusively or primarily from volunteers. Where the labor is paid, it becomes more difficult to balance the trade-offs between the resolution benefits of mediating small claims against the cost to the state.

Data from programs in other states indicate that litigant satisfaction with ADR programs is even higher than the settlement rates would imply, suggesting that many litigants whose cases do not settle are nonetheless satisfied with the efforts. Litigants (especially plaintiffs) who went to mediation were more likely to be satisfied with the outcome of the case than litigants who went to trial.

Mediation and other alternative procedures have their own potential limitations: (1) They may require a greater investment of time on the part of both the mediator and the parties to the dispute; (2) the coordination, supervision, and quality control of ADR services in small claims courts may require additional funding or the shifting of funds from an under-funded judicial system; and (3) alternative procedures may perpetuate, rather than eliminate, power imbalances between the parties. Any use of mediation or other ADR techniques should take these potential pitfalls into account.

The Metrocourt Project, a recent empirical study of small claims proceedings in Bernalillo County, New Mexico, concluded that, in both adjudicated and mediated cases, minority claimants received less money than nonminorities and that minority respondents paid more. Ethnicity was even more predictive of outcomes in mediated cases than in adjudicated small claims cases. However, minority claimants and respondents consistently expressed more satisfaction with mediation than with adjudication. The Metrocourt Project also found that female respondents do better than males in mediation outcomes. [*]

Power imbalances, gender differences, and ethnicity may play a larger role in mediation than in adjudication. The informality and flexibility of mediation both lend to its attractiveness and its dangers. The potential disparities in mediated outcomes are difficult to document and will, no doubt, remain the

---

[*] [Ed. note: *see* Chapter 6, *supra*, for further discussion of the Metro Court study and other issues regarding the implications of mediation for minority group members.]

subject of debate. However, the fear that informal procedures may disadvantage the less powerful is itself an issue that must be weighed in considering the greater use of mediation in lieu of adjudication.

[handwritten: what is special about family law?]

QUESTIONS

(1) What do you see as the potential benefits and disadvantages of small claims mediation as compared to litigating in small claims court?

(2) Why do you suppose so many parties seem to prefer mediation to litigation of small claims disputes?

(3) Do you think it is desirable that most small claims mediation be conducted by unpaid volunteers? Necessary?

(4) Are you troubled by the fact that most small claims mediators are not attorneys or judges? Were non-lawyer small claims mediators to give legal advice or draft an agreement, might they be said to be engaging in the unauthorized practice of law? *See* Chapter 7, Section 7[D], *supra.*

§ C   FAMILY MEDIATION

*[handwritten: * think about mandatory divorce mediation]*

THE USE OF MEDIATION AND ARBITRATION FOR RESOLVING FAMILY CONFLICTS: WHAT LAWYERS THINK ABOUT THEM

14 J. Am. Acad. of Matrimonial Law. 353, 354, 356-63, 366-75 (1997) [*]

By Mary Kay Kisthardt

The use of alternative methods for resolving family conflict has increased significantly in the past few years, but many attorneys are still wary. In an effort to discover some of the sources of this hesitation as well as identify support for "alternative" processes, the American Academy of Matrimonial Lawyers surveyed its members concerning the use of dispute resolution methods. . . .

The study that is the center of this report was mailed to 1500 members of the American Academy of Matrimonial Lawyers in the Fall of 1996. One hundred twentythree surveys were returned to the editor of the Journal of the American Academy of Matrimonial Lawyers and their results were compiled at that office. . . .

[handwritten: 123 surveys out of 1500]

. . . .

Section I. Court-Ordered Mediation

. . . .

A. Description/Scope

A total of 110, or nearly 90%, of the respondents reported that court-ordered mediation was used in their jurisdiction. Of that number, the vast majority (104) indicated that child custody issues were the subject of court-ordered mediation. In addition, approximately half of the respondents indicated that child support (50), property division (56), and spousal support (53) could also be addressed in the context of a court-ordered mediation session.

Throughout the country, child custody disputes are the most common focus of court-ordered mediation programs. The reasons for this vary but center primarily on the assumption that child custody cases, which also would include visitation disputes, are the most likely candidates for a resolution mechanism that promotes communication between the parties and attempts to preserve a relationship between them. Virtually universal sentiment exists that an adversarial proceeding is the least advisable method for promoting the long term cooperation between parents that benefits children. Indeed, the attorneys in our survey cited this as an advantage of these programs. Some typical comments included: "[W]hen children are involved, it helps parents to cooperate"; "[H]elps parents to focus on the needs of the children instead of their own needs." Other benefits for children were reflected in statements such as "[S]tops manipulation of children" and "[T]akes children out of the adversary system."

Increasingly, child support issues are being addressed in these same sessions, most likely because issues of child support and child custody are seen as significantly intertwined. Historically, the exclusive focus on child custody was viewed as a way of protecting women from custody blackmail, a theory based on the assumption that women would trade economic support for additional time with their children. Since the adoption of child support guidelines throughout the country has made the resolution of financial support disputes more predictable, this concern is lessened. This predictability may also account for the increased scope of mediations.

The use of court-ordered mediation for the resolution of property division and spousal support, however, is not as widely accepted. About half of the respondents indicated that these issues were also addressed in court-ordered mediations. Many attorneys in our survey suggested that they were more comfortable with the resolution of child custody disputes in mediation than they were with the resolution of property division and spousal support issues. This attitude most likely reflects the tendency of lawyers to see economic issues as "legal" and therefore requiring the expert skills of lawyers in traditional practice, whereas custody issues are more "emotional" and therefore may be adequately handled by mental health professionals in mediation. One attorney responding to the survey summed it up this way: "Support and property division are objective and should be resolved through attorneys."

This distinction between "legal" and "emotional" issues was implicit in many of the comments. Attorneys, quite naturally, see divorce as primarily a "legal" matter in which individuals have certain rights that are recognized by the law and which should guide the resolution of the divorce-related issues. Although lawyers recognize that divorce is a highly emotional matter for most clients, this aspect is seen as secondary to their representation. Some even go so far as to suggest that "emotionalism is most readily diffused by a fair economic resolution." This attitude of distinguishing between issues that are resolved by application of "legal" rules (i.e. procedural processes) becomes problematic for some lawyers when child custody must be considered. This may be due in part to the realization that the "legal" standard of "best interest of the child" that is used in making custody determinations is nebulous at best and that child-related issues are often significantly emotional ones. This may account for the deference sometimes given to mental health professionals when the issue is about "kids and not money."

Members of the mental health profession, the other discipline most commonly involved with divorcing couples, see divorce as primarily an "emotional" event where decisions regarding all aspects of the dissolution, including legal ones, are made in the context of an emotionally charged environment. This difference in approach to the various dimensions of divorce related issues is also reflected in the identity of the mediator. In many court-sponsored programs where the focus is most likely to be on child custody, mental-health professionals are often used as mediators. In our survey approximately one-third of the respondents indicated that mental health professionals who were approved or certified by the court were mediators in court-ordered or court-sponsored programs.

In voluntary mediation, however, where financial issues are more likely to be discussed, attorneys often view themselves as more appropriate mediators. This attitude of superior ability to deal with financial issues may also have an effect on how the mediation is conducted. At least one study found that when lawyers acted as mediators in full divorce mediation, they tended to focus on economic issues rather than issues relating to children.

B. Waiver of the Court-Ordered Mediation Requirements

Traditionally, mediation has been seen as a voluntary process. Therefore requiring parties to attend sessions is, to some, inconsistent with the basic philosophy of mediation. The reasons most often cited for requiring participation are overcoming institutionalized resistance and providing education for the parties about the process.

Even proponents of a mandatory system recognize that under certain circumstances requiring parties to attend would be counterproductive. Therefore, waiver options are gaining favor. Approximately one-third of the respondents indicated that a process existed in their jurisdiction for seeking a waiver of the mediation requirement.

The process for waiving the mediation requirement varies from jurisdiction to jurisdiction, but many common factors exist. Most significantly the grounds for waiver mentioned by the respondents included the presence of domestic violence, other forms of abuse, alcohol or substance abuse and to a lesser extent logistical restrictions such as a party living outside of the county. Although numerous jurisdictions did provide a process for seeking waiver, the respondents indicated that in many cases the requested waiver was not granted.

A significant controversy continues over the use of mediation for resolution of family conflicts in which there has been domestic violence. The past several years have witnessed changes which reflect a growing awareness of the family dynamic that takes place in this situation. Statutes or court rules use different approaches to these cases, either categorical exclusion, or ad hoc methods such as a case by case screening or exclusivity by the court upon a party's motion. These alternative approaches reflect different philosophical responses to the issue.

Some advocates take the position that cases involving domestic violence are simply inappropriate for mediation. Their concerns can be summarized under several categories. First, the culture of battering "which embodies the relationship between a battered woman and her abuser is incompatible with the practice of mediation." Adherents of this view argue that domestic violence is not the result of interpersonal conflict but of a culture of dominance and control. Mediation's focus on resolving interpersonal conflict is therefore misplaced in this context.

Second, since mediation de-emphasizes the criminal aspects of the behavior and is future-oriented, the abuser is allowed to escape responsibility for his past behavior. Third, the power imbalance that exists by virtue of the intimidation simply cannot be effectively remedied in the process. Finally, the effects of domestic violence on children are exacerbated when an abusive parent is allowed to use the children to retain control over their mother.

Others argue that domestic violence ought to provide grounds for seeking a waiver but should not result in automatic disqualification. The proponents of this approach believe that screening mechanisms to identify abuse and appropriate intervention techniques on the part of the mediator can ameliorate the harm.

Scheduling problems

C. Attorney Presence

Another important variable in court-ordered mediation is the presence of attorneys. Approximately 25% of the respondents indicated that attorneys are sometimes present at the court-ordered mediation session. The presence of the attorney appears to be optional and the timing of the attorney participation varies. In some cases attorneys are present only at the beginning. In other mediation situations the attorney meets with the mediator and then the clients meet with the mediator. If financial issues are considered it seems more likely that an attorney will be present at the mediation.

Fears have been expressed that the presence of attorneys during the mediation session will undermine the "cooperative environment" and negatively affect the mediation. In fact in some jurisdictions lawyers can be banned from the session by the mediator. In a recent study of divorce mediation in Maine, Nancy Rogers, Craig McEwen, and Richard Maiman have addressed the issue and arrived at the conclusion that the presence of lawyers does not decrease effectiveness. [Ed. note: *see* Chapter 8, Section [C] *supra*, for an excerpt of this article].

. . . .

Attorney presence at the mediation also varies depending on whether the mediation is court-ordered or not. One might expect that voluntary mediation would result in more attorneys being present at the sessions, and the AAML study did indicate some increase in percentages over the court-ordered programs (50% versus 30%). But even the 50% figure was somewhat less than expected. This may reflect the fact that in voluntary mediation the mediator is more likely to be an attorney, and, therefore, the parties' attorneys feel less of a need to actively participate.

Another factor which may influence attorney participation is the legal effects of any agreement clients make while in mediation. Perhaps the greatest concern of attorneys whose clients enter into a mediation process is that clients will make "bad deals." To insure that clients make informed choices some states require the mediator to advise the parties to seek attorney review of the agreement prior to signing it and approximately half our respondents indicated this was true for their practice. Where mediation was voluntary a higher percentage (58% versus 40%) indicated that the agreement was not binding until reviewed by an attorney. This additional "safeguard" might also explain the low percentage of attorneys who were present at the mediation.

Related to the issue of the legal effect of the agreement the attorneys were asked approximately how often the agreement reached in mediation was substantially the same as the one finally approved by the court. Respondents indicated that in more than 85% of the cases the agreement was substantially the same as that approved by the court. This may mean that courts are "rubber stamping" these agreements without much consideration. Or, it could mean the agreements are ones that are satisfactory to the parties and meet standards of fairness. . . .

D. Fees/The Cost of Mediation

Because mediation is often touted as being a less expensive means of resolving family conflict, attorneys were also asked how fees were set.

The study indicated that the fee schedule for court ordered mediation is set in a little more than half of the cases (64/110) by the mediator. Approximately one-third of the respondents (33/110) replied that the court set the fee that would be charged. In some circumstances the fee varied depending on whether court personnel provided mediation services. In voluntary mediation, the majority of fees were set by the mediator, with about 10% of the respondents indicating that the fee was set by the court. Our survey did not uncover any significant concerns about the "fee structure."

. . . .

E. Advantages of the Process

1. Efficiency issues

Many attorneys suggested that significant monetary savings occurred when the parties were able to resolve the dispute through mediation. This is consistent with the findings of other studies. Savings can be substantial when court-ordered mediation is conducted by court personnel or the fee is set by the court. Survey responses indicated that in some jurisdictions fees are set on a sliding scale depending on income level. Those using voluntary mediation had a slightly less positive response concerning cost reduction, most likely because fees are higher in voluntary mediation. Where voluntary mediation is "unsuccessful" attorneys may feel that the client has wasted too much money.

Many surveys indicated that even when a full agreement is not reached in mediation, however, costs may be reduced if agreement was reached on some issues. Likewise the process may have the positive effect of narrowing or clarifying the issues. Comments such as "saves time and money in the long run" are characteristic. . . . Approximately three quarters of the respondents also noted savings in time, and this is consistent with existing research findings.

2. Client satisfaction with the process

Attorneys reported that many of their clients were satisfied with the process. Comments such as "clients control their own case" and "clients felt more in control when they were directly involved in the making of the agreement" were common. Other research supports the finding that client control over the process increases satisfaction. It is likely that client comfort with the process is directly related to the pre-mediation preparation offered by the attorney. This initial orientation to mediation is critical in the overall representation process. It is at this point that the attorney can assist the client in understanding the dynamics of the process and set an agenda for the mediation. It is at this point that the attorney can provide assistance in preparing proposed budgets and evaluating different options for parenting. In addition proposed discovery requests and the need for temporary orders can be discussed. Clients' anxiety can be reduced when the attorney takes the time to fully orient the client.

3. Client satisfaction with the outcome

Several themes emerged that related to client satisfaction with the outcome. Several attorneys referred to the benefit of the client taking "ownership" of the agreement. Others noted that clients were more likely to comply with an agreement that they had an active part in making. As a specific advantage, one attorney wrote that mediation leads to "more satisfied clients who can still deal with each other."

Throughout the literature appears the proposition that another of mediation's assets is its ability to further agreements that are more closely tailored to the needs of the clients. This is especially true when the agreement relates to the day-to-day activities of family living. The comments to the survey were consistent with this proposition. When both parents continue to be involved in their children's lives, it is even more important that expectations are clear. The importance of this is reflected in state statutes that require parents to create a child care plan when joint custody will be set by the decree. Parents are seen as being in the best position to know what will or will not work for their children.

One final advantage survey respondents noted with respect to mediation outcome was predictability. Some comments reflected the uncertainty associated with allowing a judicial officer to make a decision. The difficulty associated with the use of vague standards such as "best interests of the child" has been well documented. . . .

4. Emotional issues

Respondents saw the ability to more adequately address the emotional aspects of dissolution as mediation's greatest strength. A significant number of comments related to the improvement of communication between the parties and the extent to which this ultimately improved settlement opportunities. In cases involving children, many attorneys felt that the process encouraged clients to put their children's needs over their own. Evidence supports the conclusion that a process that reduces acrimony between the parents is associated with improved child mental health.

. . . .

F. Disadvantages of the Process

. . . .

1. Inefficiency concerns

Approximately 20% of the respondents indicated that the court-ordered mediation process added to the costs of their cases. Further clarification was found in comments in which some attorneys suggested that in situations where it was clear to them that clients were not going to reach an agreement, the requirement created additional expense. Although listed as a factor to be considered as a disadvantage, it is noteworthy that only 20% (23/110) of the respondents viewed increased cost as a disadvantage compared to about 80% (87/110) of the respondents who indicated that the process resulted in decreased cost to the client. A similar discrepancy can be found in the area of efficiency with respect to time. While approximately 30% (32/110) of the respondents said the mediation requirement caused delay, 70% (77/110) indicated that the process saved time. With respect to voluntary mediation a lower percentage of respondents expressed concern about delay.

It is not surprising that a greater percentage of attorneys had concerns about delay than they did about expenses. The fees for court-ordered programs are generally not high, while the requirement in some jurisdictions that the mediation process be complete before a case can be docketed for a hearing results in the perception that the requirement almost always causes a delay. What is not clear, of course, is whether the case would otherwise have been ready for hearing even absent the mediation requirement.

2. Mediator skills

When asked whether dissatisfaction with the skills of the mediator was a perceived disadvantage, fully half (55/110) of the respondents answered in the affirmative. This may reflect the fact that court-ordered mediations are more likely to be conducted by court personnel (over 50% of the survey respondents indicated this) or mediators who were appointed as opposed to being chosen by the parties. The inability to choose a mediator may predispose some attorneys to a more harsh assessment of the mediator's skills. Training and certification of mediators also varies significantly from jurisdiction to jurisdiction. Common requirements include some type of educational degree, and/or experience as well as specialized mediation training.

Even in voluntary mediations where the attorneys select the mediator, there was a significant level of dissatisfaction with "skills." It may be that attorneys have a different standard for evaluating a "skilled mediator." A mental health mediator who focuses more on the emotional aspect of the dissolution while helping the parties arrive at their own agreement may be seen as "unskilled." In the same light, a mediator who facilitates the parties setting their own standards for determining fairness, as opposed to those that are presumed to be fair because they are "legal," may also be viewed as inept.

3. Power imbalances

Consistent with other commentaries on the process, a widely cited disadvantage of the court-ordered mediation process was the inability of the mediator to appropriately address power imbalances. Among other things, power imbalances may result in "unfair agreements." One attorney summed up this concern by writing "the [p]urpose of mediation is to resolve issues, not do justice, so the more dominant spouse usually prevails." Power imbalances may result from a lack of negotiating skills, domestic violence or the use of intimidation. It is, however, striking to note that when asked whether they thought that mediation disadvantaged clients with fewer economic resources or less sophistication, only 30% (32/110) of the respondents indicated that they thought this was true.

Because clients vary in their abilities to represent themselves well, attorneys are justifiably concerned that some may be taken advantage of in a process where they have no "advocate." Some attorneys dealt with this problem by indicating that they would not let certain clients attend mediation without them. Commentators have suggested that when the process will not involve direct attorney participation, legislatures have responded by enacting "protective" or highly regulatory procedures for the process. Included in those are requirements that mediators advise parties to have the agreement reviewed by an attorney prior to signing.

Perhaps the most interesting comment in the study concerned whether this attorney review acted as a check on "unfair" agreements. Several attorneys commented that even though the agreement was not binding until they reviewed it, it was difficult to get clients to change their minds. Clients become emotionally invested in the agreement they made and do not want to change it. This was particularly troubling if the attorney thought the client was intimidated into making the agreement in the first place. A related concern was that when attorneys advise against an agreement made by the client, the attorney is viewed as the "problem." Perhaps some of these concerns would be eliminated if the attorney and client spent time preparing for the mediation by anticipating outcomes and potential problems with them and further providing for consultation opportunities throughout the process.

. . . .

NOTES AND QUESTIONS

(1) For additional information on family mediation, see Donald T. Saposnek, *Mediating Child Custody Disputes: A Strategic Approach* (1998); Robert Coulson, *Family Mediation: Managing Conflict, Resolving Disputes* (2d ed. 1996); Jessica Pearson & Nancy Thoennes, *Divorce Mediation: Reflections on a Decade of Research in Mediation Research*, *in* Kenneth Kressel & Dean C. Pruitt, eds. *Mediation Research: The Process and Effectiveness of Third-Party Intervention* (1989); Jay Folberg & Ann Milne, eds., *Divorce Mediation: Theory and Practice* (1988); John Haynes, *Divorce Mediation* (1981).

(2) Kisthardt reports that many attorneys are more enthusiastic about using mediation to resolve custody disputes, than to resolve economic issues surrounding divorce. Do you think such an attitude is well-founded? If not, how might attorneys best be educated about the broader potential of mediation?

(3) Note that the Kisthardt reading discusses the views of attorneys, not parties, toward family mediation. How do you think parties' views would compare? What do you see as the advantages and disadvantages of having the parties' attorneys participate in a family mediation?

(4) Is mediation used differently in the family context than in other contexts? Consider, for example, the likelihood that mediators will evaluate, rather than facilitate. (*See* Chapter 4, Section 4[C], *supra*.) Also compare the roles that lawyers and clients play in family mediations as compared to other types of mediation.

(5) What qualifications do you believe should be held by a family mediator?

(6) Do you feel differently about mandatory mediation in the family context than in any other context?

(7) As noted in the above reading, and as discussed in Chapter 6, *supra*, the use of mediation in cases involving a possible history of domestic violence has been extremely controversial. For two articles that provide case studies illustrating some of the potential problems, see Scott H. Hughes, *Elizabeth's Story: Exploring Power Imbalances in Divorce Mediation*, 8 Geo. J. Legal Ethics 553 (1995), and Penelope Bryan, *Killing Us Softly: Divorce Mediation and the Politics of Power*, 40 Buff. L. Rev. 441 (1992). For a more general critique of mandatory mediation from a feminist perspective, see Trina Grillo, *The Mediation Alternative: Process Dangers for Women*, 100 Yale L.J. 1545 (1991).

§ D BUSINESS MEDIATION

BUSINESS MEDIATION: ALL IN THE FAMILY

Disp. Resol. J., Oct. 1996, at 51 [*]

By Lawrence I. Drath

The three patriarchs of the Benson, Miller and Reisler families had jointly developed, nurtured and supported a successful group of hospitality properties. Their portfolio consists of 15 hotels and four restaurants located along the eastern seaboard. They pooled capital, know-how and guts and in 1965 acquired two Holiday Inns located in Virginia. More recently they were considering entering into an area-wide franchise for a new budget concept. During their 30 years in business they delegated among themselves responsibility for operations, finance, purchasing, maintenance, administration and particular locations. From time to time, changes of responsibility were implemented without resentment or rancor.

Each patriarch had three children who were invited to and accepted positions in the business. As each "junior" came on board they were introduced to the operations and, by design or chance, were assigned responsibilities for specific geographical areas. As the juniors reached their late 20 and early 30s, certain resentments arose. Some didn't want to travel monthly to their assigned properties. A few didn't want the company to enter into an area franchise for a new budget concept and instead argued for the purchase of a luxury hotel. Others felt that they were making a greater contribution in sales, operations or financing than others and were therefore entitled to a greater slice of the pie. Arguments over who was, or was not, carrying his or her own weight or was "getting in the way" of the others became frequent. It got to the point that business issues were determined along family lines.

The patriarchs tried unsuccessfully to respond to the resentments and concerns. Meetings resulted in heated diatribes and shouting matches. While the silent treatment became the main weapon during office hours, employees could not avoid getting caught in the crossfire of countermanded instructions.

I had recently spoken at a hotel seminar attended by two of the fathers. During the course of my discussion I had mentioned the success I had achieved resolving a disagreement between a hotel owner and its management company through the use of the mediation process. Later, the patriarchs asked me to consult with them for what they described as their sorry state of affairs.

As a practicing attorney, my traditional reaction to such a narrative of the facts would have been, in the past, to offer to represent one family and attempt to achieve a "winning" outcome for them. However, having experienced enough battles and witnessed the damage that most often results from traditional posturing and antagonistic confrontations in business relationships, I have enthusiastically become an advocate of alternative dispute resolution as a

---

means of preventing all-out war and preserving the equity of a viable enterprise. Clearly, this family situation cried out for such relief.

Moving Toward Mediation

I met with the fathers on a number of occasions during which they briefed me about the evolution of the business, peculiarities of each property, specifics about geographic areas and local conditions. They shared with me the relative strength of the staffs and how they saw the personality clashes. I had just facilitated a resolution of a commercial dispute with which they were familiar and they were hopeful that I could suggest a method to resolve this dispute so that each of them could retire with a feeling of closure as to the continuity of the enterprise.

I proposed to the fathers that we send a letter to the nine children suggesting a new format to attempt to resolve their business differences. The letter introduced the children to the basic concepts and goals of mediation, including a clear message that the parties, not the mediator, formulate the agreement and that the focus would be on their specific interests and needs rather than legal principles. Unlike arbitration, mediation is a compromise procedure and is non-binding until the agreement is executed by all parties. I also emphasized the benefits of alternative dispute resolution: economy, speed, confidentiality and control. We wanted to assure each child that they held a veto as to the outcome, since I had the feeling that such assurance would be essential here.

Finally, they were asked to commit to the following:

1. Each would stick with the process as long as the mediator believed that it was worthwhile.

2. Each would conduct themselves in good faith.

3. Each would respect the confidentiality of the proceeding. The letter provided them with details of my professional background as it related to commercial transactions and alternative dispute resolution proceedings in order to gain their confidence and allay any concern as to impartiality. Ultimately, they all agreed to participate in the process.

Mediation Strategy

While an initial joint meeting is often preferable in the mediation process, I chose to meet with each group separately in order to evaluate whether the greater need was to assist in the process of communicating and issue defining or in formulating substantive concepts for the terms of a deal. Often the mediator's greatest worth is to unblock the process and allow the parties, who are already familiar with the business, to decide the issues.

I began by asking them if they thought the business could be divided into three independent businesses. If so, three separate packages of properties (including the new area franchise under consideration) would be developed. They were also asked to rank their preference by areas, to describe the extent to which they would need the cooperation of the other two groups to accomplish this process and what restrictions against competition would be necessary or desirable. I also wanted to know how they perceived and reacted to the grievances of the other groups. Finally, I asked them whether they would choose to keep the business intact as one unit (notwithstanding the current levels of antagonism), rather than work out a separation with the inherent financial risks of spinoffs. There was unanimity for a breakup. Their answers enabled me to evaluate a number of substantive and relationship issues, the relative strengths and weaknesses of each group, and where the blockages existed.

To get the ball rolling we needed to focus on:

1. The parties' lack of ability to "listen" to each other (this can be overcome through the use of a mediator).

2. Their mutual respect for all of the "patriarchs" (to be used as a "melding agent").

3. Their resentment that some work harder than others (no longer an issue after separation).

4. Sibling-like rivalries that evoke a "we against them" or clan behavior (to be recognized as a cause and then mutually discarded).

In due course, I would apply various concepts to overcome these barriers.

I reviewed the written responses, and with the assistance of the patriarchs as well as the accountant, began to assign values or points to such assets as preferable geographic areas, condition of each property and equipment, comparable profitability of each operation, book values and mortgage debt.

The next step was another series of individual group meetings to discuss what they would "pay" to purchase the segment of the business they indicated as their first choice. I obtained authority from them to allow me to show the other groups the various "purchase prices" without identifying the bidder. This allowed each group to "throw darts" at other proposals without a hostile response. It also allowed me a chance to question some of their exaggerated notions of any aspect of the business.

Two of the groups were primarily interested in the same package, so I asked each of those what they would "pay" to purchase their second choice if the first one couldn't be delivered. Their responses were encouraging since there seemed to be a consensus as to the values of particular assets, the relative degree of competition, and the potential for growth in a particular market area. The result was the production of three "packages" of assets and businesses, not currently identified with any branch of the families. I asked each group to indicate whether they thought the packages were materially different.

It was now time to hold joint meetings to refine each "package," agree on dollar adjustments, time periods for payments, and terms of restrictive covenants against competition The parties subsequently agreed that each group's selection of one of the packages would be made by picking lots out of a hat.

With the assistance of their counsel, an agreement was drafted and 90 days from the time we first met, the deal was done.

Why Mediation Worked → *Emphasized*

Most family business relationships are not formed by consensual negotiations. The parties are appointed successors in interest to the originators of the business or have been encouraged to take a position by family members. Under such circumstances parties are often hesitant to openly question business decisions. A disagreement over the purchase of a truck can culminate in a battle along family lines, while a critical comment concerning a sales approach may be squelched in order not to embarrass a cousin.

It was quite clear to me that this particular family business dispute was the result of years of hostility and lack of communication which raised barriers to a dialogue about their interests, needs and concerns for the business.

In this case the disputants were hesitant to disclose their ultimate interest and instead employed various positional bargaining devices, attempting to arrive at a "win-win result." This attitude usually leads directly to adversarial processes in the courtroom where rules and customs allow and encourage the parties to exercise combative techniques (even though 95% of those who take a dispute to trial leave the courthouse disappointed). The object of mediation is an agreement by parties resulting from "interest-based" bargaining. Mediation tends to focus on the "interest" and how to satisfy the perceived rights of the parties. The goal is to get the parties to agree and, unlike arbitration, not to impose the mediator's standard of fairness.

By highlighting each party's exaggerated claims, mediation provides feedback which is not tainted with emotions or history. Since the mediator is not empowered to render a decision, the parties can openly disclose facts that they would otherwise conceal from a decision-maker. Yet, mediation allows the parties to uncover underlying interests that may shape resolutions far broader than those available in an adversarial win-lose process.

In this case study, each group needed to cooperate with the others to maximize the value of the assets created before the separation. For example, the people who now oversee the North Carolina properties would be at a loss if not for an open line with those who had previously been responsible for that area. This cooperation would not have happened had they been forced to litigate their dispute in an adversarial form.

Parties often remain locked in positional bargaining merely because they are not aware of the alternative means available. Hopefully, more and more decision-makers will turn to the mediation process as a means of settling their grievances.

One year later each of the separate businesses is functioning with some success and growing pains, while the patriarchs remain in happy retirement.

NOTES AND QUESTIONS

(1) Do you agree with the author that mediation achieved a better result than would have been achieved through litigation?

(2) What kinds of business disputes do you believe are well suited to mediation? Can you think of any kinds of business disputes that are not well suited to mediation?

(3) What sort of role did the mediator play in helping to resolve this dispute? Did the mediator facilitate? Evaluate?

(4) What kind of background do you believe a mediator should have to resolve this type of dispute?

(5) For an article urging that companies involved in high technology business should employ mediation to resolve their disputes, see Todd B. Carver, *Mediating Communications and High Tech Disputes*, Disp. Resol. J., Spring 1997, at 34.

§ E LABOR AND EMPLOYMENT MEDIATION

In the collective bargaining context, although binding arbitration has traditionally been the primary means for resolving grievances between union members and management, mediation is becoming increasingly popular. For a description of one particular grievance mediation, see William Hobgood, *Conditioning Parties in Labor Grievances*, in Deborah Kolb, *When Talk Works* (1994). *See also* Deborah A. Schmedemann, *Reconciling Differences: The Theory and Law of Mediating Labor Grievances*, 9 Indus. Rel. L.J. 523 (1987) (examining pros and cons of using mediation to resolve labor grievances).

Mediation is being used increasingly in the individual employment context as well. More and more employers are setting up programs that either permit or require their employees to resolve employment disputes through mediation. Such programs may cover claims for employment discrimination on the basis of race, gender, ethnicity, age or disability. Such programs may also cover claims regarding workplace health and safety, entitlement to family or medical leave, entitlement to overtime pay, and disputes that may arise between co-employees.

One example of an employment mediation program is the REDRESS (Resolve Employment Disputes, Reach Equitable Solutions Swiftly) program establish by the United States Postal Service. The mediators in this program are trained in transformative mediation. Early reports on this mediation conclude that it has been quite successful. *See* Jonathan F. Anderson & Lisa Bingham, *Upstream Effects from Mediation of Workplace Disputes: Some Preliminary Evidence from the USPS*, 48 Lab. L.J. 601 (Oct. 1997). For further discussion of REDRESS see *infra* Ch. 9[D].

The reading below discusses the use of mediation to resolve sexual harassment disputes.

PRIVATIZING WORKPLACE JUSTICE: THE ADVENT OF MEDITAION IN RESOLVING SEXUAL HARASSMENT DISPUTES

34 Wake Forest L. Rev. 135, 136, 148–49, 156–64 (1999)*

By Jonathan R. Harkavy

A remarkable confluence of developments in the law may foreshadow a profound change in the way employees resolve their sexual harassment claims. Mediation has emerged as a dispute resolution technique just as public awareness of sexual harassment has reached a zenith with the impeachment of President Clinton and the Supreme Court's recent attention to workplace harassment. Whether this alignment of phenomena marks the dawning of an age of sexual harassment mediation remains to be seen. . . .

This Essay posits the notion that, despite some legitimate concerns about privatizing justice in the workplace, lawyers are now in an opportune position to take the lead in utilizing mediation to handle sexual harassment disputes. Based on the evidence available so far, mediation appears to offer a uniquely suitable method for pursuing the overriding purposes of federal sexual harassment law—namely, eradicating sex discrimination, compensating the victims of such discrimination, and permitting all individuals to have an equal opportunity for success in the workplace.

. . . .

Despite its recent attempts at clarification, the Supreme Court has left open a number of important questions ranging from what is actionable as sexual harassment to what responsibility employers bear for certain types of harassment. Among the most important unresolved issues are the following: First, how can the courts distinguish between conduct that is offensive and conduct that is actionable as hostile and abusive? Second, what constitutes "tangible employment action"? Third, is there a way to measure objectively when an employee's terms, conditions, and privileges of employment are altered to her detriment in the absence of a tangible employment action? Fourth, what liability should an employer bear for harassment perpetrated by a co-employee or other individual with no supervisory power over the victim? Fifth, what liability should an employer bear for harassment perpetrated in a non-hierarchical workplace? Sixth, what kind of complaint procedures will satisfy the first prong of an employer's affirmative defense to a hostile environment claim? Seventh, under what circumstances may a victim be excused from invoking an employer's complaint procedure under the second prong of that affirmative defense?

These questions and others engendered by the Supreme Court's sporadic forays into this field make litigation an uncertain enterprise for employees and employers alike. . . . Thus, finding alternatives to the vagaries of litigation is in the best interest of employers and employees alike.

. . . .

Although mediation may not be a panacea for the problems that beset the American judicial system generally, when applied to sexual harassment claims the advantages of mediation appear to outweigh its disadvantages. . . .

A. Advantages of Mediation in Sexual Harassment Disputes

1. Mediation provides a comfortable forum for all parties and thus is more likely to facilitate a workable resolution to a dispute than a more adversarial process involving rights adjudicated in a formal setting under a fixed set of rules. From the employee's standpoint, the safety of a mediated settlement conference permits her to assert her claims and confront her employer with less apprehension about being further victimized and with some (though not guaranteed) protection against retaliation. From the standpoint of the alleged harasser, the mediated settlement conference is also a safe forum for trying to explain (if not deny) the conduct at issue. Even from the standpoint of the employer, mediation offers an opportunity to meet a problem head-on and obtain feedback about it without fear of its position being misconstrued by either the victim or the harasser, both of whom may be productive, valued employees.

2. Mediation provides a confidential forum for resolving disputes without revealing publicly the intimate and embarrassing details of conduct that might otherwise have to be disclosed in adjudication. Particularly from the standpoint of the victim, the confidentiality of mediation offers a considerable advantage over adjudicatory proceedings where intimacies and degradations would likely be revealed for public consumption and consequent personal embarrassment. Indeed, if mediation becomes the norm for resolving sexual harassment complaints, the very fact of making such a claim may only be disclosed to a few lawyers, employer managers, and some experts if the parties try to resolve their dispute prior to filing an action or even a charge of discrimination. Finally, most accused harassers will assuredly prefer the confidentiality offered by mediation, particularly if the alleged conduct might have an impact on their own marriages, other familial relationships, and employment opportunities.

3. The prospect of settlement at an early stage offers substantial advantages to all parties. The victim, who may be quite traumatized by the harassment, will be permitted to obtain appropriate treatment which she might not otherwise have been able to afford and will generally be able to get on with her life. Indeed, the advantage to putting a personally demeaning event behind her may better enable the victim to regain her personhood and her ability to be a productive employee and a functioning family member and adult. Likewise, the accused harasser can be brought to justice more quickly, punished more appropriately, and trained or sensitized more effectively through early intervention. Or, if the dispute is resolved without any attribution of responsibility, the accused harasser will be able to resume his employment with a minimum of interruption and embarrassment. From the standpoint of the employer, early settlement offers the obvious advantages of both

cost savings and minimal diversion from the employer's ordinary business. Finally, given the cost of litigation, and particularly the financial, emotional, and lost opportunity costs of discovery, early settlement through mediation offers all parties a significant incentive to participate substantially and in good faith.

4. Mediation provides an opportunity to redirect emotions in a productive manner. In contrast to the courtroom or the arbitral forum, where the adversarial process puts parties under stress by subjecting them to cross-examination in the context of rights and rules, mediation is designed to put the parties at ease in the context of exploring their interests and needs. That is not to say that emotions in a sexual harassment case are left outside the door of the conference room. Indeed, both the general session and the private caucuses may involve displays of emotion by all sides. Such displays are sometimes therapeutic and may ultimately be useful to mediators in ferreting out a victim's true concerns and interests. Whether emotional displays at mediation are as useful to victims in working through their problems is less clear and is a subject begging for attention from psychologists, counselors, and psychiatrists. In any event, what is clear is that in a sexual harassment case the unhealthy aspects of the participants' emotions can best be controlled, while the positive aspects of these emotions can best be utilized in a setting where the parties are in control of the proceeding and are made to feel that way. Among the commonly used ADR alternatives, only mediation offers this opportunity.

5. Adaptability of procedures and flexibility of outcomes are among mediation's primary advantages in sexual harassment cases. Aside from the obvious adjustability of procedures allowing mediation to be physically and emotionally comfortable, the range of remedies available to the parties is bounded only by their creativity. In contrast to judicial or arbitral forums, mediation allows parties to craft remedies without regard to the confines of Title VII or other statutes. Thus, a requirement that a sexual predator undergo training and be subject to monitoring may be easier to achieve in a mediated settlement agreement than in a court judgment or arbitral award. Indeed, much of what courts cannot do or are not likely to do can be accomplished in mediation if the parties are sufficiently motivated and creative. Employers can also be attracted to mediation because of its remedial flexibility. Requirements that flow from a private agreement may be easier to swallow than the same or even less rigorous requirements embodied in a judgment or a consent decree. Employers, in fact, may regard negotiated obligations as a form of insurance against future claims, although the law may not recognize them as such. In any event, employers are less likely to be subject to punitive damages for "intentional" conduct after they have voluntarily undertaken obligations beyond what Title VII requires in a mediated settlement agreement. Finally, from the accused harasser's standpoint, a mediated settlement may offer the opportunity to keep one's job, albeit under close monitoring and serious probationary obligations not otherwise provided for in an employer's personnel policy. So long as the victim is comfortable with the resulting strictures on a harasser, the predator may yet retain his livelihood in a way that might not have been possible if the case were litigated.

6. Although there does not appear to be any hard evidence to affirm or deny it, there is considerable anecdotal evidence to suggest that both victims and their employers in sexual harassment cases can benefit financially from mediating these disputes. My own observation is that employers can avoid liability at the high end of the damage scale in mediated settlements, but are more likely to pay something in a greater number of cases. On the other hand, victims of sexual harassment can expect a more certain recovery through mediation, though they may have to forego the prospect of the maximum possible relief which is always available (though not often attainable) in court. Continued experience with mediation of sexual harassment cases will provide more complete data so that, from a pure financial standpoint, parties can assess mediation's impact on the monetary value of harassment claims. For the time being, however, there certainly does not appear to be any significant financial disincentive to mediate sexual harassment cases, and the anecdotal evidence suggests the opposite.

7. The avoidance of troublesome precedent is a positive consequence of mediation's inherent privacy. Victims, of course, may not care about the effect of their own settlements on other situations, although there is often a desire to change an employer's practices so that future disputes will not arise. On the other hand, employers are understandably concerned about the precedential effect of any disposition of an employment discrimination claim, and particularly in the area of sexual harassment, where valuing a claim is so difficult and non-standardized. The fact that an employer may have paid one employee a certain amount of money to settle her claim may, in the mind of an employer's human resources manager, put a floor on future claims of the same kind, even though the surrounding circumstances might suggest a markedly different outcome. Mediated settlements, conceived in private negotiations and effectuated by the parties themselves outside of a public forum, minimize the risk that such settlements will be regarded as precedential by anyone else. Certainly, the absence of any judicial, administrative, or arbitral determination of fault, responsibility, fact, or law eliminates the prospect that a mediated settlement can have any preclusive effect in any other legal proceeding.

8. One of the principal values of mediation—the resolution of a dispute in a manner so that the parties can continue their business, professional, or personal relationships—makes mediation appear superior to adjudicatory forms of dispute resolution. Judicial litigation and private arbitration, with their emphasis on adversary procedures, tend to drive parties further apart, thus making continuance of the employer-employee relationship much more difficult. Mediation, by contrast, emphasizes a non-adversarial exploration of the parties' common interests and personal concerns, thereby making it far less likely that the employment relationship becomes irreparably fractured. In terms of Title VII's overriding purpose of making the workplace hospitable for women so that women and men alike can share in the bounty of our nation's employment opportunities, non-adjudicatory ADR devices like mediation are the most promising means of handling sexual harassment cases. To put it otherwise, if the Supreme Court is correct that employees are interested primarily in securing and maintaining employment, mediation offers a considerable advantage over adjudicatory forms of dispute resolution.

9. Another of mediation's advantages has a special meaning in the field of sexual harassment. The shift of focus in mediation away from the technical legal merits of a dispute lessens the impact that undecided legal issues may have on resolving a dispute. As noted above, questions abound concerning what is actionable and who is liable in Title VII cases, despite the Supreme Court's recent effort to bring some order to how these issues are determined. By directing the parties' attention to their interests instead of to their legal positions, a mediator can sidestep the uncertainties in Title VII law to a far greater extent than is possible with other ADR techniques.

10. Perhaps the most significant advantage mediation has to offer in sexual harassment cases is personal empowerment and recognition. After all, in mediation it is a party herself, not some outside determinative force such as a jury, judge, or arbitrator, who decides whether or not to resolve her dispute and on what terms. Particularly for victims of sexual harassment, the prospect of controlling a situation instead of being controlled by it may be critical to recovering self-esteem, continuing employment, and stabilizing personal situations. In this regard, personal autonomy is recognized and rewarded in mediation. Recognition of personhood is, of course, at the heart of Title VII's promise. Self-resolution through mediation thus advances Title VII's goal of eradicating discrimination in a poignant and powerful way.

Empowerment, of course, carries with it the germ of its own destruction, for the parties can halt the process at any time and resort to adjudication. But mediators trained in facilitation and experienced in the general area of sexual harassment law can use a number of techniques to remind the parties about considering their interests and needs instead of dwelling on the differences in their legal positions. In the end, however, the parties will do what they will. Personal empowerment and recognition should thus be regarded as advantageous, whether the case actually settles or not.

B. Disadvantages of Mediation in Sexual Harassment Cases

1. Mediation may impair the orderly development of a coherent sexual harassment jurisprudence. To the extent that it is successful in resolving large numbers of disputes, the cases left for adjudication may involve such unique factual situations that the resultant body of case law will be shaped—and possibly warped—by mediation's leftovers. Success in resolving so many sexual harassment cases out of court may thus spawn an unclear, inconsistent, and aberrant set of rules that will neither advance the aims of Title VII nor provide employers with the clarity needed for efficient self-enforcement. The familiar refrain that "hard cases make bad law" may turn out to be more of an unwelcome reality than a distant aphorism.

2. The absence of public vindication is a distinct disadvantage of mediation. Particularly for victims of sexual harassment, personal vindication—being believed in a "he said/she said" situation—may be important to one's marriage, one's family, and one's self-esteem. A decision by an impartial adjudicator, whether a judge, jury, arbitrator, or evaluator, provides the kind of third-party vindication that mediation cannot. Moreover, to the extent that a victim of sexual harassment needs public approbation of her own behavior, the confidential nature of mediation cannot satisfy that need. Public vindication also

may be important from the employers' standpoint. One often hears that certain cases simply cannot be settled because the other employees are looking to the employer to defend its position. Particularly after a dispute becomes common knowledge among other employees, the employer may need to pursue public vindication in order to maintain morale in the workplace.

3. Some parties, typically employers, but occasionally employees, believe that proposing or even agreeing to mediation is a sign of weakness or an admission of responsibility. Whatever disadvantage may be entailed by that perception, the increased use of mediation as an ADR device required by court rules will render that argument less substantial and virtually moot. Also, as mediation moves toward being the norm in resolving employment disputes, the worry about agreeing to mediate before the dispute reaches litigation will dissipate—or, at least, it will have less substance to it.

4. Disclosure of unrevealed information that may be used at trial is another perceived disadvantage of mediation. Mediators often hear experienced trial counsel lament the prospect of having to deal with "trial secret" type of information during a mediation. Sexual harassment cases appear no different in this regard from other forms of civil litigation. Indeed, the kind of intimate, personal, and potentially embarrassing information about parties to a sexual harassment dispute magnifies the disadvantage that some parties and trial lawyers believe mediation entails. Responsible mediators can minimize much of the worry about secret information and trial strategies through scrupulous adherence to their duty of confidentiality. Of course, the parties have to make clear what they do and do not want the other side to know. Ultimately, the parties have to decide whether revealing undisclosed material information will be more helpful in resolving a dispute than keeping it secret will be in litigating the case if it is not resolved.

5. Mediated settlements may not fully serve the deterrence objective of Title VII. The lack of public disapproval, the prospect of cheaper and quicker settlements, and other advantageous aspects of privately negotiated and confidentially performed settlements may, in effect, provide an insufficient incentive to employers to control the conduct of supervisors. That is, some employers are more likely to obey the law fully if their feet are held to the fire of a public trial of a sexual harassment dispute. Mediation may, therefore, disserve a central objective of Title VII by permitting and encouraging employers to resolve their way out of a dispute instead of facing the cost and humiliation of a trial. Experience with mediation will measure the substance of this concern. As the jurisprudence of employer liability matures and a body of settlements grows, mediated resolutions should reflect in rough terms the economic merits of individual cases. If mediation does not provide economic justice, it will resolve fewer cases, and the parties will turn to adjudication to obtain that justice.

6. The confidentiality of most mediated settlements of individual sexual harassment cases deprives the community of information about what the law actually is, who is violating the law, and what the costs of illegal conduct are. Some prominent members of the academic community see this aspect of mediation—and of settlement in general—as a substantial departure from sound public policy. Whether respect for the law in such a high-profile area

as sexual harassment will suffer materially as a result of non-adjudicatory dispositions seems more doubtful than the abstract jurisprudential proposition that settlement generally is bad for the law. As a practical matter, the debate about "settlement or not" appears moot for the present because ADR generally and mediation in particular are on a fast track of implementation in federal and state courts alike. With the passage of time the philosophical debate may become more informed and more pertinent. For now, at least, this disadvantage to mediation is outside the circle of concern.

7. The absence of public scrutiny of how sexual harassment law is being developed and applied may be a significant disadvantage of privatizing workplace justice. Not only is there little assurance about how the careful framework of employer liability is being construed and applied at the negotiating table, but the lack of public control and reporting of negotiations and outcomes makes it unlikely that the law can be applied in any uniform way across the country. These criticisms impelled the EEOC to oppose arbitration agreements covering statutory claims. Moreover, justice achieved in private may be regarded by some as an abdication by our overworked court system to an essentially unregulated profession of mediators. Whatever force these arguments about public oversight may have in other areas, Congress long ago expressed a legislative preference in Title VII sexual harassment cases for methods of conference, conciliation, and persuasion to resolve these disputes. And, most importantly, the fact that resolution by mediation is entirely consensual and is backed up by an adjudicatory system to handle disputes that do not settle, is some assurance that privatization is not being pursued in a way that offends either our system of public justice or the manner in that Congress said Title VII should be enforced.

[The author goes on to discuss several potential obstacles to the use of mediation to resolve sexual harassment disputes: the emergence of employment practices insurance; attorneys who may possess a "gunslinger" mentality; mediators who may be either overly facilitative or overly evaluative; and changes in the work force that may affect the impact of mediation in the employment discrimination area.]

————

power imbalances can be a disadvantage

NOTES AND QUESTIONS

(1) Do you agree with Mr. Harkavy that mediation is a very promising means with which to resolve sexual harassment disputes? Can you imagine a mediated solution to the dispute between Paula Jones and President Clinton?

(2) If you were a victim of sexual harassment, how do you believe you would feel about mediating your claim? If you were a defendant charged with sexual harassment?

(3) When sexual harassment claims are mediated, who do you think should participate in the mediation? Should the alleged harasser and the alleged victim sit across the table from one another? For further reading, see Carrie

A. Bond, *Shattering the Myth: Mediating Sexual Harassment Disputes in the Workplace*, 65 Fordham L. Rev. 2489 (1997), and Andrea Kupfer Schneider, *The Intersection of Therapeutic Jurisprudence, Preventive Law & ADR*, Pub. Pol'y & L. 1084 (Dec. 1999).

(4) Apart from sexual harassment claims, do you think mediation has much to offer in the labor and employment context? As a representative of an individual employee, a labor union, or management, what advantages might you see to mediation?

(5) When employers attempt to build mediation into their human resources programs, they face such issues as how to assure the independence and neutrality of the mediator, and how to maintain employee confidence in the program. Employers must also decide whether or not to mandate mediation of employment disputes, who should pay the costs of the mediator, or whether volunteer mediators should be used. How would you advise an employer interested in setting up a program to mediate employee disputes? See Chapter 9[D], *infra*, for discussion of some such programs.

§ F   MEDIATION AND CRIMINAL LAW

As was discussed in Chapter 1, *supra*, neighborhood justice centers founded in the 1960's and 1970's handled minor criminal, as well as civil, disputes. Such neighborhood programs, also known as citizen dispute settlement centers or community dispute resolution centers, still exist today in many cities. Sometimes they are sponsored by elements of the justice system, including courts, prosecutors, police, or sheriff's departments. At other times such programs are sponsored by city or county agencies or by private organizations. For good discussions of such programs, including the variations among their approaches, see Daniel McGillis, *Community Mediation Programs : Developments and Challenges* (1997), Daniel McGillis, *Community Dispute Resolution Programs and Public Policy* (1986), and Daniel McGillis, *Neighborhood Justice Centers: An Analysis of Potential Models* (1977).

More recently, a focus on how crime impacts both its victims and society at large have led some to advocate greater use of "victim-offender" mediation. The following reading discusses this trend.

VICTIM EXPERIENCE OF MEETING ADULT VS. JUVENILE OFFENDERS: A CROSS-NATIONAL COMPARISON

61 Fed. Probation 33 (December 1997) *

By Mark S. Umbreit & William Bradshaw

Criminal Justice policymakers throughout North America increasingly have tried to respond to the needs of victims of crime, particularly during the last two decades. With the focus upon crime being a violation of the state, individual victims are most often left entirely out of the process, with few

* Copyright © 1997 by Federal Probation. Reprinted with permission.

opportunities to express their needs for information about the crime, to let the offender know how the crime affected their life, or to obtain some form of restitution. Victim impact statements, legislatively mandated victim rights, victim panels that present their stories to offenders, and increased participation in the court process are among the many reforms of recent years.

One of the more unusual but potentially beneficial victim services to develop widely throughout North America and Europe in recent years is victim-offender mediation. Through meeting the offender and engaging in a process of dialogue, victims are able to play an active role in holding their offender accountable and receiving both emotional and material assistance. . . .

Victim-offender mediation and dialogue is a process that provides interested victims of primarily property crimes and minor assaults the opportunity to meet offenders, in a safe and structured setting, with the goal of holding offenders directly accountable for their behavior while providing importance [sic] assistance and compensation to victims. With the assistance of a trained mediator, victims are able to let offenders know how the crime affected them, to receive answers to questions they may have, and to be involved directly in developing a restitution plan for offenders to be accountable for the losses victims incurred. Offenders are able to take direct responsibility for their behavior, to learn the full impact of what they did, and to develop a plan for making amends to the person(s) they violated. Some victim-offender mediation programs are called "victim-offender reconciliation," "victim-offender meetings," or "victim-offender conferences."

In some programs, cases primarily are referred to victim-offender mediation as a diversion from prosecution, and if the agreement is successfully completed charges are dropped. In other programs, cases are referred primarily after the court has accepted a formal admission of guilt, with the mediation being a condition of probation (if the victim is interested). Some programs receive case referrals at both the diversion and post-adjudication level. Most cases are referred by officials involved in the juvenile justice system, although some programs also receive referrals from the adult criminal justice system. Judges, probation officers, victim advocates, prosecutors, defense attorneys, or police can make referrals to victim-offender mediation programs.

Victim-offender mediation is different from other types of mediation. . . .

In victim-offender mediation, the involved parties are not "disputants." One clearly has committed a criminal offense and has admitted doing so. The other clearly has been victimized. Therefore, the issue of guilt or innocence is not mediated. Nor is there an expectation that crime victims compromise and request less than what they need to address their losses. While many other types of mediation are largely "settlement driven," victim-offender mediation is primarily "dialogue driven," with the emphasis upon victim healing, offender accountability, and restoration of losses.

Most victim-offender mediation sessions do in fact result in a signed restitution agreement. Many programs report an agreement rate of 95 percent or more. This agreement, however, is secondary to the importance of the initial dialogue between the parties that addresses the victims' emotional and informational needs that are central to their healing and to the offenders'

development of victim empathy, which can lead to less criminal behavior in the future. Studies consistently have found that the restitution agreement is less important to crime victims than the opportunity to talk directly with the offender about how the victims felt about the crime.

The practice of victim-offender mediation is grounded in restorative justice theory, which emphasizes that crime first should be perceived as an act against individuals within the context of community, rather than a violation of a legal abstraction called the state. While not denying that the state clearly also has an interest in preventing and resolving criminal conflict, restorative justice offers a process by which those most directly affected by crime—the victim, community, and offender—have an opportunity to be involved directly in responding to the incident, holding the offender accountable, offering emotional and material assistance to the victim, and working toward the development of a safe and caring community for victim and offender.

From the inception in 1974 in Kitchener, Ontario, of the first victim-offender mediation program, many criminal justice officials have been quite skeptical about victim interest in meeting the offender. Victim-offender mediation clearly is not appropriate for all crime victims. In all cases, practitioners are trained to present it as a voluntary choice to the victim. With more than 20 years of mediating many thousands of cases throughout North America, experience has shown that the majority of victims presented with the option of mediation choose to enter the process. A recent statewide public opinion poll in Minnesota found that 82 percent of a random sample of citizens from throughout the state would consider participating in a victim-offender program if they were the victim of a property crime. A multi-state study found that, of 280 victims who participated in victim-offender mediation programs in four states, 91 percent felt their participation was totally voluntary.

The process of allowing selected victims of crime to meet with the offender, in the presence of a mediator, is being offered in a growing number of communities throughout North America and Europe. In the mid to late 1970s only a handful of victim-offender mediation programs were being initiated. Today, there are more than 290 programs developing in the United States, approximately 26 in Canada, and more than 700 programs in Europe, with a total of 293 programs in Germany alone. The vast majority of programs in North America work with juvenile offenders and their victims. A recent survey in the United States, however, found that 38 percent of programs worked with adult offenders. While many victim-offender mediation programs continue to be administered by private community-based agencies, an increasing number of probation departments are developing programs, usually in conjunction with trained community volunteers who serve as mediators. Many thousands of primarily property-related offenses and minor assaults, involving both juveniles and adults, have been mediated during the past two decades.

Studies of juvenile and adult victim-offender mediation programs in North America and Europe consistently have found high levels of victim satisfaction with the mediation process. . . .

NOTES AND QUESTIONS

(1) Some additional resources on "victim-offender" mediation and restorative justice include Mark S. Umbreit, *Victim Meets Offender: The Impact of Restorative Justice and Mediation* (1994); Howard Zehr, *Changing Lenses: A New Focus for Crime and Justice* (1990); William R. Nugent & Jeffrey B. Paddock, *The Effect of Victim-Offender Mediation on Severity of Reoffense*, 12 Mediation Q. 353 (1995); Harry Mika, *The Practice and Prospect of Victim-Offender Programs*, 46 SMU L. Rev. 2191 (1993)

(2) For critiques of victim-offender mediation, see Jennifer Gerarda Brown, *The Use of Mediation to Resolve Criminal Cases: A Procedural Critique*, 43 Emory L.J. 1247 (1994); Sharon Levrant et al., *Reconsidering Restorative Justice: The Corruption of Benevolence Revisited?*, 45 Crime & Delinq. 3 (1999).

(3) What do you see as some of the potential advantages of victim-offender mediation? Do you see any potential disadvantages?

(4) Some have suggested that use of mediation in the criminal context might pose Constitutional problems. Can you see any possible issues? Does it depend in part on the way in which the mediation is initiated and by whom?

§ G PEER MEDIATION IN SCHOOLS

CONFLICT RESOLUTION IN AMERICA'S SCHOOLS: DEFUSING AN APPROACHING CRISIS

Disp. Resol. J., Jan. 1997, at 67 [*]

By Kay O. Wilburn & Mary Lynn Bates

This country is currently experiencing a "violence epidemic," say the authors, particularly among young people. Left unchecked, this wave of aggression could lead to even more disastrous consequences 10 or 20 years down the road when these adolescents become adults. One potential solution with a proven success rate is mediation at the elementary, middle and high schools levels, say Wilburn and Bates. Peer mediation programs enable disputants to vent frustration or anger in a controlled setting and "concentrate on identifying the problem instead of establishing blame or seeking revenge." The students then formulate their own solution to the conflict. Innumerable statistics pronounce this country is suffering a violence epidemic. Too often, the violence is being committed by children against children. According to the National Center for Health Statistics, shootings represent a leading cause of death for children under 19. James A. Fox, dean of the College of Criminal

Justice at Northeastern University, states that murders committed by adolescents aged 14 to 17 have increased by 165% in the past decade and that the number will continue to rise dramatically as children grow into their teens. Fox predicts that unless measures are taken now, this country will experience a "blood bath in 10 years when all these kids grow up."[1]

While the problem seems overwhelming at times, many communities are beginning to take proactive approaches to deal with the crisis, including the initiation of conflict resolution programs in kindergarten, middle and high school (K-12) classes. These programs often are not originated by the school board or administrators; rather, various community segments are stepping in to encourage the implementation of K-12 conflict resolution training. The programs are producing benefits in the schools and the communities. Attorneys trained in alternative dispute resolution can, by forming partnerships with their communities, provide invaluable support for programs that can make significant inroads against the rise in violence by and against America's children. Further, the tools given to adolescents to handle conflicts during their school years will be carried into their adult lives to handle disputes on the job and in their neighborhoods. As a result, the current generation of children as they mature into adults may be more likely to employ ADR measures rather than to rely exclusively on the court system to resolve all their disputes. Accordingly, attorneys can help accomplish these concomitant goals by their involvement in K-12 conflict resolution programs.

Peer Mediation in the Classroom

The process of peer mediation used in K-12 schools is similar to that used in mediating a legal dispute in that it involves third-party neutrals-mediators to assist the students in resolving their dispute. The mediators do not issue a decision as to how the students should handle the problem, they guide the students in exploring solutions to resolve the dispute. Since students typically serve as the mediators for K-12 disputes, two mediators are typically recommended for each session so that no one student will shoulder the full responsibility of moving the process along. Furthermore, if any serious problem were to arise during the mediation session, one student could go for assistance while the other would remain to keep control. Also, in the relatively small world of a school, one mediator who will be perceived as neutral by both parties may be hard to find, but two mediators with opposing perceived biases may together form a neutral team. While an adult is not present at the mediation, one must be accessible during the session. Using students as mediators brings other students to the table who might not otherwise discuss the particular problem with a teacher or administrator.

As in the legal arena, submission to the peer mediation process should be voluntary. When a dispute arises, the teacher or principal can give the students the option either to use mediation or be subject to the decision of the intervening adult. The latter course could include disciplinary measures. Most students will prefer the mediation option. Peer mediation is appropriate for most types of disputes except those involving weapons, drugs or physical

---

[1] *The Birmingham News*, February 19, 1995.

or sexual abuse. While many school systems permit mediation of disputes where fighting occurred, some do not. Each school must establish its own policy about what disputes can be mediated.

To begin the mediation, the mediator introduces the disputants and describes the process. The peer mediators also explain the rules that each participant must agree to follow in order to use the process. Common rules for mediation (depending upon the curricula adopted) include: (1) maintain confidentiality of what is stated during the session; (2) show willingness to resolve the dispute; (3) show respect to the other participants; and (4) promise compliance with the agreement reached during the mediation session. The mediators do not takes sides but must ensure that the rules are followed and that one disputant does not take unfair advantage of another. The disputants are typically seated across from each other (to avoid contact), and the two mediators usually sit at opposite ends of the table.

After the process is explained, the peer mediators allow each disputant to "tell his/her story" in an uninterrupted manner. The mediators ask about each disputant's feelings to allow the parties to vent frustration or anger in the controlled setting. As the accounts are told, the mediators attempt to identify the problem and the real interests of the disputants. Peer mediators are trained to practice effective listening skills and to paraphrase each disputant's account to obtain a better understanding of the disputant's concerns. The mediators guide the parties to concentrate on identifying the problem instead of establishing blame or seeking revenge.

Once the problem is identified, the disputants are asked to "brainstorm" for all possible options to resolve the conflict. The parties are limited only by their imagination and creativity in devising possible solutions to the problem. Implementation, of course, will depend on school rules. The mediator lists each proposed option, withholding judgment until all options are given.

If the parties initially find it difficult to create options, the mediator can assist in the brainstorming process but the mediator does not impose a solution on the parties. The disputants, in analyzing each option, discuss their feelings and concerns. Based on the discussions, the mediators assist the disputants in devising a mutually acceptable solution which then may be written down and signed by the disputants. Peer mediators are encouraged to have the participants discuss ways to avoid similar conflicts in the future. Finally, the mediators congratulate the disputants on resolving the conflict through mediation and encourage the disputants to tell others that the process was successful (while maintaining confidentiality as to what was said). Most schools provide mediator report forms to indicate whether the dispute was resolved through mediation.

Selection and Training of Mediators

Students selected as peer mediators in elementary school are usually in the fourth or fifth grade. They can serve as mediators for their peers and for the younger children in the school. Peer mediators in the middle and high schools can be from any grade, but selecting the older students lends credibility to the program as the older students can serve as role models for others. The counselors or teachers typically select the mediators based upon various criteria. The top academic students should not automatically be chosen. Many schools have discovered that the average student frequently "steps up" to the responsibility and gains more confidence and self-esteem as a result of being involved in the mediation program. In fact, some student mediators with a history of disciplinary problems have significantly improved their behavior after training in peer mediation. Most schools dismiss peer mediators if they are involved in fighting so the program provides an incentive to students to adopt non-aggressive ways to resolve conflicts.

Some of the criteria used in selecting mediators are:

— Ability to respect others and be neutral

— Ability to gain the trust and respect of the participants

— Ability to maintain self-control

— Ability to listen effectively and process nonverbal communications

— Ability to understand the real problems and issues

— Ability to communicate (frequently through paraphrasing) each disputant's concerns

— Ability to help create options

— Ability to guide the disputants to a successful resolution

— Ability to maintain confidentiality

While it is helpful if the students already have such skills, the students selected are trained in the peer mediation process before they provide any mediation services. Age-appropriate curricula have been developed by various organizations, . . . and many of these organizations also provide training programs in designated cities or where a trainer comes to the school. Most of the training programs involve a "train-to-train" format where the principal, a counselor and at least one lead teacher are trained in the principles of conflict resolution and peer mediation and this "team" goes back to the school and provides training (or support as in the case of principals) for other teachers and students.

Ultimately, all teachers and students should receive instruction. Conflict resolution techniques can easily be incorporated into most, if not all, subjects. For example, math teachers could require students to calculate how much the parties owe when a dispute arises after several families rent a condominium together for a summer; history teachers could have students mediate historical disputes or current disputes between countries; English teachers could have the students write essays on conflict resolution. The drama department of the Alabama School of Fine Arts, with the assistance of a local attorney trained in mediation, instructed its students in the principles of conflict resolution and peer mediation in preparing for a collaborative drama project requiring an unusual degree of cooperation among competing talents and interests. The instruction has proved useful to student stage managers and to the entire drama company. When the play was not "coming together," the students initiated problem-solving sessions to focus on the conflicts and brainstormed for solutions utilizing the peer mediation skills they had learned.

Community Role

Lawyers and business professionals familiar with mediation and its advantages in the legal setting should recognize the benefits that peer mediation and conflict resolution training can produce in schools and, in turn, support the development of these programs. For example, Ben and Jerry's Ice Cream business, in conjunction with the Resolving Conflict Creatively Program (RCCP) in Cambridge, Massachusetts, awarded each participating student a free ice cream cone for essays about an act of peace they initiated or witnessed. Massachusetts Attorney General Scott Harshbarger won the 1994 Innovation in State Government Award for his commitment to conflict resolution/mediation programs in the state's schools. The Ohio Commission on Dispute Resolution and Conflict Management coordinates the implementation of various forms of alternative dispute resolution in the state, including school peer mediation programs and community education programs. The New Mexico Center for Dispute Resolution initiated a school mediation program which requires the parents of the disputants also to be involved in the problem-solving session when their teenagers have been in serious fights. One principal is quoted as stating that the program was "without a doubt the most effective conflict resolution process that has ever been implemented at this site."[4]

Judges, too, can offer significant credibility to peer mediation programs. For example, as a result of the encouragement of a state judge and several attorneys from the Alabama State Bar's Alternative Dispute Resolution Committee, one high school in Montgomery, Alabama, initiated a "drop everything for peace" program which involved an extensive two-day training in conflict resolution and peer mediation for every student in the school. The Alabama State Bar Center for Dispute Resolution, assisting with the implementation of the program, provided the facilities for the earlier teacher training.

Attorneys can bring the business, legal and academic sectors together to promote K-12 mediation programs on a local basis. For instance, the authors initiated a peer mediation pilot program involving urban schools with the School of Education of the University of Alabama at Birmingham (UAB) and obtained initial "seed" funding from the business and legal community. The School of Education will compile data on the effectiveness of the program and will seek additional funding through grants for the expansion of the program. In connection with the pilot, members of the Birmingham Bar Association's Community Education Committee and other local attorneys trained in mediation recently provided a five-day (two hours per day) training program for 15 fifth grade students at North Birmingham Elementary School. The training was so well-received by the school that the committee anticipates similar requests for assistance from other schools in the area. Responsibilities for the training were divided among the attorneys so that no one attorney had to attend more than a session or two, but some did anyway! The clear consensus among the participating attorneys was that they received much more than they gave. The appreciation of the students in the forms of hugs and heartfelt "I'll miss you" remarks is a reward not easily attained within the confines of

---

[4] NIDR News, November/December 1994, at 6.

the typical law practice. As more attorneys begin to provide assistance to peer mediation programs, communities will benefit from the ripple effect of their efforts for years to come.

Conclusion

Initial research indicates that peer mediation programs are successful in reducing disciplinary problems and in improving overall school climate. One middle school, almost immediately after implementing conflict resolution programs initiated by the Ohio Commission on Dispute Resolution and Conflict Management, began to see suspensions (for fighting, unruliness and truancy) decline dramatically. A decrease in violence, physical fighting and other serious conflicts is commonly reported by schools. Just as encouraging, school administrators and teachers are reporting that the programs have had a general positive impact on adolescents by improving their attitudes, behavior and even grades. Teachers are afforded more time to teach instead of having to handle disruptive conduct such as name-calling, intimidation and threats.

Mediation can resolve conflicts without further exacerbating the tensions among disputants. The process affords the disputants an opportunity to fashion a more workable and satisfactory solution to the conflict than the typical alternative of suspension or even detention. Peer mediation programs are needed for all schools as today's children grow up in a society which glamorizes violence and aggression. The programs have been utilized successfully in suburban communities, inner-city schools and even in gang prevention and intervention programs. Teaching nonviolent ways to deal with conflict is a priority that must not be ignored by parents, schools and community leaders.

NOTES & QUESTIONS

(1) For what kinds of disputes do you believe peer mediation would be most effective? Least effective?

(2) Do you believe any kinds of alleged student misconduct would be inappropriate for peer mediation?

(3) Should peer mediation be used to resolve disputes between a student and a teacher or administrator, as well as disputes between students? If so, who should be the "peer" mediator?

(4) Do you believe peer mediation could be used to resolve any kinds of disputes among law students?

(5) Would it be appropriate to use mediation to resolve honor code or other disciplinary issues in a law school? If so, who should be the mediators?

(6) What role might law students play in helping to set up peer mediation in local schools?

(7) Could a public school mandate that students resolve disputes through mediation? Would doing so raise any Constitutional concerns?

(8) For additional readings on peer mediation, see William S. Haft & Elaine R. Weiss, *Peer Mediation in the Schools: Expectations and Evaluations*, 3 Harv. Negotiation. L. Rev. 213 (1998), and Kelly Rozmus, *Peer Mediation Programs in Schools: Resolving Classroom Conflict but Raising Ethical Concerns?*, 26 J.L. & Educ. 69 (1997).

§ H   MEDIATION OF HEALTH CARE DISPUTES

[1]   MEDICAL MALPRACTICE DISPUTES

TRANSFORMATIVE POWER: MEDICAL MALPRACTICE MEDIATIONS MAY HELP IMPROVE PATIENT SAFETY

Disp. Resol. Mag., Spring 1999, at 9 [*]

By Edward A. Dauer, Leonard J. Marcus, & George O. Thomasson

The two objectives usually assigned to the law of civil liability are compensation for the injured claimant, and deterrence for potential wrongdoers.

For much of its recent history, mediation has been offered as an efficient and more satisfying way to achieve the first of these goals. There is good reason to believe that in the special case of medical malpractice, mediation may have the potential for advancing the second as well. In health care circles that goal is known as "patient safety."

It has in recent years become increasingly apparent that the conventional procedures for processing medical liability claims—litigation and the settlement negotiations that are shaped in their image—have not been as effective as we might expect in promoting patient safety. Rather, the substantive aspects of liability law—such as its attention to the acts of individuals rather than the features of whole systems—are inconsistent with the requisites of quality improvement and error reduction in general. This is an incongruity that may explain much of why the deterrent effect has not been observed.

We believe it is equally useful to examine how the procedural aspects of the conventional process affect physicians who are implicated in malpractice claims, for as we suspect these features of the legal system may also be having untoward and unexpected effects. If that is so, then it is also appropriate to consider whether alternatives to those procedures are able to avoid the adverse consequences while effectively achieving the parties' individual objectives.

Mediation in particular may be able to overcome those artifacts of the litigation-based system that have prevented it from being more successful, as several converging lines of inquiry taken together suggest.

---

[*] Copyright © 1999 by the American Bar Association. Reprinted with permission.

Negative Effects of Litigation

Copic Insurance Co. is the medical liability carrier for 75 percent of Colorado's physicians, and a company that has made risk management an integral part of its operations. Copic's earliest efforts to analyze the malpractice litigation process began by recognizing the importance of physician decision making, a process frequently occurring in an environment of high uncertainty.

A database approach to studying medical liability claims combined with analyses taken from the analogous field of airline pilot error led to an illuminating correlation among pilot errors, physician errors and human-factor analysis in decision making. Some research suggests that the stress of a medical liability claim could be a significant risk factor adversely affecting a physician's ability to make decisions. That raises the possibility that some of the errors contributing to patient injuries might be avoidable by attending to the circumstances of how the claim process itself was affecting physicians.

Copic therefore investigated among its insured physicians the impact that the stress of liability claims has on the health of physicians, and their ability to make effective decisions. These inquiries confirmed the suggestion that the litigation process accentuates in a negative fashion characteristic physician behavior patterns, such as: not discussing the circumstances of the alleged error with anyone including colleagues, a significant increase in self doubt, and a tendency to withdraw from interpersonal contacts that in turn accentuates stress and increases the risk of further errors.

These effects are further exacerbated by anger generated by the personal accusations and professional disparagement inherent in conventional litigation. They also contribute to excessive and dysfunctional rumination and other ineffective stress avoidance behaviors, decreasing the physician's ability to give full attention to current patients and to focus on effective problem solving, useful management plans and the application of effective judgment.

Data developed by the airline industry about pilots and crew training also suggest the likelihood that decision making under this kind of stress may increase the risk of otherwise avoidable errors. Empirical support for these phenomena in health care was found in studies indicating that physicians experience an increased risk of incurring a second medical liability claim during the first year following a pervious claim.

The stress of dealing with malpractice claims was thus identified as a major risk for additional errors in physician decision making and led Copic to investigate a variety of risk management strategies. In contrast to the environment of conventional litigation, physicians appeared to benefit from programs that allowed them to reestablish their personal ego strength and to resolve questions about their decision-making effectiveness.

Thus was discovered one additional way in which the *process* of the conventional legal process inhibits rather than advances the goal of future patient safety. The aftermath of a medical error, which could be an opportunity for learning and correction, becomes instead a threat and a source of unproductive defensiveness, stress and disbelief.

Mediation's Potential

Advocates of voluntary mediation have proposed that it is well suited to medical malpractice disputes, as an alternative to much of the conventional legal process. Still, mediation has nevertheless not been widely used.

Surveys of hospitals, physicians and managed-care organizations we conducted in 1993 and updated through focus group studies in 1997 evidenced both underutilization and a widespread misunderstanding of the process. A majority of the relevant actors view mediation solely as a technique for settling lawsuits along conventional monetary lines. Seen that way, many physicians and their insurers avoid using the process, believing that expressing a willingness to mediate is equivalent to conceding liability.

A broader perspective of mediation, which is not unfamiliar to mediators experienced in other fields, is that it is a process by which communication is restored between the disputing parties. Because it is confidential and in most states legally privileged, mediation offers a safe harbor for introspection and discussion—and correction and learning. Trained mediators work to move the parties away from the advocacy of competing positions and toward the appreciation of underlying needs.

Moreover, while mediation is not an intentionally therapeutic process, its practice and results are often similar to therapeutic interventions. In addition, unlike litigation which results in monetary outcomes, and unlike conventional settlement, which also results in "solutions" expressed in dollars, the range of solutions available in mediation is unlimited.

Based on these ideas, and on the views of others about the substantive anomalies of liability law, we have hypothesized that medical malpractice mediation, taken in its more capacious guise, is better able than the conventional system is to use the claiming aftermath of a medical error as an opportunity to prevent additional errors.

Mediation Experiments

In 1995, a mediation program was put in place at the Massachusetts Board of Registration in Medicine. The process was tailored in part to further the policies of that public agency, though principally to offer a means of private dispute resolution for patients who brought to the Board claims or complaints against physicians. Protocols were established for screening and processing the cases, and mediators were trained in the program's procedures.

The pilot project was of necessity a limited one. The kinds of cases that could be mediated were constrained by the political visibility of the Board—concerns, for example, that mediation would be criticized as the board "going easy on doctors." While these concerns have not been realized, the range of cases submitted to mediation excluded those in which actionable violations or serious misconduct have been alleged.

A parallel program developed by researchers in Toronto also addresses that problem in a particularly intriguing way. In that program, when there is a case of severe misconduct or malpractice a member of the agency staff participates in the mediation as a representative of the public interest and does not agree to any resolution unless concerns of public safety are addressed. By contrast, in Massachusetts the mediations at present include only the patients and their families and the implicated physician.

Despite its limitations, the Massachusetts program offered encouraging insights into the potential of medical malpractice mediation. Of the first 10 cases mediated, nine were resolved. (The tenth involved a patient whose emotional instabilities rendered her unable to assess the resolution offered.) Of the nine cases resolved, only four involved paying money, and one of those also included a corrective action.

One patient agreed to accept half of the out-of-pocket expenses incurred for unsatisfactory complications resulting from a surgery. In another, a cosmetic surgeon agreed to return the amount the patient paid for uninsured elective surgery whose deficiencies required a corrective operation. A physician who inappropriately hit a child during an examination agreed to establish a college fund for the child. And a claim by the child of a patient who died from a late-diagnosed cancer was resolved by the urologist's making a contribution to the American Cancer Society, *and* taking refresher education in oncology.

Of greater interest, however, is that the larger number of cases involved no money payment. In two cases the patients agreed to resolutions in which the physicians changed their methods of practice—one through staff training, the other through changes in communicating information to reduce the risk of misunderstandings that could affect the quality of care.

In another case the physician and patient agreed to work together to change hospital research protocols to avoid future miscommunication between two research projects that had exposed that patient to a life-threatening drug interaction risk. In the remaining two cases the patient was satisfied with a discussion and explanation of what had happened during the procedure, often with the physician's apology or expression of regret.

These kinds of outcomes were predictable for mediation. It seems fair to say they would not have been predicted for the conventional legal process.

The pilot project's results, though derived from a regulatory setting rather than that of civil litigation, are consistent with other studies of the liability process showing that the motivations of patients who bring malpractice claims are not predominantly financial. Patients who feel injured by medical error are more significantly moved by other things—anger, confusion, a need to learn what happened and a wish to see that the error is not repeated.

Litigation offers only surrogates for these goals. Mediation allows these more productive objectives to dominate the aftermath of an injury and to replace the stress-inducing artifacts of the conventional process.

No physicians in the pilot to whom mediation was offered declined to participate after the process was explained. The program offered a confidential avenue for communication with the patient, and the prospect that explanation along with agreement to modify practices, procedures or capabilities where warranted could end what otherwise might be a punitive regulatory action.

A Promising Start

Thus far the outcomes of the cases presented to the Massachusetts mediation program support the hypothesized expectations about mediation and medical malpractice. They are fully consistent with theoretical models of voluntary mediation when it is applied to resolve—rather than merely settle—malpractice claims. They replicate in a field trial several earlier studies about patient motivations. And they exhibit the process features that distinguish this form of dispute management from the conventional legal form, thereby removing what Copic found to be among the adverse effects—and the adverse consequences for patient safety—of the current adversarial system.

Field trials in this area are extraordinarily difficult to establish. The results of this modest, and in several ways limited, effort are not proof of the hypothesis. The cases have not yet been followed to see whether these physicians, compared to some control group, have more effectively avoided the risks of additional medical errors.

Nevertheless, what does stand out clearly in this first investigation is the fact that the majority of resolutions included *explicit* attention to correction and improvements that should have beneficial effects on patient safety. This fact, together with removing one mechanism by which the liability process inhibits rather than furthers future error reduction, marks a very promising beginning.

[2] BIOETHICAL DISPUTES

HEROIC CARE CASES: WHEN DIFFICULT DECISIONS ABOUT CARE ARE NEAR, MEDIATION CAN HELP BRIDGE COMMUNICATIONS GAP

Disp. Resol. Mag., Spring 1999, at 7 *

By Nancy Neveloff Dubler

Radio shows, print media and television shows are increasingly focusing on stories about the intersection of medicine and ethics. Consider, for example, recent stories about:

— a mother who produced eight fetuses (is there a conflict of interest between the mother and her offspring?);

— a spouse of 60 years who helps his disabled wife to die (do loyalty and suffering justify assisted suicide?);

— a California prisoner who wants to donate his one remaining kidney to his daughter (what is the obligation of the state and does the prisoner have sufficient freedom to choose risk?).

Many of these personal events lead to public policy debates about individual rights and community obligations. Other stories, however—ones that almost never receive media attention—involve private, often anguished, decisions by patients, family members and beloved others who must choose among medical options for care. Inevitably, one of the paths leads to death, disability or the risk of suffering. These are the unfolding events that often lead to calls by members of the hospital team—physicians, nurses, social workers and medical students—to the Bioethics Consultation Service (BCS).

Decision-making Support

The BCS was established in the late 1970s at Montefiore Medical Center as a support for the process of decision-making in hard cases. The members of the service—two attorneys (one of whom is also a nurse) and one philosopher—all of whom have been trained in dispute resolution and mediation, respond to requests for assistance.

They come to help participants in the dispute clarify the issues, examine relevant scholarly approaches in law, medicine and bioethics, fashion an array of options for care and reach a consensus about what is the best path and why. Early in the history of the service, the team identified the process as one that "creates neutral turf" and provides the opportunity for all of the participants to reassess and revise previously staked positions. Later we added the description of a "mediative process" to describe more properly the intervention, and to distinguish it from more recognizable forms of mediation.

When coming into any consult, the team asks: Who are the parties to this conflict? What are their interests? Are those interests in conflict and, if so, how might the conflict be resolved or consensus forged? This formulation grew out of the clinical finding that most of the events that were labeled "bioethical dilemmas" were really "conflicts" that pitted members of the hospital team against each other, or members of the team against some or all of the patient/ family constellation.

The conflicts were often fueled by different perceptions of the medical facts, different understandings of the prognosis, different interpretations of patient behavior (generally relating to whether the patient was experiencing pain and suffering) and different personal value hierarchies. As we searched for ways to help patients, family members and staff understand the clashing cultures and discordant assumptions that animated their arguments, we realized that the substantive parts of our interventions were more than outweighed by the process elements. Searching for the right theoretical model steered us to the frame and the techniques of mediation.

A Tragic Example

Consider the following case:

> Frankie was a 37-year-old, HIV-positive patient with a history of drug abuse that had resulted in endocarditis and a subsequent heart valve replacement. He then contracted CLM, a form of leukemia. While in the hospital for leukemia treatment, he developed bleeding in his right kidney, which was surgically removed. He was transferred to the Intensive Care Unit (ICU), placed on a ventilator and

started on dialysis to support, and hopefully save, the remaining kidney.

Upon arriving at the ICU, Frankie's parents were shocked to see the status of their son, the number of tubes and machines to which he was tethered. They requested a "do not resuscitate" order (DNR) that would ensure that Frankie would be permitted to die in the event of cardiac or pulmonary arrest. They also requested that all aggressive treatment, including dialysis, be stopped—a decision that would permit death.

The oncologist argued that Frankie's condition was entirely reversible and that he would withdraw from the case, as he disagreed with the family's plans for the care of the patient. Frankie's AIDS doctor and renal service physician remained involved in the case. The ICU nurse called the BCS.

This case involved two physicians, the parents of the patient, a social worker, the ICU nurse and the bioethics consultant, all of whom gathered in a room off of the ICU for a discussion of the issues and the possible plan of care.

The bioethics mediator began by asking both physicians to describe what they thought was going on medically in the case, the likely prognosis and the options for care. It quickly became clear that the oncologist was relatively hopeful for a full recovery and the HIV physician less so, as continued dialysis depended upon the ability of the ICU to stabilize blood pressure, a task that was not proceeding well.

The first part of the discussion addressed the question of terminating care, given the medical status and likely outcome. The parents were adamantly in favor of discontinuing care. With probing, however, it became clear that their real issue was suffering rather than continued treatment, and they began to soften once they were assured that Frankie would receive sufficient analgesia. Indeed, they began to talk about Frankie and what a fighter he was, always wanting to take the chance to live, wanting to see his daughter grow up.

The bioethics mediator had begun the discussion assuming that this was yet one more case of an over-optimistic specialist wanting to "treat the condition" and not address the status and needs of the whole patient. Her opening assumption was that this was a dying patient, with a health care proxy (his dad) who should be able to decide whether to continue care. The discussion, however, led to the values and preferences of the patient, which became the dominant theme in the second part of the mediation. (As in traditional mediation, early in the discussion the bioethics consultant stated the first relevant theme and articulated the new relevant principle when it changed.)

The family decided against discontinuing care, opting instead to work with the team, at least for the moment. Frankie was discharged home some two months later and was still doing well five years after discharge.

Process Unique

This case illustrates some of the peculiarities and idiosyncracies of process involved in mediating bioethical disputes. First of all, it is not classical mediation as the neutral is a member of the hospital staff, although not a member of any of the care teams. She explains at the outset that her role is to try to reach a solution about the plan of care that everyone is comfortable with.

She possesses sufficient information about the hospital hierarchy and power structure, the medical and ethical issues, and the cast of characters, to form working hypotheses to guide later phases of the process. She is aware of the disparities of power that separate families and physicians, the intimidating nature of the setting (especially in the ICU), the general confusion about medical facts—so often, differential diagnosis actually means "we don't know"—and the vagaries of recovery that demand supporting the patient or family in the discussions.

The process begins with an assessment phase that identifies all of the parties and their interests, and tries to develop a common understanding of the medical facts and options. Patients and family members must understand the probabilistic reasoning that underlies "medical facts" and the notion of "medical uncertainty." It may also be appropriate to call in consultants to establish patient capacity or more finely hone the prognosis.

The second phase is a development phase that begins to explore common interests and identify those areas of agreement and disagreement. It is also the time to identify who will be the decision-maker—either the capacitated patient, a proxy or a formal or informal surrogate. The salient legal and ethical principles that are relevant to the resolution of the case should be suggested.

The resolution, phase three, requires a decision about who has authority to decide and what are the limits, if any, of that authority. The "principled solution" needs to be articulated, discussed by all and accepted. Whereas the mediator must always remain neutral regarding the actual outcome of any case, the boundaries of the inquiry must be constrained by the legal and ethical principles that undergird decisions by patients and surrogates.

The fact that patients who are capable of making medical decisions are free to consent to or refuse care, or that the proxy of an incapacitated patient is empowered to decide, is critical legal right that helps frame the process [sic]. But the fact that the outcome might be assumed or intuited at the outset does not abrogate the need for the process, or dictate the particular configuration of any individual solution. Preexisting notions of appropriate outcome are only part of the final resolution because of the massive ambiguity and uncertainty that surround many care situations and effectively preclude judgment before some mediative intervention.

In sum, the process of mediating or addressing conflict provides the opportunity for staff, patient and family members to vent their fears, articulate their concerns and share their sorrows—all steps in reaching a principled resolution.

―――――――

NOTES AND QUESTIONS

(1) What potential advantages and disadvantages do you see to using mediation to resolve medical malpractice disputes?

(2) What is the significance of the fact that defendants in medical malpractice suits are almost inevitably covered by malpractice insurance? How might this impact the mediation?

(3) If you conclude that the use of mediation is desirable in the medical malpractice context, how do you believe such mediation can or should be institutionalized?

(4) What do you see as the potential advantages of using mediation to resolve bioethical disputes? Do you see any disadvantages?

(5) Ms. Dubler states that "the boundaries of the inquiry must be constrained by the legal and ethical principles that undergird decisions by patients and surrogates." What does this mean? Does the mediation she describes differ in this respect from other forms of mediation that you have examined?

(6) In the mediation Ms. Dubler describes, the mediator is a bioethical consultant who has been retained by the hospital. Do you believe this poses any concerns in terms of the neutrality of the mediator?

(7) What kind of background or expertise do you think a mediator would need to possess to conduct a bioethical mediation?

(8) In the mediation described by Ms. Dubler, does the mediator provide information or legal advice to the parties? Do you believe this is appropriate? Desirable?

(9) For another article on using mediation to resolve bioethical disputes, see *Using Mediation for Bioethical Dilemmas*, 13 Alternatives to High Cost Litig. 159 (1995). *See also* Spring 1999 issue of Dispute Resolution Magazine, which is devoted to the issue of health care and ADR.

§ I MEDIATION OF COMMUNITY DISPUTES

A TALE OF TWO CITIES: DAY LABOR AND CONFLICT RESOLUTION FOR COMMUNITIES IN CRISIS

Disp. Resol. Mag., Fall 1997, at 8 [*]

By Lela P. Love & Cheryl B. McDonald

When written in Chinese, the word "crisis" is composed of two characters. One represents "danger" and the other represents "opportunity."

―――――――――――――――――――――――――――――――――――

A social crisis influences both individuals and groups within a community. How a government and key interest groups respond to the crisis has a similar impact on both the parties and the community-at-large. Therefore, it is important to develop an approach to the conflict that will best move society forward while limiting the danger and costs of discord.

Advocates of litigation passionately champion the value of creating binding precedents that clarify and protect the rights of individuals and groups. However, if a government exists to facilitate its community's economic and social well-being, as well as its constituents' personal safety and fundamental liberties, then enlarging the scope of issues addressed by a conflict resolution process may hold greater promise for recognizing the opportunity inherent in a crisis. In this "tale of two cities" we will describe two remarkably similar situations involving day laborers and argue that one community's choice of mediation after the commencement of litigation resulted in outcomes that addressed and satisfied a wider range of constituency interests than those realized by the community that chose litigation alone.

Gathering at the Corner

Glen Cove, N.Y., is a small city on the north shore of Long Island. Agoura Hills, Calif., is a comfortable residential suburb of Los Angeles. As the 1980s drew to a close, each community became aware of an increasing number of men who began congregating at specific "shaping points" to seek daily employment from landscapers and other contractors. In Glen Cove, the shaping point was a deli; in Agoura Hills, it was an intersection.

The men were generally Hispanic; 50-100 Central and South American immigrants. The casual labor they might find represented their only means of livelihood. Some were refugees who had fled the political violence of their home countries. Their labor allowed the surrounding middle and upper-middle class communities to enjoy well-tended lawns and gardens, and well-maintained homes at affordable prices.

The presence of these men and their activities also caused conflict in these communities. Local merchants and neighbors expressed concerns about noise, litter, public urination, catcalling to women and other disorderly behavior. Traffic safety was compromised by men running into the streets to negotiate with potential employers; vehicles would unexpectedly stop in traffic or pull up to or away from the curb as employers made their choices and picked up workers.

Two Cities, Two Responses

As tensions mounted, the cities stepped up their enforcement of traffic laws. Glen Cove city officials urged the U.S. Immigration and Naturalization Service to round up and detain illegal aliens at the shaping point. In Agoura Hills, city officials worked with local businesses to set up a hiring site in a commercial parking lot. While the site provided public toilets, drinking water and a volunteer coordinator, few men actually got jobs through the facility—although it is not clear why this was the case. It was eventually replaced with a telephone exchange, but the informal hiring practice continued.

In both cities, the workers complained that the law enforcement officers used harassing and abusive tactics, unfairly targeting them as criminals while at the same time ignoring their claims or treating them as perpetrators when in fact they were the victims of criminal activities. Both cities attempted to address the problem by holding public hearings, which only engendered strident debate and a hardening of positions.

In 1990, both cities enacted substantially similar ordinances prohibiting solicitation either to or from occupants of vehicles that are traveling on public streets or from cars parked in unauthorized areas of commercial parking lots. The Glen Cove ordinance more broadly prohibited occupants of stopped or parked vehicles from hiring or attempting to hire a worker.

Seeing these ordinances as unconstitutionally targeted against the Hispanic workers and violating First Amendment rights, civil libertarians and members of the Hispanic community in each city joined to file lawsuits, which in the case of Glen Cove included a class action seeking $3 million from the city. Plaintiffs in both cities sought preliminary injunctions against the enforcement of the new ordinances.

Here the tales of the two cities begin to diverge.

Agoura Hills

In Agoura Hills, representatives of the workers attempted to negotiate with the city, but made no progress. Following the denial of their preliminary injunction, the workers appealed. The California Court of Appeals denied the appeal in a published decision upholding the ordinance and finding no evidence of its unconstitutional application to the plaintiffs.

Three years later, while crowds of 100 men no longer congregate in one place, the nature of the situation depends on who you ask. The City of Agoura Hills contends the problem has gone away. While a few transients still gather to seek work, the "regulars" seem to have moved elsewhere. The Los Angeles County Sheriff's Department, with whom Agoura Hills contracts for police services, has assigned a bilingual ordinance enforcement officer in order to improve communication with the day-laborer population. As of July 1, 1997, the telephone exchange was shut down.

Representatives of the day laborers tell a different story, however. They report that 60-80 workers still solicit work each day in Agoura Hills, but do so in smaller, geographically scattered groups of 8 to 10 men. With a penalty of $271 per citation, the workers are cautious and disperse when a sheriff's vehicle comes into sight. Moreover, they contend that the sheriff continues to hassle workers and that the presence of a bilingual officer has neither eased the distrust held by the workers toward the city and police officials nor substantially improved communication. In some cases, the sheriff has used back-up units and helicopters to round up workers.

Glen Cove

As with Agoura Hills, a state court denied a preliminary injunction against the Glen Cove city ordinance. Facing the prospect of laborious and possibly unsuccessful litigation that would leave broader concerns unaddressed, plaintiff CARECEN (Central American Refugee Center) was receptive to alternatives. The city was also open to alternatives, having hired outside counsel to defend the lawsuit and facing sizeable legal expenses if litigation continued. In early 1992, Hofstra University Law School Professor Baruch Bush suggested mediation and recommended a possible mediator. Both sides agreed to participate.

The mediation was held in April 1992, in a conference room at the Glen Cove Public Library. In two full-day sessions, which were spaced a week apart, the parties raised and addressed a broad range of issues. By the end of the second session, they reached an understanding as to the general substance of an acceptable accord. In December 1992, many drafts and conference calls later, the parties signed a final agreement, which included an amended ordinance.

The structure and timing of the sessions were designed to create an environment that would foster understanding and collaboration, and comport with political realities. In the first session, the parties were invited to describe their perspectives and concerns in an effort to gain—for the entire group—a more comprehensive understanding of the situation. No solutions or proposals were to be put forward at this session.

Many first-session presentations included the sharing of perspectives and stories that may not have been heard in a litigation context. Two day laborers, for example, described the hardship created by the hostile environment. The deputy chief of police and a city council member talked about the situation's impact on the police and town residents. An anthropology professor described how the Salvadorans' historical experience with repressive governments and brutal police tactics made them particularly vulnerable to perceived or actual hostility from the government. This first session not only educated the participants about each other's realities, but also humanized and connected the parties. This reduced the prior acrimony that the litigation and press coverage had inflamed, and set the stage for tackling the issues.

The week between sessions gave the parties the opportunity to explore with their respective constituents possible proposals to address the issues raised. In the second session, the parties discussed and shaped proposals, and the Glen Cove mayor's visit to the working session enhanced a growing spirit of collaboration.

Notably, the agreement between the parties addressed concerns much broader than those raised by the litigation. These included:

— posting city notices in Spanish as well as English;

— use of the city soccer field by the Salvadoran community;

— collaboration between the city and advocacy groups to create an alternate site for employers to connect with day workers;

— hosting of community meetings by CARECEN to educate the day laborers about community responsibilities;

— cultural awareness and Spanish language training for members of the police force;

— the institution of a police protocol for interventions in which a party does not speak English; and

— the collaborative drafting of an amended ordinance that both promoted the City's traffic safety concerns and satisfied CARECEN's concerns about discrimination and the protection of constitutional rights.

The agreement became a final judgment of the court in the lawsuit and terminated the litigation. Since many of its provisions required ongoing collaboration between the parties, the dialogue between them continued past the mediation sessions.

Today, Hispanic advocacy groups in Glen Cove report a working "shaping point" with toilet facilities provided by the city and a variety of supportive services for the day laborers. While the shaping point took several years to materialize, the mediation was a component of the change in climate that resulted in the new facility.

Keys for Success

In one sense, each community achieved its desired goal of eliminating both a substantial traffic hazard and dispersing the large conglomeration of men and vehicles. However, Glen Cove was also able to improve understanding and relationships among parties who shared a common community by making effective use of mediation to resolve the conflict. Government officials and key interest groups began to collaborate in a problem-solving process to address the troubling issues they faced. A host of issues were addressed rather than just legal causes of action. The costs and risks of further litigation, for both sides, were eliminated.

Despite these attractive advantages, multi-party public policy mediation poses some problems. Elected officials are directly accountable to their constituents for their success or failure in managing social problems. When their approach to crisis deviates from the orthodox, they increase their risk. While multi-party negotiations are certainly somewhat commonplace, more formalized multi-party mediations still are not yet widely used, particularly at the local levels. Therefore, participants may be vulnerable to criticism for bargaining about presumptively established rights and obligations. As a result, difficult questions must be thoughtfully answered before such a mediation begins, including:

Who will the mediator be? The mediator must be comfortable and skilled in managing multiple parties with diverse interests. He or she must be knowledgeable about critical dimensions of the controversy without being identified with either side. Critically, too, all parties must trust the mediator. In the Glen Cove situation, the mediator was an academic, which in that case helped establish both credibility and neutrality. It is also important to remember in this regard that the way the mediator is defined and selected can affect whether interested parties choose to participate. While the absence of some players may not derail the mediation process in its entirety, it may limit the scope of the problems that can be effectively addressed.

How will the mediator be paid? In situations in which some parties are unable or unwilling to pay for the mediation, there is a tension between the potential perception of mediator bias and the need for unrestricted access to the process for all stakeholders. In the Glen Cove mediation, the mediator served pro bono. This solution is not always viable and may not be optimal, as financial contributions may increase commitment to the process. Where parties cannot equally contribute to the mediation, however, alternative sources of funding should be explored.

Who are the stakeholders and who represents them? In the two cities here, stakeholders included: workers (citizens, legal and illegal immigrants), city officials (both elected and law enforcement officials), residents (homeowners and rental tenants), the business community (both retailers and contractors), community groups (legal advocacy groups and churches), and motorists.

Critically, though, someone must take the lead in deciding who needs to be brought to the table. Not infrequently, advocacy groups and various individuals will vie with each other to be the designated spokesperson. Such issues must be resolved thoughtfully, both before the mediator is selected and as the process moves forward.

Even when these hurdles are successfully negotiated, one must also remember that mediation does not create legally binding precedents. Fundamental interests acknowledged and addressed in a mediated resolution are not automatically transferable to others who are similarly situated. While a mediation may stimulate positive shifts in culture, its impact on other communities will depend on informal transmission, or the "ripple effect."

Also, unless the process creates structures to carry the parties' vision beyond changes in political administration or other shifts in leadership, benefits derived from mediation may be lost. Parties must be concerned both about the resolution of the issues at hand, as well as their continued capacity to address the interests which have been brought to light.

Clearly, there is no single process or approach appropriate for every social crisis. Important community interests and values must shape the response of all participants, particularly that of city officials. However, in a democratic society, the principles of participation and dialogue that we hold dear should incline government officials toward institutionalizing processes that bring multiple affected parties together when challenges arise like those faced by Glen Cove and Agoura Hills. Thoughtfully constructed, mediation offers the chance to seize the opportunity inherent in community crisis.

§ J ENVIRONMENTAL MEDIATION

RUN, RIVER, RUN: MEDIATION OF A WATER-RIGHTS DISPUTE KEEPS FISH AND FARMERS HAPPY—FOR A TIME

67 U. Colo. L. Rev. 259, 284–91, 300–15, 320–24, 330–32 (1996) [*]

By Janet C. Neuman

[Ed: Mediation was used to resolve disputes over uses of water from the Umatilla River, a tributary of the Columbia River in northeastern Oregon. Some wanted the water to be used to support a fishery restoration project, while others favored use of the water for agricultural purposes. Disputants included the Confederated Tribes of the Umatilla Indian Reservation, the downstream farmers, the U.S. Bureau of Reclamation, the U.S. Environmental Protection Agency, the Oregon State Water Resources Department, the Oregon Department of Fish and Wildlife, and several environmental protection groups (WaterWatch and Oregon Trout). The parties selected two co-mediators: Chapin Clark (an Oregon water law expert and law professor); and Elaine Hallmark (a lawyer and experienced mediator with a Portland mediation firm).]

. . . .

B. The Mediation Process

The formal mediation sessions began on December 4, 1991. Some of the ground rules established at the first mediation session are typical of most mediations. They included, among other things: "Leave weapons of war at home, or at least at the door. Cooperate with each other as a means to avoid litigation. Treat each other with respect. Listen to understand. Share your views and interests as clearly as possible. Make decisions by consensus."

Two other crucial agreements were reached that were somewhat tailor-made for this particular mediation. One concerned the press. Just before the mediation began, a series of newspaper articles ran in area newspapers, serving to inflame the controversy. Some of the parties felt strongly that other parties might "try their case" in the media, and that such efforts would be very damaging to the mediation. The parties were also concerned that the media themselves might cover the dispute in such a manner as to damage the negotiation process, because a good fight "sells more papers" than a reasoned compromise. Therefore, the subject of press coverage was a touchy issue at the first meeting. In fact, when a reporter came to the meeting, the parties' first inclination was to ban the media entirely from their proceedings. However, the mediators managed to lead the parties through a discussion of their concerns, in the presence of the reporter, and to an agreement on how media coverage would be handled. The parties agreed not to try to use the press to affect the mediation process and to speak only for themselves when speaking to the media. They could represent their own positions and discuss the mediation process, but they would not attempt to characterize any other party's views or conduct, and any statements for the whole group would be developed by the group and released by the mediators. This initial consensus on a sensitive procedural issue probably helped set the tone for further constructive discussion and agreement on more substantive issues.

Another agreement reached at the first session was perhaps not as successful, at least in retrospect. The parties officially attending the first session included the Tribes, the Bureau, the Oregon Water Resources Department, WaterWatch, the Oregon Department of Fish and Wildlife, and the three irrigation districts that would receive the exchange water from the Bureau (Stanfield, Hermiston, and Westland, through their joint manager and counsel). Observers, in addition to a number of other party representatives, included individuals named Chet Prior and Tony Amstead, as representatives of the Teel Irrigation District ("Teel").

The Teel Irrigation District was in a curious position. Technically, Teel was not directly involved in the project at all. It would not receive any of the Columbia River water from the exchange. Nor did it hold a current water delivery contract from the Bureau of Reclamation. Yet Teel was probably the most intensely interested in the water-spreading issue that was underlying the immediate controversy because it relied on water allegedly being "spread" to it by the Westland Irrigation District. The West Extension Irrigation District ("West Extension") was also interested in the water-spreading issue. Although recognizing these significant interests, the other parties decided that because Teel and West Extension were not directly part of the current exchange, which was legally what the mediation was about, they did not need to participate as formal parties. They were invited to come to the mediation as observers, which they did, attending nearly every session. This decision not to include the Teel district as a formal participant eventually came back to haunt the mediation.

The assembled parties did agree that Oregon Trout, the other party that had filed a formal objection to the Bureau's state exchange application, should be invited to join as a party, along with the Bonneville Power Administration ("BPA"). BPA was included because the Umatilla Basin Project Act obligated BPA to provide the electricity for pumping the exchange water from the Columbia River up into the Umatilla Basin reservoirs.

The parties initially identified thirteen issues to be addressed in the mediation. They later eliminated some issues and collapsed the rest into three main categories. The parties described these categories as follows: "Full state enforcement of water rights, BOR taking no action with adverse impacts on the objectives of the Umatilla Basin Project, [and] BOR actions taken will follow the full [National Environmental Policy Act or 'NEPA'] process . . . ." Although the wording is awkward, what these really boiled down to is a distillation of the objections raised by WaterWatch and Oregon Trout. The mediation would deal with two angles of the water-spreading concerns: (1) whether water was currently being "spread" beyond the allowable amounts and/or land covered by a valid state water right and a Bureau contract; and (2) how to comply with the legal requirements, under either federal or state law, for any change or expansion of any irrigation district's service boundaries. By addressing those specific issues, the mediation would thereby deal with the general concern that the terms of the exchange needed to be strictly monitored and enforced in order to ensure that all of the replaced Umatilla water really stayed in the stream for the fish.

Five mediation sessions were held from early December to mid-February. The sessions began with a significant amount of mistrust and frustration expressed by all parties. There were particularly bad feelings by the locals, who had been working hard to reach consensus and obtain federal cooperation and funding for the project for so long, towards the "outsider" environmental groups' intervention in the approval process. However, after a tense beginning and several difficult, late-hour negotiating sessions, the parties came to an agreement on February 12, 1992, less than three months after the first session.

After reaching final agreement in concept, the parties circulated proposed final documents drafted to capture the agreement, and they then gathered for a signing ceremony on February 27 at the Tribes' Yellowhawk Administration Building on the Umatilla Indian Reservation. The parties signed three written agreements binding the various parties to specific actions. They also signed a stipulation to be submitted to the State Water Resources Department, in which WaterWatch and Oregon Trout agreed to withdraw their objections, and that included a proposed form of transfer order and permit to be issued by the State to the Bureau.

C. The Mediated Agreement

The parties' agreements are deceptively simple on the surface. For example, the agreement of the Hermiston Irrigation District consists of only four short paragraphs, as follows:

1. As soon as possible, Hermiston Irrigation District and the Bureau of Reclamation, hereafter BOR, will enter good faith negotiations for a contract to implement P.L. 100-557. Hermiston will not attempt to include any benefits for any other district in their negotiations with BOR.

2. The basis of the contract to implement P.L. 100-557 between Hermiston Irrigation District and BOR is the equal exchange of irrigation water for water from the Columbia River through the Exchange Project, resulting in delivery of the amount of water from the Umatilla and Columbia Rivers as is authorized under Oregon water law to all of those lands that received irrigation water from Hermiston Irrigation District prior to 10-1-88.

3. BOR will contract with Hermiston Irrigation District for delivery of water on an interim basis to lands with a surface water right and served by Hermiston as of 10-1-88, but outside district boundaries. Hermiston will apply for boundary expansion to include these lands. BOR will complete the boundary expansion process.

4. Each of the parties to this agreement shall support and cooperate in the protection of releases of water from McKay Reservoir for

instream flow use for fish purposes including, but not limited to, supporting any changes under federal and state law which may be necessary to ensure protection of this water for this use.

However, the apparent simplicity belies the underlying complexity and the difficult issues that were hammered out. The major components of the parties' agreements were essentially the provisions of the Umatilla Basin Project Act, but they were fleshed out with some critical details. For instance, the Bureau committed to enter into new contracts with the irrigation districts to supply water to those lands that had been legally receiving water as of October 1, 1988. But the water would come from the Columbia River instead of the Umatilla, as required by the Act. Then the stipulated order and permit went further to establish how each district's water use would be measured because there was significant disagreement on the amount of water the districts were legally entitled to, how much they had actually been using, and how to measure and monitor future uses.

The mediation handled the issue of "water spreading" in several ways. The agreements made it clear that no new irrigation would be supported with the Columbia River water and that all exchanged water would go to support instream flows for fish. This promise was also supported by the monitoring requirements so that it could be assured that the project was in fact accomplishing its purpose.

The districts, however, were assured of receiving the amount of water that they had used on October 1, 1988 on an "interim" basis, even for lands outside of the districts' official boundaries, if that water use was authorized by state law. These out-of-district lands were not guaranteed continued delivery of water beyond the interim, however. The Bureau promised to proceed with a proposal to expand the districts' boundaries to include all lands actually receiving water, but only after full NEPA review. The districts also committed to proceed under state law requirements to seek boundary changes.

Thus, what the mediated agreement really did with the water-spreading issue was first to affirm that both state law and federal contracts limit the use of water to specific lands and that only formal amendment of the state water rights and federal contracts could legitimize use on different lands. In other words, the Project Act by itself did not expand anyone's water rights. Second, the agreement committed the parties to seek the necessary approvals and gave them a grace period in which to do so.

An interesting provision of the agreement obligated the parties to "contact, to the extent feasible, every person or group to whom they had previously expressed concern about this project and assure them (1) that these concerns have been dealt with, and (2) that all parties to this agreement now support the Umatilla Basin Project completely and wholeheartedly." This provision, of course, was designed primarily to demonstrate to Congress that the project was back on track, thereby breaking loose the federal funds. But actually, this promise, along with many of the provisions that seem simply to restate the Project Act's requirements, illustrates how much this mediation was really about trust and betrayal.

At the risk of oversimplifying the agreement, it is probably fair to say that what the parties agreed upon in the mediation was to "seal" the promise of the federal legislation. "We *will* comply with all applicable laws, we *will* help the fish, and we *will* give the farmers only their legal due, cross our hearts and hope to die."

. . . .

IV. Analysis of the Results and Lessons Learned

When I began this case study, it appeared that the mediation had been successful. Final agreements had been signed by all parties after five mediation sessions, and the signing ceremony had been a celebration. Over the course of my examination, however, the parties were in and out of post-mediation negotiation several times, often teetering on the brink of litigation. A few difficult issues deferred in the initial mediation and not completely covered by the signed agreements caused a new and bitter round of disagreements, threatening to undo the original consensus. The reasons for this became clear as I surveyed the parties and reviewed their responses.

A. Survey Results: The Inside View

. . . .

Several significant conclusions can be drawn from the surveys.

This mediation delivered fairly high quality justice in terms of the participants' personal satisfaction with the process and the outcome. The parties generally found the process fair and conducive to open discussion of their real interests and the underlying facts. Many of the parties felt they saved time and money and came out with a more fair and creative solution than either litigation or the administrative process would have allowed. They felt that they had sufficient control over the process and the outcome and that the solution met their own needs. Furthermore, the parties recognized some improvement in their relationships overall as a result of working together in this mediation. Finally, the parties gave a lot of credit to good mediators for making the process work. . . .

The parties elaborated on their survey responses in the individual interviews. All of the parties expressed clear satisfaction with the mediation process. The parties commented that the process was helpful in "fleshing out the parties' real agendas," that mediation is good because it "focuses on dealmaking and making everybody happy," and that people "feel better at the end" of a mediation than with other more adversarial processes. One party put it succinctly: the process was good because it "got to agreement."

The participants also confirmed that the mediation saved them both time and money, although some noted that perhaps the "jury was still out on that question" because the matter could yet end up in litigation or a contested case. One respondent said that mediation does require a lot of time in a concentrated period, but that overall it saves time and money, especially because it can be done without attorneys.

The parties had some good words for the kind of communication that mediation can foster. Across the board, they stressed that their own views and interests were fully expressed and heard and that they developed an understanding of the other parties' concerns and positions. One person said, "All the parties learned how to communicate better; they practiced it. The first meetings were stilted, but by the last meetings, they could joke about it."

However, when asked directly whether the mediation process encouraged full and open exchange of information and development of the facts, the parties were not so sure. When this issue was probed in individual interviews, the reason for the lower ratings was revealed. The responses on information exchange boiled down to frustration over certain requests that were made early in the mediation sessions for data from one of the parties. This information was apparently never fully produced, or at least so the other parties believed, and all of them noted their frustration with this perceived withholding.

Aside from the criticism expressed about this particular data request, the parties had many positive comments about the exchange of information. "Everyone learned a lot about how this system [the Umatilla River and its dams] actually worked." The process had "educational value." "It was invaluable for a public interest group to discuss and understand the [irrigation] districts." The discussions "enlightened some parties as to water law, [reclamation] contract law," and other subjects.

The parties generally felt that the process of mediation allows for creative solutions and that the final outcome here incorporated such creative solutions. One said, "The approach itself encourages creativity. It's more relaxed and informal. The group controls its own fate. Every paragraph was a battle, but creative things came out." Several parties emphasized that the particular solutions crafted into the mediated agreements were not even possible in either litigation or an administrative contested case.

The parties all gave relatively high ratings when asked if they had sufficient control over both the process and the outcome; yet, they also noted that some parties seemed to have excessive power or procedural advantage. When this was explored in the interviews, it appeared that the parties who felt more over a barrel in terms of the substantive law thought that the other parties had more power. The feelings of imbalance were not a fault of the process but a perceived weakness by certain parties in their substantive rights that formed the basis of their bargaining position. . . .

Some of the respondents felt that the mediation process helped educate the parties in dispute resolution skills, but they were less sure that the process "empowered" the individual parties. The mediation participants answered fairly consistently that the process and outcome reduced conflict and improved the relationships among the parties. One party said, "I don't think you can help but better a relationship if you've sat in a room together and really listened. The parties become real people with a point of view. You gain respect for each other. Maybe if I were in their shoes, I'd feel the same way." Another said that "it was good for water users to be sitting in a room with instream concerned parties." The mediation created a "process of knowing how to deal with each other, even though not a happy, rosy relationship."

One party noted that, even after the mediation, the locals continued to harbor some animosity toward the two state-wide environmental groups for "sticking their noses in" where they had "no business" doing so. Nevertheless, as a result of the mediation, those groups could now "pick up the phone" and call the Tribes and the irrigation districts. "When you get to know someone, it makes a difference, even if you agree to disagree."

The parties gave mixed answers when asked to rate how important it was to them to avoid an administrative contested case proceeding or litigation. . . . Those who most wanted to continue a cooperative relationship and get the project back on track (primarily, those who lived in the Basin) were more concerned about this than the others.

The parties were all quite clear in affirming the importance of the particular mediators in helping to reach consensus. The parties noted, too, that in this case, having two mediators was quite helpful because the two complemented each other. Chapin Clark, as an expert in water law, was an "important resource in explaining the intricacies of the water law issues" involved and in "suggesting creative solutions" to some of the tricky legal problems, while Elaine Hallmark "focused on traditional facilitation and process techniques." In another party's words, Hallmark provided the "overall framework," while Clark helped with the "nuts and bolts." Some of the parties also felt it was important that Clark, as an "elder statesman" of water law, commanded the respect of some of the other water lawyers involved in the negotiations. Finally, one individual commented that good mediators are "essential" and that "poor ones would be worse than none."

Much of the foregoing discussion concerns the process of mediation; but the parties also expressed clear satisfaction with the outcome in their survey responses. The parties felt that the outcome generally met their individual needs and was also fair and in the public interest. The parties stressed that the resolution got the federally funded project back on track and was, in the words of one party, "good for fish," and yet it did so while trying to provide some security for the farmers as well. Everyone received most of what they needed in order to reaffirm their support for the project.

So far, so good. In all of the areas discussed thus far, the parties expressed a rather high level of satisfaction with how this mediation progressed and what it accomplished. Then why is it that not long after the mediation the parties were fighting again? A few clues can be found in some of the parties' written survey responses and further understood by some of the comments in the follow-up interviews.

Although the survey responses and initial interview comments expressed satisfaction with the outcome, probing deeper into the parties' comments in personal interviews revealed a bit more ambivalence. One noted that the "paper" outcome was good but that the agreement broke down after the process had ended. Another party described the feelings as "warm and fuzzy" at the end of the mediation but said that after the process shut down, tempers flared again and those feelings were lost. The frustration expressed by the parties related to the breakdown in interim-flow negotiations and the differences in interpretation that arose in trying to implement the agreements.

One of the loose threads that began to unravel the mediated agreement is revealed in the parties' answers to the questions about whether the mediation resolved the dispute fully and comprehensively and whether the parties have complied with the agreement. The parties' ratings on these two questions were among the lowest of any on the survey. Probing these ratings in interviews also brought out the most dissatisfied and bitter comments from almost all of the parties. One respondent said that the "most generous explanation" he could give for what had happened since the end of the formal mediation was that the "parties have strayed from the agreements," while the "nastiest" version was that they "bought what they wanted then, but then saw other opportunities and took advantage of them." Another party representative described it similarly: certain parties "may think they're technically complying with the agreement," but they are at least "violating the spirit." The parties "may have had some reluctance to agree to agree. Maybe they sort of went along to get it done, but maybe they really didn't like it." Some of the parties had a "larger agenda" that they really could not drop, and they "lost sight of focusing on this exchange." Indeed, at least in retrospect, some of the parties distinctly felt that not all of the other parties had negotiated in good faith.

Discussions with the parties revealed that when the first round of interim negotiations took place to determine how much irrigation water would be released for fish flows before the exchange project was fully operational (during construction of the pumping facilities), the parties had some basic disagreements about what they had agreed to. This issue had been deferred to the last mediation session because it was one of the more contentious disagreements. At a break in the formal mediation, two of the parties held a separate side caucus on this issue. They emerged, saying that they had agreed upon how to handle the issue and that the agreement simply needed to state that interim flows would be established by negotiation. Later, it became clear that the districts believed that the agreement essentially legitimized existing water use, at least for the interim, regardless of whether any technically illegal water spreading was occurring. The Tribes and Water-Watch believed that even in the interim, the districts were only entitled to "legal" water, and anything else should be freed up for fish. At least one district believed it would be paid for any interim water releases, which was apparently surprising and distressing news to the other parties. Finally, even as to the longer-term process agreed to (NEPA review for any boundary expansion), the parties had different understandings. The districts expected a short and sweet, uncontested environmental assessment process; the instream advocates expected full-scale Environmental Impact Statement ("EIS") review. Because of these different versions of how the mediated agreements were to be implemented, within a few months of the signing ceremony, the parties were already looking back at the recent mediation with something other than rose-colored glasses. Meanwhile, Teel, the district that had not participated but that relied entirely on allegedly "spread" water, filed suit against the State to enjoin cutting off its water use.

In spite of Teel's later challenge, the parties themselves were quite sure that everyone was involved in this mediation who needed to be involved. But when they were asked if the outcome was harmful to any third parties, they were not as sure, with an average answer about halfway between a no and a yes. In interviews, some parties acknowledged that all of the affected irrigation districts (including Teel and West Extension) probably should have been involved in order to ensure that their slightly different interests were represented.

When asked to rate the outcome as to a substantive decision for the management of the Umatilla River, the numerical ratings given were also mixed, and the interview comments revealed even more ambivalent feelings. Almost all of the parties recognized that the Umatilla Basin Project and the mediated agreements were simply a beginning in terms of solving larger water-management problems. The parties said this was a "good beginning," but it is only "one step in a much larger and more complicated process." This project did not begin to consider "groundwater, Columbia River system endangered species, a full review of treaty rights, or the westwide water-spreading issue." Even as to the Umatilla alone, this is a "capital intensive solution," and "electric pumping may not be the best environmental solution." The exchange did not really tackle the issues of "efficiency and conservation" in arid-land agriculture either. One party summed up by saying, "If anyone thinks we're home on this, we're just kidding ourselves."

. . . .

B. Lessons Learned: The Outside View

. . . .

1. General Mediation Lessons

a. Mediation is useful where the solution available from litigation or other formal process, such as an administrative contested case proceeding, is rigid and inflexible. Whenever parties use the court system to resolve a dispute, someone has to win and someone has to lose (unless, of course, they settle before a final decision). An administrative agency is similarly constrained to resolve contested cases in favor of one party or another. It is simply not possible for a court or an agency to say, "Okay, let's lay everything on the table. What do you people *really* want? How can we fashion a solution that gives something to everyone?"

It is this potential for fashioning a composite solution that makes mediation so attractive in certain kinds of disputes. What kinds of disputes? Likely candidates are those in which the "official" legal rights are black and white (i.e., either one party or the other gets something—money, property, or water—depending on the resolution of certain basic legal issues) but it is not a foregone conclusion which outcome is most likely. . . .

For example, in this case, the parties were able to fashion a compromise solution that gave water to both the fish and the farmers, rather than to only one or the other. Furthermore, they were able to make the nuts and bolts (measurement, monitoring, and so forth) part of the larger agreement, to ensure that the project would operate as planned. The precise result achieved in the Umatilla Basin Project mediation could not have been issued as a court or agency order. It took building trust and communicating openly about sensitive issues to establish the details of the exchange agreement and to convince finally the parties that this project could go forward and work effectively.

b. A mediated solution allows parties to recognize and incorporate into their final agreement their real interests, even though legally speaking those interests might not be directly relevant to resolving the dispute at hand. Mediating parties can incorporate "non-legal values" or put different priorities on their interests than the legal system would. These values or priorities might involve psychological, social, or ethical concerns, in addition to strictly legal or economic matters. In this case, the parties were able to deal with their shared concerns for protecting the health and diversification of the regional economy. They could focus on their common goal of maximizing the water supply and allocating it to both farmers and fish, rather than on fighting over who had the better legal entitlement to a limited and finite water supply.

c. Mediation is particularly useful as a dispute resolution device when the parties need or want to maintain a working relationship. In this particular dispute, key parties placed a high value on "living together" in the Umatilla Basin, and it was thus important to them to avoid winners and losers and to try to craft a win-win solution. The Tribes, though they knew they had a strong case to take to federal court, also knew that they did not want their claims for water for fish to destroy the local farming economy. In addition, the farmers could have fought to the bitter end to keep the water on the fields and away from the fish, but they, too, felt that mutual coexistence and cooperative reallocation of water were important goals. . . .

If a mediated agreement itself contains a provision governing resolution of future disagreements, then a formal structure for ongoing problem-solving also exists. However, even if no such formal provision is incorporated, an ongoing relationship will likely be fostered informally. Parties who have sat together through mediation sessions, hashing things out, have a ready framework for a future working relationship. At the very least, they know whom to call as the representatives of other parties when future issues or problems crop up. They have "practiced" solving problems by negotiating with each other and are thus more likely to pick up the phone or arrange a meeting with each other than to fire off angry letters or initiate further legal action. It is noteworthy that all of the Umatilla parties, in the individual interviews, noted that such informal working relationships were a product of the mediation. . . .

d. A corollary lesson is that it is critical to include a provision for future dispute resolution in the mediated agreement itself. Although successful mediations generally end on an "up" note, with the parties having fashioned a consensus out of difficult and controversial issues, it is important to recognize that even consensus agreements may be subject to future disputes about interpretation, implementation, or compliance. When the inevitable problems do arise, the parties need not despair that everything is falling apart. Instead, they can say, "Oh yes, we anticipated this," and call the mediator back without feeling like the agreement has failed. The absence of such a provision here has hampered the parties in handling their post-mediation disagreements.

e. It is important to agree to ground rules and stick to them, and to push for consensus by all parties, even on the hard issues and even at the eleventh hour. Deferring particularly thorny matters, especially without a dispute resolution method specified in the agreement, can serve to undermine an otherwise successful mediation. Thus, in the Umatilla case, treatment of the interim-flow issue with a vague clause that simply said the matter would be "negotiated" later dealt a serious, though hopefully not fatal, blow to the overall consensus. . . . As noted earlier, external deadlines can help create both an incentive to mediate and the impetus to reach consensus. But, if externally imposed timetables are too short, those deadlines create unreasonable pressures for deferring hard issues, failing to clarify key terms, and reaching premature or incomplete agreements.

f. One of the most challenging and critical decisions in conducting a mediation is determining who the parties will be. Including too many parties can overly complicate the process and prevent reaching a workable consensus. Omitting parties who should have been included can rob the agreement of its clout and implementability. In retrospect, it was probably a mistake not to encourage the Teel and West Extension Irrigation Districts to participate as formal parties in the Umatilla mediation. By not participating, Teel, at least, felt that it was sold out by the mediated agreements, and it had the ability to prevent smooth implementation of the agreement. In other words, in deciding who needs to be part of the mediation, it is always helpful to ask who could block implementation of the agreement. . . .

g. Mediation requires a different attitude of participants than does litigation or administrative action. In order for a mediation to be completely successful, the parties must learn to trust each other. Mediation cannot simply be used strategically. If parties go into a mediation to see what they can get from the negotiation but then refuse to comply if the final agreement is not to their liking or if an opportunity arises to get more, then the whole process becomes a charade.

     . . . .

In this case, it appears that the parties did participate initially in good faith but that they failed to define adequately key terms and provisions associated with resolving the most difficult issues. If they had taken a bit more time to discuss the interim-flow, boundary-expansion, and EIS issues, they would have discovered that they were not in consensus, giving them a chance to try to resolve these issues before signing an agreement. When they did discover their remaining problems on these issues, they were no longer using a neutral facilitator to help discuss differences. As a result, the parties fell back into their former patterns of mistrust, cross-accusations in the newspaper, and adversarial negotiations, if they even negotiated at all.

h. Good mediators are critical to the success of any mediation. It is the neutral mediator, with no vested stake in the outcome, who can help parties with real and bitter disagreements move beyond their differences and affronts to fashion a consensus that meets their underlying needs. A good mediator can keep focusing the discussion on common interests and goals rather than on posturing and positions. But who is a good mediator? Presumably, she is someone who can listen, understand, translate, and interpret—someone (or perhaps a combination of people, as here) with both process skills and substantive knowledge of the issues in dispute. And finally, in difficult high-profile public disputes, a good mediator may need to be a known commodity—someone with a reputation or clout whom the parties will respect, listen to, and work with.

The mediators here seemed to meet all these criteria. . . .

3. Public-policy Mediation Lessons

a. Mediation can work well for public agencies, both in resolving specific disputes and in developing general policies. The Umatilla mediation involved four public agencies, two federal and two state. All of them were generally satisfied with both the mediation process and its outcome. Mediation works to resolve disputes involving public agencies for the same reasons it works for other parties; it allows the parties to get their real issues and concerns out on the table and fashion a solution that truly meets these needs. Mediation can also be useful to an agency when it is making a policy choice of some sort rather than simply settling a dispute; the open process allows for more cross-education among parties and mutual searches for solutions than might occur in a more formal process such as rulemaking. However, there are specific lessons for public officials from this particular case study.

b. Public agencies must be sure they have sufficient legal authority to use mediation. Public agencies, both federal and state, have numerous legal requirements constraining their activities. Many times these requirements cannot be bargained away. Since the heart of mediation is working together toward a consensual solution, an agency must be sure that it has enough room to maneuver in order to negotiate in that fashion. Generally, in a specific dispute, as long as an agency has the legal authority to settle a lawsuit or a contested case, it probably has the authority to use mediation to come up with a proposed settlement. In a more general policy decision, agencies are usually operating with broad latitude and discretion, so that they can use any process, as long as it is sufficiently public, to inform themselves of the range of options and to decide upon one.

At the time of this mediation, the State Water Resources Department ("Department") had sufficient authority in its statutes and administrative rules to adjourn a contested case for up to a year and to negotiate a stipulated order. Since then, the Department has promulgated even more explicit rules for using mediation. The other agencies, because they were essentially participating as parties in the State's contested case proceeding, had sufficient negotiating authority as well, as long as they complied with other explicit mandates, such as those instigated by NEPA.

c. Agencies also need to integrate carefully mediation with legal and administrative requirements. This is closely related to the basic question of whether an agency has sufficient authority to mediate.

The Department had to act formally on the exchange application and the objections before it. The way that it accommodated both the mediation and its statutory and administrative rule requirements was to follow a three-step procedure. First, the Department officially initiated a contested case proceeding. A hearings officer was assigned, but the matter was then adjourned so the mediation sessions could take place. The hearings officer did not participate in the mediation sessions. Step two was for the Department to participate fully in the mediation, through key policy-level staff, to represent the Department's interests and to make sure that the agreement being crafted was something the Department could adopt in its order. During the pendency of the mediation the hearings officer conducted regular status conferences to make sure the parties were proceeding diligently with the mediation. The mediators also submitted written and oral status reports to the Water Resources Commission during the pendency of the mediation to inform the Department of the issues being addressed, the progress being made, and the expected time of completing a final agreement. Finally, step three was for the Department to adopt the terms of the mediated agreement as its official order in resolving the contested case.

Integration with other legally required decisions was more difficult for the Bureau of Reclamation. The Bureau had both federal legislation and a completed EIS on the Umatilla Basin Exchange Project, so when its application to the state for the exchange order was protested, it had to negotiate a solution to hammer out the details of the exchange without compromising the basic terms of the proposed project and authorizing legislation. Because the project's basic components stayed the same, the Bureau could do so consistent with the Project Act and without needing to revise the EIS.

However, the Bureau could not substitute the mediated agreement for future NEPA compliance and could not bargain away EIS requirements on the boundary changes needed to address the water-spreading problem. Furthermore, the water-spreading matter was a westwide issue, not limited to the Umatilla Basin, so the Bureau had to be careful not to lock itself into any arrangement that would prejudge or constrain resolution of the larger issue. In this regard, its job of assessing its authority and integrating the mediated solution with other legal requirements was much trickier than that of the state water agency.

d. Public agencies using mediation must pay close attention to clarifying their role in any mediation. Can an agency be a full participant, laying its cards on the table and negotiating freely, or must it hold back, observing the other parties and "saving" its authority for later official action? If the agency is too active in negotiating and compromising, it may be accused of abdicating its legal responsibilities. . . . If an agency carefully walks the line between these extremes, it can effectively use mediation as a helpful tool of governance. . . .

All of the agencies in the Umatilla mediation achieved a good balance. They used the process both to educate and to learn from the other parties, and they participated as equal parties to the extent allowed by law. At the same time, they clearly reserved final authority where they had to for separate formal decisions. . . .

e. The challenge of party identification and representation is especially critical for public-policy makers desiring to use mediation. Because agencies are accountable generally to the "public," it is sometimes difficult for them to cut specific deals with individual parties. This is not so much of a problem when a particular adjudication is involved because in that case the central parties that the agency must deal with are clear and identified. In a more general public-policy mediation, the challenge will be greater to identify appropriate and representative interest groups.

In this case, the parties that Water Resources needed to respond to were clearly identified by the formal administrative process itself—the Bureau as the exchange applicant, the two protesters, and the other parties who requested party status. For the Bureau, the problem was a bit more complex. The irrigators served by this project and the Tribes impacted by the project were clearly important parties, as were the objectors to the Bureau's application. But because of the westwide impact of the Bureau's resolution of the water-spreading controversy, other parties, such as thousands of other irrigators and many other environmental groups, were certainly interested, though not directly involved. It would have been quite unworkable for these other interests to become part of this mediation, and yet the Umatilla solution cannot truly be final until those other matters are resolved. . . .

. . . .

5. Relationships Between the Lessons Learned and the Desired Public Goods

. . . .

a. Decision Comporting with Law and Public Values/Justice and Public Interest

The flexibility of mediation to depart from or supplement the law may produce a decision that comports well with certain public values and the public interest (at least where the public is adequately represented through the parties) but, in fact, does not comport with the law. Indeed, this is often the very reason for using mediation—to craft a solution that goes beyond what existing law prescribes, especially where the law and existing procedures are rigid or do not fully account for the parties' interests. This aspect of mediation is somewhat problematic; presumably we do not want wholesale avoidance of "the law" even when we think the law needs to be reformed. As long as this potential problem is recognized and understood by mediators, parties, and scholars, it should not detract from mediation's usefulness. When the formal law represents society's best approximation of how things should be, then perhaps mediation is not the most desirable form of dispute resolution because it allows the parties to ignore the law. But when the law is actually part of the problem because it has not evolved as fast or in the same direction as other important public values, the general public interest, or overall notions of justice (including the simple justice of preserving an ongoing relationship), then mediation can be an effective solution.

Thus, in water-rights disputes, where the law favors consumptive uses and rigidly assigns rights based on the arbitrary parameter of priority date, mediation can allow the parties to improve on the law and allocate the water more flexibly, incorporating instream needs and other important values. The same can be true for other complex multiparty natural-resource disputes, where parties can use mediation to craft creative resource allocation schemes not envisioned by existing law.

b. Precedent

The formal court system automatically produces precedent because results are officially recorded, reported, and generally adhered to in subsequent cases. However, since most disputes are settled out of court, this official precedent comes from only a few cases. Thus, diversion of additional cases to mediation would not appreciably affect the justice system's "output" of precedent.

Furthermore, mediation, particularly public-policy mediation, can produce precedent in its own right. When a public agency resolves a dispute through consensus and then implements the resolution through normal legal or administrative channels, the decision is publicly known and available as a model for use in other disputes as appropriate.

When no public agency is involved, there is the possibility of a "secret" resolution with no precedential value, but this is certainly no worse than the many formal disputes that settle out of court.

c. Fair Process and Outcome/System Credibility

It is clear that in order for a mediated solution to be more "just" than a legal solution, the process must include all necessary parties and be carefully integrated with all appropriate legal requirements. Further, it must resolve all disputed issues, and it must be conducted by skillful mediators adept at helping the parties deal fairly with each other and reach a truly just solution. When the mediation involves a public agency, the agency must take special care to assure that the process ascertains the public interest by fully airing all necessary issues.

NOTES AND QUESTIONS

(1) For additional materials on environmental mediation, see Gail Bingham, *Resolving Environmental Disputes: A Decade of Experience* (1986); Allan R. Talbot, *Settling Things: Six Case Studies in Environmental Mediation* (1983); Lawrence E. Susskind, *Environmental Diplomacy: Negotiating More Effective Global Agreements* (1994); Lawrence Susskind, Lawrence Bacow & Michael Wheeler, eds., *Resolving Environmental Regulatory Disputes* (1983). For additional discussion of public policy mediations, see Lawrence Susskind, Sarah McKearnan & Jennifer Thomas-Larmer eds., *The Consensus Building Handbook: A Comprehensive Guide to Reaching an Agreement* (1999); Lawrence Susskind & Jeffrey Cruikshank, *Breaking the Impasse: Consensual Approaches to Resolving Public Disputes* (1987).

(2) What are some of the things that are special about the mediation of environmental disputes?

(3) What commonalities do you see between mediation of environmental disputes and mediation of the type of community dispute described by Lela Love and Cheryl McDonald?

(4) Do you agree with Ms. Neuman's assessment about the successes and failures of the Umatilla River mediation?

§ K MEDIATION IN OTHER SOCIETIES

HO'OPONOPONO: SOME LESSONS FROM HAWAIIAN MEDIATION

11 Negotiation J. 45 (1995)[*]

By James A. Wall, Jr. & Ronda Roberts Callister

Are you willing to kala your brother?
Free him entirely of this entanglement of your anger?
Remember, as you loosen your brother from his trespasses,
you loosen yourself, too.
As you forgive, you are forgiven

— Mediator's questions in ho'oponopono
(Pukui, Haertig and Lee 1982: 63)

. . . .

Overview

Ho'oponopono is an integral and ancient part of Polynesian culture. The Polynesians, it is believed, migrated from central Asia, through the islands east of China into Polynesia. They migrated to the Tonga-Samoa region where the roots of the Polynesian culture emerged. From there they migrated through the Marquesas, probably landing in Hawaii between 100 and 750 A.D. Since they had no written language and were migrating to unoccupied islands or to ones whose inhabitants were also illiterate, the Polynesians left no precise records of these routes.

As they settled some islands and explored many others, the Polynesians became skilled at fishing, hunting and farming. Men had their tasks—mainly hunting and fishing—and women theirs; however, there were no specific day-to-day routines or strong divisions of labor within the sexes. The Polynesian social organization stressed blood kinship and accorded high status to the elders (chiefs) as well as to the priests.

For Hawaiians, Western contact first occurred in 1778 with Captain Cook's arrival. Christian missionaries followed in the 1820's and 1830's, and many Hawaiians eventually converted to Christianity. However, their religious practices typically were semi-Christian, involving a blend of traditional Hawaiian religion, superstition, and Christian rituals.

Because they had no writing, the Polynesians, at the time of Western contact, were heavily dependent on oratory in their day-to-day lives and for recording their history. Public speaking was used to welcome guests, as well as to solve fishing issues, to coordinate with neighboring villages, and to resolve disputes.

As they migrated and fished, the Polynesian Hawaiians developed skills as navigators and sailors. . . .

Conflict and Its Resolution

Sailing, linked with the Polynesian oral tradition, gave rise to a strong use of metaphors. One most relevant to the study of conflict resolution is "entanglement." To the fisherman, sailor, or navigator, "entanglement" has an unequivocally negative connotation. A tangled fishing line requires hours of tedious unraveling, probably a lost fish or two, and the potential loss of the entire fishing line or net. When tacking, a tangled rope can snap a boat's mast. And for a sea turtle, entanglement in the net means death.

Drawing from these observations, the Hawaiians began using the term "entanglement" to describe interpersonal conflict. Accordingly, conflict resolution was referred to as ho'oponopono, "disentangling" or "putting things right." For the most part, ho'oponopono was intended and used for resolving intra-family disputes. A survey conducted in 1976 reported that in households containing persons of self-defined Hawaiian ancestry, more than one-third engaged in ho'oponopono. However, over the years ho'oponopono has been used frequently to resolve any interpersonal conflict. It is also currently used to establish the penalties and restitution for repeat criminal offenders.

Like the process of mediation in any society, ho'oponopono is highly variant. Its users—both today and in the past—employ many different techniques and vary the combinations and sequencing to fit the situation. This being the case, the unique archetype of ho'oponopono cannot be specified. However, numerous reports and case studies of ho'oponopono have been collected, which yield a representative example of the steps that are typically used. In general, ho'oponopono consists of twelve steps (see table 1), each having a distinct origin or purpose.

Table 1

> ### Steps in Ho'oponopono
>
> 1. Gathering of the disputants by a "high status" family or community member who knows the parties.
> 2. Opening prayer to the gods (or God).
> 3. A statement of the problem to be solved or prevented from growing worse.
> 4. Questioning of involved participants by the leader.
> 5. Replies to the leader and a discussion channeled through the leader.
> 6. Periods of silence.
> 7. Honest confession to the gods (or God) and to each of the disputants.
> 8. Immediate restitution or arrangements to make restitution as soon as possible.
> 9. The "setting to right" of each successive problem that becomes apparent as ho'oponopono proceeds. (Repeating the above steps if necessary).
> 10. Mutual forgiveness of the other and releasing him or her from guilt, grudges and tensions from the wrong-doing.
> 11. Closing prayer.
> 12. A meal or snack.

Rationale for the Steps

For the first step, the goal is straightforward: to address the dispute that is generating stress, hard feelings, ill will, etc. Not only does this dispute have undesirable outcomes for each party, it is also thought to bind or "tangle" the disputants in anger or guilt, which in turn causes them to become ill. Moreover there is also the fear that the gods or family guardians (amuakua) may be offended by the conflict.

Step 2 as well as Steps 7 to 11 have distinct religious connotations. Early Hawaiians believed in gods who played an active part in the world. After they were "converted" to Christianity, the Hawaiians tended, more or less, to believe in one God who also was an active player in their daily lives. For years following conversion to Christianity, Hawaiians would try Western ways of solving problems (or illnesses) but if these were unsuccessful, they would revert to traditional approaches.

In modern times, we generally consider superstition and belief in a variety of nature gods to be pagan; for Hawaiians, it was quite logical and functional. When watching a seed grow, hoping for fish to bite, or experiencing heavy seas, ancient Hawaiians tried to comprehend nature as godlike forces. Lacking scientific explanations, they interpreted nature as godlike forces. And as other early people, they attempted to understand, obey, and draw assistance from these gods.

This superstitious approach was in many ways beneficial, for it assisted the ancients in adapting to their environments. For example, the ancient Hawaiians selected farming that Laka liked; that is, land that was already supporting wild vegetation. They planted sweet potatoes in the months when they grew best, months that belonged to Kane-puaa, the special sweet potato god.

The Hawaiians, as they sought to obey and pacify the gods, were actually learning and remembering how to adapt to natural forces. In addition, invoking the gods' names strengthened generation-to-generation oral traditions. Consider, for example, the information about potato-planting, which is rather dull and could easily be forgotten. But a dictum from a priest or elder that Kane-puaa will be angry if you fail to plant correctly is more memorable. And to repeat stories of those who angered Kane-puaa and lost their crops—by planting at the wrong time—further anchors the memory.

Just as it assisted the Hawaiians in their agricultural, superstition aided them in their interpersonal relations. Harmony and cooperation were necessary in their society—for fishing, building ships, or sailing long distances. The ancients probably could recognize this and passed it along to future generations, via religion and superstition. Consider, for example the message that "harmony is good; and conflict is bad." Like objective potato-planting information, this is dull and easily forgotten. On the other hand, the belief that the gods did not like social entanglements and thereby punished disputing— entangled—people with physical illness is both compelling and memorable.

As Steps 2, 7 and 11 reveal, the Hawaiians' superstitions and religion serve as strong cleats for ho'oponopono. The traditional process begins with an opening prayer (step 2) wherein the gods are recognized and asked for assistance in identifying and resolving the problem(s). This prayer also reminds those present that there are powers and goals greater than themselves.

The honest confession to the gods of the wrongdoing, grievances, grudges, or resentments may perplex an outsider. Granted, gods are significant players and can be called upon for assistance. But why must the disputants confess to them? There are several plausible replies to this question.

One is that the gods do not like conflict or entanglements. In nature, entanglement is bad, and analogously, parties who socially entangle themselves offend the gods. The offense must therefore be acknowledged, and forgiveness must be sought. As the disputant takes these steps, the transgressions against the spirits, gods, and other humans disappear.

A more secular explanation is that conflict and the resultant guilt disrupt social activities. Such disruptions, perhaps because of supernatural nudgings, lead to failed turtle-hunting, injury, or illness to the disputants or to third parties. The gods, it is felt, can rectify these social and physical problems; however, confession is necessary before they will do so. That is, some form of coaxing or reciprocity is in order.

A final explanation is one of catharsis. Expressing one's guilt in a public forum and asking for forgiveness releases tensions. For the Hawaiians this public forum encompasses more than the grievant and the observing family members; it also includes the transcendental, observing, gods.

In step 11, the closing prayer is offered to thank the gods for their assistance and to verify the process or outcome. It also pressures the disputants to hold to the agreement, that is, to close the door on the evil, to keep it from returning.

Complementing these three supernatural steps are four procedural ones: namely Step 3, statement of the problem; Step 4, questioning of the participants; Step 5, controlled discussion; and Step 6, periods of silence.

The common element in these four steps is the leader's dominant role. She or he states the problem, questions the participants, requires that all replies and discussion be channeled through her or him, and requires silence. The roots or beginning of this structuring are somewhat ambiguous. It could stem from the leader's high status or manna (personal power and effectiveness). Or it could surface from the idea that the leader is the intermediary between the human disputants and the gods. Since all human-god communication must be channeled through him, the leader has the right to serve the same role between mortals.

While the genesis of this strong leader-as-intermediary procedure will probably never be known, the current intent of Steps 3-5 is quite clear. They maintain control. One of the core presumptions or requirements of ho'oponopono is that the participants maintain control over their aggressive feelings. Disputants can cry, express guilt, or accuse the other party, but they must also control displays of temper and hostility.

The periods of silence (Step 6) promote self-reflection and cool tempers. But more importantly, they are intended to pool emotional-spiritual forces for a common—dispute resolution—process. The roots for this step can be traced to three different factors. First, the Hawaiians have learned perhaps through trial and error that periods of silence do assist conflict resolution. Secondly, Polynesians and Hawaiians believe in an individual "force" or spiritual forces that can be utilized or combined to solve (or exacerbate) problems. Finally, recall that the Hawaiians extrapolate heavily from their nature experiences. Early Polynesians no doubt learned the value of silently contemplating the ebb and flow of the waves or patiently studying the currents. Such silent reflections guided them, helped them learn, and consequently kept them from being washed to sea. Given its value in the natural order silent reflection came to be a guide in interpersonal affairs.

Three of the later steps have a more interpersonal orientation. In Step 8 the immediate restitution—setting things right—or evening the keel corrects the current problem and sets the stage for continued harmony. The word "immediate" is significant. Since the Polynesian society was verbal, agreement or contracts were not written down. Therefore, the more immediate the restitution, the less confusion or forgetting, and thereby a reduction of future conflict.

Step 9 is thought of as "peeling the onion" (*mahiki*) dealing with each layer of difficulty one at a time; usually it involves repeating earlier steps several times. Ho'oponopono may last for several hours or even several days, ending in resolution. Or, it may be left incomplete.

Many times, the paring reveals lengthy cause-and-effect chains of events. For example, in finding one person burned a neighbor's field because he was angry the elder might discover the anger stemmed from the neighbor's insult to the arsonist's wife, who previously had allowed her children to romp in the neighbor's garden. As this example illustrates, mahiki detects submerged currents in the conflict: some are peripheral, others flow from the original conflict, a few are not related. During ho'oponopono, all of these issues are brought to the surface.

In Step 10, the emphasis is on mutual forgiveness and releasing the other from entanglement. For complete conflict resolution, the restitution and the objectively setting things right is not sufficient. Ho'oponopono requires that everything must be set right spiritually as well as interpersonally. Accompanying this alignment must be a freeing of the other—the forgiven one—from the entanglement of one's anger.

From a Western perspective, this forgiveness serves a useful purpose for the offending party. She or he feels better because she knows the party ceases to hold a grudge. From a Polynesian perspective there is an additional payoff: the forgiveness also frees the offending party from potential harm. Recall that the ancients felt that misconduct was punished by physical illness. In a similar vein, they believed that holding a grudge could be damaging, because the wrongdoer, along with the transgression and the wronged, are all linked together—entangled—until the transgression and grudges are dispelled.

In the final step comes the capstone meal, which is a thanksgiving to the gods for their assistance. Originally this was a feast, but today, a simple meal is considered adequate. No alcohol is permitted here or at any other phase of ho'oponopono, because of the belief that people will not adequately control their feelings while under the influence of alcohol.

Lessons for the Western Mediator

Extrapolation from ho'oponopono to other cultures yields dual benefits, the first of which is a broader perspective toward mediation. Typically, Westerners view mediation from a logical perspective, one which stems in part from our written tradition. A look at ho'oponopono reveals how a society reliant on oral tradition can also develop and maintain effective community mediation.

A second and more practical payoff is that several steps of ho'oponopono could be adapted by Western mediators as part of their regular procedure. Of particular interest would be the three "process" steps—Step 4. Questioning of involved participants by the leader; Step 5. Replies to the leader and discussion channeled through the leader; and Step 6. Periods of silence.

The first two steps allow emotions to be expressed. In most conflicts, emotions play a central role, serving as causes, effects, and as critical elements of the core process; however, the dominant practice in mediations in the United States and other Western nations is to downplay the emotional facet, emphasizing the logical aspects. Allowing the disputants to discuss the conflict with the leader provides a more balanced approach; it allows an emotional release, but it is controlled: the questions, replies, and periods of silence regulate the catharsis. Consequently, there is a balance between the emotional release and process control.

Step 9—the "setting to right" of each successive problem that becomes apparent as ho'oponopono proceeds—also has potential payoffs for Western mediations.

Western conflict resolution is generally legalistic; that is, Western mediators tend to slice away peripheral issues, driving to the point. In ho'oponopono these adjacent issues are always explored as the parties explain their overall actions and emotions. For example, in the dispute about the burned field, the conversation might drift to the idea that the wife's own garden was not a very good one. Or the neighbor's father had given the garden to him just before he died and asked him to care diligently for it. Such drifting to adjacent, perhaps irrelevant, topics does have benefits: like Steps 4 and 5, it allows for catharsis. At times such conversations may unearth some significant but neglected components of the conflict. Even if it fails to reveal hidden primary elements, the "peeling back" can provide useful information to mediators (e.g., which facets of the conflict are most important to the disputants). And it affords the mediator or the opponent an opportunity to hear and openly empathize with the disputants' concerns.

A final potential application of ho'oponopono is more easily advised than administered. Step 10—mutual forgiveness of the other and releasing him or her from guilt, grudges and tensions from the wrong doing—is not a tack a mediator can necessarily institute. Typically in Western mediations, apologies are avoided because they cause embarrassment and imply that one person is "good" and the other "bad." Our mediators simply help to fabricate an agreement that both sides purport to support. But many of these agreements are not implemented successfully because one party dislikes the other, holds a grudge, or believes the other party, because of rancor, will eventually seek retribution.

Sincere mutual forgiveness will reduce such impediments. In China and South Korea, this approach is easily executed because an apology, especially mutual apology, saves face rather than embarrasses. In Western cultures, people tend to link apology with admission of fault, shame and embarrassment; therefore, implementation of this step will be difficult. But it is not an impossible goal, as is shown by victim-offender mediations, where offenders generally express regret and offer an apology to the victim. When the apology is accepted, the offender often feels released from the guilt, and the victim, in turn, harbors less enmity toward the offender.

Conclusion

In closing, we offer some words of caution to our prescriptions. Most of the steps in ho'oponopono require mediators to hold substantial power, and implementation of these steps increases this power. When empowered, the mediators must avoid a variety of power-based pitfalls; namely, they should not disrupt a conflict that is moving toward resolution on its own; they should not press their own interests; and they should not impose an agreement.

Failure to heed this caution will teach our mediators a lesson the Polynesians learned centuries ago: Applying force to an entanglement—be it a rope or relationship—appears initially to improve the problem. Yet it usually makes it worse.

ENHANCING AUTONOMY FOR BATTERED WOMEN: LESSONS FROM NAVAJO PEACEMAKING

*47 UCLA L. Rev. 1, 34-38 (1999)**

By Donna Coker

Traditional Navajo thinking does not separate religious and secular life; rather, all of life is sacred and imbued with spiritual meaning. The concept of *k'e*, fundamental to Navajo common law, expresses an interdependence and respect for relationships between humans, the natural world, individuals and family, and individuals and clan members. This interdependence operates to define Navajo common law, which derives from relational frameworks in which "responsibilities to clan members are part of a sophisticated system that defines rights, duties, and mutual obligations." "The individual and the community are part of the kinship that exists among all life forms and the environmental elements. Harmony is the desired result of the relationship with all life forms, including humans, animals, and plants." Relational justice does not necessitate the subordination of the individual, however. Traditional Navajo thought and law are radically egalitarian and eschew coercion. Individuals do not speak for others, not even for members of their own family.

These concepts of relational justice provide the foundation for the practice of Peacemaking. In Peacemaking, parties meet with a peacemaker and others who have either a special relationship to the parties (e.g., family and friends) or relevant expertise (e.g., alcohol treatment counselors and hospital social workers). Each participant is given a chance to describe the problem that the petitioner has identified as the reason for the session. The peacemaker then leads the group in developing recommendations and agreements designed to ameliorate or solve the problem.

Peacemaking is structured around procedural steps. It begins with an opening prayer in both Navajo and English. After the peacemaker has explained the rules, the petitioner is allowed to explain his or her complaint. The respondent is then asked to respond to the petitioner's complaint. Next, the peacemaker provides a "[b]rief overview of the problem as presented by the disputants." Family members and other participants, including traditional teachers, may then join the discussion, providing their description or explanation of the problem(s).

The peacemaker, usually chosen by his or her chapter, is a respected person with a demonstrated knowledge of traditional Navajo stories. He or she must be someone who possesses the power of persuasion, because peacemakers do not judge or decide cases. Their power lies in their words and their influence. Peacemakers "show a lot of love, they use encouraging words, [when you] use [Navajo] teaching to lift [participants] up you can accomplish a lot, [if you] are very patient."

Peacemaking may be hard for outside observers to understand, because it seems to combine so many different things: mediation, restorative justice, therapeutic intervention, family counseling, and Navajo teaching. Under-standing is also made more difficult because of the significant differences in the practice of various peacemakers and the different approaches used for different kinds of problems. Peacemaking practice is fluid, flexible, and thoroughly practical, fitting the process to the situation. As Phil Bluehouse, coordinator for the Peacemaker Division, relates:

> [I]f there's no flexibility [in Peacemaking], we'll be doing a disserv-ice. . . . [I] prefer [the] middle ground leaning more towards flexibil-ity, because to me, that's the nature of the human being. . . . I encouraged fluidity over the process. Be dynamic, be explorative. . . . The court[s] compartmentalize, its this kind of case or that kind of case. I say, we're dealing with human beings . . . .

The *Peacemaker Court Manual* also stresses the need for flexibility:

> It cannot be stressed, repeated or urged enough that the Peacemaker Court . . . is not frozen in its present form forever. As an experiment which has been carefully built upon Navajo custom and tradition, we will have to see whether it meets the needs of the Navajo People . . ., and we will have to see what changes need to be made.

Peacemaking is a formal part of the Navajo legal system, developed and overseen by the Navajo Nation judiciary. There are two primary routes by which cases reach Peacemaking: court referral and self-referral. Criminal cases may be referred by the court as the result of diversion or as a condition of probation. The Domestic Abuse Protection Act creates special rules for domestic violence protection order cases: A referral to Peacemaking must be approved by the petitioner, and the peacemaker must have received special domestic violence training. In all other civil cases, the rules allow courts to refer cases to Peacemaking over a party's objection, but in practice judges seldom refer civil cases involving allegations of domestic violence unless both parties agree to the referral. In addition to court referral, Peacemaking may be initiated by a petitioner on a claim that he or she has been "injured, hurt or aggrieved by the actions of another." Self-referred cases make up the majority of Peacemaking cases. In a self-referred case, the peacemaker liaison seeks authorization from the district court to subpoena the respondent and all other necessary parties identified by the petitioner.

NOTES AND QUESTIONS

(1) After extensively analyzing domestic violence and the Navajo Peacemak-ing process, Professor Coker concludes that "Peacemaking is not perfect—no domestic violence intervention is perfect—but Peacemaking offers possibilities for women that are largely unavailable in other intervention strategies." She emphasizes that peacemakers define themselves as "fair but interested intervenors," which allows them to introduce norms, such as anti-misogny. The peacemaking process can also directly attack abusers' victimblaming and excusive statements. As well, peacemaking can increase victims' material and

spiritual resources by, for example, improving ties with family and providing referrals to counseling and social services. Professor Coker also examines lessons that can be learned from the Peacemaking process when we design informal domestic violence intervention strategies.

(2) In your view, what are some of the key similarities and differences between the Hawaiian Ho'oponopono process and mediation as it is practiced in other contexts in the United States?

(3) In your view, what are some of the key similarities and differences between the Navajo Peacemaking process and mediation as it is practiced in other contexts in the United States?

(4) How do the Hawaiian and Navajo processes compare to one another?

§ L   ON-LINE MEDIATION

TAKING MEDIATION ONLINE

Disp. Resol. Mag., Summer 1998, at 25 [*]

By Jeffrey Krivis

There have been a few breakthroughs in this century that have changed the course of our lives. Consider the automobile. It allowed us to travel from place to place faster, opening up many new opportunities for learning and growth. The telephone was another breakthrough. We could now communicate in an instant with our friends, neighbors and business associates wherever they were at any time. How about television and radio? Now we see information being transmitted in an entertaining and immediate manner. Get the picture?

Is it always in our best interest to apply these technological breakthroughs in every environment of our lives? For example, would it make sense for car manufacturers to install televisions in every car that comes off the assembly line? How about putting televisions in workplace cubicles of the Dilberts of the world? Some might say these applications are good things for society, others might argue that they are destructive and inappropriate.

Consider the latest and perhaps most notable discovery of this century, the microchip. This little Pacman-like object needs constant nourishment to survive, stopping off at various industries to snack on whatever needs improvement. On the way, the little bugger serves notice that we better use it or else there will be consequences to our personal fortunes.

What are we as an ADR community going to do with this little creature? As we look into the crystal ball of the future, does it make sense to bring the microchip into the mediation room, or will it be more of a hindrance than a useful tool to help mediators solve problems?

At this point in the development of digital technology, the computers are way ahead of the mediators and lawyers. Though the computer can do lots of interesting things such as putting someone's face on the screen at the same time we are asking probing questions, the marketplace hasn't shown enough interest in the technology to encourage the microchip handlers to promote these tools to lawyers on a mass scale. They would rather have us focus on the simple things the chip can do, such as word processing.

At the same time, the mediation community is training people in skills and techniques in person to person communication—active listening, questioning and facilitating negotiations which occur spontaneously. This requires warm bodies to work with, not a computer screen. The mediation community might argue that body language and other non-verbal techniques are critical to the success of a mediation, and cannot be achieved through computers.

Others might say that we cannot use computers to mediate because of the fear that confidential communications might never be secure. While that certainly is a consideration, has anybody ever wondered whether a tape device might be secretly planted in a mediation conference room? Or whether a phone that a mediator is using to speak privately with a party has been tapped? While I do not subscribe to this type of paranoia, the same response would hold true for computers.

Either we embrace the digital technology in ADR practice or we don't. If we do embrace the technology, how can it be effective to help a mediator sort through a litigated case?

I propose that many clients are truly interested in achieving closure in the most cost effective, efficient manner available. That might require substantial litigation with its commensurate costs, or it might just involve a little creativity on the part of the attorney.

Let us assume the client wants an early resolution to the dispute out of court, and the principals are located in different parts of the country. Would it not make sense to have the mediator use whatever technology is available to communicate and help solve the case? Certainly the telephone might be a first choice. Asking the attorneys to submit position statements over the Internet could also be considered.

After preliminary information is exchanged, it would be valuable to allow the mediator to converse with the parties privately, as in caucus, through either electronic mail or the instant messenger system currently available on America Online. For the cost of a local phone call, a tremendous amount of communication takes place and allows the mediator to diagnose the problem and come up with suggested approaches to solving the case.

First Things First

The first step in the online process is to send the parties a mediation agreement which should include not only the standard confidentiality language, but specific rules about responding to email, including: (1) that all communications shall go through the mediator and not to communicate with each other without permission from the mediator; (2) that the mediator shall be notified of all times when a party will be away from the computer for more than 24 hours.

The Position Statements

Next, ask all parties to submit to you a brief, confidential position statement which you will use to analyze the issues and set an agenda. This is the first critical piece of information in the case for the mediator and sets the tone for the rest of the online mediation. Based on the position statements, your job is to come up with a concise, balanced summary of the dispute. This is quite difficult because you will be tempted to lean toward one side or the other. Your statement should be accompanied by an agenda of issues.

You then ask each side to approve your statement of the case and agenda. They have the right to make comments or changes. This might require some back and forth communication until you arrive at a frame for the case to which both sides agree. The success of getting both sides to agree on the statement and agenda is the key to unlocking the dispute.

Select Your Style

I have found that in cases where the mediation is being conducted strictly through email (not teleconferencing), it is critical to be extremely facilitative, defining the issues in a narrow sense and focusing primarily on the legal issues. This initial approach gathers the most information for the mediator and helps the parties feel comfortable. Under no circumstances would it be useful to yield to the temptation to give an advisory opinion or predict the outcome too soon, or you may lose one or more of the parties.

Gathering Information

At this stage, gathering information requires thoughtful, articulate questions which allow the parties time to carefully analyze their responses. Indeed, the mediator must be especially skilled and knowledgeable in the area of law in which the parties are operating, since the personal dynamics usually available in an "in person" mediation are not be available. As a result, the mediator must follow up each answer with a more in depth question which reflects both the mediator's knowledge of the law and a sense of understanding or compassion about the parties' positions. At the same time, it is important to help the parties become realistic about their chances of success by asking the tough questions.

During this ongoing stage, there will be opportunities to learn more about the driving forces behind the positions taken by the parties. Though it is useful to learn about those forces and they could assist in crafting an ultimate settlement, it is easy to get off track with matters that might not be relevant to the dispute and will not help you reach agreement. Be careful as you drift into this area but don't be afraid to test the waters. The goal is to ask questions that lead to a common goal, and then to float trial balloons that might be used later in the mediation as the subject of a proposal.

Synthesize Materials

As you begin to synthesize and understand the information that you have gathered, the case will start to turn on an issue or two which will become readily apparent after a short period of asking questions. As the issues start to unfold, one approach I have used successfully is to ask the parties the following questions:

1. Where do you think you disagree most strongly?

2. In those areas where you disagree, is there any objective criteria you can suggest to develop a fair and constructive voluntary resolution?

3. From your perspective, what important understandings did you think you had when you originally got involved with the other party? (Time, money, allocation of risk, division of responsibilities, rights and duties, etc).

4. What important shifts in these understandings happened as the situation developed, and where do you think their perspective differs from yours?

5. In areas where you have sharply different perspectives, what evidence could you present that would be credible to the other party to help them see your view? (Written industry standards, notes, witnesses, etc.).

6. What criteria will you use to determine when an agreement proposed in this case is "fair?"

7. How do you think the other party realistically views their chances of success in this case?

8. What do you think the other party views as a fair outcome in this case for both sides?

These questions can be asked all at once or at strategic intervals depending on the progress of the case. The goal is to keep the conversation moving forward and to search for clues so that you can begin to develop a proposal for settlement.

The Neutral Evaluation

At this point, the parties will be looking to the mediator for direction and leadership. Your role as a facilitative mediator is over. It's time to become evaluative and to ask each side if they would permit you to make a neutral recommendation to which each party can confidentially respond. Tell them that if both parties agree with the recommendation, you have a deal. If not, you continue the process.

Parties can feel comfortable agreeing with part or all of the recommendation. The evaluation should be specific and supported extensively with facts and law if applicable. The timing of this recommendation is important because it has to be done only after the parties have total confidence in the mediator, and at a moment in the process where there is a sense of not wanting to lose the opportunity to settle.

Final Thoughts

Life is sometimes difficult, particularly in the civil justice system, and the process of confronting and solving litigated problems is not always perfect. As lawyers, we have an obligation to the client to look for tools that will aid us in achieving the client's goals. A good mediator with a willingness to explore the use of digital communication in a case where the parties are geographically challenged could provide the key that unlocks the dispute.

NOTES AND QUESTIONS

(1) For another good article discussing some of the existing online ADR providers, see Ethan Katsh, *Online ADR Becoming a Global Priority*, Disp. Resol. Mag., Winter 2000, at 6. Some of the mediation websites discussed are: www.internetneutral.com, www.ombuds.org, and www.onlinemediators.com. For additional articles discussing online dispute resolution, see a series of articles on ADR in Cyberspace contained in Vol. 15, No. 3 of the Ohio St. J. on Disp. Resol. (2000).

(2) Mr. Krivis suggests that mediators employ evaluative mediation online, during later stages of the mediation. Do you think evaluative mediation is any more or less appropriate online than in person?

(3) What do you see as the potential benefits of on-line dispute resolution ("odr") for mediation? Do you think odr poses any risks to mediation as we have known it?

Mediation Certification

- not required <u>usually</u>
- may be needed for some court programs

- P.P.↑ = consumer protection

  = protect reputation of the field

- cert. is not liscensing

- p.p. ↓ = inappropriate barriers

  = meaningless rubber stamp

Chapter 11

MEDIATION'S PROMISE

§ A   INTRODUCTION

For more than three decades, mediation has been used to respond to some of the most serious policy and social challenges of our times. Some initiatives were experimental only; other efforts led to systematically incorporating mediation's use into multiple settings. This sustained activity raises two important considerations: do career opportunities exist for persons who want to devote their professional lives to mediating? and (2) is mediation's use, and the need for mediators, likely to continue?

§ B   CAREERS IN MEDIATION

[1]   INDEPENDENT MEDIATION PRACTICES

All parties to a mediation wants an *experienced* mediator to assist them. But the Catch-22 is: how does one gain that experience? Unlike a traditional legal practice in which law firm partners utilize associates to assist in the research and presentation of a case, mediating is a solo activity. How can a mediator and potential client become linked?

There are several avenues: a person who participates in an established law practice or business activity can, over time, develop relationships with clients and other persons who might have a future need for a mediator. A mediator, much like other professionals and business personnel, may engage in networking activities by participating actively in social or community activities. Many courts, governmental agencies (both federal and state), and not-for-profit organizations develop "panels" of mediators. In some instances, the governing agency appoints a panel member to mediate a case, while in other situations it provides the parties with a list of selected panel members and leaves it to the parties to choose their mediator; under either scenario, becoming a panel member is the critical avenue for gaining service as a mediator. Finally, a person often gains significant experience and recognition by providing pro bono mediation services for community-based mediation programs, school peer mediation projects, or Court-sponsored "Settlement Week" activities.

Developing an independent mediation practice requires energy and patience; because parties understandably seek mediators with experience, one must not underestimate the challenge of embarking on a solo mediation practice. While Section [2], *infra*, describes more bountiful, though less direct, avenues for gaining employment opportunities in the mediation field, it is important to affirm that there is no one established avenue for pursuing this professional calling. The excerpts from Galton, Gonzalez, Curtis, and Chernick reflect the many different motivations, backgrounds, and roads they traveled to become respected practitioners.

James J. Alfini and Eric R. Galton, ADR PERSONALITIES AND PRACTICE TIPS

pp. 99, 101--02, 104--06

Eric R. Galton

American Bar Association—Section of Dispute Resolution (1998)[*]

Eric Galton is a mediator, arbitrator, and lecturer recognized throughout the United States as a leader in the Alternative Dispute Resolution field. . . .

My Personal Journey

. . . .

Upon reflection, I realize now that my entire early life history prepared me for my work as a neutral. . . .

In the summer before my senior year of high school, my then hometown of Plainfield, New Jersey experienced a terrible race riot. The National Guard was called in. The town was divided. People were afraid. Many of us never saw some of our friends again. Certain parts of town were off limits. I created a project called the Plainfield Reading Program. Black and white high school seniors, at first with police escorts, would go into an inner city youth center and work with seventh and eighth graders upgrading their reading skills. I still remember my seventh grade student, David. I helped him learn to write better and six months later David handed me a wonderful "book" of his poems. David taught me about diversity and how difficult and important it is to walk in someone else's shoes. I also remember our last month at the center. The police escorts were no longer necessary. Peace felt like a merciful and welcome rain and was so palpable that you could almost touch it and feel it.

A year later, I entered Duke at the height of the Vietnam war protests. I saw buildings taken over, the campus shut down, got on a bus to participate in the march in Washington D.C., and got tear gassed while waiting in a church for our bus ride back to North Carolina. I understood from that experience the curse of polarization and how even fair-minded people often failed to communicate effectively; i.e., a lot of talking and not much listening.

. . . .

My Professional Journey

If my personal experiences molded me to be a neutral, the kindness and inspiration of others and sheer dumb luck and good timing allowed me to become a neutral.

. . . .

In Texas, our founding father of ADR, and my mentor, was the Honorable Frank B. Evans, then Justice of the 14th Court of Appeals in Houston. Judge

Evans was my vice-chair of the State Bar of Texas Citizens Legal Education Committee.

A visionary State Bar of Texas President, Cullen Smith, appointed me, a five-year lawyer, to chair that committee and, recognizing I needed help, gave me Frank Evans as a vice-chair. One day, Frank asked me if I knew what ADR was. I did not. Frank explained ADR to me and asked me to sit in on the initial State Bar ADR planning meetings. Somehow, Judge Evans, through his sheer force of will and determination, managed to get our comprehensive ADR Act passed. I was with him the day the Governor signed the bill. Perhaps today it is passe' to have heroes; but, Judge Evans was and is mine. He inspired Texas lawyers and judges to give mediation a chance. And, Judge Evans opened the door which allowed me to transition from an eleven year litigator to a full-time mediator.

On a local level, the Honorable Joseph Hart, judge of the 126th Judicial District Court of Travis County, Texas, determined that Austin needed Settlement Week before it was legislatively mandated. Settlement Week is a process in which the courthouse shuts down for a week and docketed cases receive pro bono mediation from volunteer neutrals. Judge Hart named Paul Knisely and myself co-chairs of our first Settlement Week. We were generally clueless of what to do (but our colleagues in Tarrant County, who had already done several, helped us) and worried whether lawyers would submit cases and if they would settle. As it turned out, over 160 cases were submitted and well over 70% of those cases settled. Because of Judge Hart's determination and belief in the value of ADR to our citizens, Settlement Week proved to Austin lawyers that mediation actually worked. Thus, the mediation movement in Austin, and throughout Texas, was truly born.

. . . .

Mediation "Markets"

Basically, you will enter one of three distinct ADR markets: first, a "no market situation" in which no one makes a living doing "ADR"; second, a developing ADR market; or, third, an over saturated ADR market (yes, they really do exist). The realities of developing an ADR practice depend upon which sort of market you are entering.

. . . .

Over Saturated Market

An over saturated market is one in which several generations of mediators have entrenched themselves. This market has already ferreted out mediators who are deemed "unsuccessful." The remaining mediators have identifiable sectors of loyal clients. This market may have even, perhaps not expressly, identified mediators by style and the grade of complexity of a case (routine, complex, impossible). Mediators may be perceived as interchangeable within these subgroups or strata. I am also assuming that in such a market and in court annexed cases the *lawyers* select the mediator (in some venues, this is not the case).

In such markets, I see two wildly different approaches. They are as follows:

Develop a Niche. Certain types of disputes require a neutral with specific skills or expertise; i.e. family law, intellectual property, tax, etc. Or, certain services, even in an over saturated market, may not be available.

. . . .

Patience: Cream Rises to the Top. Alternatively, you do not want to be identified in a niche and you believe that you can compete heads up with the local talent. I would suggest the following plan:

- Be patient. Do not quit your day job.

- Contact lawyers you really know well, advise them of your training and commitment, and ask for a tryout. Inevitably, their preferred neutrals will have scheduling conflicts.

- When you finally get the call, excel and resolve the dispute. As a general rule, each successful mediation creates four new ones. . . .

Developing Market

In a developing market, others have gone before you, created the potential for the market, and have developed something of a following.

Assuming you have received your training and made an informed decision that mediation is for you, I would suggest the following approach:

- Keep your day job. You do not know how the market will respond to your efforts nor do you know whether you will succeed as a mediator or enjoy the practice.

- Do a direct mail piece to those colleagues you really know. Outline your training, your commitment, and specify your fee structure.

. . . .

- Should the courts in your jurisdiction maintain a list of qualified mediators, do what is necessary to get on such a list.

- Consider developing an identity as a "specialist" in a particular area.

No Market

If you think about it, the maximum opportunity and greatest difficulty in creating a mediation practice exists in a venue in which no one has established a viable mediation practice.

In these venues, most people will advise you that you cannot succeed. Depending upon your personality, such naysaying may be music to your ears. But, you need to exercise your communication skills and find out why people believe you will not succeed.

Again, my frame of reference is court-annexed mediation, so the questions I would ask are in that context and are as follows:

- Are the local judges opposed to mediation and why? If judges are opposed, you need to educate the judges about the value of the mediation process.

- Are local lawyers opposed to mediation and why? Most lawyers oppose what they do not understand. Again, your mission is to educate lawyers and explain that mediation is good for both their clients and them.

- Have others before you attempted to develop a mediation practice and failed? If so, why?

Your primary job will be to educate those who are in a position to refer cases. Anticipate skepticism, distrust, and ignorance. But, as a bright beacon in the fog, keep this one unmistakable truth in mind—most of the greatest skeptics and naysayers about the process become the most outspoken proponents of the process after a successful mediation.

James J. Alfini and Eric R. Galton, ADR PERSONALITIES AND PRACTICE TIPS

pp. 19–21, 23–27

STEVEN GONZALES

American Bar Association—Section of Dispute Resolution (1998) [*]

Steven Gonzales is deputy city attorney of Peoria, Arizona. He had three gubernatorial administrative law judge appointments with Senate confirmation by the age of 34, serving in Arizona, Colorado, and Michigan. . . . He is chair of the ABA Section of Dispute Resolution's Diversity Committee and participates in the ABA's Project Outreach, a school mediation project. Mr. Gonzales received his J.D. from Wayne State University and his M.A./B.A. from Michigan State University.

. . . .

I began my legal career as most attorneys, eager to gain courtroom seasoning. In time I became a prosecuting attorney, foe to hardened criminals in Battle Creek, Michigan, home of serial killers and far from my native and peaceful Detroit. My future distaste of litigation was signaled by one of my first cases as a young prosecutor. The case involved a riotous mob infuriated with a scrappy dog whose owner let him roam free despite his affection for scaring the bejeebers out of everyone in the county.

Unfortunately for the prisoner pooch, Michigan law permitted a judge to execute hairy felons, making this my first capital case. As fate would have it, he got off when a surprise witness, a French poodle named Fifi, testified to a hushed courtroom that he had been with *her* that night.

. . . .

Then I moved to Arizona, first living on the Navajo Indian Reservation, a land of immense beauty. As counsel to the Navajo Nation, I witnessed the impressive focus on unity of thought stressed by America's largest Indian Nation. This was a far cry from the old saying that there is not enough business in a small town for one lawyer, but there is always enough for two! Mediation it turns out, is a close cousin of Indian consultation.

. . . .

Of course there will always be a need for courts, lawyers and due process of law. That is not seriously in question. But our Republic is not so fragile that we must settle all disputes with judicial officers. The real issue is why offer a one-size-fits-all system? If every case is procedurally treated the same, then the neighborhood barking dog, requiring social unity, or a child custody case, needing sensitivity and other professional resources, are handled the same as insurance fender bender cases. Moreover, this has the effect of aggravating some smaller conflicts into bigger ones.

All this may have been tolerable when our population was smaller, lawsuits comparatively rare, and time not so precious. But it certainly is not designed for the coming century.

Yet legal professionals are leading the way, despite the reluctance of a few. It is probably fair to state that conflict resolution would never have gained such strength if it were not for many supportive lawyers, judges and legal scholars over the past 25 years.

So once you have accepted that mediation is generally beneficial to communities, for the legal profession and that it can become part of your legal skill-bank as well as a service your firm or organization can offer, how do you go about establishing the practice? Lawyers, never a dull lot, are learning to adapt to the changing practice.

Before practicing mediation the first lesson should be one of professional humility. Do not assume that because you have attended twenty years of settlement conferences, negotiated countless contracts, or even have judicial experience, that you are a trained mediator.

Mediation has its own training, language, professional associations, customs, ethical schemes and delivery systems. An experienced mediator can usually determine in an exchange of a few sentences whether a lawyer is trained in mediation or is deluded into thinking he or she learned mediation from participating in settlement conferences.

Start with professional training, at a minimum, the standard forty-hour basic course offered by many community mediation centers, some professional mediation firms, and a few public agencies. Then, do some volunteer mediation with another mediator, known as "co-mediation," preferably one who is well-experienced.

. . . .

Once trained, there are a variety of ways to incorporate mediation into your practice. One way I have enjoyed has been as counsel to a municipality in suburban Phoenix. This city is replete with all the familiar disputes of a rapidly growing community of 90,000.

Some of the "best" conflicts from which to learn are those neighborhood disputes that drive local police crazy. It is amazing how similar are the processes of conflict and resolution, whether involving neighborhood barking dogs (the City of Phoenix's mediation office fields an average of just over 100 barking dog complaints per month), contentious commercial disputes, or international tensions.

. . . .

Perhaps one of the most practical uses of mediation is between disputing employees. More and more employers are complementing the old ombudsperson office or even older grievance procedures with trained in-house mediators. In one large county government in Arizona, the procedure permits every single grievance to ultimately work its way up to the county CEO. Stacks of grievances pile up, overwhelming the senior staff. The county recently hired a lawyer-mediator to try to resolve this cumbersome procedure.

Services such as these enabled my practice to expand to include mediating neighborhood and employee disputes, citizen complaints, and negotiating on behalf of the city. In effect, it created a market within existing systems, inserted before matters get to court, rather than a court connected system.

. . . .

Attorneys may also maintain a mediation practice. When this route is selected a formalized office procedure should be developed. At the outset, mediation clients must be carefully educated to understand they are not retaining you as their lawyer and you cannot provide them legal advice or later serve as their attorney in the same case. . . .

Lawyers experienced in court administration and related disciplines can become involved in research, design and administration of conflict resolution systems. In between my departure from Michigan and move to Arizona, I served two years as an administrative law judge and manager of Colorado's workers' compensation system. During these years I co-designed a multi-tiered mediation and pre-hearing procedure for workers' compensation cases. The program was generally very well received by the bench, bar and parties. This should be no surprise to those who have had the pleasure of working with Colorado's outstanding and progressive bar.

Legal professionals trained and well-experienced in mediation can also teach or train. Although the market may be shaky and varies from community to community, there are many great opportunities. In addition to my legal and mediation practice, I am a visiting professor at a university in Europe. Several times a year I must sacrifice and go to Switzerland to teach American style mediation to graduate students. I have also trained eager judges in mediation in South America.

Attorneys, particularly with business, management or related experience or advanced degrees, can develop a business consultant practice. Conflict resolution is a perfect complement to business consultant training seminars.

Once your forms are printed and you are ready to foster peace among even the most inveterate of disputants, how do you find a market? There are options supplementing the obvious use of the yellow pages and local advertisement. One of my favorites is use of pro bono time. This both serves and gets you out into the community.

In my case I have trained high school students in peer mediation, taught mediation at a local community forum and helped design mediation programs for mayors, city councils and neighborhood associations. Some municipal and occasionally higher courts use lawyer mediators and maintain a list of approved neutrals, for mediating cases.

Experienced lawyers are best advised to build on contacts and strengths already established. Creating a specialized niche, especially in larger population centers, is one of the most time-honored forms of American business strategy. Mediation, at least in a widespread and formal fashion, is still new in most areas of commerce.

James J. Alfini and Eric R. Galton, ADR PERSONALITIES AND PRACTICE TIPS

pp. 49–52

DANA L. CURTIS

American Bar Association—Section of Dispute Resolution (1998) [*]

Dana L. Curtis mediates civil disputes with the American Arbitration Association Mediation Center in San Francisco in a wide range of substantive areas, . . . She began practice as a full-time mediator in 1991 with Mediation Law Offices in Mill Valley and served as Circuit Mediator with the U.S. Court of Appeals for the Ninth Circuit in San Francisco until 1997. . . .

I knew I wanted to be a mediator when I was introduced to mediation in a second-year law school course. My other courses, though interesting intellectually, minimized the role of the human being behind the legal claims. Mediation focused on the individuals involved and on the meaning they attached to the dispute. The parties' priorities could be the most important reference point for resolution. In addition to, or instead of, the rule of law, their concerns, needs, fears, hopes and desires all mattered. As well as seeing how mediation could better meet the needs of the parties than a litigated resolution, I realized that mediation better utilized my strengths. As a mediator, I could use relationship and communication skills I had developed in my first career as a teacher.

Full of enthusiasm for mediation, I asked my professor where to learn about mediating as a career. He referred me to Gary Friedman, a pioneer lawyer mediator and Director of the Center for Mediation in Law in Mill Valley, California. I sought Gary's advice about mediating employment and other commercial disputes. He encouraged me, but warned that such a career would be difficult to forge, as the application of mediation in civil disputes was uncommon at that time. He also noted that I seemed to have what it would take—the commitment to mediation and an entrepreneurial spirit, evidenced by the fact that I had entered law school as a single mother after moving to California from Idaho with my three children.

Gary advised me to remain committed, to be patient and to get litigation experience to enhance my credibility with lawyers and my understanding of

---

the legal process. Following his advice, after law school I clerked for a California Supreme Court associate justice and thereafter joined a large San Francisco law firm, practicing commercial and employment litigation in San Jose and San Francisco. I began as an enthusiastic associate and during much of my first year of practice seriously considered a long-term litigation career. Before long, my enthusiasm abated. The enormity of financial and human resources spent on litigation astounded me. The inefficiency of the discovery process (where the object, it seemed to me, was to provide the other side with as little information as possible), the lack of predictability and fairness of jury trials, and the failure of litigation to address the clients' true needs all left me disaffected.

In addition, the demands of big firm practice, the often sixty and sometimes eighty hour work weeks, and the isolation I experienced among 200 other big firm lawyers convinced me that I was not willing to sacrifice more years of "being" for "becoming." The idea of partnership became unthinkable. As one of my law school friends put it, partnership is like a pie eating contest where the prize is more pie.

I dreamed of mediating. Although I had trained as a mediator and had been teaching mediation for several years, I was unable to see a way to make the transition. During this time of profound dissatisfaction with my career, I spent an evening with four dear women friends, as I had been doing on a bimonthly basis for several years. That night I spoke of my life consumed with work, of the months without a day off, of the weeks in a hotel room, of the frustrations of a difficult trial and of the day-to-day failure of my career to provide deep, personal meaning for me. What followed caused me finally to initiate change in my life. One of my friends looked me in the eye and said, "Dana, you will die if you don't leave your job." I knew she was right. If not physically, I was dying spiritually. The next day, without knowing what else I would do, I gave notice that I would be leaving the firm.

A few days later, I ran into Gary Friedman on the street in San Francisco. When he discovered I was leaving my law practice, he invited me to meet with him. Over a series of meetings, I learned that he was becoming increasingly interested in mediation of civil disputes and would like to work closely with lawyers who were pursuing commercial mediation. Within a few months, I hung out my mediation shingle (literally!) at Gary's office in Mill Valley. There, I practiced mediation for two years with Laura Farrow, another lawyer who left the firm at the same time I did. It was an exciting time—the invigoration of moving from a high-rise Financial District office to a renovated house with rose bushes, even an apple tree, in the yard, where at last my whole heart was in my work, as well as the uncertainty of whether a mediation practice could actually support my family.

The years I spent at Mediation Law Offices enabled me to develop a successful practice and to build a foundation that has been important in my practice and in my teaching. By working closely with Gary, I became more effective and more reflective. Following most mediations, I would write a critique of the process and meet with Gary to reflect on the dynamic between the parties and within myself. I was also able to consult with Gary on the spot. At the outset of one early divorce mediation, for example, a couple told me they had come to ask me to write up an agreement they had already reached. Essentially, the agreement provided the husband would have custody of the children and all but $10,000 of their community property assets, which totaled about $300,000. I had been ready to launch into the first phase of mediation, discussing the process and helping the parties to decide if they wanted to go forward, but I was thrown by this request. Excusing myself to get some papers, I ducked into Gary's office and in three minutes worked out an approach that engaged the parties in discussion about the efficacy of their agreement without compromising my neutrality.

After two years at Mediation Law Offices, I had the opportunity to become a Circuit Court Mediator for the U.S. Court of Appeals for the Ninth Circuit in San Francisco. I was persuaded to leave private practice by the promise of an endless array of Federal cases to mediate and steady paychecks. In the Ninth Circuit Mediation Program, I worked with five other full-time mediators to resolve cases on appeal. It was a mediator's dream come true. We selected our caseload from hundreds of diverse civil appeals. On any day, we might conduct a telephone mediation in a securities case, an employment discrimination dispute, a products liability matter, an IRS appeal, a bankruptcy case or an insurance coverage dispute. Several times a month, I would mediate in person, often in complex multi-party disputes. It was a time of applying my experience and knowledge of a face-to-face mediation model, where the parties could reach understanding in order to craft a resolution that addressed their priorities, not just their assessment of their legal positions. I sought to provide more than a settlement conference. In fact, when I began to speak of legal argument in mediation as an *option*, not a *given*, I was surprised by how frequently the parties, and even their lawyers, agreed that discussing the law would not be productive. The first time I suggested that we may not want to discuss the law, the plaintiff (in an employment discrimination case) said, "Thank God! If I had to listen for five more minutes to the company's lawyer telling me what a rotten case I have, I'd leave!"

During the three years I worked at the Ninth Circuit, I mediated hundreds of appeals. I learned that it is never too late for mediation. It was not unusual for a case to have been in litigation for ten years or more—and still settle! I also learned the approach required of an appellate mediator: how to unravel a long history of misunderstanding; how to address the harm the parties inflict upon one another in litigation, which often eclipses the original grievance; how to use the parties' experience with numerous failed negotiations, settlement conferences and mediations to structure a mediation process that avoids repeating their failures. On a more practical note, I learned how to discuss the law, and especially legal issues unique to appeals, without crowding out other reference points for decision; I learned about effective facilitation of both distributional and interest-based negotiations; and I learned how to turn mandatory mediation into a voluntary process—and to believe in it!

A year ago, I left the Ninth Circuit to return to private mediation practice and to join the Negotiation and Mediation Program at Stanford Law School, where I am a lecturer teaching two mediation courses a year.

James J. Alfini and Eric R. Galton, ADR PERSONALITIES AND PRACTICE TIPS

pp. 43–46

RICHARD CHERNICK

American Bar Association—Section of Dispute Resolution (1998) ·

Richard Chernick is an arbitrator and a mediator. He is a member of the American Arbitration Association President's Panel for the Mediation of High-Stakes Cases and the Mass Tort Panel (both national) and the California Statewide Panel of Neutrals. He was formerly a partner at Gibson, Dunn & Crutcher where he specialized in commercial litigation and domestic and international arbitration. . . .

History

I was an associate and then a partner at Gibson, Dunn & Crutcher in Los Angeles, California from 1970 through 1994. My interest in dispute resolution grew out of a commercial litigation practice which emphasized "non-traditional" forms of litigation. As a young lawyer, I found that I was able to get significant trial experience which was not easily available to associates in large firms by working on commercial arbitrations. I was "first chair" in moderate-sized construction, commercial and entertainment arbitrations at a time when my peers were getting almost no courtroom experience at all.

I was drawn to the flexibility and informality of the arbitration process. I became familiar with the procedural rules governing arbitration, developed a reputation within my firm as having answers to difficult questions in the arbitration field and became our first ADR resource person before the term "ADR" had been coined.

Because of this expertise, I was consulted on many litigation assignments not involving traditional court processes. For example, when private judging became popular in California in the late 1970's, I was most often the person who was able to provide advice on process and procedural issues.

In the 1980's, I began to expand my arbitration practice to international matters. This was a direct outgrowth of my domestic arbitration practice. I conducted arbitrations under various institutional rules and in ad hoc (non-administered) processes. I tried several matters before the Iran-U.S. Claims Tribunal in The Hague.

As part of my work in arbitration and private judging proceedings I became skilled in drafting arbitration clauses and, later, dispute resolution clauses. Here again I became a resource for my firm in drafting and reviewing clauses; I provided some informal training to the transactional lawyers on do's and don'ts of clause drafting. I came to realize that the most effective pre-dispute agreements are a cooperative effort of the responsible transactional lawyer and an experienced litigator who understands the intricacies of arbitration and other process choices. I tried (with limited success) to sell this concept to my partners at every opportunity.

As my firm's expert on dispute resolution, I became its liaison with the Center for Public Resources (now the CPR Legal Institute); I was an early participant in CPR's excellent educational programs and seminars and was exposed to some of the best neutrals and trainers in the United States through CPR. It was there that I first learned, systematically, negotiation and mediation skills. (My law school curriculum included a then-innovative trial practice course, but it would be years before law schools began to teach negotiation, mediation and "ADR.")

The more I participated in ADR processes as a lawyer, the more the role of the neutral intrigued me. I began to volunteer as a settlement officer and mediator in court programs in the Los Angeles courts and as an arbitrator at the American Arbitration Association (as well as a judge *pro tem* in the Los Angeles Municipal and Superior Courts). I found that my skills as a trial lawyer were helpful to me as a neutral and that I was comfortable in that role.

I began to be selected occasionally by lawyers who knew me for assignments as a neutral in larger matters, and was actually compensated for my work in most of these cases. It was about this time that the AAA inaugurated its Large Complex Case Program, and I was selected for the Los Angeles Panel of Neutrals. . . .

Becoming a Neutral

It was in the early stages of this program, as I began to be selected somewhat regularly for cases as a sole arbitrator and occasionally as a mediator, that I began to think about neutral work as a full-time occupation. My firm had always been generous in allowing me to serve on volunteer panels and had voiced no objection to my increasing work as a compensated neutral in these cases. But as my calendar began to be more and more filled with neutral assignments, I realized that the potential for conflicts of interest in a firm as large as mine, and the lack of opportunity to leverage my time as a neutral, were eventually going to put me on a collision course with some of my partners who rightfully were responsible for promoting the firm's bottom line. I began to explore the possibility of withdrawing from my firm and setting up a free-standing arbitration and mediation practice.

I had been on the AAA National Board of Directors for several years and was aware of the changes that esteemed organization was undergoing. I spoke with the leadership at AAA to inform them of my intentions, and that conversation led quickly to a discussion of an exclusive relationship with AAA as a full-time neutral. Simply put, I would commit to bring all of my business to AAA and AAA would in turn agree to market my services, along with other AAA panelists, and to provide extra effort on my behalf because of my commitment of exclusivity.

I have never had a written agreement with AAA, but the relationship has been mutually beneficial from day one. I attract substantial mediation business which AAA administers for me and some arbitration submission cases; AAA promotes me through its California and National panels and provides, through the customary selection process, much of my arbitration business.

I also consult on dispute resolution issues with lawyers (clause drafting, process development, neutral selection) and companies (dispute system design); I also testify occasionally as an expert witness on dispute resolution issues. I do this work separate from AAA by mutual agreement.

Marketing

When I decided to become a neutral, I decided not to continue to practice law. Many neutrals edge into the field by trying over time to shift their practice from lawyering to neutral work in increments. I find this "straddle" to detract from the neutral's attractiveness as a neutral. Such a person seems not to be fully committed to the practice (or not successful enough to do it exclusively), the neutral also may be in the position of seeking business on Monday from colleagues who will be litigation adversaries on Tuesday. This is particularly problematic if the neutral is an arbitrator. Moreover, many lawyers will be reluctant to recommend a competitor for a neutral assignment because the neutral will often appear in a particularly favorable light to the referring lawyers' client.

As a result of this belief, I do not use "Esq." on my stationery or business cards. I am Richard Chernick—"Arbitrator and Mediator;" not "Richard Chernick, Esq.: Lawyer—arbitrator—mediator."

I market myself to lawyers by speaking and writing on dispute resolution issues. This is how I demonstrate my competence and knowledge as a neutral. My inclusion on many AAA specialty panels in areas in which I had litigation experience (commercial, employment, entertainment, real property, and law practice disputes) provides additional credibility.

I market myself to businesses, usually through their general counsel, much as described above. I also try to speak on programs which include business people in the audience. I teach ADR to non-lawyers and train mediators in the Los Angeles County Bar Association Dispute Resolution Services program, which includes a fair number of non-lawyers.

My most effective marketing tool is to impress the participants in each mediation and arbitration that I know my stuff: that I am experienced and comfortable in the particular process, that I am able to guide the parties through the process efficiently and effectively, and that with my assistance their objectives will be achieved. As I tried to do as a lawyer, I hope to convey the impression to each person who comes into contact with me that I am dedicated to a successful outcome.

NOTES AND QUESTIONS

(1) When trying to develop one's practice, what types of ethical dilemmas might a mediator encounter advertising one's services? Would sending

potential clients a complimentary ball-point pen or calendar bearing the mediator's name violate any ethical norms for mediators? If a mediator created a web-site, containing, among other things, her client list, would that be acceptable? *See* Chapter 8, Section D, *supra*, for additional challenges posed when mediators engage in business development activities.

(2) Given what you know about the mediation environment where you are currently attending school, or in your home town, what do you think would be the best way of trying to establish yourself as a mediator in either of those settings?

[2] ORGANIZATION-BASED EMPLOYMENT OPPORTUNITIES

Many persons interested in pursuing employment opportunities in mediation do not want to operate independent practices but rather prefer salaried jobs connected with institutions. Two types of such options exist: staff mediator positions with agencies or organizations, and staff positions with dispute resolution programs which include, but are not limited to, serving as a mediator. The method for gaining entry to each realm differs significantly.

[a] Agency-based Mediator Positions

There are some organizations, mostly governmentally-based, that hire persons onto their staff to serve as full-time mediators. Historically, most of these positions have been affiliated with those governmental units that provide mediation and technical assistance to participants in union-management relations. The Federal Mediation and Conciliation Service (FMCS), for example, employs staff mediators to assist private-sector labor-management representatives conduct their collective bargaining sessions. Beginning in the late 1960s, with the explosive growth of formal union-management relations involving public sector employees, affected states created agencies comparable in scope to FMCS to service collective bargaining needs involving public sector unions and management; these are variously referred to as Public Employment Relations Boards (PERBs) or Public Employment Relations Commissions (PERCs). A limited number of governmental agencies exist at both the federal and state level to provide mediators and conciliators to help resolve controversies involving civil rights or civil disturbances; the leading example is the Community Relations Service (CRS) of the U.S. Department of Justice. Other state government agencies, such as Worker Compensation Offices, now routinely recruit for staff mediators. Finally, many state court systems have hired staff persons to serve as mediators in subject-specific areas; staff mediator positions exist, for example, to handle controversies typically arising in family or juvenile court settings.

These agencies, in their recruiting process, seek individuals who have earned experience in the projected domain of service. Persons hired as staff mediators for agencies servicing union-management collective bargaining normally have employment experience related to that area; persons who have held union leadership positions, served in labor-relations offices in either the private or public sector, or have represented unions or management in grievance arbitration cases are typically the kinds of persons who qualify for consideration as staff mediators with agencies such as FMCS. As is true for those persons seeking to establish an independent mediation practice, the route to gain appointment is indirect; one must first acquire experience in the relevant practice area in a non-mediator capacity before the mediation career becomes a viable option.

[b] Agency-based Positions in Dispute Resolution Agencies

There are multiple employment options for persons who want to enter this field immediately following their formal educational training. However, most of these opportunities involve working in settings in which one performs multiple organizational activities, not just mediating. There are two basic types of organizational-employment opportunities in this category.

[i] Dispute Resolution Agencies that Provide Direct Service

Many governmental and not-for-profit organizations provide multiple services to constituents, including mediation services. More than one-half of our states have created "State Offices of Dispute Resolution;" while their mandates are not identical, they share the purpose of providing educational and direct mediation services to multiple constituencies within state governmental institutions and communities at large. Staff personnel participate in designing and implementing educational programs discussing when mediation's use is most appropriate, training public employees or interested citizens in mediation skills, and designing dispute resolution systems for agencies. Such dispute resolution agencies recruit to their staffs persons who are trained in mediation skills and are knowledgeable about multiple dispute resolution systems.

Similarly, many not-for-profit organizations exist to provide mediation and other dispute resolution services to their communities. Some of these organizations are free-standing, privately-financed programs, such as the Community Boards Program in San Francisco. Other not-for-profit organizations have created contractual relationships with their local court systems, pursuant to which the court refers all cases involving neighborhood controversies or family matters to the agency which then provides mediation services. Such programs are often supported by state laws. Staff members of these organizations, such as New York's and Michigan's Community Dispute Resolution Centers Program, serve as mediators of such disputes as well as recruit and train community residents to serve as mediators. Many not-for-profit organizations develop conflict resolution programs for other community agencies, including schools and neighborhood organizations. It is common for these programs to recruit staff members whose qualifications are predicated more heavily on their formal educational training than dispute resolution experience.

Persons who enter the field in this manner rapidly develop multiple employment skills, including supervisory and budgeting experience, staff training and development skills, and program development experience; with this combination of skills, particularly in conjunction with formal legal training, a person enjoys a competitive advantage in pursuing employment opportunities in organizational settings, traditional law practices, or in the development of an independent mediation practice.

[ii] Dispute Resolution Agencies that Provide Administrative Services

Some agencies and organizations provide education, technical assistance, and administrative support services to appropriate agencies or parties who are seeking dispute resolution services. While such institutions seek staff persons who are knowledgeable about mediation theory and practice, staff persons do not themselves perform any official mediating role. Such a position enables a person interested in mediation to begin working in the field of dispute resolution and to interact with multiple participants, including parties to a controversy and mediators. For example, there are dispute resolution programs placed organizationally within the administrative offices of a state's Supreme Court; persons employed in these offices conduct research about experimental programs in mediation, assist in developing prototype mediation programs, and provide technical assistance and training to courts, bar associations, judicial conferences, and community organizations who are interested in promoting mediation's use.

There are also entities referred to as "provider" organizations. The structure and operation of the American Arbitration Association (AAA), the oldest of such organizations, is characteristic: the AAA develops "panels" of mediators and arbitrators. When parties to a controversy seek the assistance of a mediator, they can contact the AAA and, with appropriate compensation for its administrative services, engage AAA to identify possible mediators (or select one for the parties), arrange for the conference meeting place and time, handle the transmission of all documents among the parties and mediator, and, at the case's end, close out the file by sending appropriate billings. Obtaining an administrative position with such a provider organization enables a person with an interest in mediation to begin working in the field of dispute resolution and to gain valuable insights into how parties and their representatives conduct themselves and how mediators perform their work. The staff member's important contribution to the proceeding, though, is procedural. While the AAA and CPR Institute for Dispute Resolution are not-for-profit provider organizations, such entities as Judicial, Arbitration, and Mediation Services are operated on a for-profit basis.

§ C MEDIATION'S PROMISE

Barring dramatic social and political changes, most United States residents can be reasonably confident that our country's basic legal institutions and processes shall continue to operate in predictable form well into the future.

As discussed in Chapter 9, *supra*, many signs point to sustained mediation activity: expansion of mandatory court-annexed mediation programs in state and local courts; state and federal legislation supporting mediation's use in various sectors; courses on mediation at universities and law schools throughout the country; and a social climate in which persons and businesses demand that their dispute resolution budgets support flexible, efficient, and varied dispute resolution processes.

But, a contrary vision is also plausible. Despite more than thirty years of mediation activity, most persons still believe suing someone is the most desirable way of resolving controversies. As depicted in television shows, movies, and "courtroom novels," our role model of the heroic problem solver is the strong, aggressive courtroom advocate. Few if any television shows, movies, or novels effectively portray the power and skills of negotiators and mediators; and many lawyers continue to view mediation as only an incidental, required hurdle to jump in the litigation process.

Several dominant lessons emerge from the mediation story, though, that provide powerful reasons for believing that mediation's place in our democratic society is both vital and secure. What are they?

First, there will always be areas of our social life in which mediation's use can be vital. And it is folly to believe that such efforts are relevant only in those countries outside the United States in which movement from totalitarian to democratic governmental forms have recently occurred; wherever there is a need for democratic-institution building measures—wherever persons want to participate responsibly in resolving controversies in which they are a stakeholder—using mediation can help make that happen. Significant practices within our own country are ripe for reconstruction: health care delivery, public school systems, and our juvenile justice systems are three examples of fundamental institutions in our society that will undergo substantial change in the 21st century. Trained mediators can be a force for creating constructive dialogue on such pivotal matters.

Second, we are becoming better educated about mediation. Unlike their predecessors, today's law students most probably attended a middle school or high school in which there was a peer mediation program; they might very well have served as mediators themselves. Persons at an early age are being taught fundamental concepts about constructive intervention practices. But the education initiative is much broader than law school curriculum: university certificate programs in dispute resolution abound; workshops at professional and business organizations are replete with topics relating to negotiation skills and consensus-building; and academic programs at both the undergraduate level and graduate levels are expanding their dispute resolution focus. Students in units as diverse as business, nursing, and natural resources are increasingly being required to take mediation and facilitation courses. There is a slow, steady climate change occurring with respect to how persons choose to deal with differences, and the study and use of mediation is a part of that change.

Finally, as the biographical excerpts above so poignantly display, the persons who are drawn to this work, by and large, are remarkably strong, energetic, thoughtful, and resourceful individuals. Their energy in, and commitment to, this work has been shaped by personal experiences and perspectives that give them confidence in the integrity and value of mediation. They are persistent, imaginative, and committed to serving the parties at the highest standards of excellence. They experience an extraordinary sense of satisfaction in helping parties overcome what had previously been perceived as insuperable barriers. They know that each mediation session involves persons with distinctive aspirations, values, and priorities—and that fact mandates their treating each party with dignity and respect. Engaging talented, compassionate individuals to do the work of mediation plays a significant role in shaping its future. As long as persons seek to be treated with dignity and respect, and as long as persons of character and conviction continue to assume the mediator's role, there will be a role for mediation.

Alfini suggest more training to deal w/ special family law issues like power imbalance *adopted by ABA*

X ethical standards

Model Standards of Practice for Family and Divorce Mediation *

[DRAFT August 2000]

Overview and Definitions

Family and divorce mediation ("family mediation" or "diation") is a process in which a mediator, an impartial third party, facilitates the resolution of family disputes by promoting the participants' voluntary agreement. The family mediator assists communication, encourages understanding and focuses the participants on their individual and common interests. The family mediator works with the participants to explore options, make decisions and reach their own agreements.

Family mediation is not a substitute for the need for family members to obtain independent legal advice or counseling or therapy. Nor is it appropriate for all families. However, experience has established that family mediation is a valuable option for many families because it can:

- increase the self-determination of participants and their ability to communicate;

- promote the best interests of children; and

- reduce the economic and emotional costs associated with the resolution of family disputes.

Effective mediation requires that the family mediator be qualified by training, experience and temperament; that the mediator be impartial; that the participants reach their decisions voluntarily; that their decisions be based on sufficient factual data; that the mediator be aware of the impact of culture and diversity; and that the best interests of children be taken into account. Further, the mediator should also be prepared to identify families whose history includes domestic abuse or child abuse.

These *Model Standards of Practice for Family and Divorce Mediation ("Model Standards")* aim to perform three major functions:

---

* The Model Standards are the product of an effort by mediation-interested organizations and individuals to create a unified set of standards. The following organizations were among those involved in the drafting: The Family Law Section of the American Bar Association and the National Council of Dispute Resolution Organizations (an umbrella organization which includes the Academy of Family Mediators, the American Bar Association Section of Dispute Resolution, AFCC, Conflict Resolution Education Network, the National Association for Community Mediation, the National Conference on Peacemaking and Conflict Resolution, and the Society of Professionals in Dispute Resolution).

1. to serve as a guide for the conduct of family mediators;

2. to inform the mediating participants of what they can expect; and

3. to promote public confidence in mediation as a process for resolving family disputes.

The *Model Standards* are aspirational in character. They describe good practices for family mediators. They are not intended to create legal rules or standards of liability.

The *Model Standards* include different levels of guidance:

- Use of the term "may" in a *Standard* is the lowest strength of guidance and indicates a practice that the family mediator should consider adopting but which can be deviated from in the exercise of good professional judgment.

- Most of the *Standards* employ the term "should" which indicates that the practice described in the *Standard* is highly desirable and should be departed from only with very strong reason.

- The rarer use of the term "shall" in a *Standard* is a higher level of guidance to the family mediator, indicating that the mediator should not have discretion to depart from the practice described.

Standard I

A family mediator shall recognize that mediation is based on the principle of self-determination by the participants.

A. Self-determination is the fundamental principle of family mediation. The mediation process relies upon the ability of participants to make their own voluntary and informed decisions.

B. The primary role of a family mediator is to assist the participants to gain a better understanding of their own needs and interests and the needs and interests of others and to facilitate agreement among the participants.

C. A family mediator should inform the participants that they may seek information and advice from a variety of sources during the mediation process.

D. A family mediator shall inform the participants that they may withdraw from family mediation at any time and are not required to reach an agreement in mediation.

E. The family mediator's commitment shall be to the participants and the process. Pressure from outside of the mediation process shall never influence the mediator to coerce participants to settle.

Standard II

A family mediator shall be qualified by education and training to undertake the mediation.

A. To perform the family mediator's role, a mediator should:

1. have knowledge of family law;

2. have knowledge of and training in the impact of family conflict on parents, children and other participants, including knowledge of child development, domestic abuse and child abuse and neglect;

3. have education and training specific to the process of mediation;

4. be able to recognize the impact of culture and diversity.

B. Family mediators should provide information to the participants about the mediator's relevant training, education and expertise.

Standard III

A family mediator shall facilitate the participants' understanding of what mediation is and assess their capacity to mediate before the participants reach an agreement to mediate.

A. Before family mediation begins a mediator should provide the participants with an overview of the process and its purposes, including:

1. informing the participants that reaching an agreement in family mediation is consensual in nature, that a mediator is an impartial facilitator, and that a mediator may not impose or force any settlement on the parties;

2. distinguishing family mediation from other processes designed to address family issues and disputes;

3. informing the participants that any agreements reached will be reviewed by the court when court approval is required;

4. informing the participants that they may obtain independent advice from attorneys, counsel, advocates, accountants, therapists or other professionals during the mediation process;

5. advising the participants, in appropriate cases, that they can seek the advice of religious figures, elders or other significant persons in their community whose opinions they value;

6. discussing, if applicable, the issue of separate sessions with the participants, a description of the circumstances in which the mediator may meet alone with any of the participants, or with any third party and the conditions of confidentiality concerning these separate sessions;

7. informing the participants that the presence or absence of other persons at a mediation, including attorneys, counselors or advocates, depends on the agreement of the participants and the mediator, unless a statute or regulation otherwise requires or the mediator believes that the presence of another person is required or may be beneficial because of a history or threat of violence or other serious coercive activity by a participant.

[handwritten in right margin: X beyond the joint Standards]

8. describing the obligations of the mediator to maintain the confidentiality of the mediation process and its results as well as any exceptions to confidentiality;

9. advising the participants of the circumstances under which the mediator may suspend or terminate the mediation process and that a participant has a right to suspend or terminate mediation at any time.

B. The participants should sign a written agreement to mediate their dispute and the terms and conditions thereof within a reasonable time after first consulting the family mediator.

C. The family mediator should be alert to the capacity and willingness of the participants to mediate before proceeding with the mediation and throughout the process. A mediator should not agree to conduct the mediation if the mediator reasonably believes one or more of the participants is unable or unwilling to participate.

D. Family mediators should not accept a dispute for mediation if they cannot satisfy the expectations of the participants concerning the timing of the process.

Standard IV

A family mediator shall conduct the mediation process in an impartial manner. A family mediator shall disclose all actual and potential grounds of bias and conflicts of interest reasonably known to the mediator. The participants shall be free to retain the mediator by an informed, written waiver of the conflict of interest. However, if a bias or conflict of interest clearly impairs a mediator's impartiality, the mediator shall withdraw regardless of the express agreement of the participants.

A. Impartiality means freedom from favoritism or bias in word, action or appearance, and includes a commitment to assist all participants as opposed to any one individual.

B. Conflict of interest means any relationship between the mediator, any participant or the subject matter of the dispute, that compromises or appears to compromise the mediator's impartiality.

C. A family mediator should not accept a dispute for mediation if the family mediator cannot be impartial.

D. A family mediator should identify and disclose potential grounds of bias or conflict of interest upon which a mediator's impartiality might reasonably be questioned. Such disclosure should be made prior to the start of a mediation and in time to allow the participants to select an alternate mediator.

E. A family mediator should resolve all doubts in favor of disclosure. All disclosures should be made as soon as practical after the mediator becomes aware of the bias or potential conflict of interest. The duty to disclose is a continuing duty.

F. A family mediator should guard against bias or partiality based on the participants' personal characteristics, background or performance at the mediation.

G. A family mediator should avoid conflicts of interest in recommending the services of other professionals.

H. A family mediator shall not use information about participants obtained in a mediation for personal gain or advantage.

I. A family mediator should withdraw pursuant to *Standard IX* if the mediator believes the mediator's impartiality has been compromised or a conflict of interest has been identified and has not been waived by the participants.

Standard V

A family mediator shall fully disclose and explain the basis of any compensation, fees and charges to the participants.

A. The participants should be provided with sufficient information about fees at the outset of mediation to determine if they wish to retain the services of the mediator.

B. The participants' written agreement to mediate their dispute should include a description of their fee arrangement with the mediator.

C. A mediator should not enter into a fee agreement that is contingent upon the results of the mediation or the amount of the settlement.

D. A mediator should not accept a fee for referral of a matter to another mediator or to any other person.

E. Upon termination of mediation a mediator should return any unearned fee to the participants.

Standard VI

A family mediator shall structure the mediation process so that the participants make decisions based on sufficient information and knowledge.

A. The mediator should facilitate full and accurate disclosure and the acquisition and development of information during mediation so that the participants can make informed decisions. This may be accomplished by encouraging participants to consult appropriate experts.

B. Consistent with standards of impartiality and preserving participant self-determination, a mediator may provide the participants with information that the mediator is qualified by training or experience to provide. The mediator shall not provide therapy or legal advice.

C. The mediator should recommend that the participants obtain independent legal representation before concluding an agreement.

D. If the participants so desire, the mediator should allow attorneys, counsel or advocates for the participants to be present at the mediation sessions.

E. With the agreement of the participants, the mediator may document the participants' resolution of their dispute. The mediator should inform the participants that any agreement should be reviewed by an independent attorney before it is signed.

Standard VII

A family mediator shall maintain the confidentiality of all information acquired in the mediation process, unless the mediator is permitted or required to reveal the information by law or agreement of the participants.

A. The mediator should discuss the participants' expectations of confidentiality with them prior to undertaking the mediation. The written agreement to mediate should include provisions concerning confidentiality.

B. Prior to undertaking the mediation the mediator should inform the participants of the limitations of confidentiality such as statutory, judicially or ethically mandated reporting.

C. As permitted by law, the mediator shall disclose a participant's threat of suicide or violence against any person to the threatened person and the appropriate authorities if the mediator believes such threat is likely to be acted upon.

D. If the mediator holds private sessions with a participant, the obligations of confidentiality concerning those sessions should be discussed and agreed upon prior to the sessions.

E. If subpoenaed or otherwise noticed to testify or to produce documents the mediator should inform the participants immediately. The mediator should not testify or provide documents in response to a subpoena without an order of the court if the mediator reasonably believes doing so would violate an obligation of confidentiality to the participants.

Standard VIII

A family mediator shall assist participants in determining how to promote the best interests of children.

A. The mediator should encourage the participants to explore the range of options available for separation or post divorce parenting arrangements and their respective costs and benefits. Referral to a specialist in child development may be appropriate for these purposes. The topics for discussion may include, among others:

1. information about community resources and programs that can help the participants and their children cope with the consequences of family reorganization and family violence;

2. problems that continuing conflict creates for children's development and what steps might be taken to ameliorate the effects of conflict on the children;

3. development of a parenting plan that covers the children's physical residence and decision-making responsibilities for the children, with appropriate levels of detail as agreed to by the participants;

4. the possible need to revise parenting plans as the developmental needs of the children evolve over time; and

5. encouragement to the participants to develop appropriate dispute resolution mechanisms to facilitate future revisions of the parenting plan.

B. The mediator should be sensitive to the impact of culture and religion on parenting philosophy and other decisions.

C. The mediator shall inform any court-appointed representative for the children of the mediation. If a representative for the children participates, the mediator should, at the outset, discuss the effect of that participation on the mediation process and the confidentiality of the mediation with the participants. Whether the representative of the children participates or not, the mediator shall provide the representative with the resulting agreements insofar as they relate to the children.

D. Except in extraordinary circumstances, the children should not participate in the mediation process without the consent of both parents and the children's court-appointed representative.

E. Prior to including the children in the mediation process, the mediator should consult with the parents and the children's court-appointed representative about whether the children should participate in the mediation process and the form of that participation.

F. The mediator should inform all concerned about the available options for the children's participation (which may include personal participation, an interview with a mental health professional, the mediator interviewing the child and reporting to the parents, or a videotaped statement by the child) and discuss the costs and benefits of each with the participants.

Standard IX

A family mediator shall recognize a family situation involving child abuse or neglect and take appropriate steps to shape the mediation process accordingly.

A. As used in these Standards, child abuse or neglect is defined by applicable state law.

B. A mediator shall not undertake a mediation in which the family situation has been assessed to involve child abuse or neglect without appropriate and adequate training.

C. If the mediator has reasonable grounds to believe that a child of the participants is abused or neglected within the meaning of the jurisdiction's child abuse and neglect laws, the mediator shall comply with applicable child protection laws.

1. The mediator should encourage the participants to explore appropriate services for the family.

2. The mediator should consider the appropriateness of suspending or terminating the mediation process in light of the allegations.

Standard X

A family mediator shall recognize a family situation involving domestic abuse and take appropriate steps to shape the mediation process accordingly.

A. As used in these Standards, domestic abuse includes domestic violence as defined by applicable state law and issues of control and intimidation.

B. A mediator shall not undertake a mediation in which the family situation has been assessed to involve domestic abuse without appropriate and adequate training.

C. Some cases are not suitable for mediation because of safety, control or intimidation issues. A mediator should make a reasonable effort to screen for the existence of domestic abuse prior to entering into an agreement to mediate. The mediator should continue to assess for domestic abuse throughout the mediation process.

D. If domestic abuse appears to be present the mediator shall consider taking measures to insure the safety of participants and the mediator including, among others:

   1. establishing appropriate security arrangements;

   2. holding separate sessions with the participants even without the agreement of all participants;

   3. allowing a friend, representative, advocate, counsel or attorney to attend the mediation sessions;

   4. encouraging the participants to be represented by an attorney, counsel or an advocate throughout the mediation process;

   5. referring the participants to appropriate community resources;

   6. suspending or terminating the mediation sessions, with appropriate steps to protect the safety of the participants.

E. The mediator should facilitate the participants' formulation of parenting plans that protect the physical safety and psychological well-being of themselves and their children.

Standard XI

A family mediator shall suspend or terminate the mediation process when the mediator reasonably believes that a participant is unable to effectively participate or for other compelling reason.

A. Circumstances under which a mediator should consider suspending or terminating the mediation, may include, among others:

1. the safety of a participant or well-being of a child is threatened;

2. a participant has or is threatening to abduct a child;

3. a participant is unable to participate due to the influence of drugs, alcohol, or physical or mental condition;

4. the participants are about to enter into an agreement that the mediator reasonably believes to be unconscionable;

5. a participant is using the mediation to further illegal conduct;

6. a participant is using the mediation process to gain an unfair advantage;

7. if the mediator believes the mediator's impartiality has been compromised in accordance with *Standard IV*.

B. If the mediator does suspend or terminate the mediation, the mediator should take all reasonable steps to minimize prejudice or inconvenience to the participants which may result.

Standard XII

A family mediator shall be truthful in the advertisement and solicitation for mediation.

A. Mediators should refrain from promises and guarantees of results. A mediator should not advertise statistical settlement data or settlement rates.

B. Mediators should accurately represent their qualifications. In an advertisement or other communication, a mediator may make reference to meeting state, national, or private organizational qualifications only if the entity referred to has a procedure for qualifying mediators and the mediator has been duly granted the requisite status.

Standard XIII

A family mediator shall acquire and maintain professional competence in mediation.

A. Mediators should continuously improve their professional skills and abilities by, among other activities, participating in relevant continuing education programs and should regularly engage in self-assessment.

B. Mediators should participate in programs of peer consultation and should help train and mentor the work of less experienced mediators.

C. Mediators should continuously strive to understand the impact of culture and diversity on the mediator's practice.

Special Policy Considerations for State Regulation of Family Mediators and Court Affiliated Programs

The *Model Standards* recognize the *National Standards for Court Connected Dispute Resolution Programs* (1992). There are also state and local regulations governing such programs and family mediators. The following principles of organization and practice, however, are especially important for regulation of mediators and court-connected family mediation programs. They are worthy of separate mention.

A. Individual states or local courts should set standards and qualifications for family mediators including procedures for evaluations and handling grievances against mediators. In developing these standards and qualifications, regulators should consult with appropriate professional groups, including professional associations of family mediators.

B. When family mediators are appointed by a court or other institution, the appointing agency should make reasonable efforts to insure that each mediator is qualified for the appointment. If a list of family mediators qualified for court appointment exists, the requirements for being included on the list should be made public and available to all interested persons.

C. Confidentiality should not be construed to limit or prohibit the effective monitoring, research or evaluation of mediation programs by responsible individuals or academic institutions provided that no identifying information about any person involved in the mediation is disclosed without their prior written consent. Under appropriate circumstances, researchers may be permitted to obtain access to statistical data and, with the permission of the participants, to individual case files, observations of live mediations, and interviews with participants.

CHAPTER 1

AUERBACH, Jerold S. (1983) *Justice without Law?* New York: Oxford University Press.

BUSH, Robert A. Baruch, and FOLGER, Joseph (1994) *The Promise of Mediation.* San Francisco: Jossey-Bass.

CARPENTER, Susan C., and KENNEDY, W.J.D. (1988) *Managing Public Disputes.* San Francisco: Jossey-Bass.

DANZIG, Richard. (1973) *Toward the Creation of a Complementary, Decentralized System of Criminal Justice,* 26 Stan. L. Rev. 1

DEUTSCH, Martin. (1973) *The Resolution of Conflict.* New Haven: Yale University Press.

FELSTINER, William, ABEL, Richard L., and SARAT, Austin. (1980-81) *The Emergence and Transformation of Disputes: Naming, Blaming, Claiming,* 15 L. & Soc'y. Rev. 631.

FISHER, Roger, and URY, William. (1981) *Getting to Yes.* Boston: Houghton Mifflin.

FOLBERG, Jay, and TAYLOR, Alison. (1984) *Mediation.* San Francisco: Jossey-Bass.

FULLER, Lon. (1971) *Mediation: Its Forms and Functions,* 44 S. Cal. L. Rev. 305.

GOLANN, Dwight. (1997) *Mediating Legal Disputes: Effective Strategies for Lawyers and Mediators.* New York: Aspen Publishers.

GOLDMANN, Robert. (1980) *Roundtable Justice.* Boulder, Colo.: Westview Press.

HAYNES, John. (1994) *The Fundamentals of Family Mediation.* Albany: State University of New York Press.

KATSH, Ethan, RIFKIN, Janet, and GAITENBY, Alan. (2000) *E-Commerce, E-Disputes, and E-Dispute Resolution: In the Shadow of 'eBay Law',* 15 Ohio St. J. on Disp. Resol. 705.

LAX, David, and SEBENIUS, James. (1986) *The Manager as Negotiator.* New York: The Free Press.

MAGGIOLO, Walter. (1985) *Techniques of Labor Mediation.* New York: Oceana Publications.

MCGILLIS, Daniel, and MULLEN, Joan. (1977) *Neighborhood Justice Centers: An Analysis of Potential Models.* Washington, D.C.: U.S. Department of Justice.

MOORE, Christopher. (1996) *The Mediation Process* (2nd edition) San Francisco: Jossey-Bass.

RAIFFA, Howard. (1982) *The Art and Science of Negotiation.* Cambridge: MA: Harvard University Press.

ROGERS, Nancy, and McEWEN, Craig. (1994) *Mediation: Law, Policy, Practice* (2nd ed.). St. Paul: West Publishing Co.

SCHELLING, Thomas. (1960) *The Strategy of Conflict.* Cambridge: MA: Harvard University Press.

SIMKIN, William, and FIDANDIS, Nicolas. (1986) *Mediation and the Dynamics of Collective Bargaining* (2nd ed.). Washington, D.C.: Bureau of National Affairs

STULBERG, Joseph B. (1987) *Taking Charge/Managing Conflict.* Lexington, MA: Lexington Press.

SUSSKIND, Lawrence, and CRUIKSHANK, Jeffrey. (1985) *Breaking the Impasse.* New York: Basic Books.

WALTON, Richard, and MCKERSIE, Robert. (1991) *A Behavioral Theory of Labor Negotiations (2nd ed.).* Ithaca, N.Y.: ILR Press.

WAHRHAFTIG, Paul, and ASSEFA, Hizkias (1988) *Extremist Groups and Conflict Resolution: the MOVE crisis in Philadelphia.* New York: Praeger.

CHAPTER 2

ALFINI, James J. (1999) *Settlement Ethics and Lawyering in ADR Proceedings: A Proposal to Revise Rule 4.1,* 19 N. Ill. U. L. Rev. 255.

AMERICAN BAR ASSOCIATION, *Model Rules of Professional Conduct, Rule 4.1.,* Chicago: American Bar Association.

ARROW, Kenneth, ed. (1995) *Barriers to Conflict Resolution.* New York: W. W. Norton.

BIRKE, Richard, and FOX, Craig R. (1999) *Psychological Principles in Negotiating Civil Settlements,* 4 Harv. Negotiation L. Rev. 1.

BOK, Sissela. (1978) *Lying: Moral Choice in Public and Private Life.* New York: Pantheon Books.

BRESLIN, J. William, and RUBIN, Jeffrey Z., eds. (1991) *Negotiation Theory and Practice.* Cambridge, MA.: Program on Negotiation.

BROWN, Jennifer Gerarda. (1997) *The Role of Hope in Negotiation,* 44 UCLA L. Rev. 1661.

BUSH, Robert A. Baruch. (1997) *What Do We Need a Mediator For?: Mediation's Value-Added for Negotiators,* 12 Ohio St. J. on Disp. Resol. 1.

CIALDINI, Robert B. (1993) *Influence: The Psychology of Persuasion (rev. ed.).* New York: Morrow.

CONDLIN, Robert J. (1992) *Bargaining in the Dark: The Normative Incoherence of Lawyer Dispute Bargaining Role,* 51 Md. L. Rev. 1.

CRAVER, Charles. (1997) Symposium: *The Lawyer's Duties and Responsibilities in Dispute Resolution: Article: Post-Conference Reflection: Negotiation Ethics: How to be Deceptive Without Being Dishonest / How to be Assertive Without Being Offensive,* 38 S. Tex. L. Rev. 713.

CRAVER, Charles B. (1997) *Effective Legal Negotiation and Settlement (3rd ed.).* Charlottesville: Michie.

DAU-SCHMIDT, Kenneth. (1990) *An Economic Analysis of the Criminal Law as a Preference-Shaping Policy,* 1990 Duke L.J. 1.

EISENBERG, Melvin. (1976) *Private Ordering Through Negotiations: Dispute Settlement and Rulemaking,* 89 Harv. L. Rev. 637.

FELSTINER, William L., and SARAT, Austin. (1992) *Enactments of Power: Negotiating Reality and Responsibility in Lawyer-Client Interactions,* 77 Cornell L. Rev. 1447.

FISHER, Roger, URY, William, and PATTON, Bruce. (1981, 1991) *Getting to Yes: Negotiating Agreement Without Giving In (2nd. ed.).* New York: Penguin Books.

FISHER, Roger. (1984) *Comment,* 34 J. Legal. Educ. 120.

FRIED, Charles. (1976) *The Lawyer as Friend: The Moral Foundation of the Lawyer-Client Relation,* 85 Yale L.J. 1060.

GIFFORD, Donald G. (1989) *Legal Negotiation.* St. Paul: West Publishing Co.

GOODPASTER, Gary. (1996) *A Primer on Competitive Bargaining,* 1996 J. Disp. Resol. 325.

HOFLING, Charles, et al. (1966) *An Experimental Study of Nurse-Physician Relationships,* 143 J. Nervous & Mental Disease 171.

KAHNEMAN, Daniel, et al., eds. (1982) *Judgment Under Uncertainty: Heuristics and Biases.* Cambridge: Cambridge University Press.

KAHNEMAN, Daniel, and TVERSKY, Amos. (1995) *Conflict Resolution: Cognitive Perspective,* in *Barriers to Conflict Resolution* (K. Arrow, ed.). New York: W. W. Norton.

KOROBKIN, Russell, et al. (1997) *Psychology, Economics, and Settlement: A New Look at the Role of the Lawyer,* 76 Tex. L. Rev. 77.

KOROBKIN, Russell, and GUTHRIE, Chris. (1994) *Psychological Barriers to Litigation Settlement: An Experimental View,* 93 Mich. L. Rev. 107.

KRITEK, Phyllis Beck. (1994) *Negotiating at an Uneven Table: A Practical Approach to Working with Difference and Diversity.* San Francisco: Jossey-Bass.

LAX, David A., and SEBENIUS, James K. (1986) *The Manager as Negotiator: Bargaining for Cooperation & Competitive Gain.* New York: Free Press.

LUBAN, David. (1988) *The Quality of Justice, Institute for Legal Studies,* Working Papers Series 8.

MENKEL-MEADOW, Carrie. (1984) *Toward Another View of Legal Negotiation: The Structure of Problem Solving,* 31 UCLA L. Rev. 754.

MEYERSON, Bruce. (1997) *Telling the Truth in Mediation: Mediator Owed Duty of Candor,* 4 Disp. Resol. Mag. 17.

MILGRAM, Stanley. (1974) *Obedience to Authority: An Experimental View.* New York: Harper & Row.

MNOOKIN, Robert H., PEPPET, Scott, and TULUMELLO, Andrew. (2000) *Beyond Winning: Negotiating to Create Value in Deals and Disputes.* Cambridge: MA.: Belknap Press of Harvard Univeristy.

MNOOKIN, Robert H., and ROSS, Lee. (1995) *Introduction* to *Barriers to Conflict Resolution* 3 (Kenneth J. Arrow, ed.). New York: W. W. Norton.

MNOOKIN, Robert H., and GILSON, Ronald J. (1994) *Disputing through Agents: Cooperation and Conflict Between Lawyers in Litigation.* 94 Colum. L. Rev. 509.

MNOOKIN, Robert H. (1993) *Why Negotiations Fail: An Exploration of Barriers to the Resolution of Conflict,* 8 Ohio St. J. on Disp. Resol. 235.

MNOOKIN, Robert H., and WILSON, Robert R. (1989) *Rational Bargaining and Market Efficiency: Understanding Pennzoil v. Texaco,* 75 Va. L. Rev. 295.

PRUITT, Dean G., and LEWIS, Steven A. (1977) *The Psychology of Integrative Bargaining* (in) *Negotiations: Social-Psychological Perspectives* (D. Druckman, ed.). Beverly Hills: Sage.

RACHLINSKI, Jeffrey J. (1996) *Gains, Losses, and the Psychology of Litigation,* 70 S. Cal. L. Rev. 113.

RAIFFA, Howard. (1982) *The Art & Science of Negotiation.* Cambridge: MA.: Harvard University Press.

ROBINSON, Rob J., et al. (June 1990) *Misconstruing the Views of the "Other Side": Real and Perceived Differences in Three Ideological Conflicts,* Stanford Center on Conflict and Negotiation Working Paper No. 18.

ROEMER, John. (1986) *The Mismarriage of Bargaining Theory and Distributive Justice,* 97 Ethics 88.

ROSS, Lee, and STILLINGER, Constance. (Oct. 1991) *Barriers to Conflict Resolution,* 7 Negotiation J. 389.

RUBIN, Alvin B. (1975) *A Causerie on Lawyers' Ethics in Negotiation,* 35 La. L. Rev. 577.

SCHELLING, Thomas C. (1984) *Choice and Consequence.* Cambridge, MA.: Harvard University Press.

SCHNEIDER, Andrea Kupfer. (1994) *Effective Responses to Offensive Comments,* 1994 Negotiation J. 107.

SIMONS, Herbert W. (1976) *Persuasion: Understanding, Practice and Analysis.*

STERNLIGHT, Jean R. (1999) *Lawyers' Representation of Clients in Mediation: Using Economics and Psychology to Structure Advocacy in an Nonadversarial Setting,* 14 Ohio St. J. on Disp. Resol. 259.

STILLINGER, Constance A., et al. (1988) *The Reactive Devaluation Barrier to Conflict Resolution,* Stanford Center on Conflict and Negotiation, Working Paper No. 3..

THURMAN, Ruth Fleet. (1990) *Chipping Away at Lawyer Veracity: The ABA's Turn Toward Situation Ethics in Negotiations,* 1990 J. Disp. Resol. 103.

TVERSKY, Amos, et al. (March 1990) *The Causes of Preference Reversals,* 80 Am. Econ Rev. 204.

TVERSKY, Amos, and KAHNEMAN, Daniel. (1991) *Loss Aversion in Riskless Choice: A Reference-Dependent Model,* 106 Q.J. Econ. 1038.

TVERSKY, Amos, and THALER, Richard. (Spring 1990) *Anomalies: Preference Reversals,* 4 J. Econ. Perspectives 201.

WETLAUFER, Gerald B. (1990) *The Ethics of Lying in Negotiations,* 75 Iowa L. Rev. 1219.

WHITE, James J. (1984) *The Pros and Cons of Getting to Yes,* 34 J. Legal Educ. 115.

WHITE, James. (1980) *Machiavelli & the Bar: Ethical Limitations on Lying in Negotiation,* Am. B. Found. Res. J. 926.

WHITE, Sally Blount, and NEALE, Margaret A. (1994) *The Role of Negotiator Aspirations and Settlement Expectancies in Bargaining Outcomes,* 57 Organizational Behav. & Hum. Decision Processes 303.

WILLIAMS, Gerald R. (1983) *Legal Negotiation and Settlement.* St. Paul: West Publishing Co.

CHAPTER 3

BUSH, Robert A. Baruch, and FOLGER, Joseph P. (1996) *Transformative Mediation and Third-Party Intervention: Ten Hallmarks of a Transformative Approach to Practice,* 13 Mediation Q. 263.

FOLBERG, Jay, and TAYLOR, Alison. (1988) *Mediation: A Comprehensive Guide to Resolving Conflicts without Litigation.* San Francisco: Jossey-Bass.

GALTON, Eric. (1993) *Mediation: A Texas Practice Guide.* Dallas, TX: Texas Lawyer Press.

GOLANN, Dwight. (1997) *Benefits and Dangers of Mediation Evaluation, Part One,* 15 Alternatives to the High Cost of Litigation 35 (March 1997).

GOLANN, Dwight. (1997) *Benefits and Dangers of Mediation Evaluation, Part Two,* 15 Alternatives to the High Cost of Litigation 49 (April 1997).

HAYNES, John M., and HAYNES, Gretchen L. (1989) *Mediating Divorce.* San Francisco: Jossey-Bass.

MOFFITT, Michael L. (1998) *Mediation "Transparency" Helps Parties See Where They're Going,* 16 Alternatives to the High Cost of Litigation 6 (June 1998).

MOORE, Christopher W. (1991) *The Mediation Process: Practical Strategies for Resolving Conflict.* San Francisco: Jossey-Bass.

PRESS, Sharon, and KOSCH, Kimberly. (2000) *County Mediator's Manual.* Tallahassee, FL: Florida Dispute Resolution Center.

STULBERG, Joseph B. (1987) *Taking Charge/Managing Conflict.* Cambridge, MA: Lexington Books.

THE TEST DESIGN PROJECT. (1995) *Performance-Based Assessment: A Methodology, for use in selecting, training and evaluating mediators.* Washington, DC: National Institute for Dispute Resolution.

CHAPTER 4

AARON, Marjorie Corman. (1996) *Evaluation in Mediation* (in) Mediating Legal Disputes (Dwight Golann, ed.). New York: Aspen Law and Business.

ALFINI, James J. (1991) *Trashing, Bashing, and Hashing It Out: Is This The End of "Good Mediation?,"* 19 Fla. St. U. L. Rev. 47.

BERNARD, Sydney E., et al. (1984) *The Neutral Mediator: Value Dilemmas in Divorce Mediation,* 4 Mediation Q. 61.

BICKERMAN, John. (1996) *Evaluative Mediator Responds,* 14 Alternatives to the High Cost of Litigation 70.

BRETT, Jeanne M., et al. (1986) *Mediator Style and Mediation Effectiveness,* 1986 Negotiation J. 277.

BUSH, Robert A. Baruch, and FOLGER, Joseph. (1994) *The Promise of Mediation: Responding to Conflict Through Empowerment and Recognition.* San Francisco: Jossey-Bass.

BUSH, Robert A. Baruch. (1989) *Efficiency and Protection, or Empowerment and Recognition?: The Mediator's Role and Ethical Standards in Mediation,* 41 Fla. L. Rev. 253.

COBB, Sara, and RIFKIN, Janet. (1991) *Practice and Paradox: Deconstructing Neutrality in Mediation,* 16 L. & Soc. Inquiry 35.

FOLBERG, Jay, and TAYLOR, Alison. (1984) *Mediation: A Comprehensive Guide to Resolving Conflicts Without Litigation.* San Francisco: Jossey-Bass.

FOLGER, Joseph P., and BUSH, Robert A. Baruch. (1996) *Transformative Mediation and Third Party Intervention: Ten Hallmarks of a Transformative Approach to Practice,* 13 Mediation Q. 263.

FRIEDMAN, Gary J. (1993) *A Guide to Divorce Mediation.* New York: Workman Publications.

FULLER, Lon L. (1971) *Mediation: Its Forms and Functions,* 44 S. Cal. L. Rev. 305.

GOLANN, Dwight, ed. (1996) *Mediating Legal Disputes.* New York: Aspen Law and Business.

HAYNES, John M. (1992) *Mediation and Therapy: An Alternative View,* 10 Mediation Q. 21.

KOLB, Deborah. (1983) *The Mediators.* Cambridge, MA: MIT Press.

KOLB, Deborah. (1994) *When Talk Works: Profiles of Mediators.* San Francisco: Jossey-Bass.

KOVACH, Kimberlee, and LOVE, Lela. (1996) *Evaluative Mediation is an Oxymoron,* 14 Alternatives to the High Cost of Mediation 31.

KRESSEL, Kenneth, et al. (1994) *The Settlement-Orientation vs. the Problem-Solving Style in Custody Mediation,* 50 J. Soc. Issues 67.

KRESSEL, Kenneth. (1994) *Frances Butler: Questions That Lead to Answers in Child Custody Mediation* (in) *When Talk Works: Profiles of Mediators* (Deborah M. Kolb ed.). San Francisco: Jossey-Bass.

LOVE, Lela P. (1997) *The Top Ten Reasons Why Mediators Should Not Evaluate,* 24 Fla. St. U. L. Rev. 937.

MATHER, L., and YNGVESSON, B. (1980-81) *Language, Audience and The Transformation of Disputes.* 15 L. & Soc'y Rev. 775.

MAUTE, Judith. (1991) *Public Values and Private Justice: A Case for Mediator Accountability,* 4 Geo. J. Legal Ethics 503.

MENKEL-MEADOW, Carrie. (1995) *The Many Ways of Mediation: The Transformation of Traditions, Ideologies, Paradigms, and Practices,* 11 Negotiation. J. 217.

NOLAN-HALEY, Jacqueline. (1999) *Informed Consent in Mediation: A Guiding Principle for Truly Educated Decisionmaking,* 74 Notre Dame L. Rev. 775.

RISKIN, Leonard L. (1996) *Understanding Mediators' Orientations, Strategies, and Techniques: A Grid for the Perplexed,* 1 Harv. Negotiation L. Rev. 7.

RISKIN, Leonard L. (1994) *Mediator Orientations, Strategies and Techniques,* 12 Alternatives to the High Cost of Litigation 111.

RISKIN, Leonard L. (1984) *Toward New Standards for the Neutral Lawyer in Mediation,* 26 Ariz. L. Rev. 329.

SIBLEY, Susan S., and MERRY, Sally E. (1986) *Mediator Settlement Strategies,* 8 L. & Pol'y 7.

STARK, James. (1997) *The Ethics of Mediation Evaluation: Some Troublesome Questions and Tentative Proposals, From an Evaluative Lawyer Mediator,* 38 S. Tex. L. Rev. 769.

STIPANOWICH, Thomas J. (1998) *The Multi-Door Contract and Other Possibilities,* 13 Ohio St. J. on Disp. Resol. 303.

STULBERG, Joseph B. (1987) *Taking Charge/Managing Conflict.* Lexington, MA: Lexington Books.

STULBERG, Joseph B. (1981) *The Theory and Practice of Mediation: A Reply to Professor Susskind,* 6 Vt. L. Rev. 85.

SUSSKIND, Lawrence. (1981) *Environmental Mediation and the Accountability Problem,* 6 Vt. L. Rev. 1.

CHAPTER 5

BROWN, Jennifer Gerarda, and AYRES, Ian. (1994) *Economic Rationales for Mediation,* 80 Va. L. Rev. 323.

BRUNET, Edward. (1987) *Questioning the Quality of Alternative Dispute Resolution,* 62 Tul. L. Rev. 1.

COBEN, James R., and THOMPSON, Peter N. (1999) *The Haghighi Trilogy and the Minnesota Civil Mediation Act: Exposing a Phantom Menace Casting a Pall Over the Development of ADR in Minnesota,* 20 Hamline J. Pub. L. & Pol'y 299.

EHRHARDT, Charles W. (1999) *Confidentiality, Privilege and Rule 408: the Protection of Mediation Proceedings in Federal Court,* 60 La. L. Rev. 91.

FREEDMAN, Lawrence R., and PRIGOFF, Michael. (1986) *Confidentiality in Mediation: The Need for Protection,* 2 Ohio St. J. on Disp. Resol. 37.

HARTER, Phillip J. (1989) *Neither Cop Nor Collection Agent: Encouraging Administrative Settlements by Ensuring Mediator Confidentiality,* 41 Admin. L. J. 315.

HUGHES, Scott H. (1998) *A Closer Look: The Case for a Mediation Confidentiality Privilege Still Has Not Been Made,* Disp. Resol. Mag. 14 (Winter 1998).

IZUMI, Carol. (1995) Remarks in *Symposium on Standards of Professional Conduct in Alternative Dispute Resolution,* 1995 J. of Disp. Resol. 95.

KATZ, Lucy V. (1988) *Enforcing an ADR Clause—Are Good Intentions All You Have?,* 26 Am. Bus. L.J. 575.

KIRTLEY, Alan. (1995) *The Mediation Privilege's Transition from Theory to Implementation: Designing a Mediation Privilege Standard to Protect Mediation Participants, the Process and the Public Interest,* 1995 J. Disp. Resol. 1.

KLINTWORTH, Tim K. (1995) *The Enforceability of an Agreement to Submit to a Non-Arbitral Form of Dispute Resolution: The Rise of Mediation and Neutral Fact-Finding,* 1995 J. Disp. Resol. 181.

MENKEL-MEADOW, Carrie. (1991) *Pursuing Settlement in an Adversary Culture: A Tale of Innovation Co-opted or "The Law of ADR",* 19 Fla. St. U. L. Rev. 1.

MURR, George B. (1997) *In the Matter of Marriage of Ames and the Enforceability of Alternative Dispute Resolution Agreements: A Case for Reform,* 28 Tex. Tech L. Rev. 31.

NADER, Laura. (1984) *The Recurrent Dialectic Between Legality and its Alternatives: The Limits of Binary Thinking,* 132 U. Pa. L. Rev. 621.

PAYNE, Cathleen Cover. (1986) *Enforceability of Mediated Agreements,* 1986 J. Disp. Resol. 385.

PERINO, Michael A. (1995) *Drafting Mediation Privileges: Lessons from the Civil Justice Reform Act,* 26 Seton Hall L. Rev. 1.

RISKIN, Leonard. (1982) *Mediation and Lawyers,* 43 Ohio St. L.J. 29.

ROGERS, Nancy, and McEWEN, Craig R. (1994) *Mediation: Law, Policy and Practice.* New York: Clark, Boardman, and Callaghan.

STONE, Katherine V. W. (2000) *Private Justice: The Law of Alternative Dispute Resolution.* Westbury, NY: Foundation Press.

WELLER, Steven. (1992) *Court Enforcement of Mediated Agreements: Should Contract Law Be Applied?,* 31 Judge's J. 13.

CHAPTER 6

AUGSBURGER, D.W.(1992). *Conflict Mediation Across Cultures.* Louisville, KY: Westminister/John Knox Press.

BARNES, Bruce. (1994) *Conflict Resolution Across Cultures: A Hawaii Perspective and a Pacific Mediation Model,* 12 Mediation Q. 117.

BRYAN, Penelope E. (1992) *Killing Us Softly: Divorce Mediation and the Politics of Power,* 40 Buff. L. Rev. 441.

CHALMERS, W. Ellison. (1974) *Racial Negotiations: Potentials & Limitations.* Ann Arbor: Institute of Labor and Industrial Relations.

COKER, Donna. (1999) *Enhancing Autonomy for Battered Women: Lessons from Navajo Peacemaking,* 47 UCLA L. Rev. 1.

DAHL, Robert A. (1989) *Democracy and Its Critics.* New Haven: Yale University Press.

DODD, Carley H. (1987) *Dynamics of Intercultural Communication.* Dubuque: W.C. Brown.

FULLER, Lon. (1958) *Positivism and Fidelity to Law—A Reply to Professor Hart,* 71 Harv. L. Rev. 630.

GULLIVER, P.H. (1979) *Disputes and Negotiations: A Cross-Cultural Perspective.*

GUTMANN, Amy, and THOMPSON, Dennis. (1996) *Democracy and Disagreement.* Cambridge, MA: Belknap Press.

HALL, Edward T., and Mildred R. (1987) *Hidden Differences.* Garden City, N.Y.: Anchor Press.

HART, H.L.A. (1994) *The Concept of Law (2nd ed.).* Oxford: Clarendon Press.

HART, H.L.A. (1958) *Positivism and the Separation of Law and Morals,* 71 Harv. L. Rev. 593.

LUBAN, David. (1995) *Settlement and the Erosion of the Public Realm,* 83 Geo. L.J. 2619.

PEARSON, Jessica. (1997) *Mediating When Domestic Violence is a Factor: Policies and Practices in Court-Based Divorce Mediation Programs,* 14 Mediation Q. 319.

RUBIN, Jeffrey Z., and SANDER, Frank E.A. (1991) *Culture, Negotiation, and the Eye of the Beholder,* 7 Negotiation J. 249.

STULBERG, Joseph B. (1998) *Mediation and Fairness,* 13 Ohio St. J. on Disp. Resol. 909

CHAPTER 7

BARRETT, Robert. (1996) *Mediator Certification: Should California Enact Legislation?*, 30 U.S.F. L. Rev 619.

BUSH, Robert A. Baruch. (1992) *The Dilemmas of Mediation Practice: A Study of Ethical Dilemmas and Policy Implications,* National Institute for Dispute Resolution.

Florida Rules for Certified and Court-appointed Mediators, Fla. Stats. Ann. §§ 10.100 et. seq., effective April 1, 2000.

HONEYMAN, Christopher. (1990) *On Evaluating Mediators,* 6 Negotiation J. 23.

MAUTE, Judith. (1991) *Public Values and Private Justice: a Case for Mediator Accountability,* 4 Geo. J. Legal Ethics 503.

MENKEL-MEADOW, Carrie. (1996) *Is Mediation the Practice of Law?* 14 Alternatives 57.

MEYERSON, Bruce. (1996) *Lawyers Who Mediate Are Not Practicing Law,* 14 Alternatives 74.

Standards of Conduct For Mediators (1994), American Arbitration Association, American Bar Association, Society of Professionals in Dispute Resolution.

NICOLAU, George. (1988) *A SPIDR Commission on Qualifications Presents Report at Annual Meeting,* 2 Alt. Disp. Res. Rep. 392.

PRESS, Sharon. (1988) *Florida Explains Court Rules, In Face of Continuing Controversy,* 2 Alt. Disp. Res. Rep. 434.

RAVINDRA, Geetha. (2000) *The Response: The Goal is to Inform, Not Impede, ADR,* 18 Alternatives 124.

SPIDR COMMISSION ON QUALIFICATIONS. (May 1989) *Qualifying Neutrals: The Basic Principles,* Dispute Resolution Forum.

STEMPEL, Jeffrey W. (1997) *Beyond Formalism and False Dichotomies: The Need for Institutionalizing a Flexible Concept of the Mediator's Role,* 24 Fla. St. U. L. Rev. 949.

THE TEST DESIGN PROJECT. (1995) *Performance-Based Assessment: A Methodology, for Use in Selecting, Training and Evaluating Mediators.* Washington, DC: National Institute for Dispute Resolution.

WALDMAN, Ellen. (1996) *The Challenge of Certification: How to Ensure Mediator Competence While Preserving Diversity* 30 U.S.F. L. Rev. 723.

WECKSTEIN, Donald T. (1996) *Mediator Certification: Why and How* 30 U.S.F. L. Rev. 757.

WELSH, Nancy. (expected publication 2001) *The Thinning Vision of Self-Determination in Court-Connected Mediation: the Inevitable Price of Institutionalization?* 6 Harv. Negot. L. Rev. ___ (2001).

CHAPTER 8

Arnold, Tom. (1995) *20 Common Errors in Mediation Advocacy,* 13 Alternatives to the High Cost of Litigation 69.

Breger, Marshall J. (2000) *Should an Attorney be Required to Advise a Client of ADR Options?,* 13 Geo. J. Legal Ethics 427.

Cochran, Robert F., Jr. (1990) *Legal Representation and the Next Steps Toward Client Control: Attorney Malpractice for the Failure to Allow the Client to Control Negotiation and Pursue Alternatives to Litigation,* 47 Wash. & Lee L. Rev. 819.

COCHRAN, Robert F. Jr. (1999) *ADR, the ABA, and Client Control: A Proposal that the Model Rules Require Lawyers to Present ADR Options to Clients,* 41 S. Tex. L. Rev. 183

COHEN, Jonathan R. (1999) *Advising Clients to Apologize,* 72 S. Cal. L. Rev. 1009

COOLEY, John W. (1996) Mediation Advocacy. South Bend, Indiana: National Institute for Trial Advocacy

COOLEY, John W. (1997) *Mediation Magic: Its Use and Abuse,* 29 Loy. U. Chi. L.J. 1

DAUER, Edward A. (1996) *Manual of Dispute Resolution: ADR Law and Practice,* § 11

GALTON, Eric. (1994) *Representing Clients in Mediation.* Dallas, Texas: American Lawyer Media

GILSON, Ronald J., and MNOOKIN, Robert H. (1994) *Disputing Through Agents: Cooperation and Conflict Between Lawyers in Litigation,* 94 Colum. L. Rev. 509.

KOROBKIN, Russell, and GUTHRIE, Chris. (1997) *Psychology, Economics and Settlement: A New Look at the Role of the Lawyer,* 76 Tex. L. Rev. 77

LANDE, John. (1997) *How Will Lawyering and Mediation Transform Each Other?* 24 Fla. St. U. L. Rev. 839.

McEWEN, Craig A. et al. (1995) *Bring in the Lawyers: Challenging the Dominant Approaches to Ensuring Fairness in Divorce Mediation,* 79 Minn. L. Rev. 1317.

McEWEN, Craig A. et al. (1994) *Lawyers, Mediation, and the Management of Divorce Practice,* 28 L. & Soc'y Rev. 149.

MENDELSON, Gary. (1996) *Lawyers as Negotiators,* 1 Harv. Negotiation L. Rev. 139.

MENKEL-MEADOW, Carrie. (1997) *Ethics in Alternative Dispute Resolution: New Issues, No Answers From the Adversary Conception of Lawyers' Responsibilities,* 38 S. Tex. L. Rev. 407.

MEYERSON, Bruce E. (1997) *Telling the Truth in Mediation: Mediator Owed Duty of Candor,* 2 Disp. Res. Mag. 17.

MNOOKIN, Robert H., PEPPET, Scott, and TULUMELLO, Andrew, (2000) *Beyond Winning: Negotiating to Create Value in Deals and Disputes.* Cambridge, MA: Belknap Press of Harvard University.

MNOOKIN, Robert H. and SUSSKIND, Lawrence eds. (1999) *Negotiating on Behalf of Others: Advice to Lawyers, Business Executives, Sports*

Agents, Diplomats, Politicians, and Everybody Else. Thousand Oaks, California: Sage Publications

MNOOKIN, Robert H., and KORNHAUSER, Lewis. (1979) *Bargaining in the Shadow of the Law: The Case of Divorce,* 88 Yale L.J. 950.

MNOOKIN, Robert H. (1993) *Why Negotiations Fail: An Exploration of Barriers to the Resolution of Conflict,* 8 Ohio St. J. on Disp. Resol. 235.

MOORE, Loretta W. (1996) *Lawyer Mediators: Meeting the Ethical Challenges,* 30 Fam. L.Q. 679.

NOLAN-HALEY, Jacqueline M. (1998) *Lawyers, Clients and Mediation,* 73 Notre Dame L. Rev. 1369.

PEDONE, Nicole. (1998) *Lawyer's Duty to Discuss Alternative Dispute Resolution: In the Best Interest of Children,* 36 Fam. & Conciliation Cts. Rev. 65.

PLIMPTON, David. (2000) *Liability Pitfalls May Be Waiting for Lawyer-Neutrals,* 18 Alternatives to the High Cost of Litigation 65.

PRIGOFF, Michael L. (1990) At Issue: *Professional Responsibility: Should There Be a Duty to Advise of ADR Options? NO: An Unreasonable Burden,* A.B.A. J. (Nov. 1990, at 51.)

ROGERS, Nancy H., and McEWEN, Craig A. (1998) *Employing the Law to Increase the Use of Mediation and to Encourage Direct and Early Negotiations,* 13 Ohio St. J. on Disp. Resol. 831.

RUTHERFORD, Mark C. (1986) *Lawyers and Divorce Mediation: Designing the Role of "Outside Counsel",* Mediation Q. (June, 1986, at 17).

SANDER, Frank E.A. (1990) At Issue: *Professional Responsibility Should There Be a Duty to Advise of ADR Options? Yes: An Aid to Clients,* A.B.A. J. (Nov. 1990, at 50).

SCHMITZ, Suzanne J. (1999) *Giving Meaning to the Second Generation of ADR Education: Attorney's Duty to Learn about ADR and What They Must Learn,* 1999 J. Dispute Resol. 29.

SPIEGEL, Mark. (1979) *Lawyering and Client Decisionmaking: Informed Consent and the Legal Profession,* 128 U. Pa. L. Rev. 41.

STERNLIGHT, Jean R. (1999) *Lawyers' Representation of Clients in Mediation: Using Economics and Psychology to Structure Advocacy in a Nonadversarial Setting,* 14 Ohio St. J. on Disp. Resol. 269.

STERNLIGHT, Jean R. (2000) *What's a Lawyer to Do in Mediation?* 18 Alternatives to the High Cost of Litigation 1.

WATSON, Lawrence M., Jr. (1995) *Effective Legal Representation in Mediation* (in) 2 *Alternative Dispute Resolution in Florida* 2-1 (2d ed.).

CHAPTER 9

BINGHAM, Lisa B. (1997) *Mediating Employment Disputes: Perceptions of REDRESS at the United States Postal Service,* 20 Rev. of Pub. Personnel Admin. 20.

BROSTEK, Michael. (1997) *Alternative Dispute Resolution: Employers' Experiences With ADR in the Workplace* (Letter Report, 8/12/97, GAO/GGD-97-157).

BUSH, Robert A. Baruch. (1989) *Mediation and Adjudication, Dispute Resolution and Ideology: An Imaginary Conversation* 3 J. of Contemp. Legal Issues 1.

CHANTILIS, Peter S. (1996) *Mediation U.S.A.,* 26 U. Mem. L. Rev. 3.

McADOO, Barbara, and WELSH, Nancy. (1997) *Does ADR Really Have a Place on the Lawyer's Philosophical Map?* 18 Hamline J. of Pub. L. & Pol'y 376.

McCRORY, John P. (1999) *Mandated Mediation of Civil Cases in State Courts: A Litigant's Perspective on Program Model Choices,* 14 Ohio St. J. on Disp. Resol. 813.

MENKEL-MEADOW, Carrie. (1991) *Pursuing Settlement in an Adversary Culture: a Tale of Innovation Co-opted or "The Law of ADR",* 19 Fla. St. L. Rev. 1.

PHILLIPS, Barbara A. (1997) *Mediation: Did We Get it Wrong?,* 33 Willamette L. Rev. 649.

PRESS, Sharon. (1992-93) *Building and Maintaining a Statewide Mediation Program: A View from the Field,* 81 Ken. L.J. 1029.

PRESS, Sharon. (1997) *Institutionalization: Savior or Saboteur of Mediation?,* 24 Fla. St. U. L. Rev. 903.

ROGERS, Nancy Frank E.A., and McEWEN, Craig. (1994) *Mediation: Law, Policy & Practice,* (2d Ed.) New York: Clark, Boardman, and Callaghan.

SANDER, Frank E.A. (2000) *The Future of ADR,* 2000 J. Disp. Resol. 3.

SENGER, Jeffrey M. (2000) *Turning the Ship of State,* 2000 J. Disp. Resol. 79.

STIFTEL, Bruce, and SIPE, Neil G. (1992) *Mediation of Environmental Enforcement: Overcoming Inertia,* 1992 J. Disp. Resol. 303.

STIPANOWICH, Thomas J. (1996) *Beyond Arbitration: Innovation and Evolution in the United States Construction Industry,* 31 Wake Forest L. Rev. 65.

CHAPTER 10:

References for Chapter 10 have been incorporated into the Notes and Questions sections of the chapter.

CHAPTER 11:

References for Chapter 11 have been incorporated into the Notes and Questions sections of the chapter.

TABLE OF CASES

[Principal cases are capitalized, with page references italicized.]

[Principal cases are capitalized, with page references italicized.]

INDEX

[References are to pages.]

A

AAA (See AMERICAN ARBITRATION ASSO-CIATION (AAA))

ABA (See AMERICAN BAR ASSOCIATION (ABA))

ACADEMY OF FAMILY MEDIATORS (AFM)
Divorce mediation . . . 21

ADMINISTRATIVE ACT OF 1966
Institutionalization of mediation . . . 457

ADMINISTRATIVE DISPUTE RESOLU-TION ACT
Enactment of . . . 481-482
Purpose of . . . 481-482

ADVERTISING
Attorney-mediator . . . 452-453
Mediators . . . 375; 380; 452-453

AFM (See ACADEMY OF FAMILY MEDIA-TORS (AFM))

AIR FORCE
ADR, use of . . . 487-489

ALTERNATIVE DISPUTE RESOLUTION ACT OF 1998
Privileged communications . . . 217; 218-219
Purpose of . . . 30

AMERICAN ARBITRATION ASSOCIA-TION (AAA)
Generally . . . 9
Negotiation, Model Rules of Professional Conduct provisions for . . . 69-85

AMERICAN BAR ASSOCIATION (ABA)
Special Committee on resolution of minor disputes . . . 13

AMERICAN INDIANS (See NATIVE AMERI-CANS)

ARBITRATION
Enforcement of arbitration clause . . . . . .
244-250

ATTORNEYS
Generally . . . 32-33
Advantages and disadvantages of attorney participation in mediation . . . 412
Advertising as mediator . . . 452-453
Advising clients about mediation, duty of . . . 405-411
Advocating for client . . . 426-429

ATTORNEYS—Cont.
Business concerns for attorney-mediator . . . 453
Conflict of interest . . . 444-451
Cooperative lawyers, selecting . . . 417-420
Decisionmaking responsibilities . . . 424-425
Disadvantages and advantages of attorney participation in mediation . . . 412
Dishonesty . . . 440-442
Divorce mediation . . . 413-417
Ethical considerations
    Generally . . . 443-444
    ADR, attorney's obligation to learn and understand . . . 409-411
    Advertising as mediator . . . 452-453
    Advising clients about mediation, duty of . . . 405-411
    Advocating for client . . . 426-429
    Business concerns . . . 453
    Conflict of interest . . . 444-451
    Decisionmaking responsibilities 424-425
    Dishonesty . . . 440-442
    False statements . . . 440-442
    Fee sharing issues . . . 451
    Good faith requirement in mediation and . . . 260-266
    Representative in mediation, attorney's role as . . . 404-405
    Solicitation . . . 452-453
    Truthfulness standards . . . 440-442
False statements . . . 440-442
Fee sharing issues . . . 451
Good faith requirement in mediation and attorney ethics . . . 260-266
Guidelines for mediation . . . 430-440
Initiating mediation . . . 398-404
Legal scholarships . . . 27-28
Mediator, role in selection of . . . 421-425
Negotiation (See NEGOTIATION)
Practice of law and mediation . . . 387-390
Preparation for mediation, guidelines for . . . 430-440
Relationship between litigation and mediation . . . 397-404
Representative in mediation, role as 404-405
Selection of mediator, role in . . . 421-425
Solicitation . . . 452-453
Truthfulness standards . . . 440-442

B

BAD FAITH (See GOOD FAITH REQUIRE-MENT)

I–1

[References are to pages.]

[References are to pages.]

[References are to pages.]

[References are to pages.]

[References are to pages.]